Popular Series Fiction for Middle School and Teen Readers

Recent Titles in the
Children's and Young Adult Literature Reference Series
Catherine Barr, Series Editor

Best Books for High School Readers, Grades 9-12
John T. Gillespie and Catherine Barr

Popular Series Fiction for K-6 Readers: A Reading and Selection Guide
Rebecca L. Thomas and Catherine Barr

Popular Series Fiction for Middle School and Teen Readers

A Reading and Selection Guide

Rebecca L. Thomas and Catherine Barr

Children's and Young Adult Literature Reference Series

LIBRARIES
UNLIMITED
A Member of the Greenwood Publishing Group

Westport, Connecticut ● London

British Library Cataloguing in Publication Data is available.

ISBN: 1-59158-202-4

First published in 2005

Libraries Unlimited, 88 Post Road West, Westport, CT 06881
A Member of the Greenwood Publishing Group, Inc.
www.lu.com

Printed in the United States of America

∞™

The paper used in this book complies with the Permanent Paper Standard issued by the National Information Standards Organization (Z39.48-1984).

10   9   8   7   6   5   4   3   2   1

CONTENTS

PREFACE

Series fiction is more popular than ever. The YA market is hot. In his essay "Dude, Where's My Year?" (*Booklist*, Jan. 1 & 15, 2004), Michael Cart wrote: "More and more books—mainly series that stores are marketing under the (patronizing?) rubric 'chick lit'—are being targeted at a consumer audience composed of teens themselves. A lot of these books are about as enduring as a snowflake (the Gossip Girl series, for example), but some (the Sammy Keyes mysteries, Phyllis Reynolds Naylor's Alice books) are established series of enduring value that kids are willing to pay for out of their own pockets . . . . Madison Avenue tells us the average teen now has a weekly disposable income of $100 or more!" Clearly, staying current with popular books is crucial if libraries want to attract and serve teen readers.

Series books with media tie-ins (such as Princess Diaries and all the Star Wars entries) or about dating and school (A-List and Gossip Girl) try to capitalize on this profitable area. Fantasy books are extremely popular thanks in part to Harry Potter and The Lord of the Rings. Many established authors—Laurence Yep, Phyllis Reynolds Naylor, and Todd Strasser, to name just a few—have contributed series books that focus on issues and topics that are of interest to teens.

Graphic novels, manga, cine-manga, and other illustrated novels have greatly increased in availability and popularity. *Popular Series Fiction for Middle School and Teen Readers: A Reading and Selection Guide* includes a selection of these materials, chosen with the help of professional reference sources. Publishers' catalogs and Web sites were also examined, although these were often more hype then help. Assigning a grade level was problematic as sources varied widely on what was suitable for younger readers. A sentence is included in the annotation to alert users to any concerns about content. As these materials become more established, more selection information should be available.

And a new marketing niche has been created—'tweens. These are the young teens who are almost old enough to drive, work, and date. The series books for this group focus on preparation for their upcoming independence. Lizzie McGuire, That's So Raven, and Winning Season are among the series that fit into this category.

Keeping up with these materials is a challenge. *Popular Series Fiction for Middle School and Teen Readers* provides guidance for professionals—and for parents—seeking to encourage young people to read. Teachers work to find series books that meet the needs of the variety of readers in their classrooms. Librarians frequently hear questions such as "Do you know any mystery books that will attract reluctant readers?" and "What fantasy books do you recommend for middle school students?" With this book, librarians and teachers will find it easier to keep tabs on new titles in existing series and to evaluate new series (and each re-packaging).

Popular Series Fiction for Middle School and Teen Readers is a companion to *Popular Series Fiction for K–6 Readers*. These books evolved from *Reading in Series* (Bowker, 1999).

RESEARCH AND SELECTION

One of our first considerations was how to identify the series. To create our initial listing, we looked at current reviewing sources such as *Booklist* and *School Library Journal* and at reference compilations including *Best Books for Middle School and Junior High Readers* and *Best Books for High School Readers* (both from Libraries Unlimited) and Wilson's *Middle and Junior High School Library Catalog* and *Senior High School Library Catalog*. In addition, we made use of online sources including publisher and author Web sites, teen sites (www.teenreads.com/ in particular), booksellers amazon.com and barnesandnoble.com, series sites such as those at Mid-Continent Public Library (http://www.mcpl.lib.mo.us) and Bettendorf Public Library (http://www.bettendorflibrary.com/teen/), and other specialized library sites.

As we searched libraries and bookstores for the books themselves, the following criteria were applied:

1. The series we selected would be content-based groupings of books with a consistent theme, setting, or group of characters.

2. A series generally needed three or more books. However, we have included some developing series that promise to become popular. These are also listed in a special appendix. Some "future titles" were included in an effort to be as current as possible. Titles for 2005 books may end up being changed (remember *Harry Potter and the Doomspell Tournament?*), but their inclusion will alert librarians that additions to the series are forthcoming.

3. The grade range of the books in this volume is from grades 6 through 12. A selection of adult books read by young adults have been included. Decisions about grade levels are based on knowledge of the audience, examination of the books, consultation of professional resources, and library experience.

4. As we annotated each series, every effort was made to examine several books, hoping to offer better insight to librarians making purchasing decisions or recommending these books to readers.

5. Older series were included, too, especially those considered "classics." In selecting the "older" series to include, we relied on our judgment and on the judgment of our contributors and on our ability to find copies of several titles in libraries and bookstores.

6. We focused on including series books with some of the titles still in print. This was a problem, especially for many paperback series. Some very popular books that were published only a few years ago are no longer available, but we decided to include these series because they can still be found in many libraries. Librarians and teachers who want to update their collections can use the Genre/Subject Index to find newer, similar books.

We scoured libraries, bookstores, publishers' catalogs, and Web sites looking for new series and the newest titles in existing series. But this is not a comprehensive listing. Many of these series have spawned a number of offshoots—Star Wars is a prime example—often spanning generations of characters. We have attempted to include a sampling of some of the most important. *Popular Series Fiction for Middle School and Teen Readers* is a work in progress and we anticipate that each successive edition will grow.

ANATOMY OF AN ENTRY

Each entry provides the following information:

Series title: Cross-referenced as needed

Author: If individual books within a series have different authors, they are listed with the books.

Publisher: Many series have had several publishers over the years. The publisher shown is the most recent publisher. In some cases both hardback and paperback publishers are listed.

Grade level: This volume covers series for grades 6–YA (grades K–6 are covered in the companion volume). There is some overlap between the two volumes. Series suitable for readers in grades 5 through 8, for example, will appear in both.

Genres: These are broad thematic areas that will help link similar series. The genres included are: Adventure, Animal Fantasy, Family Life, Fantasy, Historical, Horror, Humor, Mystery, Real Life, Recreation, Science Fiction, and Values.

Accelerated Reader: The notation A/R indicates that Accelerated Reader resources are available for some or all of the titles in the series.

Annotation: This descriptive examination of the series provides information about important characters, plots, themes, and issues in the series. Specific books are often described in detail.

List of titles in the series: This list was compiled using the books themselves and the selection sources mentioned above, as well as Books in Print (R. R. Bowker), the CLEVNET database (which serves a large number of member libraries in northeast Ohio including the Cleveland Public Library), and literature sites including NoveList. These resources (along with the publisher catalogs and Web sites) often provided conflicting information about exact titles and copyright dates, so there may be some inconsistencies; however, every effort has been made to be as complete and accurate as possible. Book titles are shown in chronological order by year of publication. Numbered series are shown in number order, which is usually also chronological. Where series include prequels or alternative reading orders, this is mentioned in the annotation.

INDEXES AND APPENDIXES

Author and Title indexes will help the user who is searching for new series by a given author or who knows only one title in a series. The Genre/Subject Index gives access by genre and by more specific topics. Thus, the fan of horror can easily find more series in that genre; and readers can quickly identify series about horses. The addition of grade levels after the series titles allows users to pinpoint grade-appropriate series quickly. To make access easier, real animals and fantasy animals (mice that wear clothes and go to school, for example) are listed together.

In addition, there are lists of series of special interest to boys or girls and for reluctant readers. These are not comprehensive lists; series were selected for their current appeal to readers. The books for boys often feature as the main characters a group of boys who are involved in mysteries, sports, school problems, friendship, and the supernatural. The books for girls often feature one or more girls involved in mysteries, sports (horseback riding and skating, in particular), school problems, friendship, and growing up. The books for reluctant readers were chosen for their popular appeal, and often feature media tie-ins, monsters, and creatures.

A final appendix lists series that are still developing and currently only include one or two titles.

There are many ways for librarians and teachers to use *Popular Series Fiction*. The Genre/Subject Index points the way to series on topics of interest. The genre Fantasy, for example, makes it easy to identify series of interest. For readers who want legends of King Arthur and Merlin, consult the subject Arthurian Legends to find T. A. Barron's Merlin as well as the classic series from T. H. White and the recent Arthur Trilogy by Kevin Crossley-Holland.

Popular Series Fiction is also a selection guide. Librarians may want to add new series or update titles in series that have already been purchased. If your students like mysteries, look at the P.C. Hawke Mysteries. For sports, there is Dream Series. For adventure, there is Alex Rider. Add the newer titles to existing series or fill in titles you may have missed. The annotations allow you to compare series and make decisions about which will best fit your needs.

Popular Series Fiction builds on the earlier *Reading in Series*. Compilation of that book involved the efforts of librarians and teachers who are well qualified in fiction for children:

Connie Parker	Cuyahoga County (Ohio) Public Library
Deanna McDaniel	Westerville (Ohio) City Schools
Jacqueline Albers	Cuyahoga County (Ohio) Public Library
Karen Breen	Program Officer, New Visions for Public Schools, New York, NY
Doris Gebel	Northport (NY) Public Library
Debbie Gold	Cuyahoga County (Ohio) Public Library

We would like to thank Barbara Ittner of Libraries Unlimited for her encouragement and support and Julie Miller, Christine Weisel McNaull, and Bette Phillips for their work on the database, design and composition, and research.

SERIES A–Z

A-List

Dean, Zoey
LITTLE, BROWN
GRADES 9–12 ◆ A/R
REAL LIFE

Anna Percy adjusts to moving from Manhattan to Los Angeles. She hooks up with a privileged crowd that takes risks with drugs, boys, and other indulgences. One reviewer compared this popular series to the teen programs on the WB television network.

1. The A-List ◆ 2003
2. Girls on Film: An A-List Novel ◆ 2004
3. Blonde Ambition: An A-List Novel ◆ 2004
4. Tall Cool One: An A-List Novel ◆ 2005

ABARAT

Barker, Clive
HARPERCOLLINS
GRADES 7–12 ◆ A/R
FANTASY

Candy Quackenbush is bored in Chickentown, MN. While wandering in a field, she is transported to Abarat, an archipelago of 25 islands. There she becomes involved in a power struggle between the Lord of Midnight and Rojo Pixler of Commexo City. Numerous unusual, moody paintings by the author extend the vision of this strange place.

1. Abarat ◆ 2002
2. Abarat: Days of Magic, Nights of War ◆ 2004

ABBY'S SOUTH SEAS ADVENTURES

Walls, Pamela
TYNDALE HOUSE
GRADES 5–8 ◆ A/R
ADVENTURE | VALUES

In Hawaii in the mid-1800s, Abby and her family face many challenges to their safety and to their values. One adventure features Abby and her friend Luke searching for an arsonist before there is another fire. Their faith and their willingness to love and forgive sustain them.

1. Lost at Sea ◆ 2000
2. Quest for Treasure ◆ 2000
3. California Gold ◆ 2001
4. Secret at Cutter Grove ◆ 2001
5. King's Ransom ◆ 2001
6. Into the Dragon's Den ◆ 2001
7. Trouble in Tahiti ◆ 2002
8. Maui Mystery ◆ 2002

ABHORSEN

Nix, Garth

HARPERCOLLINS

GRADES 7–12

FANTASY

This trilogy features a classic confrontation between good and evil. Characters include Lirael, formerly Second Assistant Librarian and now Abhorsen-in-Waiting, Prince Sam, and Disreputable Dog in a struggle to save the Old Kingdom.

1. Sabriel ◆ 1996
2. Lirael: Daughter of the Clayr ◆ 2001
3. Abhorsen ◆ 2003

ACORNA

McCaffrey, Anne

HARPERCOLLINS

GRADES 10–12 ◆ A/R

FANTASY | SCIENCE FICTION

The orphan Acorna, a pretty child with a horn on her forehead and other odd features, is discovered drifting in an escape pod. With the help of her rescuers, she grows into a strong, independent young woman who cares for the downtrodden. In *Acorna's Quest* and *Acorna's People* she searches for—and finds—her own people. But, as always, there are dangers and challenges that test Acorna's powers and resolve.

1. Acorna: The Unicorn Girl ◆ 1997
2. Acorna's Quest ◆ 1998
3. Acorna's People ◆ 1999
4. Acorna's World ◆ 2000
5. Acorna's Search ◆ 2002
6. Acorna's Rebels ◆ 2003
7. Acorna's Triumph ◆ 2004

THE ADEPT

Kurtz, Katherine, and Deborah Turner Harris
ACE BOOKS
GRADES 10–12
FANTASY | MYSTERY

Sir Adam Sinclair, a physician who assists the police with some of their more mysterious crimes, is a man of many talents. His interest in magic and the occult gives him an insight into the unknown. Set in present-day Scotland, these books are filled with evil groups seeking to release dangerous, forbidden powers. Druids, the Knights Templar, and occult experiences make for exciting, fast-paced reading. This series was reissued in the early 2000s.

1. The Adept ◆ 1991
2. The Lodge of the Lynx ◆ 1992
3. The Templar Treasure ◆ 1993
4. Dagger Magic ◆ 1995
5. Death of an Adept ◆ 1996

ADVENTURES IN ODYSSEY: PASSAGES
see Passages

ADVENTURES OF MARY-KATE AND ASHLEY *see* Mary-Kate and Ashley: Adventures of Mary-Kate and Ashley

AERIEL TRILOGY *see* Darkangel Trilogy

AGAINST THE ODDS

Strasser, Todd
ALADDIN
GRADES 6–9
ADVENTURE

In *Gator Prey*, a small plane crashes in the Everglades and the two teen characters, Justin and Rachel, are the ones whose actions save the group. Along with Justin's mom and Rachel's dad, they face dangers from alligators and fire. In *Grizzly Attack*, Tyler runs away to Alaska, where he faces his own problems and a dangerous bear.

1. Shark Bite ◆ 1998
2. Grizzly Attack ◆ 1998
3. Buzzard's Feast ◆ 1999
4. Gator Prey ◆ 1999

AGE OF MAGIC TRILOGY

McGowen, Tom
LODESTAR/DUTTON
GRADES 5–9
FANTASY

The troll wizard Gwolchmig foresees an invasion from beyond the sky and the destruction of Earth. He puts aside lifelong animosities to unite the five races of Earth: trolls, humans, little people, Alfar (elves), and dragons. Twelve-year-old Lithim faces fierce opposition from the Atlan domain and devises a plan that will save the planet.

1. The Magical Fellowship ◆ 1991
2. The Trial of Magic ◆ 1992
3. The Question of Magic ◆ 1993

THE AGE OF UNREASON

Keyes, J. Gregory
BALLANTINE DEL REY
GRADES 10–12
FANTASY | HISTORICAL

History and fantasy are intertwined in these alternate views of 18th-century Europe and America featuring well-known individuals including Benjamin Franklin and Isaac Newton working with fictionalized characters to save society from the threat of destruction. These threats come both from ruthless individuals and from an invisible world.

1. Newton's Cannon ◆ 1998
2. A Calculus of Angels ◆ 1999
3. Empire of Unreason ◆ 2000
4. The Shadows of God ◆ 2001

AKIRA

Otomo, Katsuhiro
DARK HORSE
GRADES 8–12
FANTASY

In post-apocalyptic Tokyo in 2019, two teenagers—Tetsuo and Kaneda—may hold the future of the world in their hands. They develop their paranormal skills to confront an unknown power known as Akira. This series reproduces the stunning black-and-white art of the original classic series.

1. Volume 1 ◆ 2000
2. Volume 2 ◆ 2001
3. Volume 3 ◆ 2001
4. Volume 4 ◆ 2001
5. Volume 5 ◆ 2001
6. Volume 6 ◆ 2002

AKSUM *see* Arthurian-Aksumite Cycle

AL (ALEXANDRA)

Greene, Constance C.
VIKING; PUFFIN
GRADES 5–8
FAMILY LIFE | REAL LIFE

Al is the new kid, "a little on the fat side," with glasses and pigtails, and a self-proclaimed nonconformist. She becomes the best friend of the unnamed seventh-grade narrator. Their friendship grows and helps them deal with the problems they face. Al's mother, divorced for several years, begins to date; her father visits for the first time in years; and Al sacrifices a summer visit at her father's farm to take care of her sick mother. Together, the friends face life's ups and downs with humor.

1. A Girl Called Al ◆ 1969
2. I Know You, Al ◆ 1975
3. Your Old Pal, Al ◆ 1979
4. Alexandra the Great ◆ 1982
5. Just Plain Al ◆ 1986
6. Al's Blind Date ◆ 1989

ALBRIGHT FAMILY *see* Sterling Family

ALDEN ALL STARS

Hallowell, Tommy, and David Halecroft
PENGUIN
GRADES 4–8
REAL LIFE | RECREATION

Soccer, baseball, basketball, and football are all featured in this sports series. Three seventh- and eighth-grade boys star in separate books. Nick is the wise guy; Dennis is the leader and captain of the basketball team. Justin's sport is soccer, but Alden Junior High doesn't have a team, so he goes to a camp and stands out there. All of the books in the series are loaded with sports details, but there are also some points made about relationships and the importance of studying. Fans of Matt Christopher's books will enjoy this series.

1. Duel on the Diamond ◆ 1990
2. Jester in the Back Cover ◆ 1990
3. Shot from Midfield ◆ 1990
4. Last Chance Quarterback ◆ 1990
5. Blindside Blitz ◆ 1991
6. Breaking Loose ◆ 1991
7. Championship Summer ◆ 1991
8. Hotshot on Ice ◆ 1991
9. Power Play ◆ 1991
10. Setting the Pace ◆ 1991
11. Wild Pitch ◆ 1991
12. Benched! ◆ 1991

ALEX BALFOUR

Appel, Allen

BANTAM DOUBLEDAY DELL

GRADES 10–12

FANTASY

Alex Balfour, a time-traveling young history professor, has exciting adventures in 1917 Russia and 1876 Philadelphia, among other destinations, in this series for mature teens.

1. Time After Time ◆ 1985
2. Twice Upon a Time ◆ 1988
3. Till the End of Time ◆ 1990
4. In Time of War ◆ 2003

ALEX MACK *see* Secret World of Alex Mack

ALEX RIDER

Horowitz, Anthony

PHILOMEL/PENGUIN

GRADES 6–10 ◆ A/R

ADVENTURE

Alex Rider is a teenager who has been recruited to be a spy. The British espionage agency, MI6, contacts him for special assignments, such as saving the world from a nuclear attack (*Skeleton Key*). In *Eagle Strike*, Air Force One has been hijacked in a plot to steal the President's fingerprints and access top security files. Alex uses many gadgets and technological innovations that will fascinate readers. These thrillers are packed with adventure and lots of cliff-hanging action.

1. Stormbreaker ◆ 2001
2. Point Blank ◆ 2002
3. Skeleton Key ◆ 2003
4. Eagle Strike ◆ 2003

ALEXANDER COLD AND NADIA SANTOS

Allende, Isabel
HARPERCOLLINS
GRADES 6–10
ADVENTURE

In the first book, Alexander Cold, 15, and Nadia Santos, 12, are on an expedition in the Amazon rain forest where Alex's grandmother, Kate, is looking for a mysterious "beast." They encounter snakes, poison, and the murderous beast itself. The next book takes them to the Himalayas where they become involved with thieves who are looking for the Golden Dragon. One review compared these books to Indiana Jones adventures. Teen readers will be caught up in these exciting stories.

1. City of the Beasts ◆ 2002
2. Kingdom of the Golden Dragon ◆ 2004
3. Forest of the Pygmies ◆ 2005

ALIAS

Various authors
BANTAM
GRADES 8–12
ADVENTURE

Sydney Bristow is uncertain about her future. A recruiter offers her a job with a secret government agency, SD-6, but things are not what they seem. Sydney takes the job knowing there is no way out if she changes her mind. Having a secret life takes its toll as Sydney becomes more distant from her friends and everyday activities. As the series progresses, she leaves her normal life behind and faces more secretive and dangerous assignments. These books are based on the popular television program.

1. Recruited: An Alias Prequel (Mason, Lynn) ◆ 2002
2. A Secret Life (Roberts, Laura Peyton) ◆ 2003
3. Disappeared (Mason, Lynn) ◆ 2003
4. Sister Spy (Roberts, Laura Peyton) ◆ 2003
5. The Pursuit (Skurnick, Elizabeth) ◆ 2003
6. Close Quarters (Harrison, Emma) ◆ 2003
7. Father Figure (Roberts, Laura Peyton) ◆ 2003
8. Free Fall (Roberts, Christa) ◆ 2004
9. Infiltration (Frazier, Breen) ◆ 2004
10. Vanishing Act (Gerace, Sean) ◆ 2004

11. Skin Deep (Hapka, Cathy) ◆ 2004
12. Shadowed (Skurnick, Elizabeth) ◆ 2004

ALICE

Naylor, Phyllis Reynolds
ATHENEUM; DELL
GRADES 5–8 ◆ A/R
FAMILY LIFE | HUMOR

Affectionate and humorous, these stories feature Alice getting into all kinds of funny scrapes, mostly because of her good intentions. Putting up with the boys at school, getting her first boyfriend, making and keeping friends, and dealing with her father and older brother Lester are all part of the fun. As Alice matures, the books deal with more mature topics, such as her questions about sexuality and intimacy.

1. The Agony of Alice ◆ 1985
2. Alice in Rapture, Sort of ◆ 1989
3. Reluctantly Alice ◆ 1991
4. All But Alice ◆ 1992
5. Alice in April ◆ 1993
6. Alice In-Between ◆ 1994
7. Alice the Brave ◆ 1995
8. Alice in Lace ◆ 1996
9. Outrageously Alice ◆ 1997
10. Achingly Alice ◆ 1998
11. Alice on the Outside ◆ 2000
12. The Grooming of Alice ◆ 2000
13. Alice Alone ◆ 2001
14. Simply Alice ◆ 2002
15. Patiently Alice ◆ 2003
16. Including Alice ◆ 2004

ALLIANCE-UNION

Cherryh, C. J.
WARNER
GRADES 10–12
SCIENCE FICTION

Earth loses control over its colonies, partly through failures in judgment and partly through sheer distance. The colonies grow more independent, some choosing to remain allied with Earth. But Cyteen rebels and founds a runaway colony. When faster-than-light travel is discovered, the tensions between Earth and the colonies increase. These novels are complex and show strong characters trying to resolve typical human problems with lots of action and intrigue.

1. Serpent's Reach ◆ 1980
2. Downbelow Station ◆ 1981
3. Merchanter's Luck ◆ 1982
4. Forty Thousand in Gehenna ◆ 1983
5. Voyager in Night ◆ 1984
6. Angel with the Sword ◆ 1985
7. Cyteen ◆ 1988
8. Rimrunners ◆ 1989
9. Heavy Time ◆ 1991
10. Hellburner ◆ 1992
11. Tripoint ◆ 1994
12. Finity's End ◆ 1997

ALOHA COVE

Kelly, Theresa
CONCORDIA HOUSE
GRADES 7–10 ◆ A/R
FAMILY LIFE | REAL LIFE | VALUES

Cass, 17, is upset by the upheaval in her life. Her mother has remarried and Cass has a stepfather and a stepsister her own age—Tabitha. Now her mother is pregnant. At first, Cass and Tabitha have a strained relationship, but their faith brings them together. As they become closer, Cass and Tabitha reach out to others, including a friend with a violent boyfriend and another friend with anorexia. They follow God's way as they face each problem.

1. Living on Nothing Atoll ◆ 1999
2. Seaside High ◆ 1999
3. Tomorrow I'll Miss You ◆ 1999
4. Stand by Me ◆ 1999
5. Forget Me Not ◆ 2000
6. A Place in the Heart ◆ 2000
7. Dream a Little Dream ◆ 2000
8. Good-Bye Is Not Forever ◆ 2000

THE ALPHABETICAL HOOKUP LIST TRILOGY

McPhee, Phoebe
MTV/POCKET
GRADES 9–12
REAL LIFE

College freshmen Jodi, Celeste, and Ali share a dorm room. In an effort to boost their social life, they dare themselves to kiss 26 boys—boys whose names begin with each letter of the alphabet. They even continue the dare in Paris.

1. The Alphabetical Hookup List A–J ◆ 2002
2. The Alphabetical Hookup List K–Q ◆ 2002
3. The Alphabetical Hookup List R–Z ◆ 2002

ALTERNAMORPHS *see* Animorphs: Alternamorphs

AMERICAN ADVENTURE

Roddy, Lee
BETHANY HOUSE
GRADES 5–8 ◆ A/R
HISTORICAL | VALUES

Hildy Corrigan faces many challenges during the Great Depression as she and her family move, hoping for a better life. The different locations of this series put Hildy in situations that test her faith. Searching for a thief, adjusting to a new home, helping a girl whose father is a thief, and being accused of stealing a watch give Hildy opportunities to realize God's strength, love, and power of forgiveness. Readers looking for books in which characters struggle to be true to their values will want to read this series and other books by Lee Roddy.

1. The Overland Escape ◆ 1989
2. The Desperate Search ◆ 1989
3. Danger on Thunder Mountain ◆ 1989
4. The Secret of the Howling Cave ◆ 1990

5. The Flaming Trap ◆ 1990
6. Terror in the Sky ◆ 1991
7. Mystery of the Phantom Gold ◆ 1991
8. The Gold Train Bandits ◆ 1992
9. High Country Ambush ◆ 1992

AMERICAN DREAMS

Various authors

ALADDIN

GRADES 8–10

REAL LIFE

The first two books in this series parallel the opening episodes of the television program. Meg Pryor is a teenager in the turbulent 1960s. There are civil rights marches, riots, and protests against the Vietnam War. Meg's life, however, is focused on music and her friends. One friend, Roxanne, is on *American Bandstand* and she helps Meg get on too. Popular music of the era is featured. Fans of the television series of the same name will enjoy these books.

1. End of Summer (Tigelaar, Liz) ◆ 2004
2. Dance with Me (Oz, Emily) ◆ 2004
3. Count on Me (Beechen, Adam) ◆ 2004
4. Star Maps (Tigelaar, Liz) ◆ 2004
5. Fair Play (Shaw, Deirdre) ◆ 2005

AMERICAN DREAMS

Various authors

AVON

GRADES 9–12

HISTORICAL

These books feature young women who are spirited and adventurous and destined to fall in love. In the first book, Sarah is on a ship to Jamestown Colony in 1620. When she arrives there, she tutors children. Her unhappiness leads her to plant tobacco with the hope of earning enough money to return to England. Her plans change when she finds love and marries. Fans of historical romance will enjoy the action in this series.

1. Sarah on Her Own (Coombs, Karen M.) ◆ 1996
2. Plainsong for Caitlin (Rees, Elizabeth M.) ◆ 1996
3. Into the Wind (Ferris, Jean) ◆ 1996

4. Song of the Sea (Ferris, Jean) ◆ 1996
5. Weather the Storm (Ferris, Jean) ◆ 1996
6. The Innkeeper's Daughter (Kassem, Lou) ◆ 1996
7. Reyna's Reward (Dionne, Wanda) ◆ 1996
8. Sofia's Heart (Cadwallader, Sharon) ◆ 1996
9. Heart of the Hills (Ritthaler, Shelly) ◆ 1996
10. With Love, Amanda (Ritthaler, Shelly) ◆ 1997
11. Carrie's Gold (Zach, Cheryl) ◆ 1997

AMERICAN EMPIRE *see* The Great War

AMERICAN GIRLS: GIRLS OF MANY LANDS

Various authors
PLEASANT COMPANY
GRADES 4–8 ◆ **A/R**
HISTORICAL | REAL LIFE

This historical series features 12-year-old girls during times of change. Cecile is a servant in the French court of Louis XIV. What begins as an opportunity becomes a challenge. Neela lives in India during the independence movement (1939). In 1846, Saba is kidnapped from her home in Ethiopia and taken to the court of the emperor. Girls who like books about female characters facing challenges will enjoy this series. As with other books from this publisher, historical facts follow each story.

1. Cecile: Gates of Gold, 1711 (Casanova, Mary) ◆ 2002
2. Isabel: Taking Wing, 1592 (Dalton, Annie) ◆ 2002
3. Minuk: Ashes in the Pathway, 1890 (Hill, Kirkpatrick) ◆ 2002
4. Neela: Victory Song, 1939 (Divakaruni, Chitra Banerjee) ◆ 2002
5. Spring Pearl: The Last Flower, 1857 (Yep, Laurence) ◆ 2002
6. Saba: Under the Hyena's Foot, 1846 (Kurtz, Jane) ◆ 2003
7. Kathleen: The Celtic Knot, 1937 (Parkinson, Siobhan) ◆ 2003
8. Leyla: The Black Tulip, 1720 (Croutier, Alev Lytle) ◆ 2003

AMERICAN GIRLS: HISTORY MYSTERIES

Various authors
PLEASANT COMPANY
GRADES 4–7 ◆ **A/R**
HISTORICAL | MYSTERY

Louisiana during the War of 1812; the Pony Express trail in 1860 Nebraska; San Francisco after the 1906 earthquake. These are just some of the places and times presented in this series. In each book, a girl who is around 12 years old becomes involved in a mysterious situation. There are concerns about spies, pirates, the Ku Klux Klan, and kidnappers. The intrepid behavior of the main characters saves the day. Historical information follows each novel. This is a good choice for girls who enjoy action.

1. The Smuggler's Treasure (Buckey, Sarah Masters) ◆ 1999
2. Hoofbeats of Danger (Hughes, Holly) ◆ 1999
3. The Night Fliers (Jones, Elizabeth McDavid) ◆ 1999
4. Voices at Whisper Bend (Ayres, Katherine) ◆ 1999
5. Secrets on 26th Street (Jones, Elizabeth McDavid) ◆ 1999
6. Mystery of the Dark Tower (Coleman, Evelyn) ◆ 2000
7. Trouble at Fort La Pointe (Ernst, Kathleen) ◆ 2000
8. Under Copp's Hill (Ayres, Katherine) ◆ 2000
9. Watcher in the Piney Woods (Jones, Elizabeth McDavid) ◆ 2000
10. Shadows in the Glasshouse (McDonald, Megan) ◆ 2000
11. The Minstrel's Melody (Tate, Eleanora E.) ◆ 2001
12. Riddle of the Prairie Bride (Reiss, Kathryn) ◆ 2001
13. Enemy in the Fort (Buckey, Sarah Masters) ◆ 2001
14. Circle of Fire (Coleman, Evelyn) ◆ 2001
15. Mystery on Skull Island (Jones, Elizabeth McDavid) ◆ 2001
16. Whistler in the Dark (Ernst, Kathleen) ◆ 2002
17. Mystery at Chilkoot Pass (Steiner, Barbara) ◆ 2002
18. The Strange Case of Baby H (Reiss, Kathryn) ◆ 2002
19. Danger at the Wild West Show (Hart, Alison) ◆ 2003
20. Gangsters at the Grand Atlantic (Buckey, Sarah Masters) ◆ 2003
21. Ghost Light on Graveyard Shoal (Jones, Elizabeth McDavid) ◆ 2003
22. Betrayal at Cross Creek (Ernst, Kathleen) ◆ 2004

AMONG THE . . . *see* Shadow Children

ANGEL

Various authors
SIMON & SCHUSTER
GRADES 7–12
HORROR

This popular spin-off from Buffy the Vampire Slayer features Angel, a troubled young vampire whose love for Buffy seems doomed. He moves to Los Angeles, where he seeks to right wrongs and seek redemption. The two volumes of *Angel: The Casefiles* (2002 and 2004) are official companions to the television show. *Angel: The Longest Night, Volume 1* (2002) is a collection of short stories.

1. City of Angel (Holder, Nancy) ◆ 1999
2. Not Forgotten (Holder, Nancy) ◆ 2000
3. Redemption (Odom, Mel) ◆ 2000
4. Close to the Ground (Mariotte, Jeff) ◆ 2000
5. Shakedown (DeBrandt, Don) ◆ 2000
6. Hollywood Noir (Mariotte, Jeff) ◆ 2001
7. Avatar (Passarella, John) ◆ 2001
8. Soul Trade (Sniegoski, Thomas E.) ◆ 2001
9. Bruja (Odom, Mel) ◆ 2001
10. The Summoned (Dokey, Cameron) ◆ 2001
11. Haunted (Mariotte, Jeff) ◆ 2002
12. Image (Odom, Mel) ◆ 2002
13. Stranger to the Sun (Mariotte, Jeff) ◆ 2002
14. Vengeance (Ciencin, Scott, and Dan Jolley) ◆ 2002
15. Endangered Species (Holder, Nancy, and Jeff Mariotte) ◆ 2002
16. Impressions (Durgin, Doranna) ◆ 2003
17. Sanctuary (Mariotte, Jeff) ◆ 2003
18. Fearless (Durgin, Doranna) ◆ 2003
19. Solitary Man (Mariotte, Jeff) ◆ 2003
20. Nemesis (Ciencin, Denise, and Scott Ciencin) ◆ 2004
21. Dark Mirror (Gardner, Craig Shaw) ◆ 2004
22. Monolith (Passarella, John) ◆ 2004
23. Book of the Dead (McConnell, Ashley) ◆ 2004
24. Love and Death (Mariotte, Jeff) ◆ 2004

ANGEL (GRAPHIC NOVELS)

Various authors

DARK HORSE

GRADES 8–12

HORROR

This popular spin-off from Buffy the Vampire Slayer follows the adventures of Angel, a vampire with a soul. After he leaves Sunnydale (and Buffy) and heads to Los Angeles, Angel seeks to overcome his past and confront the evil demons that threaten society.

1. The Hollower (Golden, Christopher, Hector Gomez, and Sandu Florea) ◆ 2000
2. Surrogates (Golden, Christopher, Tom Sniegoski, et al.) ◆ 2000
3. Earthly Possessions (Golden, Christopher, Tom Sniegoski, et al.) ◆ 2001
4. Hunting Ground (Golden, Christopher, Tom Sniegoski, et al.) ◆ 2001

5. Strange Bedfellows and Other Stories (Golden, Christopher, Tom Sniegoski, et al.) ◆ 2002
6. Autumnal (Golden, Christopher, Tom Sniegoski, et al.) ◆ 2002
7. Long Night's Journey (Matthews, Brett, Joss Whedon, et al.) ◆ 2002

ANGEL ON THE SQUARE

Whelan, Gloria
HARPERCOLLINS
GRADES 6–9
HISTORICAL

Katya's mother is a lady in waiting for the Empress of Russia. At the palace, Katya, 12, becomes a companion to the Grand Duchess Anastasia. The discontent and unrest in Russia leads to the Russian Revolution and brings changes for Katya. She leaves the palace and lives with her cousin, Misha, a revolutionary who helps Katya see beyond her childish, romanticized view of royalty. Katya's children continue the story in the second book, which takes place after the Revolution. Marya, 13, and her younger brother try to reunite with their mother, who has been exiled to Siberia.

1. Angel on the Square ◆ 2001
2. The Impossible Journey ◆ 2003

ANGELS UNLIMITED

Dalton, Annie
AVON
GRADES 4–7 ◆ A/R
FANTASY

Mel is 13 when she enters the Angel Academy. Mel and her schoolmates, including Orlando and Lola, travel to Earth to help with problems, arriving in different regions and centuries. These kids still party and gossip even as they face dangers from the Opposition.

1. Winging It ◆ 2001
2. Losing the Plot ◆ 2001
3. Flying High ◆ 2001
4. Calling the Shots ◆ 2002
5. Fighting Fit ◆ 2003
6. Making Waves ◆ 2003
7. Budding Star ◆ 2004
8. Keeping It Real ◆ 2005

ANIMORPHS

Applegate, K. A.
SCHOLASTIC
GRADES 4–8 ◆ A/R
ADVENTURE | SCIENCE FICTION

This fast-paced series involves the Yeerk—who have infected the brains of humans to control them—and the Animorphs, who have been given special powers by a dying Andalite. A special group of five friends find satisfaction in fighting the evil Yeerk. The Animorphs are able to "thought speak" and morph (for a period of two hours) into any animal they touch. A detailed discussion of the change process will hook readers as will the eye-catching covers. Short sentences plus continuous drama will keep readers involved. An *Animorph* television series and videos helped make this popular.

1. The Invasion ◆ 1996
2. The Visitor ◆ 1996
3. The Encounter ◆ 1996
4. The Message ◆ 1996
5. The Predator ◆ 1996
6. The Capture ◆ 1997
7. The Stranger ◆ 1997
8. The Alien ◆ 1997
9. The Secret ◆ 1997
10. The Android ◆ 1997
11. The Forgotten ◆ 1997
12. The Reaction ◆ 1997
13. The Change ◆ 1997
14. The Unknown ◆ 1998
15. The Escape ◆ 1998
16. The Warning ◆ 1998
17. The Underground ◆ 1998
18. The Decision ◆ 1998
19. The Departure ◆ 1998
20. The Discovery ◆ 1998
21. The Threat ◆ 1998
22. The Solution ◆ 1998
23. The Pretender ◆ 1998
24. The Suspicion ◆ 1998
25. The Extreme ◆ 1999
26. The Attack ◆ 1999
27. The Exposed ◆ 1999
28. The Experiment ◆ 1999
29. The Sickness ◆ 1999
30. The Reunion ◆ 1999
31. The Conspiracy ◆ 1999

32. The Separation ◆ 1999
33. The Illusion ◆ 1999
34. The Prophecy ◆ 1999
35. The Proposal ◆ 1999
36. The Mutation ◆ 1999
37. The Weakness ◆ 2000
38. The Arrival ◆ 2000
39. The Hidden ◆ 2000
40. The Other ◆ 2000
41. The Familiar ◆ 2000
42. The Journey ◆ 2000
43. The Test ◆ 2000
44. The Unexpected ◆ 2000
45. The Revelation ◆ 2000
46. The Deception ◆ 2000
47. The Resistance ◆ 2000
48. The Return ◆ 2000
49. The Diversion ◆ 2001
50. The Ultimate ◆ 2001
51. The Absolute ◆ 2001
52. The Sacrifice ◆ 2001
53. The Answer ◆ 2001
54. The Beginning ◆ 2001

ANIMORPHS: ALTERNAMORPHS

Applegate, K. A.
SCHOLASTIC
GRADES 4–8 ◆ A/R
ADVENTURE | SCIENCE FICTION

Choose your own adventure in these related Animorphs books.

1. The First Journey ◆ 1999
2. The Next Passage ◆ 2000

ANIMORPHS: ANIMORPH CHRONICLES

Applegate, K. A.
SCHOLASTIC
GRADES 4–8 ◆ A/R
ADVENTURE | SCIENCE FICTION

This is a prequel series to the Animorphs. It describes how Elfango, an Andalite war-prince, gave five young humans the ability to morph into any animal they touch. Readers learn about other adventures of the Andalites.

1. The Andalite Chronicles ◆ 1997
2. The Hork-Bajir Chronicles ◆ 1998
3. Visser ◆ 1999
4. The Ellimist Chronicles ◆ 2000

ANIMORPHS: MEGAMORPHS

Applegate, K. A.
SCHOLASTIC
GRADES 5–8 ◆ A/R
ADVENTURE | SCIENCE FICTION

Animorphs can morph into any animal, present-day or extinct, which can be a challenge if you choose to be a dinosaur. In these books, the Animorphs battle the Yeerk. In the fourth book, a decision is made to undo the creation of the Animorphs by traveling back in time and changing the original decision.

1. The Andalite's Gift ◆ 1997
2. In the Time of Dinosaurs ◆ 1998
3. Elfangor's Secret ◆ 1999
4. Back to Before ◆ 2000

ANNABEL ANDREWS

Rogers, Mary
HARPERCOLLINS
GRADES 5–7
FANTASY | HUMOR

Annabel wakes up one morning to find she has turned into her mother. Annabel and her mother reverse roles for a day, and each gains a more sympathetic understanding of the other's life. Annabel blunders her way through the day and comes to appreciate her mother's daily trials, while her mother experiences life from her 13-year-old daughter's perspective. In the sequel, *A Billion for Boris*, Annabel and her 15-year-old boyfriend Boris discover a TV set that broadcasts tomorrow's news. And in *Summer Switch* it is brother Ben's turn to switch bodies with his father.

1. Freaky Friday ◆ 1972

2. A Billion for Boris ◆ 1974
3. Summer Switch ◆ 1982

ANNE SHIRLEY *see* Avonlea

ANTHONY MONDAY

Bellairs, John
DIAL
GRADES 5–7
ADVENTURE | MYSTERY

Fourteen-year-old Anthony and his friend, librarian Miss Eells, search for a treasure rumored to have been hidden by wealthy eccentric Alpheus Winterborn. Anthony follows the clues to the Winterborn mansion and then back to the public library, where he outwits the efforts of another person who is seeking the treasure. In *The Lamp from the Warlock's Tomb*, Miss Eells buys an antique lamp and mysterious events begin to occur. There are strange voices, odd behavior, and an encounter with a ghost. These are suspenseful stories featuring supernatural events and puzzling mysteries.

1. The Treasure of Alpheus Winterborn ◆ 1978
2. The Dark Secret of Weatherend ◆ 1984
3. The Lamp from the Warlock's Tomb ◆ 1988
4. The Mansion in the Mist ◆ 1992

ANTRIAN

Wisler, G. Clifton
DUTTON
GRADES 6–8
SCIENCE FICTION

Scott looks like an ordinary teenager, but he is not. Scott is an alien with the ability to see into the future. In these books, he discovers his powers and learns their limits. He also struggles to adapt to living on Earth and to keep his abilities a secret, especially from those who would exploit him. Readers who like the Animorphs series should enjoy this series too.

1. The Antrian Messenger ◆ 1986

2. The Seer ◆ 1988
3. The Mind Trap ◆ 1990

ARABUS FAMILY SAGA

Collier, James Lincoln, and Christopher Collier
DELL; DELACORTE
GRADES 5–8
HISTORICAL

Daniel Arabus struggles to be free during the uncertain times of the Revolutionary War. Daniel's late father was granted freedom for his service to the Continental Army, but unscrupulous men want to deny that freedom to Daniel and his mother. Two related books feature young African American women—Willy Freeman and Carrie—who are involved in the conflicts of the war and their desire for personal freedom. The lives of Daniel and his family intersect with each young woman. Entertaining reading that aptly describes the plight of African Americans during this period.

1. Jump Ship to Freedom ◆ 1981
2. War Comes to Willy Freeman ◆ 1983
3. Who Is Carrie? ◆ 1984

THE ARCHIVES OF ANTHROPOS

White, John
INTERVARSITY
GRADES 4–8 ◆ A/R
FANTASY

The strange land of Anthropos is the setting for much of the action of these stories. Cousins Mary, Wesley, Lisa, and Kurt magically travel to Anthropos—a land of kings, sorcerers, and magic—to assist in the High Emperor's fight against evil. This series is modeled after the Chronicles of Narnia series and will appeal to children who enjoy allegorical fantasy stories.

1. The Tower of Geburah ◆ 1978
2. The Iron Sceptre ◆ 1981
3. The Sword Bearer ◆ 1986
4. Gaal the Conqueror ◆ 1989
5. Quest for the King ◆ 1995
6. The Dark Lord's Demise ◆ 2001

ARE YOU AFRAID OF THE DARK?

Various authors

MINSTREL/POCKET BOOKS

GRADES 5–8

HORROR

Based on the Nickelodeon television series, these books are similar to Goosebumps and other books in the scary-stories genre. In one book, Duncan Evans is given three wishes and finds that the adage "be careful what you wish for" is very true. Another book features Glynis Barrons, who makes a rash statement that she lives to regret. There are sinister statues, ghost riders, secret mirrors, and a virtual nightmare. This is sure to be a hit with fans of horror books.

1. The Tale of the Sinister Statues (Peel, John) ◆ 1995
2. The Tale of Cutter's Treasure (Seidman, David L.) ◆ 1995
3. The Tale of the Restless House (Peel, John) ◆ 1995
4. The Tale of the Nightly Neighbors (Machale, D. J., and Kathleen Derby) ◆ 1995
5. The Tale of the Secret Mirror (Strickland, Brad) ◆ 1995
6. The Tale of the Phantom School Bus (Strickland, Brad) ◆ 1996
7. The Tale of the Ghost Riders (Vornholt, John) ◆ 1996
8. The Tale of the Deadly Diary (Strickland, Brad) ◆ 1996
9. The Tale of the Virtual Nightmare (Pedersen, Ted) ◆ 1996
10. The Tale of the Curious Cat (Gallagher, Diana G.) ◆ 1996
11. The Tale of the Zero Hour (Peel, John) ◆ 1997
12. The Tale of the Shimmering Shell (Weiss, David Cody, and Bobbi J. G. Weiss) ◆ 1997
13. The Tale of the Three Wishes (Peel, John) ◆ 1997
14. The Tale of the Campfire Vampires (Emery, Clayton) ◆ 1997
15. The Tale of the Bad-Tempered Ghost (Mitchell, V. E.) ◆ 1997
16. The Tale of the Souvenir Shop (Cohen, Alice E.) ◆ 1997
17. The Tale of the Ghost Cruise (Weiss, David Cody, and Bobbi J. G. Weiss) ◆ 1998
18. The Tale of the Pulsating Gate (Gallagher, Diana G.) ◆ 1998
19. The Tale of the Stalking Shadow (Weiss, Bobbi J. G., and David Cody Weiss) ◆ 1998
20. The Tale of the Egyptian Mummies (Mitchell, Mark) ◆ 1998
21. The Tale of the Terrible Toys (Byers, Richard Lee) ◆ 1998
22. The Tale of the Mogul Monster (Weiss, David Cody, and Bobbi J. G. Weiss) ◆ 1998
23. The Tale of the Horrifying Hockey Team (Rodriguez, K. S.) ◆ 1999

ARTEMIS FOWL

Colfer, Eoin
MIRAMAX KIDS
GRADES 5–8 ◆ A/R
FANTASY

Artemis Fowl, 12, comes from a criminal family, so his larcenous talents are not surprising. He captures an elf and demands a ransom only to be confronted by the fairy police force. Later, Artemis takes action to find his father but he needs help from the fairies. Once his father is home, Artemis commits to a life without crime . . . after one more caper.

1. Artemis Fowl ◆ 2001
2. The Arctic Incident ◆ 2002
3. The Eternity Code ◆ 2003

ARTHUR TRILOGY

Crossley-Holland, Kevin
SCHOLASTIC
GRADES 6–9 ◆ A/R
FANTASY

Arthur de Caldicot, 13, lives in 12th-century England. His life is linked with the ancient Arthur (of Camelot fame), especially after he receives a "seeing stone." The stone gives him insight into the life of his namesake. In the second book, Arthur is now 14 and eager to participate in the crusades.

1. The Seeing Stone ◆ 2001
2. At the Crossing Places ◆ 2002
3. King of the Middle March ◆ 2004

ARTHURIAN-AKSUMITE CYCLE

Wein, Elizabeth
VIKING
GRADES 7–12
FANTASY

As this cycle begins, Lleu is the heir to King Artos's throne in 6th-century Britain. His illegitimate brother, Medraut, is jealous and plots against him. Their relationship is complicated by the sorcery of Medraut's mother, Morgause, who is also Artos's sister. The second book follows King Artos's daughter, Princess Goewin, to Aksum (a region in Africa that is now Ethiopia), where she uses her power to protect her young nephew Telemakos. In *The Sunbird*, Telemakos attempts to spy for the emperor on the salt smugglers of the Aksumite Empire, but is captured and enslaved in the salt mines.

1. The Winter Prince ◆ 1993
2. The Coalition of Lions ◆ 2003
3. The Sunbird ◆ 2004

ARTHURIAN KNIGHTS

Sutcliff, Rosemary
Dutton
Grades 6–8
Fantasy | Historical

The well-known legend of King Arthur—from the intrigue surrounding Arthur's conception to the quest for the Holy Grail—is dramatically retold in this series. Based on history, ballads, and Malory's *Le Morte d'Arthur*, these books explain what happens to Arthur, Lancelot, Guinevere, and the others. Vivid detail describes feats of valor along with grave errors in judgment.

1. The Light Beyond the Forest: The Quest for the Holy Grail ◆ 1980
2. The Sword and the Circle: King Arthur and the Knights of the Round Table ◆ 1981
3. The Road to Camlann: The Death of King Arthur ◆ 1982

ASTEROID WARS

Bova, Ben
Tor
Grades 10–12 ◆ A/R
Science fiction

Commerce plays an unusually strong role in this engrossing saga of a race to save Earth from environmental disaster.

1. The Precipice ◆ 2001

2. The Rock Rats ◆ 2002
3. The Silent War ◆ 2004

ASTRO BOY

Tezuka, Osamu

DARK HORSE

GRADES 8–12

FANTASY

Astro Boy is an incredible super hero created by the late Osamu Tezuka, who has been considered the Walt Disney of Japan. This classic manga series is full of exciting adventures.

1. Volume 1 ◆ 2002
2. Volume 2 ◆ 2002
3. Volume 3 ◆ 2002
4. Volume 4 ◆ 2002
5. Volume 5 ◆ 2002
6. Volume 6 ◆ 2002
7. Volume 7 ◆ 2002
8. Volume 8 ◆ 2002
9. Volume 9 ◆ 2002
10. Volume 10 ◆ 2002
11. Volume 11 ◆ 2003
12. Volume 12 ◆ 2003
13. Volume 13 ◆ 2003
14. Volume 14 ◆ 2003
15. Volume 15 ◆ 2003
16. Volume 16 ◆ 2003
17. Volume 17 ◆ 2003
18. Volume 18 ◆ 2003
19. Volume 19 ◆ 2003
20. Volume 20 ◆ 2003
21. Volume 21 ◆ 2003
22. Volume 22 ◆ 2003
23. Volume 23 ◆ 2004

@CAFE

Craft, Elizabeth

SIMON & SCHUSTER

GRADES 7–10

REAL LIFE

The Internet cafe serves up coffee, computers, and romance. Six teens, three boys and three girls, work there. The friendships become complicated when two of the guys, Sam and Dylan, like the same girl, Natalie.

1. Love Bytes ◆ 1997
2. I'll Have What He's Having ◆ 1997
3. Make Mine to Go ◆ 1998
4. Flavor of the Day ◆ 1998

AUSTIN FAMILY *see* Vicky Austin

AVALON 1: WEB OF MAGIC

Various authors
SCHOLASTIC
GRADES 4–7 ◆ A/R
FANTASY

Three girls—Emily, Kara, and Adriane—explore deep into the woods. There they find a passage to another world. While some who travel through the passage come in peace, others have sinister plans. The girls face trials by earth, water, air, and fire as they confront the evil.

1. Circles in the Stream (Roberts, Shelly) ◆ 2001
2. All That Glitters (Roberts, Rachel) ◆ 2001
3. Cry of the Wolf (Roberts, Rachel) ◆ 2001
4. The Secret of the Unicorn (Roberts, Rachel) ◆ 2002
5. Spellsinger (Roberts, Rachel) ◆ 2002
6. Trial by Fire (Roberts, Rachel) ◆ 2002

AVALON 2: QUEST FOR MAGIC

Roberts, Rachel
CDS BOOKS
GRADES 4–7 ◆ A/R
FANTASY

The adventures continue for the three girls who have found Ravenswood—Emily, Kara, and Adriane. In one book, Adriane faces the Spider Witch that is threatening the woods. In another, Kara finds a mysterious portal. Fans of the Avalon: Web of Magic series may want to continue with these books.

1. Song of the Unicorns ◆ 2003
2. All's Fairy in Love and War ◆ 2003
3. Ghost Wolf ◆ 2004
4. Heart of Avalon ◆ 2004
5. The Dark Mage ◆ 2004

AVONLEA

Montgomery, Lucy Maud
RANDOM HOUSE
GRADES 5–8
FAMILY LIFE | HISTORICAL | REAL LIFE

Red-haired, imaginative Anne Shirley is mistakenly sent from an orphanage to live with the Cuthberts, who requested a boy to help on their farm. This series details the results. Montgomery tells Anne's life story from age 11 until well into her married years. Readers watch Anne blossom from an impetuous child into a mature woman, gaining not only physical beauty but a sense of self. Though the setting of these books is small-town Canada in the early 20th century, the themes of maturity, community, and friendship will surely resonate with today's readers. Girls who enjoy imagination and creativity will become fast friends with Anne.

1. Anne of Green Gables ◆ 1908
2. Anne of Avonlea ◆ 1909
3. Chronicles of Avonlea ◆ 1912
4. Anne of the Island ◆ 1915
5. Anne's House of Dreams ◆ 1917
6. Rainbow Valley ◆ 1919
7. Further Chronicles of Avonlea ◆ 1920
8. Rilla of Ingleside ◆ 1921
9. Anne of Windy Poplars ◆ 1936
10. Anne of Ingleside ◆ 1939

BABY-SITTER

Stine, R. L.
SCHOLASTIC
GRADES 6–8
HORROR

Mr. Hagen hates babysitters. He tries to kill Jenny when she is babysitting for him, but she kills him instead. The experience overwhelms her. Just as she is starting to recover, she takes another babysitting job in a haunted house. This time she confronts her fears and exorcises the ghosts. Stine's characteristic chapter endings range from the absurd to the really terrifying, and his fans will find just what they expect in this series.

1. The Baby-Sitter ◆ 1989
2. The Baby-Sitter II ◆ 1991
3. The Baby-Sitter III ◆ 1993
4. The Baby-Sitter IV ◆ 1995

BABY-SITTERS CLUB

Martin, Ann M.

SCHOLASTIC

GRADES 4–7 ◆ A/R

REAL LIFE

The Baby-Sitters Club of Stoneybrook, Connecticut, is a group of five 8th-grade girls who are best friends and meet three times a week to take calls from parents who need sitters. Hardworking Kristy formed the club and tries to keep everyone in line. Quiet, sensitive Mary Anne is the secretary and sets up appointments. Stacey is the sophisticated one and has a great sense of style because she comes from New York City. The club's meetings are held at Claudia's house because she has a private phone in her room. She is the artistic member of the group and a junk-food addict. Each book in the series focuses on a different girl, and as the series goes on, Dawn moves to California, divorced parents remarry (two of the girls become stepsisters), and the girls deal with problems. Stacey is diabetic, Mary Anne's father won't let her grow up, and they all occasionally have difficulty getting along with the children they babysit or the parents they work for. In every story, they work together to resolve problems with good will and humor.

1. Kristy's Great Idea ◆ 1986
2. Claudia and the Phantom Phone Calls ◆ 1986
3. The Truth About Stacey ◆ 1986
4. Mary Anne Saves the Day ◆ 1987
5. Dawn and the Impossible Three ◆ 1987
6. Kristy's Big Day ◆ 1987
7. Claudia and Mean Janine ◆ 1987
8. Boy-Crazy Stacey ◆ 1987
9. The Ghost at Dawn's House ◆ 1988
10. Logan Likes Mary Anne! ◆ 1988
11. Kristy and the Snobs ◆ 1988
12. Claudia and the New Girl ◆ 1988
13. Good-bye Stacey, Good-bye ◆ 1988
14. Hello, Mallory ◆ 1988
15. Little Miss Stoneybrook . . . and Dawn ◆ 1988

16. Jessi's Secret Language ◆ 1988
17. Mary Anne's Bad Luck Mystery ◆ 1988
18. Stacey's Mistake ◆ 1988
19. Claudia and the Bad Joke ◆ 1988
20. Kristy and the Walking Disaster ◆ 1989
21. Mallory and the Trouble with the Twins ◆ 1989
22. Jessi Ramsey, Pet-Sitter ◆ 1989
23. Dawn on the Coast ◆ 1989
24. Kristy and the Mother's Day Surprise ◆ 1989
25. Mary Anne and the Search for Tigger ◆ 1989
26. Claudia and the Sad Good-bye ◆ 1989
27. Jessi and the Superbrat ◆ 1989
28. Welcome Back, Stacey! ◆ 1989
29. Mallory and the Secret Diary ◆ 1989
30. Mary Anne and the Great Romance ◆ 1990
31. Dawn's Wicked Stepsister ◆ 1990
32. Kristy and the Secret of Susan ◆ 1990
33. Claudia and the Great Search ◆ 1990
34. Mary-Anne and Too Many Boys ◆ 1990
35. Stacey and the Mystery of Stoneybrook ◆ 1990
36. Jessi's Baby-Sitter ◆ 1990
37. Dawn and the Older Boy ◆ 1990
38. Kristy's Mystery Admirer ◆ 1990
39. Poor Mallory! ◆ 1990
40. Claudia and the Middle School Mystery ◆ 1991
41. Mary Anne vs. Logan ◆ 1991
42. Jessi and the Dance School Phantom ◆ 1991
43. Stacey's Emergency ◆ 1991
44. Dawn and the Big Sleepover ◆ 1991
45. Kristy and the Baby Parade ◆ 1991
46. Mary Anne Misses Logan ◆ 1991
47. Mallory on Strike ◆ 1991
48. Jessi's Wish ◆ 1991
49. Claudia and the Genius of Elm Street ◆ 1991
50. Dawn's Big Date ◆ 1992
51. Stacey's Ex-Best Friend ◆ 1992
52. Mary Anne + 2 Many Babies ◆ 1992
53. Kristy for President ◆ 1992
54. Mallory and the Dream Horse ◆ 1992
55. Jessi's Gold Medal ◆ 1992
56. Keep Out, Claudia! ◆ 1992
57. Dawn Saves the Planet ◆ 1992
58. Stacey's Choice ◆ 1992
59. Mallory Hates Boys (and Gym) ◆ 1992
60. Mary Anne's Makeover ◆ 1993
61. Jessi and the Awful Secret ◆ 1993
62. Kristy and the Worst Kid Ever ◆ 1993
63. Claudia's—Freind—Friend ◆ 1993
64. Dawn's Family Feud ◆ 1993

65. Stacey's Big Crush ◆ 1993
66. Maid Mary Anne ◆ 1993
67. Dawn's Big Move ◆ 1993
68. Jessi and the Bad Baby-Sitter ◆ 1993
69. Get Well Soon, Mallory! ◆ 1993
70. Stacey and the Cheerleaders ◆ 1993
71. Claudia and the Perfect Boy ◆ 1994
72. Dawn and the We Love Kids Club ◆ 1994
73. Mary Anne and Miss Priss ◆ 1994
74. Kristy and the Copycat ◆ 1994
75. Jessi's Horrible Prank ◆ 1994
76. Stacey's Lie ◆ 1994
77. Dawn and Whitney, Friends Forever ◆ 1994
78. Claudia and Crazy Peaches ◆ 1994
79. Mary Anne Breaks the Rules ◆ 1994
80. Mallory Pike, #1 Fan ◆ 1994
81. Kristy and Mr. Mom ◆ 1995
82. Jessi and the Troublemaker ◆ 1995
83. Stacey vs. the BSC ◆ 1995
84. Dawn and the School Spirit War ◆ 1995
85. Claudia Kishi, Live from WSTO! ◆ 1995
86. Mary Anne and Camp BSC ◆ 1995
87. Stacey and the Bad Girl ◆ 1995
88. Farewell, Dawn ◆ 1995
89. Kristy and the Dirty Diapers ◆ 1995
90. Welcome to BSC, Abby ◆ 1995
91. Claudia and the First Thanksgiving ◆ 1995
92. Mallory's Christmas Wish ◆ 1995
93. Mary Anne and the Memory Garden ◆ 1996
94. Stacey McGill, Super Sitter ◆ 1996
95. Kristy + Bart = ? ◆ 1996
96. Abby's Lucky Thirteen ◆ 1996
97. Claudia and the World's Cutest Baby ◆ 1996
98. Dawn and Too Many Baby-Sitters ◆ 1996
99. Stacey's Broken Heart ◆ 1996
100. Kristy's Worst Idea ◆ 1996
101. Claudia Kishi, Middle School Dropout ◆ 1996
102. Mary Anne and the Little Princess ◆ 1996
103. Happy Holidays, Jessi ◆ 1996
104. Abby's Twin ◆ 1997
105. Stacey the Math Whiz ◆ 1997
106. Claudia, Queen of the Seventh Grade ◆ 1997
107. Mind Your Own Business, Kristy! ◆ 1997
108. Don't Give Up, Mallory ◆ 1997
109. Mary Anne to the Rescue ◆ 1997
110. Abby the Bad Sport ◆ 1997
111. Stacey's Secret Friend ◆ 1997
112. Kristy and the Sister War ◆ 1997
113. Claudia Makes Up Her Mind ◆ 1997

114. The Secret Life of Mary Anne Spier ◆ 1998
115. Jessi's Big Break ◆ 1998
116. Abby and the Best Kid Ever ◆ 1998
117. Claudia and the Terrible Truth ◆ 1998
118. Kristy Thomas, Dog Trainer ◆ 1998
119. Stacey's Ex-Boyfriend ◆ 1998
120. Mary Anne and the Playground Fight ◆ 1998
121. Abby in Wonderland ◆ 1998
122. Kristy in Charge ◆ 1998
123. Claudia's Big Party ◆ 1998
124. Stacey McGill . . . Matchmaker? ◆ 1998
125. Mary Anne in the Middle ◆ 1998
126. The All-New Mallory Pike ◆ 1999
127. Abby's Un-Valentine ◆ 1999
128. Claudia and the Little Liar ◆ 1999
129. Kristy at Bat ◆ 1999
130. Stacey's Movie ◆ 1999
131. The Fire at Mary Anne's House ◆ 1999

BABY-SITTERS CLUB FRIENDS FOREVER

Martin, Ann M.

SCHOLASTIC

GRADES 4–7 ◆ A/R

REAL LIFE

The girls have more babysitting adventures.

1. Kristy's Big News ◆ 1999
2. Stacey vs. Claudia ◆ 1999
3. Mary Anne's Big Breakup ◆ 1999
4. Claudia and the Friendship Feud ◆ 1999
5. Kristy Power! ◆ 2000
6. Stacey and the Boyfriend Trap ◆ 2000
7. Claudia Gets Her Guy ◆ 2000
8. Mary Anne's Revenge ◆ 2000
9. Kristy and the Kidnapper ◆ 2000
10. Stacey's Problem ◆ 2000
11. Welcome Home, Mary Anne ◆ 2000
12. Claudia and the Disaster Date ◆ 2000

BABY-SITTERS CLUB FRIENDS FOREVER SPECIAL EDITIONS

1. Everything Changes ◆ 1999
2. Graduation Day ◆ 2000

BABY-SITTERS CLUB MYSTERIES

Martin, Ann M.

SCHOLASTIC

GRADES 4–7 ◆ A/R

MYSTERY | REAL LIFE

The five girls from Stoneybrook, Connecticut, who formed the Baby-Sitters Club have their own mystery series. Kristy, founder and president of the group, Dawn the Californian, sophisticated Stacey, shy Mary Anne, and artistic Claudia run into mysteries involving empty houses that aren't really empty, missing rings, counterfeit money, and more—mysteries that they try to solve Nancy Drew style.

1. Stacey and the Missing Ring ◆ 1991
2. Beware Dawn! ◆ 1991
3. Mallory and the Ghost Cat ◆ 1992
4. Kristy and the Missing Child ◆ 1992
5. Mary Anne and the Secret in the Attic ◆ 1992
6. The Mystery at Claudia's House ◆ 1992
7. Dawn and the Disappearing Dogs ◆ 1993
8. Jessi and the Jewel Thieves ◆ 1993
9. Kristy and the Haunted Mansion ◆ 1993
10. Stacey and the Mystery Money ◆ 1993
11. Claudia and the Mystery at the Museum ◆ 1993
12. Dawn and the Surfer Ghost ◆ 1993
13. Mary Anne and the Library Mystery ◆ 1994
14. Stacey and the Mystery at the Mall ◆ 1994
15. Kristy and the Vampires ◆ 1994
16. Claudia and the Clue in the Photograph ◆ 1994
17. Dawn and the Halloween Mystery ◆ 1994
18. Stacey and the Mystery at the Empty House ◆ 1994
19. Kristy and the Missing Fortune ◆ 1995
20. Mary Anne and the Zoo Mystery ◆ 1995
21. Claudia and the Recipe for Danger ◆ 1995
22. Stacey and the Haunted Masquerade ◆ 1995
23. Abby and the Secret Society ◆ 1996
24. Mary Anne and the Silent Witness ◆ 1996
25. Kristy and the Middle School Vandal ◆ 1996
26. Dawn Schafer, Undercover Babysitter ◆ 1996
27. Claudia and the Lighthouse Ghost ◆ 1996
28. Abby and the Mystery Baby ◆ 1997
29. Stacey and the Fashion Victim ◆ 1997
30. Kristy and the Mystery Train ◆ 1997
31. Mary Anne and the Music Box Secret ◆ 1997
32. Claudia and the Mystery in the Painting ◆ 1997
33. Stacey and the Stolen Hearts ◆ 1998
34. Mary Anne and the Haunted Bookstore ◆ 1998

35. Abby and the Notorious Neighbor ◆ 1998
36. Kristy and the Cat Burglar ◆ 1998

SUPER MYSTERIES

1. Baby-Sitters' Haunted House ◆ 1995
2. Baby-Sitters Beware ◆ 1995
3. Baby-Sitters' Fright Night ◆ 1996
4. Baby-Sitters' Christmas Chiller ◆ 1997

BABY-SITTERS CLUB PORTRAIT COLLECTION

Martin, Ann M.
SCHOLASTIC
GRADES 4–7 ◆ A/R
REAL LIFE

Vignettes from other books provide insight into the personality and behavior of each girl.

1. Stacey's Book ◆ 1994
2. Claudia's Book ◆ 1995
3. Dawn's Book ◆ 1995
4. Kristy's Book ◆ 1996
5. Mary Anne's Book ◆ 1996
6. Abby's Book ◆ 1997

BABY-SITTERS CLUB SUPER SPECIALS

Martin, Ann M.
SCHOLASTIC
GRADES 4–7 ◆ A/R
REAL LIFE

The Super Specials are about twice as long as the regular Baby-Sitters Club books and deal with events such as weddings or a group visit to see Dawn when she moves to California. The books are narrated by all five girls, taking different chapters in turn. There are also special Super Chillers books.

1. Baby-Sitters on Board! ◆ 1988
2. Baby-Sitters' Summer Vacation ◆ 1989
3. Baby-Sitters' Winter Vacation ◆ 1989
4. Baby-Sitters' Island Adventure ◆ 1990

5. California Girls! ◆ 1990
6. New York, New York! ◆ 1991
7. Snowbound ◆ 1991
8. Baby-Sitters at Shadow Lake ◆ 1992
9. Starring the Baby-Sitters Club ◆ 1992
10. Sea City, Here We Come! ◆ 1993
11. The Baby-Sitters Remember ◆ 1994
12. Here Come the Bridesmaids ◆ 1994
13. Aloha, Baby-Sitters! ◆ 1996
14. BSC in the USA ◆ 1997
15. Baby-Sitters' European Vacation ◆ 1998

BAD GIRLS

Voigt, Cynthia
SCHOLASTIC; ATHENEUM
GRADES 6–9 ◆ A/R
HUMOR | REAL LIFE

When this series starts, Michelle and Margalo are in fifth grade. They are both new and feel like outsiders. They team up and get a reputation for being aggressive. They are high-spirited girls whose humorous antics will appeal to many readers. By the time the girls are 14 and in the eighth grade (in *Bad Girls in Love*), they are still best friends and still outsiders. Then, they each fall in love. These books capture the pace, language, issues, and emotions of early adolescents.

1. Bad Girls ◆ 1996
2. Bad, Badder, Baddest ◆ 1999
3. It's Not Easy Being Bad ◆ 2000
4. Bad Girls in Love ◆ 2002

BAKER STREET IRREGULARS

Dicks, Terrance
DUTTON
GRADES 4–7
MYSTERY

Four London youngsters recover a lost painting and become known as "The Baker Street Irregulars" after Sherlock Holmes's gang of street kids. The youngest, Mickey, welcomes all the attention and publicity and wants to solve another crime. Dan, the leader of the group, and

Jeff, the one with the most common sense, are reluctant to get involved again. When a crime wave hits their neighborhood, Dan, Jeff, and Mickey, along with their friend Liz, find themselves drawn in almost in spite of themselves. Dan is capable of drawing conclusions by intuitive leaps, Jeff sometimes plays the Dr. Watson role, and Liz and Mickey are fearless in dangerous situations. Don, a young police detective, comes to rely on their expertise as the young quartet takes on more cases. Lots of action and fairly complex clues for young mystery fans.

1. The Case of the Missing Masterpiece ◆ 1978
2. The Case of the Fagin File ◆ 1978
3. The Case of the Blackmail Boys ◆ 1979
4. The Case of the Cinema Swindle ◆ 1980
5. The Case of the Ghost Grabbers ◆ 1981
6. The Case of the Cop Catchers ◆ 1981
7. The Case of the Disappearing Diplomat ◆ 1986
8. The Case of the Comic Crooks ◆ 1986
9. The Case of the Haunted Holiday ◆ 1987
10. The Case of the Criminal Computer ◆ 1987

BALLAD

McCrumb, Sharyn
DUTTON
GRADES 10–12
MYSTERY

Appalachia and County Sheriff Arrowwood are central characters in this series of mysteries that are rich in atmosphere and suspense. In the first book, a famous 1960s folksinger comes home to Hamelin, Tennessee, 20 years later in search of peace and inspiration. Instead she is threatened and a young woman who bears a resemblance to her younger self is murdered. A 20-year high school reunion taking place in the background and echoes of Vietnam add to the story. In the second book, the sheriff investigates the murder of four members of a single family and suicide of a fifth.

1. If Ever I Return, Pretty Peggy-O ◆ 1990
2. The Hangman's Beautiful Daughter ◆ 1993
3. She Walks These Hills ◆ 1994
4. The Rosewood Casket ◆ 1996
5. The Ballad of Frankie Silver ◆ 1998
6. The Songcatcher ◆ 2001
7. Ghost Riders ◆ 2003

BARDIC VOICES

Lackey, Mercedes
BAEN
GRADES 10–12 ◆ A/R
FANTASY

Music and magic are at the core of this series. In the first book, Rune is an outsider with a musical gift. The Bardic Guild offers her a way out of the poverty of life in her village. Supernatural elements including ghosts, mages, and elves are apparent as the characters cope with medieval life. *Free Bards* is a compilation of the first three books.

1. The Lark and the Wren ◆ 1991
2. The Robin and the Kestrel ◆ 1993
3. The Eagle and the Nightingales ◆ 1995
4. Four and Twenty Blackbirds ◆ 1997

THE BARTIMAEUS TRILOGY

Stroud, Jonathan
HYPERION/MIRAMAX KIDS
GRADES 5–9 ◆ A/R
FANTASY

Bartimaeus is a djinn (genie) called forth by a 10-year-old magician, Nathaniel. Nathaniel orders Bartimaeus to steal the Amulet of Samarkand from Simon Lovelace. In the second book, Nathaniel is 14 and is responsible for capturing members of the Resistance. Readers will be intrigued by this magical fantasy series.

1. The Amulet of Samarkand ◆ 2003
2. The Golem's Eye ◆ 2004

BASEBALL CARD ADVENTURES

Gutman, Dan
HARPERCOLLINS
GRADES 4–8 ◆ A/R
FANTASY | RECREATION

Joe Stoshack, 12, travels back through time to meet star baseball players of the past. The first adventure happens when Joe finds a valuable Honus Wagner card. That night, Honus Wagner appears in Joe's bedroom and they time-travel to the 1909 World Series. In the Babe Ruth story, Joe's dad comes too. They plan to have Babe Ruth autograph items to take back to the present and sell, but their plans hit a snag.

1. Honus and Me ◆ 1997
2. Jackie and Me ◆ 1999
3. Babe and Me ◆ 2000
4. Shoeless Joe and Me ◆ 2002
5. Mickey and Me ◆ 2003
6. Abner and Me ◆ 2005

BEACON STREET GIRLS

Bryant, Annie
B'TWEEN PRODUCTIONS
GRADES 6–9
REAL LIFE

Char is just feeling settled in seventh grade. She has a new group of friends who call themselves the Beacon Street Girls. But now Char's father may move the family to England.

1. Worst Enemies/Best Friends ◆ 2004
2. Bad News/Good News ◆ 2004
3. Letters from the Heart ◆ 2004
4. Out of Bounds ◆ 2004

THE BELGARIAD

Eddings, David
BALLANTINE
GRADES 10–12 ◆ A/R
FANTASY

Garion's journey from farm boy to sorcerer is explored in this series set in a mythical land. Garion disdains magic and sorcery. On a quest for the stolen Orb, he begins to realize his powers. Belgarath, a sorcerer, and his daughter Polgara also search for the Orb. As the series continues, Garion becomes king and must face the evil God Torak. The Malloreon series continues the story of Garion. There is a prequel to both series, *Belgarath the Sorcerer* (1995), and a final volume to both, *Polgara the Sorceress* (1997).

1. Pawn of Prophecy ◆ 1982

2. Queen of Sorcery ◆ 1982
3. Magician's Gambit ◆ 1983
4. Castle of Wizardry ◆ 1984
5. Enchanters' End Game ◆ 1984

BELLES OF LORDSBURG

Bly, Stephen
CROSSWAY BOOKS
GRADES 9–12
HISTORICAL | VALUES

This is a Christian western series. In the first book, Grace Denison runs away from her senator father's home and finds adventure and romance in a New Mexico town. In *The Outlaw's Twin Sister*, friends of a renegade try to persuade his twin sister to help him escape from jail.

1. The Senator's Other Daughter ◆ 2001
2. The General's Notorious Widow ◆ 2001
3. The Outlaw's Twin Sister ◆ 2002

BELLTOWN MYSTERY

Murphy, T. M.
J. N. TOWNSEND PUBLISHING
GRADES 6–9
MYSTERY

Orville Jacques, 16, is a teen detective who becomes involved in mysteries on Cape Cod. In one book, Orville wonders if one elderly woman's death was really an accident. In another book, he travels to Ireland and finds clues that may lead to a missing treasure. There are some romantic moments as well as detailed crime descriptions. The books listed here are reissues.

1. The Secrets of Belltown ◆ 2001
2. The Secrets of Cranberry Beach ◆ 2001
3. The Secrets of Cain's Castle ◆ 2001
4. The Secrets of Pilgrim Pond ◆ 2001
5. The Secrets of Code Z ◆ 2001
6. The Secrets of the Twisted Cross ◆ 2002

BELOVED DEARLY

Cooney, Doug
SIMON & SCHUSTER
GRADES 4–7
HUMOR

Ernie Castellano, 12, has lots of ideas. One is providing funeral services for pets. His friends help—Dusty designs coffins, Swimming Pool cries for the deceased, and so forth. When Ernie suffers a loss and needs to use the services of his own business, he starts to see things differently. In the second book, Ernie and the gang get involved in a baseball team and a charm school.

1. The Beloved Dearly ◆ 2001
2. I Know Who Likes You ◆ 2004

BERNIE MAGRUDER (*see also* Bessledorf Hotel)

Naylor, Phyllis Reynolds
ATHENEUM; ALADDIN
GRADES 4–7 ◆ A/R
FAMILY LIFE | HUMOR | MYSTERY

The Magruder family's exploits described in the Bessledorf Hotel series are repackaged and reissued in this series.

1. Bernie Magruder and the Haunted Hotel ◆ 2001
2. Bernie Magruder and the Case of the Big Stink ◆ 2001
3. Bernie Magruder and the Disappearing Bodies ◆ 2001
4. Bernie Magruder and the Bus Station Blow Up ◆ 2001
5. Bernie Magruder and the Pirate's Treasure ◆ 2001
6. Bernie Magruder and the Parachute Peril ◆ 2001
7. Bernie Magruder and the Drive-Thru Funeral Parlor ◆ 2003
8. Bernie Magruder and the Bats in the Belfry ◆ 2003

BERSERKER

Saberhagen, Fred
BALLANTINE
GRADES 9–12
SCIENCE FICTION

Berserkers are life-destroying machines that are found throughout the galaxy. In *Berserker Prime*, these robots arrive just as the ruler of the Twin Planets of Prairie and Timber is deciding the fate of Huvean hostages. But do these hostages hold the secret to defeating the Berserkers?

1. Berserker ◆ 1967
2. Brother Assassin ◆ 1969
3. Berserker's Planet ◆ 1975
4. Berserker Man ◆ 1979
5. The Ultimate Enemy ◆ 1979
6. Berserker Wars ◆ 1981
7. Berserker Base ◆ 1985
8. The Berserker Throne ◆ 1985
9. Berserker: Blue Death ◆ 1985
10. The Berserker Attack ◆ 1987
11. Berserker Lies ◆ 1991
12. Berserker Kill ◆ 1993
13. Berserker Wars ◆ 1994
14. Berserker Fury ◆ 1997
15. Berserkers: The Beginning ◆ 1998
16. Shiva in Steel ◆ 1998
17. Berserker's Star ◆ 2003
18. Berserker Prime ◆ 2004
19. Rogue Berserker ◆ 2005

BESSLEDORF HOTEL (*see also* Bernie Magruder)

Naylor, Phyllis Reynolds
SIMON & SCHUSTER
GRADES 5–7 ◆ A/R
FAMILY LIFE | HUMOR | MYSTERY

The Magruder family lives in an apartment at the Bessledorf Hotel. The father, Theodore, manages the hotel. Alma helps out, but she dreams of writing romance novels. Son Joseph goes to veterinary college, and daughter Delores works at a parachute factory. Bernie likes to solve mysteries, and the old hotel provides plenty of them to solve. A ghost appears to Bernie in one book and he must figure out what it wants so that it will rest in peace.

1. The Mad Gasser of Bessledorf Street ◆ 1983
2. The Bodies in the Bessledorf Hotel ◆ 1986
3. Bernie and the Bessledorf Ghost ◆ 1990
4. The Face in the Bessledorf Funeral Parlor ◆ 1993
5. The Bomb in the Bessledorf Bus Depot ◆ 1996

6. The Treasure of Bessledorf Hill ◆ 1997
7. Peril in the Bessledorf Parachute Factory ◆ 1999

BEVERLY HILLS, 90210

Various authors
HARPERCOLLINS
GRADES 7–10
REAL LIFE

Beverly Hills, 90210 was a popular 1990s television series that focused on teen problems. The show is still seen on cable channels, which keeps teens interested in these books.

1. Beverly Hills, 90210 (Gilden, Mel) ◆ 1991
2. Exposed! (Mills, Bart) ◆ 1991
3. No Secrets (Gilden, Mel) ◆ 1992
4. Which Way to the Beach? (Gilden, Mel) ◆ 1992
5. Fantasies (Smith, K. T.) ◆ 1992
6. 'Tis the Season (Gilden, Mel) ◆ 1992
7. Two Hearts (Gilden, Mel) ◆ 1993
8. Where the Boys Are (Gilden, Mel) ◆ 1993
9. More than Words (Gilden, Mel) ◆ 1993
10. Summer Love (Gilden, Mel) ◆ 1993
11. Senior Year (Gilden, Mel) ◆ 1993
12. Graduation Day (Gilden, Mel) ◆ 1994
13. College Bound (Gilden, Mel) ◆ 1994

BINGO BROWN

Byars, Betsy
VIKING
GRADES 4–7
HUMOR | REAL LIFE

Bingo Brown is in sixth grade at the beginning of this series and is just discovering "mixed-sex conversations." He falls in and out of love many times but ends up being in love with Melissa. He is devastated when she moves to Oklahoma. That summer, he racks up a huge phone bill calling her and is pursued by her best friend. His parents go through a crisis of their own when his mother discovers she is pregnant. As Bingo enters seventh grade, he has a new baby brother, and is an acknowledged authority on romance among his friends.

1. The Burning Questions of Bingo Brown ◆ 1988
2. Bingo Brown and the Language of Love ◆ 1989
3. Bingo Brown, Gypsy Lover ◆ 1990
4. Bingo Brown's Guide to Romance ◆ 1992

BIONICLE ADVENTURES

Farshtey, Greg

SCHOLASTIC

GRADES 4–7 ◆ A/R

FANTASY

Six Toas guard the city of Metru Nui. These warriors protect the Matoran. When the city is attacked, the Toa face unexpected dangers. There are related items including a sticker book, an *Official Guide to Bionicles*, and comic books. These stories are based on LEGO action figures.

1. Mystery of Metru Nui ◆ 2004
2. Trial by Fire ◆ 2004
3. Darkness Below ◆ 2004
4. Legends of Metru Nui ◆ 2004
5. Voyage of Fear ◆ 2004
6. Maze of Shadows ◆ 2004

BIONICLE CHRONICLES

Various authors

SCHOLASTIC

GRADES 4–7 ◆ A/R

FANTASY

Mata Nui is an ancient land that has been peaceful until Makuta brings fear and darkness. Who will face the darkness? Six Toa, mighty warriors, are destined to rescue the land of Mata Nui. The Bionicle Chronicles describe the arrival of the Toa and their battles. Related items include a sticker book, an *Official Guide to Bionicles*, and comic books. These stories are based on LEGO action figures.

1. Tale of the Toa (Hapka, C. A.) ◆ 2003
2. Beware the Bohrok (Hapka, C. A.) ◆ 2003
3. Makuta's Revenge (Hapka, C. A.) ◆ 2003
4. Tales of the Masks (Farshtey, Greg) ◆ 2003

THE BITTERBYNDE

Dart-Thornton, Cecilia
WARNER
GRADES 10–12
FANTASY

A poor mute child named Imrhein escapes from a miserable life inside the Isse Tower, learns handspeech, and sets out to learn about her origins. In the second book, she regains the power of speech and her beauty even as she uncovers secrets and is pursued by dark forces. This is a rich fantasy full of folklore and tall tales.

1. The Ill-Made Mute ◆ 2001
2. The Lady of the Sorrows ◆ 2002
3. The Battle of Evernight ◆ 2003

BLACK BOOK (DIARY OF A TEENAGE STUD)

Black, Jonah
AVON
GRADES 8–12
HUMOR | REAL LIFE

Jonah Black is repeating eleventh grade and living with his mother in Pompano Beach, Florida. (That boarding school in Pennsylvania just didn't work out). Through his journal, Jonah describes his life. His mother is a sex expert who has written a popular book. The girl he has a crush on is attracted to a jerk. Jonah's reflections are regularly interrupted by fantasies, often sexual imaginings about Sophie, a girlfriend he left in Pennsylvania.

1. Volume 1: Girls, Girls, Girls ◆ 2001
2. Volume 2: Stop, Don't Stop ◆ 2001
3. Volume 3: Run, Jonah, Run ◆ 2001
4. Volume 4: Faster, Faster, Faster ◆ 2002

THE BLACK MAGICIAN TRILOGY

Canavan, Trudi
EOS
GRADES 10–12
FANTASY

The magicians of Imardin assemble yearly to cleanse the city of undesirable elements. Sonea stands up to them and discovers her own magical powers. She is taken to the magicians' guild to improve her skills. At the guild, she is a novice, but she gets support from High Lord Akkarin, who has his own secret.

1. The Magicians' Guild ◆ 2004
2. The Novice ◆ 2004
3. The High Lord ◆ 2004

BLACK STALLION

Farley, Walter
RANDOM HOUSE
GRADES 5–8 ◆ A/R
ADVENTURE

On his way home from visiting his missionary uncle, Alec is shipwrecked along with a wild black stallion. They are rescued, and Alec takes the horse back to New York and boards him at a nearby farm to be trained by Henry Dailey. Because there are no official papers on "the Black," Alec cannot enter him in races. However, in a special race for the fastest horse in the country, Alec and "the Black" earn the respect they deserve. In another book, Alec travels to Arabia to research the claim of a man who is trying to take away his horse. The series continues as the stallion sires foals that Alec and Henry train and race. Walter Farley wrote the early books in the series. Walter and Steven Farley wrote *The Young Black Stallion*, and Steven Farley is continuing the series. The Island Stallion series features another young man and a horse; the Young Black Stallion series by Steven Farley also features Alec Ramsey.

1. The Black Stallion ◆ 1941
2. The Black Stallion Returns ◆ 1945
3. Son of the Black Stallion ◆ 1947
4. The Black Stallion and Satan ◆ 1949
5. The Blood Bay Colt (retitled The Black Stallion's Blood Bay Colt) ◆ 1950
6. The Black Stallion's Filly ◆ 1952
7. The Black Stallion Revolts ◆ 1953
8. The Black Stallion's Sulky Colt ◆ 1954
9. The Black Stallion's Courage ◆ 1956
10. The Black Stallion Mystery ◆ 1957
11. The Black Stallion and Flame ◆ 1960
12. The Black Stallion Challenged ◆ 1964

13. The Black Stallion's Ghost ◆ 1969
14. The Black Stallion and the Girl ◆ 1971
15. The Black Stallion Legend ◆ 1983
16. The Young Black Stallion (Farley, Walter, and Steven Farley) ◆ 1989
17. The Black Stallion's Shadow (Farley, Steven) ◆ 1996

BLACK STALLION: YOUNG BLACK STALLION

Farley, Steven
RANDOM HOUSE
GRADES 5–8
REAL LIFE

Danielle Connor, 13, is upset that Alec Ramsay has turned her family's farm into a Thoroughbred training center. Her own horse, Redman, has been sold and Danielle now works in the stables that her family owned.

1. The Promise ◆ 1998
2. A Horse Called Raven ◆ 1998
3. The Homecoming ◆ 1999
4. Wild Spirit ◆ 1999
5. The Yearling ◆ 1999
6. Hard Lessons ◆ 1999

BLOOD OF THE GODDESS

Dalkey, Kara
TOR
GRADES 10–12
FANTASY

A historical fantasy in which a 16th-century English apothecary named Thomas Chinnery discovers in the Portuguese colony of Goa, in India, a powder that can revive the dead. In the sequel, Chinnery takes a dangerous journey deep into the interior in search of the source of this powder. Fact, lore, magic, and religious tenets are interwoven in these books.

1. Goa ◆ 1996
2. Bijapur ◆ 1997
3. Bhagavati ◆ 1998

BLOSSOM CULP

Peck, Richard

DELL

GRADES 5–7 ◆ A/R

FANTASY | MYSTERY

Blossom Culp lives on the wrong side of the tracks in a small midwestern town at the turn of the century. Her mother is a fortune teller, who is jealous when it seems that Blossom has "the gift." Alexander, the son of a wealthy and prominent family, lives right across the tracks, and his barn is right in Blossom's back yard. The barn is inhabited by a ghost that Blossom can see. Alexander is reluctantly drawn into this adventure, only the first of many inspired by Blossom's gift. Blossom's contacts with the dead bring her fame and a certain social standing in the town. She moves into her high school years and has more encounters with the beyond, including an Egyptian princess and time travel 70 years into the future.

1. The Ghost Belonged to Me ◆ 1975
2. Ghosts I Have Been ◆ 1977
3. The Dreadful Future of Blossom Culp ◆ 1983
4. Blossom Culp and the Sleep of Death ◆ 1986

THE BLOSSOM FAMILY

Byars, Betsy

DELL

GRADES 4–7 ◆ A/R

FAMILY LIFE | HUMOR

Maggie, Junior, and Vern Blossom live with their mother, Vicki, and their grandfather, Pap. Their father, Cotton, was killed riding a bull in the rodeo when the children were small. Vicki is a trick rider and goes out on the rodeo circuit, leaving the children behind with Pap in a rural section of the eastern United States. They make friends with a lady who lives a hermit's life in a cave. One of the boys almost drowns making a raft to float on the river. Two of the children break into prison when Pap is arrested, and Maggie makes her debut in trick riding. In each book, the stories of all the family members intersect.

1. The Not-Just-Anybody Family ◆ 1986
2. The Blossoms Meet the Vulture Lady ◆ 1986
3. The Blossoms and the Green Phantom ◆ 1987
4. A Blossom Promise ◆ 1987
5. Wanted—Mud Blossom ◆ 1991

BLUE AVENGER

Howe, Norma
HOLT
GRADES 7–10 ◆ A/R
REAL LIFE

David Schumacher likes to draw superhero comics. On his sixteenth birthday, he decides to stop drawing and take action. He creates a costume and names himself the Blue Avenger—and he really does bring about changes. Teens frustrated by social inequities will appreciate the way David tries to make a difference in the world.

1. The Adventures of the Blue Avenger ◆ 1999
2. Blue Avenger Cracks the Code ◆ 2000
3. Blue Avenger and the Theory of Everything ◆ 2002

BLUE-EYED SON TRILOGY

Lynch, Chris
HARPERCOLLINS
GRADES 7–10
REAL LIFE

Living on the mean streets of Boston's Irish American community, Mick, 15, faces a world of alcoholism, abuse, and violence. He feels alienated in his dysfunctional family. His father is aggressive, his mother is weak, and his older brother is a brutally cruel bully.

1. Mick ◆ 1996
2. Blood Relations ◆ 1996
3. Dog Eat Dog ◆ 1996

BODY OF EVIDENCE

Various authors
SIMON & SCHUSTER
GRADES 9–12 ◆ A/R
MYSTERY

Jenna Blake is attending Somerset University near Boston. Her interests in medicine (her mother is a doctor) and in crime (her father is a criminologist) lead her to take a job in the medical examiner's office. This job puts her in danger. Mysteries include a dead congressional aide whose diseased brain contains insect larvae, a series of ritual killings, and "zombie crimes."

1. Body Bags (Golden, Christopher) ◆ 1999
2. Thief of Hearts (Golden, Christopher) ◆ 1999
3. Soul Survivor (Golden, Christopher) ◆ 1999
4. Meets the Eye (Golden, Christopher) ◆ 2000
5. Head Games (Golden, Christopher) ◆ 2000
6. Skin Deep (Golden, Christopher) ◆ 2000
7. Burning Bones (Golden, Christopher, and Rick Hautala) ◆ 2001
8. Brain Trust (Golden, Christopher, and Rick Hautala) ◆ 2001
9. Last Breath (Golden, Christopher, and Rick Hautala) ◆ 2004

BONE

Smith, Jeff
CARTOON BOOKS
GRADES 6–10
FANTASY

This graphic novel series describes the antics of the three Bone cousins. Fone Bone is the hero, Phoney Bone is a schemer, and Smiley Bone is silly. After they are run out of Boneville, they enter a world of dragons and monsters. They meet the beautiful Thorn and begin adventures to find their destiny. The nine books listed are three trilogies.

1. Out from Boneville ◆ 1996
2. The Great Cow Race ◆ 1996
3. Eyes of the Storm ◆ 1997
4. The Dragonslayer ◆ 1998
5. Rock Jaw, Master of the Eastern Border ◆ 1998
6. Old Man's Cave ◆ 1999
7. Ghost Circles ◆ 2001
8. Treasure Hunters ◆ 2004
9. Crown of Horns ◆ 2004

BONE CHILLERS

Haynes, Betsy
HARPERCOLLINS
GRADES 5–8 ◆ A/R
HORROR I HUMOR

The covers of these books make statements like "Bone Chillers: They'll make your skin crawl!" and "Bone Chillers: They'll scare the words right out of your mouth!" With spooky situations and creepy creatures, this series is similar to others in the horror genre. The books feature different characters. Azie Appleton always tells lies until one day her claim about giant termites comes true. Isabella Richmond thinks that gargoyles are kidnapping neighborhood kids. Some books are not just spooky but gross: Jeremy Wilson sneezes and his mucus becomes a slimy green glob. Readers who want horror and humor will devour this series.

1. Beware the Shopping Mall! ◆ 1994
2. Little Pet Shop of Horrors ◆ 1994
3. Back to School ◆ 1994
4. Frankenturkey ◆ 1994
5. Strange Brew ◆ 1995
6. Teacher Creature ◆ 1995
7. Frankenturkey ◆ 1995
8. Welcome to Alien Inn ◆ 1995
9. Attack of the Killer Ants ◆ 1996
10. Slime Time ◆ 1996
11. Toilet Terror ◆ 1996
12. Night of the Living Clay ◆ 1996
13. The Thing Under the Bed ◆ 1997
14. A Terminal Case of the Uglies ◆ 1997
15. Tiki Doll of Doom ◆ 1997
16. The Queen of the Gargoyles ◆ 1997
17. Why I Quit the Baby-Sitter's Club ◆ 1997
18. blowtorch@psycho.com ◆ 1997
19. The Night Squawker ◆ 1997
20. Scare Bear ◆ 1997
21. The Dog Ate My Homework ◆ 1997
22. Killer Clown of Kings County ◆ 1998
23. Romeo and Ghouliette ◆ 1998

BONNETS AND BUGLES

Morris, Gilbert
MOODY PRESS
GRADES 5–7 ◆ A/R
HISTORICAL | VALUES

The Civil War splits neighbors and friends and provides opportunities for spiritual growth for five young people and their families. Tom and Jeff and their parents decide to move to Virginia and fight for the Confederacy, leaving Leah and Sarah and their parents in Kentucky as Union sympathizers. Mrs. Majors dies giving birth to Esther, and, with all the men off to war, there is no one to care for the baby. They turn to the Carters, who take her in to raise as their own. Throughout the course of the war, Jeff is a drummer boy and the other two boys are soldiers seeing action in major battles. They manage to get back to the girls often as Jeff courts Leah and Tom and Sarah become engaged. Tom loses his leg in Gettysburg and comes close to losing his faith in God, but the others help him back to spiritual health.

1. Drummer Boy at Bull Run ◆ 1995
2. Yankee Belles in Dixie ◆ 1995
3. The Secret of Richmond Manor ◆ 1995
4. The Soldier Boy's Discovery ◆ 1996
5. Blockade Runner ◆ 1996
6. The Gallant Boys of Gettysburg ◆ 1996
7. The Battle of Lookout Mountain ◆ 1996
8. Encounter at Cold Harbor ◆ 1997
9. Fire over Atlanta ◆ 1997
10. Bring the Boys Home ◆ 1997

BOOK OF THE GODS

Saberhagen, Fred
TOR
GRADES 10–12
FANTASY

Characters from Greek and Norse (*Gods of Fire and Thunder*) mythology are revisited in these action-packed books written for adults.

1. The Face of Apollo ◆ 1998
2. Ariadne's Web ◆ 2000
3. The Arms of Hercules ◆ 2000
4. God of the Golden Fleece ◆ 2001
5. Gods of Fire and Thunder ◆ 2002

BOOK OF WORDS

Jones, J. V.
WARNER
GRADES 10–12
FANTASY

Melliandra, a young noblewoman rejecting an evil prince's offer of marriage, and a baker's apprentice named Jack who has magical powers run away from Castle Harvell. When the prince seizes power, these two become the only hope for the people of the land and Jack must test the strength of his magic.

1. The Baker's Boy ◆ 1995
2. A Man Betrayed ◆ 1996
3. Master and Fool ◆ 1996

BOOKS OF MAGIC

Jablonski, Carla
HARPERCOLLINS
GRADES 9–12 ◆ A/R
FANTASY

Tim Hunter, 13, seems like a regular teenager but he is not. Four strangers lead him toward his destiny as a wizard, perhaps the greatest wizard ever. These books are based on the graphic novel series developed by Neil Gaiman and John Bolton.

1. The Invitation ◆ 2003
2. Bindings ◆ 2003
3. The Children's Crusade ◆ 2003
4. Consequences ◆ 2004
5. Lost Places ◆ 2004
6. Reckonings ◆ 2004

BORDERLANDS

Shetterly, Will
HARCOURT; TOR
GRADES 8–12 ◆ A/R
FANTASY

Bordertown lies on the line between human and faerie worlds, and attracts misfits and runaways from both. Ron arrives in Bordertown while searching for his brother Tony and finds a kind of home among the strange inhabitants of Castle Pup. However, he has to confront his own demons and the spell that has turned him into Wolfboy. Fast-paced action continues throughout this cyberpunk fantasy as Wolfboy seeks to protect an orphan elf. *Finder: A Novel of the Borderlands* by Emma Bull (Tor, 1994), written for adults, is also set in Bordertown. There are also collections of short stories written by various authors.

1. Elsewhere ◆ 1991
2. Nevernever ◆ 1993

BOSTON JANE

Holm, Jennifer L.
HARPERCOLLINS
GRADES 7–10 ◆ A/R
HISTORICAL

Jane Peck, 16, finds that her lessons in manners and polite society in Boston have not prepared her for a long sea voyage or life on the frontier in 1854. She is traveling to Washington Territory to marry William, her father's former apprentice. That relationship becomes strained by William's attitudes toward the native people and by Jane's growing independence.

1. Boston Jane: An Adventure ◆ 2001
2. Boston Jane: Wilderness Days ◆ 2002
3. Boston Jane: The Claim ◆ 2004

BRATZ

Various authors
GROSSET & DUNLAP
GRADES 6–9 ◆ A/R
HUMOR | REAL LIFE

'Tweens will enjoy the activities of Yasmin, Cloe, Jade and Sasha. The girls love fashion, dancing, parties, and fun. Sometimes, they even focus on school. In one book, the Homecoming Dance is coming and the girls are trapped in the mall. In another book, Cloe's artistic talent brings her some special attention. There are related materials with stickers and activities, like a guide to slumber party ideas. These are breezy books with lots of attitude.

1. Keepin' It Real: Bratz, the Video (O'Connor, Charles) ◆ 2004
2. Model Friendship (Krulik, Nancy) ◆ 2004
3. All-Night Mall Party! (O'Connor, Charles) ◆ 2004
4. Will Work for Fashion (Krulik, Nancy) ◆ 2004

THE BREADWINNER TRILOGY

Ellis, Deborah
GROUNDWOOD BOOKS
GRADES 6–9 ◆ A/R
REAL LIFE

Set in Afghanistan during the rule of the Taliban, these books describe the experiences of a young girl, Parvana. Beginning when she is 11, Parvana watches as her father is arrested. To earn money for her family, she disguises herself as a boy. Her family moves away and Parvana is reunited with her father, only to have him die. With another girl who has been disguised, Shauzia, Parvana goes on a quest to find her family. The third book in the trilogy focuses on Shauzia, 14, and her experiences in an Afghan refugee camp.

1. The Breadwinner ◆ 2001
2. Parvana's Journey ◆ 2002
3. Mud City ◆ 2003

BRIAN ROBESON

Paulsen, Gary
DELACORTE
GRADES 4–8
ADVENTURE | REAL LIFE

In *Hatchet*, 13-year-old Brian Robeson is stranded in the Canadian wilderness after a plane crash. He struggles to survive before being rescued just as winter approaches. *The River* features Brian returning to the site of his adventure with a psychologist, Derek Holtzer, who plans to observe and record the experience. Their trip turns into another struggle to survive. *Brian's Winter* is a continuation of *Hatchet*, but with the premise that Brian is not rescued before winter arrives and must struggle to survive even harsher circumstances. Fast-paced action—told in short, direct sentences—could appeal to reluctant readers. A related book is *Guts: The True Stories Behind Hatchet and the Brian Books* (2001).

1. Hatchet ◆ 1987
2. Brian's Return ◆ 1989
3. The River ◆ 1991
4. Brian's Winter ◆ 1996
5. Brian's Hunt ◆ 2004

BRIDES OF WILDCAT COUNTY

Watson, Jude
SIMON/ALADDIN
GRADES 7–10
REAL LIFE

This series features women who take chances to find love and independence. One woman leaves an unhappy arranged marriage. In *Audacious*, Ivy escapes from her father's misfortunes in Maine and becomes a teacher in a frontier school in Wildcat County, California. These books combine romance with a Wild West setting.

1. Dangerous: Savannah's Story ◆ 1995
2. Scandalous: Eden's Story ◆ 1996
3. Audacious: Ivy's Story ◆ 1995
4. Impetuous: Mattie's Story ◆ 1995
5. Tempestuous: Opal's Story ◆ 1996

BRIO GIRLS

Johnson, Lissa Halls
BETHANY HOUSE
GRADES 6–10 ◆ A/R
REAL LIFE | VALUES

Jacie, Solana, Hannah, and Becca are in high school in Colorado. Three of the girls are Christian and their faith plays an important part in their dealings with family and friends. In *Fast Forward to Normal*, Becca is not happy that her parents plan to adopt a Guatemalan boy. In *Croutons for Breakfast*, Hannah and Jacie are on a mission trip to Venezuela and question God's plans for them.

1. Stuck in the Sky ◆ 2001
2. Fast Forward to Normal ◆ 2001
3. Opportunity Knocks Twice ◆ 2002
4. Double Exposure ◆ 2002
5. Good-Bye to All That ◆ 2002
6. Grasping at Moonbeams ◆ 2002
7. Croutons for Breakfast ◆ 2003
8. No Lifeguard on Duty ◆ 2003
9. Dragonfly on My Shoulder ◆ 2003
10. Going Crazy Till Wednesday ◆ 2003

THE BROADWAY BALLPLAYERS

Holohan, Maureen
ALADDIN
GRADES 4–7 ◆ A/R
RECREATION

Five girls who live on Broadway Avenue participate in a variety of sports. As in the Matt Christopher books, there are many dramatic moments involving injuries, family issues, jealousy, and "making the team." Each book features a different girl—Molly, Penny, Rosie, Wil, and Angel. In one book, Angel's feet are hurting but she won't tell anyone because she does not want to be left out of the big race. Sports fans will enjoy the action.

1. Friday Nights, by Molly ◆ 1998
2. Everybody's Favorite, by Penny ◆ 1998
3. Left Out, by Rosie ◆ 1998
4. Sideline Blues, by Wil ◆ 1998
5. Don't Stop, by Angel ◆ 1998
6. Ice Cold, by Molly ◆ 1999
7. Catch Shorty, by Rosie ◆ 1999

BROKEN SKY

Wooding, Chris

SCHOLASTIC

GRADES 6–9

FANTASY

Ryushi is a prisoner. The Fane Aracq are trying to get him to reveal a secret that will allow Princess Aurin to defeat his people.

1. Broken Sky # 1 ◆ 2001
2. Broken Sky # 2 ◆ 2001
3. Broken Sky # 3 ◆ 2001
4. Broken Sky # 4 ◆ 2001
5. Broken Sky # 5 ◆ 2001
6. Broken Sky # 6 ◆ 2001
7. Broken Sky # 7 ◆ 2001

BROMELIAD

Pratchett, Terry

DELACORTE

GRADES 6–9 ◆ A/R

FANTASY

A tiny race of beings called nomes came from outer space to earth centuries ago and showed man how to use metal. Then they forgot everything they knew. Some of them ended up living in the floorboards of a department store and developed a religion based on the founders of the store. "Outside" is a myth, they believe, and the whole universe is the store. Then one day everything changes, when nomes from the Outside show up carrying the Thing, the on-board computer from the spaceship. Fans of all kinds of fantasy will love the satire and inventiveness of this series.

1. Truckers ◆ 1989
2. Diggers: The Second Book of the Bromeliad ◆ 1992
3. Wings: The Last Book of the Bromeliad ◆ 1991

BRUNO AND BOOTS

Korman, Gordon

SCHOLASTIC

GRADES 6–8 ◆ A/R

HUMOR

Bruno and Boots are pranksters at an exclusive boys' boarding school in Canada. They replace the Canadian flag with the flag of Malbonia and steal a rival school's mascot. The school's headmaster, Mr. Sturgeon ("The Fish"), knows they are the culprits and decides to separate them. But when they manage to rescue the son of the Malbonian ambassador, who is stuck in a tree in a hot-air balloon, the boys are allowed to room together again. In their further adventures, they drive "The Fish" crazy, delight their classmates, and plan mayhem with the girls from the finishing school across the street.

1. This Can't Be Happening at Macdonald Hall! ◆ 1990
2. Beware the Fish! ◆ 1991
3. The Zucchini Warriors ◆ 1991
4. Go Jump in the Pool ◆ 1991
5. Macdonald Hall Goes Hollywood ◆ 1991
6. Something Fishy at Macdonald Hall ◆ 1995

BUFFY THE VAMPIRE SLAYER

Various authors

ARCHWAY/POCKET BOOKS

GRADES 6–10

ADVENTURE | HORROR

Buffy the Vampire Slayer has an intensely loyal following among preteens and adolescents who enjoy violent encounters involving vampires and their victims. Buffy Summers leads a group of high school friends to try to destroy the creatures that have targeted Sunnydale. These books parallel some of the episodes from the television series by the same name. The teens, aided by Giles, the school librarian, try to stop the zombies, vampires, and other ghouls. This is not for the faint-hearted. Buffy uses her wits and her physical skills to protect her friends and the world.

BUFFY THE VAMPIRE SLAYER—NUMBERED TITLES

1. The Harvest (Cusick, Richie Tankersley) ◆ 1997
2. Halloween Rain (Golden, Christopher, and Nancy Holder) ◆ 1997
3. Coyote Moon (Vornholt, John) ◆ 1998
4. The Night of the Living Rerun (Cover, Arthur) ◆ 1998
5. Blooded (Golden, Christopher, and Nancy Holder) ◆ 1998
6. Visitors (Gilman, Laura Anne, and Josepha Sherman) ◆ 1999
7. Unnatural Selection (Odom, Mel) ◆ 1999
8. Power of Persuasion (Massie, Elizabeth) ◆ 1999
9. Deep Water (Gilman, Laura Anne, and Josepha Sherman) ◆ 2000
10. Here Be Monsters (Dokey, Cameron) ◆ 2000
11. Ghoul Trouble (Passarella, John) ◆ 2000
12. Doomsday Deck (Gallagher, Diana G.) ◆ 2000
13. Sweet Sixteen (Ciencin, Scott) ◆ 2002
14. Crossings (Odom, Mel) ◆ 2002
15. Little Things (Moesta, Rebecca) ◆ 2002

BUFFY THE VAMPIRE SLAYER—ADDITIONAL TITLES

1. Child of the Hunt (Golden, Christopher, and Nancy Holder) ◆ 1998
2. Return to Chaos (Gardner, Craig Shaw) ◆ 1998
3. Obsidian Fate (Gallagher, Diana G.) ◆ 1999
4. Immortal (Golden, Christopher, and Nancy Holder) ◆ 2000
5. Sins of the Father (Golden, Christopher, and Nancy Holder) ◆ 2000
6. Resurrecting Ravana (Garton, Ray) ◆ 2000
7. Prime Evil (Gallagher, Diana G.) ◆ 2000
8. The Evil that Men Do (Holder, Nancy) ◆ 2000
9. How I Survived My Summer Vacation, Volume 1 (Holder, Nancy, Yvonne Navarro, et al.) ◆ 2000
10. Paleo (Navarro, Yvonne) ◆ 2000
11. Spike and Dru: Pretty Maids All in a Row (Golden, Christopher) ◆ 2001
12. The Faith Trials, Volume 1 (Laurence, James) ◆ 2001
13. Revenant (Odom, Mel) ◆ 2001
14. The Book of Fours (Holder, Nancy) ◆ 2002
15. Tempted Champions (Navarro, Yvonne) ◆ 2002
16. Oz (Golden, Christopher, and Logan Lubera) ◆ 2002
17. The Wisdom of War (Golden, Christopher) ◆ 2002
18. These Our Actors (Koogler, Dori, and Ashley McConnell) ◆ 2002
19. Blood and Fog (Holder, Nancy) ◆ 2003
20. Chaos Bleeds (Moore, James A.) ◆ 2003
21. Mortal Fear (Ciencin, Scott, and Denise Ciencin) ◆ 2003
22. Apocalypse Memories (Metz, Melinda, and Laura J. Burns) ◆ 2004

BUFFY THE VAMPIRE SLAYER

Various authors

DARK HORSE

GRADES 6–10

ADVENTURE | HORROR

The popularity of the television program about Buffy the Vampire Slayer and her friends has led to many spinoffs, including graphic novels. This list is from the 2004 Dark Horse catalog; dates vary because of reissues and compiled volumes.

SEASON ONE AND BEFORE

1. Slayer, Interrupted (Lobdell, Scott, Fabian Nicieza, et al.) ◆ 2003
2. Viva Las Buffy (Lobdell, Scott, Fabian Nicieza, and Cliff Richards) ◆ 2003
3. Tales of the Slayers (Whedon, Joss, Tim Sale, et al.) ◆ 2002
4. The Origin (Golden, Christopher, Dan Brereton, and Joe Bennett) ◆ 1999

SEASON TWO

1. Ring of Fire (Petrie, Doug, and Ryan Sook) ◆ 2000

SEASON THREE

1. The Dust Waltz (Brereton, Dan, and Rick Ketcham) ◆ 1998
2. Uninvited Guests (Watson, Andi, and Dan Brereton) ◆ 1999
3. Food Chain (Petrie, Doug, Christopher Golden, et al.) ◆ 2001
4. Bad Blood (Watson, Andi, Joe Bennett, and Rick Ketcham) ◆ 2000
5. Crash Test Demons (Watson, Andi, Cliff Richards, and Joe Pimentel) ◆ 2000
6. Pale Reflections (Watson, Andi, Doug Petrie, et al.) ◆ 2000
7. Haunted (Espenson, Jane, Cliff Richards, and Julio Ferreira) ◆ 2002

SEASON FOUR

1. Blood of Carthage (Golden, Christopher, Cliff Richards, and Joe Pimentel) ◆ 2001
2. Oz (Golden, Christopher, and Logan Lubera) ◆ 2002
3. Autumnal (Boal, Chris, Tom Fassbender, et al.) ◆ 2001
4. Past Lives (Golden, Christopher, Tom Sniegoski, et al.) ◆ 2001
5. Out of the Woodwork (Fassbender, Tom, Jim Pascoe, et al.) ◆ 2002

SEASON FIVE

1. False Memories (Fassbender, Tom, Jim Pascoe, et al.) ◆ 2002

2. Ugly Little Monsters (Fassbender, Tom, Jim Pascoe, et al.) ◆ 2002
3. The Death of Buffy (Nicieza, Fabian, Tom Fassbender, and Jim Pascoe) ◆ 2002

SEASON SIX

1. Creatures of Habit (Fassbender, Tom, Jim Pascoe, et al.) ◆ 2002
2. Note from the Underground (Lobdell, Scott, Fabian Nicieza, et al.) ◆ 2003

BUFFY THE VAMPIRE SLAYER: BUFFY AND ANGEL

ARCHWAY/POCKET BOOKS

GRADES 6–10

ADVENTURE I HORROR

These books feature Buffy and Angel confronting vampires and other demons.

1. Cursed (Odom, Mel) ◆ 2003
2. Seven Crows (Vornholt, John) ◆ 2003
3. Heat (Holder, Nancy) ◆ 2004
4. Monster Island (Golden, Christopher, and Thomas E. Sniegoski) ◆ 2004

BUFFY THE VAMPIRE SLAYER: BUFFY AND ANGEL: THE UNSEEN TRILOGY

ARCHWAY/POCKET BOOKS

GRADES 6–10

ADVENTURE I HORROR

Buffy and Angel are in another reality ruled by monsters and they must find the portal to return to Sunnydale.

1. The Burning: The Unseen Trilogy Book 1 (Holder, Nancy, and Jeff Mariotte) ◆ 2001
2. Door to Alternity: The Unseen Trilogy Book 2 (Holder, Nancy, and Jeff Mariotte) ◆ 2001
3. Long Way Home: The Unseen Trilogy Book 3 (Holder, Nancy, and Jeff Mariotte) ◆ 2001

BUFFY THE VAMPIRE SLAYER: THE ANGEL CHRONICLES

Various authors

ARCHWAY/POCKET BOOKS

GRADES 6–10

ADVENTURE | HORROR

This trilogy explores Buffy's relationship with Angel. She is a vampire slayer; he is a vampire. Their passion for each other is doomed.

1. The Angel Chronicles, Volume 1 (Holder, Nancy) ◆ 1998
2. The Angel Chronicles, Volume 2 (Tankersley, Rick) ◆ 1998
3. The Angel Chronicles, Volume 3 (Holder, Nancy) ◆ 1999

BUFFY THE VAMPIRE SLAYER: THE GATEKEEPER TRILOGY

ARCHWAY/POCKET BOOKS

GRADES 6–10

ADVENTURE | HORROR

New demons are arriving in Sunnydale. Buffy and her friends must destroy the creatures and close the time/space Gatehouse. But first, Buffy must rescue her mother, Joyce, from the demons.

1. Out of the Madhouse: The Gatekeeper Trilogy Book 1 (Golden, Christopher, and Nancy Holder) ◆ 1999
2. Ghost Roads: The Gatekeeper Trilogy Book 2 (Golden, Christopher, and Nancy Holder) ◆ 1999
3. Sons of Entropy: The Gatekeeper Trilogy Book 3 (Golden, Christopher, and Nancy Holder) ◆ 1999

BUFFY THE VAMPIRE SLAYER: THE LOST SLAYER SERIAL NOVEL

Golden, Christopher

ARCHWAY/POCKET BOOKS

GRADES 6–10

ADVENTURE | HORROR

Buffy's mother Joyce has been killed and her corpse is controlled by evil forces. Spike and Faith are also gone. Buffy created this grim future and she must retrace her actions to find the way to undo the horror.

1. Part 1: Prophecies ◆ 2001
2. Part 2: The Dark Times ◆ 2001
3. Part 3: King of the Dead ◆ 2001
4. Part 4: Original Sins ◆ 2001

BUFFY THE VAMPIRE SLAYER: THE WILLOW FILES

Navarro, Yvonne

ARCHWAY/POCKET BOOKS

GRADES 6–10

ADVENTURE | HORROR

Willow's role has expanded during the Buffy series. Now she stands on her own and begins a romance with Oz while dealing with a witch hunt in Sunnydale.

1. The Willow Files, Volume 1 ◆ 1999
2. The Willow Files, Volume 2 ◆ 2001

BUFFY THE VAMPIRE SLAYER: THE XANDER YEARS

Mariotte, Jeff

ARCHWAY/POCKET BOOKS

GRADES 6–10

ADVENTURE | HORROR

Xander Harris has never been popular at school or with girls but he has played an important role with the Slayers and seemed to be content. After a field trip to the zoo, he begins to behave strangely.

1. The Xander Years, Volume 1 ◆ 2000
2. The Xander Years, Volume 2 ◆ 2000

BUFFY THE VAMPIRE SLAYER: WICKED WILLOW

Navarro, Yvonne
ARCHWAY/POCKET BOOKS
GRADES 6–10
ADVENTURE | HORROR

Willow has decided to practice magic on her own, forming her own coven. She has been working on a resurrection spell for her friend, the Ghost of Tara. Willow is upset when the Ghost disappears and she discovers that Buffy and the old gang are responsible.

1. Volume 1: The Darkening ◆ 2004
2. Volume 2: Shattered Twilight ◆ 2004
3. Volume 3: Broken Sunrise ◆ 2004

B.Y. TIMES

Klein, Leah
TARGUM/FELDHEIM
GRADES 4–8
REAL LIFE

A group of girls attend the same middle school, Bais Yaakov, and work on their school newspaper, the *B.Y. Times*. The staff of the paper changes as students leave the school. In an early book, Shani Baum is the editor-in-chief; in a later book, Chani Kaufman has that job. There are references to school events and to Jewish events and holidays. An issue of the *B.Y. Times* is printed at the end of each book.

1. Shani's Scoop ◆ 1991
2. Batya's Search ◆ 1991
3. Twins in Trouble ◆ 1991
4. War! ◆ 1991
5. Spring Fever ◆ 1992
6. Party Time ◆ 1992
7. Changing Times ◆ 1992
8. Summer Daze ◆ 1992
9. Here We Go Again ◆ 1992
10. The New Kids ◆ 1992
11. Dollars and Sense ◆ 1993
12. Talking It Over ◆ 1993
13. Flying High ◆ 1993
14. Nechama on Strike ◆ 1993

15. Secrets! ◆ 1993
16. Babysitting Blues ◆ 1994
17. Jen Starts Over ◆ 1994
18. Who's Who ◆ 1994

CALIBAN *see* Isaac Asimov's Caliban

CALIFORNIA DIARIES

Martin, Ann M.
SCHOLASTIC
GRADES 6–8
REAL LIFE

These books feature various girls who are facing problems that will be familiar to young teens. Sunny's family is struggling to cope with her mother's cancer. Even with this trauma, Sunny must deal with issues involving school, boys, and friends. Maggie wants to weigh 90 pounds. That means she must lose 13 pounds. She also must face her mother's drinking problem and her father's frequent absence from home. The girls mention each other in their diaries, and the format, which sometimes includes hand-printed words, may attract reluctant readers.

1. Dawn ◆ 1997
2. Sunny ◆ 1997
3. Maggie ◆ 1997
4. Amalia ◆ 1997
5. Ducky ◆ 1998
6. Sunny, Diary Two ◆ 1998
7. Dawn, Diary Two ◆ 1998
8. Maggie, Diary Two ◆ 1998
9. Amalia, Diary Two ◆ 1998
10. Ducky, Diary Two ◆ 1998
11. Dawn, Diary Three ◆ 1999
12. Sunny, Diary Three ◆ 1999
13. Maggy, Diary Three ◆ 1999
14. Amalia, Diary Three ◆ 2000
15. Ducky, Diary Three ◆ 2000

CATHERINE MARSHALL'S CHRISTY *see* Christy

CELIA REES SUPERNATURAL TRILOGY

Rees, Celia
HODDER
GRADES 6–8
FANTASY

Eleven-year-old Davey, his sister, and twin cousins Tom and Elinor visit historic ruins in their English town and find themselves transported into a parallel world of good and evil ghosts. In the final suspenseful installment, they work to save their ghost friends from a ghostbusting machine.

1. City of Shadows ◆ 2002
2. A Trap in Time ◆ 2002
3. The Host Rides Out ◆ 2002

CHANTERS OF TREMARIS TRILOGY

Constable, Kate
SCHOLASTIC
GRADES 6–10
FANTASY

Calwyn sings magic. Along with the other Chanters, she uses her skills to protect their world, Tremaris. Samis is a dangerous sorcerer who is seeking to expand his power by learning the nine powers of chantment. Calwyn's destiny is to be a priestess in Antaris, but she longs for adventure outside the walls of her kingdom.

1. The Singer of All Songs ◆ 2004
2. The Waterless Sea ◆ 2005
3. The Tenth Power ◆ 2005

CHARLIE BONE *see* Children of the Red King

CHARMED

Various authors
SIMON & SCHUSTER
GRADES 7–12
FANTASY

Once the Halliwell sisters—Prue, Piper, and Phoebe—discover their powers, they are in danger. Creatures want to steal their strength or kill them. As the series evolves, the witches continue to defend themselves from supernatural attacks on their power. The books parallel many episodes from the television shows. In later books, Prue has left and Paige becomes one of the Charmed Ones. *Seasons of the Witch* (2003) is a special book that features a story for each woman.

1. The Power of Three (Burge, Constance M.) ◆ 1999
2. Kiss of Darkness (Alexandra, Belinda) ◆ 2000
3. The Crimson Spell (Dokey, Cameron) ◆ 2000
4. Whispers from the Past (Noonan, Rosalind) ◆ 2000
5. Voodoo Moon (Burge, Constance M.) ◆ 2000
6. Haunted by Desire (Burge, Constance M.) ◆ 2000
7. The Gypsy Enchantment (Jablonski, Carla) ◆ 2001
8. The Legend of Merlin (Flood, E. L.) ◆ 2001
9. Soul of the Bride (Lenhard, Elizabeth) ◆ 2001
10. Beware What You Wish (Burge, Constance M.) ◆ 2001
11. Charmed Again (Lenhard, Elizabeth) ◆ 2002
12. Spirit of the Wolf (Gallagher, Diana G.) ◆ 2002
13. Garden of Evil (Harrison, Emma) ◆ 2002
14. Date with Death (Lenhard, Elizabeth) ◆ 2002
15. Dark Vengeance (Gallagher, Diana G.) ◆ 2002
16. Shadow of the Sphinx (Jablonski, Carla) ◆ 2003
17. Something Wiccan This Way Comes (Harrison, Emma) ◆ 2003
18. Mist and Stone (Gallagher, Diana G.) ◆ 2003
19. Mirror Image (Mariotte, Jeff) ◆ 2003
20. Between Worlds (Weiss, Bobbi J. G., and Jacklyn Weiss) ◆ 2003
21. Truth and Consequences (Dokey, Cameron) ◆ 2003
22. Luck Be a Lady (Ciencin, Scott) ◆ 2004
23. Inherit the Witch (Burns, Laura J.) ◆ 2004
24. The Book of Three (Gallagher, Diana G., and Paul Ruditis) ◆ 2004
25. A Tale of Two Pipers (Harrison, Emma) ◆ 2004
26. The Brewing Storm (Ruditis, Paul) ◆ 2004
27. Survival of the Fittest (Mariotte, Jeff) ◆ 2004

CHEER SQUAD

Singleton, Linda Joy
AVON CAMELOT
GRADES 6–8
REAL LIFE | RECREATION

Oh, no! Darlene and her megapopular friends have been chosen to be seventh-grade cheerleaders. Will Wendi and Tabby always be popularity rejects? Not when a new cheer squad is formed for the basketball team. Now Wendi and Tabby and their classmates Krystal, Anna,

Celine, and Rachel have a chance. Girls who like to read about regular girls who succeed against the "in" crowd will enjoy this series. There is even a bit of budding romance when boys join the cheer squad.

1. Crazy for Cartwheels ◆ 1996
2. Spirit Song ◆ 1996
3. Stand Up and Cheer ◆ 1996
4. Boys Are Bad News ◆ 1997
5. Spring to Stardom ◆ 1997
6. Camp Confessions ◆ 1997

Cheer USA!

Betancourt, Jeanne

SCHOLASTIC

GRADES 6–9

REAL LIFE | RECREATION

At Claymore Middle School in Florida, making the cheer squad is a big deal. Four girls try out successfully and show lots of school spirit. They get involved in pre-game pranks and then go out and cheer their team to victory. They even compete in the regional cheering competition.

1. Go, Girl, Go ◆ 1999
2. Fight, Bulldogs, Fight! ◆ 1999
3. Ready, Shoot, Score! ◆ 1999
4. We've Got Spirit! ◆ 1999

Cheerleaders

Various authors

SCHOLASTIC

GRADES 7–9

RECREATION

Who will win the big game? Can the cheer team win the state competition? How will the varsity captain confront the rumor that she is shoplifting? These questions and more are explored in this series. Dating, jealousy, clothes, body image, and more will delight readers. Fans of the Sweet Valley books will enjoy these.

1. Trying Out (Cooney, Caroline B.) ◆ 1984
2. Getting Even (Pike, Christopher) ◆ 1984
3. Rumors (Cooney, Caroline B.) ◆ 1984
4. Feuding (Norby, Lisa) ◆ 1984
5. All the Way (Cooney, Caroline B.) ◆ 1985
6. Splitting (Sarasin, Jennifer) ◆ 1985
7. Flirting (Hoh, Diane) ◆ 1985
8. Forgetting (Norby, Lisa) ◆ 1985
9. Playing Games (Sorenson, Jody) ◆ 1985
10. Betrayed (Hoh, Diane) ◆ 1985
11. Cheating (Sarasin, Jennifer) ◆ 1985
12. Staying Together (Hoh, Diane) ◆ 1985
13. Hurting (Norby, Lisa) ◆ 1986
14. Living It Up (Sarasin, Jennifer) ◆ 1986
15. Waiting (Sorenson, Jody) ◆ 1986
16. In Love (Stanley, Carol) ◆ 1986
17. Taking Risks (Reynolds, Anne) ◆ 1986
18. Looking Good (Ellis, Carol) ◆ 1986
19. Making It (Blake, Susan) ◆ 1986
20. Starting Over (Aks, Patricia) ◆ 1986
21. Pulling Together (Hoh, Diane) ◆ 1986
22. Rivals (Steinke, Ann E.) ◆ 1986
23. Proving It (Hoh, Diane) ◆ 1986
24. Going Strong (Ellis, Carol) ◆ 1986
25. Stealing Secrets (Steinke, Ann E.) ◆ 1987
26. Taking Over (Sarasin, Jennifer) ◆ 1987
27. Spring Fever (Hoh, Diane) ◆ 1987
28. Scheming (Norby, Lisa) ◆ 1987
29. Falling in Love (Steinke, Ann E.) ◆ 1987
30. Saying Yes (Cooney, Caroline B.) ◆ 1987
31. Showing Off (Ellis, Carol) ◆ 1987
32. Together Again (Sarasin, Jennifer) ◆ 1987
33. Saying No (Steinke, Ann E.) ◆ 1987
34. Coming Back (Norby, Lisa) ◆ 1987
35. Moving Up (Davis, Leslie) ◆ 1987
36. Changing Loves (Weber, Judith) ◆ 1987
37. Acting Up (Sarasin, Jennifer) ◆ 1988
38. Talking Back (Norby, Lisa) ◆ 1988
39. All or Nothing (Davis, Leslie) ◆ 1988
40. Getting Serious (Sarasin, Jennifer) ◆ 1988
41. Having It All (Steinke, Ann E.) ◆ 1988
42. Fighting Back (Ellis, Carol) ◆ 1988
43. Telling Lies (Norby, Lisa) ◆ 1988
44. Pretending (Davis, Leslie) ◆ 1988
45. Here to Stay (Sarasin, Jennifer) ◆ 1988
46. Overboard (Schurfranz, Vivian) ◆ 1988
47. Dating (Weber, Judith) ◆ 1989

CHEETAH GIRLS

Gregory, Deborah
HYPERION/JUMP AT THE SUN
GRADES 6–9
REAL LIFE

Galleria Garibaldi, 14, is from a multicultural home—African American and Italian American. Her friend Chanel has a mixed Caribbean heritage. The two girls are headed for the Fashion Industries High School in Manhattan. They form a musical group with three other friends (Dorinda, Anginette, and Aquanette) and begin a search for fame. Related materials include videos.

1. Wishing on a Star ◆ 1999
2. Shop in the Name of Love ◆ 1999
3. Who's 'Bout to Bounce? ◆ 1999
4. Hey, Ho, Hollywood! ◆ 1999
5. Woof, There It Is ◆ 2000
6. It's Raining Benjamins ◆ 2000
7. Dorinda's Secret ◆ 2000
8. Growl Power ◆ 2000
9. Showdown at the Okie-Dokie ◆ 2001
10. Cuchifrita, Ballerina ◆ 2001
11. Dorinda Gets a Groove ◆ 2001
12. In the House with Mouse! ◆ 2001
13. Oops, Doggy, Dog! ◆ 2002

CHILDREN OF THE RED KING

Nimmo, Jenny
SCHOLASTIC
GRADES 4–7 ◆ A/R
FANTASY

Charlie Bone, 10, is from a seemingly ordinary family. When he begins to hear the people in photographs speaking to him, he is identified as having the Yewbeam gift. He is sent to Bloor's Academy to develop and to meet other gifted children. In the second book, Charlie encounters Henry Yewbeam, a young ancestor who disappeared in 1916. These books have been popular with Harry Potter fans.

1. Midnight for Charlie Bone ◆ 2003
2. Charlie Bone and the Time Twister ◆ 2003
3. Charlie Bone and the Invisible Boy ◆ 2004

CHINA BAYLES MYSTERY

Albert, Susan Wittig
BERKLEY BOOKS
GRADES 9–12
MYSTERY

China Bayles is a former high-powered Houston attorney who has embraced a quieter life. Even as the owner of Thyme and Seasons Herbs in Pecan Springs, Texas, however, she cannot escape mysteries. In one book, her best friend Ruby Wilcox disappears. During the course of the series, China meets and marries Mike McQuaid, who joins her in solving some mysteries. This is an adult series that is recommended for young adults.

1. Thyme of Death ◆ 1992
2. Hangman's Root ◆ 1994
3. Rosemary Remembered ◆ 1995
4. Rueful Death ◆ 1996
5. Love Lies Bleeding ◆ 1997
6. Chile Death ◆ 1998
7. Lavender Lies ◆ 1999
8. Mistletoe Man ◆ 2000
9. Indigo Dying ◆ 2003
10. A Dilly of a Death ◆ 2004

CHINA TATE

Johnson, Lissa Halls
FOCUS ON THE FAMILY
GRADES 5–8
REAL LIFE | VALUES

At Camp Crazy Bear, China Tate and her best friend Deedee Kiersey have adventures involving bear cubs, a lost dog, and the beginning of romance. China is the daughter of missionaries and many of her actions are guided by her faith in God. In one book, China befriends a charismatic young man and her interest in him makes her question the importance of her beliefs. In another book, China and Deedee learn a lesson about disobedience after they feed some wild bear cubs. Values and Christian beliefs are incorporated into each story.

1. Sliced Heather on Toast ◆ 1994
2. The Secret in the Kitchen ◆ 1994
3. Project Black Bear ◆ 1994
4. Wishing Upon a Star ◆ 1995

5. Comedy of Errors ◆ 1995
6. The Ice Queen ◆ 1996
7. The Never-Ending Day ◆ 1997

CHINATOWN MYSTERY

Yep, Laurence
HARPERCOLLINS
GRADES 5–8 ◆ A/R
MYSTERY

Lily Lew's great aunt is a former movie star who appeared as "Tiger Lil." On the set of a television show, the two work as a team to help an actor under suspicion of using real bullets in a prop gun. In an earlier book, they team up to find out who is trying to sabotage a new restaurant. Details about their Chinese heritage are incorporated into these books.

1. The Case of the Goblin Pearls ◆ 1997
2. The Case of the Lion Dance ◆ 1998
3. The Case of the Firecrackers ◆ 1999

CHIP HILTON SPORTS SERIES

Bee, Coach Clair
BOARDMAN & HOLMAN
GRADES 5–8 ◆ A/R
RECREATION

This series, which began in the 1940s, has been updated and reissued. A new title, *Fiery Fullback*, has also been released. Cynthia Bee Farley, the author's daughter, writes that the values and honesty of these books have connected with generations of readers. Like the Matt Christopher books, these cover a variety of sports and feature athletes in conflicts both on and off the field.

1. Touchdown Pass ◆ 1998
2. Championship Ball ◆ 1998
3. Strike Three! ◆ 1998
4. Clutch Hitter! ◆ 1998
5. A Pass and a Prayer ◆ 1999
6. Hoop Crazy ◆ 1999
7. Pitchers' Duel ◆ 1999
8. Dugout Jinx ◆ 1999
9. Freshman Quarterback ◆ 1999

10. Backboard Fever ◆ 1999
11. Fence Busters ◆ 1999
12. Ten Seconds to Play! ◆ 1999
13. Fourth Down Showdown ◆ 2000
14. Tournament Crisis ◆ 2000
15. Hardcourt Upset ◆ 2000
16. Pay-Off Pitch ◆ 2000
17. No-Hitter ◆ 2001
18. Triple-Threat Trouble ◆ 2001
19. Backcourt Ace ◆ 2001
20. Buzzer Basket ◆ 2001
21. Comeback Cagers ◆ 2001
22. Home Run Feud ◆ 2002
23. Hungry Hurler ◆ 2002
24. Fiery Fullback ◆ 2002

CHOOSE YOUR OWN ADVENTURE

Various authors

BANTAM

GRADES 4–8

ADVENTURE | MYSTERY

With nearly 200 titles, this series has attracted a large audience. The format allows readers to make choices at key moments in the plot. Should you go left? Go right? Should you turn around? Each choice leads to a different page, more choices, and your own story. Then you can go back to an earlier choice, make different selections, and create a different story. Newer adventures feature ninjas, computers, aliens, cyberhacking, and mutant spider ants. This is a popular series with a fairly accessible reading level. See also the Choose Your Own Nightmare series.

1. Journey Under the Sea (Mountain, Robert) ◆ 1977
2. Deadwood City (Packard, Edward) ◆ 1978
3. The Cave of Time (Packard, Edward) ◆ 1979
4. By Balloon to the Sahara (Terman, Douglas) ◆ 1979
5. Your Code Name Is Jonah (Packard, Edward) ◆ 1979
6. Third Planet from Altair (Packard, Edward) ◆ 1979
7. Space and Beyond (Montgomery, Raymond) ◆ 1980
8. Mystery of Chimney Rock (Packard, Edward) ◆ 1980
9. Who Killed Harlowe Thrombey? (Packard, Edward) ◆ 1981
10. Lost Jewels of Nabooti (Montgomery, Raymond) ◆ 1981
11. Mystery of the Maya (Montgomery, Raymond) ◆ 1981
12. Inside UFO 54-40 (Packard, Edward) ◆ 1982
13. Abominable Snowman (Montgomery, Raymond) ◆ 1982
14. Forbidden Castle (Packard, Edward) ◆ 1982

15. House of Danger (Montgomery, Raymond) ◆ 1982
16. Survival at Sea (Packard, Edward) ◆ 1983
17. Race Forever (Montgomery, Raymond) ◆ 1983
18. Underground Kingdom (Packard, Edward) ◆ 1983
19. Secret of the Pyramids (Brightfield, Richard) ◆ 1983
20. Escape (Montgomery, Raymond) ◆ 1983
21. Hyperspace (Packard, Edward) ◆ 1983
22. Space Patrol (Goodman, Julius) ◆ 1983
23. Lost Tribe (Foley, Louise Munro) ◆ 1983
24. Lost on the Amazon (Montgomery, Raymond) ◆ 1983
25. Prisoner of the Ant People (Montgomery, Raymond) ◆ 1983
26. Phantom Submarine (Brightfield, Richard) ◆ 1983
27. Horror of High Ridge (Goodman, Julius) ◆ 1983
28. Mountain Survival (Packard, Edward) ◆ 1984
29. Trouble on Planet Earth (Montgomery, Raymond) ◆ 1984
30. Curse of Batterslea Hall (Brightfield, Richard) ◆ 1984
31. Vampire Express (Koltz, Tony) ◆ 1984
32. Treasure Diver (Goodman, Julius) ◆ 1984
33. Dragons' Den (Brightfield, Richard) ◆ 1984
34. Mystery of the Highland Crest (Foley, Louise Munro) ◆ 1984
35. Journey to Stonehenge (Graver, Fred) ◆ 1984
36. Secret Treasure of Tibet (Brightfield, Richard) ◆ 1984
37. War with the Evil Power Master (Montgomery, Raymond) ◆ 1984
38. Sabotage (Liebold, Jay) ◆ 1984
39. Supercomputer (Packard, Edward) ◆ 1984
40. Throne of Zeus (Goodman, Deborah Lerne) ◆ 1985
41. Search for the Mountain Gorillas (Wallace, Jim) ◆ 1985
42. Mystery of Echo Lodge (Foley, Louise Munro) ◆ 1985
43. Grand Canyon Odyssey (Liebold, Jay) ◆ 1985
44. Mystery of Ura Senke (Gilligan, Shannon) ◆ 1985
45. You Are a Shark (Packard, Edward) ◆ 1985
46. Deadly Shadow (Brightfield, Richard) ◆ 1985
47. Outlaws of Sherwood Forest (Kushner, Ellen) ◆ 1985
48. Spy for George Washington (Liebold, Jay) ◆ 1985
49. Danger at Anchor Mine (Foley, Louise Munro) ◆ 1985
50. Return to the Cave of Time (Packard, Edward) ◆ 1985
51. Magic of the Unicorn (Goodman, Deborah Lerne) ◆ 1985
52. Ghost Hunter (Packard, Edward) ◆ 1986
53. Case of the Silk King (Gilligan, Shannon) ◆ 1986
54. Forest of Fear (Foley, Louise Munro) ◆ 1986
55. Trumpet of Terror (Goodman, Deborah Lerne) ◆ 1986
56. Enchanted Kingdom (Kushner, Ellen) ◆ 1986
57. Antimatter Formula (Liebold, Jay) ◆ 1986
58. Statue of Liberty Adventure (Kushner, Ellen) ◆ 1986
59. Terror Island (Koltz, Tony) ◆ 1986
60. Vanished! (Goodman, Deborah Lerne) ◆ 1986
61. Beyond Escape! (Montgomery, Raymond) ◆ 1986
62. Sugarcane Island (Packard, Edward) ◆ 1986
63. Mystery of the Secret Room (Kushner, Ellen) ◆ 1986

64. Volcano! (Siegman, Meryl) ◆ 1987
65. Mardi Gras Mystery (Foley, Louise Munro) ◆ 1987
66. Secret of the Ninja (Liebold, Jay) ◆ 1987
67. Seaside Mystery (Hodgman, Ann) ◆ 1987
68. Secret of the Sun God (Packard, Andrea) ◆ 1987
69. Rock and Roll Mystery (Wallace, Jim) ◆ 1987
70. Invaders of Planet Earth (Brightfield, Richard) ◆ 1987
71. Space Vampire (Packard, Edward) ◆ 1987
72. Brilliant Doctor Wogan (Montgomery, Raymond) ◆ 1987
73. Beyond the Great Wall (Liebold, Jay) ◆ 1987
74. Longhorn Territory (Newman, Marc) ◆ 1987
75. Planet of the Dragons (Brightfield, Richard) ◆ 1988
76. Mona Lisa Is Missing (Montgomery, Raymond) ◆ 1988
77. First Olympics (Baglio, Ben) ◆ 1988
78. Return to Atlantis (Montgomery, Raymond) ◆ 1988
79. Mystery of the Sacred Stones (Foley, Louise Munro) ◆ 1988
80. Perfect Planet (Packard, Edward) ◆ 1988
81. Terror in Australia (Gilligan, Shannon) ◆ 1988
82. Hurricane! (Brightfield, Richard) ◆ 1988
83. Track of the Bear (Montgomery, Raymond) ◆ 1988
84. You Are a Monster (Packard, Edward) ◆ 1988
85. Inca Gold (Beckett, Jim) ◆ 1988
86. Knights of the Round Table (Kushner, Ellen) ◆ 1988
87. Exiled to Earth (Montgomery, Richard) ◆ 1989
88. Master of Kung Fu (Brightfield, Richard) ◆ 1989
89. South Pole Sabotage (Johnson, Seddon) ◆ 1989
90. Mutiny in Space (Packard, Edward) ◆ 1989
91. You Are a Superstar (Packard, Edward) ◆ 1989
92. Return of the Ninja (Liebold, Jay) ◆ 1989
93. Captive! (Hampton, Bill) ◆ 1989
94. Blood on the Handle (Montgomery, Raymond) ◆ 1989
95. You Are a Genius (Packard, Edward) ◆ 1989
96. Stock Car Champion (Montgomery, Raymond) ◆ 1989
97. Through the Black Hole (Packard, Edward) ◆ 1990
98. You Are a Millionaire (Liebold, Jay) ◆ 1990
99. Revenge of the Russian Ghost (Liebold, Jay) ◆ 1990
100. Worst Day of Your Life (Packard, Edward) ◆ 1990
101. Alien, Go Home! (Johnson, Seddon) ◆ 1990
102. Master of Tae Kwon Do (Brightfield, Richard) ◆ 1990
103. Grave Robbers (Montgomery, Raymond) ◆ 1990
104. Cobra Connection (Foley, Louise Munro) ◆ 1990
105. Treasure of the Onyx Dragon (Gilligan, Alison) ◆ 1990
106. Hijacked! (Brightfield, Richard) ◆ 1990
107. Fight for Freedom (Liebold, Jay) ◆ 1990
108. Master of Karate (Brightfield, Richard) ◆ 1990
109. Chinese Dragons (Montgomery, Raymond) ◆ 1991
110. Invaders from Within (Packard, Edward) ◆ 1991
111. Smoke Jumper (Montgomery, Raymond) ◆ 1991
112. Skateboard Champion (Packard, Edward) ◆ 1991

113. Lost Ninja (Liebold, Jay) ◆ 1991
114. Daredevil Park (Compton, Sara) ◆ 1991
115. Island of Time (Montgomery, Raymond) ◆ 1991
116. Kidnapped! (Packard, Edward) ◆ 1991
117. Search for Aladdin's Lamp (Liebold, Jay) ◆ 1991
118. Vampire Invaders (Packard, Edward) ◆ 1991
119. Terrorist Trap (Gilligan, Shannon) ◆ 1991
120. Ghost Train (Foley, Louise Munro) ◆ 1992
121. Behind the Wheel (Montgomery, R. A.) ◆ 1992
122. Magic Master (Packard, Edward) ◆ 1992
123. Silver Wings (Montgomery, Raymond) ◆ 1992
124. Superbike (Packard, Edward) ◆ 1992
125. Outlaw Gulch (Montgomery, Ramsey) ◆ 1992
126. Master of Martial Arts (Brightfield, Richard) ◆ 1992
127. Showdown (Brightfield, Richard) ◆ 1992
128. Viking Raiders (Packard, Edward) ◆ 1992
129. Earthquake! (Gilligan, Alison) ◆ 1992
130. You Are Microscopic (Packard, Edward) ◆ 1992
131. Surf Monkeys (Liebold, Jay) ◆ 1993
132. Luckiest Day of Your Life (Packard, Edward) ◆ 1993
133. The Forgotten Planet (Wilhelm, Doug) ◆ 1993
134. Secret of the Dolphins (Packard, Edward) ◆ 1993
135. Playoff Champion (Von Moschzisker, Felix) ◆ 1993
136. Roller Star (Packard, Edward) ◆ 1993
137. Scene of the Crime (Wilhelm, Doug) ◆ 1993
138. Dinosaur Island (Packard, Edward) ◆ 1993
139. Motocross Mania (Montgomery, R. A.) ◆ 1993
140. Horror House (Packard, Edward) ◆ 1993
141. The Secret of Mystery Hill (Wilhelm, Doug) ◆ 1993
142. The Reality Machine (Packard, Edward) ◆ 1993
143. Project UFO (Montgomery, R. A.) ◆ 1994
144. Comet Crash (Packard, Edward) ◆ 1994
145. Everest Adventure (Montgomery, Anson) ◆ 1994
146. Soccer Star (Packard, Edward) ◆ 1994
147. The Antimatter Universe (Mueller, Kate) ◆ 1994
148. Master of Judo (Brightfield, Richard) ◆ 1994
149. Search the Amazon! (Wilhelm, Doug) ◆ 1994
150. Who Are You? (Packard, Edward) ◆ 1994
151. Gunfire at Gettysburg (Wilhelm, Doug) ◆ 1994
152. War with the Mutant Spider Ants (Packard, Edward) ◆ 1994
153. Last Run (Montgomery, R. A.) ◆ 1994
154. Cyberspace Warrior (Packard, Edward) ◆ 1994
155. Ninja Cyborg (Liebold, Jay) ◆ 1995
156. You Are an Alien (Packard, Edward) ◆ 1995
157. U.N. Adventure (Brightfield, Richard) ◆ 1995
158. Sky-jam! (Packard, Edward) ◆ 1995
159. Tattoo of Death (Montgomery, R. A.) ◆ 1995
160. The Computer Takeover (Packard, Edward) ◆ 1995
161. Possessed! (Montgomery, R. A.) ◆ 1995

162. Typhoon! (Packard, Edward) ◆ 1995
163. Shadow of the Swastika (Wilhelm, Doug) ◆ 1995
164. Fright Night (Packard, Edward) ◆ 1995
165. Snowboard Racer (Montgomery, Anson) ◆ 1995
166. Master of Aikido (Brightfield, Richard) ◆ 1995
167. Moon Quest (Montgomery, Anson) ◆ 1996
168. Hostage! (Packard, Edward) ◆ 1996
169. Terror on the Titanic (Brightfield, Richard) ◆ 1996
170. Greed, Guns, and Gold (Packard, Edward) ◆ 1996
171. Death in the Dorm (Montgomery, R. A.) ◆ 1996
172. Mountain Biker (Packard, Edward) ◆ 1996
173. The Gold Medal Secret (Wilhelm, Doug) ◆ 1996
174. The Power Dome (Packard, Edward) ◆ 1996
175. The Underground Railroad (Wilhelm, Doug) ◆ 1996
176. Master of Kendo (Brightfield, Richard) ◆ 1997
177. Killer Virus (Montgomery, Raymond) ◆ 1997
178. River of No Return (Lahey, Vince) ◆ 1997
179. Ninja Avenger (Liebold, Jay) ◆ 1997
180. Stampede! (Hill, Laban Carrick) ◆ 1997
181. Fire on Ice (Packard, Edward) ◆ 1998
182. Fugitive (Packard, Edward) ◆ 1998
183. CyberHacker (Montgomery, Anson) ◆ 1998
184. Mayday! (Packard, Edward, and Andrea Packard) ◆ 1998

CHOOSE YOUR OWN NIGHTMARE

Various authors

BANTAM

GRADES 4–8

ADVENTURE | HORROR

A spin-off of the Choose Your Own Adventure series, these books capitalize on the popularity of horror fiction. From *Night of the Werewolf* on, they are filled with venomous snakes, killer insects, mummies, and haunted babies. With twists and turns, doom and demons, they are sure to appeal to the scary-story crowd.

1. Night of the Werewolf (Packard, Edward) ◆ 1995
2. Beware the Snake's Venom (McMurtry, Ken) ◆ 1995
3. Island of Doom (Brightfield, Richard) ◆ 1995
4. Castle of Darkness (Montgomery, R. A.) ◆ 1995
5. The Halloween Party (Jakab, E. A. M.) ◆ 1995
6. Risk Your Life Arcade (McMurtry, Ken) ◆ 1995
7. Biting for Blood (Packard, Edward) ◆ 1996
8. Bugged Out! (Hill, Laban Carrick) ◆ 1996
9. The Mummy Who Wouldn't Die (Jakab, E. A. M.) ◆ 1996

10. It Happened at Camp Pine Tree (Montgomery, R. A., and Janet Hubbard-Brown) ◆ 1996
11. Watch Out for Room 13 (Hill, Laban Carrick) ◆ 1996
12. Something's in the Woods (Brightfield, Richard) ◆ 1996
13. The Haunted Baby (Packard, Edward) ◆ 1997
14. The Evil Pen Pal (Hill, Laban Carrick) ◆ 1997
15. How I Became a Freak (Brightfield, Richard) ◆ 1997
16. Welcome to Horror Hospital (Hill, Laban Carrick) ◆ 1997
17. Attack of the Living Mask (Hirschfeld, Robert) ◆ 1997
18. The Toy Shop of Terror (Hill, Laban Carrick) ◆ 1997

CHOOSE YOUR OWN STAR WARS ADVENTURES

Golden, Christopher
BANTAM
GRADES 4–8
ADVENTURE | SCIENCE FICTION

This series links two popular items: the *Star Wars* movies, plots, and characters and the Choose Your Own Adventure format. The familiar characters—Luke Skywalker, Princess Leia, Han Solo, and Darth Vader—are embroiled in more intergalactic intrigues, and the reader gets to make choices about which direction the plot will take. Will there be rebellion or destruction? Will you be loyal to the Jedi or embrace the dark side? The 3-D hologram on the cover of each book will attract many readers. This is sure to be a great choice for fans of movies and participatory fiction.

1. Star Wars: A New Hope ◆ 1998
2. Star Wars: The Empire Strikes Back ◆ 1998
3. Star Wars: Return of the Jedi ◆ 1998

CHRESTOMANCI

Jones, Diana Wynne
BEECH TREE
GRADES 6–9 ◆ A/R
FANTASY

This series begins with several characters with the promise of magical powers. They are sent to further their skills at Chrestomanci Castle. Gwendolyn is a young witch who shakes things up at the castle. Christopher Chant comes from a family that is skilled at sorcery and enchantment. When he finally realizes his own powers. he goes to the castle and develops into a powerful leader. The other books are filled with magical feuds and threats to those with supernatural powers. This series was first released in the 1970s and 1980s and has been reissued.

1. Charmed Life ◆ 1998
2. The Lives of Christopher Chant ◆ 1998
3. The Magicians of Caprona ◆ 1999
4. Witch Week ◆ 2001

CHRISTIE & COMPANY

Page, Katherine Hall

AVON

GRADES 5–7

MYSTERY

Three girls—Christie, Maggie, and Vicky—meet at the boarding school where they begin eighth grade. They are from different backgrounds but they share an in interest in mysteries. Christie Montgomery is the main character and she directs the trio's activities, solving thefts at school, finding those responsible for the sabotage of an inn owned by Maggie's parents, and helping a family being threatened by a Chinese gang. While seeking solutions to these mysteries, the girls continue to grow and mature. There is lots of dialogue, making this fairly accessible. Children who enjoy mystery and adventure books featuring girls will like this series.

1. Christie & Company ◆ 1996
2. Christie & Company Down East ◆ 1997
3. Christie & Company in the Year of the Dragon ◆ 1998
4. Bon Voyage, Christie & Company ◆ 1999

CHRISTY

Marshall, Catherine

TOMMY NELSON WORDKIDS

GRADES 5–8

HISTORICAL | REAL LIFE | VALUES

Christy Huddleston, 19, goes to teach in the Great Smoky Mountains, where she finds hardships, heartache, and hope. Christy's idealism and energy often put her in conflict with people in the community, but she has the ongoing support of Dr. Neil MacNeill and the admiration of David Grantland. Christy meets Miss Alice, a veteran missionary who understands the mountain people and helps her adjust to their ways. The stories have an element of romance and are filled with Christy's commitment to her religion and her values. The series follows the format of the popular television series. Catherine Marshall based these stories on the real life of her mother around the turn of the century.

1. The Bridge to Cutter Gap ◆ 1995
2. Silent Superstitions ◆ 1995
3. The Angry Intruder ◆ 1995
4. Midnight Rescue ◆ 1995
5. The Proposal ◆ 1995
6. Christy's Choice ◆ 1996
7. The Princess Club ◆ 1996
8. Family Secrets ◆ 1996
9. Mountain Madness ◆ 1997
10. Stage Fright ◆ 1997
11. Goodbye, Sweet Prince ◆ 1997
12. Brotherly Love ◆ 1997

CHRISTY MILLER

Gunn, Robin Jones
FOCUS ON THE FAMILY
GRADES 6–8 ◆ A/R
REAL LIFE | VALUES

Christy Miller's faith in God and the support of her family help her deal with many teenage traumas. Making new friends in California, expressing her interest in Todd, being attracted by another boy (Rick), and almost losing her best friend Katie are some of Christy's concerns. Christy seeks guidance from the Lord as she tries to reconcile her personal wants with the needs of her faith. Opportunities for Biblical explications are provided as the characters attend study groups and seek guidance. Christy's romantic dilemmas will appeal to many girls. This series will connect with other values-related books. It was reissued in the late 1990s with new covers. *From the Secret Place in My Heart (Christy Miller's Diary)* (Bethany House, 1999) describes Christy's adjustment to a new life in California and her relationship with Todd.

1. A Summer Promise ◆ 1988
2. A Whisper and a Wish ◆ 1989
3. Yours Forever ◆ 1990
4. Surprise Endings ◆ 1991
5. Island Dreamer ◆ 1992
6. A Heart Full of Hope ◆ 1992

7. True Friends ◆ 1993
8. Starry Night ◆ 1993
9. Seventeen Wishes ◆ 1993
10. A Time to Cherish ◆ 1993
11. Sweet Dreams ◆ 1994
12. A Promise Is Forever ◆ 1994

CHRISTY MILLER: CHRISTY AND TODD: THE COLLEGE YEARS

Gunn, Robin Jones
BETHANY HOUSE
GRADES 9–12 ◆ A/R
REAL LIFE

Christy is studying in Switzerland in the first book; Katie and Todd, Christy's boyfriend, come to visit but things don't go as well as expected. In the second book, Christy is back in California and dating Todd. But she is also attracted to an old friend. In *I Promise*, Christy and Todd are planning their wedding.

1. Until Tomorrow ◆ 2000
2. As You Wish ◆ 2000
3. I Promise ◆ 2001

CHRONICLES OF CONAN

Various authors
DARK HORSE
GRADES 9–12
FANTASY

This graphic novel series collects the adventures of Conan the Barbarian, a popular comic series from the 1970s.

1. Tower of the Elephant and Other Stories (Thomas, Roy, and Barry Windsor) ◆ 2003
2. Rogues in the House and Other Stories (Thomas, Roy, and Barry Windsor) ◆ 2003
3. The Monster of the Monoliths and Other Stories (Thomas, Roy, Barry Windsor, and Gil Kane Smith) ◆ 2004
4. The Song of Red Sonja and Other Stories (Thomas, Roy) ◆ 2004
5. The Shadow in the Tomb and Other Stories (Thomas, Roy) ◆ 2004
6. The Curse of the Golden Skull and Other Stories (Thomas, Roy) ◆ 2004

CHRONICLES OF DERYNI

Kurtz, Katherine
BALLANTINE
GRADES 9–12
FANTASY

Kelson, 14, lives in the kingdom of Gwynedd. He is destined to be king but his heritage may block his succession. Kelson is half Deryni, a magical people who have been forced into hiding. Yet the Eleven Kingdoms are being threatened and only Kelson's powers as a sorcerer and the help of the Deryni can meet this danger. Later, Kelson is King and his power is again in jeopardy. There are many spin-off Deryni sagas and a guidebook to the land of Deryni: *The Eleven Kingdoms: A Map of the Deryni World.* This series has been read for more than 30 years; *Deryni Rising* has been reissued (Ace, 2004).

1. Deryni Rising ◆ 1970
2. Deryni Checkmate ◆ 1972
3. High Deryni ◆ 1973

CHRONICLES OF NARNIA

Lewis, C. S.
MACMILLAN
GRADES 4–8 ◆ A/R
FANTASY

Lucy, Peter, Susan, and Edmund are British schoolchildren during World War II in this series of fantasy adventures. Entering a mirrored wardrobe, they find a magical world called Narnia peopled by fauns, witches, nymphs, dwarves, and talking animals. The children fight many battles against evil and eventually become rulers of the land. Quirks in the chronicles include the facts that Narnia's inhabitants have always supposed humans to be mythical creatures and that the adventures that seem to last forever in Narnia only fill a split second at home. There is debate about the best order in which to read these books. Many prefer the order in which they were published, but boxed sets now present the books in chronological sequence: *The Magician's Nephew; The Lion, the Witch, and the Wardrobe; The Horse and His Boy; Prince Caspian, The Voyage of the Dawn Treader; The Silver Chair; and The Last Battle.*

1. The Lion, the Witch, and the Wardrobe ◆ 1950
2. Prince Caspian ◆ 1951
3. The Voyage of the Dawn Treader ◆ 1952

4. The Silver Chair ◆ 1953
5. The Horse and His Boy ◆ 1954
6. The Magician's Nephew ◆ 1955
7. The Last Battle ◆ 1956

CIRCLE OF MAGIC

Pierce, Tamora
SCHOLASTIC
GRADES 6–9 ◆ A/R
FANTASY

Four children are gifted with magical talents. They are unaware of their heritage but others are interested in their development. Niko, a powerful mage, brings them to Discipline Cottage to develop their powers. As they train, their special skills are enhanced. Sandry is interested in weaving; Daja in metal; Briar in plants; and Tris in the weather. Each young mage is featured in a book in the series.

1. Sandry's Book ◆ 1997
2. Tris's Book ◆ 1998
3. Daja's Book ◆ 1998
4. Briar's Book ◆ 2000

CIRCLE OF MAGIC: THE CIRCLE OPENS

Pierce, Tamora
SCHOLASTIC
GRADES 6–9 ◆ A/R
FANTASY

The characters from the Circle of Magic series are now older and facing new adventures as they assist young mages. Sandry, 14, realizes that the magical skills of a young boy may be the key to stopping a murderer. Briar, 14, befriends a child from the streets of Chammur. He helps her develop her magical gift with stones. Daja's apprentices are twins whose magical specialties must be discovered. Tris assists Keth, a glassblower whose magical powers are needed to seek The Ghost.

1. Magic Steps ◆ 2000
2. Street Magic ◆ 2002
3. Cold Fire ◆ 2002
4. Shatterglass ◆ 2003

CIRCLE OF THREE

Bird, Isobel

AVON

GRADES 7–10 ◆ A/R

FANTASY

Kate Morgan is a sophomore at Beecher Falls High School. While researching the Salem Witch Trials, she finds a book on spells and charms. She casts a spell to get a date to the dance and gets more than she bargained for. In additional adventures, Kate is joined by her friends Annie and Cooper.

1. So Mote It Be ◆ 2001
2. Merry Meet ◆ 2001
3. Second Sight ◆ 2001
4. What the Cards Said ◆ 2001
5. In the Dreaming ◆ 2001
6. Ring of Light ◆ 2001
7. Blue Moon ◆ 2001
8. The Five Paths ◆ 2001
9. Through the Veil ◆ 2001
10. Making the Saint ◆ 2001
11. House of Winter ◆ 2001
12. Written in the Stars ◆ 2001
13. And It Harm None ◆ 2002
14. The Challenge Box ◆ 2002
15. Initiation ◆ 2002

CIRQUE DU FREAK

Shan, Darren

LITTLE, BROWN

GRADES 6–9 ◆ A/R

FANTASY

When Darren Shan and two friends get tickets to Cirque du Freak, they find that this is no ordinary circus. These freaks are really freaky, including a vampire who lures Darren into a dangerous deal. Darren becomes the vampire's assistant and faces numerous trials as the series progresses. Book 1, *Cirque du Freak*, has been reprinted with the title *A Living Nightmare*.

1. Cirque du Freak ◆ 2000
2. The Vampire's Assistant ◆ 2002

3. Tunnels of Blood ◆ 2002
4. Vampire Mountain ◆ 2002
5. Trials of Death ◆ 2003
6. The Vampire Prince ◆ 2003
7. Hunters of the Dusk ◆ 2004
8. Allies of the Night ◆ 2004

CITY OF EMBER

DuPrau, Jeanne
RANDOM HOUSE
GRADES 6–8
SCIENCE FICTION

The underground city of Ember was built to offer protection from a disaster on the surface. More than 200 years later the city structures are deteriorating. Lina and Doon, both 12, have received their job assignments and they begin to see the extent of the damage and the danger it portends. They search for a way out of Ember. When they find the secret path, they lead 400 residents to the surface where they discover another community, Sparks. At first, the newcomers are welcomed, but conflict develops between the agrarian people of Sparks and the technological people of Ember.

1. The City of Ember ◆ 2003
2. The People of Sparks ◆ 2004

CLAIDI JOURNALS

Lee, Tanith
DUTTON
GRADES 6–9 ◆ A/R
FANTASY

Claidi, 16, records her adventures in her journals. Stifled by her life as a maid in the House, she helps a prisoner escape and travels with him to his home in the Waste. There, she rebels against the oppressive Rules and is rescued by the bandit Argul. Their adventures together continue and they marry in the fourth book.

1. Wolf Tower ◆ 2000
2. Wolf Star ◆ 2001
3. Wolf Queen ◆ 2001
4. Wolf Wing ◆ 2003

CLAMP SCHOOL DETECTIVES

Ohkawa, Ageha, team leader
TOKYOPOP
GRADES 4–8
FANTASY

CLAMP School is a school for geniuses. Three teens at the school create an investigative agency to protect their fellow students, especially the girls. Nokoru, a sixth-grader, founded the group and is joined by his friends Akira and Suoh. They look into unusual situations including a ghost in the art department.

1. Volume 1 ◆ 2004
2. Volume 2 ◆ 2004
3. Volume 3 ◆ 2004

CLASS SECRETS

Baker, Jennifer
SIMON & SCHUSTER
GRADES 6–10
REAL LIFE

This series features Hillcrest High in suburban Connecticut. Suzanne is new and feels left out so she takes an audacious risk. Nikki is having problems with her boyfriend, Luke. Victoria wants to get her way and doesn't care who she hurts.

1. Most Likely to Deceive ◆ 1995
2. Just Like Sisters ◆ 1995
3. Sworn to Silence ◆ 1995
4. The Lying Game ◆ 1996

CLEARWATER CROSSING

Roberts, Laura Peyton
BANTAM DOUBLEDAY DELL
GRADES 6–9 ◆ A/R
REAL LIFE | VALUES

In this series, good friends Melanie, Peter, Jenna, Jesse, Nicole, Miguel, Ben, and Leah face high school with the support of each other and their faith in God. Concerns including boyfriends, sports, school events—even hardship and tragedy—are resolved through the guidance of Christian friends and family. Modern photographic covers give these books an appeal similar to that of the Sweet Valley series.

1. Get a Life ◆ 1998
2. Reality Check ◆ 1998
3. Heart and Soul ◆ 1998
4. Promises, Promises ◆ 1998
5. Just Friends ◆ 1998
6. Keep the Faith ◆ 1998
7. New Beginnings ◆ 1998
8. One Real Thing ◆ 1999
9. Skin Deep ◆ 1999
10. No Doubt ◆ 1999
11. More Than This ◆ 1999
12. Hope Happens ◆ 2000
13. Dream On ◆ 2000
14. Love Hurts ◆ 2000
15. What Goes Around ◆ 2000
16. Tried and True ◆ 2000
17. Just Say Yes ◆ 2001
18. Prime Time ◆ 2001
19. Now and Always ◆ 2001
20. Don't Look Back ◆ 2001

CLEARWATER CROSSING DIARY SPECIAL

1. The Diaries ◆ 2000

CLIQUE

Harrison, Lisi
LITTLE, BROWN
GRADES 6–9 ◆ A/R
REAL LIFE

Clair Lynons, a seventh-grader, is a victim of The Clique. Massie Block and the other popular girls at Octavian Country Day School decide to ostracize the new girl from Florida. They verbally abuse her and take every opportunity to embarrass her. This series focuses on teen issues such as body image, clothes, boys, school, and, of course, cliques.

1. The Clique ◆ 2004
2. Best Friends for Never: A Clique Novel ◆ 2004
3. Revenge of the Wannabes: A Clique Novel ◆ 2005

CLUELESS

Various authors
ARCHWAY
GRADES 6–9
REAL LIFE

This series is based on the movie that evolved into a television program. Cher was named for the famous singer and actress. She is the ultimate princess, daughter of an indulgent and busy father. Her goals while in high school include dressing appropriately in designer fashions, hanging out at the mall, and keeping up with popular friends. The plots change a little from title to title, but the theme remains the same.

1. Cher Negotiates New York (Baker, Jennifer) ◆ 1995
2. Cher's Guide to . . . Whatever (Gilmour, H. B., and Amy Heckerling) ◆ 1995
3. Clueless: A Novel (Gilmour, H. B.) ◆ 1995
4. Achieving Personal Perfection (Gilmour, H. B.) ◆ 1996
5. An American Betty in Paris (Reisfeld, Randi) ◆ 1996
6. Cher Goes Enviro-mental (Reisfeld, Randi) ◆ 1996
7. Cher's Furiously Fit Workout (Reisfeld, Randi) ◆ 1996
8. Friend or Faux (Gilmour, H. B.) ◆ 1996
9. Baldwin from Another Planet (Gilmour, H. B.) ◆ 1996
10. Cher and Cher Alike (Gilmour, H. B.) ◆ 1997
11. Romantically Correct (Gilmour, H. B.) ◆ 1997
12. Too Hottie to Handle (Reisfeld, Randi) ◆ 1997
13. True Blue Hawaii (Reisfeld, Randi) ◆ 1997
14. Babes in Boyland (Gilmour, H. B.) ◆ 1998
15. Cher's Frantically Romantic Assignment (Gilmour, H. B.) ◆ 1998
16. Chronically Crushed (Reisfeld, Randi) ◆ 1998
17. Dude with a 'Tude (Reisfeld, Randi) ◆ 1998
18. A Totally Cher Affair (Gilmour, H. B.) ◆ 1998
19. Extreme Sisterhood (Reisfeld, Randi) ◆ 1999
20. Bettypalooza (Lenhard, Elizabeth) ◆ 1999
21. Southern Fried Makeover (Jablonski, Carla) ◆ 1999

COLONIAL CAPTIVES

Hunt, Angela Elwell
TYNDALE HOUSE
GRADES 6–8
HISTORICAL

In 1627, Kimberly Hollis is traveling with her mother on a ship to Jamestown Colony. There, they will rejoin Kimberly's father. The other passengers on the boat include children who are to become indentured servants. Dangers on the voyage include pirates and bad weather. Kimberly's faith in God helps her deal with the difficulties.

1. Kimberly and the Captives ◆ 1996
2. The Deadly Chase ◆ 1996
3. Pirate's Revenge ◆ 1996
4. Lost in the Fog ◆ 1996

COLONIZATION

Turtledove, Harry

BALLANTINE DEL REY

GRADES 9–12

SCIENCE FICTION

An alternate history of post-World War II Earth, set in the turbulent 1960s. It is 20 years since the first aliens arrived but they have failed to take control. So when their colonization fleet turns up, they meet unexpected resistance. The series is full of historical characters and anecdotes. In *Homeward Bound*, the aliens must decide whether humanity can be allowed to survive. This series is linked to Turtledove's earlier alternate World War II saga, in which the alien lizards make their debut.

1. Colonization: Second Contact ◆ 1999
2. Colonization: Down to Earth ◆ 2000
3. Colonization: Aftershocks ◆ 2001
4. Colonization: Homeward Bound ◆ 2004

CONCRETE

Chadwick, Paul

DARK HORSE

GRADES 7–10

FANTASY

Ron Lithgow is a speechwriter trapped in an alien body made of stone. Despite his bulk, Concrete is able to help his friends and protect the world. In one graphic novel, a film crew hires Concrete to be like a special effect come to life. When accidents begin to happen, Concrete intervenes.

1. The Complete Short Stories, 1986–1989 ◆ 1990
2. Fragile Creatures ◆ 1994

3. Killer Smile ◆ 1995
4. The Complete Short Stories, 1990–1995 ◆ 1996
5. Think Like a Mountain ◆ 1997
6. Strange Armor ◆ 1998

CONFESSIONS OF A TEENAGE DRAMA QUEEN

Sheldon, Dyan
CANDLEWICK
GRADES 7–10
REAL LIFE

Mary Elizabeth Cep must adjust to her family's move from New York City to New Jersey. To do so, she reinvents herself, becoming Lola and devising a plan to shake up suburbia. Her classmates are not interested. They already have a "drama queen" to worship—Carla Santini. Lola and Carla become rivals and the games begin.

1. Confessions of a Teenage Drama Queen ◆ 1999
2. My Perfect Life ◆ 2002

CONFESSIONS OF GEORGIA NICOLSON

Rennison, Louise
HARPERCOLLINS
GRADES 7–10
HUMOR | REAL LIFE

In her diary, Georgia Nicolson reflects on her teenage anxieties. She writes about her bra and about kissing. She dates a "Sex God" until he tells her she should date a younger boy. Set in England, the novels contain British terms and phrases but American teens have connected with this irreverent series. The first book received a Michael L. Printz Award for young adult literature.

1. Angus, Thongs and Full Frontal Snogging: Confessions of Georgia Nicolson ◆ 2000
2. On the Bright Side, I'm Now the Girlfriend of a Sex God: Further Confessions of Georgia Nicolson ◆ 2001
3. Knocked Out by My Nunga-Nungas: Further, Further Confessions of Georgia Nicolson ◆ 2002

4. Dancing in My Nuddy Pants: Even Further Confessions of Georgia Nicolson ◆ 2003
5. Away Laughing on a Fast Camel: Even More Confessions of Georgia Nicolson ◆ 2004

THE CONTENDER

Lipsyte, Robert
HARPERCOLLINS
GRADES 6–8
REAL LIFE

Alfred is an orphaned inner-city boy who lives with his aunt and three cousins. When the series opens, he has dropped out of school and works in a grocery store. His best friend has fallen in with a crowd of punks and gets arrested for robbing a store. Alfred decided to start working out at Donatelli's Gym to become a boxer. Donatelli convinces him to try to become a contender. As the series continues, Alfred succeeds as a boxer, becomes a policeman, and teaches a young Native American, Sonny, the lessons he learned from Donatelli.

1. The Contender ◆ 1967
2. The Brave ◆ 1991
3. The Chief ◆ 1998

COUNTDOWN

Parker, Daniel
ALADDIN
GRADES 7–10
FANTASY

As the millennium approaches, a strange space phenomenon destroys the children and adults on Earth. Only young adults survive and some of them are now searching for the Chosen One. Each month brings new dangers, culminating in *December* when the Chosen One faces the Demon.

1. January ◆ 1998
2. February ◆ 1998
3. March ◆ 1999
4. April ◆ 1999

5. May ◆ 1999
6. June ◆ 1999
7. July ◆ 1999
8. August ◆ 1999
9. September ◆ 1999
10. October ◆ 1999
11. November ◆ 1999
12. December: Time's Up ◆ 1999

THE CRIMSON SHADOW

Salvatore, R. A.
WARNER
GRADES 7–12
FANTASY

When the land of Eriador is enslaved by the Wizard-King Greensparrow, a young nobleman named Luthien Bedwyr becomes an outlaw. He always leaves behind the crimson mark of his shadow. Aided by elves, dwarves, and other humans, Luthien battles the evil, magical army of Belsen Krieg.

1. The Sword of Bedwyr ◆ 1995
2. Luthien's Gamble ◆ 1996
3. The Dragon King ◆ 1996

CROSSROADS TRILOGY

O'Donohoe, Nick
ACE
GRADES 8–12
FANTASY

Medical detail, mythology, and fantasy are intertwined in these stories of the magical world of Crossroads where veterinarian B. J. Vaughn treats beasts of legend. In the second book, she becomes romantically involved with a faun and teaches centaurs about first aid and wellness. In the last book, B. J. must protect her animal friends from outside threats.

1. The Magic and the Healing ◆ 1994
2. Under the Healing Sign ◆ 1995
3. The Healing of Crossroads ◆ 1996

THE CULTURE

Banks, Iain M.

POCKET

GRADES 11–12

SCIENCE FICTION

Epic space adventures are the focus of this well-written adult series that will challenge and interest older teens. The Culture is a technologically advanced giant civilization (31 trillion inhabitants) that values its own freedoms but is careless with those of others. In the first book, the Idirans hire an alien shape changer to battle against the Culture. In *The Player of Games,* the Culture's star player will compete in a contest that holds the key to the future.

1. Consider Phlebas ◆ 1987
2. The Player of Games ◆ 1988
3. Use of Weapons ◆ 1990
4. The State of the Art ◆ 1991
5. Excession ◆ 1996
6. Look to Windward ◆ 2000

CYBERSURFERS

Pedersen, Ted, and Mel Gilden

PRICE STERN SLOAN

GRADES 6–9

ADVENTURE

Mr. Madison, the computer lab teacher at Fort Benson High School, engages two young computer students to explore the Internet in a special program. Fourteen-year-old techno-wizard Athena Bergstrom and computer hacker Jason Kane share adventures both dangerous and exciting. Internet notes plus a user-friendly glossary explain terms for "Newbies" to the technology. This series would have a particular appeal to kids with an interest in computers.

1. Pirates on the Internet ◆ 1995
2. Cyberspace Cowboy ◆ 1995
3. Ghost on the Net ◆ 1996
4. Cybercops and Flame Wars ◆ 1996

DALEMARK QUARTET

Jones, Diana Wynne
HARPERCOLLINS
GRADES 6–9 ◆ A/R
FANTASY

Dalemark is a land divided. Each book in this quartet features a young person who confronts dangerous magic and evil. In *The Crown of Dalemark*, Maewen time travels to Dalemark where she impersonates Noreth, a teen who believes she is destined to unite her land. Books in this series were first published in the 1970s. The recent popularity of fantasy may have helped prompt these reissues.

1. Cart and Cwidder ◆ 2001
2. Drowned Ammet ◆ 2001
3. The Spellcoats ◆ 2001
4. The Crown of Dalemark ◆ 2001

DAMAR CHRONICLES

McKinley, Robin
GREENWILLOW
GRADES 6–10 ◆ A/R
ADVENTURE | FANTASY

Two of the three books in this wonderful fantasy series are Newbery award-winning titles. *The Blue Sword* is the story of Harry Crewe, who travels to the Homelander empire when her father dies. She is kidnapped by a native king with mysterious powers. *The Hero and the Crown* is the prequel to *The Blue Sword*, and gives the reader historical background on the magical powers of the kingdom. Aerin, the main character of this story, wins her birthright with the help of a wizard and the blue sword. The third volume in the series is a collection of short stories set in the kingdom of Damar. Maddy, the main character of *The Stone Fey*, is as strong-willed and independent as the women in the earlier books. Maddy's fascination with the Fey threatens her future.

1. The Blue Sword ◆ 1982
2. The Hero and the Crown ◆ 1984
3. A Knot in the Grain and Other Stories ◆ 1994
4. The Stone Fey ◆ 1998

DANGER BOY

Williams, Mark London
CANDLEWICK
GRADES 6–9 ◆ A/R
FANTASY

When scientific research on "spacetime spheres" results in the death of his mother, Eli, 12, and his father leave Princeton, New Jersey, and move to Sonoma, California. It is 2019, and Eli's father wants to abandon his research but is coerced into continuing and using Eli as his test subject. Eli's time travel adventures begin. Clyne, a dinosaur, and Thea, a librarian from ancient Egypt, join him. Candlewick Press reissued the first two books in 2004, retitling the second book *Dragon Sword.*

1. Ancient Fire ◆ 2001
2. Dino Sword ◆ 2001
3. Trail of Bones ◆ 2005

DANGER.COM

Cray, Jordan
ALADDIN
GRADES 6–9 ◆ A/R
ADVENTURE | MYSTERY

These books use communication on the Internet to establish the plots and then have the characters solve the mystery. In one book, Annie and her brother Nick send messages to a cute girl who has stolen Annie's boyfriend. When the messages fall into the wrong hands, there is danger, and Annie and Nick must use their computer skills to prevent even more trouble. Annie and Nick return in another book to solve a murder while on vacation in Florida. Internet dating, cyber terrorists, chat rooms, and a web of lies enhance the action-packed stories in this series.

1. Gemini 7 ◆ 1997
2. Firestorm ◆ 1997
3. Shadow Man ◆ 1997
4. Hot Pursuit ◆ 1997
5. Stalker ◆ 1998
6. Bad Intent ◆ 1998

7. Most Wanted ◆ 1998
8. Dead Man's Hand ◆ 1998
9. Shiver ◆ 1998

DARK GROUND TRILOGY

Cross, Gillian
DUTTON
GRADES 6–9
FANTASY

Teens who fall, faint, or collapse undergo strange transformations. When they awake, they are as small as mice. The familiar world becomes dangerous and distant when you are small. Robert is one of those struggling to find his way back to his own reality. This is the first book in a proposed trilogy.

1. The Dark Ground ◆ 2004

DARK IS RISING

Cooper, Susan
COLLIER
GRADES 4–8 ◆ A/R
ADVENTURE | FANTASY

This is a classic fantasy series. Two of the five books are Newbery award winners. The story starts out with the three Drew children: Simon, Jane, and Barney. While on holiday, they discover an ancient manuscript that will reveal the true story of King Arthur. In the second book, Will Stanton, age 11, discovers that he is the last of the Old Ones who are able to triumph over the evil forces of the Dark. In *Greenwitch*, Jane and her brothers help the Old Ones uncover the grail. As the quest continues, Will and his companions must uncover the items necessary to vanquish the rising forces of the Dark. Fantasy lovers will be absorbed by this series and will also enjoy C. S. Lewis's Chronicles of Narnia and Tolkien's Lord of the Rings trilogy, which plunge readers into mysterious fantasy worlds.

1. Over Sea, Under Stone ◆ 1965
2. The Dark Is Rising ◆ 1973
3. Greenwitch ◆ 1974
4. The Grey King ◆ 1975
5. Silver on the Tree ◆ 1977

DARK SECRETS

Chandler, Elizabeth
SIMON & SCHUSTER
GRADES 7–10 ◆ A/R
FANTASY

In the first book of the series, Megan, 16, visits her grandmother in Maryland. They have been estranged for years, but now Megan feels the need to reestablish contact. Once she is there, Megan knows she has been there before . . . in her dreams. Megan has visions of Avril, her grandmother's sister who died years ago when she was 16. The other books feature other teens in mysterious, supernatural situations.

1. Legacy of Lies ◆ 2000
2. Don't Tell ◆ 2001
3. No Time to Die ◆ 2001
4. The Deep End of Fear ◆ 2003
5. The Back Door of Midnight ◆ 2004

DARK TOWER

King, Stephen
VIKING, SCRIBNER
GRADES 9–12 ◆ A/R
FANTASY

Roland of Gilead is a gunslinger. The world is a wasteland and Roland is on a quest for the Dark Tower. Along the way he meets murderers, drug dealers, and other dangerous humans. He also encounters nonhuman characters including a cyborg bear and a demonic woman from a parallel world. Time travel, horror, fantasy, and supernatural events will keep YA readers enthralled. This series has evolved over several decades and the first volume has been revised for the 2003 reissue. There is a related guide to the characters, places, and events in the series.

1. The Gunslinger ◆ 2003
2. The Drawing of the Three ◆ 2003
3. The Waste Lands ◆ 2003
4. Wizard and Glass ◆ 2003
5. Wolves of the Calla ◆ 2003
6. Song of Susannah ◆ 2004
7. The Dark Tower ◆ 2004

DARK VISIONS

Smith, L. J.
SIMON & SCHUSTER
GRADES 9–12
FANTASY | HORROR

Kaitlyn Fairchild has psychic powers that have resulted in her receiving a scholarship to the Zetes Institute. Strange, threatening things are happening at the institute even as the students form romantic attachments. Kaitlyn teams up with four other teens to escape the dangerous experiment that has been devised for them.

1. The Strange Power ◆ 1994
2. The Possessed ◆ 1995
3. The Passion ◆ 1995

DARKANGEL TRILOGY

Pierce, Meredith Ann
LITTLE, BROWN
GRADES 6–10 ◆ A/R
FANTASY

Aeriel sets out on a quest to destroy the vampyre Irrylath. However, she cannot resist the fatal allure of this creature and chooses to love him rather than destroy him. Though mortal again, Irrylath is still tormented by the witch through the pull of dreams, and once again Aeriel must fight the dark forces, gathering the gargoyles to do battle with the witch. It is with the aid of a shimmering pearl that Aeriel is able to wage the last battle with the powerful white witch and break the spell cast on her husband.

1. Darkangel ◆ 1982
2. Gathering of the Gargoyles ◆ 1984
3. Pearl of the Soul of the World ◆ 1990

DAUGHTER OF THE LIONESS

Pierce, Tamora
RANDOM HOUSE
GRADES 10–12
FANTASY

Aliane, 16, the intelligent and rebellious daughter of Alanna the Lioness (see Song of the Lioness Quartet), manages to outwit the trickster god Kyprioth. In the second book, Aly is at the center of a rebellion against colonial rulers.

1. Trickster's Choice ◆ 2003
2. Trickster's Queen ◆ 2004

DAUGHTERS OF THE MOON

Ewing, Lynne
HYPERION
GRADES 9–12 ◆ A/R
FANTASY | HORROR

A group of high school girls discover they have magical powers. Catty can travel through time. Serina is a mind reader. Vanessa can become invisible. They must battle the evil of Atrox and the Followers. The multicultural characters will expand the appeal of this series. The combination of mythology and horror should attract the fans of the Buffy books.

1. Goddess of the Night ◆ 2000
2. Into the Cold Fire ◆ 2000
3. Night Shade ◆ 2001
4. The Secret Scroll ◆ 2001
5. The Sacrifice ◆ 2001
6. The Lost One ◆ 2001
7. Moon Demon ◆ 2002
8. Possession ◆ 2002
9. The Choice ◆ 2003
10. The Talisman ◆ 2003
11. The Prophecy ◆ 2004
12. The Becoming ◆ 2004

DAVID BRIN'S OUT OF TIME

Various authors
AVON
GRADES 6–8
FANTASY

In a future Utopian world, conflict and danger no longer exist. It is peaceful. The people are not equipped to deal with problems such as aliens who want to destroy them. Instead, they pull teens from the past to confront terrors. The three books in this series feature different teens who have been "yanked" into the future. In the third book, Adam O'Connor is summoned to face the K'lugu and Devlins, dangerous warlike creatures.

1. Yanked (Kress, Nancy) ◆ 1999
2. Tiger in the Sky (Finch, Sheila) ◆ 1999
3. The Game of Worlds (Allen, Roger MacBride) ◆ 1999

DAWSON'S CREEK

Various authors

SIMON & SCHUSTER

GRADES 7–12

REAL LIFE

Dawson and his friends Joey, Jen, and Pacey share their fears and dreams in these spin-off books from the popular television show. In *Lighthouse Legend*, Joey believes she hears voices in the abandoned lighthouse. Another book follows the teens on a ski weekend. Jack and Andie appear in later books. These books are filled with suspense, romance, and teen anxieties. There are companion materials including a scrapbook, a fan book (with cast biographies and episode guides), and a book about the production of the show.

1. Long Hot Summer (Rodriguez, K. S.) ◆ 1998
2. Calm Before the Storm (Baker, Jennifer) ◆ 1998
3. Shifting into Overdrive (Anders, C. J.) ◆ 1998
4. Major Meltdown (Rodriguez, K. S.) ◆ 1999
5. Double Exposure (Anders, C. J.) ◆ 1999
6. Trouble in Paradise (Anders, C. J.) ◆ 1999
7. Too Hot to Handle (Anders, C. J.) ◆ 1999
8. Don't Scream (Anders, C. J.) ◆ 1999
9. Tough Enough (Anders, C. J.) ◆ 2000
10. Running on Empty (Anders, C. J.) ◆ 2000
11. A Capeside Christmas (Anders, C. J.) ◆ 2000
12. Lighthouse Legend (Teglaar, Liz, and Holly E. Henderson) ◆ 2001
13. Bayou Blues (Fricke, Anna, and Barbara Sieberetz) ◆ 2001
14. Mysterious Boarder (Henderson, Holly E., and Liz Teglaar) ◆ 2001
15. Playing for Keeps (Anders, C. J.) ◆ 2001

DAYSTAR VOYAGES

Morris, Gilbert, and Dan Meeks
MOODY PUBLISHERS
GRADES 6–9 ◆ A/R
SCIENCE FICTION | VALUES

Captain Edge commands the Daystar, a shabby starship with a crew of teens who are dubbed the Junior Space Rangers. As they travel across the galaxy, they work on secret assignments, visit a planet with only children as inhabitants, and defeat wizards who want to control planets. These characters struggle with good and evil; they also deal with circumstances that test their faith.

1. Secret of the Planet Makon ◆ 1998
2. Wizards of the Galaxy ◆ 1998
3. Escape From the Red Comet ◆ 1998
4. Dark Spell Over Morlandria ◆ 1998
5. Revenge of the Space Pirate ◆ 1998
6. Invasion of the Killer Locusts ◆ 1999
7. Dangers of the Rainbow Nebula ◆ 1999
8. Frozen Space Pilot, The ◆ 1999
9. White Dragon of Sharnu, The ◆ 2000
10. Attack of the Denebian Starship ◆ 2000

DAYWORLD

Farmer, Philip José
PUTNAM, TOM DOHERTY ASSOCIATES
GRADES 10–12
SCIENCE FICTION

This futuristic series focuses on the New Era. To cope with overpopulation, suspended animation is used. There are seven groups of people and each group "lives" for one day each week and is suspended for the others. One man, who can transform his appearance, lives every day. When he is discovered, he escapes and finds there are secret groups organizing to rebel against the government.

1. Dayworld ◆ 1985
2. Dayworld Rebel ◆ 1987
3. Dayworld Breakup ◆ 1990

DEAR DIARY

Various authors

BERKLEY

GRADES 7–12

REAL LIFE

In *Runaway*, Cassie is pregnant and Zach is the father. Cassie's father is outraged and sends her to a Home for Girls. Zach finds her and the two run away. Cassie's diary reveals her fears and hopes for her future and her baby. Other books use the diary format to focus on teens in trouble. Shoplifting, Internet "romance," and a girl's search for her biological mother are among the problems described.

1. Runaway (Zach, Cheryl) ◆ 1995
2. Remember Me (Lanham, Cheryl) ◆ 1996
3. Family Secrets (Zach, Cheryl) ◆ 1996
4. Secret Admirer (Zach, Cheryl) ◆ 2000
5. Dying Young (Lanham, Cheryl) ◆ 2000
6. Fighting Back (Lanham, Cheryl) ◆ 2000
7. Shadow Self (Zach, Cheryl) ◆ 2000

DEAR MR. PRESIDENT

Various authors

WINSLOW PRESS

GRADES 5–7 ◆ A/R

HISTORICAL

These books use historical documents—maps, timelines, archival sources—to illuminate a fictional correspondence between a young person and a famous historical figure. Through the letters, the reader learns about the events of the era: FDR and the Great Depression, Lincoln and slavery/the Civil War, and so forth. Readers who enjoy historical fiction books with a diary format, like the Dear America books, will connect with this series.

1. Thomas Jefferson: Letters from a Philadelphia Bookworm (Armstrong, Jennifer) ◆ 2000
2. Theodore Roosevelt: Letters from a Young Coal Miner (Armstrong, Jennifer) ◆ 2001
3. John Quincy Adams: Letters from a Southern Planter's Son (Kroll, Steven) ◆ 2001
4. Franklin Delano Roosevelt: Letters from a Mill Town Girl (Winthrop, Elizabeth) ◆ 2001

5. Abraham Lincoln: Letters from a Slave Girl (Pinkney, Andrea Davis) ◆ 2001
6. Dwight D. Eisenhower: Letters from a New Jersey Schoolgirl (Karr, Kathleen) ◆ 2003

DEEP SPACE NINE *see* Star Trek: Deep Space Nine

DEGREES OF GUILT

Various authors
TYNDALE HOUSE
GRADES 7–10
REAL LIFE

Three teens may be heading for destruction. Kyra, 17, struggles to cope with the pressures of school, the play, and preparing for college. She begins to abuse prescription drugs. Miranda is a senior who decides to be a "party girl." Tyrone, 18, wonders how he might have influenced a friend who overdosed.

1. Kyra's Story (Mackall, Dandi Daley) ◆ 2003
2. Miranda's Story (Carlson, Melody) ◆ 2003
3. Tyrone's Story (Brouwer, Sigmund) ◆ 2003

DELTORA: DELTORA QUEST

Rodda, Emily
SCHOLASTIC
GRADES 4–7 ◆ A/R
FANTASY

Deltora is being threatened by the evil Shadow Lord. The magic belt of Deltora could overcome the evil but only if all seven stones are in the belt. Lief, 16, Barda, and Jasmine seek the stones.

1. The Forests of Silence ◆ 2000
2. The Lake of Tears ◆ 2000
3. City of the Rats ◆ 2000
4. The Shifting Sands ◆ 2001
5. Dread Mountain ◆ 2001
6. The Maze of the Beast ◆ 2001
7. The Valley of the Lost ◆ 2001
8. Return to Del ◆ 2001

DELTORA: DELTORA SHADOWLANDS

Rodda, Emily
SCHOLASTIC
GRADES 4–7 ◆ A/R
FANTASY

Even though the Shadow Lord has been defeated, his evil still reigns over Deltora captives in the Shadowlands. In this new quest, Lief, Barda, and Jasmine seek the Pirran Pipe. This trilogy follows the adventures in the Deltora Quest series.

1. Cavern of the Fear ◆ 2002
2. The Isle of Illusion ◆ 2002
3. The Shadowlands ◆ 2002

DELTORA: DRAGONS OF DELTORA

Rodda, Emily
SCHOLASTIC
GRADES 4–7
FANTASY

Another series set in Deltora and again featuring Lief, Jasmine, and Barda. Now they must get help from seven dragons to save Deltora from the seeds of death that are controlled by the Four Sisters. If they fail, the Shadow Lord will return.

1. Dragons of Deltora ◆ 2004
2. Shadowgate ◆ 2004

THE DEMONWARS

Salvatore, R. A.
BANTAM DOUBLEDAY DELL
GRADES 10–12 ◆ A/R
FANTASY

Elbryan Wyndon and Jilseponie (Pony) Ault, orphans in league with elves, find themselves in conflict with a variety of beings who seek to rule the world. *Mortalis* (2000), a related book, features Pony's efforts to combat a plague. The Second DemonWars Saga starts with *Ascendance* and continues Pony's story. *Highwayman* (2004) begins a new series set in Corona.

1. The Demon Awakes ◆ 1997
2. The Demon Spirit ◆ 1998
3. The Demon Apostle ◆ 1999

THE SECOND DEMONWARS SAGA

1. Ascendance ◆ 2001
2. Transcendence ◆ 2002
3. Immortalis ◆ 2003

THE DENIZENS OF CAMELOT

Morris, Gerald

HOUGHTON MIFFLIN

GRADES 6–9

FANTASY

Tales of Camelot are told from the viewpoint of peripheral characters—for example, Sir Tristram's younger brother Sir Dinadan, an 11-year-old page to Sir Parsifal, and an aristocratic lady seeking aid for her sister.

1. The Squire's Tale ◆ 1998
2. The Squire, His Knight and His Lady ◆ 1999
3. The Savage Damsel and the Dwarf ◆ 2000
4. Parsifal's Page ◆ 2001
5. The Ballad of Sir Dinadan ◆ 2003
6. The Princess, the Crone, and the Dung-Cart Knight ◆ 2004

DEPTFORD MICE

Jarvis, Robin

SEA STAR

GRADES 5–8 ◆ A/R

ANIMAL FANTASY

Fans of the Redwall books by Brian Jacques will connect with this British import about the mice of the London borough of Deptford. They are a quiet group of mice who enjoy a simple life. But when Audrey Brown's father goes missing, the young mouse searches for him in the dangerous sewers. She is followed by her brother and some other brave young mice. In the sewers, the evil cat Jupiter controls the rats with a mysterious power. In the second book, the mice move to the country but the evil follows them. There is a series of prequels called the Deptford Mice Histories.

1. The Dark Portal ◆ 2000
2. The Crystal Prison ◆ 2001
3. The Final Reckoning ◆ 2002

DEPTFORD MICE HISTORIES

Jarvis, Robin
SEA STAR
GRADES 5–8 ◆ A/R
FANTASY

This series provides background information about the events in the Deptford Mice Trilogy. How did Jupiter the cat gain his power over the sewer rats? Originally published in England, the first book of the series is available from Sea Star. Two additional books are in print from Hodder Wayland publishers—*The Oaken Throne* (1993) and *Thomas* (1995).

1. The Alchemist's Cat ◆ 2003

DERYNI *see* Chronicles of Deryni

DEVERRY

Kerr, Katharine
BANTAM
GRADES 10–12 ◆ A/R
FANTASY

This fantasy based on Celtic mythology features a sorcerer named Nevyn and a long battle between good and evil. The first book introduces Nevyn's urge to atone for a wrong he committed. In the second book, Nevyn and companions Rhodry and Jill combat sorcerers who would introduce new vices to the humans of Deverry.

1. Daggerspell ◆ 1986
2. Darkspell ◆ 1987
3. The Bristling Wood ◆ 1989
4. The Dragon Revenant ◆ 1990
5. A Time of Exile ◆ 1991
6. A Time of Omens ◆ 1992
7. Days of Blood and Fire ◆ 1993

8. Days of Air and Darkness ◆ 1994
9. The Red Wyvern ◆ 1997
10. The Black Raven ◆ 1999
11. The Fire Dragon ◆ 2001

DIADEM

Peel, John
SCHOLASTIC
GRADES 6–8 ◆ A/R
ADVENTURE | FANTASY

Three characters from diverse backgrounds and eras are drawn into adventures in another dimension. Score is an orphan from the streets of New York. Renald is a girl warrior from medieval times. Pixel exists in virtual reality. They are kidnapped by an unknown force and drawn toward the Diadem. To survive, they seek the help of magicians, both good and evil, and they try to understand the reason for their selection.

1. Book of Names ◆ 1997
2. Book of Signs ◆ 1997
3. Book of Magic ◆ 1997
4. Book of Thunder ◆ 1997
5. Book of Earth ◆ 1998
6. Book of Nightmares ◆ 1998

THE DIAMOND BROTHERS

Horowitz, Anthony
PHILOMEL
GRADES 5–8 ◆ A/R
HUMOR | MYSTERY

Tim and Nick are the Diamond Brothers. Tim is the older brother and he is not a very good detective. Nick, 13, manages to keep them both one step ahead of trouble and to solve the mystery too. In *The Falcon's Malteser*, Tim has been framed and is in jail for murder. Nick tries to deal with a mysterious package and find the real killer. These books have humorous moments that reflect on the genre of detective fiction.

1. The Falcon's Malteser ◆ 2004
2. Public Enemy, Number Two ◆ 2004

DIARY OF A TEENAGE GIRL

Carlson, Melody
MULTNOMAH
GRADES 9–12
REAL LIFE | VALUES

The first four books in this series feature Caitlin O'Connor, who is 16. As she approaches adulthood, she searches to understand her place in the world. She struggles with her changing role with her family, her friends, and her boyfriend, Josh Miller. Her growing commitment to Christ provides a foundation for her decisions. Using her diary, Caitlin explores her feelings and the issues she faces. Books five through eight are told from the perspective of Chloe Miller, Josh's younger sister. *I Do* returns the focus to Caitlin and her marriage to Josh.

1. Becoming Me ◆ 2000
2. It's My Life ◆ 2002
3. Who I Am ◆ 2002
4. On My Own ◆ 2002
5. My Name Is Chloe ◆ 2003
6. Sold Out ◆ 2003
7. Road Trip ◆ 2003
8. Face the Music ◆ 2004
9. I Do ◆ 2005

DIDO TWITE *see* Wolves Chronicles

DINOTOPIA

Various authors
RANDOM HOUSE
GRADES 6–9 ◆ A/R
FANTASY

Dinotopia Island is a peaceful world where humans and dinosaurs exist as friends. The first book is set in the 1860s and two boys, Raymond and Hugh, are shipwrecked on the island and try to adjust. Subsequent books feature other humans and dinosaurs facing a variety of problems such as a threat to Waterfall City and a journey into the Rainy Basin jungles.

1. Windchaser (Ciencin, Scott) ◆ 1995
2. River Quest (Vornholt, John) ◆ 1995
3. Hatchling (Snyder, Midori) ◆ 1995

4. Lost City (Ciencin, Scott) ◆ 1995
5. Sabertooth Mountain (Vornholt, John) ◆ 1996
6. Thunder Falls (Ciencin, Scott) ◆ 1996
7. Firestorm (DeWeese, Gene) ◆ 1997
8. The Maze (David, Peter) ◆ 1999
9. Rescue Party (Garland, Mark A.) ◆ 1999
10. Sky Dance (Ciencin, Scott) ◆ 2000
11. Chomper (Glut, Don) ◆ 2000
12. Return to Lost City (Ciencin, Scott) ◆ 2000
13. Survive! (Strickland, Brad) ◆ 2001
14. The Explorers (Ciencin, Scott) ◆ 2001
15. Dolphin Watch (Vornholt, John) ◆ 2002
16. Oasis (Hapka, Cathy) ◆ 2002

DINOVERSE

Ciencin, Scott
RANDOM HOUSE
GRADES 6–9 ◆ A/R
FANTASY

It all started when Bertram's science fair project went wacko. He and three junior high classmates—Mike, Candayce, and Janine—travel back to prehistoric times and become dinosaurs. They have to figure out how to survive in their new environment. As the series progresses, other teens have prehistoric adventures. And in one book, Bertram travels back in time while the dinosaurs come to our time. Talk about trouble!

1. I Was a Teenage T. Rex ◆ 2000
2. The Teens Time Forgot ◆ 2000
3. Raptor Without a Cause ◆ 2000
4. Please Don't Eat the Teacher! ◆ 2000
5. Beverly Hills Brontosaurus ◆ 2000
6. Dinosaurs Ate My Homework ◆ 2000

DISCWORLD

Pratchett, Terry
HARPERCOLLINS
GRADES 6–12 ◆ A/R
FANTASY | HUMOR

The Amazing Maurice and His Educated Rodents (winner of the 2001 Carnegie Medal) and the other two titles listed here were written for readers in middle and junior high school. Older readers (grades 10 and up) will enjoy the many absorbing adult installments in this humorous fantasy set on a flat earth populated by everything from dragons to robots.

1. The Amazing Maurice and His Educated Rodents ◆ 2001
2. The Wee Free Men ◆ 2003
3. A Hat Full of Sky: The Continuing Adventures of Tiffany Aching and the Wee Free Men ◆ 2004

Adult Discworld Books

1. The Color of Magic ◆ 1983
2. The Light Fantastic ◆ 1986
3. Equal Rites ◆ 1987
4. Mort ◆ 1987
5. Wyrd Sisters ◆ 1988
6. Sourcery ◆ 1989
7. Pyramids ◆ 1989
8. Guards! Guards! ◆ 1989
9. Eric ◆ 1990
10. Moving Pictures ◆ 1990
11. Reaper Man ◆ 1991
12. Witches Abroad ◆ 1991
13. Lords and Ladies ◆ 1992
14. Small Gods ◆ 1992
15. Men at Arms ◆ 1993
16. Interesting Times ◆ 1994
17. Soul Music ◆ 1995
18. Maskerade ◆ 1995
19. Feet of Clay ◆ 1996
20. Hogfather ◆ 1996
21. Jingo ◆ 1997
22. The Last Continent ◆ 1998
23. Carpe Jugulum ◆ 1999
24. The Fifth Elephant ◆ 2000
25. The Truth ◆ 2000
26. Thief of Time ◆ 2001
27. The Last Hero ◆ 2001
28. Night Watch ◆ 2002
29. The Monstrous Regiment ◆ 2003
30. Going Postal ◆ 2004

DISTRESS CALL 911

Carey, D. L.
SIMON & SCHUSTER
GRADES 7–10
REAL LIFE

These books feature teenagers who have volunteered for emergency services. As "Yellowjackets," they end up in life-and-death situations. One volunteer is trapped in a basement during a flood. Another tries to distance himself from his former gang as they commit arson on Devil's Night. Readers who like adventure where the teens are right in the middle of the action will enjoy these books.

1. Twist of Fate ◆ 1996
2. Buried Alive ◆ 1996
3. Danger Zone ◆ 1996
4. Worth Dying For ◆ 1996
5. Million Dollar Mistake ◆ 1996
6. Roughing It ◆ 1996
7. Promise Me You'll Stop Me ◆ 1997

DIVE

Korman, Gordon
SCHOLASTIC
GRADES 7–10 ◆ A/R
ADVENTURE

On a summer expedition to study marine habitats, four teens find themselves in an exciting and dangerous adventure. Kaz, Star, Adriana, and Dante find a shipwreck with a sunken treasure. Will they be able to recover the treasure? Will the sharks stop them or will human predators reach the treasure first?

1. The Discovery ◆ 2003
2. The Deep ◆ 2003
3. The Danger ◆ 2003

DOGTOWN GHETTO

Bonham, Frank
DELL
GRADES 6–8
REAL LIFE

This series depicts the tough lives of children who grow up in housing projects. Keeny is proud of his Mexican heritage and wants to live up to his dead father's expectations, but he is often led astray by circumstances in his environment. The theme of feeling misunderstood will resonate with readers, and the near-journalistic depiction of street life is admirable, but readers may find much of the material dated. The first book was reissued in 1999.

1. Durango Street ◆ 1965
2. Mystery of the Fat Cat ◆ 1968
3. Golden Bees of Tulami ◆ 1974

DOLLANGANGER

Andrews, V. C.
SIMON & SCHUSTER
GRADES 8–12
HORROR

Four children have been locked away. Their own mother has sinister plans for them. Now they will have their revenge. This series has had a following among teen fans of horror and violence. *Garden of Shadows* is a prequel.

1. Flowers in the Attic ◆ 1979
2. Petals on the Wind ◆ 1980
3. In There Be Thorns ◆ 1981
4. Seeds of Yesterday ◆ 1984
5. Garden of Shadows ◆ 1987

DON'T GET CAUGHT

Strasser, Todd
SCHOLASTIC
GRADES 6–9 ◆ A/R
REAL LIFE

Three middle school boys—Kyle, Dusty, and Wilson—play pranks that put them in danger of being caught. Of course, they narrowly escape the attention of the bumbling adults in their school, which should add to the appeal of this series.

1. Don't Get Caught Driving the School Bus ◆ 2000
2. Don't Get Caught in the Girls' Locker Room ◆ 2001
3. Don't Get Caught in the Teachers' Lounge ◆ 2001
4. Don't Get Caught Wearing the Lunch Lady's Hairnet ◆ 2001

DON'T TOUCH THAT REMOTE!

Abbott, Tony
MINSTREL
GRADES 5–7 ◆ A/R
REAL LIFE

Slapstick situations are commonplace when the middle school becomes the site for a sitcom. Spencer Babbitt and his friends must come up with enough action to keep the cameras rolling. They succeed with immature, even gross, antics that should appeal to 'tween readers.

1. Sitcom School ◆ 1999
2. The Fake Teacher ◆ 1999
3. Stinky Business ◆ 1999

DRAGON BALL

Toriyama, Akira
VIZ COMMUNICATIONS
GRADES 7–10
FANTASY

Goku is a monkey-tailed boy who joins Bulma on a quest for seven Dragon Balls to give to the Eternal Dragon. This act will be rewarded with one wish. Goku and Bulma team up with Kuririn and face many enemies including ghouls, a robot, a giant octopus, Commander Blue, and the Great Demon King Piccolo. Related materials include drawing/tracing books and strategy guides.

1. Volume 1 ◆ 2003
2. Volume 2 ◆ 2003
3. Volume 3 ◆ 2003
4. Volume 4 ◆ 2003
5. Volume 5 ◆ 2003
6. Volume 6 ◆ 2003

7. Volume 7 ◆ 2003
8. Volume 8 ◆ 2003
9. Volume 9 ◆ 2003
10. Volume 10 ◆ 2003
11. Volume 11 ◆ 2003

12. Volume 12 ◆ 2003
13. Volume 13 ◆ 2003
14. Volume 14 ◆ 2004
15. Volume 15 ◆ 2004

DRAGON BALL Z

Toriyama, Akira
VIZ COMMUNICATIONS
GRADES 7–10
FANTASY

Goku grows and faces many dangers in this manga series from Japan. He discovers that one enemy is his brother, Raditz. Another danger comes from Cell, a creature from the future that destroys cities and eats people. Throughout the adventures, there are time travels, special training, and magical maneuvers that help Goku and his colleagues. Related materials include drawing/tracing books and strategy guides.

1. Volume 1 ◆ 2003
2. Volume 2 ◆ 2003
3. Volume 3 ◆ 2003
4. Volume 4 ◆ 2003
5. Volume 5 ◆ 2003
6. Volume 6 ◆ 2003
7. Volume 7 ◆ 2003
8. Volume 8 ◆ 2003

9. Volume 9 ◆ 2003
10. Volume 10 ◆ 2003
11. Volume 11 ◆ 2003
12. Volume 12 ◆ 2003
13. Volume 13 ◆ 2003
14. Volume 14 ◆ 2003
15. Volume 15 ◆ 2004

DRAGON CHRONICLES

Fletcher, Susan
ATHENEUM
GRADES 6–9
ADVENTURE | FANTASY

With her strange green eyes, Kaeldra, 15, is an outsider. The king of Elythian uses her ability to communicate with dragons to arrange for dragons to be killed. Kara is heartsick and runs away, joining a "Kyn" (family) of dragons. In a later book, the dragons are aided by Lyf, Kaeldra's foster sister. *Flight of the Dragon Kyn* is a prequel to *Dragon's Milk*.

1. Dragon's Milk ◆ 1989
2. Flight of the Dragon Kyn ◆ 1993
3. Sign of the Dove ◆ 1996

DRAGON OF THE LOST SEA

Yep, Laurence
HARPERCOLLINS
GRADES 6–9 ◆ A/R
FANTASY

Shimmer is able to leave the human world and transform herself into dragon form. In the first novel, she tries to redeem herself by capturing a witch with the help of Thorn, her human companion. In each book, there is a quest or adventure that Shimmer and her companions must experience.

1. Dragon of the Lost Sea ◆ 1982
2. Dragon Steel ◆ 1985
3. Dragon Cauldron ◆ 1991
4. Dragon War ◆ 1992

THE DRAGON QUARTET

Kellogg, Marjorie
DAW
GRADES 7–12
FANTASY

Four dragons—Earth, Water, Fire, and Air—may hold the future of the world in their hands in this series with an environmental focus on a future America. In the third book, Fire rebels and in the last book Earth and Water struggle to rescue Air and to control Fire's dangerous actions.

1. The Book of Earth ◆ 1995
2. The Book of Water ◆ 1997
3. The Book of Fire ◆ 2000
4. The Book of Air ◆ 2003

DRAGONCROWN WAR CYCLE

Stackpole, Michael A.
BANTAM
GRADES 10–12
FANTASY

An evil sorceress named Chytrine rules the city of Yslin. Will, a young thief, discovers to his surprise that he holds the key to overthrowing this brutal regime. In the second book, Will and a varied cast of rebels band together to resist Chytrine's renewed attacks in her search for pieces of the DragonCrown. This adult series is recommended for mature teens.

1. Fortress Draconis ◆ 2001
2. When Dragons Rage ◆ 2002
3. The Grand Crusade ◆ 2003

DRAGONFLIGHT BOOKS

Various authors

IPICTUREBOOKS

GRADES 7–10

FANTASY

The books in this series all have a supernatural element that adds to the danger and mystery: shape shifters, time travel, mind transfers, nightmares, spirit visions, encounters with a vampire, and more. Three of the books—*Black Unicorn*, *Gold Unicorn*, and *Red Unicorn*—feature a character named Tanaquil, who is the daughter of a sorceress.

1. Letters from Atlantis (Silverberg, Robert) ◆ 1990
2. Black Unicorn (Lee, Tanith) ◆ 1991
3. The Sleep of Stone (Cooper, Louise) ◆ 1991
4. Child of an Ancient City (Williams, Tad) ◆ 1992
5. Dragon's Plunder (Strickland, Brad) ◆ 1992
6. The Dreaming Place (De Lint, Charles) ◆ 1992
7. Wishing Season (Friesner, Esther M.) ◆ 1993
8. The Wizard's Apprentice (Somtow, S. P.) ◆ 1993
9. Gold Unicorn (Lee, Tanith) ◆ 1994
10. Born of Elven Blood (Anderson, Kevin J.) ◆ 1995
11. The Monster's Legacy (Norton, Andre) ◆ 1996
12. The Orphan's Tent (De Haven, Tom) ◆ 1996
13. Monet's Ghost (Yarbro, Chelsea Quinn) ◆ 1997
14. Red Unicorn (Lee, Tanith) ◆ 1997

DRAGONLANCE DEFENDERS OF MAGIC

Kirchoff, Mary L.

WIZARDS OF THE COAST

GRADES 9–12

FANTASY

The land of Krynn has three moons. When they form a line in the sky, it is the Night of the Eye. On this night, Guerrand DiThon leaves his betrothed to begin a search for wizardly powers in the Tower of Wayreth. Eventually, he becomes the High Defender of Bastion, but evil forces seek to destroy him. There are many Dragonlance books connected with the role-playing games.

1. Night of the Eye ◆ 1994
2. The Medusa Plague ◆ 1994
3. The Seventh Sentinel ◆ 1995

DRAGONLANCE DWARVEN NATIONS TRILOGY

Parkinson, Dan
WIZARDS OF THE COAST
GRADES 9–12
FANTASY

Fans of the Dragonlance role-playing games will read these books set in the land of Krynn. The dwarven clans come together to secure the survival of their race. There are many Dragonlance books connected with the role-playing games.

1. The Covenant of the Forge ◆ 1993
2. Hammer and Axe ◆ 1993
3. The Swordsheath Scroll ◆ 1994

DRAGONMASTER

Bunch, Chris
ORBIT BOOK CO
GRADES 9–12
FANTASY

As this series begins, Hal Kailas, 13, is fascinated with dragons. Years pass and Hal becomes a Dragonmaster and joins the dragon fliers. His goal is to avenge the deaths of his comrades in the war against the Roche.

1. Storm of Wings ◆ 2003
2. Knighthood of the Dragon ◆ 2003
3. The Last Battle ◆ 2004

DRAGONS OF DELTORA *see* Deltora: Dragons of Deltora

DREAM SERIES

Various authors
SCOBRE PRESS
GRADES 6–12 ◆ A/R
RECREATION

Each of these books features characters involved in sports who are also trying to deal with problems in their own lives. In *The Highest Stand*, Dede is on the outside until he begins to run in hurdle races. He hopes to win the race and the acceptance of his peers. *Hoop City* features African American twins who confront a tragedy when Mike is paralyzed. His brother, Tony, is inspired to achieve. Different sports (including soccer, tennis, football, golf, and more) involving males and females provide the foundation for these inspiring stories. The grade level varies among the books from middle school through young adults.

1. The Road to the Majors (Blumenthal, Scott) ◆ 2001
2. Hoop City (Blumenthal, Scott) ◆ 2002
3. Keeper (Sloan, Holly Goldberg) ◆ 2002
4. Chasing the King (Stein, Joshua) ◆ 2003
5. The Green (Reichman, Justin) ◆ 2003
6. The Highest Stand (Campbell, Tonie) ◆ 2003
7. The Kid from Courage (Berman, Ron) ◆ 2003
8. Long Shot (Fowler, Marie) ◆ 2003
9. The Long Way Around (Hand, Jimmie) ◆ 2003

EARTHSEA

Le Guin, Ursula K.
ATHENEUM
GRADES 7–8 ◆ A/R
FANTASY

Readers who enjoy Tolkien's Middle Earth books and the Narnia books by C. S. Lewis will enjoy this journey into the realm of wizards and dragons. This fantasy world is full of strong characters and powerful language and features Sparrowhawk, apprentice to a master wizard. As in many fantasies, there is a confrontation with the powers of darkness, and the realization that some of the most dangerous evils come from within. *Tales of Earthsea* (2001) is a collection of five Earthsea stories.

1. A Wizard of Earthsea ◆ 1968
2. The Tombs of Atuan ◆ 1971
3. The Farthest Shore ◆ 1972
4. Tehanu ◆ 1990
5. The Other Wind ◆ 2001

ECHORIUM SEQUENCE

Roberts, Katherine

CHICKEN HOUSE

GRADES 6–9 ◆ A/R

FANTASY

Echorium is the Land of Echoes. Three students—Rialle, Kherron, and Frenn—are learning to be Singers so their songs will influence the thoughts and feelings of other beings. The world is filled with strange creatures and conflicts. The events in the second and third books take place decades after those in the first.

1. Song Quest ◆ 2001
2. Crystal Mask ◆ 2001
3. Dark Quetzal ◆ 2003

EDGAR AND ELLEN

Ogden, Charles

TRICYCLE PRESS

GRADES 4–7 ◆ A/R

HUMOR

Edgar and Ellen are 12-year-old twins. They live in a dilapidated mansion and enjoy creating chaos. For example, they decorate the neighbor's pets and try to sell them as exotic animals. This series might be a choice for the fans of Lemony Snicket.

1. Rare Beasts ◆ 2003
2. Tourist Trap ◆ 2004
3. Under Town ◆ 2004

EERIE INDIANA

Various authors

AVON CAMELOT

GRADES 5–8

HORROR | MYSTERY

Marshall Teller and his family have left the crowded, noisy, crime-filled streets of a New Jersey city to live the bucolic small-town life in Eerie, Indiana. What a mistake! This town is not normal. Weird things happen here, like the release of characters from a cryogenic store—including Jesse James. Then, there is a dollhouse that looks like a real house and a doll that looks like a real girl and Marshall seems to be getting smaller. This series mixes the horror genre with bizarre situations that many readers will find amusing.

1. Return to Foreverware (Ford, Mike) ◆ 1997
2. Bureau of Lost (Peel, John) ◆ 1997
3. The Eerie Triangle (Ford, Mike) ◆ 1997
4. Simon and Marshall's Excellent Adventure (Peel, John) ◆ 1997
5. Have Yourself an Eerie Little Christmas (Ford, Mike) ◆ 1997
6. Fountain of Weird (Shahan, Sherry) ◆ 1998
7. Attack of the Two-Ton Tomatoes (Ford, Mike) ◆ 1998
8. Who Framed Alice Prophet? (Ford, Mike) ◆ 1998
9. Bring Me a Dream (James, Robert) ◆ 1998
10. Finger-Lickin' Strange (Roberts, Jeremy) ◆ 1998
11. The Dollhouse that Time Forgot (Ford, Mike) ◆ 1998
12. They Say (Ford, Mike) ◆ 1998
13. Switching Channels (Ford, Mike) ◆ 1998
14. The Incredible Shrinking Stanley (James, Robert) ◆ 1998
15. Halloweird (Ford, Mike) ◆ 1998
16. Eerie in the Mirror (James, Robert) ◆ 1998
17. We Wish You an Eerie Christmas (James, Robert) ◆ 1998

EGERTON HALL NOVELS

Geras, Adèle

HARCOURT

GRADES 9–12

REAL LIFE

Megan, Bella, and Alice become friends at an exclusive British girls' school in the early 1960s. The clash between their secluded school surroundings and the often harsh nature of the outside world provides the basis for many of the plots. The girls confront jealous stepmothers, family curses, and first loves over the course of the series, which uses fairy tales as a foundation. *Pictures of the Night*, for example, is based on the story of Snow White.

1. The Tower Room ◆ 1990
2. Watching the Roses ◆ 1991
3. Pictures of the Night ◆ 1992

ElfQuest

Pini, Wendy, and Richard Pini
DC COMICS
GRADES 9–12
FANTASY

This graphic novel fantasy series first appeared in the 1970s and has been reissued in small, manga-sized paperbacks. The series focuses on Chief Cutter, a tribal leader whose mythological heritage provides guidance for his people. The elves have been isolated and secure. The problems begin when humans move too close to the elves.

1. EflQuest: Wolfrider: Vol. 1 ◆ 2003
2. ElfQuest: Archives: Vol. 1 ◆ 2003
3. ElfQuest: The Grand Quest: Vol. 1 ◆ 2004
4. ElfQuest: The Grand Quest: Vol. 2 ◆ 2004
5. ElfQuest: The Grand Quest: Vol. 3 ◆ 2004
6. ElfQuest: The Grand Quest: Vol. 4 ◆ 2004
7. ElfQuest: The Grand Quest: Vol. 5 ◆ 2004
8. ElfQuest: The Grand Quest: Vol. 6 ◆ 2004
9. ElfQuest: The Grand Quest: Vol. 7 ◆ 2004
10. ElfQuest: The Grand Quest: Vol. 8 ◆ 2004
11. ElfQuest: The Searcher and the Sword ◆ 2004

THE ELLIOTT COUSINS

Thesman, Jean
AVON
GRADES 7–8
REAL LIFE

Jamie, Meredith, and Teresa are cousins and very close friends. They meet at an annual family reunion and help each other with problems, especially those with boys. Teresa is shy and her mother is overprotective, so when she meets a new boy named Ian her insecurities almost keep her from making friends with him and getting her first kiss. Jamie is afraid to tell her boyfriend that she wants to see other people.

Meredith is still getting over being betrayed by her boyfriend and her (former) best friend. These are romances that will appeal to junior high girls.

1. Jamie ◆ 1998
2. Meredith ◆ 1998
3. Teresa ◆ 1998

EMORTALITY

Stableford, Brian
ST. MARTIN'S PRESS
GRADES 9–12
SCIENCE FICTION

In a 22nd-century world of plenty, Damon Hart, son of the inventor of the artificial womb, is under attack from those who accuse his father of wrongdoing. This series, written for adults, looks at biotechnology, longevity, and the spread of the human race. In *Dark Ararat*, colonists arriving on a supposedly habitable planet tackle a number of challenges.

1. Inherit the Earth ◆ 1998
2. Architects of Emortality ◆ 1999
3. The Fountains of Youth ◆ 2000
4. The Cassandra Complex ◆ 2001
5. Dark Ararat ◆ 2002
6. The Omega Expedition ◆ 2002

ENCHANTED FOREST CHRONICLES

Wrede, Patricia C.
HARCOURT; SCHOLASTIC
GRADES 4–7 ◆ A/R
FANTASY

Sensing the boredom that awaits her if she marries Prince Therandil as her parents require, reluctant princess Cimorene escapes to the Enchanted Forest to meet Kazul, King of the Dragons. With the dragons, Cimorene finally experiences the adventure she craves. Throughout the series, Cimorene and Kazul confront wicked wizards to save the forest.

1. Dealing with Dragons ◆ 1990

2. Searching for Dragons ◆ 1991
3. Calling on Dragons ◆ 1993
4. Talking to Dragons ◆ 1993

ENCHANTED HEARTS

Various authors

AVON

GRADES 7–12

FANTASY

Romance with a touch of the supernatural is the focus of these books. Gina realizes her family's house is haunted. Emily gets some help with a witch. Colleen must choose between Kevin and Luke—will hypnosis help?

1. The Haunted Heart (Bennett, Cherie) ◆ 1999
2. Eternally Yours (Baker, Jennifer) ◆ 1999
3. Lost and Found (Dokey, Cameron) ◆ 1999
4. Love Potion (Quin-Harkin, Janet) ◆ 1999
5. Spellbound (Karas, Phyllis) ◆ 1999
6. Love Him Forever (Bennett, Cherie) ◆ 1999

ENDER WIGGIN

Card, Orson Scott

TOM DOHERTY ASSOCIATES

GRADES 9–12 ◆ A/R

SCIENCE FICTION

Ender Wiggin is selected to attend a special school that will hone his computer talents. Although he is just a child, he has the skills to command the Earth fleet that is the last defense against an alien race. After these experiences, Ender tries to prevent war from starting in *Speaker for the Dead. First Meetings in the Enderverse* (Tor, 2003) includes *Ender's Game* and three novellas about Ender.

1. Ender's Game ◆ 1985
2. Speaker for the Dead ◆ 1986
3. Xenocide ◆ 1991
4. Children of the Mind ◆ 1996
5. Ender's Shadow ◆ 1999
6. Shadow of the Hegemon ◆ 2001
7. Shadow Puppets ◆ 2002

ENDLESS QUEST

Various authors

TSR; WIZARDS OF THE COAST

GRADES 9–12

FANTASY

You are Caric, a fighter lured into a dungeon of treasure; you are Landon, an elf . . . ; you are Jaimie, a villager . . . . These are some of the scenarios in these books that connect to the Dungeons and Dragons game worlds. Elves, goblins, ogres, and other creatures try to keep you from your mission. Readers make choices (as in Choose Your Own Adventure books). In the first series, most of the books use Dungeons and Dragons settings. In the second series, most of the settings are from Advanced Dungeon and Dragons games. Both series contain books that link to other game worlds.

THE FIRST SERIES

1. Dungeon of Dread (Estes, Rose) ◆ 1982
2. Mountain of Mirrors (Estes, Rose) ◆ 1982
3. Pillars of Pentegarn (Estes, Rose) ◆ 1982
4. Return to Brookmere (Estes, Rose) ◆ 1982
5. Revolt of the Dwarves (Estes, Rose) ◆ 1983
6. Revenge of the Rainbow Dragons (Estes, Rose) ◆ 1983
7. Hero of Washington Square (Estes, Rose) ◆ 1983
8. Villains of Volturnus (Blashfield, Jean) ◆ 1983
9. Robbers and Robots (Carr, Mike) ◆ 1983
10. Circus of Fear (Estes, Rose) ◆ 1983
11. Spell of the Winter Wizard (Lowery, Linda) ◆ 1983
12. Light on Quests Mountain (Kirchoff, Mary L.) ◆ 1983
13. Dragon of Doom (Estes, Rose) ◆ 1983
14. Raid on Nightmare Castle (McGuire, Catherine) ◆ 1983
15. Under Dragon's Wing (Kendall, John) ◆ 1983
16. Dragon's Ransom (French, Laura) ◆ 1983
17. Captive Planet (Simon, Morris) ◆ 1984
18. King's Quest (McGowen, Tom) ◆ 1984
19. Conan the Undaunted (Ward, James Michael) ◆ 1984
20. Conan and the Prophecy (Moore, Roger E.) ◆ 1984
21. Duel of the Masters (Martindale, Chris) ◆ 1984
22. Endless Catacombs (Weis, Margaret Baldwin) ◆ 1984
23. Blade of the Young Samurai (Simon, Morris) ◆ 1984
24. Trouble on Artule (McGuire, Catherine) ◆ 1984
25. Conan the Outlaw (Moore, Roger E.) ◆ 1985

26. Tarzan and the Well of Slaves (Niles, Douglas) ◆ 1985
27. Lair of the Lich (Algozin, Bruce) ◆ 1985
28. Mystery of the Ancients (Simon, Morris) ◆ 1985
29. Tower of Darkness (Fultz, Regina Oehler) ◆ 1985
30. Fireseed (Simon, Morris) ◆ 1985
31. Tarzan and the Tower of Diamonds (Reinsmith, Richard) ◆ 1986
32. Prisoner of Elderwood (Algozin, Bruce) ◆ 1986
33. Knights of Illusion (Kirchoff, Mary L.) ◆ 1986
34. Claw of the Dragon (Algozin, Bruce) ◆ 1986
35. Vision of Doom (Kirchoff, Mary L.) ◆ 1987
36. Song of the Dark Druid (Sherman, Josepha) ◆ 1987

THE SECOND SERIES

1. Dungeon of Fear (Andrews, Michael) ◆ 1994
2. Castle of the Undead (Baron, Nick) ◆ 1994
3. Secret of the Djinn (Rabe, Jean) ◆ 1994
4. Siege of the Tower (Antilles, Kem) ◆ 1994
5. A Wild Ride (Anderson, Louis) ◆ 1994
6. Forest of Darkness (Andrews, Michael) ◆ 1994
7. American Knights (Pollotta, Nick) ◆ 1995
8. Night of the Tiger (Rabe, Jean) ◆ 1995
9. Galactic Challenge (Varney, Allen) ◆ 1995
10. Bigby's Curse (Brown, Anne) ◆ 1995
11. The 24-Hour War (Pollotta, Nick) ◆ 1995
12. The Test (Nicholson, Wes) ◆ 1996
13. Sands of Deception (Rabe, Jean) ◆ 1996

EVEREST

Korman, Gordon
SCHOLASTIC
GRADES 6–9 ◆ A/R
ADVENTURE

Climbing Mount Everest. It's dangerous. It's deadly. Especially if you are one of four teens hoping to be the youngest to reach the summit. It's even more difficult when one member of the expedition is a saboteur.

1. The Contest ◆ 2002
2. The Climb ◆ 2002
3. The Summit ◆ 2002

EVERWOOD

Various authors
SIMON & SCHUSTER
GRADES 7–12
REAL LIFE

Ephram Brown is a teenager whose life seems normal. He's close to his mom and distant from his dad, a neurosurgeon who is busy with work. When his mom dies in an accident, Ephram's father moves the family to Everwood, Colorado. After living in New York City, this small town seems dull . . . until he meets Amy. But Amy has a boyfriend who is in a coma and Dr. Brown is going to operate on him. This series parallels the popular television series.

1. First Impressions (Burns, Laura J., and Melinda Metz) ◆ 2004
2. Moving On (Harrison, Emma) ◆ 2004
3. Love Under Wraps (Harrison, Emma) ◆ 2004
4. Making Choices (Burns, Laura J., and Melinda Metz) ◆ 2004
5. Slipping Away (Harrison, Emma) ◆ 2005

EVERWORLD

Applegate, K. A.
SCHOLASTIC
GRADES 7–12 ◆ A/R
FANTASY

Five high schoolers are drawn into adventures in a parallel universe. They encounter monsters, mythological characters, and magic. In the first book, Senna has been captured by a wolflike creature. David and his friends enter a strange and dangerous place to try to rescue her.

1. Search for Senna ◆ 1999
2. Land of Loss ◆ 1999
3. Enter the Enchanted ◆ 1999
4. Realm of the Reaper ◆ 1999
5. Discover the Destroyer ◆ 2000
6. Fear the Fantastic ◆ 2000
7. Gateway to the Gods ◆ 2000
8. Brave the Betrayal ◆ 2000
9. Inside the Illusion ◆ 2000
10. Understand the Unknown ◆ 2000
11. Mystify the Magician ◆ 2001
12. Entertain the End ◆ 2001

EXTREME TEAM

Christopher, Matt

LITTLE, BROWN

GRADES 4–7 ◆ A/R

RECREATION

Mark Goldstein and his friends enjoy skateboarding and doing kick-flips and ollies. But Mark is embarrassed because he is not as coordinated as the others. Taking kung fu classes helps improve his control and gives him insights into his feelings. In all the books, there is a nice mix of sports and character interaction.

1. One Smooth Move ◆ 2004
2. Day of the Dragon ◆ 2004
3. Roller Hockey Rumble ◆ 2004
4. On Thin Ice ◆ 2004
5. Rock On ◆ 2004
6. Into the Danger Zone ◆ 2004
7. Wild Ride ◆ 2005

EXTREME ZONE

Sumner, M. C.

SIMON & SCHUSTER

GRADES 7–12 ◆ A/R

HORROR

Kathleen "Harley" Davisidaro got her nickname because she rides a Harley. With her friend, Noah Templer, she investigates a mysterious research facility. They end up in the Extreme Zone—a creepy world where they can trust no one.

1. Night Terrors ◆ 1997
2. Dark Lies ◆ 1997
3. Unseen Powers ◆ 1997
4. Deadly Secrets ◆ 1997
5. Common Enemy ◆ 1997
6. Inhuman Fury ◆ 1997
7. Lost Soul ◆ 1997
8. Dead End ◆ 1998

FAB 5

Rushton, Rosie
HYPERION
GRADES 7–10 ◆ A/R
REAL LIFE

Chelsea, Laura, Jemma, Jon, and Sumitha are five British teens who want to establish their independence. In one book, Sumitha lies to her father, who adheres to his Bengali traditions. Will she be found out? Jemma's mother is overly protective. The friends struggle with serious issues such as anorexia and depression along with more usual concerns about dating and romance.

1. Just Don't Make a Scene, Mum! ◆ 1999
2. Think I'll Just Curl Up and Die ◆ 1999
3. How Could You Do This To Me, Mum? ◆ 1999
4. Where Do We Go From Here? ◆ 1999
5. Poppy ◆ 2000
6. Olivia ◆ 2000
7. Sophie ◆ 2000
8. Melissa ◆ 2000

FABULOUS FIVE

Haynes, Betsy
BANTAM
GRADES 6–9
REAL LIFE

Five junior high girls experience ups and downs in relationships with boys, school activities, other groups, and in their friendships with each other. Each book features one of the girls, who all excel in different areas. This is the same group that united in elementary school against the snobby Taffy Sinclair in the series by that name.

1. Seventh Grade Rumors ◆ 1988
2. The Trouble with Flirting ◆ 1988
3. The Popularity Trap ◆ 1988
4. Her Honor, Katie Shannon ◆ 1988
5. The Bragging War ◆ 1989
6. Parent Game ◆ 1989
7. The Kissing Disaster ◆ 1989
8. The Runaway Crisis ◆ 1989

9. The Boyfriend Dilemma ◆ 1989
10. Playing the Part ◆ 1989
11. Hit and Run ◆ 1989
12. Katie's Dating Tips ◆ 1989
13. The Christmas Countdown ◆ 1989
14. Seventh-Grade Menace ◆ 1989
15. Melanie's Identity Crisis ◆ 1990
16. The Hot-line Emergency ◆ 1990
17. Celebrity Auction ◆ 1990
18. Teen Taxi ◆ 1990
19. Boys Only Club ◆ 1990
20. The Witches of Wakeman ◆ 1990
21. Jana to the Rescue ◆ 1990
22. Melanie's Valentine ◆ 1991
23. Mall Mania ◆ 1991
24. The Great TV Turnoff ◆ 1991
25. Fabulous Five Minus One ◆ 1991
26. Laura's Secret ◆ 1991
27. The Scapegoat ◆ 1991
28. Breaking Up ◆ 1991
29. Melanie Edwards, Super Kisser ◆ 1992
30. Sibling Rivalry ◆ 1992
31. The Fabulous Five Together Again ◆ 1992
32. Class Trip Calamity ◆ 1992

THE FACE ON THE MILK CARTON *see* Janie

THE FAIRY GODMOTHER

Scarborough, Elizabeth Ann
BERKLEY/ACE
GRADES 7–12
FANTASY | HUMOR

In Seattle, Rosalie gets what she wants: a fairy godmother. Although this godmother's abilities are somewhat limited, she succeeds in some of her goals and provides entertainment and a review of some classic fairy tales in the process. In *The Godmother's Apprentice*, Snohomish Quantrill ("Sno"—or Snow White) travels to Ireland to learn from Dame Felicity Fortune.

1. The Godmother ◆ 1994
2. The Godmother's Apprentice ◆ 1995
3. The Godmother's Web ◆ 1998

THE FALLEN

Sniegoski, Thomas E.
SIMON & SCHUSTER
GRADES 8–12
FANTASY

Aaron Corbet, 18, discovers he has special powers. He wonders why and learns he is a Nephilim—an offspring of an angel and an earth woman. Aaron must face "the Powers" that want to kill him. The series follows Aaron's encounters with those who want to keep him from fulfilling the prophecy that he is the one who will reunite the fallen angels with Heaven.

1. The Fallen ◆ 2003
2. Leviathan ◆ 2003
3. Aerie ◆ 2003
4. Reckoning ◆ 2004

FARSALA TRILOGY

Bell, Hilari
SIMON & SCHUSTER
GRADES 6–10
FANTASY

This fantasy is set in Farsala, a Persia-like culture that is under threat of attack. The Hrum army, which has characteristics of the ancient Roman military, plans to take over the country and add it to the Hrum empire. Three teens play pivotal roles in the conflict: Jiaan, the illegitimate son of the High Commander of the Farsala Army; Soraya, the High Commander's daughter; and Kavi, a traveling merchant. Watch for the remaining volume of this intricate trilogy.

1. Flame ◆ 2003
2. Fall of a Kingdom ◆ 2005

FAT GLENDA

Perl, Lila
CLARION
GRADES 4–8
REAL LIFE

Overweight Glenda struggles with her weight over the course of the series. She loses pounds and finds a boyfriend, only to gain the weight back when he doesn't call. Later, she meets an even more obese teen who interests her in plus-size modeling, Throughout, her mother makes things more difficult for her by denying that she has a problem.

1. Me and Fat Glenda ◆ 1972
2. Hey, Remember Fat Glenda? ◆ 1981
3. Fat Glenda's Summer Romance ◆ 1986
4. Fat Glenda Turns Fourteen ◆ 1991

FEAR STREET

Stine, R. L.
SIMON & SCHUSTER
GRADES 7–10 ◆ A/R
HORROR

Evil, danger, creatures, murders, and more are featured in these books from the master of horror. In *Into the Dark*, Paulette Fox is blind and in love with Brad Jones. But her friends are sure he committed a horrible crime. Can Paulette trust her heart? In *Trapped*, there is a sinister red mist in the tunnels under Shadyside High School. When a group of teens explore the tunnels, their escape is blocked by the skeletons of teens who died there years ago.

1. The New Girl ◆ 1989
2. The Surprise Party ◆ 1989
3. The Overnight ◆ 1989
4. Missing ◆ 1989
5. The Wrong Number ◆ 1990
6. The Sleepwalker ◆ 1990
7. Haunted ◆ 1990
8. Halloween Party ◆ 1990
9. The Stepsister ◆ 1990
10. Ski Weekend ◆ 1990
11. The Fire Game ◆ 1990
12. Lights Out ◆ 1991
13. The Secret Bedroom ◆ 1992
14. The Knife ◆ 1992
15. Prom Queen ◆ 1992
16. First Date ◆ 1992
17. The Best Friend ◆ 1992
18. The Cheater ◆ 1993
19. Sunburn ◆ 1993
20. The New Boy ◆ 1993
21. The Dare ◆ 1994
22. Bad Dreams ◆ 1994
23. Double Date ◆ 1994
24. The Thrill Club ◆ 1994

25. One Evil Summer ◆ 1994
26. The Mind Reader ◆ 1994
27. Wrong Number 2 ◆ 1994
28. Truth or Dare ◆ 1994
29. Dead End ◆ 1995
30. Final Grade ◆ 1995
31. Switched ◆ 1995
32. College Weekend ◆ 1995
33. The Stepsister 2 ◆ 1995
34. What Holly Heard ◆ 1995
35. The Face ◆ 1995
36. Secret Admirer ◆ 1996
37. The Perfect Date ◆ 1996
38. The Confession ◆ 1996
39. The Boy Next Door ◆ 1996
40. Night Games ◆ 1996
41. The Runaway ◆ 1996
42. Killer's Kiss ◆ 1997
43. All-Night Party ◆ 1997
44. The Rich Girl ◆ 1997
45. Cat ◆ 1996
46. Who Killed the Homecoming Queen ◆ 1997
47. Into the Dark ◆ 1997
48. The Best Friend 2 ◆ 1997
49. Midnight Diary ◆ 1997
50. Trapped ◆ 1997
51. The Stepbrother ◆ 1998
52. Camp Out ◆ 1998
53. Let's All Kill Jennifer ◆ 1998

FEAR STREET: FEAR STREET CHEERLEADERS

Stine, R. L.

SIMON & SCHUSTER

GRADES 7–10

HORROR

An evil spirit is lurking, waiting to take control of unsuspecting teens and make them kill. Corky Corcoran thought she destroyed the spirit (and she died in the process). Will Amanda open the wooden box that Corky left behind?

1. First Evil ◆ 1992
2. Second Evil ◆ 1992
3. Third Evil ◆ 1992
4. The New Evil ◆ 1994

FEAR STREET: FEAR STREET SAGAS

Stine, R. L.
SIMON & SCHUSTER
GRADES 7–10
HORROR

The town of Shadyside is controlled by the evil power of the curse of the Fear family. In *A New Fear*, Nora Goode married Daniel Fear, hoping to escape the curse. But the pair died in a fire on their wedding day and their son was the only survivor. Will he follow the evil of the Fears?

1. A New Fear ◆ 1996
2. House of Whispers ◆ 1996
3. Forbidden Secrets ◆ 1996
4. The Sign of Fear ◆ 1996
5. The Hidden Evil ◆ 1997
6. Daughters of Silence ◆ 1997
7. Children of Fear ◆ 1997
8. Dance of Death ◆ 1997
9. Heart of the Hunter ◆ 1997
10. The Awakening Evil ◆ 1997
11. Circle of Fire ◆ 1998
12. Chamber of Fear ◆ 1998
13. Faces of Terror ◆ 1998
14. One Last Kiss ◆ 1998
15. Door of Death ◆ 1998
16. Hand of Power ◆ 1998

FEAR STREET SAGAS TRILOGY

1. The Betrayal ◆ 1993
2. The Secret ◆ 1993
3. The Burning ◆ 1993

FEAR STREET: FEAR STREET SENIORS

Stine, R. L.
GOLDEN BOOKS
GRADES 7–10
HORROR

Trisha's party turns sinister when she has a premonition that her classmates will not survive their senior year.

1. Let's Party ◆ 1998
2. In Too Deep ◆ 1998

3. The Thirst ◆ 1998
4. No Answer ◆ 1998
5. Last Chance ◆ 1998
6. The Gift ◆ 1998
7. Fight, Team, Fight ◆ 1999
8. Sweetheart, Evil Heart ◆ 1999
9. Spring Break ◆ 1999
10. Wicked ◆ 1999
11. Prom Date ◆ 1999
12. Graduation Day ◆ 1999

FEAR STREET: FEAR STREET SUPER CHILLERS

Stine, R. L.
SIMON & SCHUSTER
GRADES 7–10
HORROR

Teens face more danger in this series. Josie is receiving threatening Valentines. Billy is chasing vampires. And one by one, the lifeguards are disappearing. There are many cliff-hanging moments in these fast-paced thrillers.

1. Party Summer ◆ 1991
2. Silent Night ◆ 1991
3. Goodnight Kiss ◆ 1992
4. Broken Hearts ◆ 1993
5. Silent Night 2 ◆ 1993
6. The Dead Lifeguard ◆ 1993
7. The New Evil: Cheerleaders ◆ 1994
8. Bad Moonlight ◆ 1995
9. The New Year's Party ◆ 1995
10. Goodnight Kiss 2 ◆ 1996
11. Silent Night 3 ◆ 1996
12. High Tide ◆ 1997
13. The Evil Lives! Cheerleaders ◆ 1997

FEAR STREET: GHOSTS OF FEAR STREET

Stine, R. L.
POCKET BOOKS
GRADES 4–8 ◆ A/R
HORROR

Shadow people, ooze, the bugman, the werecat, ghouls, ghosts, and other creatures populate these horror books. The unsuspecting characters experience nightmares; they encounter body switchers and screaming jokers; they have frightening Christmas celebrations and are attacked by aqua apes. There are many cliff-hangers—chapters ending with a scream or with fingers grabbing the character's neck—so readers enjoy lots of scary moments.

1. Hide and Shriek ◆ 1995
2. Who's Been Sleeping in My Grave? ◆ 1995
3. The Attack of the Aqua Apes ◆ 1995
4. Nightmare in 3-D ◆ 1996
5. Stay Away from the Treehouse ◆ 1996
6. The Eye of the Fortuneteller ◆ 1996
7. Fright Knight ◆ 1996
8. The Ooze ◆ 1996
9. The Revenge of the Shadow People ◆ 1996
10. The Bugman Lives! ◆ 1996
11. The Boy Who Ate Fear Street ◆ 1996
12. Night of the Werecat ◆ 1996
13. How to Be a Vampire ◆ 1996
14. Body Switchers from Outer Space ◆ 1996
15. Fright Christmas ◆ 1996
16. Don't Ever Get Sick at Granny's ◆ 1997
17. House of a Thousand Screams ◆ 1997
18. Camp Fear Ghouls ◆ 1997
19. Three Evil Wishes ◆ 1997
20. Spell of the Screaming Jokers ◆ 1997
21. The Creature from Club Lagoona ◆ 1997
22. Field of Screams ◆ 1997
23. Why I'm Not Afraid of Ghosts ◆ 1997
24. Monster Dog ◆ 1997
25. Halloween Bugs Me! ◆ 1997
26. Go to Your Tomb—Right Now! ◆ 1997
27. Parents from the 13th Dimension ◆ 1997
28. Hide and Shriek II ◆ 1998
29. The Tale of the Blue Monkey ◆ 1998
30. I Was a Sixth-Grade Zombie ◆ 1998
31. Escape of the He-Beast ◆ 1998
32. Caution: Aliens at Work ◆ 1998
33. Attack of the Vampire Worms ◆ 1998
34. Horror Hotel: The Vampire Checks In ◆ 1998
35. Horror Hotel: Ghost in the Guest Room ◆ 1998
36. Funhouse of Dr. Freek ◆ 1998

GHOSTS OF FEAR STREET CREEPY COLLECTION

1. Happy Hauntings ◆ 1998
2. Beastly Tales ◆ 1998
3. The Scream Tea ◆ 1998

    4. Big Bad Bugs ◆ 1998
    5. Ghoul Friends ◆ 1998
    6. Weird Science ◆ 1998

FEAR STREET: 99 FEAR STREET

Stine, R. L.
SIMON & SCHUSTER
GRADES 6–9 ◆ A/R
HORROR

Don't move into any house on Fear Street! Ever! Especially not 99 Fear Street. Cally and Kody Frasier moved there and faced the evil in the house. Then Cally's ghost threatened the next inhabitant. Finally, Kody returns to make a movie of her life, which quickly becomes a horror-filled experience.

    1. The First Horror ◆ 1994
    2. The Second Horror ◆ 1994
    3. The Third Horror ◆ 1994

FEARLESS

Pascal, Francine
SIMON & SCHUSTER
GRADES 8–12 ◆ A/R
ADVENTURE

Gaia Moore, 17, is different from other high school seniors. She has a black belt in karate and she has no "fear gene." She faces dangerous situations, including terrorists and drug dealers. As the series progresses, Gaia becomes disenchanted with her situation.

    1. Fearless ◆ 1999
    2. Sam ◆ 1999
    3. Run ◆ 1999
    4. Twisted ◆ 2000
    5. Kiss ◆ 2000
    6. Payback ◆ 2000
    7. Rebel ◆ 2000
    8. Heat ◆ 2000
    9. Blood ◆ 2000
  10. Liar ◆ 2000
  11. Trust ◆ 2000
  12. Killer ◆ 2000

13. Bad ◆ 2001
14. Missing ◆ 2001
15. Tears ◆ 2001
16. Naked ◆ 2001
17. Flee ◆ 2001
18. Love ◆ 2001
19. Twins ◆ 2002
20. Sex ◆ 2002
21. Blind ◆ 2002
22. Alone ◆ 2002
23. Fear ◆ 2002
24. Betrayed ◆ 2002
25. Lost ◆ 2003
26. Escape ◆ 2003
27. Shock ◆ 2003
28. Chase ◆ 2003
29. Lust ◆ 2003
30. Freak ◆ 2003
31. Normal ◆ 2004
32. Terror ◆ 2004
33. Wired ◆ 2004
34. Fake ◆ 2004
35. Exposed ◆ 2004
36. Gone ◆ 2004

SUPER EDITIONS

1. Before Gaia ◆ 2002
2. Gaia Abducted ◆ 2003

FERRET CHRONICLES

Bach, Richard
SCRIBNER
GRADES 7–10 ◆ A/R
ANIMAL FANTASY

The human race is in trouble, and riding to the rescue are ferrets. They have left their own perfect world on another planet to deal with the chaos on Earth. In *Rescue Ferrets at Sea*, Bethany Ferret achieves her dream of becoming part of the sea rescue ferrets. In *The Last Wars*, two ferrets search for a future-changing object that may help them contact their home planet.

1. Air Ferrets Aloft ◆ 2002
2. Rescue Ferrets at Sea ◆ 2002
3. Writer Ferrets Chasing the Muse ◆ 2002

    4. Rancher Ferrets on the Range ◆ 2003
    5. The Last Wars: Detective Ferrets and the Case of the Golden Deed ◆ 2003

FIENDLY CORNERS

Leroe, Ellen W.
HYPERION
GRADES 5–8
HORROR

In this small town, strange things happen. Like when the pizza parlor sends out toy robots with each pizza. The robots turn the residents into *Pizza Zombies* and Bryan Hartley must try to undo the damage and save the town. Another book features Jamie, who receives the contact lenses of a dead magician and is haunted by his ghost. A werewolf and an evil snowman cause problems in other books. Action, suspense, horror, and creatures make these a choice for the Goosebumps and Fear Street fans.

    1. Monster Vision ◆ 1996
    2. Pizza Zombies ◆ 1996
    3. Revenge of the Hairy Horror ◆ 1996
    4. Nasty the Snowman ◆ 1996

FINGERPRINTS

Metz, Melinda
AVON
GRADES 7–10 ◆ A/R
FANTASY

Rae is hospitalized for having delusions. She realizes that her "visions" come from touching objects. She uses this ability to investigate a mysterious bombing. As the series progresses, Rae develops her power, touching fingerprints to find out the inner thoughts of others.

    1. Gifted Touch ◆ 2001
    2. Haunted ◆ 2001
    3. Trust Me ◆ 2001
    4. Secrets ◆ 2001
    5. Betrayed ◆ 2001

6. Revelations ◆ 2001
7. Payback ◆ 2002

FINNEGAN ZWAKE

Dahl, Michael
SIMON & SCHUSTER
GRADES 6–9 ◆ A/R
ADVENTURE | MYSTERY

Finnegan Zwake, 13, encounters mysteries and adventure. His parents disappeared in Iceland but they could be anywhere. With his Uncle Stoppard, a mystery writer, Finnegan travels the world searching for them. They come across pirates in Australia and mysterious events in Iceland. There are humorous moments in these books and readers of A Series of Unfortunate Events will enjoy them.

1. The Horizontal Man ◆ 1999
2. The Worm Tunnel ◆ 1999
3. The Ruby Raven ◆ 1999
4. The Viking Claw ◆ 2001
5. The Coral Coffin ◆ 2002

FIRE-US TRILOGY

Armstrong, Jennifer, and Nancy Butcher
HARPERCOLLINS
GRADES 6–12 ◆ A/R
FANTASY

This post-apocalyptic trilogy describes the survivors of a virus ("fire-us") that seems to have destroyed the adult population. A group of children in Florida band together to become the Family and take on roles of protectors, nurturers, and needy. As they learn to survive, they decide to travel and discover that they are not alone. Eventually, they realize that there are dangerous adults at the Crossroads. These adults survived by going underground before the virus hit and they are led by a power-hungry madman.

1. The Kindling ◆ 2002
2. The Keepers of the Flame ◆ 2002
3. The Kiln ◆ 2003

FIREBALL

Christopher, John
DUTTON
GRADES 5–7
FANTASY

Two cousins encounter a "fireball," which proves to be an entry into a parallel, "what-if" world in which the Roman Empire has endured and European society has been static for two thousand years. In our hemisphere, without interference from the white man, the Aztecs have conquered the Incas and taken over North and South America. Brad and Simon travel all over this world having one adventure after another. They provoke a revolution against the Empire in Britain, but then are victims of persecution by the new regime. They flee to the New World and become the heroes of an Aztec game. Then they run into a Chinese civilization that has also remained static. In all their adventures, they use their superior technical knowledge to come out on top. In the end, given the opportunity to go home, they decide to explore other possible worlds.

1. Fireball ◆ 1981
2. New Found Land ◆ 1983
3. Dragon Dance ◆ 1986

FIREBRINGER TRILOGY

Pierce, Meredith Ann
FIREBIRD
GRADES 7–10 ◆ A/R
FANTASY

The world of unicorns is the setting for this series. Aljan, a unicorn whose name means "Dark Moon," is the son of Prince Korr. Jan's destiny is to become a Firebringer. To achieve this, he must face dangers, overcome his own reckless nature, and confront the dark secret that haunts his father.

1. Birth of the Firebringer ◆ 1985
2. Dark Moon ◆ 1992
3. The Son of Summer Stars ◆ 2003

FIRST PERSON FICTION

Various authors

SCHOLASTIC

GRADES 6–10 ◆ A/R

REAL LIFE

This series looks at the difficulties of leaving homelands and coming to America. Early books describe the experiences of characters from Korea, Cambodia, Cuba, and Haiti. The stories take place in different eras. Yara and her family are from 1967 Cuba (*Flight to Freedom*). Nakri and her family leave Cambodia in the 1970s. In *Call Me Maria*, Maria tries to adjust to life in New York City. She misses her mother, who is still in Puerto Rico. Her father is busy as the super in their apartment building. Out of her sense of loneliness, Maria finds a voice through poetry.

1. Finding My Hat (Son, John) ◆ 2003
2. The Stone Goddess (Ho, Minfong) ◆ 2003
3. Flight to Freedom (Veciana-Suarez, Ana) ◆ 2004
4. Behind the Mountains (Danticat, Edwidge) ◆ 2004
5. Call Me María (Cofer, Judith Ortiz) ◆ 2004

FLAMBARDS

Peyton, K. M.

PHILOMEL

GRADES 7–8

FAMILY LIFE | HISTORICAL

This saga of the Russell family and Flambards, their historic mansion in rural England, begins in 1908. Christina comes to the family as an orphan, sent to live at Flambards with her uncle and two cousins. The series is filled with historical details and provides a glimpse into social conventions of the era. This saga is still popular with many readers, especially those who enjoy English historical fiction.

1. Flambards ◆ 1967
2. The Edge of the Cloud ◆ 1969
3. Flambards in Summer ◆ 1969
4. Flambards Divided ◆ 1981

FORBIDDEN DOORS

Myers, Bill
TYNDALE HOUSE
GRADES 7–9 ◆ A/R
HORROR | VALUES

After living in Brazil, Scott and Becka are back in school in the United States. They encounter many problems with supernatural events and the occult. In *The Society*, they discover a cult that is trying to entice students to participate. Scott and Becka intervene, getting guidance from the Bible and trusting their faith. Other books feature Scott and Becka and other students of faith coping with mysterious, supernatural situations.

   1. The Society ◆ 2001
   2. The Deceived ◆ 2001
   3. The Spell ◆ 2001
   4. The Haunting ◆ 2001
   5. The Guardian ◆ 2001
   6. The Encounter ◆ 2002
   7. The Curse ◆ 2002
   8. The Undead ◆ 2002
   9. The Scream ◆ 2002
  10. The Ancients ◆ 2003
  11. The Wiccan ◆ 2003
  12. The Cards ◆ 2003

FORBIDDEN GAME

Smith, L. J.
SIMON & SCHUSTER
GRADES 7–10
HORROR

In the tradition of Buffy, the Vampire Slayer, this series pits teens against a demonic spirit named Julian. In the first book, Jenny and her friends are transported to Julian's mansion, where they face frightening events. In the second and third books, the Shadow Man appears, putting the teens in even greater danger.

   1. The Hunter ◆ 1994
   2. The Chase ◆ 1994
   3. The Kill ◆ 1994

FOREIGNER

Cherryh, C. J.
DAW
GRADES 10–12
SCIENCE FICTION

Mature readers of science fiction will enjoy this complex and well-written series about the colonization of an alien world. The occupants of this planet are the Atevi, a people who look like humans but have quite different characteristics. Bren Cameron is chosen to lead the humans in their efforts to befriend the Atevi and avoid further misunderstandings and violence.

1. Foreigner ◆ 1994
2. Invader ◆ 1995
3. Inheritor ◆ 1996
4. Precursor ◆ 1999
5. Defender ◆ 2001
6. Explorer ◆ 2002

FORGOTTEN REALMS—THE LAST MYTHAL

Baker, Richard
WIZARDS OF THE COAST
GRADES 9–12
FANTASY

A society of elves who have lived apart from the Forgotten Realms want to return to the mainstream. They face threats and danger as they try to complete their journey. Forgotten Realms is one of the original settings for Dungeons and Dragons.

1. Forsaken House: Wizards of the Coast ◆ 2004
2. Farthest Reach: Wizards of the Coast ◆ 2005

FOUNDATION

Asimov, Isaac
HARPERCOLLINS
GRADES 10–12
SCIENCE FICTION

Asimov first wrote in the 1940s about the collapse of a galactic empire and the establishment by a psychohistorian called Hari Seldon of a Foundation to limit the impact of the empire's demise. As the empire dies, the Foundation is left exposed to invading warlords. Asimov's early stories were collected in the first three volumes. *Prelude to Foundation* is a prequel that describes the birth of psychohistory. *Forward the Foundation* was published after Asimov's death. This series has been published in many editions.

1. Foundation ◆ 1951
2. Foundation and Empire ◆ 1952
3. Second Foundation ◆ 1953
4. Foundation's Edge ◆ 1982
5. Foundation and Earth ◆ 1986
6. Prelude to Foundation ◆ 1988
7. Forward the Foundation ◆ 1993

THE SECOND FOUNDATION TRILOGY

1. Foundation's Fear (Benford, Gregory) ◆ 1997
2. Foundation and Chaos (Bear, Greg) ◆ 1998
3. Foundation's Triumph (Brin, David) ◆ 1999

FOXFIRE *see* Golden Mountain Chronicles

THE FRIENDSHIP RING

Vail, Rachel
SCHOLASTIC
GRADES 6–9 ◆ A/R
REAL LIFE

A group of seventh-grade friends are the focus of this series. Each story is told from one of the friends' perspectives and looks at family and social problems. The friends have very different backgrounds, very different talents, and very different likes and dislikes. Preteen and adolescent girls will particularly enjoy these stories about friendship and growing awareness of the differences between the sexes.

1. If You Only Knew ◆ 1998
2. Please, Please, Please ◆ 1998
3. Not That I Care ◆ 1998
4. What Are Friends For? ◆ 1999
5. Popularity Contest ◆ 2000
6. Fill in the Blank ◆ 2000

FROM THE FILES OF MADISON FINN

Dower, Laura
HYPERION
GRADES 6–8 ◆ A/R
REAL LIFE

At Far Hills Junior High, Madison Finn and her friends Fiona and Aimee are looking forward to new activities. They enjoy their classes, friends, field trips, and concerts. In *Give Me a Break*, Maddie is going on a skiing trip with her dad and can only take one friend. How can she choose?

1. Only the Lonely ◆ 2001
2. Boy, Oh Boy! ◆ 2001
3. Play It Again ◆ 2001
4. Caught in the Web ◆ 2001
5. Thanks for Nothing ◆ 2001
6. Lost and Found ◆ 2001
7. Save the Date ◆ 2001
8. Picture Perfect ◆ 2002
9. Just Visiting ◆ 2002
10. Give and Take ◆ 2002
11. Heart to Heart ◆ 2003
12. Lights Out ◆ 2003
13. Sink or Swim ◆ 2003
14. Double Dare ◆ 2003
15. Off the Wall ◆ 2004
16. Three's a Crowd ◆ 2004
17. On the Case ◆ 2004
18. Give Me a Break ◆ 2005

GALAXY OF FEAR *see* Star Wars Galaxy of Fear

GENERATION GIRL

Stewart, Melanie
GOLDEN BOOKS
GRADES 7–10
REAL LIFE

Lara, Barbie, Chelsie, Tori, and Nichelle are some of the girls involved in the activities at International High in New York City. Barbie is featured in several books as she makes friends and finally gets a chance to do some acting.

1. New York, Here We Come ◆ 1999
2. Bending the Rules ◆ 1999
3. Pushing the Limits ◆ 1999
4. Singing Sensation ◆ 1999
5. Picture Perfect? ◆ 1999
6. Secrets of the Past ◆ 1999
7. Stage Fright ◆ 1999
8. Taking a Stand ◆ 1999
9. Hitting the Slopes ◆ 1999
10. Taking Charge! ◆ 1999
11. First Crush ◆ 2000
12. Campaign Chaos ◆ 2000

GHOST

Various authors

DARK HORSE

GRADES 10–12

HORROR

Elisa Cameron is Ghost, the protector of Arcadia. She faces zombies, an evil villainess named Dr. October, and other demonic forces. As she faces these dark threats, she searches for those who killed her and tries to understand her special powers.

1. Nocturnes (Luke, Eric) ◆ 1996
2. Exhuming Elisa (Luke, Eric) ◆ 1997
3. Black October (Luke, Eric) ◆ 1999
4. Painful Music (Luke, Eric) ◆ 1999
5. No World So Dark (Warner, Chris) ◆ 2000

THE GHOST IN THE TOKAIDO INN

Hoobler, Dorothy, and Thomas Hoobler

PUTNAM

GRADES 7–9

HISTORICAL | MYSTERY

In dramatic stories set in 18th-century Japan, 14-year-old Seikei, a resourceful boy who dreams of becoming a samurai, becomes involved in solving mysteries. In *The Demon in the Teahouse*, Seikei investigates murders and arson that are connected with popular geishas, and in the third book, he tangles with a ninja.

1. The Ghost in the Tokaido Inn ◆ 1999

    2. The Demon in the Teahouse ◆ 2001
    3. In Darkness, Death ◆ 2004

GHOSTS OF FEAR STREET *see* Fear Street: Ghosts of Fear Street

GILMORE GIRLS

Various authors
HARPERCOLLINS
GRADES 7–10
FAMILY LIFE

Based on the popular television program, these books feature a mom, Lorelai, and daughter, Rory, who are best friends. Raising Rory as a single parent has not been easy for Lorelai. It has even led to estrangement from her parents. Now, Lorelai has borrowed money from her parents so that Rory can go to a private prep school. Fans of the television show will enjoy these books.

    1. I Do, Don't I? (Clark, Catherine) ◆ 2002
    2. I Love You, You Idiot (Dubowski, Cathy East) ◆ 2002
    3. Like Mother, Like Daughter (Clark, Catherine) ◆ 2002
    4. The Other Side of Summer (Pai, Helen) ◆ 2002

GIRLS OF MANY LANDS *see* American Girls: Girls of Many Lands

THE GIRLS QUARTET

Wilson, Jacqueline
DELACORTE
GRADES 6–9 ◆ A/R
REAL LIFE

Ellie feels like an ugly duckling. Her friends Magda and Nadine are stunning while Ellie is flabby. She diets and works out and begins to look fit, but she is cranky. Can she look great and be a good friend too? This series is set in England.

    1. Girls in Love ◆ 2002
    2. Girls Under Pressure ◆ 2002

3. Girls Out Late ◆ 2002
4. Girls in Tears ◆ 2003

GIRLS R.U.L.E.

Lowe, Kris
BERKLEY
GRADES 6–8
ADVENTURE | REAL LIFE

Cayenga Park is adding a girls' division of junior rangers. The tryouts will be difficult, especially since the boys' division is not totally in favor of this new group. Five girls—Kayla Adams, Carson McDonald, Sophie Schultz, Becca Fisher, and Alex Loomis-Drake—tell their own stories about their lives and interest in the park program. The first book established the personality of each girl and her strengths, insecurities, and special needs. Sophie is stubborn and outspoken; Carson does not let her hearing disability limit her accomplishments; Becca's jokes and sarcasm sometimes cause problems. This adventure series will appeal to girls who like intrepid, strong-willed, female main characters.

1. Girls R.U.L.E. ◆ 1998
2. Trail of Terror ◆ 1998
3. Seal Island Scam ◆ 1998

THE GIVER

Lowry, Lois
HOUGHTON MIFFLIN
GRADES 6–10
SCIENCE FICTION

These companion books may not be a true series but they are connected by the strength of the young main characters in worlds that have gone wrong. Jonas (in *The Giver*), Kira (in *Gathering Blue*), and Matty (in *Messenger*) face cruelty, oppression, and hostility. Each responds with creativity, independence, and courage. *The Giver* received the Newbery Award for its depiction of Jonas's life in a society that has repressed emotions, colors, senses, and memory. Jonas's Assignment is to be the Receiver of Memories and he begins to uncover everything that has been hidden from him.

1. The Giver ◆ 1993
2. Gathering Blue ◆ 2000
3. Messenger ◆ 2004

GLORY

Lynn, Jodi
PUFFIN
GRADES 6–9 ◆ **A/R**
REAL LIFE

Glory, 13, lives in Dogwood, West Virginia, in a strict religious sect that shuns modern ways. After becoming drunk with her friend Katie (who dies in an accident), Glory is cast out. She struggles to survive as she tries to reach Boston. But there is an added danger. She has been given a slow poison and she must return to Dogwood to confront her transgressions.

1. Glory ◆ 2003
2. Shadow Tree ◆ 2003
3. Blue Girl ◆ 2003
4. Forget Me Not ◆ 2003

GODDESSES

Hantman, Clea
HARPERCOLLINS
GRADES 6–9 ◆ **A/R**
FANTASY | HUMOR

In a fit of temper, Zeus banishes his daughters—Polly, Era, and Thalia—but accidentally sends them to present-day Athens, Georgia. There the girls try to fit in at school and in their social life, learning about contemporary customs and language. The Furies are also there, in disguise, and Thalia's boyfriend Apollo turns up in *Three Girls and a God*. In the last book, the trio find themselves in Hades.

1. Heaven Sent ◆ 2002
2. Three Girls and a God ◆ 2002
3. Muses on the Move ◆ 2002
4. Love or Fate ◆ 2002

GOLDEN FILLY SERIES

Snelling, Lauraine
BETHANY HOUSE
GRADES 6–9 ◆ A/R
REAL LIFE

Tricia Evanston wants to train and race horses. Her mother disapproves and her father is too ill to intervene (in *Shadow over San Mateo*, her father dies). When Tricia gets the horse Spitfire, she begins to succeed. Trish and Spitfire are the surprise winners of the Santa Anita Derby. What's next . . . the Kentucky Derby! The series follows Trish through high school where she deals with horse racing, dating, and a stalker.

1. The Race ◆ 1991
2. Eagle's Wing ◆ 1991
3. Go for the Glory ◆ 1991
4. Kentucky Dreamer ◆ 1992
5. Call for Courage ◆ 1992
6. Shadow over San Mateo ◆ 1993
7. Out of the Mist ◆ 1993
8. Second Wind ◆ 1994
9. Close Call ◆ 1994
10. The Winner's Circle ◆ 1995

GOLDEN MOUNTAIN CHRONICLES

Yep, Laurence
HarperCollins
GRADES 7–8 ◆ A/R
HISTORICAL

Each of these books has a different main character, but they are all intertwined by family ties. In the first book, *The Serpent's Children*, Foxfire and Cassia are a brother and sister in China whose father, Gallant, has gone to war against the British invaders. Cassia struggles to hold her family together. In the second novel, *Mountain Light*, another character, Squeaky, loses his home in one of the rebellions and goes off to America to seek his fortune. Finally, in *Dragon's Gate*, Otter goes to join his Uncle Foxfire in America to become rich and then return to China and continue fighting against the Manchu. Instead, he discovers that Foxfire is not the man he thought he was and that the Chinese working on the railroad are little more than slaves. With much historical detail, these books make for great reads.

1. Dragonwings: 1903 ◆ 1975
2. Child of the Owl: 1965 ◆ 1977
3. Sea Glass: 1970 ◆ 1979
4. The Serpent's Children: 1849 ◆ 1984
5. Mountain Light: 1855 ◆ 1985
6. Dragon's Gate: 1867 ◆ 1993
7. Thief of Hearts: 1995 ◆ 1995
8. The Traitor: 1885 ◆ 2003

GOLDSTONE TRILOGY

Lawson, Julie
STODDART
GRADES 5–7
FANTASY | REAL LIFE

In early 20th-century British Columbia, 12-year-old Karin, a girl of Swedish descent, inherits a goldstone pendant when her mother is killed in an avalanche. This necklace allows Karin to dream of the future. In the first book, she foresees a second avalanche. In *Turns on a Dime*, set in the 1950s, lonely and uncertain 11-year-old Jo inherits the pendant and finds it gives her strength and self-confidence. In the final volume, Jo passes the pendant on to her niece Ashley, who is challenged by a ghost seeking to return the goldstone to its original home.

1. Goldstone ◆ 1998
2. Turns on a Dime ◆ 1999
3. The Ghost of Avalanche Mountain ◆ 2000

GOOSEBUMPS

Stine, R. L.
SCHOLASTIC
GRADES 4–8 ◆ A/R
HORROR

According to the publisher, more than 200 million copies of Goosebumps have been sold. There are spin-off series, television tie-ins, and a Web site (http://www.scholastic.com/goosebumps). The books are filled with creatures and gore, with implausible situations and frightening circumstances. The characters are often unsuspecting innocents—just like your neighbors and friends, or even yourself—caught in the clutches of gnomes, werewolves, monsters, vampires, and other creatures. The locations include a mummy's tomb, Camp Nightmare, Horrorland, and the Haunted School. This popular series brings the horror genre to a younger audience, giving them dripping blood, shrunken heads, and monsters awaiting their next victim.

1. Welcome to Dead House ◆ 1992
2. Stay Out of the Basement ◆ 1992
3. Monster Blood ◆ 1992
4. Say Cheese and Die! ◆ 1992
5. Curse of the Mummy's Tomb ◆ 1993
6. Let's Get Invisible! ◆ 1993
7. Night of the Living Dummy ◆ 1993
8. The Girl Who Cried Monster ◆ 1993
9. Welcome to Camp Nightmare ◆ 1993
10. The Ghost Next Door ◆ 1993
11. The Haunted Mask ◆ 1993
12. Be Careful What You Wish For ◆ 1993
13. Piano Lessons Can Be Murder ◆ 1993
14. The Werewolf of Fever Swamp ◆ 1993
15. You Can't Scare Me! ◆ 1994
16. One Day at Horrorland ◆ 1994
17. Why I'm Afraid of Bees ◆ 1994
18. Monster Blood II ◆ 1994
19. Deep Trouble ◆ 1994
20. The Scarecrow Walks at Midnight ◆ 1994
21. Go Eat Worms! ◆ 1994
22. Ghost Beach ◆ 1994
23. Return of the Mummy ◆ 1994
24. Phantom of the Auditorium ◆ 1994
25. Attack of the Mutant ◆ 1994
26. My Hairiest Adventure ◆ 1994
27. A Night in Terror Tower ◆ 1995
28. The Cuckoo Clock of Doom ◆ 1995
29. Monster Blood III ◆ 1995
30. It Came from Beneath the Sink! ◆ 1995
31. Night of the Living Dummy II ◆ 1995
32. The Barking Ghost ◆ 1995
33. The Horror at Camp Jellyjam ◆ 1995
34. Revenge of the Lawn Gnomes ◆ 1995
35. A Shocker on Shock Street ◆ 1995
36. The Haunted Mask II ◆ 1995
37. The Headless Ghost ◆ 1995
38. The Abominable Snowman of Pasadena ◆ 1995
39. How I Got My Shrunken Head ◆ 1996
40. Night of the Living Dummy III ◆ 1996
41. Bad Hare Day ◆ 1996
42. Egg Monsters from Mars ◆ 1996
43. The Beast from the East ◆ 1996
44. Say Cheese and Die—Again! ◆ 1996

45. Ghost Camp ◆ 1996
46. How to Kill a Monster ◆ 1996
47. Legend of the Lost Legend ◆ 1996
48. Attack of the Jack-O'-Lanterns ◆ 1996
49. Vampire Breath ◆ 1996
50. Calling All Creeps! ◆ 1996
51. Beware, the Snowman ◆ 1997
52. How I Learned to Fly ◆ 1997
53. Chicken Chicken ◆ 1997
54. Don't Go to Sleep! ◆ 1997
55. The Blob That Ate Everyone ◆ 1997
56. The Curse of Camp Cold Lake ◆ 1997
57. My Best Friend Is Invisible ◆ 1997
58. Deep Trouble II ◆ 1997
59. The Haunted School ◆ 1997
60. Werewolf Skin ◆ 1997
61. I Live in Your Basement! ◆ 1997
62. Monster Blood IV ◆ 1998

GOOSEBUMPS: GIVE YOURSELF GOOSEBUMPS

Stine, R. L.

SCHOLASTIC

GRADES 4–8

HORROR

What do you get when you cross the incredibly popular horror stories of Goosebumps with the popular format of Choose Your Own Adventure? You get Give Yourself Goosebumps. The cover of each book announces "Choose from over 20 different scary endings," giving readers many different ways to direct the adventures. Like the basic Goosebumps books, these are scary stories where characters try to escape from weird creatures or are attacked by monsters or lost in a swamp. You meet werewolves, vampires, and terrible toys. You visit such places as the Carnival of Horrors and the Dead-End Hotel. Depending on the choices, the reader can triumph over the evil creatures, just barely escape, or be swallowed by a sea monster. The two popular genres represented in this series are sure to capture the interest of even the most reluctant readers.

1. Escape from the Carnival of Horrors ◆ 1995
2. Tick Tock, You're Dead! ◆ 1995
3. Trapped in Bat Wing Hall ◆ 1995
4. The Deadly Experiments of Dr. Eek ◆ 1996
5. Night in Werewolf Woods ◆ 1996
6. Beware of the Purple Peanut Butter ◆ 1996

7. Under the Magician's Spell ◆ 1996
8. The Curse of the Creeping Coffin ◆ 1996
9. The Knight in Screaming Armor ◆ 1996
10. Diary of a Mad Mummy ◆ 1996
11. Deep in the Jungle of Doom ◆ 1996
12. Welcome to the Wicked Wax Museum ◆ 1996
13. Scream of the Evil Genie ◆ 1997
14. The Creepy Creations of Professor Shock ◆ 1997
15. Please Don't Feed the Vampire! ◆ 1997
16. Secret Agent Grandma ◆ 1997
17. Little Comic Shop of Horrors ◆ 1997
18. Attack of the Beastly Baby-Sitter ◆ 1997
19. Escape from Camp Run-for-Your-Life ◆ 1997
20. Toy Terror: Batteries Included ◆ 1997
21. The Twisted Tale of Tiki Island ◆ 1997
22. Return to the Carnival of Horrors ◆ 1997
23. Zapped in Space ◆ 1997
24. Lost in Stinkeye Swamp ◆ 1997
25. Shop 'Til You Drop . . . Dead ◆ 1998
26. Alone in Snakebite Canyon ◆ 1998
27. Checkout Time at the Dead-End Hotel ◆ 1998
28. Night of a Thousand Claws ◆ 1998
29. Invaders from the Big Screen ◆ 1998
30. You're Plant Food! ◆ 1998
31. The Werewolf of Twisted Tree Lodge ◆ 1998
32. It's Only a Nightmare ◆ 1998
33. It Came from the Internet ◆ 1999
34. Elevator to Nowhere ◆ 1999
35. Hocus-Pocus Horror ◆ 1999
36. Ship of Ghouls ◆ 1999
37. Escape from Horror House ◆ 1999
38. Into the Twister of Terror ◆ 1999
39. Scary Birthday to You! ◆ 1999
40. Zombie School ◆ 2000
41. Danger Time ◆ 2000
42. All-Day Nightmare ◆ 2000

GIVE YOURSELF GOOSEBUMPS SPECIAL EDITIONS

1. Into the Jaws of Doom ◆ 1998
2. Return to Terror Tower: The Nightmare Continues ◆ 1998
3. Power Play: Trapped in the Circus of Fear ◆ 1998
4. The Ultimate Challenge: One Night in Payne House ◆ 1998
5. The Curse of the Cave Creatures ◆ 1999
6. Revenge of the Body Squeezers ◆ 1999

7. Trick or . . . Trapped ◆ 1999
8. Weekend at Poison Lake ◆ 1999

GOOSEBUMPS SERIES 2000

Stine, R. L.

SCHOLASTIC

GRADES 4–8 ◆ A/R

HORROR

Advertised as having a "scarier edge," Goosebumps 2000 capitalizes on the popularity of the horror genre and the familiar name of Goosebumps. The danger in these books is a bit more intense and could appeal to an older audience and provide a transition to YA horror titles. As with the related series, there are weird creatures and slime, ghosts and gore.

1. Cry of the Cat ◆ 1998
2. Bride of the Living Dummy ◆ 1998
3. Creature Teacher ◆ 1998
4. Invasion of the Body Squeezers, Part 1 ◆ 1998
5. Invasion of the Body Squeezers, Part 2 ◆ 1998
6. I Am Your Evil Twin ◆ 1998
7. Revenge R Us ◆ 1998
8. Fright Camp ◆ 1998
9. Are You Terrified Yet? ◆ 1998
10. Headless Halloween ◆ 1998
11. Attack of the Graveyard Ghouls ◆ 1998
12. Brain Juice ◆ 1998
13. Return to Horrorland ◆ 1999
14. Jekyll and Heidi ◆ 1999
15. Scream School ◆ 1999
16. The Mummy Walks ◆ 1999
17. The Werewolf in the Living Room ◆ 1999
18. Horrors of the Black Ring ◆ 1999
19. Return to Ghost Camp ◆ 1999
20. Be Afraid—Be Very Afraid! ◆ 1999
21. The Haunted Car ◆ 1999
22. Full Moon Fever ◆ 1999
23. Slappy's Nightmare ◆ 1999
24. Earth Geeks Must Go! ◆ 1999
25. Ghost in the Mirror ◆ 2000

GORDY SMITH

Hahn, Mary Downing
CLARION
GRADES 5–7
FAMILY LIFE | HISTORICAL

This series begins during World War II when best friends Elizabeth and Margaret spy on their sixth-grade classmate—a bully named Gordy Smith. They discover that he is hiding his brother Stu, who is an Army deserter. This is a grave moral dilemma for these patriotic friends. The sequels focus on Gordy as he is separated from his abusive family and sent to live with a grandmother in North Carolina. On her sudden death, Gordy returns to his hometown and the lingering perceptions that he is a bully from a "trashy" family. These are thoughtfully written books with realistic insights into the era and the characters.

1. Stepping on the Cracks ◆ 1991
2. Following My Own Footsteps ◆ 1996
3. As Ever, Gordy ◆ 1998

GOSSIP GIRL

von Ziegesar, Cecily
LITTLE, BROWN
GRADES 9–12 ◆ A/R
REAL LIFE

These books feature teens who have it all—money, good schools, and beauty. But they also have serious problems with alcohol, drugs, and sex. The core group of kids includes Blair, her ex-boyfriend Nate, Serena, Dan, and Vanessa. They attend posh prep schools in Manhattan and are sometimes friends and sometimes rivals. One review called these books "soap operalike," but they are among the most popular with teens right now.

1. Gossip Girl ◆ 2002
2. You Know You Love Me ◆ 2002
3. All I Want Is Everything ◆ 2003
4. Because I'm Worth It ◆ 2003
5. I Like It Like That ◆ 2004
6. You're the One That I Want ◆ 2004

GRAVEYARD SCHOOL

Stone, Tom B.

BANTAM

GRADES 4–7 ◆ A/R

HORROR

Grove School is right next to a graveyard. So naturally the kids call it Graveyard School. Park, who considers himself a detective, and his friend Stacey solve mysteries and get into some terrifying situations. At the beginning of their sixth-grade year, the principal, Dr. Morehouse, introduces a new lunch room supervisor who promises tasty meals at low cost. Soon after, pets start disappearing all over town. The series continues as the friends solve more scary mysteries at the school.

1. Don't Eat the Mystery Meat ◆ 1994
2. The Skeleton on the Skateboard ◆ 1994
3. The Headless Bicycle Rider ◆ 1994
4. Little Pet Werewolf ◆ 1995
5. Revenge of the Dinosaurs ◆ 1995
6. Camp Dracula ◆ 1995
7. Slime Lake ◆ 1995
8. Let's Scare the Teacher to Death ◆ 1995
9. The Abominable Snow Monster ◆ 1995
10. There's a Ghost in the Boy' s Bathroom ◆ 1996
11. April Ghoul's Day ◆ 1996
12. Scream, Team! ◆ 1996
13. Tales Too Scary to Tell at Camp ◆ 1996
14. The Tragic School Bus ◆ 1996
15. The Fright Before Christmas ◆ 1996
16. Don't Tell Mummy ◆ 1997
17. Jack and the Beanstalker ◆ 1997
18. The Dead Sox ◆ 1997
19. The Gator Ate Her ◆ 1997
20. Creature Teacher ◆ 1997
21. The Skeleton's Revenge ◆ 1997
22. Boo Year's Eve ◆ 1998
23. The Easter Egg Haunt ◆ 1998
24. Scream Around the Campfire ◆ 1998
25. Escape from Vampire Park ◆ 1998
26. Little School of Horrors ◆ 1998
27. Here Comes Santa Claws ◆ 1998
28. The Spider Beside Her ◆ 1998

THE GREAT BRAIN

Fitzgerald, John D.

DIAL

GRADES 5–7 ◆ A/R

HISTORICAL | HUMOR | REAL LIFE

Tom, Sweyn, and J.D. are three brothers growing up in a small Utah town in the late 1800s. Tom has a great brain and an insatiable love for money, a combination that leads him to concoct endless schemes for swindling his friends and family. One of his first enterprises is to charge the neighborhood kids to see his family's toilet, the first in town. Occasionally, he has fits of conscience and promises to reform, most notably when the neighborhood kids decide to stop speaking to him. Sweyn, the oldest brother, is amused by Tom's schemes, but J.D., the youngest brother and narrator, always seems to be taken in.

1. The Great Brain ◆ 1967
2. More Adventures of the Great Brain ◆ 1969
3. Me and My Little Brain ◆ 1971
4. The Great Brain at the Academy ◆ 1972
5. The Great Brain Reforms ◆ 1973
6. The Return of the Great Brain ◆ 1974
7. The Great Brain Does It Again ◆ 1975
8. The Great Brain Is Back ◆ 1995

THE GREAT WAR

Turtledove, Harry

BALLANTINE DEL REY

GRADES 10–12

SCIENCE FICTION

Trench warfare reaches America in this alternate history that starts when the U.S. sides with Germany and the Confederate States of America sides with France and Great Britain. *How Few Remain* (1997), in which the Confederate States of America has won the Civil War but conflicts persist, serves as a prequel to this series and to *American Empire*, a trilogy of turmoil across the North American continent. Volumes in that series are *Blood and Iron* (2001), *The Center Cannot Hold* (2002), and *The Victorious Opposition* (2003).

1. American Front ◆ 1998
2. Walk in Hell ◆ 1999
3. Breakthroughs ◆ 2000

GREEN KNOWE

Boston, L. M.
HARCOURT
GRADES 4–8 ◆ A/R
FANTASY

An ancient house in Great Britain is rich with history and stories of the children who have lived there over the centuries. Lonely young Tolly goes to live there with his Great-Grandmother Oldknow in the early 1930s. Tolly soon discovers that his great-grandmother's stories about the children who used to live there literally come to life. We are not sure at first whether he is time-traveling or seeing the children's ghosts, but it soon becomes clear that all time blends together in this house. The series continues with more stories of children from different eras and with mysteries about the house itself, including hidden treasure.

1. The Children of Green Knowe ◆ 1954
2. The Treasure of Green Knowe ◆ 1958
3. The River at Green Knowe ◆ 1959
4. A Stranger at Green Knowe ◆ 1961
5. An Enemy at Green Knowe ◆ 1964
6. The Stones of Green Knowe ◆ 1976

THE GROO

Aragones, Sergio, and Mark Evanier
DARK HORSE
GRADES 6–12
FANTASY | HUMOR

Groo is a barbarian swordsman with strength but little sense. With his dog, Rufferto, he wanders the world encountering magic, confronting evil, and bumbling through adventures. Some of the books may be appropriate for a younger audience while others are more satirical. Reviewers tend to place these in YA collections.

1. The Groo: Most Intelligent Man in the World ◆ 1998
2. The Groo: Inferno ◆ 1999
3. The Groo: Houndbook ◆ 1999
4. The Groo: Jamboree ◆ 2000
5. Groo and Rufferto ◆ 2000
6. The Groo: Library ◆ 2001
7. The Groo: Mightier than the Sword ◆ 2001
8. The Groo: Kingdom ◆ 2001

9. The Groo: Death and Taxes ◆ 2002
10. The Groo: Nursery ◆ 2002
11. The Groo: Odyssey ◆ 2002
12. The Groo: Maiden ◆ 2002

GUARDIANS OF GA'HOOLE

Lasky, Kathryn
SCHOLASTIC
GRADES 4–8 ◆ A/R
FANTASY

The Academy for Orphaned Owls is not a kind place. Soren, a barn owl, discovers that when he arrives and is given a number to replace his name. All the young owls are made to follow the very strict rules. With the help of an old owl, Soren and his friends subvert the rules. They learn to fly and to confront the evil that surrounds them. Fans of Avi's books about Poppy and Brian Jacques's Redwall should try this series.

1. The Capture ◆ 2003
2. The Journey ◆ 2003
3. The Rescue ◆ 2003
4. The Siege ◆ 2004
5. The Shattering ◆ 2004
6. The Burning ◆ 2004

GWYN GRIFFITHS TRILOGY

Nimmo, Jenny
TROLL
GRADES 4–7
FANTASY

Gwyn's sister has disappeared in the Welsh mountains. Gwyn's grandmother gives him five magic gifts to help him solve this mystery. In the second book, Gwyn and a girl called Nia save Gwyn's cousin Emlyn from the creatures that snatched Gwyn's sister. The series concludes as Gwyn uses his magical powers to capture an evil spirit.

1. The Snow Spider ◆ 1987
2. Orchard of the Crescent Moon ◆ 1989
3. The Chestnut Soldier ◆ 1991

HAGWOOD TRILOGY

Jarvis, Robin
SILVER WHISTLE BOOKS
GRADES 6–9 ◆ A/R
FANTASY

The Werling folk live in Hagwood Forest and are skilled at shape shifting. Gamaliel is perfecting the skills he will need when the High Lady attacks. The High Lady is searching for her heart, which is hidden in a golden casket. Thorn ogres, monsters, magic, and adventure will attract fantasy fans.

    1. Thorn Ogres of Hagwood ◆ 2002

HAMILTON HIGH

Reynolds, Marilyn
MORNING GLORY PRESS
GRADES 8–12
REAL LIFE

This series focuses on typical teen problems. In *Telling*, a 12-year-old girl confides to her teenage cousin about being sexually molested by the father of the children she is babysitting. Other books deal with teen sexuality, pregnancy, drug addiction, and more. *Beyond Dreams* is a collection of six short stories.

    1. Detour for Emily ◆ 1993
    2. Too Soon for Jeff ◆ 1994
    3. Beyond Dreams ◆ 1995
    4. But What About Me? ◆ 1996
    5. Telling ◆ 1996
    6. Baby Help ◆ 1997
    7. If You Loved Me ◆ 1999
    8. Love Rules ◆ 2001

HAMLET CHRONICLES

Maguire, Gregory
CLARION
GRADES 4–7 ◆ A/R
FANTASY

In Hamlet, Vermont, problems arise when seven frozen prehistoric Siberian snow spiders thaw. Each imprints on a different girl in the Tattletale Club. Things are fine while the spiders are small. But when they begin to grow, they become mean and have plans for the boys in the Copycat Club and their teacher, Miss Earth. The same students return in other books as the Tattletales and Copycats continue their rivalry.

1. Seven Spiders Spinning ◆ 1994
2. Six Haunted Hairdos ◆ 1997
3. Five Alien Elves ◆ 1998
4. Four Stupid Cupids ◆ 2000
5. Three Rotten Eggs ◆ 2002
6. Couple of April Fools ◆ 2004

A HANDFUL OF MEN

Duncan, David

BALLANTINE DEL REY

GRADES 9–12

FANTASY

Readers of fantasy will be attracted to this lively, detailed series set in the world of Pandemia. Magic, trolls, gnomes, sorcerers, and battles against evil forces fill each book. In the concluding book, Zinixo, a dwarf, has enslaved many magicians. Rap, the faun king, struggles to confront Zinixo and free the magicians. Fans of the Fellowship of the Ring could follow up with these books. Duncan has a previous series about Pandemia, A Man of His Word.

1. The Cutting Edge ◆ 1992
2. Upland Outlaws ◆ 1993
3. The Stricken Field ◆ 1993
4. The Living God ◆ 1994

HARD CASH

Cann, Kate

SIMON & SCHUSTER

GRADES 9–12

REAL LIFE

Rich, 17, is obsessed with money. His life at home has been a struggle. Now he is on the way to financial success. His job at an ad agency pays incredibly well, although he has to use his art talent on banal accounts. With his new income status, Rich begins to buy the things he has dreamed about and goes beyond his resources. After he loses his job, he tries to go back to college and begins to date a vapid beauty, Portia, ignoring Bonny, who clearly would like to have his attention. This British series will be enjoyed by readers of Louise Rennison's books.

1. Hard Cash ◆ 2003
2. Shacked Up ◆ 2004
3. Speeding ◆ 2004

HARDY BOYS

Dixon, Franklin W.
SIMON & SCHUSTER
GRADES 5–7 ◆ A/R
MYSTERY

Frank and Joe Hardy, the sons of famous detective Fenton Hardy, have become well-known detectives in their own right, even though they are still in their teens. In each book, the two boys are pursuing their various interests when they are confronted with a crime or mystery. After much action and adventure, the mystery is solved, the criminal caught, and all is well again in Bayport. Frank is cast as the serious and thoughtful one, while Joe is more athletic and impulsive. They are aided occasionally by their friend Chet and their father's sister Gertrude.

1. The Tower Treasure ◆ 1927
2. The House on the Cliff ◆ 1927
3. The Secret of the Old Mill ◆ 1927
4. The Missing Chums ◆ 1928
5. Hunting for Hidden Gold ◆ 1928
6. The Shore Road Mystery ◆ 1928
7. Secret of the Caves ◆ 1929
8. Mystery of Cabin Island ◆ 1929
9. Great Airport Mystery ◆ 1930
10. What Happened at Midnight? ◆ 1931
11. While the Clock Ticked ◆ 1932
12. Footprints Under the Window ◆ 1933
13. The Mark on the Door ◆ 1934
14. The Hidden Harbor Mystery ◆ 1935
15. Sinister Signpost ◆ 1936
16. Figure in Hiding ◆ 1937
17. Secret Warning ◆ 1938
18. The Twisted Claw ◆ 1939
19. The Disappearing Floor ◆ 1940

20. Mystery of the Flying Express ◆ 1941
21. The Clue of the Broken Blade ◆ 1942
22. The Flickering Torch Mystery ◆ 1943
23. The Melted Coins ◆ 1944
24. Short-Wave Mystery ◆ 1945
25. The Secret Panel ◆ 1946
26. The Phantom Freighter ◆ 1947
27. The Secret of Skull Mountain ◆ 1948
28. The Sign of the Crooked Arrow ◆ 1949
29. The Secret of the Lost Tunnel ◆ 1950
30. The Wailing Siren Mystery ◆ 1951
31. The Secret of Wildcat Swamp ◆ 1952
32. The Yellow Feather Mystery ◆ 1953
33. The Crisscross Shadow ◆ 1953
34. The Hooded Hawk Mystery ◆ 1954
35. The Clue in the Embers ◆ 1955
36. The Secret of Pirates' Hill ◆ 1957
37. The Ghost at Skeleton Rock ◆ 1957
38. Mystery at Devil's Paw ◆ 1959
39. Mystery of the Chinese Junk ◆ 1960
40. Mystery of the Desert Giant ◆ 1961
41. Clue of the Screeching Owl ◆ 1962
42. The Viking Symbol Mystery ◆ 1963
43. Mystery of the Aztec Warrior ◆ 1964
44. The Haunted Fort ◆ 1965
45. Mystery of the Spiral Bridge ◆ 1966
46. Secret Agent on Flight 101 ◆ 1967
47. Mystery of the Whale Tattoo ◆ 1968
48. The Arctic Patrol Mystery ◆ 1969
49. Bombay Boomerang ◆ 1970
50. Danger on Vampire Trail ◆ 1971
51. The Masked Monkey ◆ 1972
52. The Shattered Helmet ◆ 1973
53. The Clue of the Hissing Serpent ◆ 1974
54. The Mysterious Caravan ◆ 1975
55. The Witchmaster's Key ◆ 1976
56. The Jungle Pyramid ◆ 1977
57. Firebird Rocket ◆ 1978
58. The Sting of the Scorpion ◆ 1979
59. Night of the Werewolf ◆ 1979
60. The Mystery of the Samurai Sword ◆ 1979
61. The Pentagon Spy ◆ 1980
62. The Apeman's Secret ◆ 1980
63. The Mummy Case ◆ 1980
64. Mystery of Smuggler's Cove ◆ 1980
65. The Stone Idol ◆ 1981
66. The Vanishing Thieves ◆ 1981
67. The Outlaw's Silver ◆ 1981
68. Deadly Chase ◆ 1981

69. The Four-Headed Dragon ◆ 1981
70. The Infinity Clue ◆ 1981
71. The Track of the Zombie ◆ 1982
72. The Voodoo Plot ◆ 1982
73. The Billion Dollar Ransom ◆ 1982
74. Tic-Tac Terror ◆ 1982
75. Trapped at Sea ◆ 1982
76. Game Plan for Disaster ◆ 1982
77. The Crimson Flame ◆ 1983
78. Cave-In! ◆ 1983
79. Sky Sabotage ◆ 1983
80. The Roaring River Mystery ◆ 1984
81. The Demon's Den ◆ 1984
82. The Blackwing Puzzle ◆ 1984
83. The Swamp Monster ◆ 1985
84. Revenge of the Desert Phantom ◆ 1985
85. The Skyfire Puzzle ◆ 1985
86. The Mystery of the Silver Star ◆ 1987
87. Program for Destruction ◆ 1987
88. Tricky Business ◆ 1988
89. Sky Blue Frame ◆ 1988
90. Danger on the Diamond ◆ 1988
91. Shield of Fear ◆ 1988
92. The Shadow Killers ◆ 1988
93. The Serpent's Tooth Mystery ◆ 1988
94. Breakdown in Axeblade ◆ 1989
95. Danger on the Air ◆ 1989
96. Wipeout ◆ 1989
97. Cast of Criminals ◆ 1989
98. Spark of Suspicion ◆ 1989
99. Dungeon of Doom ◆ 1989
100. The Secret of the Island Treasure ◆ 1990
101. The Money Hunt ◆ 1990
102. Terminal Shock ◆ 1990
103. The Million-Dollar Nightmare ◆ 1990
104. Tricks of the Trade ◆ 1990
105. The Smoke Screen Mystery ◆ 1990
106. Attack of the Video Villains ◆ 1991
107. Panic on Gull Island ◆ 1991
108. Fear on Wheels ◆ 1991
109. The Prime-Time Crime ◆ 1991
110. Secret of Sigma Seven ◆ 1991
111. Three-Ring Terror ◆ 1991
112. The Demolition Mission ◆ 1992
113. Radical Moves ◆ 1992
114. Case of the Counterfeit Criminals ◆ 1992
115. Sabotage at Sports City ◆ 1992
116. Rock 'n' Roll Renegades ◆ 1992
117. The Baseball Card Conspiracy ◆ 1992

118. Danger in the Fourth Dimension ◆ 1993
119. Trouble at Coyote Canyon ◆ 1993
120. Case of the Cosmic Kidnapping ◆ 1993
121. The Mystery in the Old Mine ◆ 1993
122. Carnival of Crime ◆ 1993
123. The Robot's Revenge ◆ 1993
124. Mystery with a Dangerous Beat ◆ 1993
125. Mystery on Makatunk Island ◆ 1994
126. Racing with Disaster ◆ 1994
127. Reel Thrills ◆ 1994
128. Day of the Dinosaur ◆ 1994
129. The Treasure at Dolphin Bay ◆ 1994
130. Sidetracked to Danger ◆ 1995
131. Crusade of the Flaming Sword ◆ 1995
132. Maximum Challenge ◆ 1995
133. Crime in the Kennel ◆ 1995
134. Cross-Country Crime ◆ 1995
135. The Hypersonic Secret ◆ 1995
136. The Cold Cash Caper ◆ 1996
137. High-Speed Showdown ◆ 1996
138. The Alaskan Adventure ◆ 1996
139. The Search for the Snow Leopard ◆ 1996
140. Slam Dunk Sabotage ◆ 1996
141. The Desert Thieves ◆ 1996
142. Lost in the Gator Swamp ◆ 1997
143. The Giant Rat of Sumatra ◆ 1997
144. The Secret of Skeleton Reef ◆ 1997
145. Terror at High Tide ◆ 1997
146. The Mark of the Blue Tattoo ◆ 1997
147. Trial and Terror ◆ 1998
148. The Ice-Cold Case ◆ 1998
149. The Chase for the Mystery Twister ◆ 1998
150. The Crisscross Crime ◆ 1998
151. The Rocky Road to Revenge ◆ 1998
152. Danger in the Extreme ◆ 1998
153. Eye on Crime ◆ 1998
154. The Caribbean Cruise Caper ◆ 1999
155. The Hunt for the Four Brothers ◆ 1999
156. A Will to Survive ◆ 1999
157. The Lure of the Italian Treasure ◆ 1999
158. The London Deception ◆ 1999
159. Daredevils ◆ 1999
160. A Game Called Chaos ◆ 2000
161. Training for Trouble ◆ 2000
162. The End of the Trail ◆ 2000
163. The Spy that Never Lies ◆ 2000
164. Skin and Bones ◆ 2000
165. Crime in the Cards ◆ 2001
166. Past and Present Danger ◆ 2001

167. Trouble Times Two ◆ 2001
168. The Castle Conundrum ◆ 2001
169. Ghost of a Chance ◆ 2001
170. Kickoff to Danger ◆ 2001
171. The Test Case ◆ 2002
172. Trouble in Warp Space ◆ 2002
173. Speed Times Five ◆ 2002
174. Hide and Sneak ◆ 2002
175. Trick-or-Trouble ◆ 2002
176. In Plane Sight ◆ 2002
177. The Case of the Psychic's Vision ◆ 2003
178. The Mystery of the Black Rhino ◆ 2003
179. Passport to Danger ◆ 2003
180. Typhoon Island ◆ 2003
181. Double Jeopardy ◆ 2003
182. The Secret of the Soldier's Gold ◆ 2003
183. Warehouse Rumble ◆ 2004
184. The Dangerous Transmission ◆ 2004
185. Wreck and Roll ◆ 2004
186. Hidden Mountain ◆ 2004
187. No Way Out ◆ 2004
188. Farming Fear ◆ 2004

HARDY BOYS CASEFILES

Dixon, Franklin W.
ARCHWAY
GRADES 6–8 ◆ A/R
MYSTERY

The Hardy Boys Casefiles series is for an older audience of readers. Frank and Joe Hardy have girlfriends and face more serious crimes than in the original series. Corruption, organized crime, hired thugs, conspiracies, and even the threat of murder are included in the action. Even though Frank and Joe always succeed, the increased realism of the danger and violence make this a choice for middle school and older.

1. Dead on Target ◆ 1987
2. Evil, Inc. ◆ 1987
3. Cult of Crime ◆ 1987
4. The Lazarus Plot ◆ 1988
5. Edge of Destruction ◆ 1988
6. The Crowning Terror ◆ 1988
7. Deathgame ◆ 1988
8. See No Evil ◆ 1988
9. The Genius Thieves ◆ 1988

10. Hostages of Hate ◆ 1988
11. Brother Against Brother ◆ 1988
12. Perfect Getaway ◆ 1988
13. The Georgia Dagger ◆ 1989
14. Too Many Traitors ◆ 1989
15. Blood Relations ◆ 1989
16. Line of Fire ◆ 1989
17. The Number File ◆ 1989
18. A Killing in the Market ◆ 1989
19. Nightmare in Angel City ◆ 1989
20. Witness to Murder ◆ 1989
21. Street Spies ◆ 1989
22. Double Exposure ◆ 1989
23. Disaster for Hire ◆ 1989
24. Scene of the Crime ◆ 1989
25. The Borderline Case ◆ 1989
26. Trouble in the Pipeline ◆ 1989
27. Nowhere to Run ◆ 1989
28. Countdown to Terror ◆ 1989
29. Thick as Thieves ◆ 1989
30. The Deadliest Dare ◆ 1989
31. Without a Trace ◆ 1989
32. Blood Money ◆ 1989
33. Collision Course ◆ 1989
34. Final Cut ◆ 1989
35. The Dead Season ◆ 1990
36. Running on Empty ◆ 1990
37. Danger Zone ◆ 1990
38. Diplomatic Deceit ◆ 1990
39. Flesh and Blood ◆ 1991
40. Fright Wave ◆ 1991
41. Highway Robbery ◆ 1990
42. The Last Laugh ◆ 1990
43. Strategic Moves ◆ 1990
44. Castle Fear ◆ 1991
45. In Self-Defense ◆ 1990
46. Foul Play ◆ 1990
47. Flight into Danger ◆ 1991
48. Rock 'n' Revenge ◆ 1991
49. Dirty Deeds ◆ 1991
50. Power Play ◆ 1991
51. Choke Hold ◆ 1991
52. Uncivil War ◆ 1991
53. Web of Horror ◆ 1991
54. Deep Trouble ◆ 1991
55. Beyond the Law ◆ 1991
56. Height of Danger ◆ 1991
57. Terror on Track ◆ 1991
58. Spiked! ◆ 1991

59. Open Season ◆ 1992
60. Deadfall ◆ 1992
61. Grave Danger ◆ 1992
62. Final Gambit ◆ 1992
63. Cold Sweat ◆ 992
64. Endangered Species ◆ 1992
65. No Mercy ◆ 1992
66. The Phoenix Equation ◆ 1992
67. Lethal Cargo ◆ 1992
68. Rough Riding ◆ 1992
69. Mayhem in Motion ◆ 1992
70. Rigged for Revenge ◆ 1992
71. Real Horror ◆ 1993
72. Screamers ◆ 1993
73. Bad Rap ◆ 1993
74. Road Pirates ◆ 1993
75. No Way Out ◆ 1993
76. Tagged for Terror ◆ 1993
77. Survival Run ◆ 1993
78. The Pacific Conspiracy ◆ 1993
79. Danger Unlimited ◆ 1993
80. Dead of Night ◆ 1993
81. Sheer Terror ◆ 1993
82. Poisoned Paradise ◆ 1993
83. Toxic Revenge ◆ 1994
84. False Alarm ◆ 1994
85. Winner Take All ◆ 1994
86. Virtual Villainy ◆ 1994
87. Dead Man in Deadwood ◆ 1994
88. Inferno of Fear ◆ 1994
89. Darkness Falls ◆ 1994
90. Deadly Engagement ◆ 1994
91. Hot Wheels ◆ 1994
92. Sabotage at Sea ◆ 1994
93. Mission: Mayhem ◆ 1994
94. A Taste for Terror ◆ 1994
95. Illegal Procedure ◆ 1995
96. Against All Odds ◆ 1995
97. Pure Evil ◆ 1995
98. Murder by Magic ◆ 1995
99. Frame-Up ◆ 1995
100. True Thriller ◆ 1995
101. Peak of Danger ◆ 1995
102. Wrong Side of the Law ◆ 1995
103. Campaign of Crime ◆ 1995
104. Wild Wheels ◆ 1995
105. Law of the Jungle ◆ 1995
106. Shock Jock ◆ 1995
107. Fast Break ◆ 1996

108. Blown Away ◆ 1996
109. Moment of Truth ◆ 1996
110. Bad Chemistry ◆ 1996
111. Competitive Edge ◆ 1996
112. Cliff-Hanger ◆ 1996
113. Sky High ◆ 1996
114. Clean Sweep ◆ 1996
115. Cave Trap ◆ 1996
116. Acting Up ◆ 1996
117. Blood Sport ◆ 1996
118. The Last Leap ◆ 1996
119. The Emperor's Shield ◆ 1997
120. Survival of the Fittest ◆ 1997
121. Absolute Zero ◆ 1997
122. River Rats ◆ 1997
123. High-Wire Act ◆ 1997
124. The Viking's Revenge ◆ 1997
125. Stress Point ◆ 1997
126. Fire in the Sky ◆ 1997
127. Dead in the Water ◆ 1998

HARPER WINSLOW

Trembath, Don
ORCA
GRADES 6–9
REAL LIFE

Harper Winslow, 15, tells his own stories in this series of books set in Canada, near Toronto. In *The Tuesday Cafe*, Harper describes his problems with his parents and his school, problems that have resulted in an appearance in juvenile court. He is assigned to write an essay about changing his life, so he enrolls in a writing class called "The Tuesday Cafe." Harper grows and changes as a character, developing insights into his personality and choices that will resonate with junior high school readers. The essay that he writes appears toward the end of the book and provides a wonderful look at a character's growth. Subsequent books allow Harper to continue to change by writing for the school newspaper and beginning a romantic friendship.

1. The Tuesday Cafe ◆ 1996
2. A Fly Named Alfred ◆ 1997
3. A Beautiful Place on Yonge Street ◆ 1998
4. The Popsicle Journal ◆ 2002

HARRY POTTER

Rowling, J. K.
SCHOLASTIC
GRADES 3–9 ◆ A/R
FANTASY

Harry Potter's adventures at Hogwart's, a school for wizards and witches, are chronicled in this series. From his initial discovery of his magical past to his developing skills at spells and Quidditch to his realization that there are dark forces at work around him, these books have attracted the attention of readers around the world. Many younger children (in grades 3 and 4) read the earlier books, especially after seeing the movies. They also have the books read to them or listen to them on audio. The optimum audience for the complete series is grades 5 and up. The books are available in many languages and the three movies (so far) have been wildly successful. There are many related items including toys, games, books about Quidditch and Beasts, puzzles, computer programs, and more.

1. Harry Potter and the Sorcerer's Stone ◆ 1998
2. Harry Potter and the Chamber of Secrets ◆ 1999
3. Harry Potter and the Prisoner of Azkaban ◆ 1999
4. Harry Potter and the Goblet of Fire ◆ 2000
5. Harry Potter and the Order of the Phoenix ◆ 2003
6. Harry Potter and the Half Blood Prince ◆ 2005

HARVEY ANGELL TRILOGY

Hendry, Diana
POCKET/MINSTREL
GRADES 4–7 ◆ A/R
FANTASY | MYSTERY

Henry, an orphan living in a depressing boarding house with his miserly Aunt Agatha, is cheered by the arrival of new resident Harvey Angell, who brings music and a kit full of magical gadgets. Henry calls for Harvey's help with mysteries in subsequent books. In the third, Henry discovers an abandoned baby that has antennae. These entertaining stories were first published in Britain.

1. Harvey Angell ◆ 2001
2. Harvey Angell and the Ghost Child ◆ 2002
3. Harvey Angell Beats Time ◆ 2002

HATCHET *see* Brian Robeson

HAUNTING WITH LOUISA

Cates, Emily
BANTAM
GRADES 5–8
MYSTERY

Dee Forest comes to Misty Island to live with her Aunt Winnifred after her mother dies and her father cannot cope with his grief. There she meets Louisa, a young ghost who must help four of her living relatives before she can go on to the next life. With Dee's help, and after many adventures, Louisa finds three of them. In the last book, they discover that Dee herself is Louisa's distant cousin, and Louisa saves her life. Meanwhile, Louisa is concerned that Dee doesn't have any living friends and urges her to make some. At the same time, Dee's father finds a new romance, which Dee comes to accept.

1. The Ghost in the Attic ◆ 1990
2. The Mystery of Misty Island Inn ◆ 1991
3. The Ghost Ferry ◆ 1991

HAVE A NICE LIFE

Macdougal, Scarlett
ALLOYBOOKS
GRADES 9–12
FANTASY | HUMOR

On prom night, fairy godfather Clarence Terence shows four girls their dismal futures. One will be an unsuccessful model, one will have a failed marriage, one will continue to live with her mother. The girls immediately decide to improve themselves and the series follows their efforts to do so. In *Score*, a rival fairy godmother turns up and advises the girls to take a different course. Which godmother is giving the right advice?

1. Start Here ◆ 2000
2. Play ◆ 2000
3. Popover ◆ 2003
4. Score ◆ 2001

HAZELWOOD HIGH

Draper, Sharon M.
ATHENEUM
GRADES 7–10
REAL LIFE

Sharon M. Draper has written a trilogy of books about African American teens who are connected by their participation on the Hazelwood High basketball team, the Tigers. These students deal with harsh issues including drug addiction, drunk driving, and abuse. In *Tears of a Tiger*, Robert Washington has been killed in an auto accident. The driver was his best friend, Andy Jackson, and all the kids in the car had been drinking. In *Darkness Before Dawn*, Keisha Montgomery tries to recover after her ex-boyfriend's suicide. That boyfriend was Andy Jackson. Draper received the Coretta Scott King Genesis Award for *Tears of a Tiger* and the Coretta Scott King Award for *Forged by Fire*. The reading order of the books is different from their chronological release.

1. Forged by Fire ◆ 1997
2. Tears of a Tiger ◆ 1994
3. Darkness Before Dawn ◆ 2001

HE-MAN WOMEN HATERS CLUB

Lynch, Chris
HARPERCOLLINS
GRADES 6–9 ◆ A/R
REAL LIFE

Four adolescent boys take guidance from Spanky and Alfalfa and form their own He-Man Women Haters Club. They don't really hate women; they are just confused about their changing relationships. Steven, 13, starts out as the leader but makes a mess of things. The second book features Jerome; Wolfgang (who is in a wheelchair) is the leader in the third book; and Ling is in charge in the fourth book. The boys go camping, play in a band, and try to deal with their developing interest in girls. There is a lot here for male reluctant readers.

1. Johnny Chesthair ◆ 1997
2. Babes in the Woods ◆ 1997
3. Scratch and the Sniffs ◆ 1997
4. Ladies' Choice ◆ 1997
5. The Wolf Gang ◆ 1998

HEAR NO EVIL

Chester, Kate
SCHOLASTIC
GRADES 9–12
MYSTERY

Most of Sara Howell's perceptions are heightened but she does not have "super powers." Sara is deaf. She uses her insights and intelligence to solve such mysteries as finding Kimberly Roth and investigating the murder of her friend Amy. The exciting action in these books should interest reluctant readers.

1. Death in the Afternoon ◆ 1996
2. Missing ◆ 1996
3. Time of Fear ◆ 1996
4. Dead and Buried ◆ 1996
5. Sudden Death ◆ 1997
6. Playing with Fire ◆ 1997

HEART BEATS

Rees, Elizabeth M.
ALADDIN
GRADES 7–8 ◆ A/R
REAL LIFE

The students at Dance Tech dream of success in dancing. They are also devoted to their friends and boyfriends. Sophy likes having Carlos as her dance partner, but she is also interested in him romantically. Ray is worried about Daly's commitment to losing weight. Can he help her and still be her boyfriend? The dance school setting provides a background for stories of jealousy, both personal and professional.

1. Moving as One ◆ 1998
2. Body Lines ◆ 1998
3. In the Spotlight ◆ 1998
4. Latin Nights ◆ 1998
5. Face the Music ◆ 1999
6. Last Dance ◆ 1999

HEARTLAND

Brooke, Lauren
SCHOLASTIC
GRADES 4–7 ◆ A/R
REAL LIFE

Heartland is a farm in Virginia that specializes in caring for horses that have been mistreated. Amy, 14, is developing her skills as a horse whisperer. Throughout the series as Amy works with horses, she also deals with different people and their problems.

1. Coming Home ◆ 2000
2. After the Storm ◆ 2000
3. Breaking Free ◆ 2000
4. Taking Chances ◆ 2001
5. Come What May ◆ 2001
6. One Day You'll Know ◆ 2001
7. Out of the Darkness ◆ 2002
8. Thicker than Water ◆ 2002
9. Every New Day ◆ 2002
10. Tomorrow's Promise ◆ 2002
11. True Enough ◆ 2003
12. Sooner or Later ◆ 2003
13. Darkest Hour ◆ 2003
14. Everything Changes ◆ 2003
15. Love Is a Gift ◆ 2004
16. Holding Fast ◆ 2004
17. A Season of Hope ◆ 2004
18. A Holiday Memory: Heartland Super Special ◆ 2004

HEARTLIGHT

Barron, T. A.
PUTNAM
GRADES 6–9
FANTASY | SCIENCE FICTION

Kate Gordon, 13, and her 80-year-old grandfather, Dr. Miles Prancer, have a special bond and an ability to journey through time and space. Dr. Prancer is an astrophysicist working on saving the planet Earth and its solar system from total destruction. In the third book, Kate and her father travel to California on a quest for a lost treasure. This fantasy with elements of science fiction includes conflicts between the forces of good and evil and features links to Arthurian legends that should appeal to many readers. Fans of L'Engle's Time Fantasy Series will enjoy these adventures, which are somewhat technical and a little more scientific.

1. Heartlight ◆ 1990
2. The Ancient One ◆ 1992
3. The Merlin Effect ◆ 1994

HELLBOY

Various authors
DARK HORSE
GRADES 10–12
HORROR

This is one of the most popular horror comics with adults and older teenagers. Hellboy is a paranormal investigator determined to save the world from mystical forces of evil. In *Wake the Devil*, his search for a missing corpse leads him to an encounter with a vampire. In another book, he faces the conqueror worm. Volumes titled *Weird Tales* (2003 and 2004), *Odd Jobs* (1999), and *Odder Jobs* (2004) contain short stories about Hellboy.

1. Seed of Destruction (Mignola, Mike, and John Byrne) ◆ 1994
2. The Lost Army (Golden, Christopher) ◆ 1997
3. Wake the Devil (Mignola, Mike) ◆ 1997
4. The Chained Coffin and Others (Mignola, Mike) ◆ 1998
5. The Right Hand of Doom (Mignola, Mike) ◆ 2000
6. The Bones of Giants Illustrated Novel (Golden, Christopher) ◆ 2001
7. Conqueror Worm (Mignola, Mike) ◆ 2002

HELLSING

Hirano, Kohta
DARK HORSE
GRADES 10–12
HORROR

Based in England, the Hellsing Organization protects the world from vampires, ghouls, and other dark forces. The secret weapon of Hellsing is Arucard, a vampire! Talk about fighting fire with fire!

1. Volume 1 ◆ 2003
2. Volume 2 ◆ 2004
3. Volume 3 ◆ 2004
4. Volume 4 ◆ 2004
5. Volume 5 ◆ 2004

HELP, I'M TRAPPED

Strasser, Todd

SCHOLASTIC

GRADES 5–8 ◆ A/R

FANTASY | HUMOR

Jake Sherman seems like an ordinary middle school student, but he has a secret. He can body switch. He has been trapped in his teacher's body, his sister's body, the President's body, and his gym teacher's body. He has even been trapped in a dog's body. In some of the books, he is trapped in repeating events. For example, he has to live through the first day of school until he makes the right choices that break the cycle. Readers will like the implausible situations and the ensuing confusion. These are entertaining books with lots of clever dialogue, albeit at the humor level of a junior high school audience.

1. Help! I'm Trapped in My Teacher's Body ◆ 1993
2. Help! I'm Trapped in the First Day of School ◆ 1994
3. Help! I'm Trapped in Obedience School ◆ 1995
4. Help! I'm Trapped in My Gym Teacher's Body ◆ 1996
5. Help! I'm Trapped in the President's Body ◆ 1996
6. Help! I'm Trapped in Obedience School Again ◆ 1997
7. Help! I'm Trapped in Santa's Body ◆ 1997
8. Help! I'm Trapped in My Sister's Body ◆ 1997
9. Help! I'm Trapped in the First Day of Summer Camp ◆ 1997
10. Help! I'm Trapped in an Alien's Body ◆ 1998
11. Help! I'm Trapped in a Movie Star's Body ◆ 1998
12. Help! I'm Trapped in My Principal's Body ◆ 1998
13. Help! I'm Trapped in My Lunch Lady's Body ◆ 1999
14. Help! I'm Trapped in a Professional Wrestler's Body ◆ 2000
15. Help! I'm Trapped in a Vampire's Body ◆ 2000
16. Help! I'm Trapped in a Supermodel's Body ◆ 2001

HERCULEAH JONES

Byars, Betsy

PENGUIN

GRADES 5–7 ◆ A/R

HUMOR | MYSTERY

Herculeah Jones is the daughter of a divorced police detective and a private investigator, so mystery solving comes naturally to her. Her friend Meat appreciates being allowed to help out, and occasionally works on his own. In *Dead Letter*, Herculeah buys a coat at a thrift store and finds a note in its hem. A woman is trapped and someone is going to kill her. Meat and Herculeah trace the note to a wealthy older woman being cared for by her nephew. In and out of danger the whole time, they are eventually responsible for the culprit's arrest. Herculeah is proud of being strong, and her hair always stands on end when there is danger. Girls will appreciate tough, smart Herculeah, and the relationship between her and Meat provides some humor.

1. The Dark Stairs ◆ 1994
2. Tarot Says Beware ◆ 1995
3. Dead Letter ◆ 1996
4. Death's Door ◆ 1997
5. Disappearing Acts ◆ 1998

HERE COMES HEAVENLY

Strasser, Todd

SIMON & SCHUSTER

GRADES 6–8 ◆ A/R

FANTASY

Heavenly Litebody is no ordinary nanny. With her piercings, tattoos, and purple hair, she looks at situations creatively. There are five children in the Rand family, so there are lots of problems to solve. Especially when the family takes a trip to Rome. Kit, 14, is the narrator.

1. Here Comes Heavenly ◆ 1999
2. Dance Magic ◆ 1999
3. Pastabilities ◆ 2000
4. Spell Danger ◆ 2000

HERMUX TANTAMOQ ADVENTURES

Hoeye, Michael
PUTNAM
GRADES 5–8 ◆ A/R
ANIMAL FANTASY | MYSTERY

Hermux Tantamoq, a mouse, is a watchmaker who enjoys a quiet and orderly life . . . until the intrepid aviatrix Linka Perflinger appears, dragging him into adventure and mystery in *Time Stops for No Mouse*. In the sequels, he continues to show courage while investigating such mysteries as the early relationship between mice and cats.

1. Time Stops for No Mouse ◆ 2002
2. The Sands of Time ◆ 2003
3. No Time like Show Time ◆ 2004

HIGH HURDLES

Snelling, Lauraine
BETHANY HOUSE
GRADES 4–7 ◆ A/R
FAMILY LIFE | REAL LIFE | VALUES

DJ Randall, 13 at the start of the series, loves horses. She lives with her mother and has never met her father. As the series progresses, her biological father makes contact for the first time in 14 years. Her mother remarries and DJ must adjust to a stepfather and stepsiblings. DJ spends a lot of time at the riding academy. Like many teens, she is busy with friends, family, and activities. She seeks God's guidance to help her with problems. As the series closes, DJ helps save the horses from a fire and is seriously burned. Her faith helps her face the challenges of her recovery.

1. Olympic Dreams ◆ 1995
2. DJ's Challenge ◆ 1995
3. Setting the Pace ◆ 1996
4. Out of the Blue ◆ 1996
5. Storm Clouds ◆ 1997
6. Close Quarters ◆ 1998
7. Moving Up ◆ 1998
8. Letting Go ◆ 1999
9. Raising the Bar ◆ 1999
10. Class Act ◆ 2000

HIGH SEAS TRILOGY

Lawrence, Iain

DELACORTE

GRADES 6–9

ADVENTURE

As ships sail along the Cornish coast, villagers deliberately wreck them to loot the cargo. It is 1799. John Spencer, 14, is on his father's merchant ship and it crashes. The villagers want to plunder the ship and cannot allow any witnesses. John manages to escape them and find his father. Their second adventure involves piracy. In the final book, John is 17 and must deal with a dangerous stranger.

1. The Wreckers ◆ 1998
2. The Smugglers ◆ 1999
3. The Buccaneers ◆ 2001

HIGHLAND HEROES

Reding, Jaclyn

NAL

GRADES 11–12

HISTORICAL

These entertaining historical romances feature women with independent spirits. In *The Pretender*, Lady Elizabeth Drayton rebels against an arranged marriage. The second book involves an enchanted stone that seems to guide Lady Isabella's introduction to an attractive adventurer. This adult romance series is recommended for mature teens.

1. The Pretender ◆ 2002
2. The Adventurer ◆ 2002
3. The Secret Gift ◆ 2003

HIS DARK MATERIALS

Pullman, Philip

KNOPF

GRADES 7–12 ◆ A/R

FANTASY

With her *daemon*, an animal manifestation of her soul, Lyra intervenes in a dangerous scheme to kidnap children. Later, with her friend Will, she searches for Will's father and discovers the Subtle Knife, a tool that cuts into other worlds. Lyra is captured and Will must find her and rescue her. But he is not alone in his search. Fantasy readers will be challenged by the complexity of this series but will appreciate the classic battle between good and evil.

1. The Golden Compass ◆ 1995
2. The Subtle Knife ◆ 1997
3. The Amber Spyglass ◆ 2000

HISTORY MYSTERIES *see* American Girls: History Mysteries

HITCHHIKER'S TRILOGY

Adams, Douglas
BALLANTINE
GRADES 7–12 ◆ A/R
FANTASY

What began as a popular BBC radio program evolved into a "trilogy" of five books following the exploits of Ford Prefect and Arthur Dent. Ford is researching a new edition of a book—*The Hitchhiker's Guide to the Galaxy*. Just as Earth is being destroyed, Ford rescues his friend, Arthur Dent. The two start their trek through the galaxy on a Vogon constructor ship. After they are thrown off that ship, they continue to hitchhike through space, often saving the universe from destruction. In the fifth book, Arthur Dent's daughter, Random, investigates her heritage. *The Salmon of Doubt* (2002) includes letters, early writings, and part of an unfinished novel left by Adams on his death.

1. The Hitchhiker's Guide to the Galaxy ◆ 1980
2. The Restaurant at the End of the Universe ◆ 1980
3. Life, the Universe and Everything ◆ 1982
4. So Long, and Thanks for All the Fish ◆ 1984
5. Mostly Harmless ◆ 1992

HOLLOW KINGDOM

Dunkle, Clare B.
HENRY HOLT
GRADES 6–9
FANTASY

Set in England in the 19th century, this series has magic and mystery. Two orphaned sisters, Kate and Emily, are sent to live at Hallow Hill. There they encounter goblins whose king, Marak, wants to marry Kate. To protect her sister, Kate agrees and she moves to Marak's underground kingdom.

1. The Hollow Kingdom ◆ 2003
2. Close Kin ◆ 2004
3. By These Ten Bones ◆ 2005

HOLLY'S HEART

Lewis, Beverly
BETHANY HOUSE
GRADES 6–9 ◆ A/R
REAL LIFE | VALUES

Romance and Christian faith play large roles in these stories of Holly Meredith and her friendships and romantic attachments at school. In *Best Friend, Worst Enemy*, Holly faints and is given mouth-to-mouth resuscitation. But her best friend won't tell her which boy was involved. In another book, Holly develops a crush on a teacher and wonders whether her affection is returned.

1. Best Friend, Worst Enemy ◆ 2001
2. Secret Summer Dreams ◆ 2001
3. Sealed with a Kiss ◆ 2002
4. The Trouble with Weddings ◆ 2002
5. California Crazy ◆ 2002
6. Second-Best Friend ◆ 2002
7. Good-Bye, Dressel Hills ◆ 2002
8. Straight-A Teacher ◆ 2003
9. No Guys Pact ◆ 2003
10. Little White Lies ◆ 2003
11. Freshman Frenzy ◆ 2003
12. Mystery Letters ◆ 2003
13. Eight Is Enough ◆ 2003
14. It's a Girl Thing ◆ 2003

HOMECOMING SAGA

Card, Orson Scott
TOR
GRADES 9–12 ◆ A/R
FANTASY | SCIENCE FICTION

On the planet Harmony, the Oversoul has kept the peace. Now the artificial intelligence system is failing. A group has been selected to leave Harmony and search for the planet Earth. Naifeh and his family are among those chosen. The journey is made even more difficult by the treachery of some of those on the starship. Eventually, they reach Earth and establish a colony there.

1. The Memory of Earth ◆ 1992
2. The Call of Earth ◆ 1993
3. The Ships of Earth ◆ 1994
4. Earthfall ◆ 1995
5. Earthborn ◆ 1995

HOMEROOM

Norton, Nancy
SCHOLASTIC
GRADES 7–10
REAL LIFE

Piper is eager to begin high school. After fixing some scheduling problems, she makes new friends—Tamara and Judd. Grades, dating, friends, and other high school concerns are featured in this series.

1. Strange Times at Fairwood High ◆ 1988
2. The Princess of Fairwood High ◆ 1988
3. Triple Trouble at Fairwood High ◆ 1988

HONOR HARRINGTON

Weber, David
BAEN
GRADES 9–12
SCIENCE FICTION

Manticoran Navy Commander Honor Harrington manages to overcome the deficiencies of her starship when attacked by the enemy. The series, written for adults but enjoyed by teens, follows her exploits in pursuit of foes and her ability to deal with political intrigues. In *Honor Among Enemies*, she is brought out of forced retirement to tackle intrepid space pirates.

1. On Basilisk Station ◆ 1993
2. The Honor of the Queen ◆ 1993
3. The Short Victorious War ◆ 1994

4. Field of Dishonor ◆ 1994
5. Flag in Exile ◆ 1995
6. Honor Among Enemies ◆ 1996
7. In Enemy Hands ◆ 1997
8. Echoes of Honor ◆ 1998
9. Ashes of Victory ◆ 2000
10. War of Honor ◆ 2002

HORSEFEATHERS

Mackall, Dandi Daley
CONCORDIA
GRADES 7–10
REAL LIFE | VALUES

Scoop, 16, is good at caring for horses. Living with her aunt and her grandfather on a struggling horse farm, Scoop's life is difficult. Her love for her horse, Orphan, and her faith in God help sustain her.

1. Horsefeathers! ◆ 2000
2. Horse Cents ◆ 2000
3. Horse Whispers in the Air ◆ 2000
4. A Horse of a Different Color ◆ 2000
5. Horse Angels ◆ 2000
6. Home Is Where Your Horse Is ◆ 2001
7. Horsefeathers' Mystery ◆ 2001
8. All the King's Horses ◆ 2001

HOUSE OF HORRORS

Various authors
HARPERCOLLINS
GRADES 5–7
HORROR

What would you do if a ghost were stalking your brother? And then, what if your Aunt Wendy came to visit and took off her head? How about if your dog turned into an angry beast and brought home a gross claw that wasn't quite dead? These are just some of the problems faced by Sara and Michael Buckner in the House of Horrors series. There are oozing eggs and a scheming gargoyle. Readers who enjoy being scared and disgusted will want to read these creepy adventures.

1. My Brother, the Ghost (Weyn, Suzanne) ◆ 1994
2. Rest in Pieces (Weyn, Suzanne) ◆ 1994
3. Jeepers Creepers (Weyn, Suzanne) ◆ 1995
4. Aunt Weird (Lloyd, Alan) ◆ 1995
5. Knock, Knock . . . You're Dead (Stine, Megan) ◆ 1995
6. Night of the Gargoyle (Lloyd, Alan) ◆ 1995
7. Evil on Board (Moore, Leslie) ◆ 1995

THE HUNGRY CITY CHRONICLES

Reeve, Philip
HarperCollins
Grades 7–10
Science fiction

Many years ago, the Sixty Minute War brought death and destruction. Now, cities move on huge tracks and consume smaller towns. Fifteen-year-old Tom is an orphan who is apprenticed to Valentine, a scavenger/historian. Tom saves Valentine from being stabbed but, inexplicably, Valentine pushes Tom off a bridge along with Hester, the disfigured girl who attacked Valentine. Tom and Hester find themselves in Out-Country and only at the beginning of their crusade to restore order to the world. In *Predator's Gold*, Tom and Hester become involved in Anchorage's effort to outrun its pursuers.

1. Mortal Engines ◆ 2003
2. Predator's Gold ◆ 2004

I, ROBOT

Asimov, Isaac
Bantam Doubleday Dell
Grades 10–12
Science fiction

Robots take on many human characteristics in these entertaining stories featuring Dr. Susan Calvin and her mechanical inventions.

1. I, Robot ◆ 1950
2. The Caves of Steel ◆ 1954
3. The Naked Sun ◆ 1957
4. The Robots of Dawn ◆ 1983
5. Robots and Empire ◆ 1985

Immortals

Pierce, Tamora

Atheneum

Grades 7–10 ◆ **A/R**

Fantasy

Daine, 13, is an orphan who has a way with animals. When the kingdom of Tortall is threatened by immortal beings, Daine's skills are needed. She works with an endangered pack of wolves and helps the emperor's dying birds. As the series progresses, Daine grows up and becomes attracted to the mage Numair.

1. Wild Magic ◆ 1992
2. Wolf-Speaker ◆ 1994
3. Emperor Mage ◆ 1995
4. The Realms of the Gods ◆ 1996

Impact Zone

Strasser, Todd

Simon & Schuster

Grades 7–12 ◆ **A/R**

Family life | Real life | Recreation

Kai, 15, has left his home in Hawaii to live with his father and stepbrother near New York City. His father is abusive, forcing Kai to work selling cheaply made T-shirts for outlandish prices. Kai finds peace when he is surfing. He begins to make friends, including a girlfriend, Shauna. Family problems, romance, and surfing should keep teen readers interested.

1. Take Off ◆ 2004
2. Cut Back ◆ 2004
3. Close Out ◆ 2004

Indigo

Cooper, Louise

Tor

Grades 7–12

Fantasy

Princess Indigo releases demons from the Tower of Regrets and she must struggle to undo this wrong in a life of continual wandering. By

Aisling, she has destroyed six of the seven demons over a 50-year period but now she loses her memory.

1. Nemesis ◆ 1989
2. Inferno ◆ 1989
3. Infanta ◆ 1990
4. Nocturne ◆ 1990
5. Troika ◆ 1991
6. Avatar ◆ 1992
7. Revenant ◆ 1993
8. Aisling ◆ 1994

INHERITANCE

Paolini, Christopher

KNOPF

GRADES 6–10 ◆ A/R

FANTASY

Eragon, 15, finds a dragon egg that hatches. Out comes a female dragon he names Saphira. The two of them have a strange psychic connection that comes to their aid as they face challenges. Eragon is a Rider, a new generation of warriors who are rising against King Galbatorix. Readers who love Tolkien will want to try this series.

1. Eragon ◆ 2003
2. Eldest ◆ 2005

ISAAC ASIMOV'S CALIBAN

Allen, Roger MacBride

ORION

GRADES 9–12

SCIENCE FICTION

This trilogy expands on Asimov's Three Laws of Robotics. Caliban is a no-law robot. He does not conform to the behavior code that keeps other robots from harming humans. As a result, he is a rogue who strives to establish his own identity in a world where robots are servants.

1. Isaac Asimov's Caliban ◆ 1994
2. Isaac Asimov's Inferno ◆ 1994
3. Isaac Asimov's Utopia ◆ 1996

ISLAND

Korman, Gordon

SCHOLASTIC

GRADES 6–9

ADVENTURE

Six trouble-prone children are part of a program called "Charting a New Course." They will spend one month on a boat in the Pacific Ocean. It is expected to be tough and it gets tougher when the boat is shipwrecked. The captain and first mate disappear, but the children are not alone on the island.

1. Shipwreck ◆ 2001
2. Survival ◆ 2001
3. Escape ◆ 2001

ISLAND TRILOGY

Whelan, Gloria

HARPERCOLLINS

GRADES 6–9 ◆ A/R

HISTORICAL

During the War of 1812, Mary O'Shea, 12, lives with her older brother and sister on Mackinac Island. Their father has left them and gone to fight against the British. Mary and her siblings are now in charge of the family farm. They face the dangers of war and the difficulty of managing the farm. There is a subplot with a Native American boy, Gavin, who has lived among the settlers. After the war, Mary travels to London, gets swept up in the social whirl, and finds romance. After she returns to Mackinac Island, she must choose between two paths for her future.

1. Once on This Island ◆ 1995
2. Farewell to the Island ◆ 1998
3. Return to the Island ◆ 2000

JACKIE CHAN ADVENTURES

Various authors
GROSSET & DUNLAP
GRADES 4–8
ADVENTURE | FANTASY

When Jackie's talisman breaks in half, he becomes two people—Jackie Light and Jackie Dark. The two must team up to rescue Jackie's niece, Jade, from the dangers of the group called the Dark Hand. The Super Special book, *Day of the Dead*, includes puzzles and a secret message from Jackie.

1. The Dark Hand (Willard, Eliza) ◆ 2001
2. Jade's Secret Power (West, Cathy) ◆ 2002
3. Sign of the Ox (Stine, Megan) ◆ 2002
4. Enter . . . the Viper (Carrol, Jacqueline) ◆ 2002
5. Shendu Escapes! (Slack, David) ◆ 2002
6. A New Enemy (Ashby, R. S.) ◆ 2002
7. Revenge of the Dark Hand (Willard, Eliza) ◆ 2002
8. The Power of the Rat (Stine, Megan) ◆ 2002
9. Stronger than Stone (Ashby, R. S.) ◆ 2002
10. Uncle's Big Surprise (Carrol, Jacqueline) ◆ 2002
11. The Jade Monkey (Katschke, Judy) ◆ 2002
12. The Strongest Evil (Carrol, Jacqueline) ◆ 2002
13. Day of the Dragon: Super Special (Willard, Eliza) ◆ 2003

JACKIE CHAN ADVENTURES (TOKYOPOP)

1. Enter the Dark Hand ◆ 2003
2. Legend of the Zodiac ◆ 2004
3. Jackie and Jade Save the Day ◆ 2004

JAMES BUDD

Carlson, Dale Bick
WESTERN PUBLISHING
GRADES 7–10
MYSTERY

James Budd, 16, is a supersleuth who takes on difficult cases. A Vietnam vet accused of murder, a classmate who is being abused, and a mad scientist are among the challenges that he faces.

1. The Mystery of the Madman at Cornwall Crag ◆ 1984
2. The Secret of Operation Brain ◆ 1984
3. The Mystery of the Lost Princess ◆ 1984
4. The Mystery of Galaxy Games ◆ 1984

JANIE

Cooney, Caroline B.

DELACORTE

GRADES 6–9

REAL LIFE

When Janie was 15, she saw her face on a milk carton as a missing child and began the search for her true identity. She discovers that she was kidnapped from her biological parents 12 years before. The couple who have raised her have their own secret. Janie is betrayed by her boyfriend when he reveals her family's secret. Ultimately, Janie discovers the mystery of her past.

1. The Face on the Milk Carton ◆ 1990
2. Whatever Happened to Janie? ◆ 1993
3. The Voice on the Radio ◆ 1996
4. What Janie Found ◆ 2000

JENNIE McGRADY MYSTERIES

Rushford, Patricia H.

BETHANY HOUSE

GRADES 7–10 ◆ A/R

MYSTERY I VALUES

Like Nancy Drew, Jennie McGrady gets involved in mysterious situations. From finding her grandmother—who is missing along with a million dollars in stolen diamonds—to discovering a classmate's secret past to traveling to Ireland where she is threatened, Jennie's life is full of adventure. Her family, friends, and faith help her face each new challenge.

1. Too Many Secrets ◆ 1993
2. Silent Witness ◆ 1993
3. Pursued ◆ 1994

4. Deceived ◆ 1994
5. Without a Trace ◆ 1995
6. Dying to Win ◆ 1995
7. Betrayed ◆ 1996
8. In Too Deep ◆ 1996
9. Over the Edge ◆ 1997
10. From the Ashes ◆ 1997
11. Desperate Measures ◆ 1998
12. Abandoned ◆ 1999
13. Forgotten ◆ 2000
14. Stranded ◆ 2001
15. Grave Matters ◆ 2002

THE JERSEY

Various authors
DISNEY PRESS
GRADES 4–7 ◆ A/R
FANTASY

A group of friends have a jersey with magical powers. When they use it, they connect with a well-known sports star. In *Fight for Your Right*, Morgan boxes with Laila Ali. Other famous sports figures who appear in these stories include skateboarder Tony Hawk, BMX star Dave Mirra, and track star Michael Johnson. Gordon Korman created the series for television and these books are adapted from several episodes.

1. It's Magic (Sinclair, Jay) ◆ 2000
2. No Girly Girls Allowed (Sinclair, Jay) ◆ 2000
3. Nick's a Chick (Selman, Matty) ◆ 2000
4. This Rocks! (Selman, Matty) ◆ 2000
5. Team Player (Mantell, Paul) ◆ 2001
6. Head over Heels (Mantell, Paul) ◆ 2001
7. Fight for your Right (Mantell, Paul) ◆ 2001
8. Need for Speed (Rees, Elizabeth M.) ◆ 2001

JESSICA DARLING

McCafferty, Megan
THREE RIVERS PRESS
GRADES 10–12
FAMILY LIFE | HUMOR | REAL LIFE

When her best friend moves away, 16-year-old Jessica Darling struggles to deal alone with her feelings of isolation at home and at school.

In the second book, Jessica is in her senior year and the poignant but humorous description of unrequited love and parental over-involvement continues.

1. Sloppy Firsts ◆ 2001
2. Second Helpings ◆ 2003

JIGGY MCCUE

Lawrence, Michael
DUTTON
GRADES 4–7 ◆ **A/R**
FANTASY | HUMOR

In the first of these entertaining adventures, Jiggy and his friends investigate what is haunting his new house and suspect it's the ghost of a goose. In the second, Jiggy and his friend Angie end up switching bodies after playing a beta version of a computer game, causing much confusion.

1. The Poltergoose ◆ 2002
2. The Killer Underpants ◆ 2002
3. Toilet of Doom ◆ 2002

JIMMY FINCHER SAGA

Dashner, James
BONNEVILLE BOOKS
GRADES 7–10
SCIENCE FICTION

Jimmy Fincher is drawn into hidden worlds of villains and danger. There are Four Gifts that will help him face the Shadow Ka and the Stompers. Will he find the Gifts in time to prevent destruction?

1. A Door in the Woods ◆ 2003
2. A Gift of Ice ◆ 2004
3. The Tower of Air ◆ 2004

JOE GREY MYSTERIES

Murphy, Shirley Rousseau
HARPERCOLLINS
GRADES 9–12
ANIMAL FANTASY | MYSTERY

Joe Grey and Dulcie, intrepid and intelligent cat investigators, use their varied feline skills to solve intricately plotted crimes.

1. Cat on the Edge ◆ 1996
2. Cat Under Fire ◆ 1997
3. Cat Raise the Dead ◆ 1997
4. Cat in the Dark ◆ 1999
5. Cat to the Dogs ◆ 2000
6. Cat Spitting Mad ◆ 2001
7. Cat Laughing Last ◆ 2002
8. Cat Seeing Double ◆ 2003
9. Cat Fear No Evil ◆ 2004

JOEY PIGZA

Gantos, Jack
FARRAR, STRAUS & GIROUX
GRADES 5–9 ◆ A/R
REAL LIFE

Joey Pigza is out of control. His hyperactivity causes him trouble at school. He can't pay attention; he can't sit still. His medication works for a while, but it wears off. He finally gets his meds balanced only to visit his father who wants him to try going without them. This series provides a revealing look at a special education student. The second book received a Newbery Honor award.

1. Joey Pigza Swallowed the Key ◆ 1998
2. Joey Pigza Loses Control ◆ 2000
3. What Would Joey Do? ◆ 2002

JOHNNY DIXON

Bellairs, John, and Brad Strickland
DIAL
GRADES 5–8 ◆ A/R
FANTASY | MYSTERY

Johnny Dixon's mother is dead and his dad is fighting in the Korean War. He lives with his grandparents across the street from the eccentric but kindly Professor Childermass. The two strike up a strange friendship, and together with Johnny's friend Fergie they solve mysteries involving ghosts, demon possession, and even time travel. Johnny is a small, almost timid boy who seems an unlikely candidate for such adventures. The professor is knowledgeable in many areas and sometimes unwillingly draws the boys into things. Fergie is a bit of a smart aleck and adds humor to the situations. Edward Gorey's black-and-white drawings add to the air of mystery. *The Drum, the Doll, and the Zombie* was completed by Strickland after Bellair's death. *The Hand of the Necromancer* and *The Bell, the Book, and the Spellbinder* are by Strickland.

1. The Curse of the Blue Figurine ◆ 1983
2. The Mummy, the Will, and the Crypt ◆ 1983
3. The Spell of the Sorcerer's Skull ◆ 1984
4. The Revenge of the Wizard's Ghost ◆ 1985
5. The Eyes of the Killer Robot ◆ 1986
6. The Trolley to Yesterday ◆ 1989
7. The Chessmen of Doom ◆ 1989
8. The Secret of the Underground Room ◆ 1990
9. The Drum, the Doll, and the Zombie ◆ 1994
10. The Hand of the Necromancer ◆ 1996
11. The Bell, the Book, and the Spellbinder ◆ 1997
12. The Wrath of the Grinning Ghost ◆ 1999

JOURNEY OF ALLEN STRANGE

Various authors
ALADDIN
GRADES 4–7
SCIENCE FICTION

Allen Strange is an alien from Xela. He was left behind by his spaceship and he has adopted the appearance of an African American human boy. He needs Robbie Stevenson's help but Robbie does not believe he is an alien until Allen appears as he really looks. Allen and

Robbie help prevent several alien invasions, including the arrival of the insect-like Arubii. This is fun for fans of science fiction.

1. The Arrival (Weiss, Bobbi J. G., and David Cody Weiss) ◆ 1999
2. Invasion (Gallagher, Diana G.) ◆ 1999
3. Split Image (Dubowski, Cathy East) ◆ 1999
4. Legacy (Odom, Mel) ◆ 1999
5. Depth Charge (Weiss, Bobbi J. G., and David Cody Weiss) ◆ 1999
6. Alien Vacation (Weiss, Bobbi J. G., and David Cody Weiss) ◆ 1999
7. Election Connection (Ponti, James) ◆ 1999
8. Changeling Diapers (Weiss, Bobbi J. G., and David Cody Weiss) ◆ 2000
9. Joyride (Vornholt, John) ◆ 2000

JULIAN ESCOBAR

O'Dell, Scott
HOUGHTON MIFFLIN
GRADES 6–8
HISTORICAL

Set in the 16th century, this series chronicles the adventures of Julian Escobar, a young seminarian from Spain who journeys to the Americas. He is captured by Mayan Indians and manages to convince them that he is Kukulcan, a god who had promised to return to them. He continues this charade in the second book when he leaves the Maya and encounters Cortez in the days when the Aztec king Moctezuma is conquered by a few hundred Spanish soldiers. In the third book, his fortunes change and he becomes a wanderer, but eventually he ends up with Francisco Pizarro in the land of the Incas.

1. The Captive ◆ 1979
2. The Feathered Serpent ◆ 1981
3. The Amethyst Ring ◆ 1983

JULIE OF THE WOLVES

George, Jean Craighead
HARPERCOLLINS
GRADES 5–8
ADVENTURE

Beginning with the Newbery-winning *Julie of the Wolves*, George explores the experiences of people and animals in the Alaskan tundra.

Julie's story follows her quest for her identity through her return to her father's home. *Julie's Wolf Pack* describes the hardships faced by Kapu, first seen as a pup in the first book. The wolves face famine, disease, rivalries, and other dangers. These are exciting, realistic adventure novels. Readers will also relate to George's series about Sam Gribley and the falcon called Frightful.

   1. Julie of the Wolves ◆ 1972
   2. Julie ◆ 1996
   3. Julie's Wolf Pack ◆ 1997

JUNEBUG

Mead, Alice

FARRAR, STRAUS & GIROUX

GRADES 4–7

REAL LIFE

These realistic novels begin when Reeve McClain, Jr., "Junebug," is 10 years old. His family lives in the projects, facing all the threats of urban life—drugs, gangs, and loneliness. In the second book, they have moved to a safer neighborhood where Junebug's mother is the supervisor of a home for the elderly. Junebug helps her and interacts with Reverend Ashford. The third book finds Junebug meeting up with his friend Robert, who still lives in the projects. Junebug faces his family problems (his father has been in jail) and makes choices about his future.

   1. Junebug ◆ 1995
   2. Junebug and the Reverend ◆ 1998
   3. Junebug in Trouble ◆ 2003

JUNIOR JEDI KNIGHTS *see* Star Wars Junior Jedi Knights

JUNIPER *see* Wise Child

JUSTICE TRILOGY

Hamilton, Virginia
GREENWILLOW

GRADES 5–8

FANTASY | SCIENCE FICTION

Justice and her two brothers discover that they are the first of a new race with extraordinary powers. Together with their friend Dorian, they form a unit that is able to travel into the distant future. Among the beings they find there is Duster, the leader of a group of young people. He is hindered, as is all of this world, by the evil Mal. When the Mal is defeated, all the friends they have made are free to be themselves. When Justice and her brothers return to their own time, they find that they have lost some of their powers but have gained maturity.

1. Justice and Her Brothers ◆ 1978
2. Dustland ◆ 1980
3. The Gathering ◆ 1981

THE KARMIDEE

Haptie, Charlotte
HOLIDAY HOUSE

GRADES 4–7

FANTASY

The City of Trees is an isolated place surrounded by mountains and magic. The Normals are in power and they make rules to control those with magical powers, the Karmidee. Otto believes he is a Normal and is surprised to learn that his father, a librarian, is actually the King of the Karmidees. Otto's life is totally upended and he faces dangers as he tries to protect the Karmidee from the prejudice of the Normals.

1. Otto and the Flying Twins: The First Book of the Karmidee ◆ 2004
2. Otto and the Bird Charmers: The Second Book of the Karmidee ◆ 2005

KATE GORDON *see* Heartlight

KEEPER MARTIN'S TALES *see* Ruin Mist: The Kingdoms and the Elves of the Reaches

THE KEEPER'S CHRONICLES

Huff, Tanya
DAW
GRADES 7–12
FANTASY

Claire Hanson is a Keeper, a protector of the universe. Accompanied by her talking cat Austin, she tackles problems including a hole to Hell. In *The Second Summoning*, she must deal with an angel and a devil who appear as teenagers and face the usual teen problems. These are entertaining stories.

1. Summon the Keeper ◆ 1998
2. The Second Summoning ◆ 2001
3. Long Hot Summoning ◆ 2003

KEYS TO THE KINGDOM

Nix, Garth
SCHOLASTIC
GRADES 5–8 ◆ A/R
FANTASY

Mister Monday wants to recover a mysterious key from Arthur Penhaligon. It turns out that Arthur is the heir to "the Will" and there are seven keys that he must acquire. The Second Key brings him into contact with Grim Tuesday. Arthur battles to save not only the Earth but also the magical worlds that have been revealed to him.

1. Mister Monday ◆ 2003
2. Grim Tuesday ◆ 2004
3. Drowned Wednesday ◆ 2005

KIDS FROM KENNEDY MIDDLE SCHOOL

Cooper, Ilene

MORROW

GRADES 5–7

REAL LIFE

Friends and foes at a middle school are the focus of this series. Robin and Veronica are friends but when Veronica creates an exclusive club, Robin is uneasy. If she speaks up, she'll be left out. Jon Rossi is a sixth-grader who plays basketball but dislikes his coach's negative approach. If he leaves the team, he'll disappoint his father. Gretchen, 12, loses weight, but she still remembers the way she was treated.

1. Queen of the Sixth Grade ◆ 1988
2. Choosing Sides ◆ 1990
3. Mean Streak ◆ 1991
4. The New, Improved Gretchen Hubbard ◆ 1992

KIM POSSIBLE (CHAPTER BOOKS)

Various authors

HYPERION, DISNEY PRESS

GRADES 4–7

FANTASY

Kim Possible will save the world. She faces the evil Drakken. She finds a kidnapped scientist. She stops DNAmy from creating a stuffed-animal army. All the while, she manages to stay involved with cheerleading, ski trips, and watching television. There are related items to this series including a puzzle book, *Code Word: Kim*.

1. Bueno Nacho (Thorpe, Kiki) ◆ 2003
2. The New Ron (Thorpe, Kiki) ◆ 2003
3. Showdown at Camp Wannaweep (Thorpe, Kiki) ◆ 2003
4. Downhill (Jones, Jasmine) ◆ 2003
5. Killigan's Island (Pascoe, Jim) ◆ 2004
6. Monkey Business (Cerasini, Marc) ◆ 2004
7. Attack of the Killer Bebes (Pascoe, Jim) ◆ 2004
8. Royal Pain (Jones, Jasmine) ◆ 2004

KIM POSSIBLE (TOKYOPOP)

Schooley, Bob, and Mark McCorkle
TOKYOPOP
GRADES 4–7
FANTASY

Kim Possible is a typical high school girl who saves the world from evil villains in her spare time.

1. Bueno Nacho and Tick Tick Tick ◆ 2003
2. Monkey Fist Strikes and Attack of the Killer Bebes ◆ 2003
3. The New Ron and Mind Games ◆ 2003
4. Royal Pain and Twin Factor ◆ 2003
5. Animal Attraction and All the News ◆ 2004
6. Sink or Swim and Number One ◆ 2004
7. Monkey Ninjas in Space and Crush ◆ 2004

KIM POSSIBLE CINE-MANGA

1. Volume 1 ◆ 2003
2. Volume 2 ◆ 2003
3. Volume 3 ◆ 2004
4. Volume 4 ◆ 2004
5. Volume 5 ◆ 2004
6. Volume 6 ◆ 2004
7. Volume 7 ◆ 2004

THE KIN

Dickinson, Peter
GROSSET & DUNLAP
GRADES 6–9 ◆ A/R
FANTASY

In a prehistoric era, five children have been separated from the Moon-hawk clan. It is dangerous for them to be on their own without food, water, shelter, or protection. They encounter a man, Tor, who is unable to speak. He uses his skill with tools to help them survive. Mythology and mysticism pervade these novels. Noli is a character with a strong spirit connection. She seems able to communicate with the group's totem animal, a hawk. Po's character is involved in a struggle to prove his bravery.

1. Suth's Story ◆ 1998
2. Noli's Story ◆ 1998
3. Mana's Story ◆ 1998
4. Po's Story ◆ 1998

KING GARION *see* Malloreon

THE KINGDOM

Voigt, Cynthia
ATHENEUM, SCHOLASTIC
GRADES 6–10 ◆ A/R
FANTASY

The books in this series are all set in an imaginary world of the past. They feature strong characters who defy expectations and face unusual challenges and choices. In the first book, Gwyn is the daughter of an innkeeper. She hears the legend of Jackaroo and decides to masquerade as the Robin Hood-like character. She realizes that she is not the only one disguised as Jackaroo. There are dramatic encounters with the Wolfers, a dangerous group that threatens the Kingdom. Readers will appreciate the classic fantasy elements in these books.

1. Jackaroo ◆ 1985
2. On Fortune's Wheel ◆ 1990
3. The Wings of a Falcon ◆ 1993
4. Elske ◆ 1999

THE KINGDOMS AND THE ELVES OF THE REACHES *see* Ruin Mist: The Kingdoms and the Elves of the Reaches

THE LAST VAMPIRE

Pike, Christopher
POCKET BOOKS
GRADES 9–12
HORROR

Alisa is a 5,000-year-old vampire. In the first book, she must enter high school in an effort to escape a threat. There she falls for a shy young man. In *Red Dice*, Alisa is the focus of a government manhunt; and in *Phantom*, Alisa becomes pregnant and the nature of her child is in question.

1. The Last Vampire ◆ 1994
2. Black Blood ◆ 1994

3. Red Dice ◆ 1995
4. The Phantom ◆ 1996
5. Evil Thirst ◆ 1996
6. Creatures of Forever ◆ 1996

LaVaughn *see* Make Lemonade Trilogy

Lechow Family

Benary-Isbert, Margot
HARCOURT
GRADES 5–8
FAMILY LIFE | HISTORICAL

Set in postwar Germany, *The Ark* begins the trilogy of the Lechow family. Mrs. Lechow is trying to keep her family alive while her husband is in a Russian prison camp. The family fortunately finds its way to Rowan Farm and makes a home in the Ark, an old railroad car. The author was born in Germany, lived under Nazi rule, and arrived in the United States in 1957. The stories, translated from German, are based on the author's childhood.

1. The Ark ◆ 1948
2. Rowan Farm ◆ 1949
3. Castle on the Border ◆ 1956

Left Behind—The Kids

Jenkins, Jerry B., and Tim LaHayes
TYNDALE HOUSE
GRADES 6–10 ◆ A/R
FANTASY | VALUES

Many thousands of people have disappeared. Those who are left behind are confused and frightened. They include four teens who try to understand what has happened. They come to realize that those who have disappeared experienced the Rapture, a time when God brings the truly faithful to be with Him. Judd, Vicki, Lionel, and Ryan have adventures that test their commitment to God. This is based on a popular religious series for adults.

1. The Vanishings ◆ 1998
2. Second Chance ◆ 1998
3. Through the Flames ◆ 1998

4. Facing the Future ◆ 1998
5. Nicolae High ◆ 1999
6. The Underground ◆ 1999
7. Busted! ◆ 2000
8. Death Strike ◆ 2000
9. The Search ◆ 2000
10. On the Run ◆ 2000
11. Into the Storm ◆ 2000
12. Earthquake! ◆ 2000
13. The Showdown ◆ 2001
14. Judgment Day ◆ 2001
15. Battling the Commander ◆ 2001
16. Fire from Heaven ◆ 2001
17. Terror in the Stadium ◆ 2001
18. Darkening Skies ◆ 2001
19. Attack of Apollyon ◆ 2002
20. A Dangerous Plan ◆ 2002
21. Secrets of New Babylon ◆ 2002
22. Escape from New Babylon ◆ 2002
23. Horsemen of Terror ◆ 2002
24. Uplink from the Underground ◆ 2002
25. Death at the Gala ◆ 2003
26. The Beast Arises ◆ 2003
27. Wildfire ◆ 2003
28. Mark of the Beast ◆ 2003
29. Breakout! ◆ 2003
30. Murder in the Holy Place ◆ 2003
31. Escape to Masada ◆ 2003
32. War of the Dragon ◆ 2003
33. Attack on Petra ◆ 2004
34. Bounty Hunters ◆ 2004
35. The Rise of the False Messiahs ◆ 2004
36. Ominous Choices ◆ 2004
37. Heat Wave ◆ 2004
38. Perils of Love ◆ 2004

LEWIS BARNAVELT

Bellairs, John, and Brad Strickland
DIAL
GRADES 5–8 ◆ A/R
FANTASY

Lewis is a 10-year-old orphan who goes to live with his Uncle Jonathan in the small town of New Zebedee. His uncle is a kind old man who practices "white magic," and his neighbor and best friend is Mrs. Zimmerman, who is a good witch. Jonathan lives in a big old house that was previously owned by an evil man who practiced black magic. Lewis makes a new friend toward the end of the first book in the series: Rose Rita, who loves baseball and lives in a nearby mansion. Some of the books in the series feature Rose Rita and Mrs. Zimmerman as they fight black magic together. The first three books were written by Bellairs; the fourth and fifth were completed by Strickland after Bellairs's death; and the remaining books were written by Strickland and are based on the characters of Bellairs.

1. The House with a Clock in its Walls ◆ 1973
2. The Figure in the Shadows ◆ 1975
3. The Letter, the Witch, and the Ring ◆ 1976
4. The Ghost in the Mirror ◆ 1993
5. The Vengeance of the Witch-Finder ◆ 1993
6. The Doom of the Haunted Opera ◆ 1995
7. The Specter from the Magician's Museum ◆ 1998
8. The Beast under the Wizard's Bridge ◆ 2000
9. The Tower at the End of the World ◆ 2001
10. The Whistle, the Grave and the Ghost ◆ 2003

LIBERTY LETTERS

LeSourd, Nancy

ZONDERKIDZ

GRADES 7–10

HISTORICAL

These books use a fictional correspondence between two teenage women to explore the impact of historical events on everyday life and faith. In the first book, Abigail Matthews has left England and settled in Virginia, first at Jamestown and then in Henricus. She writes to her friend in England, Elizabeth Walton, and describes her adventures.

1. The Personal Correspondence of Elizabeth Walton and Abigail Matthews: The Story of Pocahontas, 1613 ◆ 2003
2. The Personal Correspondence of Hannah Brown and Sarah Smith: The Underground Railroad, 1858 ◆ 2003
3. The Personal Correspondence of Emma Edmunds and Mollie Turner: Assignment: Civil War Spies, 1862 ◆ 2004
4. The Personal Correspondence of Catherine Clark and Meredith Lyons: Pearl Harbor, 1941 ◆ 2004

THE LIFE AND TIMES

Denenberg, Barry

SCHOLASTIC

GRADES 4–7

ADVENTURE | HISTORICAL

This series begins with two adventures. One features the life of a slave in a wealthy home in the Roman Republic. Although his master is kind, Atticus becomes caught up in the intrigues and plots. The second book tells the story of a young girl, Pandora, who is dreading her 14th birthday. On that day, she will be old enough to marry. Her father has already arranged an engagement for her. Pandora chafes under the restrictions of life in ancient Athens.

1. Atticus of Rome, 30 B.C. ◆ 2004
2. Pandora of Athens, 399 B.C. ◆ 2004

LIFE AT SIXTEEN

Various authors

BERKLEY PUBLISHING GROUP

GRADES 7–9

REAL LIFE

These books feature teens facing difficult situations. In *No Guarantees*, Courtney is used to having money and being a cheerleader. When her father loses his job, she must help out with the family and deal with how her friends now treat her. In *Good Intentions*, Chloe has been in a coma. As she recovers, she learns about how selfish she was in the past. Now she wants to try to change.

1. Silent Tears (Zach, Cheryl) ◆ 1997
2. Second Best (Lanham, Cheryl) ◆ 1997
3. Blue Moon (Kirby, Susan E.) ◆ 1997
4. No Guarantees (Lanham, Cheryl) ◆ 1997
5. Good Intentions (Lanham, Cheryl) ◆ 1998

LIGHTNING ON ICE

Brouwer, Sigmund
THOMAS NELSON
GRADES 8–10 ◆ A/R
RECREATION | VALUES

Ice hockey action provides a backdrop to these books that focus on teens struggling to succeed while maintaining their values. In the first book, B. T. McPhee, 17, wants to be a professional hockey player. A series of unusual accidents causes him to wonder if his team will even make the playoffs.

1. Rebel Glory ◆ 1995
2. All-Star Pride ◆ 1995
3. Thunderbird Spirit ◆ 1996
4. Winter Hawk Star ◆ 1996
5. Blazer Drive ◆ 1996
6. Chief Honor ◆ 1997

THE LILY ADVENTURES

Leppard, Lois Gladys
RANDOM HOUSE
GRADES 8–10
VALUES

While visiting England with her young sister, Lily Masterson, 16, receives word that her father has died. It is 1901 and Lily does not have enough money to return home until a mysterious packet of money is given to her. Her Christian faith supports her as she returns to South Carolina to investigate her father's death.

1. Secret Money ◆ 1995
2. Suspicious Identity ◆ 1995
3. Accidental Dreams ◆ 1996

LILY QUENCH

Prior, Natalie Jane
PUFFIN
GRADES 4–7 ◆ A/R
FANTASY

Dragons, quests, magic, and a battle with dangers from the past are all part of this fantasy series. Lily Quench has been paired with the Queen Dragon to try to protect Ashby from Gordon, the Black Count, and his army. One of their adventures helps them learn the secrets of the Eyes of Time.

1. Lily Quench and the Dragon of Ashby ◆ 2004
2. Lily Quench and the Black Mountains ◆ 2004
3. Lily Quench and the Treasure of Mote Ely ◆ 2004
4. Lily Quench and the Lighthouse of Skellig Mor ◆ 2004
5. Lily Quench and the Magician's Pyramid ◆ 2004
6. Lily Quench and the Hand of Manuelo ◆ 2004

LIONBOY TRILOGY

Corder, Zizou
DIAL
GRADES 4–8 ◆ A/R
FANTASY

Charlie Ashanti's parents have been kidnapped. With his special power to communicate with cats, Charlie begins his search for them. His journey takes him (and his lion friends) from London to various sites in Europe. This series is written by a mother and her young daughter using a pseudonym.

1. Lionboy ◆ 2003
2. Lionboy: The Chase ◆ 2004

LIVE FROM BRENTWOOD HIGH

Baer, Judy
BETHANY HOUSE
GRADES 6–9 ◆ A/R
REAL LIFE | VALUES

The school's radio news is run by a group including Darby, Sarah, Jake, Molly, and Izzy. These teens cover stories about a range of problems in the community—for example, violence, discrimination, teen parents, and graffiti—while also indulging in fun and romance.

1. Risky Assignment ◆ 1994
2. Price of Silence ◆ 1994
3. Double Danger ◆ 1994
4. Sarah's Dilemma ◆ 1995

5. Undercover Artists ◆ 1996
6. Faded Dreams ◆ 1996

LIZZIE MCGUIRE

Various authors
DISNEY PRESS
GRADES 4–7
FAMILY LIFE | REAL LIFE

Lizzie McGuire, played by actress Hilary Duff, is a popular character on the Disney television show of the same name. She hangs out with her friends at school talking about boys, family, and projects. In the first book, she is eager to go on a camping trip but is chagrined to discover her mom is a chaperone. In another book, she models in a fashion show. There is a lot of Lizzie McGuire merchandise for preteens. A Lizzie McGuire Super Special, *Code Blue!*, is planned for 2005.

1. When Moms Attack! (Ostrow, Kim) ◆ 2002
2. Totally Crushed! (Thorpe, Kiki) ◆ 2002
3. Lizzie Goes Wild (Larsen, Kirsten) ◆ 2002
4. The Rise and Fall of the Kate Empire (Larsen, Kirsten) ◆ 2002
5. Picture This (Jones, Jasmine) ◆ 2003
6. New Kid in School (Jones, Jasmine) ◆ 2003
7. Broken Hearts (Thorpe, Kiki) ◆ 2003
8. A Very Lizzie Christmas (Jones, Jasmine) ◆ 2003
9. Just Like Lizzie (Jones, Jasmine) ◆ 2003
10. Lizzie Loves Ethan (Jones, Jasmine) ◆ 2003
11. On the Job (Disney editors) ◆ 2004
12. Head over Heels (Disney editors) ◆ 2004
13. Best Dressed (Disney editors) ◆ 2004
14. Mirror, Mirror (Disney editors) ◆ 2004
15. Freaked Out (Disney editors) ◆ 2004
16. Lizzie for President (Disney editors) ◆ 2004
17. Oh, Brother! (Disney editors) ◆ 2005
18. The Importance of Being Gordo (Disney editors) ◆ 2005

LIZZIE MCGUIRE MYSTERIES

Banim, Lisa
DISNEY PRESS
GRADES 4–7
MYSTERY | REAL LIFE

Lizzie and her friends are back in these light mysteries. In the first book, Lizzie sets out to prove she is not responsible for the creepy notes kids have been getting. In the third book, Lizzie has hurt Audrey's feelings and now Audrey is missing. Gordo and Miranda go with Lizzie to a science fiction convention looking for Audrey and find some really strange characters.

1. Get a Clue! ◆ 2004
2. Case at Camp Get-Me-Out ◆ 2004
3. Case of the Missing She-Geek ◆ 2004
4. Hands Off My Crush-Boy! ◆ 2004

LIZZIE MCGUIRE (TOKYOPOP)

Minsky, Terri
TOKYOPOP
GRADES 4–7
REAL LIFE

Lizzie McGuire is in junior high and her life revolves around school. No! Her life revolves around boys and her friends! In the Disney Channel series, Lizzie is a live-action character with a cartoon alter ego. This Cine-Manga captures all the flair of this popular character.

1. Pool Party and Picture Day ◆ 2003
2. Rumors and I've Got Rhythmic ◆ 2003
3. When Moms Attack and Misadventures in Babysitting ◆ 2003
4. I Do, I Don't and Come Fly with Me ◆ 2003
5. Lizzie's Nightmare and Sibling Bonding ◆ 2004
6. Mom's Best Friend and Movin' On Up ◆ 2004
7. Over the Hill and Just Friends ◆ 2004
8. Gordo and the Girl and You're a Good Man Lizzie McGuire ◆ 2004
9. Magic Train and Grubby Longjohn's Olde Tyme Revue ◆ 2004
10. Inner Beauty and Best Dressed for Less ◆ 2005
11. In Miranda, Lizzie Does Not Trust and The Longest Yard ◆ 2005

LOGAN FAMILY

Taylor, Mildred D.
DIAL
GRADES 4–7 ◆ A/R
HISTORICAL | REAL LIFE

Cassie tells the story of the African American Logan family, living in Mississippi during the Great Depression. High taxes and the mortgage on their house have forced her father to take a job away from home on the railroad. Mrs. Logan works as a schoolteacher. Although poor, the Logans are economically self-sufficient, which makes them more fortunate than their neighbors, who are all in debt to the local store. When Mrs. Logan is fired for teaching black history and Mr. Logan loses his job when he is injured by some angry white men, the family lives in fear that they will lose their land. *Roll of Thunder, Hear My Cry* is a Newbery Award winner. *Song of the Trees* is written for younger readers. *The Land* is a prequel to *Roll of Thunder, Hear My Cry*. Members of the Logan family also appear in other books by this author.

1. Song of the Trees ◆ 1975
2. Roll of Thunder, Hear My Cry ◆ 1976
3. Let the Circle Be Unbroken ◆ 1981
4. The Road to Memphis ◆ 1990
5. The Well: David's Story ◆ 1995
6. The Land ◆ 2001

LORD OF THE RINGS

Tolkien, J. R. R.
HOUGHTON MIFFLIN
GRADES 5–8 ◆ A/R
FANTASY

When Hobbit Bilbo Baggins is visited by Gandalf the wizard, he finds himself tricked into being part of a dangerous quest. Together, they seek to recover a stolen treasure hidden in Lonely Mountain, guarded by Smaug the Dragon. *The Hobbit* is the introduction to Middle Earth and the Lord of the Rings trilogy, in which Bilbo names his cousin, Frodo Baggins, his heir. Frodo embarks on a journey to destroy the Ring of Power, a ring that would enable evil Sauron to destroy all that is good in Middle Earth. It is up to Frodo and his servant, Sam, to carry the Ring to the one place it can be destroyed. Author Tolkien was an eminent philologist and an authority on myths and sagas. *The Silmarillion* (1977) tells the story of the First Age, an ancient drama to which characters in the main trilogy look back.

1. The Fellowship of the Ring ◆ 1954
2. The Two Towers ◆ 1954
3. The Return of the King ◆ 1955

LOSERS, INC.

Mills, Claudia
FARRAR, STRAUS & GIROUX
GRADES 4–7
REAL LIFE

Ethan and Julius are both in sixth grade. They feel so left out that they form their own club—Losers, Inc. Ethan wants to be more like his smart, athletic older brother. Julius's mom tries to help him develop more confidence. Lizzie and Alex also feel like losers. These stories should give readers insights into kids on the outside.

1. Losers, Inc ◆ 1997
2. You're a Brave Man, Julius Zimmerman ◆ 1999
3. Lizzie at Last ◆ 2000
4. Alex Ryan, Stop That ◆ 2003

LOST YEARS OF MERLIN

Barron, T. A.
PHILOMEL
GRADES 6–10 ◆ A/R
FANTASY

Using the well-known Arthurian legends about Merlin as a base, Barron speculates about the unknown details of the wizard's childhood. From when he is washed onto the shores of ancient Wales and raised by Branwen, to his journey to the isle of Fincayra and his challenge to solve the riddle of the Dance of the Giants, these books weave adventure and fantasy. Merlin encounters and battles mythic creatures—Balor the ogre and a sleeping dragon; he also grapples with his own evil, greed, and desires. This fantasy will connect with readers who have read Jane Yolen's Young Merlin books and who enjoy Arthurian legends.

1. The Lost Years of Merlin ◆ 1996
2. The Seven Songs of Merlin ◆ 1997
3. The Fires of Merlin ◆ 1998
4. The Mirror of Merlin ◆ 1999
5. The Wings of Merlin ◆ 2000

LOVE STORIES

Various authors
BANTAM
GRADES 7–10 ◆ A/R
REAL LIFE

Romance novels are extremely popular with teen girls. This series portrays teens involved in the difficulties of finding true love. In one book, it's hard enough to manage schoolwork and swimming, now

Amy is also in love. Her romance with Chris complicates everything. Other books feature girls who are trying to attract boys and girls who can't choose between two boys.

1. My First Love (West, Callie) ◆ 1995
2. Sharing Sam (Applegate, K. A.) ◆ 1995
3. How to Kiss a Guy (Bernard, Elizabeth) ◆ 1995
4. The Boy Next Door (Quin-Harkin, Janet) ◆ 1995
5. The Day I Met Him (Clark, Catherine) ◆ 1995
6. Love Changes Everything (Presser, Arlynn) ◆ 1995
7. More than a Friend (Winfrey, Elizabeth) ◆ 1995
8. The Language of Love (Emburg, Kate) ◆ 1996
9. My So-Called Boyfriend (Winfrey, Elizabeth) ◆ 1996
10. It Had to Be You (Doyon, Stephanie) ◆ 1996
11. Some Girls Do (Kosinski, Dahlia) ◆ 1996
12. Hot Summer Nights (Chandler, Elizabeth) ◆ 1996
13. Who Do You Love? (Quin-Harkin, Janet) ◆ 1996
14. Three-Guy Weekend (Page, Alexis) ◆ 1996
15. Never Tell Ben (Namm, Diane) ◆ 1997
16. Together Forever (Dokey, Cameron) ◆ 1997
17. Up All Night (Michaels, Karen) ◆ 1997
18. 24/7 (Wilensky, Amy) ◆ 1997
19. It's a Prom Thing (Schwemm, Diane) ◆ 1997
20. The Guy I Left Behind (Brooke, Ali) ◆ 1997
21. He's Not What You Think (Reisfeld, Randi) ◆ 1997
22. A Kiss Between Friends (Haft, Erin) ◆ 1997
23. The Rumor About Julia (Sinclair, Stephanie) ◆ 1997
24. Don't Say Good-Bye (Schwemm, Diane) ◆ 1997
25. Crushing on You (Loggia, Wendy) ◆ 1998
26. Our Secret Love (Harry, Miranda) ◆ 1998
27. Trust Me (Scott, Kieran) ◆ 1998
28. He's the One (Alexander, Nina) ◆ 1998
29. Kiss and Tell (Scott, Kieran) ◆ 1998
30. Falling for Ryan (Taylor, Julie) ◆ 1998
31. Hard to Resist (Loggia, Wendy) ◆ 1998
32. At First Sight (Chandler, Elizabeth) ◆ 1998
33. What We Did Last Summer (Craft, Elizabeth) ◆ 1998
34. As I Am (Mason, Lynn) ◆ 1999
35. I Do (Chandler, Elizabeth) ◆ 1999
36. While You Were Gone (Scott, Kieran) ◆ 1999
37. Stolen Kisses (Abrams, Liesa) ◆ 1999
38. Torn Apart (Quin-Harkin, Janet) ◆ 1999
39. Behind His Back (Schwemm, Diane) ◆ 1999
40. Playing for Keeps (Alexander, Nina) ◆ 1999
41. How Do I Tell? (Scott, Kieran) ◆ 1999
42. His Other Girlfriend (Abrams, Liesa) ◆ 1999

LOVE STORIES: BROTHERS TRILOGY

Zimmerman, Zoe
BANTAM
GRADES 7–10
REAL LIFE

Three summer stories featuring three teen boys. In one book, Kevin's summer job is at the Surf City Beach Resort. It's fun, and made even more interesting by the boss's beautiful daughter.

1. Danny ◆ 2000
2. Kevin ◆ 2000
3. Johnny ◆ 2000

LOVE STORIES: HIS. HERS. THEIRS

Various authors
BANTAM
GRADES 7–10
REAL LIFE

Teen girls describe their romances in these first-person accounts. One girl gets a date with a senior. Another, Edie, turns down a date with a cool, popular guy. Another series for romance fans.

1. The Nine-Hour Date (Henry, Emma) ◆ 2001
2. Snag Him! (Greene, Gretchen) ◆ 2001
3. Nick and the Nerd (Hawthorne, Rachel) ◆ 2001
4. You're Dating Him? (Gersh, A.) ◆ 2001
5. The Popular One (Skurnick, Lizzie) ◆ 2001
6. The Older Guy (Hawthorne, Rachel) ◆ 2001

LOVE STORIES: PROM TRILOGY

Craft, Elizabeth
BANTAM
GRADES 7–10
REAL LIFE

The Prom! Just thinking about it sends thrills through Jane. Will she get the attention of that special boy in time for him to invite her?

These books are sure to appeal to teenage girls. The featured couples include an African American pair, Justin and Nicole.

1. Max and Jane ◆ 2000
2. Justin and Nicole ◆ 2000
3. Jake and Christy ◆ 2000

LOVE STORIES: SUPER EDITIONS

Various authors

BANTAM

GRADES 7–10

REAL LIFE

More romance and heartache are featured in these books. Jeremy falls in love with Liv. That should be great, right? Wrong! Liv is Patrick's girlfriend and Patrick is Jeremy's best friend. In another book, Noah and Meg have been friends forever. Then Noah starts to feel more than friendship for Meg.

1. Listen to My Heart (Applegate, K. A.) ◆ 1996
2. Kissing Caroline (Zach, Cheryl) ◆ 1996
3. It's Different for Guys (Leighton, Stephanie) ◆ 1997
4. My Best Friend's Girlfriend (Loggia, Wendy) ◆ 1997
5. Love Happens (Chandler, Elizabeth) ◆ 1998
6. Out of My League (Owens, Everett) ◆ 1998
7. A Song for Caitlin (Bright, J. E.) ◆ 1998
8. The "L" Word (Mason, Lynn) ◆ 1998
9. Summer Love (Loggia, Wendy) ◆ 1999
10. All That (Mason, Lynn) ◆ 1999
11. The Dance (Hillman, Craig, Kieran Scott, and Elizabeth Skurnick) ◆ 1999
12. Andy and Andie (Vallik, Malle) ◆ 2000
13. Sweet Sixteen (Raine, Allison) ◆ 2000
14. Three Princes (Mason, Lynn) ◆ 2000

LOVE STORIES: YEAR ABROAD

Hawthorne, Rachel

BANTAM

GRADES 7–10

REAL LIFE

Dana is spending her junior year in Paris and she only wants one thing—a French boyfriend. Why does she keep coming across Alex Turner, a boy from her hometown? Readers will enjoy the romantic settings for these love stories.

1. London: Kit and Robin ◆ 2000
2. Paris: Alex and Dana ◆ 2000
3. Rome: Antonio and Carrie ◆ 2000

LOVE TRILOGY

Cann, Kate
HARPERCOLLINS
GRADES 10–12
REAL LIFE

Colette, 16, and Art meet and start dating in the first book. The series follows their up-and-down relationship, the pressure to become sexually active, and the toll this pressure takes on their initial friendship.

1. Ready? ◆ 2001
2. Sex? ◆ 2001
3. Go! ◆ 2001

LUDELL

Wilkinson, Brenda
HARPERCOLLINS
GRADES 5–8
FAMILY LIFE | HISTORICAL

Ludell Wilson is an African American girl growing up in the rural town of Waycross, Georgia, in the mid-1950s. She is being raised by her loving, protective, but strict grandmother because her mother is living in New York City. *Ludell* depicts three years in a segregated southern school, Ludell's friends and family, and the people who affect her life. In *Ludell and Willie*, Ludell and her boyfriend are seniors in high school, frustrated by the standards of their small town. In *Ludell's New York Time*, Ludell moves to Harlem to plan her wedding. A strong portrait of growing up in the South in the 1950s and 1960s.

1. Ludell ◆ 1975
2. Ludell and Willie ◆ 1977
3. Ludell's New York Time ◆ 1980

LUNA BAY

Various authors
HARPERCOLLINS
GRADES 6–9 ◆ A/R
REAL LIFE

Five friends in Southern California are working as counselors at a surfing camp. Each girl deals with issues in her life. Luna wants to do her best in a surfing competition but is distracted by her interest in a new boy. Rae is worried that her parents are separating and she will have to move. In *Hawaii Five-Go!*, the girls are in Hawaii on a fashion shoot and Kanani decides to explore her heritage.

1. Pier Pressure: A Roxy Girl Series (Lantz, Francess) ◆ 2003
2. Wave Good-Bye: A Roxy Girl Series (Lantz, Francess) ◆ 2003
3. Weather or Not: A Roxy Girl Series (Lantz, Francess) ◆ 2003
4. Oh, Buoy! A Roxy Girl Series (Lantz, Francess) ◆ 2003
5. Hawaii Five-Go! A Roxy Girl Series (Lantz, Francess) ◆ 2003
6. Heart Breakers: A Roxy Girl Series (Lantz, Francess) ◆ 2004
7. Board Games: A Roxy Girl Series (Dubowski, Cathy East) ◆ 2004
8. Sea for Yourself: A Roxy Girl Series (Lantz, Francess) ◆ 2004

THE LURKER FILES

Ciencin, Scott
RANDOM HOUSE
GRADES 6–10
FANTASY

The Lurker seems to control many students and teachers at Wintervale University. Using information from the university computer network, the Lurker manipulates people and situations.

1. Faceless ◆ 1996
2. Know Fear ◆ 1996
3. Nemesis ◆ 1997
4. Incarnate ◆ 1997

LYON SAGA

Stainer, M. L.

CHICKEN SOUP PRESS

GRADES 6–9 ◆ A/R

HISTORICAL

Jessabel, 14, describes her voyage from England to Roanoke Island. As a colony is established there, the settlers struggle to survive. Of course, the Roanoke Colony does not thrive and historians have speculated about what happened. In subsequent novels, readers follow Jess's fictional adventures as she lives with the Croatoan tribe, eventually marrying a Native American and returning to England. Along the way, they encounter pirates whose violent actions destroy two Native women.

1. The Lyon's Roar ◆ 1997
2. The Lyon's Cub ◆ 1998
3. The Lyon's Pride ◆ 1998
4. The Lyon's Throne ◆ 1999
5. The Lyon's Crown ◆ 2004

MACDONALD HALL *see* Bruno and Boots

MAGICIAN TRILOGY

McGowen, Tom

PENGUIN

GRADES 4–7

FANTASY | SCIENCE FICTION

Far in the future, civilization has been destroyed by war, and the people look back at our era as the Age of Magic and call our inventions "spells." People who seek wisdom are called Sages, and they attempt to make sense of the ruins and find out what ancient objects were used for. The head of these Sages, Armindor, takes as an apprentice a boy named Tigg, who had been a pickpocket. Together they travel to the Wild Lands and find a tape recorder with a tape that they believe will help them find the key to the ancient language. First, they must fight a terrible threat from intelligent ratlike creatures bent on taking over the human race. With Jilla, an orphan girl, and Reepah, a "grubber," they travel to the city of Ingarron and lead a successful attack.

1. The Magician's Apprentice ◆ 1987
2. The Magician's Company ◆ 1988
3. The Magician's Challenge ◆ 1989

MAGICIAN'S HOUSE QUARTET

Corlett, William
POCKET BOOKS
GRADES 6–9 ◆ A/R
FANTASY

William Constant, 13, and his younger sisters, Mary and Alice, are spending Christmas in Wales with their Uncle Jack. As they investigate Uncle Jack's home, they discover a secret room in the chimney. There they meet a magician who warns them of the tests they will soon face. In subsequent books, they return to Golden House for more magical adventures. This series was originally published in England in the early 1990s.

1. The Steps Up the Chimney ◆ 2000
2. The Door in the Tree ◆ 2000
3. The Tunnel Behind the Waterfall ◆ 2001
4. The Bridge in the Clouds ◆ 2001

THE MAGICKERS

Drake, Emily
DAW
GRADES 6–10
FANTASY

In the first book, 11-year-old Jason is invited to Camp Ravenwyng, where—to his surprise—he finds that he will be trained as a Magicker and will work against evil. In the second book, Jason realizes that the Dark Hand, whom he battled at the Camp, is present in his hometown.

1. The Magickers ◆ 2001

2. The Curse of Arkady ◆ 2002
3. Dragon Guard ◆ 2003

MAIZON

Woodson, Jacqueline
DELACORTE; PUTNAM
GRADES 6–8
FAMILY LIFE | REAL LIFE

Margaret and Maizon are best friends, but they are separated when Maizon goes to boarding school. At Blue Hill, Maizon adjusts to being one of only five African American students. She misses her grandmother and her friends. Returning home, she rebuilds her friendship with Margaret and makes some new friends. Maizon even meets her father, who left when she was a baby. This series follows a character from the end of her childhood into independence and young adulthood.

1. Last Summer with Maizon ◆ 1990
2. Maizon at Blue Hill ◆ 1992
3. Between Madison and Palmetto ◆ 1993

THE MAJIPOOR CYCLE

Silverberg, Robert
HARPERCOLLINS
GRADES 10–12
FANTASY | SCIENCE FICTION

This is a rich saga—combining elements of fantasy and science fiction—about events on the planet of Majipoor, which has many medieval aspects. Valentine is an itinerant juggler until he realizes that he is in fact heir to the kingdom. Other books follow various characters as they deal with intrigue and dark forces.

1. Lord Valentine's Castle ◆ 1980
2. The Majipoor Chronicles ◆ 1982
3. Valentine Pontifex ◆ 1983
4. The Mountains of Majipoor ◆ 1995
5. Sorcerers of Majipoor ◆ 1996
6. Lord Prestimion ◆ 1999
7. The King of Dreams ◆ 2001

MAKE LEMONADE TRILOGY

Wolff, Virginia Euwer
HENRY HOLT; ATHENEUM
GRADES 7–10 ♦ A/R
REAL LIFE

In *Make Lemonade*, LaVaughn, 14, describes the difficulties faced by Jolly, a 17-year-old dropout with two children from two different fathers. LaVaughn babysits for Jolly while Jolly looks for work. The free verse poetry of LaVaughn's observations is sparse and powerful. In *True Believer*, LaVaughn's poetic writing describes her own attraction to Jody and the impact it has on her efforts to get out of the projects. A third book is planned.

1. Make Lemonade ♦ 1993
2. True Believer ♦ 2001

MAKING OUT

Applegate, K. A.
AVON
GRADES 8–12
REAL LIFE

A group of teenagers—Zoey, Jake, Benjamin, Claire, Lucas, and Nina—grow up together on an island off the coast of Maine. They remain close while developing different relationships. In the first book, the status quo is rocked when Lucas returns to the island after two years in reform school. Originally published as the Boyfriends, Girlfriends series by HarperPaperbacks.

1. Zoey Fools Around ♦ 1998
2. Jake Finds Out ♦ 1998
3. Nina Won't Tell ♦ 1998
4. Ben's in Love ♦ 1998
5. Claire Gets Caught ♦ 1998
6. What Zoey Saw ♦ 1998
7. Lucas Gets Hurt ♦ 1998
8. Aisha Goes Wild ♦ 1999
9. Zoey Plays Games ♦ 1999
10. Nina Shapes Up ♦ 1999
11. Ben Takes a Chance ♦ 1999
12. Claire Can't Love ♦ 1999
13. Don't Tell Zoey ♦ 1999
14. Aaron Let's Go ♦ 1999
15. Who Loves Kate ♦ 1999

16. Lara Gets Even ◆ 1999
17. Two-Timing Aisha ◆ 1999
18. Zoey Speaks Out ◆ 1999
19. Kate Finds Love ◆ 1999
20. Never Trust Lara ◆ 2000
21. Trouble with Aaron ◆ 2000
22. Always Loving Zoey ◆ 2000
23. Lara Gets Lucky ◆ 2000
24. Now Zoey's Alone ◆ 2000
25. Don't Forget Lara ◆ 2000
26. Zoey's Broken Heart ◆ 2000
27. Falling for Claire ◆ 2000
28. Zoey Comes Home ◆ 2000

MAKING WAVES

Applegate, K. A.
17TH STREET PRESS
GRADES 9–12
REAL LIFE

When their ex-boyfriends show up, dynamics change at the beach house that high school graduates Kate and Chelsea are sharing. Previously published by HarperCollins under the series title Ocean City.

1. Making Waves ◆ 2001
2. Tease ◆ 2001
3. Sweet ◆ 2001
4. Thrill ◆ 2001
5. Heat ◆ 2001
6. Secret ◆ 2001
7. Attitude ◆ 2001
8. Burn ◆ 2001
9. Wild ◆ 2001
10. Chill ◆ 2001
11. Last Splash ◆ 2001

MALLOREON

Eddings, David
BALLANTINE
GRADES 10–12
FANTASY

Garion is now the King of Riva. The evil God Torak is dead. Garion must face demon worshippers and later, Zandramas, the Child of the

Dark. Earlier events are described in the Belgariad. There is a prequel to both series, *Belgarath the Sorcerer* (1995), and a final volume to both, *Polgara the Sorceress* (1997).

1. Guardians of the West ◆ 1987
2. King of the Murgos ◆ 1987
3. Demon Lord of Karanda ◆ 1988
4. Sorceress of Darshiva ◆ 1989
5. The Seeress of Kell ◆ 1991

MAN OF HIS WORD

Duncan, David

BALLANTINE DEL REY

GRADES 10–12

FANTASY

From the beginning, Inos, daughter of the King, and Rap, a stable boy, were friends. As they grow up, their paths diverge. Inos is destined to be married to nobility while Rap begins to realize his magical powers. Throughout this series, Rap is there for Inos, even after she marries the evil Sultan Azak.

1. Magic Casement ◆ 1990
2. Faery Lands Forlorn ◆ 1991
3. Perilous Seas ◆ 1991
4. Emperor and Clown ◆ 1997

MARS YEAR ONE

Strickland, Brad, and Thomas E. Fuller

SIMON & SCHUSTER

GRADES 5–8 ◆ A/R

SCIENCE FICTION

It is 2085. Sean is leaving the turmoil on Earth to travel to Mars. There are only 20 teenagers in the colony and Sean must try to fit in and find a way to contribute.

1. Marooned! ◆ 2004
2. Missing! ◆ 2004
3. Marsquake! ◆ 2005

MARY-KATE AND ASHLEY: ADVENTURES OF MARY-KATE AND ASHLEY

Various authors

SCHOLASTIC

GRADES 4–7

FAMILY LIFE | MYSTERY | REAL LIFE

The Olsen twins, Mary-Kate and Ashley, have achieved great popularity on television, video, and in movies. This series capitalizes on the popularity of these appealing twins.

1. The Case of the Christmas Caper (Waricha, Jean) ◆ 1996
2. The Case of the Mystery Cruise (Thompson, Carol) ◆ 1996
3. The Case of the Fun House Mystery (Scholastic staff) ◆ 1996
4. The Case of the U.S. Space Camp Mission (Scholastic staff, and Bonnie Bader) ◆ 1996
5. The Case of the Sea World Adventure (Dubowski, Cathy East) ◆ 1996
6. The Case of the Shark Encounter (Krulik, Nancy E.) ◆ 1997
7. The Case of the Hotel Who-Done-It (O'Neil, Laura) ◆ 1997
8. The Case of the Volcano Mystery (Thompson, Carol) ◆ 1997
9. The Case of the U.S. Navy Adventure (Perlberg, Deborah) ◆ 1997
10. The Case of Thorn Mansion (Alexander, Nina) ◆ 1997

THE NEW ADVENTURES OF MARY-KATE AND ASHLEY

1. The Case of the 202 Clues (Alexander, Nina) ◆ 1998
2. The Case of the Ballet Bandit (O'Neil, Laura) ◆ 1998
3. The Case of the Blue-Ribbon Horse (Swobud, I. K) ◆ 1998
4. The Case of the Haunted Camp (Alexander, Nina) ◆ 1998
5. The Case of the Wild Wolf River (Katschke, Judy) ◆ 1998
6. The Case of the Rock and Roll Mystery (Eisenberg, Lisa) ◆ 1998
7. The Case of the Missing Mummy (Lantz, Francess Lin) ◆ 1999
8. The Case of the Surprise Call (Metz, Melinda) ◆ 1999
9. The Case of the Disappearing Princess (Eisenberg, Lisa) ◆ 1999
10. The Case of the Great Elephant Escape (Doolittle, June) ◆ 1999
11. The Case of the Summer Camp Caper (Katschke, Judy) ◆ 1999
12. The Case of the Surfing Secret (Dubowski, Cathy East) ◆ 1999
13. The Case of the Green Ghost (Ellis, Carol) ◆ 1999
14. The Case of the Big Scare Mountain Mystery (Ellis, Carol) ◆ 1999
15. The Case of the Slam Dunk Mystery (Dubowski, Cathy East) ◆ 2000
16. The Case of the Rock Star's Secret (Metz, Melinda) ◆ 2000
17. The Case of the Cheerleading Camp Mystery (Fiedler, Lisa) ◆ 2000
18. The Case of the Flying Phantom (Metz, Melinda) ◆ 2000

19. The Case of the Creepy Castle (Katschke, Judy) ◆ 2000
20. The Case of the Golden Slipper (Metz, Melinda) ◆ 2000
21. The Case of the Flapper 'Napper (Katschke, Judy) ◆ 2001
22. The Case of the High Seas Secret (Leonhardt, Alice) ◆ 2001
23. The Case of the Logical I Ranch (Preiss, Pauline) ◆ 2001
24. The Case of the Dog Camp Mystery (Katschke, Judy) ◆ 2001
25. The Case of the Screaming Scarecrow (Katschke, Judy) ◆ 2001
26. The Case of the Jingle Bell Jinx (Leonhardt, Alice) ◆ 2001
27. The Case of the Game Show Mystery (Thomas, Jim) ◆ 2002
28. The Case of the Mall Mystery (Leonhardt, Alice) ◆ 2002
29. The Case of the Weird Science Mystery (Katschke, Judy) ◆ 2002
30. The Case of Camp Crooked Lake (Ellis, Carol) ◆ 2002
31. The Case of the Giggling Ghost (Metz, Melinda) ◆ 2002
32. The Case of the Candy Cane Clue (Katschke, Judy) ◆ 2002
33. The Case of the Hollywood Who-Done-It (Metz, Melinda) ◆ 2003
34. The Case of the Sundae Surprise (Metz, Melinda) ◆ 2003
35. The Case of Clue's Circus Caper (Katschke, Judy) ◆ 2003
36. The Case of Camp Pom-Pom (Alexander, Heather) ◆ 2003
37. The Case of the Tattooed Cat (Alexander, Heather) ◆ 2003
38. The Case of the Nutcracker Ballet (Stine, Megan) ◆ 2003
39. The Case of the Clue at the Zoo (Katschke, Judy) ◆ 2004
40. The Case of the Easter Egg Race (Alexander, Heather) ◆ 2004
41. The Case of the Dog Show Mystery (not available) ◆ 2004
42. The Case of the Cheerleading Tattletale (not available) ◆ 2004
43. The Case of the Haunted Maze (not available) ◆ 2004
44. The Case of the Hidden Holiday Riddle (not available) ◆ 2004
45. The Case of the Icy Igloo Inn (not available) ◆ 2005
46. The Case of the Unicorn Mystery (not available) ◆ 2005

MARY-KATE AND ASHLEY: SO LITTLE TIME

Olsen, Mary-Kate, and Ashley Olsen

HARPERCOLLINS

GRADES 4–7 ◆ A/R

FAMILY LIFE | REAL LIFE

Based on the television series *So Little Time*, in which Mary-Kate and Ashley Olsen play Chloe and Riley Carlson. The girls enjoy being in high school, paying some attention to books and studying but spending most of their time spent on boys and dating.

1. How to Train a Boy ◆ 2002
2. Instant Boyfriend ◆ 2002
3. Too Good to Be True ◆ 2002
4. Just Between Us ◆ 2002
5. Tell Me About It ◆ 2002
6. Secret Crush ◆ 2002

7. Girl Talk ◆ 2002
8. The Love Factor ◆ 2003
9. Dating Game ◆ 2003
10. A Girl's Guide to Guys ◆ 2003
11. Boy Crazy ◆ 2003
12. Best Friends Forever ◆ 2003
13. Love Is in the Air ◆ 2003
14. Spring Breakup ◆ 2004
15. Get Real ◆ 2004
16. Surf Holiday ◆ 2004
17. The Makeover Experiment ◆ 2005

MARY-KATE AND ASHLEY: TWO OF A KIND

Various authors
HARPERCOLLINS
GRADES 4–7 ◆ A/R
FAMILY LIFE | REAL LIFE

In this series, Mary-Kate and Ashley are older and they love shopping and hanging out with their friends. They also have hopes about boys and dating. 'Tween girls will enjoy these books.

1. It's a Twin Thing (Katschke, Judy) ◆ 1999
2. How to Flunk Your First Date (Stine, Megan) ◆ 1999
3. The Sleepover Secret (Katschke, Judy) ◆ 1999
4. One Twin Too Many (Stine, Megan) ◆ 1999
5. To Snoop or Not to Snoop (Katschke, Judy) ◆ 1999
6. My Sister the Supermodel (Stine, Megan) ◆ 1999
7. Two's a Crowd (Katschke, Judy) ◆ 1999
8. Let's Party (Katschke, Judy) ◆ 1999
9. Calling All Boys (Katschke, Judy) ◆ 2000
10. Winner Take All (Banim, Lisa) ◆ 2000
11. P. S. Wish You Were Here (Stine, Megan) ◆ 2000
12. The Cool Club (Katschke, Judy) ◆ 2000
13. War of the Wardrobes (Stine, Megan) ◆ 2000
14. Bye-Bye-Boy Friend (Katschke, Judy) ◆ 2000
15. It's Snow Problem (Butcher, Nancy) ◆ 2001
16. Likes Me, Likes Me Not (Stine, Megan) ◆ 2001
17. Shore Thing (Katschke, Judy) ◆ 2001
18. Two for the Road (Butcher, Nancy) ◆ 2001
19. Surprise, Surprise! (Stine, Megan) ◆ 2001
20. Sealed with a Kiss (Katschke, Judy) ◆ 2001
21. Now You See Him, Now You Don't (Stine, Megan) ◆ 2002
22. April Fools' Rules (Katschke, Judy) ◆ 2002
23. Island Girls (Butcher, Nancy) ◆ 2002
24. Surf, Sand, and Secrets (Butcher, Nancy) ◆ 2002

25. Closer than Ever (Katschke, Judy) ◆ 2002
26. The Perfect Gift (Stine, Megan) ◆ 2002
27. The Facts About Flirting (Katschke, Judy) ◆ 2003
28. The Dream Date Debate (Stine, Megan) ◆ 2003
29. Love-Set-Match (Dubowski, Cathy East) ◆ 2003
30. Making a Splash (Stine, Megan) ◆ 2003
31. Dare to Scare (Katschke, Judy) ◆ 2003
32. Santa Girls (Gallagher, Diana G.) ◆ 2003
33. Heart to Heart (not available) ◆ 2004
34. Prom Princess (not available) ◆ 2004
35. Camp Rock 'n Roll (not available) ◆ 2004
36. Twist and Shout (not available) ◆ 2004
37. Hocus-Pocus (not available) ◆ 2004

MARY-KATE AND ASHLEY IN ACTION

Olsen, Mary-Kate, and Ashley Olsen
HARPERCOLLINS
GRADES 4–7 ◆ A/R
FAMILY LIFE | MYSTERY | REAL LIFE

There are mysteries to be solved. Mary-Kate and Ashley go undercover as secret agents Misty and Amber. They are on the spot when strange things happen and they investigate such mysteries as why a restaurant is too popular and why all the radio stations are playing the same song. There are lots of cartoon-style illustrations in these books, which add to the appeal.

1. Makeup Shake-Up ◆ 2002
2. The Dream Team ◆ 2002
3. Fubble Bubble Trouble ◆ 2002
4. Operation Evaporation ◆ 2003
5. Dog Gone Mess ◆ 2003
6. The Music Meltdown ◆ 2003
7. Password: Red Hot ◆ 2003
8. Fast Food Fight ◆ 2003

MARY-KATE AND ASHLEY STARRING IN . . .

Various authors
HARPERCOLLINS
GRADES 4–7 ◆ A/R
FAMILY LIFE | REAL LIFE

These books feature the Olsen twins in stories from their video series. In one book, the girls play twins who switch places. Emma is popular but her father gives more attention to her sister, Sam. Sam is athletic but wants to attract a cute guy. Emma and Sam switch and develop an understanding for each other. In another book, the Olsens play twins whose family has moved to Australia to escape the wrath of a jewel thief they helped to catch. Of course, the thief ends up in Australia, too.

1. Switching Goals (Fiedler, Lisa) ◆ 2000
2. Our Lips Are Sealed (Willard, Eliza) ◆ 2001
3. Winning London (Kruger, Elizabeth) ◆ 2001
4. School Dance Party (Willard, Eliza) ◆ 2001
5. Holiday in the Sun (Willard, Eliza) ◆ 2001
6. When in Rome (Stine, Megan) ◆ 2002
7. The Challenge (not available) ◆ 2003

MARY-KATE AND ASHLEY SWEET 16

Olsen, Mary-Kate, and Ashley Olsen

HARPERCOLLINS

GRADES 4–7 ◆ A/R

FAMILY LIFE | REAL LIFE

The Olsen twins turn 16! They can drive, go to parties, visit the mall, and enjoy their friends—including boyfriends.

1. Never Been Kissed ◆ 2002
2. Wishes and Dreams ◆ 2002
3. The Perfect Summer ◆ 2002
4. Getting There ◆ 2002
5. Starring You and Me ◆ 2002
6. My Best Friend's Boyfriend ◆ 2002
7. Playing Games ◆ 2003
8. Cross Our Hearts ◆ 2003
9. All that Glitters ◆ 2003
10. Keeping Secrets ◆ 2003
11. Little White Lies ◆ 2003
12. Dream Holiday ◆ 2003
13. Love and Kisses ◆ 2004
14. Spring into Style ◆ 2004
15. California Dreams ◆ 2004
16. Truth or Dare ◆ 2004
17. Forget Me Not ◆ 2005
18. I Want My Sister Back ◆ 2005

MATES, DATES, AND . . .

Hopkins, Cathy
SIMON & SCHUSTER
GRADES 6–9 ◆ A/R
REAL LIFE

Three friends, all 14, live in London and describe their adolescent concerns. Lucy worries about her self-image. Izzie realizes that a relationship is not right for her. Nesta learns that telling the truth is better than living a lie. This series was originally published in England with different titles.

    1. Mates, Dates, and Inflatable Bras ◆ 2003
    2. Mates, Dates, and Cosmic Kisses ◆ 2003
    3. Mates, Dates, and Designer Divas ◆ 2003
    4. Mates, Dates, and Sleepover Secrets ◆ 2003
    5. Mates, Dates, and Sole Survivors ◆ 2003
    6. Mates, Dates, and Mad Mistakes ◆ 2004
    7. Mates, Dates, and Sequin Smiles ◆ 2004
    8. Mates, Dates, and Tempting Trouble ◆ 2005

MED CENTER

Hoh, Diane
SCHOLASTIC
GRADES 6–8
REAL LIFE

Abby and Susannah are best friends who love their work as volunteers at the large Medical Center in Grant, Massachusetts. The two girls come from very different backgrounds. Susannah is the descendent of the town's founders and lives in the most lavish house in town. Abby comes from a more middle-class family. Each book deals with a disaster that strikes the small town and the reactions of the girls, their families, and friends.

    1. Virus ◆ 1996
    2. Flood ◆ 1996
    3. Fire ◆ 1996
    4. Blast ◆ 1996
    5. Blizzard ◆ 1997
    6. Poison ◆ 1997

THE MEDIATOR

Cabot, Meg
AVON; HARPERCOLLINS
GRADES 7–10 ◆ A/R
FANTASY

Susannah Simon, 16, is eager to get settled in California with her mom, stepdad, and stepbrothers. Before she can feel at ease, she must deal with the ghost in her bedroom. Later, there is the ghost of a dead woman who gives Suze a message about her murder. Like Buffy the Vampire Slayer, Susannah deals with her supernatural powers. She also has a normal life as a sophomore and attractive boys are included in each book.

1. Shadowland ◆ 2001
2. Ninth Key ◆ 2001
3. Reunion ◆ 2001
4. Darkest Hour ◆ 2001
5. Haunted ◆ 2003
6. Twilight ◆ 2005

MEG MURRY *see* Time Fantasy Series

MENNYMS

Waugh, Sylvia
GREENWILLOW
GRADES 5–8 ◆ A/R
FAMILY LIFE | FANTASY

This is a fantasy quintet set in England that older readers will enjoy. The Mennyms are a family of rag dolls that are able to pass quietly for human—that is to say, until various adventures happen to them. First there is the Australian owner of the house who comes to pay a visit. Then they discover that they are in the care of an antiques dealer, who, it seems, will shortly discover their secret. Readers will want to read all five books in the series.

1. The Mennyms ◆ 1994
2. Mennyms in the Wilderness ◆ 1995
3. Mennyms Under Siege ◆ 1996
4. Mennyms Alone ◆ 1996
5. Mennyms Alive ◆ 1997

MERLIN *see* Lost Years of Merlin

MERLIN CODEX

Holdstock, Robert

TOR

GRADES 9–12

FANTASY

The legend of Merlin is merged with elements of Greek mythology in this fascinating series. In *Celtika*, Merlin is a young man wandering the earth seeking enlightenment. He encounters Jason and joins him in the search for the Golden Fleece. When Medea kills Jason's sons, Jason sails away, consumed by his loss. Hundreds of years later, Merlin hears Jason's cries and uses magic to help reunite him with his sons.

1. Celtika ◆ 2003
2. The Iron Grail ◆ 2004

MIKE PILLSBURY

Mackel, Kathy

HARPERCOLLINS

GRADES 6–9

FANTASY

Mike is a geeky outsider who enjoys making up stories about encounters with aliens. As a joke, he sends a message into space asking for help and strange creatures come to rescue him. By the time they arrive, Mike does not want to be rescued. In the second book, Mike helps a friend, Scott, who has become involved in an intergalactic battle. The third book features Nick, Mike's sister Jill, and a time warp.

1. Can of Worms ◆ 1999
2. Eggs in One Basket ◆ 2000
3. From the Horse's Mouth ◆ 2002

THE MINDS SERIES

Matas, Carol, and Perry Nodelman

SIMON & SCHUSTER

GRADES 6–9

FANTASY

Princess Lenora and Prince Coren, who both have unusual powers, initially resist plans for their marriage. As the series progresses, they become engaged and together fight evil in a variety of situations including a mall in Winnipeg. These are entertaining and lively stories.

1. Of Two Minds ◆ 1998
2. More Minds ◆ 1998
3. Out of Their Minds ◆ 1998
4. A Meeting of Minds ◆ 1999

MINDWARP

Archer, Chris
MINSTREL/POCKET BOOKS
GRADES 6–8 ◆ A/R
ADVENTURE | FANTASY | HORROR

A group of friends at Metier (Wisconsin) Junior High School seem to be the only ones who are aware that there are aliens among us. Ethan Rogers is a kind of a geek until an alien force invades him. Ethan knows that something is wrong but he can't seem to convince anyone else in town, including his father, the police chief. Can Ethan save the town from the *Alien Terror*? Ashley Rose is the next victim. The aliens take over her body, giving her special powers. In another adventure, Ashley and her friends try to escape the aliens in a UFO only to enter a future world that is worse than their own. This series will interest readers of Goosebumps and Ghosts of Fear Street.

1. Alien Terror ◆ 1997
2. Alien Blood ◆ 1997
3. Alien Scream ◆ 1997
4. Second Sight ◆ 1998
5. Shape-Shifter ◆ 1998
6. Aftershock ◆ 1998
7. Flash Forward ◆ 1998
8. Face the Fear ◆ 1998
9. Out of Time ◆ 1998
10. Meltdown ◆ 1999

MIRROR IMAGE

Bennett, Cherie, and Jeff Gottesfeld
SIMON & SCHUSTER
GRADES 7–10
FANTASY

In the first book, a mysterious rock gives Callie Bailey her every wish and she goes from being a geek to being popular. Along the way, though, she alienates her friends and hurts her sister, Laurel. Subsequent books show the impact of the magic rock on other teen girls.

1. Stranger in the Mirror ◆ 1999
2. Rich Girl in the Mirror ◆ 2000
3. Star in the Mirror ◆ 2000
4. Flirt in the Mirror ◆ 2000

MISERY GUTS

Gleitzman, Morris
HARCOURT
GRADES 6–8
FAMILY LIFE | REAL LIFE

Keith worries that his parents aren't happy running a fish-and-chips shop in dreary London, so he invents all kinds of schemes to cheer them up. After convincing them to move to sunnier Australia, Keith plans to seek a fortune for his family in the opal mines. When his parents separate, Keith suggests ways for each of them to become better-looking to attract new mates. Throughout the series, Keith's humorous adventures border on the absurd.

1. Misery Guts ◆ 1991
2. Worry Warts ◆ 1991
3. Puppy Fat ◆ 1994

MISFITS, INC.

Delaney, Mark
PEACHTREE
GRADES 5–9 ◆ A/R
MYSTERY

Four high school students who are outsiders band together to solve mysteries. Jake, Peter, Byte, and Mattie have individual skills that help with each mystery. In the first book, they clear a security guard and find the real thief of a powerful computer chip.

1. The Vanishing Chip ◆ 1998
2. Of Heroes and Villains ◆ 1999
3. Growler's Horn ◆ 2000
4. The Kingfisher's Tale ◆ 2000

5. The Protester's Song ◆ 2001
6. Hit and Run ◆ 2002

MISSING PERSONS

Rabb, M. E.
SPEAK; PUFFIN
GRADES 7–10 ◆ A/R
MYSTERY

Sophie and Sam Shattenberg are Jewish sisters from Queens, New York. Circumstances cause them to leave their home and go into hiding. They end up in Venice, Indiana, where Sophie goes to high school and Sam assists a private investigator. Their specialty is missing persons. In *The Chocolate Lover*, they help Professor Shattenberg (who may be their grandfather's missing cousin) find his missing sweetheart. These books are fast and fun and should attract reluctant readers.

1. The Rose Queen ◆ 2004
2. The Chocolate Lover ◆ 2004
3. The Venetian Policeman ◆ 2004
4. The Unsuspecting Gourmet ◆ 2004

MOESHA

Various authors
ARCHWAY
GRADES 6–8
REAL LIFE

Based on the television series starring teen star Brandy, these books feature Moesha Mitchell, a 15-year-old African American girl who experiences typical teen dilemmas. Her family consists of a younger brother, father, and a new stepmother (her mother died several years ago), and there are realistic moments involving family adjustments and concerns. Moesha's friends often come to her aid with guidance and support, but they also get involved in minor scrapes and misunderstandings. With plots that are current, upbeat language, and a positive family model, this series provides solid reading that will be of special interest to girls.

1. Everybody Say Moesha! (Scott, Stefanie) ◆ 1997
2. Keeping It Real (Scott, Stefanie) ◆ 1997
3. Trippin' Out (Scott, Stefanie) ◆ 1997
4. Hollywood Hook-Up (Scott, Stefanie) ◆ 1998

5. What's Up, Brother? (Reed, Teresa) ◆ 1998
6. House Party! (Scott, Stefanie) ◆ 1998

MOONDOG

Garfield, Henry
ST. MARTIN'S
GRADES 10–12
HORROR

Three women . . . three dead bodies. The gruesome discoveries bring fear to the isolated town of Julian, California. Cyrus "Moondog" Nygerski thinks the murders may be connected. Each occurred during a full moon. Moondog believes there are supernatural elements at work, and he should know because he is a werewolf. The third book takes place in Boston during the 1967 pennant race by the Red Sox, which may attract sports fans to this series.

1. Moondog ◆ 1995
2. Room 13 ◆ 1997
3. Tartabull's Throw ◆ 2001

MRS. MURPHY

Brown, Rita Mae
BANTAM
GRADES 10–12
MYSTERY

Mary Minor ("Harry") Haristeen is postmaster in a small southern town in these books coauthored by Brown and her cat, Sneaky Pie. With her sidekicks—Mrs. Murphy the cat and Welsh corgi Tee Tucker, both of whom converse and comment on human behavior in italics—Harry investigates and solves many mysteries. These range from dead bodies to computer viruses.

1. Wish You Were Here ◆ 1990
2. Rest in Pieces ◆ 1992
3. Murder at Monticello ◆ 1994
4. Pay Dirt ◆ 1995
5. Murder, She Meowed ◆ 1996
6. Murder on the Prowl ◆ 1998
7. Cat on the Scent ◆ 1999

8. Pawing Through the Past ◆ 2000
9. Claws and Effect ◆ 2001
10. Catch as Cat Can ◆ 2002
11. Tail of the Tip-off ◆ 2003
12. Whisker of Evil ◆ 2004

MUMMY CHRONICLES

Wolverton, Dave
SKYLARK
GRADES 4–7 ◆ A/R
FANTASY

Alex O'Connell, 12, wants to be a Medjai—one who works against the forces of darkness. It is 1937 and Alex is in Egypt. He discovers that his amulet gives him special powers. Alex battles mummies and faces a special test. In the spirit of Young Indiana Jones, Alex rescues the world from evil powers.

1. Revenge of the Scorpion King ◆ 2001
2. Heart of the Pharaoh ◆ 2001
3. The Curse of the Nile ◆ 2001
4. Flight of the Phoenix ◆ 2001

MY SIDE OF THE MOUNTAIN

George, Jean Craighead
DUTTON
GRADES 4–8
REAL LIFE

Sam Gribley leaves his home in the city to spend a year in the Catskill Mountains. He survives and develops a relationship with a falcon he names Frightful. The third book is presented from Frightful's point of view. The fourth book is a picture book that focuses on Oksi, Frightful's daughter, as she grows from a hatchling to a young falcon. *My Side of the Mountain* was a Newbery Honor book.

1. My Side of the Mountain ◆ 1959
2. On the Far Side of the Mountain ◆ 1990
3. Frightful's Mountain ◆ 1999
4. Frightful's Daughter ◆ 2002

MYSTIC KNIGHTS OF TIR NA NOG

Various authors
HARPERCOLLINS
GRADES 5–8
FANTASY

Ivan, Rohan, Deirdre, and Angus confront many dangers, including dragons and other creatures. They battle the forces of the evil queen Maeve and hope to earn their armor. The stories include references to Celtic heroes and legends. A television program featured these characters.

1. The Legend of the Ancient Scroll (Teitelbaum, Michael) ◆ 1999
2. Fire Within, Air Above! (Simpson, Robert) ◆ 1999
3. Water Around, Earth Below! (Brightfield, Richard) ◆ 1999
4. The Taming of the Pyre (Whitman, John) ◆ 1999
5. Dragata Revealed! (Teitelbaum, Michael) ◆ 1999

MYTH ADVENTURES

Asprin, Robert
ACE
GRADES 5–8
FANTASY

Skeeve, a magician's apprentice, begins a series of adventures. He jumps to different dimensions and confronts characters such as the evil wizard Isstvan. Skeeve and his companions, Aahz and Tanada, have humorous, fast-paced encounters with many strange creatures. There have been a variety of editions and reissues of this series.

1. Another Fine Myth ◆ 1985
2. Myth Conceptions ◆ 1985
3. Myth Directions ◆ 1985
4. Hit or Myth ◆ 1985
5. Myth-ing Persons ◆ 1986
6. Little Myth Marker ◆ 1986
7. M.Y.T.H. Inc. Link ◆ 1986
8. Myth-Nomers and Im-Pervections ◆ 1990
9. M.Y.T.H. Inc. in Action ◆ 1990
10. Sweet Myth-tery of Life ◆ 2000
11. Something M.Y.T.H. Inc. ◆ 2002
12. Myth-ion Improbable ◆ 2002
13. Myth-told Tales ◆ 2003

14. Myth Alliances ◆ 2003
15. Myth-taken Identity ◆ 2004

NADIA SANTOS *see* Alexander Cold and Nadia Santos

NANCY DREW

Keene, Carolyn
SIMON & SCHUSTER
GRADES 4–7 ◆ A/R
MYSTERY

Nancy Drew is a teenage detective who solves crimes while her friends George and Bess tag along. In one book, Bess is working for a wedding consultant based in an old mansion on the outskirts of River Heights. During a busy week in June, she asks George and Nancy to help out. As the first wedding begins, it seems that someone is trying to sabotage it. Nancy suspects a cousin of the bride; but when a second wedding is sabotaged, suspicion shifts to the sister of the wedding manager. The history of the old house eventually helps to solve the mystery. Throughout the series, Nancy is thorough, methodical, and undistracted. Bess and George provide contrast, Bess being a food-loving flirt and George serious and athletic.

1. The Secret of the Old Clock ◆ 1930
2. The Hidden Staircase ◆ 1930
3. The Bungalow Mystery ◆ 1930
4. The Mystery at Lilac Inn ◆ 1930
5. The Secret of Shadow Ranch ◆ 1930
6. The Secret of Red Gate Farm ◆ 1931
7. The Clue in the Diary ◆ 1932
8. Nancy's Mysterious Letter ◆ 1932
9. The Sign of the Twisted Candles ◆ 1933
10. The Password to Larkspur Lane ◆ 1933
11. The Clue of the Broken Locket ◆ 1934
12. The Message in the Hollow Oak ◆ 1935
13. The Mystery of the Ivory Charm ◆ 1936
14. The Whispering Statue ◆ 1937
15. The Haunted Bridge ◆ 1937
16. The Clue of the Tapping Heels ◆ 1939
17. The Mystery of the Brass-Bound Trunk ◆ 1940
18. The Mystery of the Moss-Covered Mansion ◆ 1941
19. The Quest of the Missing Map ◆ 1942
20. The Clue in the Jewel Box ◆ 1943

21. The Secret in the Old Attic ◆ 1944
22. The Clue in the Crumbling Wall ◆ 1945
23. The Mystery of the Tolling Bell ◆ 1946
24. The Clue in the Old Album ◆ 1947
25. The Ghost of Blackwood Hall ◆ 1948
26. The Clue of the Leaning Chimney ◆ 1949
27. The Secret of the Wooden Lady ◆ 1950
28. The Clue of the Black Keys ◆ 1951
29. The Mystery at the Ski Jump ◆ 1952
30. The Clue of the Velvet Mask ◆ 1953
31. The Ringmaster's Secret ◆ 1953
32. The Scarlet Slipper Mystery ◆ 1954
33. The Witch Tree Symbol ◆ 1955
34. The Hidden Window Mystery ◆ 1957
35. The Haunted Showboat ◆ 1957
36. The Secret of the Golden Pavilion ◆ 1959
37. The Clue in the Old Stagecoach ◆ 1960
38. The Mystery of the Fire Dragon ◆ 1961
39. The Clue of the Dancing Puppet ◆ 1962
40. The Moonstone Castle Mystery ◆ 1963
41. The Clue of the Whistling Bagpipes ◆ 1964
42. The Phantom of Pine Hill ◆ 1965
43. The Mystery of the 99 Steps ◆ 1966
44. The Clue in the Crossword Cypher ◆ 1967
45. The Spider Sapphire Mystery ◆ 1968
46. The Invisible Intruder ◆ 1969
47. The Mysterious Mannequin ◆ 1970
48. The Crooked Bannister ◆ 1971
49. The Secret of Mirror Bay ◆ 1972
50. The Double Jinx Mystery ◆ 1974
51. The Mystery of the Glowing Eye ◆ 1974
52. The Secret of the Forgotten City ◆ 1975
53. The Sky Phantom ◆ 1976
54. Strange Message in the Parchment ◆ 1977
55. Mystery of Crocodile Island ◆ 1978
56. The Thirteenth Pearl ◆ 1979
57. Triple Hoax ◆ 1979
58. The Flying Saucer Mystery ◆ 1980
59. The Secret in the Old Lace ◆ 1980
60. The Greek Symbol Mystery ◆ 1981
61. The Swami's Ring ◆ 1981
62. The Kachina Doll Mystery ◆ 1981
63. The Twin Dilemma ◆ 1981
64. Captive Witness ◆ 1981
65. Mystery of the Winged Lion ◆ 1982
66. Race Against Time ◆ 1982
67. The Sinister Omen ◆ 1982
68. The Elusive Heiress ◆ 1982
69. Clue in the Ancient Disguise ◆ 1982

70. The Broken Anchor ◆ 1983
71. The Silver Cobweb ◆ 1983
72. The Haunted Carousel ◆ 1983
73. Enemy Match ◆ 1984
74. The Mysterious Image ◆ 1984
75. The Emerald-Eyed Cat ◆ 1984
76. The Eskimo's Secret ◆ 1985
77. The Bluebeard Room ◆ 1985
78. The Phantom of Venice ◆ 1985
79. The Double Horror of Fenley Place ◆ 1987
80. The Case of the Disappearing Diamonds ◆ 1987
81. Mardi Gras Mystery ◆ 1988
82. The Clue in the Camera ◆ 1988
83. The Case of the Vanishing Veil ◆ 1988
84. The Joker's Revenge ◆ 1988
85. The Secret of Shady Glen ◆ 1988
86. The Mystery of Misty Canyon ◆ 1988
87. The Case of the Rising Stars ◆ 1988
88. The Search for Cindy Austin ◆ 1988
89. The Case of the Disappearing Deejay ◆ 1989
90. The Puzzle at Pineview School ◆ 1989
91. The Girl Who Couldn't Remember ◆ 1989
92. The Ghost of Craven Cove ◆ 1989
93. The Case of the Safecracker's Secret ◆ 1990
94. The Picture-Perfect Mystery ◆ 1990
95. The Silent Suspect ◆ 1990
96. The Case of the Photo Finish ◆ 1990
97. The Mystery at Magnolia Mansion ◆ 1990
98. The Haunting of Horse Island ◆ 1990
99. The Secret at Seven Rocks ◆ 1991
100. The Secret in Time: Nancy Drew's 100th Anniversary Edition ◆ 1991
101. The Mystery of the Missing Millionaires ◆ 1991
102. The Secret in the Dark ◆ 1991
103. The Stranger in the Shadows ◆ 1991
104. The Mystery of the Jade Tiger ◆ 1991
105. The Clue in the Antique Trunk ◆ 1992
106. The Case of the Artful Crime ◆ 1992
107. The Legend of Miner's Creek ◆ 1992
108. The Secret of the Tibetan Treasure ◆ 1992
109. The Mystery of the Masked Rider ◆ 1992
110. The Nutcracker Ballet Mystery ◆ 1992
111. The Secret at Solitaire ◆ 1993
112. Crime in the Queen's Court ◆ 1993
113. The Secret Lost at Sea ◆ 1993
114. The Search for the Silver Persian ◆ 1993
115. The Suspect in the Smoke ◆ 1993
116. The Case of the Twin Teddy Bears ◆ 1993
117. Mystery on the Menu ◆ 1993
118. Trouble at Lake Tahoe ◆ 1994

119. The Mystery of the Missing Mascot ◆ 1994
120. The Case of the Floating Crime ◆ 1994
121. The Fortune-Teller's Secret ◆ 1994
122. The Message in the Haunted Mansion ◆ 1994
123. The Clue on the Silver Screen ◆ 1995
124. The Secret of the Scarlet Hand ◆ 1995
125. The Teen Model Mystery ◆ 1995
126. The Riddle in the Rare Book ◆ 1995
127. The Case of the Dangerous Solution ◆ 1995
128. The Treasure in the Royal Tower ◆ 1995
129. The Baby-Sitter Burglaries ◆ 1996
130. The Sign of the Falcon ◆ 1996
131. The Hidden Inheritance ◆ 1996
132. The Fox Hunt Mystery ◆ 1996
133. The Mystery at the Crystal Palace ◆ 1996
134. The Secret of the Forgotten Cave ◆ 1996
135. The Riddle of the Ruby Gazelle ◆ 1997
136. The Wedding Day Mystery ◆ 1997
137. In Search of the Black Rose ◆ 1997
138. Legend of the Lost Gold ◆ 1997
139. The Secret of Candlelight Inn ◆ 1997
140. The Door-to-Door Deception ◆ 1997
141. The Wild Cat Crime ◆ 1997
142. The Case of Capital Intrigue ◆ 1998
143. Mystery on Maui ◆ 1998
144. The E-Mail Mystery ◆ 1998
145. The Missing Horse Mystery ◆ 1998
146. The Ghost of the Lantern Lady ◆ 1998
147. The Case of the Captured Queen ◆ 1998
148. On the Trail of Trouble ◆ 1999
149. The Clue of the Gold Doubloons ◆ 1999
150. Mystery at Moorsea Manor ◆ 1999
151. The Chocolate-Covered Contest ◆ 1999
152. The Key in the Satin Pocket ◆ 1999
153. Whispers in the Fog ◆ 2000
154. The Legend of the Emerald Lady ◆ 2000
155. The Mystery in Tornado Alley ◆ 2000
156. The Secret in the Stars ◆ 2000
157. The Music Festival Mystery ◆ 2000
158. The Curse of the Black Cat ◆ 2001
159. The Secret of the Fiery Chamber ◆ 2001
160. The Clue on the Crystal Dove ◆ 2001
161. Lost in the Everglades ◆ 2001
162. The Case of the Lost Song ◆ 2001
163. The Clues Challenge ◆ 2001
164. The Mystery of the Mother Wolf ◆ 2002
165. The Crime Lab Case ◆ 2002
166. The Case of the Creative Crime ◆ 2002
167. Mystery By Moonlight ◆ 2002

168. The Bike Tour Mystery ◆ 2002
169. Mistletoe Mystery ◆ 2002
170. No Strings Attached ◆ 2002
171. Intrigue at the Grand Opera ◆ 2003
172. The Riding Club Crime ◆ 2003
173. Danger on the Great Lakes ◆ 2003
174. A Taste of Danger ◆ 2003
175. Werewolf in a Winter Wonderland ◆ 2003

NANCY DREW: GIRL DETECTIVE

Keene, Carolyn
SIMON & SCHUSTER
GRADES 4–7 ◆ A/R
MYSTERY

This updated series puts Nancy into more contemporary situations. She finds the money that is missing from the Bucks for Charity race. She is chosen to appear in a film and then ends the sabotage that is plaguing the production.

1. Without a Trace ◆ 2004
2. A Race Against Time ◆ 2004
3. False Notes ◆ 2004
4. High Risk ◆ 2004
5. Lights, Camera . . . ◆ 2004
6. Action! ◆ 2004
7. The Stolen Relic ◆ 2004
8. The Scarlet Macaw Scandal ◆ 2004
9. Secret of the Spa ◆ 2005
10. Riverboat Ruse ◆ 2005
11. Uncivil Acts ◆ 2005

NANCY DREW AND THE HARDY BOYS SUPER MYSTERIES

Keene, Carolyn
SIMON & SCHUSTER
GRADES 7–9 ◆ A/R
MYSTERY

Nancy teams up with Frank and Joe Hardy for mysteries. In one book, they investigate sabotage directed at the site of the Winter Olympics in Salt Lake City.

1. Dangerous Games ◆ 1989
2. Shock Waves ◆ 1989
3. Buried in Time ◆ 1990
4. Last Resort ◆ 1990
5. Mystery Train ◆ 1990
6. Paris Connection ◆ 1990
7. Best of Enemies ◆ 1991
8. A Crime for Christmas ◆ 1991
9. Double Crossing ◆ 1991
10. High Survival ◆ 1991
11. New Year's Evil ◆ 1991
12. Spies and Lies ◆ 1992
13. Tour of Danger ◆ 1992
14. Tropic of Fear ◆ 1992
15. Courting Disaster ◆ 1993
16. Evil in Amsterdam ◆ 1993
17. Hits and Misses ◆ 1993
18. Copper Canyon Conspiracy ◆ 1994
19. Desperate Measures ◆ 1994
20. Hollywood Horror ◆ 1994
21. Passport to Danger ◆ 1994
22. Danger Down Under ◆ 1995
23. Dead on Arrival ◆ 1995
24. Secrets of the Nile ◆ 1995
25. Target for Terror ◆ 1995
26. High Stakes ◆ 1996
27. Islands of Intrigue ◆ 1996
28. Murder on the Fourth of July ◆ 1996
29. A Question of Guilt ◆ 1996
30. At All Costs ◆ 1997
31. Exhibition of Evil ◆ 1997
32. Nightmare in New Orleans ◆ 1997
33. Out of Control ◆ 1997
34. Royal Revenge ◆ 1997
35. Operation: Titanic ◆ 1998
36. Process of Elimination ◆ 1998

NANCY DREW FILES

Keene, Carolyn
ARCHWAY
GRADES 6–9 ◆ A/R
MYSTERY

In the Nancy Drew Files, geared more for older readers, Nancy remains the same gutsy, smart, accomplished sleuth she has always been. In this series, Nancy goes undercover at a high school, solves a rock 'n' roll mystery and travels to exotic places, such as a ski resort or Ft. Lauderdale during spring break. A new character in this series is Brenda Carlton, an aspiring investigative reporter who thinks she can outsmart Nancy, and has the habit of messing up her investigations.

1. Secrets Can Kill ◆ 1986
2. Deadly Intent ◆ 1986
3. Murder on Ice ◆ 1986
4. Smile and Say Murder ◆ 1986
5. Hit and Run Holiday ◆ 1986
6. White Water Terror ◆ 1987
7. Deadly Doubles ◆ 1987
8. Two Points for Murder ◆ 1987
9. False Moves ◆ 1987
10. Buried Secrets ◆ 1987
11. Heart of Danger ◆ 1987
12. Fatal Ransom ◆ 1987
13. Wings of Fear ◆ 1987
14. This Side of Evil ◆ 1987
15. Trial by Fire ◆ 1987
16. Never Say Die ◆ 1987
17. Stay Tuned for Danger ◆ 1987
18. Circle of Evil ◆ 1987
19. Sisters in Crime ◆ 1988
20. Very Deadly Yours ◆ 1988
21. Recipe for Murder ◆ 1988
22. Fatal Attraction ◆ 1988
23. Sinister Parade ◆ 1988
24. Till Death Do Us Part ◆ 1988
25. Rich and Dangerous ◆ 1988
26. Playing with Fire ◆ 1988
27. Most Likely to Die ◆ 1988
28. The Black Widow ◆ 1988
29. Pure Poison ◆ 1988
30. Death by Design ◆ 1988
31. Trouble in Tahiti ◆ 1989
32. High Marks for Malice ◆ 1989
33. Danger in Disguise ◆ 1989
34. Vanishing Act ◆ 1989
35. Bad Medicine ◆ 1989
36. Over the Edge ◆ 1989
37. Last Dance ◆ 1989
38. The Final Scene ◆ 1989
39. The Suspect Next Door ◆ 1989
40. Shadow of a Doubt ◆ 1989
41. Something to Hide ◆ 1989
42. The Wrong Chemistry ◆ 1989
43. False Impressions ◆ 1990
44. Scent of Danger ◆ 1990

45. Out of Bounds ◆ 1990
46. Win, Place, or Die ◆ 1990
47. Flirting with Danger ◆ 1990
48. A Date with Deception ◆ 1990
49. Portrait in Crime ◆ 1990
50. Deep Secrets ◆ 1990
51. A Model Crime ◆ 1990
52. Danger for Hire ◆ 1990
53. Trail of Lies ◆ 1990
54. Cold as Ice ◆ 1990
55. Don't Look Twice ◆ 1991
56. Make No Mistake ◆ 1991
57. Into Thin Air ◆ 1991
58. Hot Pursuit ◆ 1991
59. High Risk ◆ 1991
60. Poison Pen ◆ 1991
61. Sweet Revenge ◆ 1991
62. Easy Marks ◆ 1991
63. Mixed Signals ◆ 1991
64. The Wrong Track ◆ 1991
65. Final Notes ◆ 1991
66. Tall, Dark, and Deadly ◆ 1991
67. Nobody's Business ◆ 1992
68. Crosscurrents ◆ 1992
69. Running Scared ◆ 1992
70. Cutting Edge ◆ 1992
71. Hot Tracks ◆ 1992
72. Swiss Secrets ◆ 1992
73. Rendezvous in Rome ◆ 1992
74. Greek Odyssey ◆ 1992
75. A Talent for Murder ◆ 1992
76. The Perfect Plot ◆ 1992
77. Danger on Parade ◆ 1992
78. Update in Crime ◆ 1992
79. No Laughing Matter ◆ 1993
80. Power of Suggestion ◆ 1993
81. Making Waves ◆ 1993
82. Dangerous Relations ◆ 1993
83. Diamond Deceit ◆ 1993
84. Choosing Sides ◆ 1993
85. Sea of Suspicion ◆ 1993
86. Let's Talk Terror ◆ 1993
87. Moving Target ◆ 1993
88. False Pretenses ◆ 1993
89. Designs in Crime ◆ 1993
90. Stage Fright ◆ 1993
91. If Looks Could Kill ◆ 1994
92. My Deadly Valentine ◆ 1994
93. Hotline to Danger ◆ 1994

94. Illusions of Evil ◆ 1994
95. An Instinct for Trouble ◆ 1994
96. The Runaway Bride ◆ 1994
97. Squeeze Play ◆ 1994
98. Island of Secrets ◆ 1994
99. The Cheating Heart ◆ 1994
100. Dance Till You Die ◆ 1994
101. The Picture of Guilt ◆ 1994
102. Counterfeit Christmas ◆ 1994
103. Heart of Ice ◆ 1995
104. Kiss and Tell ◆ 1995
105. Stolen Affections ◆ 1995
106. Flying Too High ◆ 1995
107. Anything for Love ◆ 1995
108. Captive Heart ◆ 1995
109. Love Notes ◆ 1995
110. Hidden Meanings ◆ 1995
111. The Stolen Kiss ◆ 1995
112. For Love or Money ◆ 1995
113. Wicked Ways ◆ 1996
114. Rehearsing for Romance ◆ 1996
115. Running into Trouble ◆ 1996
116. Under His Spell ◆ 1996
117. Skipping a Beat ◆ 1996
118. Betrayed By Love ◆ 1996
119. Against the Rules ◆ 1997
120. Dangerous Loves ◆ 1997
121. Natural Enemies ◆ 1997
122. Strange Memories ◆ 1997
123. Wicked for the Weekend ◆ 1997
124. Crime at the Ch@t Cafe ◆ 1997

NANCY DREW ON CAMPUS

Keene, Carolyn
SIMON & SCHUSTER
GRADES 7–10
MYSTERY

Nancy is attending Wilder University. She lives in a co-ed dorm and still solves mysteries. She finds out why a fraternity prank went out of control. And investigates the mysterious death of a photographer. Nancy's job as the co-host of a campus television show keeps her right in the thick of things.

1. New Lives, New Loves ◆ 1995
2. On Her Own ◆ 1995

3. Don't Look Back ◆ 1995
4. Tell Me the Truth ◆ 1995
5. Secret Rules ◆ 1996
6. It's Your Move ◆ 1996
7. False Friends ◆ 1996
8. Getting Closer ◆ 1996
9. Broken Promises ◆ 1996
10. Party Weekend ◆ 1996
11. In the Name of Love ◆ 1996
12. Just the Two of Us ◆ 1996
13. Campus Exposures ◆ 1996
14. Hard to Get ◆ 1996
15. Loving and Losing ◆ 1996
16. Going Home ◆ 1996
17. New Beginnings ◆ 1997
18. Keeping Secrets ◆ 1997
19. Love On-Line ◆ 1997
20. Jealous Feelings ◆ 1997
21. Love and Betrayal ◆ 1997
22. In and Out of Love ◆ 1997
23. Otherwise Engaged ◆ 1997
24. In the Spotlight ◆ 1997
25. Snowbound ◆ 1998

NASCAR POLE POSITION ADVENTURES

Calhoun, T. B.
HARPERCOLLINS
GRADES 5–8
REAL LIFE | RECREATION

This series should appeal to stock-car racing enthusiasts. Kin Travis is 15. Along with his sister Laura and his brother Laptop, Kin is involved in adventures involving cars, mysteries, and high-speed action. Throughout the books, there is information about stock cars and NASCAR racing events. The Travis kids are helped by their grandfather, Hotshoe Hunter, a famous stock-car racer. His knowledge about racing and his connections with other racers give Kin and his siblings an up-close look at these exciting events.

1. Rolling Thunder ◆ 1998
2. In the Groove ◆ 1998
3. Race Ready ◆ 1998
4. Speed Demon ◆ 1999
5. Spinout ◆ 1999
6. Hammer Down ◆ 1999

NATHAN BRAZIL *see* Watchers at the Well

NATIONAL PARKS MYSTERY

Skurzynski, Gloria, and Alane Ferguson
NATIONAL GEOGRAPHIC
GRADES 5–8
ADVENTURE | MYSTERY

Jack, 12, and his younger sister, Ashley, travel with their parents to national parks. On these trips, they encounter mysteries that they try to solve. At Yellowstone, a pack of wolves may have killed a hunting dog. Jack and Ashley find out what is really happening. At Carlsbad Caverns National Park, Jack and Ashley search for a lost boy and become lost in the caverns. This series offers fast-paced adventure and brief information about each park.

1. Wolf Stalker ◆ 2001
2. Rage of Fire ◆ 2001
3. Cliff Hanger ◆ 2001
4. Deadly Waters ◆ 2001
5. The Hunted ◆ 2001
6. Ghost Horses ◆ 2002
7. Over the Edge ◆ 2002
8. Valley of Death ◆ 2002
9. Escape from Fear ◆ 2002
10. Out of the Deep ◆ 2002
11. Running Scared ◆ 2002
12. Buried Alive ◆ 2003

NET FORCE

Clancy, Tom, and Steve Pieczenik
BERKLEY JAM BOOKS
GRADES 7–10 ◆ A/R
REAL LIFE

In this futuristic series, the Net Force Explorers track criminals who are making illegal use of computers and the Net. *Virtual Vandals* focuses on four teens who use assumed identities to create cyber chaos. Other books feature different teens investigating computer crimes.

1. Virtual Vandals ◆ 1999
2. The Deadliest Game ◆ 1999

3. One Is the Loneliest Number ◆ 1999
4. The Ultimate Escape ◆ 1999
5. The Great Race ◆ 1999
6. End Game ◆ 1999
7. Cyberspy ◆ 1999
8. Shadow of Honor ◆ 2000
9. Private Lives ◆ 2000
10. Safe House ◆ 2000
11. Gameprey ◆ 2000
12. Dual Identity ◆ 2000
13. Deathworld ◆ 2000
14. High Wire ◆ 2001
15. Cold Case ◆ 2001
16. Runaways ◆ 2001
17. Cloak and Dagger ◆ 2003
18. Death Match ◆ 2003

NEXT GENERATION: STARFLEET ACADEMY *see* Star Trek: The Next Generation: Starfleet Academy

NFL MONDAY NIGHT FOOTBALL CLUB

Korman, Gordon
HYPERION
GRADES 4–7
FANTASY | RECREATION

When Nick, 11, puts on an old football jersey, he is transported into the body of John Elway—right in the middle of a Monday Night Football game! Then, when Elliot tries on the jersey, he becomes Barry Sanders. Even Nick's sister Hilary puts on the jersey and is transformed—into Junior Seau. Football fans will like the action and humor of this series.

1. Quarterback Exchange: I Was John Elway ◆ 1997
2. Running Back Conversion: I Was Barry Sanders ◆ 1997
3. Super Brown Switch: I Was Dan Marino ◆ 1997
4. Heavy Artillery: I Was Junior Seau ◆ 1997
5. Ultimate Scoring Machine: I Was Jerry Rice ◆ 1998

NICKELODEON ARE YOU AFRAID OF THE DARK? *see* Are You Afraid of the Dark?

NIGHT WORLD

Smith, L. J.
POCKET BOOKS
GRADES 9–12
HORROR

The lives of vampires and teen girls intersect in this series with a romantic twist. In *Soulmate*, Hannah is wary of approaching danger. Is Thierry, the Lord of the Night World, her friend or her foe? In *Black Dawn*, Maggie is tempted by the delights offered by a young vampire prince but fears that he killed her brother.

1. Secret Vampire ◆ 1996
2. Daughters of Darkness ◆ 1996
3. Spellbinder ◆ 1996
4. Dark Angel ◆ 1996
5. The Chosen ◆ 1996
6. Soulmate ◆ 1997
7. Huntress ◆ 1997
8. Black Dawn ◆ 1997
9. Witchlight ◆ 1997

NIGHTMARE HALL

Hoh, Diane
SCHOLASTIC
GRADES 6–9
HORROR | MYSTERY

The Nightmare Hall series takes place in a dormitory where evil seems to lurk. A girl is found hanged in her bedroom, and her spirit tries to help incoming students find the truth about her murder. Jessica Vogt leads the group in discovering the clues. As the first novel ends, there is a sense of relief but not complete peace. This sets the mood for the sequels.

1. The Silent Scream ◆ 1993
2. The Roommate ◆ 1993
3. Deadly Attraction ◆ 1993
4. The Wish ◆ 1993
5. The Scream Team ◆ 1993
6. Guilty ◆ 1993
7. Pretty Please ◆ 1994
8. The Experiment ◆ 1994
9. The Night Walker ◆ 1994

10. Sorority Sister ◆ 1994
11. Last Date ◆ 1994
12. The Whisperer ◆ 1994
13. Monster ◆ 1994
14. The Initiation ◆ 1994
15. Truth or Die ◆ 1994
16. Book of Horrors ◆ 1994
17. Last Breath ◆ 1994
18. Win, Lose, or Die ◆ 1994
19. The Coffin ◆ 1995
20. Deadly Visions ◆ 1995
21. Student Body ◆ 1995
22. The Vampire's Kiss ◆ 1995
23. Dark Moon ◆ 1995
24. The Biker ◆ 1995
25. Captives ◆ 1995
26. Revenge ◆ 1995
27. Kidnapped ◆ 1995
28. The Dummy ◆ 1995
29. The Voice in the Mirror ◆ 1995

NIGHTMARE ROOM

Stine, R. L.
AVON
GRADES 4–7 ◆ A/R
HORROR

These stories are somewhat scary, with elements of mystery, the supernatural, and aliens. In *Liar, Liar*, Ross Arthur goes to a party and sees his twin. One problem—he does not have a twin. In another book, Alex Smith's blank journal is being written in, but not by Alex. When Alex reads the journal, he realizes he is learning about the future. Fans of creepy stories will enjoy these.

1. Don't Forget Me! ◆ 2000
2. Locker 13 ◆ 2000
3. My Name Is Evil ◆ 2000
4. Liar, Liar ◆ 2000
5. Dear Diary, I'm Dead ◆ 2001
6. They Call Me Creature ◆ 2001
7. The Howler ◆ 2001
8. Shadow Girl ◆ 2001
9. Camp Nowhere ◆ 2001
10. Full Moon Halloween ◆ 2001
11. Scare School ◆ 2001
12. Visitors ◆ 2001

NIGHTMARE ROOM THRILLOGY

Stine, R. L.
AVON
GRADES 4–7 ◆ A/R
HORROR

More chills and thrills in the Nightmare Room, where it is not safe to be alone.

1. Fear Games ◆ 2001
2. What Scares You the Most? ◆ 2001
3. No Survivors ◆ 2001

NIGHTMARES! HOW WILL YOURS END?

Wulffson, Don L.
PRICE, STERN, SLOAN
GRADES 4–7
HORROR

Your father and brother are missing in the jungles of Malaysia—which way do you choose to go? Or, you are on Earth but it has been invaded by aliens—what will you do? Readers are given scary situations and make choices to create different endings.

1. Castle of Horror ◆ 1995
2. Cave of Fear ◆ 1995
3. Planet of Terror ◆ 1995
4. Valley of the Screaming Statues ◆ 1995

NIKKI SHERIDAN

Brinkerhoff, Shirley
BETHANY HOUSE
GRADES 6–9 ◆ A/R
REAL LIFE | VALUES

Nikki becomes pregnant at the age of 16 and has to face difficult choices. As the series progresses and she finds religion, she struggles to accept her decision to give the baby up and she confronts differing views on adoption, abortion, and divorce.

1. Choice Summer ◆ 1996

2. Mysterious Love ◆ 1996
3. Narrow Walk ◆ 1998
4. Balancing Act ◆ 1998
5. Tangled Web ◆ 1999
6. Second Choices ◆ 2000

NINE CHARMS *see* Tales of the Nine Charms

THE NINE LIVES OF CHLOE KING

Thomson, Celia
SIMON & SCHUSTER
GRADES 9–12 ◆ A/R
FANTASY

Chloe King is almost 16 when she falls from the top of a tower in San Francisco. While she appears to be unharmed, there are hints that something unusual has happened. Chloe has mysterious encounters with a supernatural society and comes to realize that she now has special cat-like powers.

1. The Fallen ◆ 2004
2. The Stolen ◆ 2004
3. The Chosen ◆ 2005

99 FEAR STREET *see* Fear Street: 99 Fear Street

NO SECRETS: THE STORY OF A GIRL BAND

Krulik, Nancy
GROSSET & DUNLAP
GRADES 6–9
REAL LIFE

PCBS is the Professional Children's Boarding School and it's time for the Fall Showcase. This year, a talent agent, Eileen Kerr, is in the audience. Eight girls will make *The First Cut* but only four will be in the all-girl band.

1. The First Cut ◆ 2001
2. Sneaking Around ◆ 2001

3. Spring Fever ◆ 2001
4. In the Spotlight ◆ 2001

NORTHERN FRIGHTS

Slade, Arthur G.

ORCA

GRADES 5–8 ◆ A/R

FANTASY

Exciting adventures are interwoven with Norse mythology in this Canadian series. On Drang Island off the coast of British Columbia, Michael, 15, meets Fiona and together they encounter ghosts, spirits, and other dangers. This could be a good choice for R. L. Stine fans.

1. The Haunting of Drang Island ◆ 1998
2. Draugr ◆ 1998
3. The Loki Wolf ◆ 2000

NOSE

Scrimger, Richard

TUNDRA

GRADES 6–8

FANTASY | HUMOR

Alan Dingwell is 13 and, like many middle school boys, he struggles with schoolwork and bullies. Then Norbert, an alien from Jupiter, comes to his rescue and takes up residence in his nose! Norbert is opinionated and funny and he gets Alan into and out of trouble. Reluctant readers will find these books accessible.

1. Nose from Jupiter ◆ 1998
2. Nose for Adventure ◆ 2000
3. Noses Are Red ◆ 2002

THE O.C.

Various authors

SCHOLASTIC

GRADES 10–12

REAL LIFE

Fans of the television show will want to read these related books. Ryan Atwood, 16, goes to live with a wealthy family in Orange County, California (the O.C.) He feels out of place and has trouble relating to rich teens like Seth and Marissa Cooper. There are many related materials including cast biographies and calendars.

1. The Misfit (Wallington, Aury) ◆ 2004
2. The Outsider (Martin, Cory) ◆ 2004

OBSIDIAN CHRONICLES

Watt-Evans, Lawrence
TOR
GRADES 10–12
FANTASY

Arlian is the only survivor of a dragon attack on his village. He has vowed vengeance and for 14 years has devoted himself to slaying dragons. When he returns to the walled city of Manfort, he finds that a wild magic has been released. His treatment of dragons may be responsible and Arlian must investigate the power of dragon venom.

1. Dragon Weather ◆ 1999
2. The Dragon Society ◆ 2001
3. Dragon Venom ◆ 2003

OCEAN CITY *see* Making Waves

OH MY GODDESS!

Fujishima, Kosuke
DARK HORSE
GRADES 10–12
FANTASY

So, you want to order a pizza. When you dial for delivery, you connect with a goddess, Belldandy, who grants you one wish. That's when the adventure begins for Keiichi Morisato, who wishes that Belldandy would stay with him forever. Thus begins the classic manga adventures with magic, more goddesses, and fun. The dates for this series vary as some volumes have been reworked or repackaged. (For example, the first three books are re-created from the 1996 title *1-555-Goddess*.)

1. Wrong Number ◆ 2002

2. Leader of the Pack ◆ 2002
3. Final Exam ◆ 2002
4. Love Potion, No. 9 ◆ 1997
5. Sympathy for the Devil ◆ 1998
6. Terrible Master Urd ◆ 2001
7. The Queen of Vengeance ◆ 1999
8. Mara Strikes Back! ◆ 2000
9. Ninja Master! ◆ 2000
10. Miss Keiichi ◆ 2001
11. The Devil in Miss Urd ◆ 2001
12. The Fourth Goddess ◆ 2001
13. Childhood's End ◆ 2002
14. Queen Sayoko ◆ 2002
15. Hand in Hand ◆ 2003
16. Mystery Child ◆ 2003
17. Traveler ◆ 2003
18. Phantom Racer ◆ 2004

ON THE ROAD

Doyon, Stephanie
ALADDIN
GRADES 6–10 ◆ A/R
REAL LIFE

Miranda, 18, is tired of the routine of her life. She is bored with always doing what is expected. She decides to delay going to college and to travel across the country with her friend Kirsten. Along the way, Miranda spends some time doing volunteer work with her brother in Virginia. And she develops a romantic attraction for a boy who helps her try rock climbing.

1. Leaving Home ◆ 1998
2. Buying Time ◆ 1999
3. Taking Chances ◆ 1999
4. Making Waves ◆ 1999

ON TIME'S WING

Various authors
ROUSSAN
GRADES 5–8 ◆ A/R
HISTORICAL

This series features well-researched historical novels. In *Living Freight*, Emma has been orphaned and is waiting to go to the workhouse.

Instead, she boards a ship sailing from England to Canada. Once in Canada, she tries to sell her mother's ring to fund her journey to British Columbia, where she hopes to look for gold. The ring brings Emma to the father she believed was dead. Each book features intrepid young teens who overcome obstacles.

1. Home Child (Haworth-Attard, Barbara) ◆ 1991
2. Candles (Kositsky, Lynne) ◆ 1996
3. Dark of the Moon (Haworth-Attard, Barbara) ◆ 1996
4. Living Freight (Campbell, Gaetz Dayle) ◆ 1998
5. Love-Lies-Bleeding (Haworth-Attard, Barbara) ◆ 1999
6. Rebecca's Flame (Kositsky, Lynne) ◆ 1999
7. Run for Your Life (Alexander, Wilma E.) ◆ 1999
8. Sunflower Diary (Boraks-Nemetz, Lillian) ◆ 1999
9. Danger in Disguise (Downie, Mary Alice) ◆ 2001
10. In Search of Klondike Gold (Wilson, Lynda) ◆ 2001
11. The Lenski File (Boraks-Nemetz, Lillian) ◆ 2001
12. Virtual Zone: Titanic's Race to Disaster (Wilson, Lynda) ◆ 2001

ONCE AND FUTURE KING

White, T. H.

PUTNAM

GRADES 7–10

ADVENTURE | HISTORICAL

This classic series tells the entire glorious and tragic Arthurian legend. The first novel relates Arthur's life growing up with Kay, his older brother; Sir Ector, his father; and Merlyn, his tutor. The subsequent novels continue to unfold Arthur's life as he discovers that he is King and forms the Knights of the Round Table. Battles for power are fought and won, but Arthur's personal life unravels because of Sir Lancelot and Guinevere. This series is not merely a retelling, for White incorporates humor and fresh insights into the characters as real people with real problems. *The Book of Merlyn* was published separately in 1977, as a final chapter in the story.

1. The Sword in the Stone ◆ 1938
2. The Queen of Air and Darkness ◆ 1939
3. The Ill-Made Knight ◆ 1940
4. The Candle in the Wind ◆ 1958
5. The Book of Merlyn ◆ 1977

1-800-WHERE-R-YOU

Cabot, Meg
SIMON & SCHUSTER
GRADES 7–10 ◆ A/R
ADVENTURE

Jessica Mastriana, 16, was a struggling high school student until she walked through a thunderstorm. Before, she was troubled but normal. Now, she is changed. She has psychic powers that bring her to the attention of the government and of others who want her help. She tries unsuccessfully to hide her new abilities and is asked to help find missing children and even solve a murder. The fast-paced action and Jess's strong personality will attract many readers.

1. Code Name Cassandra ◆ 2004
2. Safe House ◆ 2004
3. Sanctuary ◆ 2004
4. When Lightning Strikes ◆ 2004

ONE LAST WISH

McDaniel, Lurlene
BANTAM
GRADES 6–9 ◆ A/R
REAL LIFE

Although several of these books feature the same characters, the linking themes are serious illness, death, love, and generosity through the awarding of gifts from the One Last Wish Foundation. In *A Season for Goodbye*, three girls who are facing difficult problems of their own work together to help a 12-year-old with leukemia.

1. A Time to Die ◆ 1992
2. Mourning Song ◆ 1992
3. Mother, Help Me Live ◆ 1992
4. Someone Dies, Someone Lives ◆ 1992
5. Sixteen and Dying ◆ 1992
6. Let Him Live ◆ 1993
7. The Legacy: Making Wishes Come True ◆ 1993
8. Please Don't Die ◆ 1993
9. She Died Too Young ◆ 1994

10. All the Days of Her Life ◆ 1994
11. A Season for Goodbye ◆ 1995
12. Reach for Tomorrow ◆ 1999

ORION THE HUNTER

Bova, Ben

TOR

GRADES 9–12

SCIENCE FICTION

Adventure, romance, and mythology are interwoven in this well-written saga about Orion the Hunter as he strives for independence from the Creators and a life with his beloved Anya.

1. Orion ◆ 1984
2. Vengeance of Orion ◆ 1988
3. Orion in the Dying Time ◆ 1990
4. Orion and the Conqueror ◆ 1994
5. Orion Among the Stars ◆ 1995

ORMINGAT

Waugh, Sylvia

DELACORTE

GRADES 5–8

FANTASY

Aliens from Ormingat living in England are collecting information on Earthlings and their behaviors. Each book in this series features a young person from Ormingat. In *Earthborn*, Nesta Gwynn, 12, learns a secret about her parents. They are aliens who planning to return to Ormingat, but Nesta does not want to go.

1. Space Race ◆ 2000
2. Earthborn ◆ 2002
3. Who Goes Home ◆ 2004

ORPHAN TRAIN ADVENTURES

Nixon, Joan Lowery
DELACORTE
GRADES 5–8 ◆ A/R
FAMILY LIFE | HISTORICAL

Originally published as a quartet of books, this series has been extend-ed to relate more adventures of the Kelly children. The first book, *A Family Apart*, sets the stage for the series, which takes place in the mid-1800s. When their mother can no longer support them, the six Kelly children are sent from New York City to Missouri on an orphan train. They are placed with different farm families across the Great Plains. The series describes their experiences from the oldest, Frances Mary Kelly, to the youngest, Peaty. In *Caught in the Act*, Michael Patrick Kelly faces cruelty and a harsh life on a Missouri farm; in a later book, he becomes a Union soldier. Though orphan trains did exist, the characters and plots in this series are fictional.

1. A Family Apart ◆ 1987
2. Caught in the Act ◆ 1988
3. In the Face of Danger ◆ 1988
4. A Place to Belong ◆ 1989
5. A Dangerous Promise ◆ 1994
6. Keeping Secrets ◆ 1995
7. Circle of Love ◆ 1997

OUTCAST

Golden, Christopher, and Thomas E. Sniegoski
ALADDIN
GRADES 4–7 ◆ A/R
FANTASY

Timothy is the son of a powerful mage. His father, now deceased, has kept Timothy hidden. Now Timothy has been discovered by Leader, a former apprentice, and he is introduced to the world of magic.

1. The Un-Magician ◆ 2004
2. Dragon Secrets ◆ 2004
3. Ghostfire ◆ 2005

OUTER BANKS TRILOGY

Taylor, Theodore
DOUBLEDAY; HARPERCOLLINS
GRADES 5–8 ◆ A/R
ADVENTURE | HISTORICAL

This adventure trilogy is by the author of *The Cay*. Teetoncey is a frail young girl whom Ben helps rescue from a shipwreck. Many mysteries surround her. Later, as Ben searches for his brother, he discovers that their fates are more closely entwined than he first thought. Harper-Collins reissued these books in 1995 with the following titles: *Stranger from the Sea: Teetoncey, Box of Treasures: Teetoncey and Ben O'Neal, Into the Wind: The Odyssey of Ben O'Neal.*

1. Teetoncey ◆ 1974
2. Teetoncey and Ben O'Neal ◆ 1975
3. The Odyssey of Ben O'Neal ◆ 1977

THE OUTER LIMITS

Peel, John
TOR KIDS!
GRADES 6–8
FANTASY | HORROR

The books in this series feature different characters in fantastic, even bizarre, situations. In *The Zanti Misfits*, the Zanti have sent their problem creatures to Earth, putting human society in danger of destruction. Deciding what to do with these dangerous misfits is a dilemma—they may destroy Earth, but killing them may bring the wrath of the Zanti. Another book features a character with telekinetic powers, and still another deals with the planet Tarnish, which is ruled by children. Recommend this series to readers who like unusual creatures and surprising plot twists.

1. The Choice ◆ 1997
2. The Zanti Misfits ◆ 1997
3. The Time Shifter ◆ 1997
4. The Lost ◆ 1997
5. The Invaders ◆ 1998
6. The Innocent ◆ 1998
7. The Vanished ◆ 1998
8. The Nightmare ◆ 1998
9. Beware the Metal Children ◆ 1999
10. Alien Invasion from Hollyweird ◆ 1999

11. The Payback ◆ 1999
12. The Change ◆ 1999

OUTERNET

Barlow, Steve
SCHOLASTIC
GRADES 6–9
SCIENCE FICTION

Jack Armstrong got just what he wanted for his birthday—a laptop.
Of course, it's not new; Jack's father got it from a man at his work-
place, a U.S. Air Force base near Cambridge, England. The surprise
comes when Jack discovers that his computer is connected to the
Outernet, an intergalactic communication network. With his friends
Loaf and Merle, Jack faces the evil Tyrant who wants to gain control
of the Server.

1. Friend or Foe? ◆ 2002
2. Control ◆ 2002
3. Odyssey ◆ 2002
4. Time Out ◆ 2003
5. The Hunt ◆ 2003
6. Weaver ◆ 2003

OUTLANDER

Gabaldon, Diana
DELACORTE
GRADES 11–12
FANTASY

With World War II over, Claire Randall, a nurse, has finally been
reunited with her husband Frank. On a trip to Scotland, Claire walks
into a circle of standing stones and travels back in time 200 years.
This is a violent era when women were subservient. Claire's nursing
skills earn her a place in the clan; her attractive features and feisty
nature earn her a place in Scots warrior James Fraser's bed. This is a
lush historical romance that spans generations as Claire leaves the past
to bear Jamie's child in the present.

1. Outlander ◆ 1991
2. Dragonfly in Amber ◆ 1992
3. Voyager ◆ 1993

4. Drums of Autumn ◆ 1997
5. The Fiery Cross ◆ 2001

Oz

Baum, Lyman Frank
MORROW; GREENWILLOW

GRADES 4–8 ◆ A/R

FANTASY

The popular *Wizard of Oz* was only the first of a great many adventures about the land of Oz, which were continued by others after Baum's death. Dorothy returns many times and fights villains; and other children, such as Peter and Betsy Bobbins, find their way to the magical land. The Tin Man and Scarecrow are involved in various battles for control of Oz, but Ozma of Oz is the rightful ruler. All the books share a rich and detailed fantasy laced with satire. The first 15 books were written by L. Frank Baum. Other authors have extended the series. Greenwillow has reissued many of these titles in its Books of Wonder series.

ORIGINAL OZ BOOKS

1. The Wonderful Wizard of Oz ◆ 1900
2. The New Wizard of Oz ◆ 1903
3. The Marvelous Land of Oz ◆ 1904
4. Ozma of Oz ◆ 1907
5. Dorothy and the Wizard of Oz ◆ 1908
6. The Road to Oz ◆ 1909
7. The Emerald City of Oz ◆ 1910
8. The Patchwork Girl of Oz ◆ 1913
9. Tik-Tok of Oz ◆ 1914
10. The Scarecrow of Oz ◆ 1915
11. Rinktink in Oz ◆ 1916
12. The Lost Princess of Oz ◆ 1917
13. The Tin Woodman of Oz ◆ 1918
14. The Magic of Oz ◆ 1919
15. Glinda of Oz ◆ 1920

OZ CONTINUED

1. The Royal Book of Oz (Thompson, Ruth Plumly) ◆ 1921
2. The Cowardly Lion of Oz (Thompson, Ruth Plumly) ◆ 1923
3. Grampa in Oz (Thompson, Ruth Plumly) ◆ 1924
4. The Lost King of Oz (Thompson, Ruth Plumly) ◆ 1925
5. The Hungry Tiger in Oz (Thompson, Ruth Plumly) ◆ 1926
6. The Gnome King of Oz (Thompson, Ruth Plumly) ◆ 1927
7. The Giant Horse of Oz (Thompson, Ruth Plumly) ◆ 1928

8. Jack Pumpkinhead of Oz (Thompson, Ruth Plumly) ◆ 1929
9. The Yellow Knight of Oz (Thompson, Ruth Plumly) ◆ 1930
10. The Pirates in Oz (Thompson, Ruth Plumly) ◆ 1931
11. Purple Prince of Oz (Thompson, Ruth Plumly) ◆ 1932
12. Ojo in Oz (Thompson, Ruth Plumly) ◆ 1933
13. Speedy in Oz (Thompson, Ruth Plumly) ◆ 1934
14. Wishing Horse of Oz (Thompson, Ruth Plumly) ◆ 1935
15. Captain Salt in Oz (Thompson, Ruth Plumly) ◆ 1936
16. Kabumpo in Oz (Thompson, Ruth Plumly) ◆ 1936
17. Handy Mandy in Oz (Thompson, Ruth Plumly) ◆ 1937
18. The Silver Princess in Oz (Thompson, Ruth Plumly) ◆ 1938
19. Ozoplaning with the Wizard of Oz (Thompson, Ruth Plumly) ◆ 1939
20. The Wonder City of Oz (Neill, John R.) ◆ 1940
21. The Scalawagons of Oz (Neill, John R.) ◆ 1941
22. Lucky Bucky in Oz (Neill, John R.) ◆ 1942
23. The Magical Mimics in Oz (Snow, Jack) ◆ 1946
24. The Shaggy Man of Oz (Snow, Jack) ◆ 1949
25. Hidden Valley of Oz (Cosgrove, Rachel) ◆ 1951
26. Merry Go Round in Oz (McGraw, Eloise Jervis) ◆ 1963
27. Yankee in Oz (Thompson, Ruth Plumly) ◆ 1972
28. Autocrats of Oz (Suter, Jon Michael) ◆ 1976
29. Enchanted Island of Oz (Thompson, Ruth Plumly) ◆ 1976
30. Orange Knight of Oz (Suter, Jon Michael) ◆ 1976
31. Forbidden Fountain of Oz (McGraw, Eloise Jervis) ◆ 1980
32. Barnstormer in Oz (Farmer, Philip Jose) ◆ 1982
33. Return to Oz (Vinge, Joan Dennison) ◆ 1982
34. Dorothy and the Magic Belt (Baum, Roger S.) ◆ 1985
35. Mister Tinker of Oz (Howe, James) ◆ 1985
36. Dorothy of Oz (Baum, Roger) ◆ 1989
37. Rewolf of Oz (Baum, Roger S.) ◆ 1990
38. How the Wizard Came to Oz (Abbott, Donald) ◆ 1991
39. SillyOzbuls of Oz (Baum, Roger S.) ◆ 1991
40. The Nome King's Shadow in Oz (Sprague, Gilbert M.) ◆ 1992
41. The SillyOzbul of Oz and the Magic Merry-Go-Round (Baum, Roger S.) ◆ 1992
42. The SillyOzbul of Oz & Toto (Baum, Roger S.) ◆ 1992
43. The Blue Witch of Oz (Shanower, Eric) ◆ 1993
44. The Enchanted Apples of Oz (Shanower, Eric) ◆ 1993
45. The Forgotten Forest of Oz (Shanower, Eric) ◆ 1993
46. The Giant Garden of Oz (Shanower, Eric) ◆ 1993
47. The Magic Chest of Oz (Abbott, Donald) ◆ 1993
48. The Patchwork Bride of Oz (Sprague, Gilbert M.) ◆ 1993
49. Queen Ann in Oz (Carlson, Karyl, and Eric Gjovaag) ◆ 1993
50. Father Goose in Oz (Abbott, Donald) ◆ 1994
51. Christmas in Oz (Hess, Robin) ◆ 1995
52. The Glass Cat of Oz (Hulan, David) ◆ 1995
53. The Magic Dishpan of Oz (Freedman, Jeff) ◆ 1995
54. Masquerade in Oz (Campbell, Bill, and Irwin Terry) ◆ 1995
55. The Runaway in Oz (Neill, John R.) ◆ 1995

56. The Speckled Rose of Oz (Abbott, Donald) ◆ 1995
57. How the Wizard Saved Oz (Abbott, Donald) ◆ 1996
58. The Lavender Bear of Oz (Campbell, Bill) ◆ 1998

P.C. HAWKE MYSTERIES

Zindel, Paul
HYPERION/VOLO
GRADES 5–8 ◆ A/R
MYSTERY

P.C. Hawke and his friend Mackenzie Riggs solve mysteries. In one book, their friend is accused of the murder of a biologist at the Natural History Museum. The investigation involves a necklace, hypnosis, and a tarantula. In another book, P.C. and Mac travel to Monaco and investigate the murder of a guest at a conference.

1. The Scream Museum ◆ 2001
2. The Surfing Corpse ◆ 2001
3. The E-Mail Murders ◆ 2001
4. The Lethal Gorilla ◆ 2001
5. The Square Root of Murder ◆ 2002
6. Death on the Amazon ◆ 2002
7. The Gourmet Zombie ◆ 2002
8. The Phantom of 86th Street ◆ 2002
9. The Houdini Whodunit ◆ 2002

PACIFIC CASCADES UNIVERSITY

Various authors
PALISADES PRESS/MULTNOMAH
GRADES 8–10 ◆ A/R
REAL LIFE | VALUES

Follow the adventures of girls as they attend college. Emily is a freshman and has to adjust to her dorm and roommate along with the food and classes. Maddy wants college to inject some stability into her mixed-up life, especially her relationship with her difficult boyfriend. Their faith in God helps them face their challenges.

1. Freshman Blues (Nentwig, Wendy Lee) ◆ 1996
2. Homeward Heart (Johnson, Lissa Halls) ◆ 1996

3. True Identity (Sheahan, Bernie) ◆ 1996
4. Spring Break (Nentwig, Wendy Lee) ◆ 1996
5. Major Changes (Brooks, Jennifer) ◆ 1997
6. Summer Song (Sheahan, Bernie) ◆ 1997
7. Overbooked (Nentwig, Wendy Lee) ◆ 1997

PAGAN

Jinks, Catherine
CANDLEWICK
GRADES 9–12 ◆ A/R
HISTORICAL

Beginning in 12th-century Jerusalem, Pagan, 16, is an orphan. He serves as a squire for a Templar Knight, Lord Roland. Together, they face Saladin's armies. Later, they return to Lord Roland's castle in France and deal with feuds and religious upheaval. As the series continues, Pagan follows Lord Roland to a monastery.

1. Pagan's Crusade ◆ 2003
2. Pagan in Exile ◆ 2004
3. Pagan's Vows ◆ 2004
4. Pagan's Scribe ◆ 2005

PAGEANT

Bennett, Cherie
BERKLEY
GRADES 7–10
REAL LIFE

Who will be "Miss Teen Spirit"? A popular teen magazine is looking across America to find that special girl. The first four books describe the regional events, giving a behind-the-scenes look at the camaraderie and competition. Teen girls will find these books entertaining.

1. The Southern Girls ◆ 1998
2. The Midwest Girls ◆ 1998
3. The Northeast Girls ◆ 1998
4. The West Coast Girls ◆ 1998
5. The National Pageant ◆ 1998
6. The Winners on the Roads ◆ 1999

PANGUR BAN

Sampson, Fay

LION

GRADES 5–8

FANTASY

In ancient Wales, Pangur, a small white cat fleeing from a group of witches and their evil spells, befriends a monk called Niall. In *Pangur Ban*, the cat struggles to rescue Niall and the Princess Finnglas when they encounter a storm at sea and their lives are imperiled by mermaids and monsters. The fight between good and evil continues in later books and in *Finnglas and the Stones of Choosing*, the princess must face seven trials before she can become queen. These books were first published in Britain in the 1980s.

1. Shape-Shifter: The Naming of Pangur Ban ◆ 2003
2. Pangur Ban: The White Cat ◆ 2003
3. Finnglas of the Horses ◆ 2003
4. Finnglas and the Stones of Choosing ◆ 2003
5. The Serpent of Senargad ◆ 2003

PARTY OF FIVE

Various authors

SIMON & SCHUSTER

GRADES 7–10

REAL LIFE

Following the death of their parents four years ago, the Salinger kids have stayed together. Charlie, the oldest, has taken charge of Claudia, Bailey, Owen, and Julia. In one book, Claudia is attracted to a cute guy named Cliff. Her friend, Jody, tells her she has no chance. That's because Jody wants Cliff for herself. These books reflect some of the episodes from the television program.

1. Too Cool for School: Claudia (Mostow, Debra) ◆ 1997
2. Welcome to My World: Claudia (Winfrey, Elizabeth) ◆ 1997
3. A Boy Friend Is Not a "Boyfriend": Claudia (Costello, Emily) ◆ 1997
4. Everything Changes: Julia (Noonan, Rosalind) ◆ 1997
5. Trouble with Guys: Claudia (Speregen, Devra Newberger) ◆ 1997
6. You Can't Choose Your Family: Claudia (Tamar, Erika) ◆ 1997
7. On My Own: Bailey (Stine, Megan) ◆ 1997
8. Don't Say You Love Me: Sarah (Noonan, Rosalind) ◆ 1998
9. Breaking the Rules: Bailey (Stine, Megan) ◆ 1998
10. Nothing Lasts Forever: Julia (Levine, Michael) ◆ 1998

11. One Step Too Far: Bailey (Stine, Megan) ◆ 1998
12. My Ex-Best Friend: Claudia (Tamar, Erika) ◆ 1998

PARVANA *see* The Breadwinner Trilogy

PASSAGES

McCusker, Paul
TOMMY NELSON/FOCUS ON THE FAMILY
GRADES 6–10
VALUES

Modern-day children slip through to another world—Marus. Using their religious knowledge they help the inhabitants deal with problems. The books retell Biblical stories in this new context and present values including faith, repentance, and salvation.

1. Darien's Rise ◆ 1999
2. Arin's Judgment ◆ 1999
3. Annison's Risk ◆ 1999
4. Glennall's Betrayal ◆ 2000
5. Draven's Defiance ◆ 2000
6. Fendar's Legacy ◆ 2000

PAXTON CHEERLEADERS

Hall, Katy
MINSTREL/POCKET BOOKS
GRADES 6–8
REAL LIFE | RECREATION

Patti wants to be one of the Paxton cheerleaders. She has been practicing with her friend Tara for the tryouts, but Tara can't do all the moves. Will Patti stick with her friend or find a way to get on the team on her own? This is the sort of dilemma found in this series. Lauren and Cassie have to deal with not always being the best while Patti has to resist being influenced by a new girl. School concerns, worries about boys, and team spirit are issues that will appeal to young teen readers.

1. Go for It, Patti! ◆ 1994
2. Three Cheers for You, Cassie! ◆ 1994
3. Winning Isn't Everything, Lauren! 1994 ◆ 1994
4. We Did It, Tara! ◆ 1995

5. We're in This Together, Patti! ◆ 1995
6. Nobody's Perfect, Cassie! ◆ 1995

PAYTON SKKY

Moore, Stephanie Perry
MOODY PRESS
GRADES 9–12 ◆ A/R
REAL LIFE | VALUES

Payton Skky is beautiful, popular, and dating a great guy. Her values are tested when he pressures her to have sex. And, as an African American, Payton faces prejudice and racism. She relies on her faith to guide her. The books follow Payton into her early years at college.

1. Staying Pure ◆ 2000
2. Sober Faith ◆ 2001
3. Saved Race ◆ 2001
4. Sweetest Gift ◆ 2001
5. Surrendered Heart ◆ 2002

PELLUCIDAR

Burroughs, Edgar Rice
BALLANTINE
GRADES 7–12
ADVENTURE | FANTASY

Pellucidar is a land under the earth's crest populated with dinosaurs, saber-toothed tigers, and other extinct animals, and lit by the earth's molten core. There are humans too, but they are the slaves of intelligent reptiles called the Mahars. The discoverers of this world—David Innes and Abner Perry—work to free these Stone Age humans in a series of exciting adventures.

1. At the Earth's Core ◆ 1922
2. Pellucidar ◆ 1923
3. Tanar of Pellucidar ◆ 1930
4. Tarzan at the Earth's Core ◆ 1930
5. Back to the Stone Age ◆ 1937
6. Land of Terror ◆ 1944
7. Savage Pellucidar ◆ 1963

PENDRAGON

MacHale, D. J.
ALADDIN
GRADES 5–8 ◆ A/R
FANTASY

Bobby Pendragon, 14, seems normal, but he's not. He is going to save the world. First, by traveling to an alternate dimension, Denduron. Later, he continues his role as a Traveler and strives to save the land of Halla from the evil Saint Dane.

1. The Merchant of Death ◆ 2002
2. The Lost City of Faar ◆ 2003
3. The Never War ◆ 2003
4. The Reality Bug ◆ 2003
5. Black Water ◆ 2004

PERN (*see also* Acorna)

McCaffrey, Anne
BALLANTINE DEL REY
GRADES 10–12
SCIENCE FICTION

From the first settlement on the planet of Pern, the colonists have lived in a world of dragons and the dreaded Thread, which falls from the sky to destroy everything it touches.

1. Moreta, Dragonlady of Pern ◆ 1983
2. Nerilka's Story ◆ 1986
3. Dragonsdawn ◆ 1988
4. Renegades of Pern ◆ 1989
5. All the Weyrs of Pern ◆ 1991
6. Chronicles of Pern: First Fall ◆ 1993
7. The Dolphins of Pern ◆ 1994
8. Dragonseye ◆ 1997
9. The Masterharper of Pern ◆ 1998
10. The Skies of Pern ◆ 2001
11. Dragon's Kin (McCaffrey, Anne, with Todd McCaffrey) ◆ 2004

DRAGONRIDERS OF PERN

1. Dragonflight ◆ 1968
2. Dragonquest ◆ 1971
3. The White Dragon ◆ 1978

PERN: THE HARPER-HALL TRILOGY

McCaffrey, Anne
SIMON & SCHUSTER
GRADES 10–12
FANTASY | SCIENCE FICTION

Menolly runs away when her parents refuse to let her sing or become a Harper. She finds a new home with a family of fire lizards. In the second book, she studies with the Masterharper, learns about music and about herself, and makes a friend, Piemur.

1. Dragonsong ◆ 2003
2. Dragonsinger ◆ 2003
3. Dragondrums ◆ 2003

PETTICOAT PARTY

Karr, Kathleen
HARPERCOLLINS
GRADES 5–8 ◆ A/R
HISTORICAL

Independence, Missouri, 1845. Twelve wagons head west for Oregon. In one wagon are Mr. and Mrs. Brown and their daughters Amelia and Phoebe. There is an accident and ten of the men are injured or killed. Now the women must take charge or the group will not survive. When the series begins, Phoebe is 12. After reaching Oregon when she is 15, she gets caught up in the Gold Rush and goes to California.

1. Go West, Young Women ◆ 1996
2. Phoebe's Folly ◆ 1996
3. Oregon, Sweet Oregon ◆ 1998
4. Gold-Rush Phoebe ◆ 1998

PHANTOM VALLEY

Beach, Lynn
ALADDIN
GRADES 7–9
FANTASY

Jason McCormack, who is blind, releases an evil spirit that has been trapped in a cave. Jason's seeing-eye dog, Erroll, tries to protect Jason from the danger.

1. The Evil One ◆ 1991
2. The Dark ◆ 1991
3. Scream of the Cat ◆ 1992
4. Stranger in the Mirror ◆ 1992
5. The Spell ◆ 1992
6. Dead Man's Secret ◆ 1992
7. In the Mummy's Tomb ◆ 1992
8. The Headless Ghost ◆ 1992
9. Curse of the Claw ◆ 1993

PHILIP HALL

Greene, Bette

DIAL, HARPERCOLLINS

GRADES 4–7

REAL LIFE

Beth Lambert lives in a small town in Arkansas. She and her girl-friends are in a group called the Pretty Penny Club. But her best friend is a boy, Philip Hall. This series shows the experiences of African American children living in rural settings.

1. Philip Hall Likes Me, I Reckon Maybe ◆ 1974
2. Get On Out of Here, Philip Hall ◆ 1981
3. I've Already Forgotten Your Name, Philip Hall ◆ 2004

PINE HOLLOW *see* Saddle Club: Pine Hollow

PIT DRAGON TRILOGY

Yolen, Jane

HARCOURT

GRADES 6–8 ◆ A/R

ADVENTURE | FANTASY

On a distant planet, a thousand years in the future, fighting pit drag-ons provide the basis for a people's way of life. Jakkin Stewart gains his freedom by training his dragon, Heart's Blood, to win in the pits. Along the way, he gains the respect and love of Akki and crusades for the destiny of his planet, Austar IV.

1. Dragon's Blood ◆ 1982
2. Heart's Blood ◆ 1984
3. A Sending of Dragons ◆ 1987

PLATT FAMILY

Levitin, Sonia
ATHENEUM
GRADES 6–9
FAMILY LIFE | HISTORICAL | REAL LIFE

In 1938, the Platts—a Jewish family—escape from Nazi Germany. Their goal is to reach America but the journey is filled with separations, uncertainty, and danger. Once they arrive in America in the 1940s, they must adjust to different customs and traditions.

1. Journey to America ◆ 1986
2. Silver Days ◆ 1992
3. Annie's Promise ◆ 1996

POPULAR

Krulik, Nancy
HYPERION
GRADES 7–10
REAL LIFE

A group of high school students and their ups and downs are the focus here. In one book, Sugar and Josh use a hidden camera to spy on the girls. What they hear is honest and surprising. These books connect with a television series that had a brief broadcast period.

1. Round One ◆ 2000
2. Boys! Boys! Boys! ◆ 2000
3. From the Mouths of Babes ◆ 2000
4. Wherefore Art Thou . . . Josh? ◆ 2001

PRAIRIE LEGACY

Oke, Janette
BETHANY HOUSE
GRADES 9–12 ◆ A/R
REAL LIFE | VALUES

Virginia Simpson is eager to be on her own. Of course, her faith and her family are important to her, but she wants to make her own choices. She begins to spend time with a new friend who encourages her to disobey her family. When a boy drowns, Virginia must face her own role in the tragedy. The series follows Virginia through her graduation from high school and, later, her marriage. Oke's Love Comes Softly series for adults describes the lives of Virginia's grandparents on the prairie.

1. The Tender Years ◆ 1997
2. A Searching Heart ◆ 1998
3. A Quiet Strength ◆ 1999
4. Like Gold Refined ◆ 2000

PRAIRIE RIVER

Gregory, Kristiana

SCHOLASTIC

GRADES 4–7 ◆ A/R

HISTORICAL | REAL LIFE

After Nessa Clemens, 14, runs away from the orphanage, she travels to Prairie River, Kansas. Against her wishes, she had been engaged to marry an older man. In Prairie River, she finds work as a schoolteacher and hopes to escape her past. In the third book, a man arrives who knows about her past. Nessa hopes the information will not cause the townspeople to turn against her.

1. A Journey of Faith ◆ 2003
2. A Grateful Harvest ◆ 2003
3. Winter Tidings ◆ 2004

PRINCE TRILOGY *see* Sword of the Spirits

PRINCESS DIARIES

Cabot, Meg

HARPERCOLLINS

GRADES 7–10 ◆ A/R

HUMOR

Mia Thermopolis is in ninth grade when her father reveals a secret. He is the prince of Genovia . . . and Mia is the crown princess! In addition to tackling the usual teenage problems and pining for a relationship with Michael, she must prepare her for her future responsibilities. This series has been made into movies and there are many other related materials including a calendar and stationery. Two companion books give girls tips about what it takes to be a princess: *Perfect Princess* and *Princess Lessons*.

1. The Princess Diaries ◆ 2000
2. Princess in the Spotlight ◆ 2001
3. Princess in Love ◆ 2003
4. Princess in Waiting ◆ 2003
5. The Princess Project ◆ 2003
6. Princess in Pink ◆ 2004
7. The Princess Present ◆ 2004

PRISCILLA HUTCHINS

McDevitt, Jack
HARPERCOLLINS
GRADES 9–12
SCIENCE FICTION

Priscilla Hutchins, a starship pilot, and archaeologist Richard Wald travel to a distant planet to examine its potential for colonization and the mysterious ruins found there. Priscilla's adventures continue in the books that follow. She investigates alien signals in *Chindi* and struggles to prevent the destruction of a planet in *Deepsix*.

1. The Engines of God ◆ 1994
2. Deepsix ◆ 2001
3. Chindi ◆ 2002
4. Omega ◆ 2003

PROBABILITY

Kress, Nancy
TOR
GRADES 10–12
SCIENCE FICTION

In the far future, humans can travel across the universe. In *Probability Moon*, members of a "research" expedition to an alien planet must hide their real intent—finding a weapon against the Fallers. The conflict with the Fallers continues in the next two books.

1. Probability Moon ◆ 2000

2. Probability Sun ◆ 2001
3. Probability Space ◆ 2002

PROMISE OF ZION

Elmer, Robert
BETHANY HOUSE
GRADES 6–9 ◆ A/R
HISTORICAL

Dov Zalinski has survived World War II but fears his parents perished in the concentration camps. His parents had hoped to migrate to Palestine and Dov now begins the dangerous journey across war-ravaged countries. With Emily Parkinson, the daughter of a British major, Dov reaches Palestine and the two become involved in the political turmoil there.

1. Promise Breaker ◆ 2000
2. Peace Rebel ◆ 2001
3. Refugee Treasure ◆ 2001
4. Brother Enemy ◆ 2001
5. Freedom Trap ◆ 2002
6. True Betrayer ◆ 2002

PROTECTOR OF THE SMALL

Pierce, Tamora
RANDOM HOUSE
GRADES 5–8 ◆ A/R
FANTASY

Keladry of Mindelan, 10, is training to be a page, an opportunity that has only been available to males. As a girl, she faces special challenges. She succeeds and wins the respect of the other pages. At age 18, Kel becomes a knight and is given an assignment to help save her homeland, Tortall.

1. First Test ◆ 1999
2. Page ◆ 2000
3. Squire ◆ 2001
4. Lady Night ◆ 2002

PROWLERS

Golden, Christopher

SIMON & SCHUSTER

GRADES 8–12

HORROR

Jack Dwyer, 19, searches for the Prowlers—werewolves that killed his best friend, Artie. With Molly Hatcher, Jack goes after the pack. Jack and Molly and their friends are aided at times by those in Ghostland, including Artie. Their efforts are hampered by the Prowlers' ability to appear as humans.

1. Prowlers ◆ 2001
2. Laws of Nature ◆ 2001
3. Predator and Prey ◆ 2001
4. Wild Things ◆ 2002

PRYDAIN CHRONICLES

Alexander, Lloyd

DELL

GRADES 5–8

FANTASY

Taran, a foundling who has no known parents, is Assistant Pig-Keeper for Hen Wen, an oracular pig who is kept in a safe, quiet place by Dallben the wizard. The country is Prydain, a fantasy land loosely based on Welsh legends. Taran dreams of adventure and longs to serve with Gwydion, a warrior of the House of Don. When Hen Wen runs away, Taran gives chase and runs into the warrior's life of which he dreamed. He meets a young enchantress named Eilonwy, and the two of them and many other friends fight against the Death Lord, who would enslave the whole land. They are finally victorious, and the House of Don decides to go to a perfect land. When Taran is invited to go with them, he decides instead to stay and take his rightful place as High King of Prydain. The *High King* won the Newbery Award. A volume of short stories about Prydain, *The Foundling, and Other Tales of Prydain* was published in 1973.

1. The Book of Three ◆ 1964
2. The Black Cauldron ◆ 1965
3. The Castle of Llyr ◆ 1966
4. Taran Wanderer ◆ 1967
5. The High King ◆ 1968

PSION

Vinge, Joan D.
WARNER
GRADES 9–12
SCIENCE FICTION

In a distant future, a slum child named Cat learns to use his telepathic powers. The government then exploits him, setting him against ruthless enemies. The sequels are more violent than the first book in the series and may be suitable only for older teens.

1. Psion ◆ 1982
2. Catspaw ◆ 1988
3. Dreamfall ◆ 1996

PURE DEAD MAGIC

Gliori, Debi
KNOPF
GRADES 5–8
FANTASY

In a Scottish castle, the Strega-Borgia children are in danger. Their father has been kidnapped and their new nanny is unusual. In the second book, their castle, StregaSchloss is being repaired and Titus, 12, Pandora, 10, and baby Damp have to move. Like the Unfortunate Events books (Snicket) and Eddie Dickens (Ardagh), this series is dark and humorous.

1. Pure Dead Magic ◆ 2001
2. Pure Dead Wicked ◆ 2002
3. Pure Dead Brilliant ◆ 2003

PYRATES

Archer, Chris
SCHOLASTIC
GRADES 5–7 ◆ A/R
FANTASY

George has always wondered about his family's heritage. Is he really descended from the famous pirate Captain Kidd? When George and his friends discover tunnels and an underground city, they face curses and creatures seeking to protect the buried treasure.

1. Secret City ◆ 2003
2. Eye of Eternity ◆ 2003
3. Dead Man's Chest ◆ 2003
4. Last Clue ◆ 2003

QUILT TRILOGY

Rinaldi, Ann
SCHOLASTIC
GRADES 6–9
FAMILY LIFE | HISTORICAL

Hannah's life has always been focused on her family. She cared for her siblings after the death of their mother. Now her siblings are older and her father is home from his sea voyages. Hannah begins to think about her future. This trilogy spans several generations of strong female characters.

1. A Stitch in Time ◆ 1994
2. Broken Days ◆ 1995
3. The Blue Door ◆ 1996

RAISE THE FLAG

Rue, Nancy N.
WATERBROOK PRESS
GRADES 7–10
REAL LIFE | VALUES

Six girls at King High School in Reno, Nevada, gather each day for prayer meetings. They are known as the "Flagpole girls." Tobey, a preacher's child, takes the leadership role. The teens confront serious problems such as Shannon's anorexia and a teacher's sexual abuse of Angelica. The girls' Christian values guide their decisions.

1. Don't Count on Homecoming Queen ◆ 1998
2. "B" Is for Bad at Getting Into Harvard ◆ 1998
3. I Only Binge on Holy Hungers ◆ 1998
4. Do I Have to Paint You a Picture ◆ 1998
5. Friends Don't Let Friends Date Jason ◆ 1999
6. When Is Perfect, Perfect Enough? ◆ 1999

RAMA

Clarke, Arthur C.

BANTAM

GRADES 10–12 ◆ A/R

SCIENCE FICTION

In 2130, a strange object enters our solar system. The crew sent to investigate finds a hollow cylindrical vessel that appears to have been made by intelligent life. In *Rama II*, a similar space ship arrives and three explorers remain on it when it leaves. *The Garden of Rama* records the 13 years the three humans spend on the space ship. The second and third books were written by Clarke and Gentry Lee. The first book won the Hugo, Nebula, and Campbell awards.

1. Rendezvous with Rama ◆ 1973
2. Rama II ◆ 1989
3. The Garden of Rama ◆ 1991
4. Rama Revealed ◆ 1993

RATHA QUARTET

Bell, Clare E.

SIMON & SCHUSTER

GRADES 7–12

ANIMAL FANTASY

Ratha, the leader of an intelligent tribe of prehistoric cats, deals with physical and emotional challenges, including the reappearance of a daughter she tried to kill, in this series of thoughtful novels.

1. Ratha's Creature ◆ 1983
2. Clan Ground ◆ 1984
3. Ratha and Thistle-Chaser ◆ 1990
4. Ratha's Challenge ◆ 1994

RAVENSCLIFF

Huntington, Geoffrey

REGAN BOOKS

GRADES 7–10 ◆ A/R

FANTASY

Devon March, 14, realizes that he has special powers and he knows that there are evil forces lurking around him, hoping to drag him into their Hellhole. Devon goes to live in a mansion, Ravenscliff. There he learns that he is a sorcerer of the Order of the Nightwing. Even at Ravenscliff the demons pursue him. Devon discovers that there is a Hellhole controlled by the Madman and that the mansion is built right over it.

1. Sorcerers of the Nightwing ◆ 2002
2. Demon Witch ◆ 2003

THE REAL DEAL

Kaye, Amy
SMOOCH
GRADES 7–10 ◆ A/R
REAL LIFE

Claire's successful appearance on a reality television show about high school has led to a spin-off show. Now the cameras will focus on her as she appears in a Broadway musical. It's exciting and stressful, putting a strain on Claire's relationship with her newly discovered older half-sister Tina (a secret from her father's past). It also endangers Claire's budding romance with Jeb, another member of the production.

1. Focus on This ◆ 2003
2. Unscripted ◆ 2004

RECLUCE

Modesitt, L. E.
TOR
GRADES 10–12
FANTASY

Good and evil. Order and chaos. Recluce is a land that has achieved perfect order. Lerris has the chance to become an order-master but he must accept responsibility and prove his devotion to order. While he strives to reach his destiny, Lerris must escape the forces of the evil wizard Antonin. The saga of Recluce spans generations. *The Towers of the Sunset* is a prequel and describes the island kingdom.

1. The Magic of Recluce ◆ 1991
2. The Towers of the Sunset ◆ 1993
3. The Magic Engineer ◆ 1995
4. The Order War ◆ 1996
5. The Death of Chaos ◆ 1996

6. Fall of Angels ◆ 1997
7. The Chaos Balance ◆ 1998
8. The White Order ◆ 1999
9. Colors of Chaos ◆ 2000
10. Magi'i of Cyador ◆ 2001
11. Scion of Cyador ◆ 2001
12. Wellspring of Chaos ◆ 2004

RED RIVER: RED RIVER OF THE NORTH

Snelling, Lauraine
BETHANY HOUSE
GRADES 9–12 ◆ A/R
REAL LIFE | VALUES

The Bjorklund family has left Norway and settled in the Dakota Territory. Life there is a struggle. Their prairie homestead is isolated and the climate is harsh. This series follows the hardships of the family, the expanding settlement, and the arrival of other family members and friends. Faith and the support of God are important elements in this series.

1. An Untamed Land ◆ 1996
2. A New Day Rising ◆ 1996
3. A Land to Call Home ◆ 1997
4. The Reapers' Song ◆ 1998
5. Tender Mercies ◆ 1999
6. A Blessing in Disguise ◆ 1999

RED RIVER: RETURN TO RED RIVER

Snelling, Lauraine
BETHANY HOUSE
GRADES 9–12 ◆ A/R
REAL LIFE | VALUES

Thorliff Bjorklund is at college studying writing. Back home, his relationship with Anji is crumbling. As the series progresses, Thorliff gets a job with a newspaper but he returns home when a disaster strikes. As in the earlier series, Red River of the North, faith and the support of God are important elements.

1. A Dream to Follow ◆ 2001
2. Believing the Dream ◆ 2002
3. More than a Dream ◆ 2003

REDWALL

Jacques, Brian

PHILOMEL

GRADES 4–8 ◆ **A/R**

ADVENTURE | ANIMAL FANTASY

Redwall Abbey is the focal point for the mice and other creatures who live in Mossflower Woods. In the first book, *Redwall,* an army of rats tries to conquer the abbey and the defending mice must find the lost sword of Martin the Warrior to save themselves and their beloved abbey. Subsequent titles introduce a changing cast of heroes, heroines, and evildoers who interact in an epic saga full of conspiracies, adventures and heroics. *The Great Redwall Feast* is a colorfully illustrated companion book directed toward a younger audience about the secret preparations by the Redwall creatures for a feast in honor of the Abbott. *A Redwall Winter's Tale* is another picture book directed at younger readers. The books can also be read following events in chronological order: *Lord Brocktree, Martin The Warrior, Mossflower, The Legend of Luke, Outcast of Redwall, Mariel of Redwall, The Bellmaker, Salamandastron, Redwall, Mattimeo, The Pearls of Lutra, The Long Patrol, Marlfox, The Taggerung, Triss, Loamhedge,* and *Rakkety Tam.*

1. Redwall ◆ 1986
2. Mossflower ◆ 1988
3. Mattimeo ◆ 1989
4. Mariel of Redwall ◆ 1991
5. Salamandastron ◆ 1992
6. Martin the Warrior ◆ 1993
7. The Bellmaker ◆ 1994
8. Outcast of Redwall ◆ 1995
9. The Pearls of Lutra ◆ 1996
10. The Long Patrol ◆ 1997
11. Marlfox ◆ 1998
12. The Legend of Luke ◆ 1999
13. Lord Brocktree ◆ 2000
14. The Taggerung ◆ 2001
15. Triss ◆ 2002
16. Loamhedge ◆ 2003
17. Rakkety Tam ◆ 2004

REGENERATION

Singleton, Linda Joy

BERKLEY

GRADES 8–10

SCIENCE FICTION

Five teens have been cloned in an experiment. Now the scientist in charge of the experiment has decided that it is a failure and the clones should die. In this series, the teens try to survive.

1. Regeneration ◆ 2000
2. The Search ◆ 2000
3. The Truth ◆ 2000
4. The Imposter ◆ 2000
5. The Killer ◆ 2001

REMNANTS

Applegate, K. A.
SCHOLASTIC
GRADES 5–9 ◆ A/R
SCIENCE FICTION

It is 2011. Earth will soon be gone, destroyed by a collision with an asteroid. A group of people are brought together and launched into space in a tube. They travel for 500 years and awake in a strange world. There are complex adventures as the survivors face dangers from the new environment and from each other.

1. The Mayflower Project ◆ 2001
2. Destination Unknown ◆ 2001
3. Then ◆ 2001
4. Nowhere Land ◆ 2002
5. Mutation ◆ 2002
6. Breakdown ◆ 2002
7. Isolation ◆ 2002
8. Mother, May I? ◆ 2002
9. No Place like Home ◆ 2002
10. Lost and Found ◆ 2002
11. Dream Storm ◆ 2003
12. Aftermath ◆ 2003
13. Survival ◆ 2003
14. Begin Again ◆ 2003

REPLICA

Kaye, Marilyn
BANTAM
GRADES 6–9 ◆ A/R
SCIENCE FICTION

Amy Candler, 12, is working on an autobiography assignment. Her mother is vague about her family's history so Amy digs deeper. She then discovers that she is one of 13 clones—all named Amy. The project that created her now wants to control her and the other Amys.

1. Amy, Number Seven ◆ 1998
2. Pursuing Amy ◆ 1999
3. Another Amy ◆ 1999
4. Perfect Girls ◆ 1999
5. Secret Clique ◆ 1999
6. And the Two Shall Meet ◆ 1999
7. The Best of the Best ◆ 1999
8. Mystery Mother ◆ 1999
9. The Fever ◆ 2000
10. Ice Cold ◆ 2000
11. Lucky Thirteen ◆ 2000
12. In Search of Andy ◆ 2000
13. The Substitute ◆ 2000
14. The Beginning ◆ 2000
15. Transformation ◆ 2000
16. Happy Birthday, Dear Amy ◆ 2001
17. Missing Pieces ◆ 2001
18. Return of the Perfect Girls ◆ 2001
19. Dreamcrusher ◆ 2001
20. Like Father, Like Son ◆ 2001
21. Virtual Amy ◆ 2001
22. All About Andy ◆ 2002
23. The War of the Clones ◆ 2002
24. Amy, On Her Own ◆ 2002

REPLICA: THE PLAGUE TRILOGY

Kaye, Marilyn
BANTAM
GRADES 6–9
SCIENCE FICTION

When a plague threatens the present, Amy journeys back in time to find a way to control the disease. When she returns to the present, she is injected into an infected human to investigate the infectious bacteria up close. The final book takes Amy on an adventure in the future.

1. Rewind ◆ 2002
2. Play ◆ 2002
3. Fast Forward ◆ 2002

RICHARD STEELE TRILOGY

Cann, Kate

SIMON & SCHUSTER

GRADES 9–12

REAL LIFE

Richard Steele is pleased when he gets a job as a graphic designer. He hopes his new prosperity will make him more attractive to Portia. In the second book, his friend Bonny moves into his apartment, and in the third, Rich realizes Bonny has grown very important to him. Fans of British series such as the Confessions of Georgia Nicolson will particularly enjoy this.

1. Hard Cash ◆ 2003
2. Shacked Up ◆ 2004
3. Speeding ◆ 2004

RIVERWORLD SAGA

Farmer, Philip José

BALLANTINE

GRADES 10–12

SCIENCE FICTION

All the humans who ever lived find themselves resurrected and living on the banks of a giant river. But why? Efforts to find out form the center of the series as a motley crew of characters, ranging from Mark Twain to Sir Richard Burton to Genghis Khan, explore their world and its origins. Confrontations erupt as characters from different eras come together and disagree.

1. To Your Scattered Bodies Go ◆ 1971
2. The Fabulous Riverboat ◆ 1971
3. The Dark Design ◆ 1977
4. The Magic Labyrinth ◆ 1980
5. Gods of Riverworld ◆ 1983
6. River of Eternity ◆ 1983

ROMA SUB ROSA

Saylor, Steven
ST. MARTIN'S
GRADES 10–12
HISTORICAL | MYSTERY

Gordianus the Finder is a detective in Rome in the first century b.c. He must investigate within the conspiracies and intrigues of Roman society. In one book, he looks into the murder of a woman who knew too many secrets. In another, he searches for his son, Meto. This series combines historical information with exciting mysteries.

1. Roman Blood ◆ 1991
2. Arms of Nemesis ◆ 1992
3. Catalina's Riddle ◆ 1993
4. The Venus Throw ◆ 1996
5. A Murder on the Appian Way ◆ 1996
6. The House of the Vestals ◆ 1997
7. Rubicon ◆ 1999
8. Last Seen in Massilia ◆ 2000
9. A Mist of Prophecies ◆ 2002
10. The Judgment of Caesar ◆ 2004

ROOKIES

Freeman, Mark
BALLANTINE
GRADES 7–10 ◆ A/R
RECREATION

Major league scouts visit the Rosemont Rockets baseball players. Glen "Scrapper" Mitchell goes to play in Chicago. Dave "DT" Green becomes a rookie power hitter for Boston. Roberto "Magic" Ramirez pitches for Los Angeles. As the series ends, DT and Magic face each other in the World Series.

1. Play Ball! ◆ 1989
2. Squeeze Play ◆ 1989
3. Spring Training ◆ 1989
4. Big-League Break ◆ 1989
5. Play-Off Pressure ◆ 1989
6. Series Showdown ◆ 1989

ROOSEVELT HIGH SCHOOL

Velasquez, Gloria
PIÑATA
GRADES 9–12 ◆ A/R
FAMILY LIFE | REAL LIFE

The problems of students at Roosevelt High School in Laguna, California, are featured in this series. Maya copes with her parents' divorce. African American Ankiza begins to date Hunter, who is white. She must deal with the disapproval of her friends and family. In *Teen Angel*, Celia, 15, becomes pregnant and realizes that Nicky is no longer interested in her. The students seek guidance from the school counselor, Dr. Sandra Martinez.

1. Juanita Fights the School Board ◆ 1994
2. Maya's Divided World ◆ 1995
3. Tommy Stands Alone ◆ 1997
4. Rina's Family Secret ◆ 1998
5. Ankiza ◆ 2001
6. Teen Angel ◆ 2003

ROSWELL HIGH

Metz, Melinda
POCKET BOOKS
GRADES 7–10 ◆ A/R
SCIENCE FICTION

Max, Isabel, and Michael have a secret. They are aliens, hatched from pods following the crash of their space ship in Roswell, New Mexico. Now they are attending Roswell High and trying to fit in. But as they interact with other teens, their secret may be discovered.

1. The Outsider ◆ 1999
2. The Wild One ◆ 1999
3. The Seeker ◆ 2000
4. The Watcher ◆ 2000
5. The Intruder ◆ 2000
6. The Stowaway ◆ 2000
7. The Vanished ◆ 2000
8. The Rebel ◆ 2000
9. The Dark One ◆ 2000
10. The Salvation ◆ 2000

NEW ROSWELL SERIES

1. No Good Deed (Smith, Dean Wesley, and Kristine K. Rusch) ◆ 2001
2. Loose Ends (Fox, Greg) ◆ 2001
3. Shades (Odom, Mel) ◆ 2002
4. Skeletons in the Closet (Mangels, Andy) ◆ 2002
5. Dreamwalk (Ruditis, Paul) ◆ 2002
6. Little Green Men (Smith, Dean Wesley, and Kristine K. Rusch) ◆ 2002
7. Quarantine (Burns, Laura J.) ◆ 2003
8. A New Beginning (Ryan, Kevin, and Jason Katims) ◆ 2003
9. Nightscape (Ryan, Kevin, and Jason Katims) ◆ 2003
10. Pursuit (Mangels, Andy, and Michael A. Martin) ◆ 2003
11. Turnabout (Mangels, Andy, and Michael A. Martin) ◆ 2003

ROWAN HOOD

Springer, Nancy
PHILOMEL; PUTNAM
GRADES 6–9 ◆ A/R
ADVENTURE | FANTASY

In the first book, 13-year-old Rosemary sets off on a search of her father, Robin Hood. She disguises herself as a boy and adopts the name of Rowan. Subsequent novels feature young people who join Rowan's band and have adventures and support each other through problems. In *Lion Claw*, Lionel learns to stand up to his father, Lord Lionclaw. In *Outlaw Princess of Sherwood*, a young girl seeking to avoid an arranged marriage hides in the forest.

1. Rowan Hood: Outlaw Girl of Sherwood Forest ◆ 2001
2. Lion Claw: A Tale of Rowan Hood ◆ 2002
3. Outlaw Princess of Sherwood: A Tale of Rowan Hood ◆ 2003
4. Wild Boy: A Tale of Rowan Hood ◆ 2004

ROXY GIRLS *see* Luna Bay

ROYAL DIARIES

Various authors
SCHOLASTIC
GRADES 3–7 ◆ A/R
HISTORICAL

Readers are introduced to different eras in history through these fictionalized diaries. Each book features events from the childhood or adolescence of a famous female. The books include historical notes, documents, maps, genealogy, and illustrations. Fans of Dear America would gain a new perspective on world history from these books.

1. Cleopatra: Daughter of the Nile, Egypt, 57 B.C. (Gregory, Kristiana) ◆ 1999
2. Elizabeth I: Red Rose of the House of Tudor, England, 1544 (Lasky, Kathryn) ◆ 1999
3. Marie Antoinette: Princess of Versailles, Austria-France, 1769 (Lasky, Kathryn) ◆ 2000
4. Isabel: Jewel of Castilla, Spain, 1466 (Meyer, Carolyn) ◆ 2000
5. Nzingha: Warrior Queen of Matamba, Angola, Africa, 1595 (McKissack, Patricia C.) ◆ 2000
6. Anastasia: The Last Grand Duchess, Russia, 1914 (Meyer, Carolyn) ◆ 2000
7. Kaiulani: The People's Princess, Hawaii, 1889 (White, Ellen Emerson) ◆ 2001
8. Lady of Ch'iao Kuo: Warrior of the South, Southern China, A.D. 531 (Yep, Laurence) ◆ 2001
9. Victoria: May Blossom of Britannia, England, 1829 (Kirwan, Anna) ◆ 2001
10. Mary: Queen of Scots, Queen Without a Country, France 1553 (Lasky, Kathryn) ◆ 2002
11. Sondok: Princess of the Moon and Stars, Korea, A.D. 595 (Holman, Sheri) ◆ 2002
12. Jahanara: Princess of Princesses, India, 1627 (Lasky, Kathryn) ◆ 2002
13. Eleanor: Crown Jewel of Aquitaine, France, 1136 (Lasky, Kathryn) ◆ 2002
14. Elisabeth: The Princess Bride, Austria-Hungary, 1853 (Denenberg, Barry) ◆ 2003
15. Kristina: The Girl King, Sweden, 1638 (Meyer, Carolyn) ◆ 2003
16. Weetamoo: Heart of the Pocassets, Massachusetts, 1653 (Smith, Patricia Clark) ◆ 2003
17. Lady of Palenque: Flower of Bacal, Mesoamerica, A.D. 749 (Kirwan, Anna) ◆ 2004
18. Kazunomiya: Prisoner of Heaven, Japan, 1858 (Lasky, Kathryn) ◆ 2004

ROYAL PAVILIONS

Chaikin, Linda
BETHANY HOUSE
GRADES 9–12
HISTORICAL

In the time of the crusades, Tancred Redwan is a rebel who rescues Helena, a courageous Byzantine heiress. Once restored to her family,

Helena is to marry a Muslim prince. Tancred again comes to her aid, taking her to his family's castle.

1. Swords and Scimitars ◆ 1996
2. Golden Palaces ◆ 1996
3. Behind the Veil ◆ 1998

RUIN MIST: THE KINGDOMS AND THE ELVES OF THE REACHES

Stanek, Robert

REAGENT PRESS

GRADES 6–9

FANTASY

Adrina is a princess whose kingdom is threatened; Seth is a warrior elf on a journey to the land of Man; Vilmos is a boy with a magical future. Keeper Martin, head of the Lore Keepers, chronicles the adventures of these three heroes. In one book, they prevent the end of the Kingdom Alliance and they save Quashan'. The events in this series are from Stanek's fantasy series for adults, Ruin Mist Chronicles.

1. Keeper Martin's Tales, Book 1 ◆ 2002
2. Keeper Martin's Tales, Book 2 ◆ 2002
3. Keeper Martin's Tales, Book 3 ◆ 2002
4. Keeper Martin's Tales, Book 4 ◆ 2003

RUIN MIST CHRONICLES

Stanek, Robert

REAGENT PRESS

GRADES 9–12

FANTASY

After the war, the kingdoms were divided. Darkness has fallen over the mortal world. The kings have proclaimed that all magic must be destroyed so that the world can be restored. Princess Adrina must fight for her kingdom while Vilmos studies to be a mage. This series is for adults and older teens and has been reissued in a series for a younger readers, Ruin Mist: The Kingdoms of the Elves and the Reaches.

1. Keeper Martin's Tale ◆ 2002
2. Elf Queen's Quest ◆ 2002
3. Kingdom Alliance ◆ 2003

RUIN MIST TALES

1. The Elf Queen and the King, Book 1 ◆ 2002
2. The Elf Queen and the King, Book 2 ◆ 2002

SADDLE CLUB: PINE HOLLOW

Bryant, Bonnie
BANTAM
GRADES 6–8 ◆ A/R
REAL LIFE

The friends from the Saddle Club series are now in high school. Stevie, Lisa, and Carole are busy with their individual activities as they begin dating, driving, and working. They still love horses and enjoy being together at Pine Hollow stables. The events in this series are more serious. For example, Stevie is involved in an accident that seriously injures another girl, Callie. Several books deal with Callie's injuries, anger, and recovery. Fans of books about horses, school, and boys will want to read this series.

1. The Long Ride ◆ 1998
2. The Trail Home ◆ 1998
3. Reining In ◆ 1998
4. Changing Leads ◆ 1999
5. Conformation Faults ◆ 1999
6. Shying at Trouble ◆ 1999
7. Penalty Points ◆ 1999
8. Course of Action ◆ 1999
9. Riding to Win ◆ 1999
10. Ground Training ◆ 2000
11. Cross-Ties ◆ 2000
12. Back in the Saddle ◆ 2000
13. High Stakes ◆ 2000
14. Headstrong ◆ 2000
15. Setting the Pace ◆ 2000
16. Track Record ◆ 2001
17. Full Gallop ◆ 2001

SAGA OF THE SKOLIAN EMPIRE

Asaro, Catherine
TOR
GRADES 10–12
SCIENCE FICTION

Romance and science fiction are intertwined in this series set in the distant future with side trips to an alternate contemporary Earth. The Skolian Empire and the Traders are longstanding rivals. The Skolians have telepathic abilities and the Traders derive pleasure from pain. In the first book, Soz, a potential leader of the Skolian Empire, meets and falls in love with the Trader heir. Soz faces difficult decisions about the future of her people. Other books feature different characters and interstellar intrigues. *The Quantum Rose* won the Nebula Award for Best Novel.

1. Primary Inversion ◆ 1995
2. Catch the Lightning ◆ 1996
3. The Last Hawk ◆ 1997
4. The Radiant Seas ◆ 1998
5. Ascendant Sun ◆ 2000
6. The Quantum Rose ◆ 2000
7. Spherical Harmonic ◆ 2001
8. Skyfall ◆ 2003

THE SAGAS OF DARREN SHAN *see* Cirque du Freak

SALLY LOCKHART TRILOGY

Pullman, Philip
KNOPF
GRADES 9–12
HISTORICAL | MYSTERY

Sally Lockhart, 16, lives in London during the Victorian era. Her first mystery is to find out who killed her father and why. She encounters many characters from the darker side of London. As the mystery evolves, Sally's search for a missing ruby places her in great danger. *The Tin Princess* (1994) is a related book that features characters from the Sally Lockhart trilogy.

1. The Ruby in the Smoke ◆ 1985
2. The Shadow in the North ◆ 1988
3. The Tiger in the Well ◆ 1990

SAM GRIBLEY *see* My Side of the Mountain

SAMMY KEYES

Van Draanen, Wendelin
KNOPF
GRADES 5–8 ◆ A/R
MYSTERY

Sammy Keyes is in seventh grade. She lives with her grandmother in an apartment. While playing with some binoculars, she observes a thief at work. Unfortunately, the thief sees her, too. Now she has real problems. Other books have mysteries at Halloween and Christmas. In one book, she helps her actress mother when she is suspected of murdering a rival for an acting part.

1. Sammy Keyes and the Hotel Thief ◆ 1998
2. Sammy Keyes and the Skeleton Man ◆ 1998
3. Sammy Keyes and the Sisters of Mercy ◆ 1999
4. Sammy Keyes and the Runaway Elf ◆ 1999
5. Sammy Keyes and the Curse of Moustache Mary ◆ 2000
6. Sammy Keyes and the Hollywood Mummy ◆ 2001
7. Sammy Keyes and the Search for Snake Eyes ◆ 2002
8. Sammy Keyes and the Art of Deception ◆ 2003
9. Sammy Keyes and the Psycho Kitty Queen ◆ 2004

SAMURAI CAT

Rogers, Mark E.
TOR; INFINITY
GRADES 10–12
ANIMAL FANTASY

Puns and satire fill these highly illustrated stories about Miaowara Tomokato and his sidekick Shiro, felines who will take on anyone— from King Arthur and his knights to Genghis Khan to characters from science fiction.

1. The Adventures of Samurai Cat ◆ 1984
2. More Adventures of Samurai Cat ◆ 1986
3. Samurai Cat in the Real World ◆ 1989
4. Samurai Cat Goes to the Movies ◆ 1994
5. Samurai Cat Goes to Hell ◆ 1998
6. Sword of the Samurai Cat ◆ 2003

SAMURAI GIRL

Asai, Carrie
SIMON & SCHUSTER
GRADES 6–10 ◆ A/R
FANTASY

As a baby, Heaven was adopted by the Kogo family whose patriarch is a Japanese crime boss. Now, at age 17, she is to be married to the son of a colleague of her adoptive father so that two Japanese families come together. Her wedding is interrupted by a man claiming to be her brother. Heaven watches as he is brutally murdered. She escapes from her family and studies to be a samurai, hoping to find her true identity and avenge her brother's death.

1. The Book of the Sword ◆ 2003
2. The Book of the Shadow ◆ 2003
3. The Book of the Pearl ◆ 2003
4. The Book of the Wind ◆ 2003
5. The Book of the Flame ◆ 2004
6. The Book of the Heart ◆ 2004

SANDY LANE STABLES

Various authors
EDC PUBLISHING
GRADES 5–8 ◆ A/R
REAL LIFE

Horses and riding are featured in this series that includes show jumping, competitions, and horses being mistreated. The series was originally published in Britain.

1. A Horse for the Summer (Bates, Michelle) ◆ 1996
2. The Runaway Pony (Leigh, Susannah) ◆ 1996
3. Strangers at the Stables (Bates, Michelle) ◆ 1996
4. The Midnight Horse (Bates, Michelle) ◆ 1998
5. Dream Pony (Leigh, Susannah) ◆ 1998
6. Ride by Moonlight (Bates, Michelle) ◆ 1998
7. Horse in Danger (Bates, Michelle) ◆ 1998
8. The Perfect Pony (Bates, Michelle) ◆ 1999
9. Racing Vacation (Bates, Michelle) ◆ 2000

SARAH'S JOURNEY

Luttrell, Wanda

CHARIOT VICTOR PUBLISHING
GRADES 10–12 ◆ A/R
HISTORICAL | VALUES

Sarah is 12 at the start of this series and the Revolutionary War is beginning. With her family, she moves from Kentucky to Williamsburg, but there is hardship as her brother leaves to fight against the British. Eventually, Sarah returns to Kentucky to open a school in a rural area. Throughout her struggles, she asks God for guidance.

1. Home on Stoney Creek ◆ 1995
2. Stranger in Williamsburg ◆ 1995
3. Reunion in Kentucky ◆ 1995
4. Whispers in Williamsburg ◆ 1997
5. Shadows on Stoney Creek ◆ 1997

SAVED BY THE BELL

Cruise, Beth

ALADDIN
GRADES 6–8 ◆ A/R
ADVENTURE

Different characters appear in the books in this series, which is linked to the television program of the same name. Some of the books feature original characters of the television show; others introduce new classmates. The focus throughout the books is on conflicts that will be familiar to teens—dating, grades, responsibilities, romance, and even social and political issues. These books will appeal especially to teenage girls.

1. Bayside Madness ◆ 1992
2. Zack Strikes Back ◆ 1992
3. California Scheming ◆ 1992
4. Girls' Night Out ◆ 1992
5. Zack's Last Scam ◆ 1992
6. Class Trip Chaos ◆ 1992
7. That Old Zack Magic ◆ 1993
8. Impeach Screech! ◆ 1993

9. One Wild Weekend ◆ 1993
10. Kelly's Hero ◆ 1993
11. Don't Tell a Soul ◆ 1994
12. Computer Confusion ◆ 1994
13. Silver Spurs ◆ 1994
14. Best Friend's Girl ◆ 1994
15. Zack in Action ◆ 1994
16. Operation: Clean Sweep ◆ 1994
17. Scene One, Take Two ◆ 1995
18. Fireside Manners ◆ 1995
19. Picture Perfect ◆ 1995
20. Surf's Up ◆ 1995
21. Screech in Love ◆ 1995
22. Ex-Zack-Ly ◆ 1995
23. Standing Room Only ◆ 1996

SAVED BY THE BELL: THE NEW CLASS

1. Trouble Ahead ◆ 1994
2. Spilling the Beans ◆ 1994
3. Going, Going, Gone! ◆ 1995
4. Breaking the Rules ◆ 1995
5. Spreading the Word ◆ 1995
6. Lights, Camera, Action! ◆ 1995
7. May the Best Team Win ◆ 1995
8. It's the Thought That Counts ◆ 1995
9. Finders, Keepers ◆ 1995
10. Franken-Bobby! ◆ 1995

SAVED BY THE BELL: THE COLLEGE YEARS

1. Freshman Frenzy ◆ 1994
2. Zack Zeroes In ◆ 1994
3. Exit, Stage Right ◆ 1994
4. Mistletoe Magic ◆ 1994

SEAFORT SAGA

Feintuch, David
ASPECT
GRADES 9–12
SCIENCE FICTION

This military science fiction saga follows the exploits of Nicholas Seafort. His colonial adventures take him across the stars as he serves as captain, then commander, and even Secretary General—the global executive of Earth. He faces intergalactic dangers and is involved in numerous battles. In his later years, he is the commandant of the

Naval Academy, where he must prepare young cadets to face alien invaders.

1. Midshipman's Hope ◆ 1994
2. Prisoner's Hope ◆ 1995
3. Challenger's Hope ◆ 1995
4. Fisherman's Hope ◆ 1996
5. Voices of Hope ◆ 1996
6. Patriarch's Hope ◆ 2000
7. Children of Hope ◆ 2001

SEBASTIAN BARTH

Howe, James
AVON
GRADES 5–7
MYSTERY

Sebastian Barth lives in rural Connecticut, where he has a weekly radio show. He becomes involved in solving mysteries as he looks for scoops for the show. He is friends with Alex, the police chief, who helps him out. In *Dew Drop Dead*, he and his friends Corrie and David befriend a homeless man when Corrie's father, a minister, begins a ministry to the homeless. At the same time, the children find a body in an abandoned inn. Clues seem to point to the homeless man, but police work determines that the man died of exposure and the confused homeless man hid the body. Other mysteries are about poisoning in the school cafeteria, and a famous actress in danger.

1. What Eric Knew ◆ 1985
2. Stage Fright ◆ 1986
3. Eat Your Poison, Dear ◆ 1986
4. Dew Drop Dead ◆ 1990

SECRET CIRCLE

Smith, L. J.
HARPERCOLLINS
GRADES 7–10
FANTASY

Cassie joins a coven of young witches in the town of New Salem and endangers everyone when she seeks to attract Adam, the coven leader. In *The Captive*, there is a struggle for power within the coven, and in *The Power*, good and evil battle each other.

1. The Initiation ◆ 1992
2. The Captive ◆ 1992
3. The Power ◆ 1992

THE SECRET COUNTRY TRILOGY

Dean, Pamela
PENGUIN
GRADES 7–10
FANTASY

For years, five cousins have played a game called "The Secret." It is a game they created involving witches, unicorns, magical events, and another world. Then their game becomes a reality. They are in the Secret Country and to save this magical place they must face three challenges. These books were originally published in the 1980s and have been reissued.

1. The Secret Country ◆ 2003
2. The Hidden Land ◆ 2003
3. The Whim of the Dragon ◆ 2003

SECRET REFUGE

Snelling, Lauraine
BETHANY HOUSE
GRADES 9–12 ◆ A/R
FAMILY LIFE | HISTORICAL | VALUES

On her family's plantation in Kentucky, Jesselynn Highwood is preparing to escape the dangers of the Civil War. With her younger brother and the family's Thoroughbred horses, she begins a journey to Missouri. Her sister, Louisa, is involved in smuggling supplies to a hospital in Richmond, Virginia. Strong family values are woven into this historical fiction series.

1. Daughter of Twin Oaks ◆ 2000
2. Sisters of the Confederacy ◆ 2000
3. The Long Way Home ◆ 2001

SECRET TEXTS

Lisle, Holly
WARNER
GRADES 11–12
FANTASY

This complex and fast-paced series features Kait Galweigh, a young diplomat who has a dark secret. If she and her companions can destroy the Mirror of Souls, they may save the people they care for.

1. Diplomacy of Wolves ◆ 1998
2. Vengeance of Dragons ◆ 1999
3. Courage of Falcons ◆ 2000

SECRET WORLD OF ALEX MACK

Various authors
MINSTREL/POCKET BOOKS
GRADES 5–8
ADVENTURE | FANTASY

Alex Mack was just an ordinary teenager until she was drenched with a strange chemical. Now she can move objects with her mind and change shapes by morphing into a liquid form. Alex and her friends—Ray Alvarado, Robyn Russo, Nicole Wilson, and boyfriend Hunter Reeves—get involved in adventures such as capturing a pet-napping ring. Alex also has to worry about keeping her special powers a secret; especially when she gets sick on a trip to New York and can't control her ability to become liquid. Readers who like the popular Nickelodeon television program will enjoy following the familiar characters in these adventures.

1. Alex, You're Glowing! (Gallagher, Diana G.) ◆ 1995
2. Bet You Can't! (Gallagher, Diana G.) ◆ 1995
3. Bad News Babysitting! (Lipman, Ken) ◆ 1995
4. Witch Hunt! (Gallagher, Diana G.) ◆ 1995
5. Mistaken Identity! (Gallagher, Diana G.) ◆ 1996
6. Cleanup Catastrophe! (Dubowski, Cathy East) ◆ 1996
7. Take a Hike! (Dubowski, Cathy East) ◆ 1996
8. Go for the Gold! (Gallagher, Diana G.) ◆ 1996
9. Poison in Paradise! (Gallagher, Diana G.) ◆ 1996

10. Zappy Holidays! (Super Edition) (Gallagher, Diana G.) ◆ 1996
11. Junkyard Jitters! (Barnes-Svarney, Patricia) ◆ 1997
12. Frozen Stiff! (Gallagher, Diana G.) ◆ 1997
13. I Spy! (Peel, John) ◆ 1997
14. High Flyer! (Barnes-Svarney, Patricia) ◆ 1997
15. Milady Alex! (Gallagher, Diana G.) ◆ 1997
16. Father-Daughter Disaster! (Emery, Clayton) ◆ 1997
17. Bonjour, Alex! (Dubowski, Cathy East) ◆ 1997
18. Close Encounters! (Weiss, David Cody, and Bobbi J. G. Weiss) ◆ 1997
19. Hocus Pocus! (Locke, Joseph) ◆ 1997
20. Halloween Invaders! (Vornholt, John) ◆ 1997
21. Truth Trap! (Dubowski, Cathy East) ◆ 1997
22. New Year's Revolution! (Gallagher, Diana G.) ◆ 1997
23. Lost in Vegas! (Peel, John) ◆ 1998
24. Computer Crunch! (Barnes-Svarney, Patricia) ◆ 1998
25. In Hot Pursuit! (Odom, Mel) ◆ 1998
26. Canine Caper! (Gallagher, Diana G.) ◆ 1998
27. Civil War in Paradise! (Stone, Bonnie D.) ◆ 1998
28. Pool Party Panic! (Mitchell, V. E.) ◆ 1998
29. Sink or Swim! (Dubowski, Cathy East) ◆ 1998
30. Gold Rush Fever! (Gallagher, Diana G.) ◆ 1998
31. New York Nightmare! (Pass, Erica) ◆ 1998
32. Haunted House Hijinks! (Vornholt, John) ◆ 1998
33. Lights Camera Action (Garton, Ray) ◆ 1998
34. Paradise Lost, Paradise Regained! (Gallagher, Diana G.) ◆ 1998

A SERIES OF UNFORTUNATE EVENTS

Snicket, Lemony
HARPERCOLLINS
GRADES 3–7 ◆ A/R
FANTASY

The lives of the Baudelaire children are full of woe. Their parents perished in a fire, leaving Violet, Klaus, and Sunny at the mercy of the villainous Count Olaf. Just when you think they may find happiness, it is snatched away. The books in this droll series include many side comments and dire predictions. Continue reading them at your own peril. There are related items including boxed sets of books, posters, puzzles, postcards, calendars, and *Lemony Snicket: The Unauthorized Autobiography*. A film has been optioned based on this series.

1. The Bad Beginning: Book the First ◆ 1999
2. The Reptile Room: Book the Second ◆ 1999
3. The Wide Window: Book the Third ◆ 2000

4. The Miserable Mill: Book the Fourth ◆ 2000
5. The Austere Academy: Book the Fifth ◆ 2000
6. The Ersatz Elevator: Book the Sixth ◆ 2001
7. The Vile Village: Book the Seventh ◆ 2001
8. The Hostile Hospital: Book the Eighth ◆ 2001
9. The Carnivorous Carnival: Book the Ninth ◆ 2002
10. The Slippery Slope: Book the Tenth ◆ 2003
11. The Grim Grotto: Book the Eleventh ◆ 2004

SEVENS

Wallens, Scott
PUFFIN
GRADES 6–12 ◆ **A/R**
REAL LIFE

Seven teens have problems ranging from life in a wheelchair to homosexuality to an obsession with good grades. These seven were all involved in a terrible experience in their pasts. This suspenseful series, which takes place over the course of seven weeks, introduces each character and his or her problems, building to a cliff-hanger ending.

1. Shattered: Week 1 ◆ 2002
2. Exposed: Week 2 ◆ 2002
3. Pushed: Week 3 ◆ 2002
4. Meltdown: Week 4 ◆ 2002
5. Torn: Week 5 ◆ 2002
6. Betrayal: Week 6 ◆ 2002
7. Redemption: Week 7 ◆ 2002

7TH HEAVEN

Various authors
RANDOM HOUSE
GRADES 4–7
FAMILY LIFE | VALUES

The Camden family—characters from the popular television series—have further adventures in these books. Readers will enjoy more stories about Rev. and Mrs. Camden and their children and their friends. In one book, Ruthie wins a trip to Hollywood. In another, Lucy and Mary have a survival adventure in New York City. Family values and a commitment to faith infuse these novels. There are related items including a scrapbook and background information about the cast.

1. Nobody's Perfect (Christie, Amanda) ◆ 1999
2. Mary's Story (Christie, Amanda) ◆ 1999
3. Matt's Story (Christie, Amanda) ◆ 1999
4. Middle Sister (Clark, Catherine) ◆ 2000
5. Mr. Nice Guy (Christie, Amanda) ◆ 2000
6. Rivals (Cerasini, Marc) ◆ 2000
7. The Perfect Plan (Christie, Amanda) ◆ 2000
8. Secrets (Christie, Amanda) ◆ 2000
9. The New Me (Christie, Amanda) ◆ 2000
10. Sister Trouble (Christie, Amanda) ◆ 2001
11. Learning the Ropes (Thomas, Jim) ◆ 2001
12. Drive You Crazy (Cerasini, Marc) ◆ 2001
13. Camp Camden (Christie, Amanda) ◆ 2001
14. Lucy's Angel (Christie, Amanda) ◆ 2001
15. Winter Ball (Christie, Amanda) ◆ 2002
16. Dude Ranch (Christie, Amanda) ◆ 2002
17. Sisters Through the Seasons (Christie, Amanda, and Marc Cerasini) ◆ 2002
18. Mary's Rescue (Christie, Amanda) ◆ 2003
19. Wedding Memories (Christie, Amanda) ◆ 2004
20. The East-West Contest (Christie, Amanda) ◆ 2004

THE SEVENTH TOWER

Nix, Garth
SCHOLASTIC
GRADES 6–9 ◆ A/R
FANTASY

Tal lives among the Chosen in the Dark World. He needs a sunstone to maintain his status. When he fails to steal one, he is expelled to the world of the Underfolk. There he joins the rebels and, with Milla, participates in a struggle to combat the evil forces.

1. The Fall ◆ 2000
2. Castle ◆ 2000
3. Aenir ◆ 2001
4. Above the Veil ◆ 2001
5. Into Battle ◆ 2001
6. The Violet Keystone ◆ 2001

SEVENWATERS

Marillier, Juliet

TOR

GRADES 10–12

FANTASY

In the first installment of this fantasy trilogy based on Celtic legend, Sorcha must rescue her six brothers from a spell cast by a sorceress. Evil is again in evidence in the *Son of the Shadows*, which features Sorcha's daughter Liadan, who has the power to heal.

1. Daughter of the Forest ◆ 2000
2. Son of the Shadows ◆ 2001
3. Child of the Prophecy ◆ 2002

SHADOW CHILDREN

Haddix, Margaret Peterson

SIMON & SCHUSTER

GRADES 5–8 ◆ A/R

FANTASY | SCIENCE FICTION

Luke, 12, is a third child in a future society that allows only two children. He must remain hidden. His family is victimized by "the Barons," the elite group of their society. Luke discovers a secret in the Baron house next door—another "shadow child." The series follows Luke and other third-born children as they struggle with being outcasts.

1. Among the Hidden ◆ 1998
2. Among the Imposters ◆ 2001
3. Among the Betrayed ◆ 2003
4. Among the Barons ◆ 2003
5. Among the Brave ◆ 2004
6. Among the Enemy ◆ 2005

SHADOW CLUB

Shusterman, Neal
PENGUIN
GRADES 8–12 ◆ A/R
REAL LIFE

Jared, Cheryl, and their friends are doing well at school and sports but they are not "the best." They form the Shadow Club to get revenge on the top students and jocks who have been arrogant and condescending. Their tricks begin as embarrassing pranks but quickly become more dangerous. Tyson, a creepy student on the outside, is suspected of torments; the club members beat him up only to discover the real culprit. In the second book, Jared is 15 and is trying to rebuild his reputation.

1. The Shadow Club ◆ 2002
2. The Shadow Club Rising ◆ 2003

SHADOWMANCER

Taylor, G. P.
PUTNAM
GRADES 7–12
FANTASY

Beginning in an English village in the 1500s, the focus is on Obadiah Demurral, a vicar who has embraced the dark world of evil. His skills as a sorcerer allow him to be a Shadowmancer. He can speak to the dead and he can command them to act. Two children, Thomas and Kate, are drawn into his dark world. The evil continues in 1756 as a star called Wormwood is destined to destroy the world. An archangel appears in both books to cast out the demons and bring salvation. This is a complex, dark, violent fantasy with mythic overtones.

1. Shadowmancer ◆ 2004
2. Wormwood ◆ 2004

THE SHAKESPEARE STEALER

Blackwood, Gary L.
DUTTON
GRADES 5–8
HISTORICAL

In London in 1601, Widge is a 14-year-old orphan boy whose master sends him to steal an unpublished play—Hamlet. Instead of stealing the manuscript, Widge becomes an acting apprentice. He has many adventures with Shakespeare's company of actors.

1. The Shakespeare Stealer ◆ 1998
2. Shakespeare's Scribe ◆ 2000
3. Shakespeare's Spy ◆ 2003

SHANNARA

Brooks, Terry

BALLANTINE

GRADES 10–12 ◆ A/R

FANTASY

The Druid Allanon needs Brin Ohmsford's skill with the magical wishsong. The Ildatch, an ancient source of evil, is protected by dense dangerous plants but Brin's wishsong can tame them. There are many classic fantasy elements in this trilogy including magic, creatures, quests, and a struggle between good and evil. This is the first Shannara series and originally was a trilogy, but an additional prequel describes some of the events that provide the foundation for the later struggles. A companion volume is *The Heritage of Shannara* (2001), written by Brooks and Teresa Patterson.

1. The Sword of Shannara ◆ 1977
2. The Elfstones of Shannara ◆ 1982
3. The Wishsong of Shannara ◆ 1985
4. First King of Shannara ◆ 1996

SHANNARA: HERITAGE OF SHANNARA

Brooks, Terry

BALLANTINE

GRADES 10–12 ◆ A/R

FANTASY

There are new threats to the Four Lands. The ghost of Druid Allanon calls for three descendants from the Ohmsfords (heroes of the first Shannara trilogy) to face the dangers from the mysterious Shadowen. A companion volume is *The Heritage of Shannara* (2001), written by Brooks and Teresa Patterson.

1. The Scions of Shannara ◆ 1990

2. The Druid of Shannara ◆ 1991
3. The Elf Queen of Shannara ◆ 1992
4. The Talismans of Shannara ◆ 1993

SHANNARA: HIGH DRUID OF SHANNARA

Brooks, Terry
BALLANTINE
GRADES 10–12 ◆ A/R
FANTASY

In the face of great danger, Penderrin Ohmsford embarks on a quest for the limb of a tree that holds the key to his imprisoned aunt's freedom and the chance of peace in the Four Lands.

1. Jarka Ruus ◆ 2003
2. Tanequil ◆ 2004

SHANNARA: THE SWORD OF SHANNARA

Brooks, Terry
BALLANTINE
GRADES 6–12 ◆ A/R
FANTASY

The three books in this "series" are really just the first Shannara book published in three installments to be accessible to younger readers. A companion volume is *The Heritage of Shannara* (2001), written by Brooks and Teresa Patterson.

1. The Secret of the Sword ◆ 2003
2. The Druid's Keep ◆ 2003
3. In the Shadow of the Warlock ◆ 2003

SHANNARA: THE VOYAGE OF THE JERLE SHANNARA

Brooks, Terry
BALLANTINE
GRADES 10–12 ◆ A/R
FANTASY

The Shannara adventures continue. Walker Boh is the last Druid. He leads a group which includes elves, Rovers, shapeshifters, and other creatures, against Antrax, an evil artificial intelligence. Once Antrax is defeated, the group faces new challenges, including the death of Walker Boh.

1. Ilse Witch ◆ 2000
2. Antrax Sky ◆ 2001
3. Morgawr ◆ 2002

SHOPAHOLIC

Kinsella, Sophie
DELTA; DIAL
GRADES 10–12
REAL LIFE

Rebecca Bloomwood, 25, has it all. Clothes, a wonderful flat (this series is from Britain), a great career, and a HUGE pile of bills. She is attracted to Luke Brandon, who is very rich, but she knows she must control her spending and debt in order to have a chance with him. In true romantic fiction style, Becky gets Luke, loses Luke and her job, gets a job at Barneys, marries Luke, and shops some more. This is an adult series that teen girls have discovered and list among their favorites.

1. Confessions of a Shopaholic ◆ 2001
2. Shopaholic Takes Manhattan ◆ 2002
3. Shopaholic Ties the Knot ◆ 2003
4. Shopaholic and Sister ◆ 2004

SIERRA JENSEN

Gunn, Robin Jones
FOCUS ON THE FAMILY, BETHANY HOUSE
GRADES 6–8 ◆ A/R
FAMILY LIFE | VALUES

Sierra lives with her sister Tawni, two younger brothers, and their parents and grandmother. Theirs is an upper-middle-class lifestyle, and Sierra is a casual teenager with a natural approach to life. This puts her in conflict with Tawni, whom Sierra believes always acts as if she is on display. On a mission trip to England, Sierra makes friends with some older teens and meets an interesting boy. He is much older but she eventually dates him.

1. Only You—Sierra ◆ 1995
2. In Your Dreams ◆ 1996
3. Don't You Wish ◆ 1996
4. Close Your Eyes ◆ 1996
5. Without a Doubt ◆ 1997
6. With This Ring ◆ 1997
7. Open Your Heart ◆ 1997
8. Time Will Tell ◆ 1998
9. Now Picture This ◆ 1998
10. Hold on Tight ◆ 1998
11. Closer Than Ever ◆ 1999
12. Take My Hand ◆ 1999

SIGMUND BROUWER'S SPORTS MYSTERY *see* Sports Mystery

SILVER CREEK RIDERS

Kincaid, Beth
JOVE BOOKS
GRADES 6–8
REAL LIFE | RECREATION

Four friends—Melissa, Jenna, Katie, and Sharon—all love horses. After they meet at the Silver Creek riding camp, they find ways to keep in touch and help each other. At camp, they help Melissa as she learns to deal with a tragic accident and her fear of riding again. In another book, Katie meets Matt and it looks like love—except that Katie is attracted to Matt's horse (at first). During the Autumn Horse Show, Melissa helps a horse that is being mistreated. The audience for these books is primarily horse-crazy girls, who will also enjoy the Saddle Club books.

1. Back in the Saddle ◆ 1994
2. True Romance ◆ 1994
3. Winning ◆ 1995

SISTERHOOD OF THE TRAVELING PANTS

Brashares, Ann
DELACORTE
GRADES 6–9
REAL LIFE

Four friends—Lena, Tibby, Bridget, and Carmen—are upset about spending the summer vacation apart. A pair of jeans that Carmen bought at a secondhand store turns out to be the way the girls stay in touch. They take turns wearing the pants (no one keeps them more than one week) and they each write about their adventures with the pants. There are ten rules governing the pants, ending with "Pants-love. Love your pals. Love yourself."

1. The Sisterhood of the Traveling Pants ◆ 2001
2. The Second Summer of the Sisterhood ◆ 2003
3. Girls in Pants: The Third Summer of the Sisterhood ◆ 2005

SISTERS

Kaye, Marilyn
GULLIVER BOOKS / HARCOURT BRACE JOVANOVICH
GRADES 6–8
FAMILY LIFE | REAL LIFE

Each book in this series is devoted to one of the four Gray sisters, each of whom has a very distinct personality. Lydia, the baby of the family, is a dreamer and content being a child; Daphne is the sensitive poet; Cassie is the self-centered beauty; Lydia, the eldest at 14, is a leader who is always taking on an important cause. Readers may find that they relate strongly to one of the sisters or maybe to individual qualities of each girl. While the individual stories stand on their own, reading the series provides the reader with a stronger sense of the individual personalities that make up a family.

1. Phoebe ◆ 1987
2. Daphne ◆ 1987
3. Cassie ◆ 1987
4. Lydia ◆ 1987
5. A Friend like Phoebe ◆ 1989

THE SIXTH SENSE: SECRETS FROM BEYOND

Benjamin, David
SCHOLASTIC
GRADES 5–7
FANTASY

Cole Sear has special powers. He sees and can communicate with the dead. There are secrets that the dead want Cole to share. These secrets will help solve mysteries surrounding their deaths. The popularity of the movie adds to the interest in these books.

1. Survivor ◆ 2000
2. Runaway ◆ 2001
3. Hangman ◆ 2001

SLAPSHOTS

Korman, Gordon
SCHOLASTIC
GRADES 5–8 ◆ A/R
RECREATION

Hockey action is featured in this series. The Stars from Mars face a variety of opponents including the dreaded Oilers. Will the Stars win the trophy cup?

1. The Stars from Mars ◆ 1999
2. All-Mars All-Stars ◆ 1999
3. The Face-Off Phony ◆ 2000
4. Cup Crazy ◆ 2000

SLAYERS

Kanzaka, Hajime
TOKYOPOP
GRADES 7–10
FANTASY

This series of books takes the popular Slayers manga comic series and expands the adventure. In one volume, Lina, a teenage sorceress, finds some stolen money and decides to keep some of it . . . actually, most of it. The people who stole the money are not amused. In another book, Lina and Gourry fight a magical battle in Atlas City. Each book includes several full-color manga illustration pages and many black-and-white pages, too.

1. Volume 1 ◆ 2004
2. Volume 2 ◆ 2004
3. Volume 3 ◆ 2005

SLIMEBALLS

Gross, U. B.
RANDOM HOUSE
GRADES 5–7
HUMOR

Two of the books in this series feature Gus, his friend Polly, and the class dullard Ray. Gus plans to win the science fair with his collection of unusual molds. The books are full of gross humor and weird characters. A wacko school nurse is fired and returns in another book as a crazed bus driver. The characters often behave in ways that will appeal to the middle school sense of humor—food fights, slime attacks, and rodents that take over a home.

1. Fun Gus and Polly Pus ◆ 1996
2. Fun Gus Slimes the Bus ◆ 1997
3. The Slithers Buy a Boa ◆ 1997

SMALLVILLE

Various authors
LITTLE, BROWN
GRADES 7–10
FANTASY

Smallville is the hometown of Clark Kent. This book series (and the television series) describe his life as a teenager. He does mundane things, like helping Lana Lang with the high school play. He also faces sinister circumstances and individuals, such as a being that kills by taking your breath away. There is another series of Smallville books for adults.

1. Arrival (Teitelbaum, Michael) ◆ 2002
2. See No Evil (Bennett, Cherie, and Jeff Gottesfeld) ◆ 2002
3. Flight (Bennett, Cherie, and Jeff Gottesfeld) ◆ 2002
4. Animal Rage (Weiss, David Cody, and Bobbi J. G. Weiss) ◆ 2003
5. Speed (Bennett, Cherie, and Jeff Gottesfeld) ◆ 2003
6. Buried Secrets (Colon, Suzan) ◆ 2003
7. Runaway (Colon, Suzan) ◆ 2003
8. Greed (Bennett, Cherie, and Jeff Gottesfeld) ◆ 2003
9. Temptation (Colon, Suzan) ◆ 2004
10. Sparks (Bennett, Cherie, and Jeff Gottesfeld) ◆ 2004

SO LITTLE TIME *see* Mary-Kate and Ashley: So Little Time

SOCK MONKEY

Millionaire, Tony

DARK HORSE

GRADES 6–12

FANTASY

Sock Monkey came from the jungles of Borneo. Now he lives in Massachusetts with a little girl named Ann-Louise. His presence brings both delight and fear. These books may be enjoyed by a younger audience, although some reviewers place them with YAs.

1. The Adventures of Tony Millionaire's Sock Monkey ◆ 2000
2. Sock Monkey: A Children's Book ◆ 2001
3. Sock Monkey: The Glass Doorknob ◆ 2002
4. Sock Monkey: Uncle Gabby ◆ 2004

SONG OF THE LIONESS QUARTET

Pierce, Tamora

ATHENEUM

GRADES 6–9 ◆ A/R

FANTASY

Alanna, 11, disguises herself as a boy to become a page and, later, a knight. She is a strong and skillful warrior who serves Prince Jonathan (who knows her secret). Her magical powers help protect the Prince from the evil sorcerer. Originally published in the 1980s, this series was reissued in the 1990s. The Immortals is set in the same world. *Trickster's Choice* (2003) is the first book in the Lioness Quartet, about Alanna's daughter, Alianne.

1. Alanna: The First Adventure ◆ 1983
2. In the Hand of the Goddess ◆ 1984
3. The Woman Who Rides Like a Man ◆ 1986
4. Lioness Rampant ◆ 1988

SOOKAN BAK

Choi, Sook Nyul
HOUGHTON MIFFLIN
GRADES 5–8
FAMILY LIFE | HISTORICAL

In the first book of this trilogy, *Year of Impossible Goodbyes*, Sookan Bak is ten. It is the 1940s and she and her family are enduring the occupation of their homeland in northern Korea. When the country is divided at the end of the war, the family emigrates to the south, hoping for a better life. *Echoes of the White Giraffe* describes Sookan's life in Pusan and her growing friendship with Junho, a boy she knows from the church choir. In the final book, Sookan is in college in the United States, where she is challenged by a new language, a different culture, and the death of her mother.

1. Year of Impossible Goodbyes ◆ 1991
2. Echoes of the White Giraffe ◆ 1993
3. Gathering of Pearls ◆ 1994

SPACE ABOVE AND BEYOND

Various authors
HARPERCOLLINS
GRADES 5–8
SCIENCE FICTION

In 2063, an Earth space station has been destroyed by aliens and now Earth is in danger. Lieutenants Vansen, West, and Hawke are thrown together to accomplish a dangerous mission and face the Artificial Intelligence (AI) creatures. There are encounters on Mars, a mutiny in space, and an electromagnetic lightning storm. Fans of Star Trek and Deep Space Nine will enjoy these books.

1. The Aliens Approach (Royce, Easton) ◆ 1996
2. Dark Side of the Sun (Anastasio, Dina) ◆ 1996
3. Mutiny (Royce, Easton) ◆ 1996
4. The Enemy (Anastasio, Dina) ◆ 1996
5. Demolition Winter (Telep, Peter) ◆ 1997

SPELL CASTERS

Warriner, Holly
ALADDIN
GRADES 5–8 ◆ A/R
FANTASY

Lucinda is a witch who is conflicted about her powers. Her evil grandmother and her sinister cousin Rafe push her to fulfill her destiny. Lucinda's friendship with Sally and her everyday school activities provide a backdrop for spells, seances, and witchcraft.

1. Witch at the Door ◆ 1998
2. Full Moon Magic ◆ 1998
3. Witches' Brew ◆ 1998
4. Julian's Jinx ◆ 1998
5. Witches on Ice ◆ 1999
6. Phoebe's Fortune ◆ 1999

THE SPELLSONG CYCLE

Modesitt, L. E.
TOR
GRADES 9–12
FANTASY

In this unusual series based on the power of music, Anna Marshall, a singer and music teacher from the Midwest, is transported to a world where songs bear the power of magic. Her talents win her a position as regent of the kingdom of Defalk. In the fourth book, Anna dies and the peace she has negotiated is threatened by Sea Priests who use magical drumming as a weapon. Anna's foster daughter and successor, Secca, must test her own powers against this new danger.

1. The Soprano Sorceress ◆ 1997
2. The Spellsong War ◆ 1998
3. Darksong Rising ◆ 1999
4. The Shadow Sorceress ◆ 2001
5. Shadowsinger ◆ 2002

SPINETINGLERS

Coffin, M. T.

AVON

GRADES 6–8

HORROR

Suppose you went to class and your teacher was a bug. When you tried to tell others about it, you realized ahat there were bugs everywhere. In fact, everyone in town is a bug. This is just one weird scenario in the Spinetingler series. There are spooky libraries (*Check It Out—and Die!*), scary schools (*Don't Go to the Principal's Office*), and spooky television (*The Monster Channel*). Bizarre creatures, zombie dogs, cursed cheerleaders, lizard people, and freaks inhabit the books, which also include cliff-hanging plot twists and breathtaking encounters. There are also humorous moments, which you would expect from an author named M. T. Coffin who claims to live in Tombstone with children named Phillip A. Coffin and Carrie A. Coffin. Fans of Goosebumps will take to these books.

1. The Substitute Creature ◆ 1995
2. Billy Baker's Dog Won't Stay Buried ◆ 1995
3. My Teacher's a Bug ◆ 1995
4. Where Have All the Parents Gone? ◆ 1995
5. Check It Out—and Die! ◆ 1995
6. Simon Says, "Croak!" ◆ 1995
7. Snow Day ◆ 1996
8. Don't Go to the Principal's Office ◆ 1996
9. Step on a Crack ◆ 1996
10. The Dead Kid Did It ◆ 1996
11. Fly by Night ◆ 1996
12. Killer Computer ◆ 1996
13. Pet Store ◆ 1996
14. Blood Red Eightball ◆ 1996
15. Escape from the Haunted Mountain ◆ 1996
16. We Wish You a Scary Christmas ◆ 1996
17. The Monster Channel ◆ 1997
18. Mirror, Mirror ◆ 1997
19. Boogey's Back for Blood ◆ 1997
20. Lights, Camera, Die! ◆ 1997
21. Camp Crocodile ◆ 1997
22. Student Exchange ◆ 1997

23. Gimme Back My Brain ◆ 1997
24. Your Turn—to Scream! ◆ 1997
25. The Curse of the Cheerleaders ◆ 1997
26. Wear and Scare ◆ 1997
27. Lizard People ◆ 1997
28. Circus F.R.E.A.K.S. ◆ 1997
29. My Dentist Is a Vampire ◆ 1998
30. Saber-Toothed Tiger ◆ 1998

SPOOKSVILLE

Pike, Christopher
POCKET BOOKS
GRADES 5–8 ◆ A/R
HORROR

Springville seems like an ordinary town, but a closer look reveals strange things going on. Cindy Mackey finds this out when her brother Neil is kidnapped by a ghost. Adam Freeman knows things are different. One of his best friends is Watch, a creature who has returned from the dead. Cindy, Adam, Watch, and their friends Sally Wilcox and Bryce Poole confront howling ghosts, aliens, witches, wicked cats, killer crabs, vampires, and other demons as they try to survive in a very strange town. This series will be a hit with readers who enjoy Goosebumps, Fear Street, and Buffy the Vampire Slayer.

1. The Secret Path ◆ 1995
2. The Howling Ghost ◆ 1995
3. The Haunted Cave ◆ 1995
4. Aliens in the Sky ◆ 1996
5. The Cold People ◆ 1996
6. The Witch's Revenge ◆ 1996
7. The Dark Corner ◆ 1996
8. The Little People ◆ 1996
9. The Wishing Stone ◆ 1996
10. The Wicked Cat ◆ 1996
11. The Deadly Past ◆ 1996
12. The Hidden Beast ◆ 1996
13. The Creature in the Teacher ◆ 1996
14. The Evil House ◆ 1997
15. Invasion of the No-Ones ◆ 1997
16. Time Terror ◆ 1997
17. The Thing in the Closet ◆ 1997
18. Attack of the Killer Crabs ◆ 1997
19. Night of the Vampire ◆ 1997
20. The Dangerous Quest ◆ 1998

21. The Living Dead ◆ 1998
22. The Creepy Creature ◆ 1998
23. Phone Fear ◆ 1998
24. The Witch's Gift ◆ 1999

SPORTS MYSTERY

Brouwer, Sigmund
TOMMY NELSON
GRADES 9–12 ◆ A/R
MYSTERY | RECREATION

In the first book, Matt, 16, investigates the disappearance of the top scorer of his soccer team. These books have the appeal of sports action and mysteries. Soccer, football, basketball, and stock car racing are among the featured sports.

1. Maverick Mania ◆ 1998
2. Tiger Heat ◆ 1998
3. Cobra Threat ◆ 1998
4. Titan Clash ◆ 1998
5. Scarlet Thunder ◆ 1998
6. Hurricane Power ◆ 1999

SPY GIRLS

Cage, Elizabeth
POCKET BOOKS
GRADES 7–10
ADVENTURE | MYSTERY

A secret agency, the Tower, has chosen three teenage girls to be spies. Caylin, Jo, and Theresa deal with dangers including terrorist plots, a missing ballerina, an international conspiracy, and more. Teens will enjoy these hip, savvy girls who travel around the world and solve crimes.

1. License to Thrill ◆ 1998
2. Live and Let Spy ◆ 1998
3. Nobody Does It Better ◆ 1999
4. Spy Girls Are Forever ◆ 1999
5. Dial 'V' for Vengeance ◆ 1999
6. If Looks Could Kill ◆ 1999

SPY HIGH

Butcher, A. J.
LITTLE, BROWN
GRADES 9–12 ◆ A/R
ADVENTURE

Deveraux Academy is no ordinary high school. Yes, there are regular classes, but then there are also lessons in martial arts, electronic eavesdropping, and shock suits. Set in 2060, the team of six teens, called the Bond team, is trained to infiltrate evil organizations and combat terrorism.

1. Spy High Mission One ◆ 2004
2. Spy High Mission Two: Chaos Rising ◆ 2004
3. Spy High Mission Three: The Serpent Scenario ◆ 2004
4. Spy High Mission Four: The Paranoia Plot ◆ 2004

SPYBOY

Various
DARK HORSE
GRADES 6-9
ADVENTURE

Alex Fleming seems to be an ordinary teenager. He goes to high school, worries about dating and bullies, and is an international super spy. A spy!!! Yes, Alex is developing his latent talents for intrigue. He trains in the martial arts and is learning to use high-tech gadgets. Alex's ordinary life is not ordinary anymore.

1. The Deadly Gourmet Affair (David, Peter) ◆ 2001
2. Trial and Terror (David, Peter) ◆ 2001
3. Bet Your Life (David, Peter) ◆ 2001
4. Undercover, Underwear (David, Peter) ◆ 2002
5. Spy-School Confidential (David, Peter) ◆ 2003
6. The M.A.N.G.A. Affair (David, Peter, Pop Mhan, and Norman Lee)
   ◆ 2003

THE SQUIRE'S TALE *see* The Denizens of Camelot

STAR POWER

Hapka, Cathy
ALADDIN
GRADES 6–8 ◆ A/R
REAL LIFE

'Tween girls should enjoy this flashy series about a 14-year-old pop star. Fame comes quickly and easily to Star Calloway, but there are problems too. Her family has been missing for two years. Still, Star focuses on her career, her competitors, and her adoring fans.

1. Supernova ◆ 2004
2. Always Dreamin' ◆ 2004
3. Never Give Up ◆ 2004
4. Together We Can Do It ◆ 2004
5. Blast from the Past ◆ 2004
6. Someday, Some Way ◆ 2005
7. Over the Top ◆ 2005

STAR TREK: DEEP SPACE NINE

Various authors
POCKET BOOKS
GRADES 4–8 ◆ A/R
ADVENTURE | SCIENCE FICTION

Fans of the television series *Deep Space Nine* will enjoy reading adventures featuring their favorite characters. Young Jake Sisko and his Ferengi friend Nog are involved in time travel, attending Starfleet Academy's summer space camp, and even a field trip through the Worm Hole. They meet unusual creatures and are often in situations that threaten the future of the world. Jake's father, Commander Benjamin Sisko, supervises the Deep Space Nine space station with the assistance of security officer Odo and first officer Major Kira Nerys. Other characters from the show, including Miles and Keiko O'Brien and the Ferengi businessman Quark, appear in the books. There is lots of action and imaginative situations that should attract science fiction fans.

1. The Star Ghost (Strickland, Brad) ◆ 1994
2. Stowaways (Strickland, Brad) ◆ 1994
3. Prisoners of Peace (Peel, John) ◆ 1994

4. The Pet (Gilden, Mel, and Ted Pedersen) ◆ 1994
5. Arcade (Gallagher, Diana G.) ◆ 1995
6. Field Trip (Peel, John) ◆ 1995
7. Gypsy World (Pedersen, Ted, and John Peel) ◆ 1996
8. Highest Score (Antilles, Kem) ◆ 1996
9. Cardassian Imps (Gilden, Mel) ◆ 1997
10. Space Camp (Pedersen, Ted, and John Peel) ◆ 1997
11. Day of Honor: Honor Bound (Gallagher, Diana G.) ◆ 1997
12. Trapped in Time (Pedersen, Ted) ◆ 1998

STAR TREK: STARFLEET ACADEMY

Various authors
POCKET BOOKS
GRADES 4–8 ◆ A/R
ADVENTURE | SCIENCE FICTION

Many fans of science fiction series want to know everything about the characters. These fans are often so enthralled with the series that publishers and media producers provide numerous spin-offs and related activities (computer games, Web sites, conventions, and so forth). *Star Trek* fans are among the most loyal and intense. The ongoing popularity of the television series, along with every related item, is a testament to that. This series examines the early lives and training of key characters: James T. Kirk, Spock, and Leonard McCoy. Their adventures at the Starfleet Academy include escaping from space pirates and saving earthquake victims on the planet Playamar. Fans will especially enjoy *Crisis on Vulcan*, in which Spock meet young Christopher Pike (who was the captain in the *Star Trek* pilot program).

1. Crisis on Vulcan (Strickland, Brad, and Barbara Strickland) ◆ 1996
2. Aftershock (Vornholt, John) ◆ 1996
3. Cadet Kirk (Carey, Diane L.) ◆ 1996

STAR TREK: THE NEXT GENERATION: STARFLEET ACADEMY

Various authors
POCKET BOOKS
GRADES 4–8 ◆ A/R
ADVENTURE | SCIENCE FICTION

Focusing on the early years of the crew of the *U.S.S. Enterprise*, this series features the Starfleet Academy training experiences of familiar characters including Picard, Worf, Geordi, and Data. In *Deceptions*, Data participates in a research investigation of ancient ruins on the planet Arunu. When the communications system is sabotaged, Data must use his powers as an android to rescue his friends. In *Survival*, Worf and several Starfleet cadets work with a group of Klingon cadets to escape from the evil of an alien force. This series will interest fans of the television programs and movies as well as readers who like fast-paced adventures.

1. Worf's First Adventure (David, Peter) ◆ 1993
2. Line of Fire (David, Peter) ◆ 1993
3. Survival (David, Peter) ◆ 1993
4. Capture the Flag (Vornholt, John) ◆ 1994
5. Atlantis Station (Mitchell, V. E.) ◆ 1994
6. Mystery of the Missing Crew (Friedman, Michael J.) ◆ 1995
7. Secret of the Lizard People (Friedman, Michael J.) ◆ 1995
8. Starfall (Strickland, Brad, and Barbara Strickland) ◆ 1995
9. Nova Command (Strickland, Brad, and Barbara Strickland) ◆ 1995
10. Loyalties (Barnes-Svarney, Patricia) ◆ 1996
11. Crossfire (Vornholt, John) ◆ 1996
12. Breakaway (Weiss, Bobbi J. G., and David Cody Weiss) ◆ 1997
13. The Haunted Starship (Ferguson, Brad, and Kathi Ferguson) ◆ 1997
14. Deceptions (Weiss, Bobbi J. G., and David Cody Weiss) ◆ 1998

STAR TREK: VOYAGER: STARFLEET ACADEMY

Various authors

POCKET BOOKS

GRADES 4–8 ◆ A/R

ADVENTURE | SCIENCE FICTION

The *Voyager* series (on television and in these books) revolves around Kathryn Janeway, daughter of Vice Admiral Edward Janeway. At the Starfleet Academy, Kathryn wants to step out from the shadow of her successful father and establish her own credentials. These adventures put her in situations involving alien animals and an outer-space quarantine that could prove deadly. There is lots of action in these books, which should be appealing to fans of the show and of science fiction. The creatures and outer-space setting may attract reluctant readers.

1. Lifeline (Weiss, Bobbi J. G., and David Cody Weiss) ◆ 1997
2. The Chance Factor (Gallagher, Diana G., and Martin R. Burke) ◆ 1997
3. Quarantine (Barnes-Svarney, Patricia) ◆ 1997

STAR WARS: A NEW HOPE—MANGA

Lucas, George
DARK HORSE
GRADES 5–10
SCIENCE FICTION

The drawings for this series are by Hisao Tamaki. The events parallel
Episode IV, which was the original *Star Wars* movie.

1. Manga #1 ◆ 1998
2. Manga #2 ◆ 1998
3. Manga #3 ◆ 1998
4. Manga #4 ◆ 1998

STAR WARS: EPISODE I THE PHANTOM MENACE—MANGA

Lucas, George
DARK HORSE
GRADES 5–10
SCIENCE FICTION

The drawings for this series are by Kia Asamiya. The story parallels
the *Phantom Menace* film.

1. Manga #1 ◆ 1999
2. Manga #2 ◆ 2000

STAR WARS: JEDI APPRENTICE

Various authors
SCHOLASTIC
GRADES 6–8
ADVENTURE | SCIENCE FICTION

Follow the early years of Obi-Wan Kenobi. As a boy, Obi-Wan was
destined to be a farmer but the force drew him to Qui-Gon Jinn, who
might allow him to become a Padawan, a future Jedi Knight. This
series explores the relationship that develops between the two as they
travel across the universe facing the forces of evil.

1. The Rising Force (Wolverton, Dave) ◆ 1999
2. The Dark Rival (Watson, Jude) ◆ 1999
3. The Hidden Past (Watson, Jude) ◆ 1999
4. The Mark of the Crown (Watson, Jude) ◆ 1999

5. The Defenders of the Dead (Watson, Jude) ◆ 1999
6. The Uncertain Path (Watson, Jude) ◆ 2000
7. The Captive Temple (Watson, Jude) ◆ 2000
8. The Day of Reckoning (Watson, Jude) ◆ 2000
9. The Fight for Truth (Watson, Jude) ◆ 2000
10. The Shattered Peace (Watson, Jude) ◆ 2000
11. The Deadly Hunter (Watson, Jude) ◆ 2000
12. The Evil Experiment (Watson, Jude) ◆ 2001
13. The Dangerous Rescue (Watson, Jude) ◆ 2001
14. The Ties that Bind (Watson, Jude) ◆ 2001
15. The Death of Hope (Watson, Jude) ◆ 2001
16. The Call to Vengeance (Watson, Jude) ◆ 2001
17. The Only Witness (Watson, Jude) ◆ 2002
18. The Threat Within (Watson, Jude) ◆ 2002

STAR WARS: THE EMPIRE STRIKES BACK—MANGA

Lucas, George
DARK HORSE
GRADES 5–10
SCIENCE FICTION

The drawings for this series are by Toshiki Kudo. The action parallels the second *Star Wars* movie.

1. Manga # 1 ◆ 1999
2. Manga #2 ◆ 1999
3. Manga #3 ◆ 1999
4. Manga #4 ◆ 1999

STAR WARS: THE RETURN OF THE JEDI—MANGA

Lucas, George
DARK HORSE
GRADES 5–10
SCIENCE FICTION

The drawings for this series are by Shin-ichi Hiromoto. The action parallels the third *Star Wars* movie, in which Han Solo is encased in carbonite by Jabba the Hutt.

1. Manga #1 ◆ 1999
2. Manga #2 ◆ 1999
3. Manga #3 ◆ 1999
4. Manga #4 ◆ 1999

STAR WARS EPISODE 1: JOURNALS

Various authors

SCHOLASTIC

GRADES 4–8

ADVENTURE | SCIENCE FICTION

First-person journal entries reveal entertaining insight into the youths of favorite characters, with discussion of early challenges and accomplishments.

1. Anakin Skywalker (Strasser, Todd) ◆ 1999
2. Queen Amidala (Watson, Jude) ◆ 1999
3. Darth Maul (Watson, Jude) ◆ 2000

STAR WARS GALAXY OF FEAR

Whitman, John

BANTAM

GRADES 4–8 ◆ A/R

ADVENTURE | SCIENCE FICTION

Tash Arranda, 13, and her brother Zak, 12, travel through space encountering creatures and circumstances that threaten the security of space communities. In *Spore*, the two children and their Uncle Hoole visit a mining community that has released an ancient, evil force. *Clones* features a visit to a remote planet that is inhabited by familiar characters who turn out to be clones. Readers who enjoy *Star Wars* will like these adventures, many of which include appearances by characters from the movies, including Luke Skywalker and Darth Vader. These are exciting adventures with gruesome creatures that link the horror genre to science fiction.

1. Eaten Alive ◆ 1997
2. City of the Dead ◆ 1997
3. Planet Plague ◆ 1997
4. The Nightmare Machine ◆ 1997
5. Ghost of the Jedi ◆ 1997
6. Army of Terror ◆ 1997
7. The Brain Spiders ◆ 1997
8. The Swarm ◆ 1998
9. Spore ◆ 1998
10. The Doomsday Ship ◆ 1998
11. Clones ◆ 1998
12. The Hunger ◆ 1998

STAR WARS JUNIOR JEDI KNIGHTS

Various authors

BERKLEY

GRADES 4–8

ADVENTURE | SCIENCE FICTION

Anakin Solo is the youngest son of Leia Organa Solo and Han Solo. In this series, Anakin attends Luke Skywalker's Jedi Academy, where he makes friends with a child of the Sand People named Tahiri. The friends go through a rigorous training program and become involved in many exciting adventures. In one book, they search the abandoned fortress of Darth Vader for Obi-Wan Kenobi's lightsaber. In another, they travel to the distant moon of Yavin 8 and try to break the curse of the Golden Globe. Readers who enjoy science fiction, especially those who like the *Star Wars* films, will be attracted to this series. The familiar characters and exciting situations should appeal to reluctant readers.

1. The Golden Globe (Richardson, Nancy) ◆ 1995
2. Lyric's World (Richardson, Nancy) ◆ 1996
3. Promises (Richardson, Nancy) ◆ 1996
4. Anakin's Quest (Moesta, Rebecca) ◆ 1997
5. Vader's Fortress (Moesta, Rebecca) ◆ 1997
6. Kenobi's Blade (Moesta, Rebecca) ◆ 1997

STAR WARS YOUNG JEDI KNIGHTS

Anderson, Kevin J., and Rebecca Moesta

BERKLEY

GRADES 4–8

ADVENTURE | SCIENCE FICTION

Jacen and Jaina are the twin children of Han Solo and Princess Leia. They are the future of the New Republic and are being trained in the powers of the Force. In one book, the twins help Anja Gallandro, who had planned to destroy their family but has become their friend. In another, Lando Calrissian takes the twins and Anja on a vacation that turns deadly. Encounters with the Dark Side and adventures across the galaxy should attract fans of Star Wars and science fiction.

1. Heirs of the Force ◆ 1995
2. Shadow Academy ◆ 1995
3. The Lost Ones ◆ 1995
4. Lightsabers ◆ 1996
5. Darkest Knight ◆ 1996

6. Jedi Under Siege ◆ 1997
7. Shards of Alderaan ◆ 1997
8. Diversity Alliance ◆ 1997
9. Delusions of Grandeur ◆ 1997
10. Jedi Bounty ◆ 1997
11. The Emperor's Plague ◆ 1998
12. Return to Ord Mantell ◆ 1998
13. Trouble on Cloud City ◆ 1998
14. Crisis at Crystal Reef ◆ 1998

STARFLEET ACADEMY *see* Star Trek: Starfleet Academy

STARRING IN . . . *see* Mary-Kate and Ashley Starring In . . .

STERLING FAMILY

Johnston, Norma
ATHENEUM
GRADES 6–8
FAMILY LIFE | HISTORICAL

These tales about the Sterlings and the Albrights are based on stories the author heard, while growing up in New Jersey, about her relatives living in Yonkers and the Bronx at the turn of the century. The first four books center on teenager Tish Sterling and the problems she and her family are coping with: Her mother is having yet another baby, her older sister marries a man with a child from a previous marriage, her grandfather dies, and the family business is in trouble. The last two books center on a child of the next generation, Saranne Albright, who experiences problems similar to her Aunt Tish's and is particularly distracted by the antics of her troubled friend Paul Hodge. The thoughtful perspectives presented by the two girls help readers to recognize similarities between their own situations and those of girls who grew up in the early part of the last century.

1. The Keeping Days ◆ 1973
2. Glory in the Flower ◆ 1974
3. A Mustard Seed of Magic ◆ 1977
4. The Sanctuary Tree ◆ 1977
5. A Nice Girl Like You ◆ 1980
6. Myself and I ◆ 1981

STRAVAGANZA

Hoffman, Mary
BLOOMSBURY
GRADES 6–12 ◆ A/R
FANTASY

Lucien, a contemporary British boy who is undergoing chemotherapy, is transported to a city resembling 16th-century Venice, where he feels renewed, makes friends, and becomes embroiled in intrigue. In *City of Stars*, horse-loving Georgia "stravagates" to Remora (Sienna). There she finds romance and competes in the annual horse race.

1. Stravaganza: City of Masks ◆ 2002
2. Stravaganza: City of Stars ◆ 2003

SUMMER

Applegate, K. A.
SIMON & SCHUSTER
GRADES 7–10
REAL LIFE

Summer is visiting the Florida Keys from Minnesota. She is attracted to three boys with very different personalities and she remembers her boyfriend back home. She returns to Minnesota and becomes engaged to Seth, but visiting Florida again throws her right into Austin's arms. Teens will find these quick, satisfying romantic reads.

1. June Dreams ◆ 1995
2. July's Promise ◆ 1995
3. August Magic ◆ 1995
4. Sand, Surf and Secrets ◆ 1996
5. Rays, Romance and Rivalry ◆ 1996
6. Beaches, Boys and Betrayal ◆ 1996

SUMMERHILL SECRETS

Lewis, Beverly
BETHANY HOUSE
GRADES 6–8 ◆ A/R
VALUES

Merry Hanson, 13, lives in Amish country and early adventures in this series involve her Amish friend, Rachel Zook. In one book, they hide a girl who is being abused at home. Lissa stays with an Amish family and finds the strength to face her problems. Prayer, faith, and family help Merry face each new challenge.

1. Whispers Down the Lane ◆ 1994
2. Secret in the Willows ◆ 1994
3. Catch a Falling Star ◆ 1995
4. Night of the Fireflies ◆ 1995
5. A Cry in the Dark ◆ 1996
6. House of Secrets ◆ 1996
7. Echoes in the Wind ◆ 1997
8. Hide Behind the Moon ◆ 1998
9. Windows on the Hill ◆ 1999
10. Shadows Beyond the Gate ◆ 2000

SUMMIT HIGH

Tullos, Matt
BROADMAN & HOLMAN
GRADES 7–10
REAL LIFE | VALUES

Teens at Summit High find strength in their values. In one book, Justin seeks to help his friends realize the power of religion, but he is rejected. His faith in Christ sustains him. In another book, Kandi deals with racism.

1. Wrong Turn in the Fast Lane ◆ 1998
2. Processing the Computer Conspiracy ◆ 1998
3. Wild Lies and Secret Truth ◆ 1999
4. Deleting the Net Threat ◆ 1999
5. Dangerous Decisions and Hidden Choices ◆ 1999
6. Friends to the End ◆ 1999

SUNSET ISLAND

Bennett, Cherie
BERKLEY
GRADES 6–9
REAL LIFE

While working as au pairs on Sunset Island for the summer, Emma, Carrie, and Samantha find romance and adventure. Related series are Sunset After Dark and Club Sunset Island.

1. Sunset Island ◆ 1991
2. Sunset Kiss ◆ 1991
3. Sunset Dreams ◆ 1991
4. Sunset Farewell ◆ 1991
5. Sunset Reunion ◆ 1991
6. Sunset Secrets ◆ 1992
7. Sunset Heat ◆ 1992
8. Sunset Promises ◆ 1992
9. Sunset Scandal ◆ 1992
10. Sunset Whispers ◆ 1992
11. Sunset Paradise ◆ 1992
12. Sunset Surf ◆ 1993
13. Sunset Deceptions ◆ 1993
14. Sunset on the Road ◆ 1993
15. Sunset Embrace ◆ 1993
16. Sunset Wishes ◆ 1993
17. Sunset Touch ◆ 1993
18. Sunset Wedding ◆ 1993
19. Sunset Glitter ◆ 1994
20. Sunset Stranger ◆ 1994
21. Sunset Heart ◆ 1994
22. Sunset Revenge ◆ 1994
23. Sunset Sensation ◆ 1994
24. Sunset Magic ◆ 1994
25. Sunset Illusions ◆ 1994
26. Sunset Fire ◆ 1994
27. Sunset Fantasy ◆ 1994
28. Sunset Passion ◆ 1994
29. Sunset Love ◆ 1995
30. Sunset Fling ◆ 1995
31. Sunset Tears ◆ 1995
32. Sunset Spirit ◆ 1995
33. Sunset Holiday ◆ 1995
34. Sunset Forever ◆ 1997

CLUB SUNSET ISLAND

1. Too Many Boys ◆ 1994
2. Dixie's First Kiss ◆ 1994
3. Tori's Crush ◆ 1994

SUNSET AFTER DARK

1. Sunset After Dark ◆ 1993
2. Sunset After Midnight ◆ 1993
3. Sunset After Hours ◆ 1993

SURVIVAL!

Duey, Kathleen, and Karen A. Bale
ALADDIN
GRADES 5–8 ◆ A/R
ADVENTURE | HISTORICAL

The sinking of the *Titanic*, the San Francisco earthquake, the Colorado blizzard—imagine that you are there. The Survival! series places young characters in the middle of exciting, even dangerous situations. In 1850, twins Jess and Will find themselves stranded in Death Valley. In 1871, the Chicago Fire places Nate Cooper and Julie Flynn in great danger from the chaotic crowds and the spreading inferno. Dramatic events are woven into the historical context, which should attract readers who want stories with adventure and courageous characters.

1. Titanic: April 14, 1912 ◆ 1998
2. Earthquake: San Francisco, 1906 ◆ 1998
3. Blizzard: Estes Park, Colorado, 1886 ◆ 1998
4. Fire: Chicago, 1871 ◆ 1998
5. Flood: Mississippi, 1927 ◆ 1998
6. Stranded: Death Valley, Circa 1850 ◆ 1998
7. Cave-in: Pennsylvania, 1880s ◆ 1998
8. Train Wreck: Kansas, 1892 ◆ 1999
9. Hurricane: Open Seas, 1784 ◆ 1999
10. Forest Fire: Hinckley, Minnesota, 1894 ◆ 1999
11. Swamp: Bayou Teche, Louisiana, 1851 ◆ 1999

SWALLOWS AND AMAZONS

Ransome, Arthur
GODINE
GRADES 6–8
ADVENTURE

The first volume in this series introduces readers to an imaginative group of children. John, Susan, Titty, and Roger Walker are allowed to sail their small boat *Swallow* to an island and camp there without their parents. They meet up here with Nancy and Peggy Blackett, who also enjoy a large amount of freedom in their boat *Amazon*. The six youngsters become embroiled in an adventure involving a stolen book. They finally solve the crime and move onto similar nautical adventures in subsequent novels. The books have been reissued many times over the years.

1. Swallows and Amazons ◆ 1930

2. Swallowdale ◆ 1931
3. Peter Duck ◆ 1932
4. Winter Holiday ◆ 1933
5. Coot Club ◆ 1934
6. Pigeon Post ◆ 1936
7. We Didn't Mean to Go to Sea ◆ 1937
8. Secret Water ◆ 1939
9. The Big Six ◆ 1940
10. Missee Lee ◆ 1941
11. The Picts and the Martyrs ◆ 1943
12. Great Northern? ◆ 1947

SWAMPLAND TRILOGY

Martin, S. R.
SCHOLASTIC
GRADES 7–10
FANTASY

Marvin thinks the new neighbors are strange. They look like creatures from the nearby swamp . . . they are creatures from the swamp! In the third book, Marvin's brother Zac enters a terrifying world of darkness. The fast pace should appeal to reluctant readers.

1. Swampland ◆ 2000
2. Tankworld ◆ 2000
3. Endsville ◆ 2000

SWEEP

Tiernan, Cate
PENGUIN
GRADES 8–10 ◆ A/R
FANTASY

High school junior Morgan, who has always felt inferior to her friend Bree, is attracted to Cal and to his Wiccan rituals and beliefs. As the series progresses, Morgan discovers that she is in fact a hereditary witch and becomes an important member of the coven and eventually the most powerful witch of her generation, active in the battle against evil.

1. Book of Shadows ◆ 2001
2. The Coven ◆ 2001
3. Blood Witch ◆ 2001
4. Dark Magick ◆ 2001

   5. Awakening ◆ 2001
   6. Spellbound ◆ 2001
   7. The Calling ◆ 2001
   8. Changeling ◆ 2001
   9. Strife ◆ 2002
   10. Seeker ◆ 2002
   11. Legacy ◆ 2002
   12. Eclipse ◆ 2002
   13. Reckoning ◆ 2002
   14. Full Circle ◆ 2002

Sweep Super Special

   1. Night's Child ◆ 2003

Sweet Dreams

Various authors

Bantam Doubleday Dell

Grades 7–9

Real life

Teen romance is the focus of this slightly old-fashioned, long-running series that deals with themes including dating, popularity, and friendship.

   1. P.S. I Love You (Conklin, Barbara P.) ◆ 1981
   2. The Popularity Plan (Vernon, Rosemary) ◆ 1981
   3. Laurie's Song (Brand, Debra) ◆ 1981
   4. Princess Amy (Pollowitz, Melinda) ◆ 1981
   5. Little Sister (Green, Yvonne) ◆ 1981
   6. California Girl (Quin-Harkin, Janet) ◆ 1981
   7. Green Eyes (Rand, Suzanne) ◆ 1982
   8. The Thoroughbred (Campbell, Joanna) ◆ 1982
   9. Cover Girl (Green, Yvonne) ◆ 1982
   10. Love Match (Quin-Harkin, Janet) ◆ 1982
   11. The Problem with Love (Vernon, Rosemary) ◆ 1982
   12. Night of the Prom (Spector, Debra) ◆ 1982
   13. The Summer Jenny Fell in Love (Vernon, Rosemary) ◆ 1982
   14. Dance of Love (Saal, Jocelyn) ◆ 1982
   15. Thinking of You (Noble, Jeanette) ◆ 1982
   16. How Do You Say Goodbye? (Burman, Margaret) ◆ 1982
   17. Ask Annie (Rand, Suzanne) ◆ 1982
   18. Ten-Boy Summer (Quin-Harkin, Janet) ◆ 1982
   19. Love Song (Park, Anne) ◆ 1982
   20. The Popularity Summer (Vernon, Rosemary) ◆ 1982
   21. All's Fair in Love (Andrews, Jeanne) ◆ 1982
   22. Secret Identity (Campbell, Joanna) ◆ 1982

23. Falling in Love Again (Conklin, Barbara P.) ◆ 1983
24. The Trouble with Charlie (Ellen, Jaye) ◆ 1983
25. Her Secret Self (Willot, Rhondi) ◆ 1983
26. It Must Be Magic (Woodruff, Marian) ◆ 1983
27. Too Young for Love (Maravel, Gailanne) ◆ 1983
28. Trusting Hearts (Saal, Jocelyn) ◆ 1983
29. Never Love a Cowboy (Dukore, Jesse) ◆ 1983
30. Little White Lies (Fisher, Lois I.) ◆ 1983
31. Too Close for Comfort (Spector, Debra) ◆ 1983
32. Daydreamer (Quin-Harkin, Janet) ◆ 1983
33. Dear Amanda (Vernon, Rosemary) ◆ 1983
34. Country Girl (Pollowitz, Melinda) ◆ 1983
35. Forbidden Love (Woodruff, Marian) ◆ 1983
36. Summer Dreams (Conklin, Barbara P.) ◆ 1983
37. Portrait of Love (Noble, Jeanette) ◆ 1983
38. Running Mates (Saal, Jocelyn) ◆ 1983
39. First Love (Spector, Debra) ◆ 1983
40. Secrets (Aaron, Anna) ◆ 1983
41. The Truth About Me and Bobby V. (Johns, Janetta) ◆ 1983
42. The Perfect Match (Woodruff, Marian) ◆ 1983
43. Tender Loving Care (Park, Anne) ◆ 1983
44. Long Distance Love (Dukore, Jesse) ◆ 1983
45. Dream Prom (Burman, Margaret) ◆ 1983
46. On Thin Ice (Saal, Jocelyn) ◆ 1983
47. Te Amo Means I Love You (Kent, Deborah) ◆ 1983
48. Dial L for Love (Woodruff, Marian) ◆ 1983
49. Too Much to Lose (Rand, Suzanne) ◆ 1983
50. Lights, Camera, Love (Maravel, Gailanne) ◆ 1983
51. Magic Moments (Spector, Debra) ◆ 1983
52. Love Notes (Campbell, Joanna) ◆ 1983
53. Ghost of a Chance (Quin-Harkin, Janet) ◆ 1983
54. I Can't Forget You (Fisher, Lois I.) ◆ 1983
55. Spotlight on Love (Pines, Nancy) ◆ 1984
56. Campfire Nights (Cowan, Dale) ◆ 1984
57. On Her Own (Rand, Suzanne) ◆ 1984
58. Rhythm of Love (Foster, Stephanie) ◆ 1984
59. Please Say Yes (Crawford, Alice O.) ◆ 1984
60. Summer Breezes (Blake, Susan) ◆ 1984
61. Exchange of Hearts (Quin-Harkin, Janet) ◆ 1984
62. Just like the Movies (Rand, Suzanne) ◆ 1984
63. Kiss Me, Creep (Woodruff, Marian) ◆ 1984
64. Love in the Fast Lane (Vernon, Rosemary) ◆ 1984
65. The Two of Us (Quin-Harkin, Janet) ◆ 1984
66. Love Times Two (Foster, Stephanie) ◆ 1984
67. I Believe in You (Conklin, Barbara P.) ◆ 1984
68. Lovebirds (Quin-Harkin, Janet) ◆ 1984
69. Call Me Beautiful (Blair, Shannon) ◆ 1984
70. Special Someone (Fields, Terri) ◆ 1984
71. Too Many Boys (Dickenson, Celia) ◆ 1984

72. Goodbye Forever (Conklin, Barbara P.) ◆ 1984
73. Language of Love (Vernon, Rosemary) ◆ 1984
74. Don't Forget Me (Gregory, Diana) ◆ 1984
75. First Summer Love (Foster, Stephanie) ◆ 1984
76. Three Cheers for Love (Rand, Suzanne) ◆ 1984
77. Ten-Speed Summer (Kent, Deborah) ◆ 1984
78. Never Say No (Capron, Jean F.) ◆ 1984
79. Star Struck! (Blair, Shannon) ◆ 1984
80. A Shot at Love (Jarnow, Jill) ◆ 1984
81. Secret Admirer (Spector, Debra) ◆ 1984
82. Hey, Good Looking! (Polcover, Jane) ◆ 1984
83. Love by the Book (Park, Anne) ◆ 1985
84. The Last Word (Blake, Susan) ◆ 1985
85. The Boy She Left Behind (Rand, Suzanne) ◆ 1985
86. Questions of Love (Vernon, Rosemary) ◆ 1985
87. Programmed for Love (Crane, Stephen) ◆ 1985
88. Wrong Kind of Boy (Blair, Shannon) ◆ 1985
89. 101 Ways to Meet Mr. Right (Quin-Harkin, Janet) ◆ 1985
90. Two's a Crowd (Gregory, Diana) ◆ 1985
91. The Love Hunt (Green, Yvonne) ◆ 1985
92. Kiss and Tell (Blair, Shannon) ◆ 1985
93. The Great Boy Chase (Quin-Harkin, Janet) ◆ 1985
94. Second Chances (Levinson, Nancy) ◆ 1985
95. No Strings Attached (Hehl, Eileen) ◆ 1985
96. First, Last and Always (Conklin, Barbara P.) ◆ 1985
97. Dancing in the Dark (Ross, Carolyn) ◆ 1985
98. Love in the Air (Conklin, Barbara P.) ◆ 1985
99. Follow that Boy (Quin-Harkin, Janet) ◆ 1985
100. One Boy Too Many (Caudell, Marian) ◆ 1985
101. Wrong for Each Other (Quin-Harkin, Janet) ◆ 1986
102. Hearts Don't Lie (Fields, Terri) ◆ 1986
103. Cross My Heart (Gregory, Diana) ◆ 1986
104. Playing for Keeps (Stevens, Janice) ◆ 1986
105. The Perfect Boy (Hapgood, Elizabeth R.) ◆ 1986
106. Mission: Love (Makris, Kathryn) ◆ 1986
107. If You Love Me (Steiner, Barbara) ◆ 1986
108. One of the Boys (Jarnow, Jill) ◆ 1986
109. No More Boys (White, Charlotte) ◆ 1986
110. Playing Games (Hehl, Eileen) ◆ 1986
111. Stolen Kisses (Reynolds, Elizabeth) ◆ 1986
112. Listen to Your Heart (Caudell, Marian) ◆ 1986
113. Private Eyes (Winfield, Julia) ◆ 1986
114. Just the Way You Are (Boies, Janice) ◆ 1986
115. Promise Me Love (Redish, Jane) ◆ 1986
116. Heartbreak Hill (MacBain, Carol) ◆ 1986
117. The Other Me (Fields, Terri) ◆ 1986
118. Heart to Heart (Curtis, Stefanie) ◆ 1987
119. Star-Crossed Love (Cadwallader, Sharon) ◆ 1987
120. Mr. Wonderful (Michaels, Fran) ◆ 1987

121. Only Make-Believe (Winfield, Julia) ◆ 1987
122. A Song for Linda (Daley, Dee) ◆ 1987
123. Love in the Wings (Smiley, Virginia) ◆ 1987
124. More than Friends (Boies, Janice) ◆ 1987
125. Parade of Hearts (Beecham, Jahnna) ◆ 1987
126. Here's My Heart (Curtis, Stefanie) ◆ 1987
127. My Best Enemy (Quin-Harkin, Janet) ◆ 1987
128. One Boy at a Time (Fields, Terri) ◆ 1987
129. A Vote for Love (Gregory, Diana) ◆ 1987
130. Dance with Me (Beecham, Jahnna) ◆ 1987
131. Hand-Me-Down Heart (Schultz, Mary) ◆ 1987
132. Winner Takes All (Lykken, Laurie) ◆ 1987
133. Playing the Field (Hehl, Eileen) ◆ 1987
134. Past Perfect (Michaels, Fran) ◆ 1987
135. Geared for Romance (Wyeth, Sharon Dennis) ◆ 1987
136. Stand by for Love (MacBain, Carol) ◆ 1987
137. Rocky Romance (Wyeth, Sharon Dennis) ◆ 1987
138. Heart and Soul (Boies, Janice) ◆ 1987
139. The Right Combination (Beecham, Jahnna) ◆ 1987
140. Love Detour (Curtis, Stefanie) ◆ 1988
141. Winter Dreams (Conklin, Barbara P.) ◆ 1988
142. Lifeguard Summer (Jarnow, Jill) ◆ 1988
143. Crazy for You (Beecham, Jahnna) ◆ 1988
144. Priceless Love (Lykken, Laurie) ◆ 1988
145. This Time for Real (Gorman, Susan) ◆ 1988
146. Gifts from the Heart (Simbal, Joanne) ◆ 1988
147. Trust in Love (Finney, Shan) ◆ 1988
148. Riddles of Love (Baer, Judy) ◆ 1988
149. Practice Makes Perfect (Beecham, Jahnna) ◆ 1988
150. Summer Secrets (Blake, Susan) ◆ 1988
151. Fortunes of Love (Schultz, Mary) ◆ 1988
152. Cross-Country Match (Richards, Ann) ◆ 1988
153. The Perfect Catch (Lykken, Laurie) ◆ 1988
154. Love Lines (Grimes, Francis Hurley) ◆ 1988
155. The Game of Love (Gorman, Susan) ◆ 1988
156. Two Boys Too Many (Bloss, Janet Adele) ◆ 1988
157. Mr. Perfect (Curtis, Stefanie) ◆ 1988
158. Crossed Signals (Boies, Janice) ◆ 1988
159. Long Shot (Simbal, Joanne) ◆ 1988
160. Blue Ribbon Romance (Smiley, Virginia) ◆ 1988
161. My Perfect Valentine (Baker, Susan) ◆ 1988
162. Trading Hearts (Blake, Susan) ◆ 1989
163. My Dream Guy (Cassidy, Carla Bracale) ◆ 1989
164. Playing to Win (Boies, Janice) ◆ 1989
165. A Brush with Love (St. Pierre, Stephanie) ◆ 1989
166. Three's a Crowd (Dale, Allison) ◆ 1989
167. Working at Love (Baer, Judy) ◆ 1989
168. Dream Date (Cassidy, Carla Bracale) ◆ 1989
169. Golden Girl (Ballard, Jane) ◆ 1991

170. Rock 'n' Roll Sweetheart (Lykken, Laurie) ◆ 1991
171. Acting on Impulse (Wallach, Susan Jo) ◆ 1991
172. Sun Kissed (St. Pierre, Stephanie) ◆ 1991
173. Music from the Heart (Laskin, Pamela L.) ◆ 1991
174. Love on Strike (Boies, Janice) ◆ 1991
175. Puppy Love (Cassidy, Carla Bracale) ◆ 1991
176. Wrong-Way Romance (South, Sherri Cobb) ◆ 1991
177. The Truth About Love (Lykken, Laurie) ◆ 1991
178. Project Boyfriend (Pierre, Stephanie St.) ◆ 1991
179. Racing Hearts (Sloate, Susan) ◆ 1991
180. Opposites Attract (Singleton, Linda Joy) ◆ 1991
181. Time Out for Love (O'Connell, June) ◆ 1991
182. Down with Love (Cassidy, Carla Bracale) ◆ 1991
183. The Real Thing (McHugh, Elisabet) ◆ 1991
184. Too Good to Be True (Kirby, Susan) ◆ 1991
185. Focus on Love (Anson, Mandy) ◆ 1991
186. That Certain Feeling (South, Sherri Cobb) ◆ 1991
187. Fair-Weather Love (Cassidy, Carla Bracale) ◆ 1991
188. Play Me a Love Song (Headapohl, Bette) ◆ 1991
189. Cheating Heart (Lykken, Laurie) ◆ 1991
190. Almost Perfect (Singleton, Linda Joy) ◆ 1992
191. Backstage Romance (Kroeger, Kelly) ◆ 1992
192. The Cinderella Game (South, Sherri Cobb) ◆ 1992
193. Love on the Upbeat (O'Connell, June) ◆ 1992
194. Lucky in Love (Hehl, Eileen) ◆ 1992
195. Comedy of Errors (Crawford, Diane M.) ◆ 1992
196. Clashing Hearts (Jenner, Caryn) ◆ 1992
197. The News Is Love (Phelps, Lauren M.) ◆ 1992
198. Partners in Love (Kirby, Susan) ◆ 1992
199. Wings of Love (Wolfe, Anne Herron) ◆ 1992
200. Love to Spare (Singleton, Linda Joy) ◆ 1992
201. His and Hers (O'Connell, June) ◆ 1992
202. Love on Wheels (Jones, Sandy) ◆ 1993
203. Lessons in Love (Headapohl, Bette) ◆ 1993
204. Picture Perfect Romance (Cooper, J. B.) ◆ 1993
205. Cowboy Kisses (Crawford, Diane M.) ◆ 1993
206. Moonlight Melody (Watts, Alycyn) ◆ 1993
207. My Secret Heart (Kirby, Susan) ◆ 1993
208. Romance on the Run (Hastings, Catt) ◆ 1993
209. Weekend Romance (Teeters, Peggy) ◆ 1993
210. Oh, Promise Me (Lykken, Laurie) ◆ 1993
211. Dreamskate (Cash, Angela) ◆ 1993
212. Highland Hearts (Hayes, Maggie) ◆ 1994
213. Finders Keepers (Washburn, Jan) ◆ 1994
214. Don't Bet on Love (South, Sherri Cobb) ◆ 1994
215. Deep in My Heart (Singleton, Linda Joy) ◆ 1994
216. Careless Whispers (Voeller, Sydell) ◆ 1994
217. Head over Heels (Sloate, Susan) ◆ 1994

218. Face Up to Love (Danner, Nikki) ◆ 1994
219. Heartstrings (Wilson, Barbara) ◆ 1994
220. My Funny Guy (Santori, Helen) ◆ 1994
221. A Little More to Love (Erlbach, Arlene) ◆ 1994
222. Fool for Love (Jones, Sandy) ◆ 1994
223. Heartthrob (Schuler, Betty J.) ◆ 1994
224. Boyfriend Blues (Phelps, Lauren M.) ◆ 1995
225. Recipe for Love (Emburg, Kate) ◆ 1995
226. Aloha Love (Kremer, Marcie) ◆ 1995
227. Dreamboat (Singleton, Linda Joy) ◆ 1995
228. Blame It on Love (South, Sherri Cobb) ◆ 1995
229. Rich in Romance (Cash, Angela) ◆ 1995
230. Happily Ever After (Hehl, Eileen) ◆ 1995
231. Love Notes (Maxwell, Janet) ◆ 1995
232. The Love Line (Kroeger, Kelly) ◆ 1995
233. Follow Your Heart (Headapohl, Bette) ◆ 1995

SWEET DREAMS SPECIALS

1. My Secret Love (Quin-Harkin, Janet) ◆ 1986
2. A Change of Heart (Blake, Susan) ◆ 1986
3. Searching for Love (Warren, Andrea) ◆ 1986
4. Taking the Lead (Kent, Deborah) ◆ 1987
5. Never Say Goodbye (Quin-Harkin, Janet) ◆ 1987
6. A Chance to Love (Foster, Stephanie) ◆ 1988

SWEET DREAMS: ON OUR OWN

Quin-Harkin, Janet
BANTAM DOUBLEDAY DELL
GRADES 7–9
REAL LIFE

Friends Jill and Toni have finished high school and are in college in this series. In the first book, Jill must cope with a difficult roommate, the newness of life on campus, and the absence of her friend Toni. In the second book, Toni is attending the local community college. She has a rocky start but then settles into her studies, friendship, and apartment.

1. The Graduates ◆ 1986
2. The Trouble with Toni ◆ 1986
3. Out of Love ◆ 1986
4. Old Friends, New Friends ◆ 1986
5. Growing Pains ◆ 1986
6. Best Friends Forever ◆ 1986

SWEET 16

Various authors

HARPERCOLLINS

GRADES 7–10 ◆ A/R

REAL LIFE

As their sixteenth birthdays approach, teens from different areas of the country get ready to celebrate. In most cases, the unexpected happens and the characters are often caught in their own lies and deceptions. Lucy decides to develop a new persona for her new school. Julia and Maggie meet at the license bureau and decide to switch places.

1. Julia (Metz, Melinda) ◆ 2000
2. Lucy (Barondes, Jessica) ◆ 2000
3. Kari (Bray, Libba) ◆ 2000
4. Trent (Parker, Daniel) ◆ 2000
5. Marisa (Pittel, Jamie) ◆ 2000
6. Sunny and Matt (Metz, Melinda) ◆ 2000

SWEET 16 (MARY-KATE AND ASHLEY)

see Mary-Kate and Ashley Sweet 16

SWEET VALLEY HIGH

Pascal, Francine, creator

BANTAM

GRADES 7–10 ◆ A/R

REAL LIFE

This series of more than 140 titles follows the lives of popular twins Jessica and Elizabeth Wakefield. Their exploits at Sweet Valley High School in California include falling in and out of love, making and losing friends, traveling, modeling, having fun, and sometimes finding themselves in dangerous situations.

1. Double Love ◆ 1983
2. Secrets ◆ 1983
3. Playing with Fire ◆ 1983
4. Power Play ◆ 1983
5. All Night Long ◆ 1984
6. Dangerous Love ◆ 1984
7. Dear Sister ◆ 1984
8. Heartbreaker ◆ 1984
9. Racing Hearts ◆ 1984

10. Wrong Kind of Girl ◆ 1984
11. Too Good to be True ◆ 1984
12. When Love Dies ◆ 1984
13. Kidnapped! ◆ 1984
14. Deceptions ◆ 1984
15. Promises ◆ 1984
16. Rags to Riches ◆ 1985
17. Love Letters ◆ 1985
18. Head over Heels ◆ 1985
19. Showdown ◆ 1985
20. Crash Landing! ◆ 1985
21. Runaway ◆ 1985
22. Too Much in Love ◆ 1985
23. Say Goodbye ◆ 1985
24. Memories ◆ 1985
25. Nowhere to Run ◆ 1986
26. Hostage! ◆ 1986
27. Lovestruck ◆ 1986
28. Alone in the Crowd ◆ 1986
29. Bitter Rivals ◆ 1986
30. Jealous Lies ◆ 1986
31. Taking Sides ◆ 1986
32. The New Jessica ◆ 1986
33. Starting Over ◆ 1987
34. Forbidden Love ◆ 1987
35. Out of Control ◆ 1987
36. Last Chance ◆ 1987
37. Rumors ◆ 1987
38. Leaving Home ◆ 1987
39. Secret Admirer ◆ 1987
40. On the Edge ◆ 1987
41. Outcast ◆ 1987
42. Caught in the Middle ◆ 1988
43. Hard Choices ◆ 1988
44. Pretenses ◆ 1988
45. Family Secrets ◆ 1988
46. Decisions ◆ 1988
47. Troublemaker ◆ 1988
48. Slam Book Fever ◆ 1988
49. Playing for Keeps ◆ 1988
50. Out of Reach ◆ 1988
51. Against the Odds ◆ 1988
52. White Lies ◆ 1989
53. Second Chance ◆ 1989
54. Two-Boy Weekend ◆ 1989
55. Perfect Shot ◆ 1989
56. Lost at Sea ◆ 1989
57. Teacher Crush ◆ 1989
58. Broken-Hearted ◆ 1989

59. In Love Again ◆ 1989
60. That Fatal Night ◆ 1989
61. Boy Trouble ◆ 1990
62. Who's Who? ◆ 1990
63. The New Elizabeth ◆ 1990
64. The Ghost of Tricia Martin ◆ 1990
65. Trouble at Home ◆ 1990
66. Who's to Blame? ◆ 1990
67. The Parent Plot ◆ 1990
68. The Love Bet ◆ 1990
69. Friend Against Friend ◆ 1990
70. Ms. Quarterback ◆ 1990
71. Starring Jessica! ◆ 1991
72. Rock Star's Girl ◆ 1991
73. Regina's Legacy ◆ 1991
74. The Perfect Girl ◆ 1991
75. Amy's True Love ◆ 1991
76. Miss Teen Sweet Valley ◆ 1991
77. Cheating to Win ◆ 1991
78. The Dating Game ◆ 1991
79. The Long-Lost Brother ◆ 1991
80. The Girl They Both Loved ◆ 1991
81. Rosa's Lie ◆ 1992
82. Kidnapped by the Cult ◆ 1992
83. Steven's Bride ◆ 1992
84. The Stolen Diary ◆ 1992
85. Soap Star ◆ 1992
86. Jessica Against Bruce ◆ 1992
87. My Best Friend's Boyfriend ◆ 1993
88. Love Letters for Sale ◆ 1993
89. Elizabeth Betrayed ◆ 1993
90. Don't Go Home with John ◆ 1993
91. In Love with a Prince ◆ 1993
92. She's Not What She Seems ◆ 1993
93. Stepsisters ◆ 1993
94. Are We in Love? ◆ 1993
95. The Morning After ◆ 1993
96. The Arrest ◆ 1993
97. The Verdict ◆ 1993
98. The Wedding ◆ 1993
99. Beware the Babysitter ◆ 1993
100. The Evil Twin ◆ 1993
101. The Boyfriend War ◆ 1994
102. Almost Married ◆ 1994
103. Operation Love Match ◆ 1994
104. Love and Death in London ◆ 1994
105. A Date with a Werewolf ◆ 1994
106. Beware the Wolfman ◆ 1994
107. Jessica's Secret Love ◆ 1994

108. Left at the Altar ◆ 1994
109. Double-Crossed ◆ 1994
110. Death Threat ◆ 1994
111. A Deadly Christmas ◆ 1994
112. Jessica Quits the Squad ◆ 1995
113. The Pom-Pom Wars ◆ 1995
114. "V" for Victory ◆ 1995
115. The Treasure of Death Valley ◆ 1995
116. Nightmare in Death Valley ◆ 1995
117. Jessica the Genius ◆ 1996
118. College Weekend ◆ 1996
119. Jessica's Older Guy ◆ 1996
120. In Love with the Enemy ◆ 1996
121. The High School War ◆ 1996
122. A Kiss Before Dying ◆ 1996
123. Elizabeth's Rival ◆ 1996
124. Meet Me at Midnight ◆ 1996
125. Camp Killer ◆ 1996
126. Tall, Dark, and Deadly ◆ 1996
127. Dance of Death ◆ 1996
128. Kiss of a Killer ◆ 1996
129. Cover Girls ◆ 1997
130. Model Flirt ◆ 1997
131. Fashion Victim ◆ 1997
132. Once Upon a Time ◆ 1997
133. To Catch a Thief ◆ 1997
134. Happily Ever After ◆ 1997
135. Lila's New Flame ◆ 1997
136. Too Hot to Handle ◆ 1997
137. Fight Fire with Fire ◆ 1997
138. What Jessica Wants ◆ 1998
139. Elizabeth Is Mine ◆ 1998
140. Please Forgive Me ◆ 1998
141. A Picture-Perfect Prom ◆ 1998
142. The Big Night ◆ 1998
143. Party Weekend! ◆ 1998

SWEET VALLEY HIGH MAGNA EDITIONS

1. The Wakefields of Sweet Valley ◆ 1991
2. The Wakefield Legacy: The Untold Story ◆ 1992
3. A Night to Remember ◆ 1993
4. The Evil Twin ◆ 1993
5. Elizabeth's Secret Diary ◆ 1994
6. Jessica's Secret Diary ◆ 1994
7. Return of the Evil Twin ◆ 1995
8. Elizabeth's Secret Diary Volume II ◆ 1996
9. Jessica's Secret Diary Volume II ◆ 1996
10. The Fowlers of Sweet Valley ◆ 1996
11. The Patmans of Sweet Valley ◆ 1997

12. Elizabeth's Secret Diary Volume III ◆ 1997
13. Jessica's Secret Diary Volume III ◆ 1997

SWEET VALLEY HIGH SUPER EDITIONS

1. Perfect Summer ◆ 1985
2. Special Christmas ◆ 1985
3. Spring Break ◆ 1986
4. Malibu Summer ◆ 1986
5. Winter Carnival ◆ 1986
6. Spring Fever ◆ 1987
7. Falling for Lucas ◆ 1996
8. Jessica Takes Manhattan ◆ 1997
9. Mystery Date ◆ 1998
10. Last Wish ◆ 1998
11. Earthquake ◆ 1998
12. Aftershock ◆ 1998

SWEET VALLEY HIGH SUPER STARS

1. Lila's Story ◆ 1989
2. Bruce's Story ◆ 1990
3. Enid's Story ◆ 1990
4. Olivia's Story ◆ 1991
5. Todd's Story ◆ 1992

SWEET VALLEY HIGH SUPER THRILLERS

1. Double Jeopardy ◆ 1987
2. On the Run ◆ 1988
3. No Place to Hide ◆ 1988
4. Deadly Summer ◆ 1989
5. Murder on the Line ◆ 1992
6. Beware the Wolfman ◆ 1994
7. A Deadly Christmas ◆ 1994
8. Murder in Paradise ◆ 1995
9. A Stranger in the House ◆ 1995
10. A Killer on Board ◆ 1995
11. "R" for Revenge ◆ 1997

SWEET VALLEY HIGH SENIOR YEAR

Pascal, Francine, creator
BANTAM
GRADES 7–10 ◆ A/R
REAL LIFE

An earthquake disrupts home and school life for Jessica and Elizabeth as they start their senior year at high school.

1. Can't Stay Away ◆ 1999
2. Say It to My Face ◆ 1999
3. So Cool ◆ 1999
4. I've Got a Secret ◆ 1999
5. If You Only Knew ◆ 1999
6. Your Basic Nightmare ◆ 1999
7. Boy Meets Girl ◆ 1999
8. Maria Who? ◆ 1999
9. The One That Got Away ◆ 1999
10. Broken Angel ◆ 1999
11. Take Me On ◆ 1999
12. Bad Girl ◆ 1999
13. All About Love ◆ 1999
14. Split Decision ◆ 2000
15. On My Own ◆ 2000
16. Three Girls and a Guy ◆ 2000
17. Backstabber ◆ 2000
18. As if I Care ◆ 2000
19. It's My Life ◆ 2000
20. Nothing Is Forever ◆ 2000
21. The It Guy ◆ 2000
22. So Not Me ◆ 2000
23. Falling Apart ◆ 2000
24. Never Let Go ◆ 2000
25. Straight Up ◆ 2001
26. Too Late ◆ 2001
27. Playing Dirty ◆ 2001
28. Meant to Be ◆ 2001
29. Where We Belong ◆ 2001
30. Close to You ◆ 2001
31. Stay or Go ◆ 2001
32. Road Trip ◆ 2001
33. Me, Me, Me ◆ 2001
34. Troublemaker ◆ 2001
35. Control Freak ◆ 2001
36. Tearing Me Apart ◆ 2001
37. Be Mine ◆ 2002
38. Get a Clue ◆ 2002
39. Best of Enemies ◆ 2002
40. Never Give Up ◆ 2002
41. He's Back ◆ 2002
42. Touch and Go ◆ 2002
43. It Takes Two ◆ 2002
44. Cruise Control ◆ 2002
45. Tia in the Middle ◆ 2002
46. Prom Night ◆ 2002
47. Senior Cut Day ◆ 2002
48. Sweet 18 ◆ 2003

SWEET VALLEY JUNIOR HIGH

Pascal, Francine, creator

BANTAM

GRADES 6–8 ◆ A/R

REAL LIFE

Twins Jessica and Elizabeth have differing expectations—and experiences—when they move from middle school to junior high.

1. Get Real ◆ 1999
2. One 2 Many ◆ 1999
3. Soulmates ◆ 1999
4. The Cool Crowd ◆ 1999
5. Boy. Friend. ◆ 1999
6. Lacey's Crush ◆ 1999
7. How to Ruin a Friendship ◆ 1999
8. Cheating on Anna ◆ 1999
9. Too Popular ◆ 1999
10. Twin Switch ◆ 1999
11. Got a Problem? ◆ 2000
12. Third Wheel ◆ 2000
13. Three Days, Two Nights ◆ 2000
14. My Perfect Guy ◆ 2000
15. Hands Off! ◆ 2000
16. Keepin' It Real ◆ 2000
17. Whatever ◆ 2000
18. True Blue ◆ 2000
19. She Loves Me . . . Not ◆ 2000
20. Wild Child ◆ 2000
21. I'm So Outta Here ◆ 2000
22. What You Don't Know ◆ 2000
23. Invisible Me ◆ 2000
24. Clueless ◆ 2000
25. Drama Queen ◆ 2001
26. No More Mr. Nice Guy ◆ 2001
27. She's Back ◆ 2001
28. Dance Fever ◆ 2001
29. He's the One ◆ 2001
30. Too Many Good-Byes ◆ 2001

SWEET VALLEY TWINS

Pascal, Francine, creator

BANTAM

GRADES 6–8 ♦ A/R

FAMILY LIFE | REAL LIFE

Jessica and Elizabeth Wakefield are identical twins who, though close and usually supportive of each other, are also individuals with their own friends, interests, and abilities. In the first title of this popular paperback series, the twins start middle school. Each of the more than 100 subsequent titles deals with typical situations and predicaments that young teens may encounter in school and at home. Occasional titles, such as *Cammi's Crush*, feature other students at Sweet Valley Middle School who are friends of Jessica and Elizabeth.

1. Best Friends ♦ 1986
2. Teacher's Pet ♦ 1986
3. Haunted House ♦ 1986
4. Choosing Sides ♦ 1986
5. Sneaking Out ♦ 1987
6. New Girl ♦ 1987
7. Three's a Crowd ♦ 1987
8. First Place ♦ 1987
9. Against the Rules ♦ 1987
10. One of the Gang ♦ 1987
11. Buried Treasure ♦ 1987
12. Keeping Secrets ♦ 1987
13. Stretching the Truth ♦ 1987
14. Tug of War ♦ 1987
15. Older Boy ♦ 1988
16. Second Best ♦ 1988
17. Boys Against Girls ♦ 1988
18. Center of Attention ♦ 1988
19. Bully ♦ 1988
20. Playing Hooky ♦ 1988
21. Left Behind ♦ 1988
22. Out of Place ♦ 1988
23. Claim to Fame ♦ 1988

24. Jumping to Conclusions ◆ 1988
25. Standing Out ◆ 1989
26. Taking Charge ◆ 1989
27. Teamwork ◆ 1989
28. April Fool! ◆ 1989
29. Jessica and the Brat Attack ◆ 1989
30. Princess Elizabeth ◆ 1989
31. Jessica's Bad Idea ◆ 1989
32. Jessica on Stage ◆ 1989
33. Elizabeth's New Hero ◆ 1989
34. Jessica's the Rock Star ◆ 1989
35. Amy's Pen Pal ◆ 1990
36. Mary Is Missing ◆ 1990
37. War Between the Twins ◆ 1990
38. Lois Strikes Back ◆ 1990
39. Jessica and the Money Mix-Up ◆ 1990
40. Danny Means Trouble ◆ 1990
41. Twins Get Caught ◆ 1990
42. Jessica's Secret ◆ 1990
43. Elizabeth's First Kiss ◆ 1990
44. Amy Moves In ◆ 1991
45. Lucy Takes the Reins ◆ 1991
46. Mademoiselle Jessica ◆ 1991
47. Jessica's New Look ◆ 1991
48. Mansy Miller Fights Back ◆ 1991
49. Twins' Little Sister ◆ 1991
50. Jessica and the Secret Star ◆ 1991
51. Elizabeth the Impossible ◆ 1991
52. Booster Boycott ◆ 1991
53. The Slime that Ate Sweet Valley ◆ 1991
54. Big Party Weekend ◆ 1991
55. Brooke and Her Rock Star Mom ◆ 1991
56. The Wakefields Strike It Rich ◆ 1991
57. Steven's in Love ◆ 1992
58. Elizabeth and the Orphans ◆ 1992
59. Barnyard Battle ◆ 1992
60. Ciao, Sweet Valley ◆ 1992
61. Jessica the Nerd ◆ 1992
62. Sarah's Dad and Sophia's Mom ◆ 1992
63. Poor Lila ◆ 1992
64. Charm School Mystery ◆ 1992
65. Patty's Last Dance ◆ 1993
66. Great Boyfriend Switch ◆ 1993
67. Jessica the Thief ◆ 1993
68. Middle School Gets Married ◆ 1993
69. Won't Someone Help Anna? ◆ 1993
70. Psychic Sisters ◆ 1993
71. Jessica Saves the Trees ◆ 1993
72. Love Potion ◆ 1993
73. Lila's Music Video ◆ 1993

74. Elizabeth the Hero ◆ 1993
75. Jessica and the Earthquake ◆ 1994
76. Yours for a Day ◆ 1994
77. Todd Runs Away ◆ 1994
78. Steven and the Zombie ◆ 1994
79. Jessica's Blind Date ◆ 1994
80. Gossip War ◆ 1994
81. Robbery at the Mall ◆ 1994
82. Steven's Enemy ◆ 1994
83. Amy's Secret Sister ◆ 1994
84. Romeo and Two Juliets ◆ 1995
85. Elizabeth the Seventh Grader ◆ 1995
86. It Can't Happen Here ◆ 1995
87. Mother-Daughter Switch ◆ 1995
88. Steven Gets Even ◆ 1995
89. Jessica's Cookie Disaster ◆ 1995
90. Cousin War ◆ 1996
91. Deadly Voyage ◆ 1996
92. Escape from Terror Island ◆ 1996
93. Incredible Madame Jessica ◆ 1996
94. Don't Talk to Brian ◆ 1996
95. Battle of the Cheerleaders ◆ 1996
96. Elizabeth the Spy ◆ 1996
97. Too Scared to Sleep ◆ 1996
98. Beast Is Watching You ◆ 1996
99. Beast Must Die ◆ 1996
100. If I Die Before I Wake ◆ 1996
101. Twins in Love ◆ 1996
102. Mysterious Doctor Q ◆ 1996
103. Elizabeth Solves It All ◆ 1996
104. Big Brother's in Love Again ◆ 1997
105. Jessica's Lucky Millions ◆ 1997
106. Breakfast of Enemies ◆ 1997
107. The Twins Hit Hollywood ◆ 1997
108. Cammi's Crush ◆ 1997
109. Don't Go in the Basement ◆ 1997
110. Pumpkin Fever ◆ 1997
111. Sisters at War ◆ 1997
112. If Looks Could Kill ◆ 1997
113. The Boyfriend Game ◆ 1998
114. The Boyfriend Mess ◆ 1998
115. Happy Mother's Day, Lila ◆ 1998
116. Jessica Takes Charge ◆ 1998
117. Down with Queen Janet! ◆ 1998
118. No Escape! ◆ 1998

SWEET VALLEY TWINS MAGNA EDITIONS

1. The Magic Christmas ◆ 1992
2. A Christmas Without Elizabeth ◆ 1994
3. BIG for Christmas ◆ 1994

SWEET VALLEY TWINS SUPER CHILLER EDITIONS

Pascal, Francine, creator
BANTAM
GRADES 6–8 ◆ A/R
HORROR

Ghosts, curses, masks that change one's character, and other scary situations are featured in this series. The books are written by Jamie Suzanne.

1. The Christmas Ghost ◆ 1989
2. The Ghost in the Graveyard ◆ 1990
3. The Carnival Ghost ◆ 1990
4. The Ghost in the Bell Tower ◆ 1992
5. The Curse of the Ruby Necklace ◆ 1993
6. The Curse of the Golden Heart ◆ 1994
7. The Haunted Burial Ground ◆ 1994
8. The Secret of the Magic Pen ◆ 1995
9. Evil Elizabeth ◆ 1995

SWEET VALLEY TWINS SUPER EDITIONS

Pascal, Francine, creator
BANTAM
GRADES 6–8 ◆ A/R
REAL LIFE

This paperback series is a spinoff of the Sweet Valley Twins and Friends series. In these books, identical twins Jessica and Elizabeth Wakefield venture away from their home turf, Sweet Valley Middle School, and become involved with extracurricular activities such as volunteering at the zoo, going on a camping trip, and taking a vacation to Paris.

1. The Class Trip ◆ 1988
2. Holiday Mischief ◆ 1998
3. The Big Camp Secret ◆ 1989
4. The Unicorns Go Hawaiian ◆ 1991
5. Lila's Secret Valentine ◆ 1995
6. The Twins Take Paris ◆ 1996
7. Jessica's Animal Instincts ◆ 1996
8. Jessica's First Kiss ◆ 1997
9. The Twins Go to College ◆ 1997

10. The Year Without Christmas ◆ 1997
11. Jessica's No Angel ◆ 1998
12. Goodbye, Middle School ◆ 1998

SWEET VALLEY UNIVERSITY

Pascal, Francine, creator
BANTAM
GRADES 7–10 ◆ A/R
REAL LIFE

Twins Jessica and Elizabeth Wakefield of the Sweet Valley series are off to college. As they get older, they are involved in more grown-up relationships and adventures, and even face life-and-death situations. Fans of the other Sweet Valley books will enjoy following the collegiate exploits of the two girls.

1. College Girls ◆ 1993
2. Love, Lies, and Jessica Wakefield ◆ 1993
3. What Your Parents Don't Know ◆ 1994
4. Anything for Love ◆ 1994
5. Married Woman ◆ 1994
6. Love of Her Life ◆ 1994
7. Good-Bye to Love ◆ 1994
8. Home for Christmas ◆ 1994
9. Sorority Scandal ◆ 1995
10. No Means No ◆ 1995
11. Take Back the Night ◆ 1995
12. College Cruise ◆ 1995
13. SS Heartbreak ◆ 1995
14. Shipboard Wedding ◆ 1995
15. Behind Closed Doors ◆ 1995
16. The Other Woman ◆ 1995
17. Deadly Attraction ◆ 1995
18. Billie's Secret ◆ 1996
19. Broken Promises, Shattered Dreams ◆ 1996
20. Here Comes the Bride ◆ 1996
21. For the Love of Ryan ◆ 1996
22. Elizabeth's Summer Love ◆ 1996
23. Sweet Kiss of Summer ◆ 1996
24. His Secret Past ◆ 1996
25. Busted! ◆ 1996
26. The Trial of Jessica Wakefield ◆ 1996
27. Elizabeth and Todd Forever ◆ 1997
28. Elizabeth's Heartbreak ◆ 1997
29. One Last Kiss ◆ 1997
30. Beauty and the Beach ◆ 1997

31. The Truth about Ryan ◆ 1997
32. The Boys of Summer ◆ 1997
33. Out of the Picture ◆ 1997
34. Spy Girl ◆ 1997
35. Undercover Angels ◆ 1997
36. Have You Heard About Elizabeth ◆ 1997
37. Breaking Away ◆ 1998
38. Good-Bye, Elizabeth ◆ 1998
39. Elizabeth Loves New York ◆ 1998
40. Private Jessica ◆ 1998
41. Escape to New York ◆ 1998
42. Sneaking In ◆ 1998
43. The Price of Love ◆ 1998
44. Love Me Always ◆ 1998
45. Don't Let Go ◆ 1999
46. I'll Never Love Again ◆ 1999
47. You're Not My Sister ◆ 1999
48. No Rules ◆ 1999
49. Stranded ◆ 1999
50. Summer of Love ◆ 1999
51. Living Together ◆ 2000
52. Fooling Around ◆ 2000
53. Truth or Dare ◆ 2000
54. Rush Week ◆ 2000
55. The First Time ◆ 2000
56. Dropping Out ◆ 2000
57. Who Knew? ◆ 2000
58. The Dreaded Ex ◆ 2000
59. Elizabeth in Love ◆ 2000
60. Secret Love Diaries: Elizabeth ◆ 2000
61. Secret Love Diaries: Jessica ◆ 2000
62. Secret Love Diaries: Sam ◆ 2000
63. Secret Love Diaries: Chloe ◆ 2000

SWEET VALLEY UNIVERSITY: ELIZABETH

Pascal, Francine, creator
BANTAM
GRADES 7–10 ◆ A/R
REAL LIFE

After quarreling with her sister Jessica, Elizabeth Wakefield decides not to return to Sweet Valley University and sets off for England. There she meets an attractive young aristocrat.

1. University, Interrupted ◆ 2001

2. London Calling ◆ 2001
3. Royal Pain ◆ 2001
4. Downstairs, Upstairs ◆ 2001
5. Max's Choice ◆ 2001
6. I Need You ◆ 2001

SWEET VALLEY UNIVERSITY THRILLER EDITIONS

Pascal, Francine, creator
BANTAM
GRADES 7–10 ◆ A/R
HORROR | REAL LIFE

Companions to the Sweet Valley High University series, these mystery-thriller books are page-turners, with Sweet Valley University students investigating murders, being threatened by stalkers, and foiling other evil plots.

1. Wanted for Murder ◆ 1995
2. He's Watching You ◆ 1995
3. Kiss of the Vampire ◆ 1995
4. The House of Death ◆ 1995
5. Running for Her Life ◆ 1996
6. The Roommate ◆ 1996
7. What Winston Saw ◆ 1997
8. Dead Before Dawn ◆ 1997
9. Killer at Sea ◆ 1997
10. Channel X ◆ 1997
11. Love and Murder ◆ 1998
12. Don't Answer the Phone ◆ 1998
13. CyberStalker: The Return of William White, Part I ◆ 1998
14. Deadly Terror: The Return of William White, Part II ◆ 1999
15. Loving the Enemy ◆ 1999
16. Killer Party ◆ 1999
17. Very Bad Things ◆ 2000
18. Face It ◆ 2000

SWITCHERS

Thompson, Kate
HYPERION
GRADES 6–9 ◆ A/R
FANTASY

Tess and Kevin are Switchers and can adopt the form of animals at will. In the face of an oncoming Ice Age, they use these powers to defeat the monsters who are responsible. In the second book, Tess must decide her future. Among the choices is immortality—as either a vampire or a phoenix. The decision is harder than she expected.

1. Switchers ◆ 1998
2. Midnight's Choice ◆ 1998
3. Wild Blood ◆ 1999

SWORD DANCER SAGA

Roberson, Jennifer
DAW BOOKS
GRADES 10–12
FANTASY

Del is a sword master from the North. Tiger is a skillful warrior from the South. They join together to face danger and to understand Tiger's past. Tiger realizes that he must find his homeland and learn about his destiny. As the series progresses, so does the romance between Del and Tiger.

1. Sword-Dancer ◆ 1986
2. Sword-Singer ◆ 1988
3. Sword-Maker ◆ 1989
4. Sword-Breaker ◆ 1991
5. Sword-Born ◆ 1998
6. Sword-Sworn ◆ 2002

SWORD OF SHADOWS

Jones, J. V.
WARNER; TOR
GRADES 10–12
FANTASY

An epic fantasy set in a subarctic landscape into which evil is intruding. Details from history, mythology, and religion add to the atmosphere. Lovers Raif and Ash face many challenges in their quest to find the Fortress of Black Ice and seek to March are separated after she is kidnapped, and he must choose between attempting her rescue and completing his quest to find the Fortress of Black Ice.

1. A Cavern of Black Ice ◆ 1999

2. A Fortress of Grey Ice ◆ 2000

3. A Sword from Red Ice ◆ 2005

SWORD OF THE SPIRITS

Christopher, John

ALADDIN

GRADES 5–8

ADVENTURE | SCIENCE FICTION

Post-apocalyptic England is the setting of this trilogy. It is a world of warriors, dwarfs, mutants and seers. Luke Perry, the future ruler, is thrown into chaos as he finds out that his world is not as it seems. He must hide after his father is murdered and his half-brother takes the throne. Continuous action, drama, and intrigue create a satisfying read for fans of science fiction.

1. The Prince in Waiting ◆ 1970
2. Beyond the Burning Lands ◆ 1971
3. The Sword of the Spirits ◆ 1972

T*WITCHES

Gilmour, H. B., and Randi Reisfeld

SCHOLASTIC

GRADES 6–9 ◆ A/R

FANTASY

Cam and Alex are identical twin sisters who have never known each other. They have been separated since birth and meet accidentally. They work together to solve the mystery of their past and to deal with strange circumstances. As the series progresses, an evil warlock, Thantos, wants to destroy them

1. The Power of Two ◆ 2001
2. Building a Mystery ◆ 2001
3. Seeing Is Deceiving ◆ 2001
4. Dead Wrong ◆ 2002
5. Don't Think Twice ◆ 2002
6. Double Jeopardy ◆ 2002
7. Kindred Spirits ◆ 2003
8. The Witch Hunters ◆ 2003
9. Split Decision ◆ 2004
10. Destiny's Twins ◆ 2004

TAG AND WALKER *see* Walker and Tag

TALES FROM THE ODYSSEY

Osborne, Mary Pope
HYPERION
GRADES 4–8 ◆ A/R
FANTASY

Homer's Odyssey is retold in this series. At the end of the Trojan War, Odysseus and his men begin the dangerous journey home. They encounter all the familiar mythical creatures including Cyclops, Circe, and Aeolus.

1. The One-Eyed Giant ◆ 2002
2. The Land of the Dead ◆ 2003
3. Sirens and Sea Monsters ◆ 2003
4. The Gray-Eyed Goddess ◆ 2003
5. Return to Ithaca ◆ 2004
6. The Final Battle ◆ 2004

TALES OF ALVIN MAKER

Card, Orson Scott
T. DOHERTY/TOR
GRADES 8–10 ◆ A/R
FANTASY

This series takes place on the American frontier in the 19th century. The author creates an alternative history with magical creatures. Alvin is the seventh son of a seventh son and is developing the powers of a mage. He faces the evil of the Unmaker using folk magic and the help of others, including a guardian angel. Alvin's love, Peggy, has the gift to see the future.

1. Seventh Son ◆ 1987
2. Red Prophet ◆ 1988
3. Prentice Alvin ◆ 1989
4. Alvin Journeyman ◆ 1995
5. Heartfire ◆ 1998
6. The Crystal City: A Tale of Alvin Maker ◆ 2003

TALES OF GOM IN THE LEGENDS OF ULM

Chetwin, Grace

LOTHROP, LEE, & SHEPARD; BRADBURY BOOKS

GRADES 6–8

FANTASY

Fantasy lovers will enjoy this series full of mountain lore, wizardry, and adventure. Gom, a mountain boy growing up in the land of Ulm, has many unusual talents. In the first book, his mother has disappeared, leaving a mysterious stone rune with Gom. This leads to his first great challenge. In the second book, he tries to return the rune to his mother while being pursued by evil forces that also want it. In the third book, he finds his mother and begins to learn about wizardry and other worlds.

1. Gom on Windy Mountain ◆ 1986
2. The Riddle and the Rune ◆ 1987
3. The Crystal Stair ◆ 1988
4. The Starstone ◆ 1989

TALES OF THE NINE CHARMS

Farber, Erica, and J. R. Sansevere

DELACORTE

GRADES 6–9 ◆ A/R

FANTASY

When Walker Crane falls into a fountain, he enters another world. There he teams up with Niko and Aurora to face the Dragons of the Dark. Zoe, 13, and Lila, 11, enter the adventure in later books.

1. Circle of Three ◆ 2000
2. The Secret in the Stones ◆ 2001
3. Islands of the Black Moon ◆ 2002

TALES OF THE OTORI

Hearn, Lian

RIVERHEAD BOOKS

GRADES 10–12 ◆ A/R

FANTASY

In an imagined feudal Japan, young Takeo becomes the ward of Lord Otori. Takeo discovers his supernatural abilities and joins the group of assassins known as The Tribe. As Takeo becomes immersed in the mysteries of The Tribe, his beloved Kaede returns to her homeland. Their separation strengthens their commitment and they reunite and secretly marry. Now they must prepare for war in their respective kingdoms.

1. Across the Nightingale Floor ◆ 2002
2. Grass for His Pillow ◆ 2003
3. Brilliance of the Moon ◆ 2004

TARRAGON ISLAND

Tate, Nikki
SONO NIS PRESS
GRADES 6–8
FAMILY LIFE | REAL LIFE

Heather Blake's family has moved from Toronto to small, isolated Tarragon Island in British Columbia. Heather misses her friends, shopping, and her writing group. She is beginning to adjust when she must face a family tragedy. Her new friends on the island help her cope.

1. Tarragon Island ◆ 1999
2. No Cafes in Narnia ◆ 2000

TARTAN MAGIC TRILOGY

Yolen, Jane
HARCOURT
GRADES 4–7 ◆ A/R
FANTASY

American twins Jennifer and Peter find Scotland to be a place full of magic in this series full of ghosts, local lore, adventure, and suspense. In the last book, they visit a graveyard and become embroiled in a 300-year-old feud between former lovers.

1. The Wizard's Map ◆ 1999
2. The Pictish Child ◆ 1999
3. The Bagpiper's Ghost ◆ 2002

TEEN ANGELS

Bennett, Cherie, and Jeff Gottesfeld
AVON
GRADES 9–12
FANTASY

In the first book, Cisco is training to become an angel by trying to help a self-destructive rock star. Later, teen angel Nicole tries to help Cisco's sister Shelby who is distraught over Cisco's death.

1. Heaven Can't Wait ◆ 1996
2. Love Never Dies ◆ 1996
3. Angel Kisses ◆ 1996
4. Heaven Help Us ◆ 1996
5. Nightmare in Heaven ◆ 1996
6. Love Without End ◆ 1996

THAT'S SO RAVEN

TOKYOPOP
GRADES 6–8
FANTASY

Raven is a teen with her own Disney Channel show—"That's So Raven." She has a special power—she can see into the future. Even though she has this gift, she often misinterprets her visions, creating chaos and fun. This Cine-manga series is sure to appeal to fans of the television show.

1. That's So Raven ◆ 2004
2. The Trouble with Boys ◆ 2004
3. Smother Dearest ◆ 2005

THOROUGHBRED

Campbell, Joanna, creator
HARPERCOLLINS
GRADES 4–7 ◆ A/R
REAL LIFE | RECREATION

Eighteen-year-old jockey Samantha McLean and her middle school-aged adopted sister live at Whitebrook, a Thoroughbred breeding and training farm in Kentucky. In addition to typical problems with school, friends, boyfriends, and parents, the girls handle the pressures of riding and racing. Girls who like horses will enjoy this series about what it's like to live on a horse farm.

1. A Horse Called Wonder ◆ 1991
2. Wonder's Promise ◆ 1991
3. Wonder's First Race ◆ 1991
4. Wonder's Victory ◆ 1991
5. Ashleigh's Dream ◆ 1993
6. Wonder's Yearling ◆ 1993
7. Samantha's Pride ◆ 1993
8. Sierra's Steeplechase ◆ 1993
9. Pride's Challenge ◆ 1994
10. Pride's Last Race ◆ 1994
11. Wonder's Sister ◆ 1994
12. Shining's Orphan ◆ 1994
13. Cindy's Runaway Colt ◆ 1995
14. Cindy's Glory ◆ 1995
15. Glory's Triumph ◆ 1995
16. Glory in Danger ◆ 1996
17. Ashleigh's Farewell ◆ 1996
18. Glory's Rival ◆ 1997
19. Cindy's Heartbreak ◆ 1997
20. Champion's Spirit ◆ 1997
21. Wonder's Champion ◆ 1997
22. Arabian Challenge ◆ 1997
23. Cindy's Honor ◆ 1997
24. The Horse of Her Dreams ◆ 1997
25. Melanie's Treasure ◆ 1998
26. Sterling's Second Chance ◆ 1998
27. Christina's Courage ◆ 1998
28. Camp Saddlebrook ◆ 1998
29. Melanie's Last Ride ◆ 1998
30. Dylan's Choice ◆ 1998
31. A Home for Melanie ◆ 1998
32. Cassidy's Secret ◆ 1999
33. Racing Parker ◆ 1999
34. On the Track ◆ 1999
35. Dead Heat ◆ 1999
36. Without Wonder ◆ 1999
37. Star in Danger ◆ 1999
38. Down to the Wire ◆ 1999
39. Living Legend ◆ 2000
40. Ultimate Risk ◆ 2000
41. Close Call ◆ 2000
42. Bad Luck Filly ◆ 2000
43. Fallen Star ◆ 2000
44. Perfect Image ◆ 2000

45. Star's Chance ◆ 2001
46. Racing Image ◆ 2001
47. Cindy's Desert Adventure ◆ 2001
48. Cindy's Bold Start ◆ 2001
49. Rising Star ◆ 2001
50. Team Player ◆ 2001
51. Distance Runner ◆ 2001
52. Perfect Challenge ◆ 2002
53. Derby Fever ◆ 2002
54. Cindy's Last Hope ◆ 2002
55. Great Expectations ◆ 2002
56. Hoofprints in the Snow ◆ 2002
57. Faith in a Long Shot ◆ 2003
58. Christina's Shining Star ◆ 2003
59. Star's Inspiration ◆ 2003
60. Taking the Reins ◆ 2003
61. Parker's Passion ◆ 2003
62. Unbridled Fury ◆ 2003
63. Starstruck ◆ 2004
64. The Price of Fame ◆ 2004
65. Bridal Dreams ◆ 2004
66. Samantha's Irish Luck ◆ 2004
67. Breaking the Fall ◆ 2004
68. Kaitlin's Wild Ride ◆ 2004
69. Melanie's Double Jinx ◆ 2004
70. Allie's Legacy ◆ 2005

THOROUGHBRED SUPER EDITIONS

1. Ashleigh's Christmas Miracle (Campbell, Joanna) ◆ 1994
2. Ashleigh's Diary (Campbell, Joanna) ◆ 1995
3. Ashleigh's Hope (Campbell, Joanna) ◆ 1996
4. Samantha's Journey (Campbell, Joanna, and Karen Bentley) ◆ 1997

THOROUGHBRED: ASHLEIGH

Campbell, Joanna
HARPERCOLLINS
GRADES 4–7 ◆ A/R
REAL LIFE | RECREATION

Before the Thoroughbred series, Ashleigh Griffen lived at her family's farm in Kentucky. This series begins when Ashleigh helps an abused horse, Lightning, back to health. When the humane society tells her that there is now a home for Lightning, Ashleigh is upset. She tries to find a way to keep Lightning. Girls who like horse stories will enjoy this series.

1. Lightning's Last Hope ◆ 1998
2. A Horse for Christmas ◆ 1998
3. Waiting for Stardust ◆ 1999
4. Goodbye, Midnight Wanderer ◆ 1999
5. The Forbidden Stallion ◆ 1999
6. A Dangerous Ride ◆ 1999
7. Derby Day ◆ 1999
8. The Lost Foal ◆ 2000
9. Holiday Homecoming ◆ 2000
10. Derby Dreams ◆ 2001
11. Ashleigh's Promise ◆ 2001
12. Winter Race Camp ◆ 2002
13. The Prize ◆ 2002
14. Ashleigh's Western Challenge ◆ 2002
15. Stardust's Foal ◆ 2003

THOROUGHBRED: ASHLEIGH'S COLLECTION

Campbell, Joanna
HARPERCOLLINS
GRADES 4–7 ◆ **A/R**
REAL LIFE | RECREATION

Here are three of Ashleigh's favorite stories. In the first book, Susan has fallen and worries about riding again. Then a mistreated horse, Evening Star, comes to the stable and begins to trust Susan. Can she overcome her fear and help Star? Fans of horse stories will enjoy this collection.

1. Star of Shadowbrook Farm ◆ 1998
2. The Forgotten Filly ◆ 1998
3. Battlecry Forever! ◆ 1998

THE THOUSAND CULTURES

Barnes, John
TOM DOHERTY ASSOCIATES
GRADES 9–12
SCIENCE FICTION

A new form of travel provides contact between two formerly isolated planets: Nou Occitan, a world in which the arts are revered, and Caledony, where the arts are regarded with disdain. The first book deals with this clash of cultures. In *Earth Made of Glass*, Giraut—former ambassador to Caledony—and Margaret Leones work to bring peace to the planet of Briand.

1. A Million Open Doors ◆ 1992
2. Earth Made of Glass ◆ 1998
3. The Merchants of Souls ◆ 2001

THREE GIRLS IN THE CITY

Betancourt, Jeanne
SCHOLASTIC
GRADES 6–9
REAL LIFE

At a summer photography class in New York City, three 13-year old girls meet and become friends. Carolyn is timid and her Wyoming background has not prepared her for such a big city. Joy is privileged and willful. Maya is from Harlem and is proud of her African American heritage.

1. Self-Portrait ◆ 2003
2. Exposed ◆ 2003
3. Black and White ◆ 2004
4. Close-Up ◆ 2004

THREE INVESTIGATORS

Various authors
RANDOM HOUSE
GRADES 5–7 ◆ A/R
ADVENTURE | MYSTERY

Jupiter Jones and his friends Pete and Bob form the Three Investigators and operate out of a secret office in the junkyard owned by Jupiter's aunt and uncle. Jupiter is a young Sherlock Holmes, never missing anything and coming to conclusions that astonish his friends and nearly always turn out to be right. The mysteries are fairly complicated, and the solutions depend on historic or scientific knowledge. Jupiter, as the First Investigator, supplies the brains, and Pete, stronger and more athletic, is the Second Investigator. Bob is in charge of research and records. Boys who like the Hardy Boys will find more depth and realism in the Three Investigators.

1. The Secret of Terror Castle (Arthur, Robert) ◆ 1964
2. The Mystery of the Stuttering Parrot (Arthur, Robert) ◆ 1964

3. The Mystery of the Whispering Mummy (Arthur, Robert) ◆ 1965
4. The Mystery of the Green Ghost (Arthur, Robert) ◆ 1965
5. The Mystery of the Vanishing Treasure (Arthur, Robert) ◆ 1966
6. The Secret of Skeleton Island (Arthur, Robert) ◆ 1966
7. The Mystery of the Fiery Eye (Arthur, Robert) ◆ 1967
8. The Mystery of the Silver Spider (Arthur, Robert) ◆ 1967
9. The Mystery of the Screaming Clock (Arthur, Robert) ◆ 1968
10. The Mystery of the Moaning Cave (Arden, William) ◆ 1968
11. The Mystery of the Talking Skull (Arthur, Robert) ◆ 1969
12. The Mystery of the Laughing Shadow (Arden, William) ◆ 1969
13. The Secret of the Crooked Cat (Arden, William) ◆ 1970
14. The Mystery of the Coughing Dragon (West, Nick) ◆ 1970
15. The Mystery of the Flaming Footprints (Carey, M. V.) ◆ 1971
16. The Mystery of the Nervous Lion (West, Nick) ◆ 1971
17. The Mystery of the Singing Serpent (Carey, M. V.) ◆ 1972
18. The Mystery of the Shrinking House (Arden, William) ◆ 1972
19. The Secret of Phantom Lake (Arden, William) ◆ 1973
20. The Mystery of Monster Mountain (Carey, M. V.) ◆ 1973
21. The Secret of the Haunted Mirror (Carey, M. V.) ◆ 1974
22. The Mystery of the Dead Man's Riddle (Arden, William) ◆ 1974
23. The Mystery of the Invisible Dog (Carey, M. V.) ◆ 1975
24. The Mystery of Death Trap Mine (Carey, M. V.) ◆ 1976
25. The Mystery of the Dancing Devil (Arden, William) ◆ 1976
26. The Mystery of the Headless Horse (Arden, William) ◆ 1977
27. The Mystery of the Magic Circle (Carey, M. V.) ◆ 1978
28. The Mystery of the Deadly Double (Arden, William) ◆ 1978
29. The Mystery of the Sinister Scarecrow (Carey, M. V.) ◆ 1979
30. The Secret of Shark Reef (Arden, William) ◆ 1979
31. The Mystery of the Scar-Faced Beggar (Carey, M. V.) ◆ 1981
32. The Mystery of the Blazing Cliffs (Carey, M. V.) ◆ 1981
33. The Mystery of the Purple Pirate (Arden, William) ◆ 1982
34. The Mystery of the Wandering Caveman (Carey, M. V.) ◆ 1982
35. The Mystery of the Kidnapped Whale (Brandel, Marc) ◆ 1983
36. The Mystery of the Missing Mermaid (Carey, M. V.) ◆ 1983
37. The Mystery of the Two-Toed Pigeon (Brandel, Marc) ◆ 1984
38. The Mystery of the Smashing Glass (Arden, William) ◆ 1984
39. The Mystery of the Trail of Terror (Carey, M. V.) ◆ 1984
40. The Mystery of the Rogues' Reunion (Brandel, Marc) ◆ 1985
41. The Mystery of the Creep-Show Crooks (Carey, M. V.) ◆ 1985
42. The Mystery of Wrecker's Rock (Arden, William) ◆ 1986
43. The Mystery of the Cranky Collector (Carey, M. V.) ◆ 1986
44. The Case of the Savage Statue (Carey, M. V.) ◆ 1987

THREE INVESTIGATORS CRIMEBUSTERS

1. Hot Wheels (Arden, William) ◆ 1989
2. Murder to Go (Stine, Megan, and H. William Stine) ◆ 1989
3. Rough Stuff (Stone, G. H.) ◆ 1989
4. Funny Business (McCay, William) ◆ 1989
5. An Ear for Danger (Brandel, Marc) ◆ 1989

6. Thriller Diller (Stine, Megan, and H. William Stine) ◆ 1989
7. Reel Trouble (Stone, G. H.) ◆ 1989
8. Shoot the Works (McCay, William) ◆ 1990
9. Foul Play (Lerangis, Peter) ◆ 1990
10. Long Shot (Stine, Megan, and H. William Stine) ◆ 1990
11. Fatal Error (Stone, G. H.) ◆ 1990

TIGER AND DEL *see* Sword Dancer Saga

TIGER'S APPRENTICE

Yep, Laurence
SCHOLASTIC
GRADES 6–9 ◆ A/R
FANTASY

In San Francisco, eighth-grader Tom has been learning magic from his Chinese grandmother. On her death, Tom must take over the defense of a mysterious coral rose that is being sought by the evil Kung Kung. Chinese mythology is woven into this exciting fantasy.

1. The Tiger's Apprentice ◆ 2003
2. Tiger's Blood ◆ 2005

TILLERMAN CYCLE

Voigt, Cynthia
ATHENEUM
GRADES 5–8 ◆ A/R
FAMILY LIFE

Two of the books in this outstanding series have won awards: *Dicey's Song*, a Newbery, and *A Solitary Blue*, a Newbery Honor. In *Homecoming*, the four Tillerman children are abandoned by their mother, and it is up to 13-year-old Dicey to get them safely to their grandmother's house, far away on Chesapeake Bay. *Dicey's Song* continues the story, with their adjustment to living with Gram. The rest of the titles are continuations of the story and companion titles about other people with whom the Tillermans come in contact.

1. Homecoming ◆ 1981
2. Dicey's Song ◆ 1982
3. A Solitary Blue ◆ 1983
4. The Runner ◆ 1985

5. Come a Stranger ◆ 1986
6. Sons from Afar ◆ 1987
7. Seventeen Against the Dealer ◆ 1989

TIME FANTASY SERIES

L'Engle, Madeleine
FARRAR, STRAUS & GIROUX; DELL
GRADES 4–8
ADVENTURE | FANTASY

The four books in this fantasy series feature different members of the Murry family in the classic struggle between good and evil in the universe. *A Wrinkle in Time*, which won the Newbery Award, chronicles Meg Murry's efforts to find her father, overcome the forces of darkness that are threatening the Earth, and recognize her own limitations and strengths. In doing these things, Meg, her brother Charles Wallace, and a friend, Calvin, travel through space and time to rescue Mr. Murry from the evil It. Later books focus on different members of the family as the struggle continues. Readers will be challenged by the intricate plot devices, including time travel and elements of classic literary tales. In all the books, there are complex issues of values, beliefs, and a connection with spiritual powers in the battle against cruelty, injustice, and intolerance.

1. A Wrinkle in Time ◆ 1962
2. A Wind in the Door ◆ 1973
3. A Swiftly Tilting Planet ◆ 1978
4. Many Waters ◆ 1986

TIME TRAVEL QUARTET

Cooney, Caroline B.
BANTAM DOUBLEDAY DELL
GRADES 6–10 ◆ A/R
FANTASY

In the first book, Annie Lockwood travels back to 1895, falls in love with Hiram Stratton Jr., and becomes involved in a murder. In the second of these stories of ill-timed romance, Annie returns to the 1890s and works to free Strat from an insane asylum. *Prisoner of Time* features Strat's sister Devonny and Annie's brother Tod. And in *For All Time*, Annie overshoots Strat's time and ends up in ancient Egypt.

1. Both Sides of Time ◆ 1995
2. Out of Time ◆ 1995
3. Prisoner of Time ◆ 1998
4. For All Time ◆ 2001

TIME TRILOGY

Anderson, Margaret J.
KNOPF
GRADES 5–8
FANTASY

In this science fantasy trilogy, Jennifer and Robert discover that they can slip through the Circle of Stones and travel through time to the year 2179. There they come upon a peaceful society trying to protect itself from a barbaric mechanized society. As the trilogy progresses, these people who refuse to meet violence with violence struggle to protect their community.

1. In the Keep of Time ◆ 1977
2. In the Circle of Time ◆ 1979
3. The Mists of Time ◆ 1984

TIME ZONE HIGH

Strasser, Todd
SIMON & SCHUSTER
GRADES 7–10
REAL LIFE

These entertaining books, set at a high school on the West Coast, concentrate mainly on romantic attachments. In *How I Spent My Life on Earth*, a rumor has spread that an asteroid is headed for Earth, and the students spend a night confronting impending doom and examining their relationships.

1. How I Changed My Life ◆ 1995
2. How I Created My Perfect Prom Date ◆ 1998
3. How I Spent My Last Night on Earth ◆ 1998

TODAYSGIRLS.COM

Various authors
THOMAS NELSON
GRADES 6–9 ◆ A/R
REAL LIFE | VALUES

Six high school girls have a Web site with a private chat room. In the first book, a stranger crashes the chat room and threatens Amber. In the second book, Jamie faces a dilemma when the painting that wins an art scholarship for her is not really her painting. Faith and values play important roles in this series.

1. Stranger Online (Smith, Carol) ◆ 1997
2. Portrait of Lies (Mackall, Dandi Daley) ◆ 2000
3. Tangled Web (Holl, Kristi) ◆ 2000
4. R U 4 Real? (Peacock, Nancy) ◆ 2000
5. Luv@First Site (Kindig, Tess Eileen) ◆ 2000
6. Chat Freak (Holl, Kristi) ◆ 2000
7. N 2 Deep (Knowlton, Laurie Lazzaro) ◆ 2001
8. Please Reply! (Mackall, Dandi Daley) ◆ 2001
9. 4Give & 4Get (Holl, Kristi) ◆ 2001
10. Power Drive (Peacock, Nancy) ◆ 2001
11. Unpredictable (Kindig, Tess Eileen) ◆ 2001
12. Fun E-Farm (Wiseman, Heather) ◆ 2001

TOM CLANCY'S NET FORCE *see* Net Force

TOM SWIFT

Appleton, Victor
SIMON & SCHUSTER
GRADES 7–8
ADVENTURE | FANTASY

Mutant sea creatures, a cyborg kick boxer, and microbots are just some of the creatures that this updated Tom Swift and his friends battle to protect our world. In *Mutant Beach*, Tom faces a giant squid and a 50-foot shark, which could be the result of his research into growth hormones. Tom battles those who are out to blame him while he tries to find out who is really responsible. *Fire Biker* features Tom and his sister Sandra. They have invented a jet-powered cycle and a suit that makes the wearer invisible, but their inventions have been stolen and now the whole world is in danger. These are action-packed books with the kinds of creatures and suspense that will attract the readers of R. L. Stine's series as well as readers who like the adventure of *Star Trek* and *Star Wars*.

1. The Black Dragon ◆ 1991
2. The Negative Zone ◆ 1991
3. Cyborg Kickboxer ◆ 1991
4. The DNA Disaster ◆ 1991
5. Monster Machine ◆ 1991
6. Aquatech Warriors ◆ 1991
7. Moonstalker ◆ 1992
8. The Microbots ◆ 1992
9. Fire Biker ◆ 1992
10. Mind Games ◆ 1992
11. Mutant Beach ◆ 1992
12. Death Quake ◆ 1993
13. Quantum Force ◆ 1993

TOMORROW

Marsden, John
HOUGHTON MIFFLIN
GRADES 8–12 ◆ A/R
ADVENTURE

A group of Australian teens return from a camping trip to find that their country has been invaded and their families imprisoned. Ellie and her friends survive in the countryside and use guerrilla tactics against the enemy. In *A Killing Frost*, they tackle a containership. In *Burning for Revenge*, they become separated from a group of New Zealand rescuers and attack an airfield.

1. Tomorrow, When the War Began ◆ 1995
2. The Dead of Night ◆ 1997
3. A Killing Frost ◆ 1998
4. Darkness, Be My Friend ◆ 1999
5. Burning for Revenge ◆ 2000
6. The Night Is for Hunting ◆ 2001
7. The Other Side of Dawn ◆ 2002

TRAIL OF THREAD

Hubalek, Linda K.
BUTTERFIELD BOOKS
GRADES 7–10
HISTORICAL

Pioneer women in the mid-19th century are featured in this atmospheric historical fiction series. In the first book, Deborah Pieratt writes letters describing her family's journey from Kentucky to the Territory of Kansas. Carefully researched details of the experiences on a wagon train and descriptions of quilting patterns make for absorbing reading.

1. Trail of Thread: A Woman's Westward Journey ◆ 1995
2. Thimble of Soil: A Woman's Quest for Land ◆ 1996
3. Stitch of Courage: A Woman's Fight for Freedom ◆ 1996

TRASH

Bennett, Cherie, and Jeff Gottesfeld
BERKLEY
GRADES 8–12
REAL LIFE

Six teens are summer interns on a new reality talk show. The antics onscreen are outrageous while behind the scenes the interns have their own problems. A show about mass murders may reveal Chelsea's secret. Lisha is being stalked. Sky's best friend is dating the woman he wants. The first book in the series has been reissued with the title *Hot Trash*.

1. Trash ◆ 1997
2. Love, Lies and Video ◆ 1997
3. Good Girls, Bad Boys ◆ 1997
4. Dirty Big Secrets ◆ 1997
5. The Evil Twin ◆ 1997
6. Truth or Scare ◆ 1998

TRAVELING PANTS *see* Sisterhood of the Traveling Pants

TRIGUN MAXIMUM

Nightow, Yasuhiro
DARK HORSE
GRADES 8–12
FANTASY

The original popular Trigun manga is continued in this series. Vash the Stampede, a super-gunslinger, is back with a bounty on his head. He moves from one violent conflict to another, confronting evil villains including Gray the Ninelives. Fans of action and manga will want to see these books.

1. The Hero Returns ◆ 2004
2. Death Blue ◆ 2004
3. His Life as a . . . ◆ 2004

TRIPODS

Christopher, John
MACMILLAN
GRADES 5–8 ◆ A/R
SCIENCE FICTION

Aliens have taken over the Earth, and every Earth boy receives a cap at age 13 so the aliens can control his thoughts. The aliens take the form of huge metal tripods, and no one knows if that is their real form or if they are just machines that aliens use. Will, Henry, and Jean Paul escape to the White Mountains and find a colony of free men. Jean Paul, Will, and a German boy named Fritz are sent on a mission to the city of the aliens to learn their ways, and Will barely escapes with his life. The aliens are completely defeated as a result of what Fritz and Will are able to learn. *When the Tripods Came* is a prequel to the series, and readers may want to read it first.

1. The White Mountains ◆ 1967
2. The City of Gold and Lead ◆ 1967
3. The Pool of Fire ◆ 1968
4. When the Tripods Came ◆ 1988

TROLLTOWN *see* The Word and the Void

TROUBLESHOOTERS

Brockmann, Suzanne
BALLANTINE
GRADES 11–12
REAL LIFE

A Navy SEAL Troubleshooter squad trained to deal with terrorists is the focus of this series of thrillers full of romance, mystery, and suspense. For mature readers.

1. The Unsung Hero ◆ 2000
2. The Defiant Hero ◆ 2001
3. Over the Edge ◆ 2001
4. Out of Control ◆ 2002
5. Into the Night ◆ 2002
6. Gone Too Far ◆ 2003
7. Hot Target ◆ 2004

TRUE-TO-LIFE *see* Hamilton High

TRUTH OR DARE

Hopkins, Cathy
SIMON & SCHUSTER
GRADES 7–10 ◆ A/R
REAL LIFE

Everyone knows the game Truth or Dare. Cat has played the game but cannot face the results. How can she tell her boyfriend that it is over? Her friend, Becca, is no help. In the second book, the two girls compete for the title of Pop Princess. These books were originally published in England.

1. White Lies and Barefaced Truths ◆ 2004
2. The Princess of Pop ◆ 2004
3. Teen Queens and Has-Beens ◆ 2004
4. Starstruck ◆ 2005

THE TUCKET ADVENTURES

Paulsen, Gary
DELACORTE
GRADES 5–8 ◆ A/R
ADVENTURE | HISTORICAL

Francis Tucket is 14 when this series begins. While heading west on the Oregon Trail, Francis is separated from his family and captured by Pawnees. He is aided by Mr. Grimes, who teaches him survival skills but also gives him a look at the violent ways of a frontiersman. Francis leaves Mr. Grimes and searches for his family only to encounter more ruthless outlaws. This is a gritty series that does not romanticize the difficulties of life on the frontier. With lots of action, this should appeal to boys and perhaps to reluctant readers.

1. Mr Tucket ◆ 1994
2. Call Me Francis Tucket ◆ 1995
3. Tucket's Ride ◆ 1997
4. Tucket's Gold ◆ 1999
5. Tucket's Home ◆ 2000

TURNING SEVENTEEN

Various authors
PARACHUTE PRESS
GRADES 7–10 ◆ A/R
REAL LIFE

Four friends—Kerri, Jessica, Erin, and Maya—experience a variety of teenage anxieties. For example, Kerri wins a bet when she gets a date with Matt. Unfortunately, Matt finds out. This series is presented in cooperation with *Seventeen* magazine.

1. Any Guy You Want (Noonan, Rosalind) ◆ 2000
2. More than This (Straub, Wendy Corsi) ◆ 2000
3. For Real (Roberts, Christa) ◆ 2000
4. Show Me Love (Craft, Elizabeth) ◆ 2000
5. Can't Let Go (Noonan, Rosalind) ◆ 2000
6. This Boy Is Mine (Straub, Wendy Corsi) ◆ 2001

7. Secrets and Lies (Roberts, Christa) ◆ 2001
8. We Have to Talk (Craft, Elizabeth) ◆ 2001
9. Just Trust Me (Noonan, Rosalind) ◆ 2001
10. Reality Check (Carrol, Jacqueline) ◆ 2001

TWO OF A KIND *see* Mary-Kate and Ashley: Two of a Kind

2099

Peel, John
SCHOLASTIC
GRADES 5–8 ◆ A/R
SCIENCE FICTION

It is 2099 and 14-year-old Tristan Connor has been working to stop the dangerous actions of Devon, only to discover that Devon is his clone. With the help of a policewoman and an Underworld crook, Tristan must stop the doomsday virus that Devon has released. With cliff-hanging endings, the books do not stand alone. The action comes to a dramatic conclusion in *Firestorm*. Fans of futuristic novels and computers will enjoy the cyber-action.

1. Doomsday ◆ 1999
2. Betrayal ◆ 1999
3. Traitor ◆ 2000
4. Revolution ◆ 2000
5. Meltdown ◆ 2000
6. Firestorm ◆ 2000

2001

Clarke, Arthur C.
NAL; BALLANTINE
GRADES 9–12
SCIENCE FICTION

The computer named Hal plays a starring role in *2001*, an allegorical story about the history and future of mankind. In *2010*, scientists race to recover the information from the deserted *2001* space ship. Humans continue to search for the secret of the strange monolith in the succeeding volumes.

1. 2001: A Space Odyssey ◆ 1968
2. 2010: Odyssey Two ◆ 1982
3. 2061: Odyssey Three ◆ 1988
4. 3001: The Final Odyssey ◆ 1997

UNCOMMON HEROES

Henderson, Dee
MULTNOMAH
GRADES 10–12
REAL LIFE | VALUES

This series about Navy SEALs combines suspense and romance with Christian values and strong female characters. *True Valor* features a feisty combat pilot named Gracie Yates whose plane crashes behind enemy lines in Iraq. She is rescued by an air force major with whom she has a long but chaste history.

1. True Devotion ◆ 2000
2. True Valor ◆ 2002
3. True Honor ◆ 2002

THE UNDERLAND CHRONICLES

Collins, Suzanne
SCHOLASTIC
GRADES 4–8
FANTASY

Gregor, 11, and his sister Boots, 2, enter the Underland and encounter unusual humans along with giant cockroaches, spiders, rats, and bats. Gregor discovers that the humans are captives and that one of them is his father. The second book follows Gregor's return to the Underland to fulfill a prophecy. More adventures are expected.

1. Gregor the Overlander ◆ 2003
2. Gregor and the Prophecy of Bane ◆ 2004

UNICORN

Lee, Tanith
MACMILLAN; TOR
GRADES 7–12
FANTASY

Tanaquil, the daughter of a sorceress, makes a unicorn from strange golden bones. and the unicorn lures her away to a seaside city and a perfect world. In the second book, Tanaquil meets her half-sister, who has a golden unicorn that must be mended. Despite her misgivings, Tanaquil brings it to life and discovers that it is not only a beast of war but provides entry to a world whose purpose is war.

1. Black Unicorn ◆ 1991
2. Gold Unicorn ◆ 1994
3. Red Unicorn ◆ 1997

UNIVERSITY HOSPITAL

Bennett, Cherie
BERKLEY
GRADES 7–10
REAL LIFE

After graduating from high school, five teens hope to enter medical school. A summer program at a hospital may earn them a scholarship. They are connected but still competitive. Tristan and Summer begin a romantic relationship but Zoey finds out. Teens will find the romance and medical details fascinating.

1. University Hospital ◆ 1999
2. Condition Critical ◆ 1999
3. Crisis Point ◆ 2000
4. Heart Trauma ◆ 2000
5. Prognosis: Heartbreak ◆ 2002

VALDEMAR: GRYPHON TRILOGY

Lackey, Mercedes
DAW
GRADES 7–12
FANTASY

Prehistoric Valdemar is the setting for this series that provides background information for three other series—Mage Wars, Magic Winds, and Mage Storms. The city of White Gryphon is threatened and the combined efforts of humans and gryphons are needed to defeat the evil.

1. The Black Gryphon ◆ 1994
2. The White Gryphon ◆ 1995
3. The Silver Gryphon ◆ 1996

VALDEMAR: MAGE STORMS

Lackey, Mercedes
DAW
GRADES 7–12 ◆ A/R
FANTASY

This series follows the events in the Mage Wars and Magic Wind series. Also set in Valdemar, it focuses on two young adults—Karal and An'desha. As they realize their talents, they join with others to face the mage storms. Eventually, they come to understand that the storms are linked to events in the prehistory of Valdemar. These events are described in the Gryphon Trilogy.

1. Storm Warning ◆ 1994
2. Storm Rising ◆ 1995
3. Storm Breaking ◆ 1996

VALDEMAR: MAGE WARS

Lackey, Mercedes
DAW
GRADES 7–12 ◆ A/R
FANTASY

Vanyel discovers his destiny—first at the High Court of Valdemar and later as a Herald-Mage. With his Companion, Yfandes, he faces the dark magic. The adventures continue with the series Magic Winds, and Mage Storms. The Gryphon Trilogy provides background information on the magical events in Valdemar.

1. Magic's Pawn ◆ 1989
2. Magic's Promise ◆ 1990
3. Magic's Price ◆ 1990

VALDEMAR: MAGE WINDS

Lackey, Mercedes
DAW
GRADES 7–12 ◆ A/R
FANTASY

Valdemar is a magical land. Elspeth Herald must develop her magical powers to become the mage needed to face the coming dangers. This series comes after the events in Mage Wars and before those in Mage Storms. The prequel series is the Gryphon Trilogy.

1. Winds of Fate ◆ 1991
2. Winds of Change ◆ 1992
3. Winds of Fury ◆ 1993

VALDEMAR: MAGEWORLDS

Doyle, Debra, and James D. MacDonald
TOR
GRADES 6–9
FANTASY

This series follows years of turmoil between the Republic and the Mageworlds. Battles, intrigue, royal feuds, supernatural powers, creatures, and more are found in these books, which one review called a space opera (like an intergalactic soap opera). In one book, Beka seeks to avenge her mother's assassination. In another, the adventure focuses on the body of a starship captain that was found on his broken-down ship. Two prequels, the fourth and seventh books, provide background information on the conflict and the early warriors.

1. The Price of the Stars ◆ 1993
2. Starpilot's Grave ◆ 1993
3. By Honor Betray'd ◆ 1994
4. The Gathering Flame: The Prequel to Mageworlds ◆ 1995
5. The Long Hunt ◆ 1996
6. A Working of Stars ◆ 2002
7. The Stars Asunder: A New Novel of the Mageworlds ◆ 2003

VAMPIRE DIARIES

Smith, L. J.

HARPERCOLLINS

GRADES 7–10

FANTASY | HORROR

Elena finds herself drawn to Stefan when she meets him at school. She later finds out that he and his brother are vampires and the series follows Elena's attraction to both brothers and her own conversion into a vampire. The books were reissued in 1999.

1. The Awakening ◆ 1991
2. The Struggle ◆ 1991
3. The Fury ◆ 1991
4. Dark Reunion ◆ 1991

THE VAMPIRE'S PROMISE

Cooney, Caroline B.

SCHOLASTIC

GRADES 6–8 ◆ A/R

HORROR

Teenagers with ordinary concerns find themselves involved with vampires. In *Fatal Bargain*, six teenagers decide to have a party in an old abandoned house and meet a hungry vampire who declares that one of them will be his victim. They need to decide which one it will be. After some failed escape attempts, and encounters with various people who stumble on the scene, they all escape, only to confront the monster again.

1. Deadly Offer ◆ 1991
2. Evil Returns ◆ 1992
3. Fatal Bargain ◆ 1993

VESPER HOLLY

Alexander, Lloyd

DUTTON

GRADES 5–7 ◆ A/R

ADVENTURE | HUMOR

Vesper is the teenage daughter of a deceased famous scholar and adventurer. Her father's best friend, Brinnie, and his wife, Mary, have become Vesper's guardians, and together they travel the world from one adventure to another. The evil Dr. Helvitius is their arch enemy, always coming up with some evil scheme against innocent people. In Central America, he is building a canal that will ruin the land of the Indian people. In Europe, he is planning for a small country to be annexed by its neighbors. Vesper and Brinnie are always one step ahead of him, with the help of various friends they collect along the way. Brinnie's pompous behavior supplies humor, while Vesper is an exciting heroine.

1. The Illyrian Adventure ◆ 1986
2. The El Dorado Adventure ◆ 1987
3. The Drackenberg Adventure ◆ 1988
4. The Jedera Adventure ◆ 1989
5. The Philadelphia Adventure ◆ 1990

VICKY AUSTIN

L'Engle, Madeleine

FARRAR, STRAUS & GIROUX; BANTAM DOUBLEDAY DELL

GRADES 4–7

FAMILY LIFE | MYSTERY | REAL LIFE

In *Meet the Austins*, Vicky is 12 and her family is faced with taking in a spoiled orphan girl. The father, a country doctor, is offered a position in New York, where they become involved in an international plot. On a cross-country camping trip, they meet a spoiled rich boy who takes a liking to Vicky. The Austins spend summers in their grandfather's house on an island off the East Coast. Here Vicky befriends a boy who is doing research on dolphins and discovers that she has a real affinity for the animals. This series tackles issues of life and death, faith and cynicism, and shows a loving family dealing intelligently with problems. A simple Christmas story, *The Twenty-Four Days Before Christmas* (1964), is a prequel written on a much easier level than the rest of the series.

1. Meet the Austins ◆ 1960
2. The Moon by Night ◆ 1963
3. The Young Unicorns ◆ 1968
4. A Ring of Endless Light ◆ 1980
5. Troubling a Star ◆ 1994

Victorian Tales of London

Blackwell, Lawana
Bethany House
Grades 9–12
Historical | Values

This series features teenage girls who are searching for true love while maintaining their virtue and values in Victorian London. In *The Maiden of Mayfair*, Sarah Matthews was raised as an orphan in the Foundling Home for Girls. A rich widow suspects that Sarah may be her granddaughter. She takes her into her own home and Sarah must adjust to the manners of London society, which provide a backdrop for these rags to riches sagas.

1. The Maiden of Mayfair ◆ 2001
2. Catherine's Heart ◆ 2002
3. Leading Lady ◆ 2004

The Viking

Tebbetts, Christopher
Puffin
Grades 6–8 ◆ A/R
Fantasy

Zack Gilman, 14, is tailgating with his father at a Minnesota Vikings game when he gets lost in a snowstorm. He travels to the time of the real Vikings (whose traits and appearance remind Zack of people in the present, including a boy who has bullied him). Zack becomes involved in the quest for Yggdrasil's Chest and in solving the Prophecy of the Lost Boy.

1. Viking Pride ◆ 2003
2. Quest for Faith ◆ 2003
3. Land of the Dead ◆ 2003
4. Hammer of the Gods ◆ 2003

VIRTUAL REALITY

Kritlow, William
THOMAS NELSON
GRADES 7–10
FANTASY

In a virtual reality chamber, Kelly and her brother Tim must use their computer skills and their faith to solve problems. In one book, they try to rescue the president and his son from an alternate, hostile virtual reality.

1. A Race Against Time ◆ 1995
2. The Deadly Maze ◆ 1995
3. Backfire ◆ 1995

VIVI HARTMAN

Feder, Harriet K.
LERNER
GRADES 6–10 ◆ A/R
MYSTERY

Vivi Hartman is a lively and intelligent teenage daughter of a rabbi. In *Mystery of the Kaifeng Scroll*, she uses her linguistic talents to track down her mother when she goes missing in Turkey. At a funeral on a Seneca reservation in *Death on Sacred Ground*, she learns that a murder may have taken place.

1. Mystery in Miami Beach ◆ 1992
2. Mystery of the Kaifeng Scroll ◆ 1995
3. Death on Sacred Ground ◆ 2001

WAKARA OF EAGLE LODGE

Shands, Linda
REVELL
GRADES 6–9
REAL LIFE | VALUES

After her mother's death in a car accident, Wakara Sheridan, 15, tries to help at her family's lodge. Wakara is skeptical about the faith shown by some of the employees of Eagle Lodge, but her beliefs change when she escapes a forest fire. In the third book, Wakara explores her Native American heritage (she is also part Irish) and she faces another test of her faith.

1. Wild Fire ◆ 2001
2. Blind Fury ◆ 2001
3. White Water ◆ 2001

WALKER AND TAG

Vick, Helen H.
HARBINGER HOUSE
GRADES 6–9
FANTASY

Walker, 15, is a Hopi Indian boy who travels 800 years back in time to the world of the Sinagua culture. A younger white boy, Tag, inadvertently travels along with him. Walker becomes involved with the people and agrees to lead them to a new home.

1. Walker of Time ◆ 1993
2. Walker's Journey Home ◆ 1995
3. Tag Against Time ◆ 1996

WARRIORS

Hunter, Erin
HARPERCOLLINS
GRADES 6–9 ◆ A/R
FANTASY

A house cat named Rusty has lived in comfort with Twolegs but leaves to enter the world of the wildcat clans. A world with four different clans—ThunderClan, ShadowClan, WindClan, and RiverClan. Rusty becomes an apprentice named Firepaw. After he proves himself, he beecomes a warrior cat in training named Fireheart. He begins a quest to be a true warrior.

1. Into the Wild ◆ 2003
2. Fire and Ice ◆ 2003
3. Forest of Secrets ◆ 2003
4. Rising Storm ◆ 2004
5. A Dangerous Path ◆ 2004
6. The Darkest Hour ◆ 2004

WATCHERS AT THE WELL

Chalker, Jack L.
BALLANTINE
GRADES 10–12
FANTASY

The Well World is a place where beings experience strange transformations. Space wanderer Nathan Brazil has become the guardian of the Well of Souls. He knows powerful secrets but has grown weary of his responsibilities. When danger threatens the Well World, Nathan and Mavra Chang work to protect the future of the world. This trilogy stands alone but there are other Well World novels dating back into the late 1970s.

1. Echoes of the Well of Souls: A Well World Novel ◆ 1993
2. Shadow of the Well of Souls: A Well World Novel ◆ 1994
3. Gods of the Well of Souls: A Well World Novel ◆ 1995

WATCHER'S QUEST

Buffie, Margaret
KIDS CAN PRESS
GRADES 7–10 ◆ A/R
FANTASY

What begins as a modern family story set in Manitoba quickly develops into an intricate fantasy with roots in Celtic mythology. Emma has been raised as a human but is really an alien, a Watcher. Emma has kept watch over her alien sister, Summer, a changeling and the queen of Argadnel. Emma joins with another Watcher, Tom, to find her mother's true daughter, Ailla. The two compete with aliens in a game to win Ailla. The relationship between Tom and Emma grows when they search for the four Wands—Earth, Wind, Water, and Fire.

1. The Watcher ◆ 2002
2. The Seeker ◆ 2002
3. The Finder ◆ 2004

WATCHING ALICE

Parker, Daniel, and Lee Miller

PUTNAM

GRADES 7–10

REAL LIFE

Tom Sinclair is 16 and he wants to begin a new life in New York City. He meets Alice Brown and is deeply attracted to her; then she disappears. Alice's diary and some mysterious e-mail messages help direct his search for her. Tom finds that his own past may have something to do with the disappearance.

1. Break the Surface ◆ 2004
2. Walk on Water ◆ 2004
3. Seek the Prophet ◆ 2004
4. Find the Miracle ◆ 2005

WATER

Dalkey, Kara

AVON

GRADES 7–10

FANTASY

Romance and adventure are interwoven into these rich fantasies featuring a 16-year-old mermyd called Nia who lives in Atlantis. Nia has ambitions that are thwarted and she comes to realize that their government is rife with intrigue and plots. In the second book, Nia becomes involved with a "dry-lander," and in the final book of the trilogy, Nia and Corwin hold the key to the survival of her city.

1. Ascension ◆ 2002
2. Reunion ◆ 2002
3. Transformation ◆ 2002

WEETZIE BAT SAGA

Block, Francesca Lia

HARPERCOLLINS

GRADES 10–12 ◆ A/R

REAL LIFE

Set in Los Angeles, these books describe the struggles, anxieties, joys, and hopes of a group of friends. Weetzie is 23 and she loves the glamour and romance of Hollywood movies. She meets Dirk, a gay man looking for love. They each find companions and move in together. Witch Baby joins the group and struggles to find her place. Two books issued in 2004 combine the earlier volumes. *Beautiful Boys* includes *Missing Angel Juan* and *Baby Be-Bop*, both featuring male heroes; *Goat Girls* includes *Witch Baby* and *Cherokee Bat and the Goat Guys*, both with female protagonists' point of views.

1. Weetzie Bat ◆ 1989
2. Witch Baby ◆ 1991
3. Cherokee Bat and the Goat Guys ◆ 1992
4. Missing Angel Juan ◆ 1993
5. Baby Be-Bop ◆ 1995

WELL OF SOULS *see* Watchers at the Well

THE WESSEX PAPERS

Parker, Daniel

AVON

GRADES 9–12

MYSTERY

Wessex Academy is a private school for privileged students, who get up to a variety of pranks and rebellions. Sunday and her friend Fred uncover a blackmail plot and their efforts to expose the perpetrators continue throughout the three books.

1. Trust Falls ◆ 2002
2. Fallout ◆ 2002
3. Outsmart ◆ 2002

WEST CREEK MIDDLE SCHOOL *see* Losers, Inc.

WESTMARK

Alexander, Lloyd
BANTAM DOUBLEDAY DELL
GRADES 5–7 ◆ A/R
ADVENTURE | FANTASY

This series is set in a world much like our own in the late Renaissance. Theo is a printer's helper who is embroiled in a revolt against a corrupt government. When his master is killed, he falls in with the scheming Count and with Mickle, a poor girl with an amazing talent for ventriloquism. They meet up with a group of revolutionaries led by the charismatic Florian, who wants to do away with the monarchy altogether. Mickle and Theo fall in love, and she is revealed to be the king's long-lost daughter. She and Theo plan to marry, and the next two books in this trilogy concern their struggles against enemies in and out of Westmark.

1. Westmark ◆ 1981
2. The Kestrel ◆ 1982
3. The Beggar Queen ◆ 1984

THE WHEEL OF TIME

Jordan, Robert
TOR
GRADES 10–12 ◆ A/R
FANTASY

The Third Age is the Age of Prophecy. A peaceful world is threatened by the Dark One. Rand al'Thor is chosen to revisit the heritage (and madness) of the Dragon on a quest to find the magical elements to rescue the world from evil.

1. Eye of the World ◆ 1990
2. The Great Hunt ◆ 1990
3. The Dragon Reborn ◆ 1991
4. The Shadow Rising ◆ 1992
5. The Fires of Heaven ◆ 1993
6. Lord of Chaos ◆ 1994
7. A Crown of Swords ◆ 1996
8. The Path of Daggers ◆ 1998
9. Winter's Heart ◆ 2000
10. Crossroads of Twilight ◆ 2003

THE WHEEL OF TIME (RELATED BOOKS)

Jordan, Robert
STARSCAPE
GRADES 7–10 ◆ A/R
FANTASY

These books from the original series are revised to be accessible to a younger audience.

1. From the Two Rivers: The Eye of the World, Book One ◆ 2002
2. To the Blight: Part Two of The Eye of the World ◆ 2002
3. The Hunt Begins: The Great Hunt, Part 1 ◆ 2003
4. New Threads in the Pattern: The Great Hunt, Part 2 ◆ 2003

WHISPERING BROOK

Bender, Carrie
HERALD PRESS
GRADES 6–9
FAMILY LIFE | REAL LIFE

The Petersheims are a large Amish family living on several farms in Lancaster County, Pennsylvania. These books focus on the struggles of different family members. In *Hemlock Hill Hideaway,* Omar and his sister work on the farm and make a home for a difficult child named Dannie. These stories provide insights into the Amish world.

1. Whispering Brook Farm ◆ 1999
2. Summerville Days ◆ 1999
3. Hemlock Hill Hideaway ◆ 2000
4. Chestnut Ridge Acres ◆ 2001
5. Woodland Dell's Secret ◆ 2002
6. Timber Lane Cove ◆ 2003

WHITE MANE KIDS

Various authors
WHITE MANE PUBLISHING
GRADES 6–10
HISTORICAL

All of these books feature characters caught up in the Civil War. In *Ghosts of Vicksburg,* Jamie Carswell is fighting in Mississippi with the

14th Wisconsin regiment. Jamie used to visit his cousins there, but their home has been destroyed. His cousins are in Vicksburg and face more destruction, which leads Jamie to question his role in the conflict. These are fast-paced books that should interest fans of this era.

1. The Secret of the Lion's Head (Hall, Beverly B.) ◆ 1995
2. The Night Riders of Harper's Ferry (Ernst, Kathleen) ◆ 1996
3. Broken Drum (Hemingway, Edith Morris) ◆ 1996
4. Brothers at War (Blair, Margaret Whitman) ◆ 1996
5. The Bravest Girl in Sharpsburg (Ernst, Kathleen) ◆ 1997
6. Shenandoah Autumn (Joslyn, Mauriel) ◆ 1998
7. House of Spies: Danger in Civil War Washington (Blair, Margaret Whitman) ◆ 1999
8. Rebel Hart (Hemingway, Edith Morris) ◆ 1999
9. Retreat from Gettysburg (Ernst, Kathleen) ◆ 2000
10. Freedom Calls (Sawyer, Kem Knapp) ◆ 2001
11. Hayfoot, Strawfoot: The Bucktail Recruits (Robertson, William P.) ◆ 2001
12. The Bucktails' Shenandoah March (Robertson, William P.) ◆ 2002
13. Ghosts of Vicksburg (Ernst, Kathleen) ◆ 2003
14. The Bucktails' Antietam Trials (Robertson, William P.) ◆ 2004
15. Anybody's Hero: The Battle of Old Men and Young Boys (Haislip, Phyllis Hall) ◆ 2004
16. The Battling Bucktails at Fredericksburg (Robertson, William P.) ◆ 2004
17. The Sand Castle: Blockade Running and the Battle of Fort Fisher (Blair, Margaret Whitman) ◆ 2004

WHY ME?

Kent, Deborah
SIMON & SCHUSTER
GRADES 6–9 ◆ A/R
REAL LIFE

Teens coping with illness and injury are the focus of this trilogy featuring unrelated characters. In the first book, 15-year-old Chloe comes down with lupus and retreats from her everyday life and her boyfriend. In *Living with a Secret,* Cassie tries to hide her diabetes. And in *Don't Cry for Yesterday,* Amber's spinal cord is severed when the car driven by her date crashes. Fans of Lurlene McDaniel will enjoy these stories.

1. The Courage to Live ◆ 2001
2. Living with a Secret ◆ 2001
3. Don't Cry for Yesterday ◆ 2002

WICKED

Holder, Nancy, and Debbie Viguie
SIMON & SCHUSTER
GRADES 9–12 ◆ A/R
FANTASY

When her parents die, 16-year-old Holly Cathers goes to live with her twin cousins Amanda and Nicole and their mother. Holly soon discovers that she and her cousins have magical powers. Her life becomes more complicated when she falls in love with Jer Deveraux, whose family are warlocks with a longstanding grudge against her own relatives. As the series progresses, Holly and her cousins must rescue each other, Jer, and relatives from dangerous situations.

1. Witch ◆ 2002
2. Curse ◆ 2002
3. Legacy ◆ 2003
4. Spellbound ◆ 2003

WILD AT HEART

Anderson, Laurie Halse
PLEASANT COMPANY
GRADES 4–7 ◆ A/R
REAL LIFE

Animal lovers will love this series. At the Wild at Heart Animal Clinic, animals are cared for and protected. Maggie, 13, lives with her grandmother who is a vet at the clinic. She resents having to train some new volunteers but she appreciates their help when animals are found in abusive situations. Issues such as animal testing and cruelty to pets are explored.

1. Fight for Life: Book 1: Maggie ◆ 2000
2. Homeless: Book 2: Sunita ◆ 2000
3. Trickster: Book 3: David ◆ 2000
4. Manatee Blues: Book 4: Brenna ◆ 2000
5. Say Good-Bye: Book 5: Zoe ◆ 2001
6. Storm Rescue: Book 6: Sunita ◆ 2001
7. Teacher's Pet: Book 7: Maggie ◆ 2001
8. Trapped: Book 8: Brenna ◆ 2001
9. Fear of Falling: Book 9: David ◆ 2001

10. Time to Fly: Book 10: Zoe ◆ 2002
11. Masks: Book 11: Sunita ◆ 2002
12. End of the Race: Book 12: Maggie ◆ 2003

WILD ROSE INN

Armstrong, Jennifer
BANTAM
GRADES 6–10
FAMILY LIFE | HISTORICAL

This series follows six generations of young women who have ties to an inn in Marblehead, Massachusetts. In the first book, Bridie comes from Scotland to join her parents in the New World and discovers that she must hide her beliefs in the Puritan community. In the second book, Ann is torn between love for her country and her attraction for a British sailor.

1. Bridie of the Wild Rose Inn, 1695 ◆ 1994
2. Ann of the Wild Rose Inn, 1774 ◆ 1994
3. Emily of the Wild Rose Inn, 1858 ◆ 1994
4. Laura of the Wild Rose Inn, 1898 ◆ 1994
5. Claire of the Wild Rose Inn, 1928 ◆ 1994
6. Grace of the Wild Rose Inn, 1944 ◆ 1994

THE WIND ON FIRE

Nicholson, William
HYPERION
GRADES 5–8 ◆ A/R
FANTASY

Twins Kestrel and Bowman, born into the regimented society of Amaranth, rebel against the focus on work and order and set off on a quest to find the voice of the Wind Singer, believing this will free their people, the Manth. In the third book, the siblings lead the Manth on a dangerous journey to a new homeland.

1. The Wind Singer: An Adventure ◆ 2001
2. Slaves of the Mastery ◆ 2001
3. Firesong ◆ 2002

WINDS OF LIGHT

Brouwer, Sigmund
VICTOR BOOKS
GRADES 6–8 ◆ A/R
FANTASY I HISTORICAL I VALUES

As an orphan in the 1300s, Thomas must search for his rightful place. Leaving the monks who raised him, Thomas struggles to regain Magnus, an English manor that has been taken from its owners. He encounters a dangerous conspiracy and he comes to realize that it is God's power, not his own anger and violence, that will restore the manor. Thomas's efforts are aided by Katherine, who loves him, and by Sir William, who had escaped the brutality of the conquest of Magnus. Once established as Thomas of Magnus, there are other tests to Thomas's faith. Evil within the leadership of the church threatens Thomas. He is enticed by a group of sorcerers to abandon his faith and enter their false world. The drama of this historical fiction series is supported by the dedication to Christian values.

1. Wings of an Angel ◆ 1992
2. Barbarians from the Isle ◆ 1992
3. Legend of Burning Water ◆ 1992
4. The Forsaken Crusade ◆ 1992
5. A City of Dreams ◆ 1993
6. Merlin's Destiny ◆ 1993
7. The Jester's Quest ◆ 1994
8. Dance of Darkness ◆ 1997

WINNING SEASON

Wallace, Rich
VIKING
GRADES 4–7
RECREATION

Sports fans, get ready. Here's a new series of books featuring popular sports. In the first book, Manny wants to play football but, because he is small, he spends a lot of time on the bench. Manny hopes to prove that he deserves to play. Basketball is featured in the second book. Jared is a great player with a bad temper. Watch for more books in this series, which should be popular with fans of Matt Christopher books.

1. The Roar of the Crowd ◆ 2004
2. Technical Foul ◆ 2004
3. Fast Company ◆ 2005

WISE CHILD

Furlong, Monica
RANDOM HOUSE
GRADES 6–8
FANTASY

After the death of her grandmother, Wise Child (who has been abandoned by her parents) struggles to survive in the poverty of her village. She is befriended by Juniper, a witch, who trains her in magic, herbs, and healing. As the series progresses, Wise Child and Juniper are threatened by Wise Child's evil aunt, Meroot, and they begin a quest to Juniper's home kingdom in Cornwall. *Juniper* is a prequel and, sequentially, comes first.

1. Juniper ◆ 1991
2. Wise Child ◆ 1987
3. Colman ◆ 2004

W.I.T.C.H.

Lenhard, Elizabeth
HYPERION/VOLO
GRADES 5–8
FANTASY

Will, Irma, Taranee, Cornelia, and Hay Lin have secret magical powers. They join together to fight the evil of Prince Phobos. Meanwhile, they go to middle school, do homework, and have ups and downs with their friends.

1. The Power of Five ◆ 2004
2. The Disappearance ◆ 2004
3. Finding Meridian ◆ 2004
4. The Fire of Friendship ◆ 2004
5. The Last Tear ◆ 2004
6. Illusions and Lies ◆ 2004
7. The Light of Meridian ◆ 2004
8. Out of the Dark ◆ 2004
9. The Four Dragons ◆ 2004
10. A Bridge Between Worlds ◆ 2004
11. The Crown of Light ◆ 2004
12. The Return of a Queen ◆ 2005
13. A Different Path ◆ 2005

WITCH

Naylor, Phyllis Reynolds

DELACORTE

GRADES 5–7

HORROR

Lynn is convinced that her neighbor, Mrs. Tuggle, is a witch; but when she and her best friend Mouse try to convince people, no one will listen. Readers will want to keep turning the pages in this suspenseful series as Mrs. Tuggle is overcome, only to return in another form and another way.

1. Witch's Sister ◆ 1975
2. Witch Water ◆ 1977
3. The Witch Herself ◆ 1978
4. The Witch's Eye ◆ 1990
5. Witch Weed ◆ 1992
6. The Witch Returns ◆ 1992

WITCH CHILD

Rees, Celia

CANDLEWICK

GRADES 8–12

FANTASY

In 1659, Mary Newbury, 14, watched as her grandmother was hung for being a witch. Mary must hide her own skills as a healer or she will suffer the same fate. She leaves England and journeys to America but she faces the suspicion of the villagers there, especially the minister who condemned her grandmother. Mary's story is told through journal entries that capture the dramatic action. The second book is set in modern times as Agnes Herne explores her connection to Mary and to her Native American beliefs.

1. Witch Child ◆ 2002
2. Sorceress ◆ 2003

WITCH SEASON

Mariotte, Jeff
SIMON & SCHUSTER
GRADES 9–12
FANTASY

Kerry's summer job is at a posh resort in California. She shares a residence with other teens working there. Daniel Blessing, a young man with a mysterious past, arrives and Kerry is attracted to him. However, his past catches up with him in the form of Season Howe, a witch. Daniel is killed and Kerry struggles to understand the evil that destroyed him.

1. Summer ◆ 2004
2. Fall ◆ 2004
3. Winter ◆ 2005
4. Spring ◆ 2005

A WIZARD IN RHYME

Stasheff, Christopher
BALLANTINE
GRADES 10–12
FANTASY

Matt is transported to a land called Merovence while reading a poem. There he helps Princess Alisande to regain her throne and is instrumental in removing other threats, including that of a ruthless khan in *The Crusading Wizard*.

1. Her Majesty's Wizard ◆ 1986
2. The Oathbound Wizard ◆ 1993
3. The Witch Doctor ◆ 1994
4. The Secular Wizard ◆ 1994
5. My Son the Wizard ◆ 1997
6. The Haunted Wizard ◆ 2000
7. The Crusading Wizard ◆ 2000
8. The Feline Wizard ◆ 2000
9. A Wizard in a Feud ◆ 2001

WIZARDRY

Cook, Rick
BAEN
GRADES 7–12
FANTASY

Wiz Zumwalt, a computer programmer and wizard, finds his high-tech skills in demand. He programs demons, battles dark forces, and is kidnapped by dragons.

1. Wizard's Bane ◆ 1989
2. Wizardry Compiled ◆ 1990
3. Wizardry Cursed ◆ 1991

WIZARDRY

Duane, Diane
HARCOURT
GRADES 5–8
ADVENTURE | FANTASY

Nita is a 13-year-old girl tormented by bullies because she chooses not to fight back. While hiding in the local library, she discovers a book of instructions in the ancient art of wizardry. She meets Kit, a boy who is also a beginning wizard, and together they go on their first quest: to find the book that holds the key to preserving the universe. In the companion books, Nita and Kit go on other adventures: becoming whales to conquer the evil Lone Power in the deepest part of the Atlantic Ocean, cloning a computer and helping Nita's sister travel through several worlds in outer space, and becoming entangled in a magic battle in Ireland. With the popularity of fantasy books, this series has been reissued and expanded.

1. So You Want to be a Wizard ◆ 1983
2. Deep Wizardry ◆ 1985
3. High Wizardry ◆ 1989
4. A Wizard Abroad ◆ 1993
5. The Wizard's Dilemma ◆ 2001
6. A Wizard Alone ◆ 2002
7. Wizard's Holiday ◆ 2003
8. Wizards at War ◆ 2005

WODAN'S CHILDREN

Paxson, Diana L.
MORROW
GRADES 10–12
FANTASY

The story of Siegfried and Brunhilde is retold in this trilogy set on the Rhine in the fifth century.

1. The Wolf and the Raven ◆ 1993
2. The Dragons of the Rhine ◆ 1995
3. The Lord of Horses ◆ 1996

WOLFBAY WINGS

Brooks, Bruce
HARPERCOLLINS
GRADES 4–8 ◆ A/R
REAL LIFE | RECREATION

The Wolfbay Wings are a Squirt A ice hockey team that has become very successful. Unfortunately, a new coach and new players make the future uncertain. Each book in this series features a different player. Dixon "Woodsie" Woods is 11 years old and is worried about the team's prospects. William Fowler, "Billy," is only 10, and he is bothered by his teammates, Coach Cooper, and his overbearing father. There are statistics about the featured player on the back of each book and a tear-out sports card in the front. With lots of details about hockey and ample action, this should be a good choice for sports fans.

1. Woodsie ◆ 1997
2. Zip ◆ 1997
3. Cody ◆ 1997
4. Boot ◆ 1998
5. Prince ◆ 1998
6. Shark ◆ 1998
7. Billy ◆ 1998
8. Dooby ◆ 1998
9. Reed ◆ 1998
10. Subtle ◆ 1999
11. Barry ◆ 1999
12. Woodsie, Again ◆ 1999

WOLVES CHRONICLES

Aiken, Joan
DELACORTE; BANTAM
GRADES 4–8 ◆ A/R
ADVENTURE | FANTASY

High melodrama and an "unhistorical" setting mark this loosely connected series. In the England of this alternate world, King James III rules, Hanoverians are constantly plotting to put Prince George on the throne, and packs of vicious wolves menace the countryside. The Wolves Chronicles begin with the story of two little girls who are left in the care of an evil woman who schemes to take their inheritance. The girls are rescued by the mysterious orphan boy Simon, who later in the series is revealed to be a duke. Simon befriends a Cockney girl, Dido, whose parents are evil Hanoverians, and the rest of the series is about their adventures, by themselves and with other friends, as they defend the true king.

1. The Wolves of Willoughby Chase ◆ 1963
2. Black Hearts in Battersea ◆ 1964
3. Nightbirds on Nantucket ◆ 1966
4. The Whispering Mountain ◆ 1968
5. The Cuckoo Tree ◆ 1971
6. The Stolen Lake ◆ 1981
7. Dido and Pa ◆ 1986
8. Is Underground ◆ 1993
9. Cold Shoulder Road ◆ 1996
10. Dangerous Games ◆ 2000
11. Midwinter Nightingale ◆ 2003
12. Witch of Clatteringshaws ◆ 2005

THE WORD AND THE VOID

Brooks, Terry
BALLANTINE DEL REY
GRADES 10–12
FANTASY

Nest Freemark, a 14-year-old with inherited magical powers, finds herself in the middle of a struggle between Knight of the Word John Ross and a force known as the Void. By the last book in the trilogy, Nest is 29 and she and John must fight evil once more.

1. Running with the Demon ◆ 1997

2. A Knight of the Word ◆ 1998
3. Angel Fire East ◆ 1999

WORLD WAR

Turtledove, Harry
BALLANTINE DEL REY
GRADES 9–12
SCIENCE FICTION

In the midst of World War II, lizard-like aliens invade Earth. They seek total control. Their arrival adds to the general turmoil, and strange alliances are created. This series is linked to Turtledove's later Colonization series, in which the aliens' colonization fleet turns up.

1. World War: In the Balance ◆ 1994
2. World War: Tilting the Balance ◆ 1995
3. World War: Upsetting the Balance ◆ 1996
4. World War: Striking the Balance ◆ 1996

X FILES

Various authors
HARPERCOLLINS
GRADES 5–10 ◆ A/R
FANTASY | HORROR

Terror in the forest, dying teenagers, a serial killer, a dead alligator man at the circus, and extraterrestrial entities—these are just a few of the problems investigated by Agents Mulder and Scully. Fans of the television program will flock to this series, which is based on teleplays of specific episodes. Like the show, these books are gritty and grim, with enough twists in the plot to leave you wondering what is really true. There are many different X Files books, including ones for young adult and adult readers.

X FILES (GRADES 5–8)

1. X Marks the Spot (Martin, Les) ◆ 1995
2. Darkness Falls (Martin, Les) ◆ 1995
3. Tiger, Tiger (Martin, Les) ◆ 1995
4. Squeeze (Steiber, Ellen) ◆ 1996
5. Humbug (Martin, Les) ◆ 1996
6. Shapes (Steiber, Ellen) ◆ 1996

7. Fear (Martin, Les) ◆ 1996
8. Voltage (Royce, Easton) ◆ 1996
9. E.B.E. (Martin, Les) ◆ 1996
10. Die Bug Die (Martin, Les) ◆ 1997
11. Ghost in the Machine (Martin, Les) ◆ 1997

X FILES (GRADES 7–10)

1. The Calusari (Nix, Garth) ◆ 1997
2. Eve (Steiber, Ellen) ◆ 1997
3. Bad Sign (Easton, Royce) ◆ 1997
4. Our Town (Elfman, Eric) ◆ 1997
5. Empathy (Steiber, Ellen) ◆ 1997
6. Fresh Bones (Martin, Les) ◆ 1997
7. Control (Owens, Everett) ◆ 1997
8. The Host (Martin, Les) ◆ 1997
9. Hungry Ghosts (Steiber, Ellen) ◆ 1998
10. Dark Matter (Easton, Royce) ◆ 1999
11. Howlers (Owens, Everett) ◆ 1999
12. Grotesque (Steiber, Ellen) ◆ 1999
13. Quarantine (Martin, Les) ◆ 1999
14. Regeneration (Owens, Everett) ◆ 1999
15. Haunted (Steiber, Ellen) ◆ 2000
16. Miracle Man (Bisson, Terry) ◆ 2000

X GAMES XTREME MYSTERIES

Hill, Laban
HYPERION
GRADES 4–8
MYSTERY | RECREATION

Fans of the X Games (on ESPN) will enjoy these fast-paced mysteries with in-line skating, snowboarding, wakeboarding, snow mountain biking and other extreme sports. In one mystery, Jamil and his friends are at a mystery party and they investigate the theft of plans for a new wakeboard. In another book, Kevin is almost lost in a man-made avalanche. Other books feature Nat and Wall, who are also part of the Xtreme detectives. Merging sports action with mysteries could attract reluctant readers.

1. Crossed Tracks ◆ 1998
2. Deep Powder, Deep Trouble ◆ 1998
3. Rocked Out: A Summer X Games Special ◆ 1998
4. Half Pipe Rip-Off ◆ 1998

5. Lost Wake ◆ 1998
6. Out of Line ◆ 1998
7. Spiked Snow: A Winter X Games Special ◆ 1999
8. Totally Snowed ◆ 1999

XANTH SAGA

Anthony, Piers
BALLANTINE; TOR
GRADES 10–12 ◆ A/R
FANTASY

Xanth is a magic world where nearly everyone—including ogres, gargoyles, and centaurs—has a special talent. The population of this world has varied adventures and embarks on assorted quests. These books for adults are popular with strong teen readers.

1. A Spell for Chameleon ◆ 1977
2. The Source of Magic ◆ 1979
3. Castle Roogna ◆ 1979
4. Centaur Aisle ◆ 1981
5. Ogre, Ogre ◆ 1982
6. Night Mare ◆ 1982
7. Dragon on a Pedestal ◆ 1983
8. Crewel Lye: A Caustic Yarn ◆ 1985
9. Golem in the Gears ◆ 1986
10. Vale of the Vole ◆ 1987
11. Heaven Cent ◆ 1988
12. Man from Mundania ◆ 1989
13. Isle of View ◆ 1990
14. Question Quest ◆ 1991
15. The Color of Her Panties ◆ 1992
16. Demons Don't Dream ◆ 1993
17. Harpy Thyme ◆ 1994
18. Geis of the Gargoyle ◆ 1995
19. Roc and a Hard Place ◆ 1995
20. Yon Ill Wind ◆ 1996
21. Faun and Games ◆ 1997
22. Zombie Lover ◆ 1998
23. Xone of Contention ◆ 1999
24. The Dastard ◆ 2000
25. Swell Foop ◆ 2001
26. Up in a Heaval ◆ 2002
27. Cube Route ◆ 2003

YORK TRILOGY

Naylor, Phyllis Reynolds
ATHENEUM; ALADDIN
GRADES 8–10 ◆ A/R
FANTASY

Dan Roberts, 15, is enjoying a vacation in York, England, but he is troubled by his parents' behavior. Why did they take this trip in the middle of the school year? Why are their moods so unpredictable? These questions are overwhelmed by strange experiences that seem to be connected with some mysterious gypsies. Dan travels to the past to try to understand why he is being haunted.

1. Shadows on the Wall ◆ 2001
2. Faces in the Water ◆ 2002
3. Footprints at the Window ◆ 2003

THE YOUNG AMERICANS

Various authors
WHITE MANE PUBLISHING
GRADES 6–8
HISTORICAL

The Civil War comes to life in these well-researched, exciting books. In *Save the Colors*, Charley Olson, 12, joins the First Minnesota Regiment as a drummer boy. His initial battle experience is at First Manassas (Bull Run) and it is frightening. Charley must maintain the cadence for the troops but he is totally unprotected. Readers will gain insight into the impact of war on individuals.

1. Rose at Bull Run: Romance and Realities of First Bull Run (Sappey, Maureen Stack) ◆ 1998
2. Yankee Spy: A Union Girl in Richmond During the Pennisular Campaign (Sappey, Maureen Stack) ◆ 1998
3. Dreams of Ships, Dreams of Julia: At Sea with the Monitor and the Merrimac, Virginia, 1862 (Sappey, Maureen Stack) ◆ 1998
4. Powder Monkey: Battle Between the Merrimac and the Cumberland, Congress, and Monitor, 1862 (Campbell, Carole R.) ◆ 1999
5. Save the Colors: A Civil War Battle Cry (Reisberg, Joanne A.) ◆ 2001

YOUNG HEROES

Yolen, Jane, and Robert J. Harris
HARPERCOLLINS
GRADES 4–7 ◆ **A/R**
FANTASY

Tales from mythology are brought to life in spirited renditions that look at heroes' younger years. In the first book, a 13-year-old Odysseus is captured by pirates and joins young prisoners Penelope and Helen in exciting adventures. Twelve-year-old Atalanta and her best friend, a bear, join in the hunt for the creature that killed her father in the third book.

1. Odysseus in the Serpent Maze ◆ 2001
2. Hippolyta and the Curse of the Amazons ◆ 2002
3. Atalanta and the Arcadian Beast ◆ 2003
4. Jason and the Gorgon's Blood ◆ 2004

YOUNG INDIANA JONES CHRONICLES: CHOOSE YOUR OWN ADVENTURE

Brightfield, Richard
BANTAM
GRADES 5–8
ADVENTURE | FANTASY

The series uses the popular Choose Your Own Adventure format in which readers turn to different pages based on what they want to happen. For example, if you decide to go to the party, turn to page 45; if you want to stay in the dorm, turn to page 51. These books feature the popular character of Indiana Jones when he is a young man and place him at the center of events around the world. The popularity of the character and the format should attract reluctant readers.

1. The Valley of the Kings ◆ 1992
2. South of the Border ◆ 1992
3. Revolution in Russia ◆ 1992
4. Masters of the Louvre ◆ 1993
5. African Safari ◆ 1993
6. Behind the Great Wall ◆ 1993

7. The Roaring Twenties ◆ 1993
8. The Irish Rebellion ◆ 1993

YOUNG ROYALS

Meyer, Carolyn
HARCOURT
GRADES 6–9 ◆ A/R
HISTORICAL

This series looks at the dramatic youths of four royal women of the 16th century: Queen Mary I, Queen Elizabeth I, Anne Boleyn, and Catherine of Aragon.

1. Mary, Bloody Mary ◆ 1999
2. Beware, Princess Elizabeth ◆ 2001
3. Doomed Queen Anne ◆ 2002
4. Patience, Princess Catherine ◆ 2004

THE YOUNG UNDERGROUND

Elmer, Robert
BETHANY HOUSE
GRADES 5–8 ◆ A/R
HISTORICAL

Peter and Elise Andersen are 11-year-old twins involved in the Resistance in Denmark during World War II. They help their Jewish friend, Henrik, escape to Sweden and then help an injured RAF pilot. By the end of the series, the twins are 14 and try to stop a plot against a group of Jews traveling to Israel.

1. A Way Through the Sea ◆ 1994
2. Beyond the River ◆ 1994
3. Into the Flames ◆ 1995
4. Far From the Storm ◆ 1995
5. Chasing the Wind ◆ 1996
6. A Light in the Castle ◆ 1996

7. Follow the Star ◆ 1996
8. Touch the Sky ◆ 1997

You're the One

Lantz, Francess
ALADDIN
GRADES 6–9 ◆ A/R
REAL LIFE

In *A Royal Kiss*, Samantha, 14, meets a prince and they fall in love. They manage to stay out of the limelight until the press finds out about their relationship. Just when it looks as if Samantha will lose Prince Sebastian, her mother comes to the rescue. Fans of improbable "girl gets the great guy" romances will enjoy this series.

1. Sing Me a Love Song ◆ 2000
2. A Royal Kiss ◆ 2000
3. Lights, Camera, Love! ◆ 2000

Yurt

Brittain, C. Dale
SIMON & SCHUSTER
GRADES 9–12
FANTASY

Daimbert is the wizard to the King of Yurt. As such, he faces all manner of unusual situations. There's a plague of horned rabbits, a zombie creature, a blue djinn, black magic, and more. Readers who like humor and fantasy will enjoy these books.

1. Bad Spell in Yurt ◆ 1991
2. The Wood Nymph and the Cranky Saint ◆ 1993
3. Mage Quest ◆ 1993
4. The Witch and the Cathedral ◆ 1995
5. Daughter of Magic ◆ 1996
6. Is This Apocalypse Necessary? ◆ 2000

ZENDA

Petti, Ken, and John Amodeo
GROSSET & DUNLAP
GRADES 4–7 ◆ A/R
FANTASY

On Azureblue, gazing balls reveal 13 messages that tell the destiny of each child. Unfortunately for Zenda, the balls are not used until a child is 12 ½ years old. But Zenda can't wait. When she takes her gazing ball too soon, it breaks. Now she must recover the 13 pieces.

1. Zenda and the Gazing Ball ◆ 2004
2. A New Dimension ◆ 2004
3. The Crystal Planet ◆ 2004
4. Lost on Aquaria ◆ 2004
5. The Impossible Butterfly ◆ 2004
6. A Test of Mirrors ◆ 2004

INDEXES
AND
APPENDIXES

AUTHOR INDEX

Authors are listed with the series to which they contributed. Series are listed in alpabetical order in the main section of this book.

A

Aaron, Anna
  Sweet Dreams
Abbott, Donald
  Oz
Abbott, Tony
  Don't Touch That Remote!
Abrams, Liesa
  Love Stories
Adams, Douglas
  Hitchhiker's Trilogy
Aiken, Joan
  Wolves Chronicles
Aks, Patricia
  Cheerleaders
Albert, Susan Wittig
  China Bayles Mystery
Alexander, Heather
  Mary-Kate and Ashley:
    Adventures of Mary-Kate
    and Ashley
Alexander, Lloyd
  Prydain Chronicles
  Vesper Holly
  Westmark
Alexander, Nina
  Love Stories
  Mary-Kate and Ashley:
    Adventures of Mary-Kate
    and Ashley
Alexander, Wilma E.
  On Time's Wing
Alexandra, Belinda
  Charmed
Algozin, Bruce
  Endless Quest
Allen, Roger MacBride
  David Brin's Out of Time
  Isaac Asimov's Caliban
Allende, Isabel
  Alexander Cold and Nadia
    Santos
Amodeo, John (jt. author)
  Zenda

Anastasio, Dina
  Space Above and Beyond
Anders, C. J.
  Dawson's Creek
Anderson, Kevin J.
  Dragonflight Books
  Star Wars Young Jedi Knights
Anderson, Laurie Halse
  Wild at Heart
Anderson, Louis
  Endless Quest
Anderson, Margaret J.
  Time Trilogy
Andrews, Jeanne
  Sweet Dreams
Andrews, Michael
  Endless Quest
Andrews, V. C.
  Dollanganger
Anson, Mandy
  Sweet Dreams
Anthony, Piers
  Xanth Saga
Antilles, Kem
  Endless Quest
  Star Trek: Deep Space Nine
Appel, Allen
  Alex Balfour
Applegate, K. A.
  Animorphs
  Animorphs: Alternamorphs
  Animorphs: Animorph
    Chronicles
  Animorphs: Megamorphs
  EverWorld
  Love Stories
  Love Stories: Super Editions
  Making Out
  Making Waves
  Remnants
  Summer
Appleton, Victor
  Tom Swift
Aragones, Sergio
  The Groo

Archer, Chris
  Mindwarp
  Pyrates
Arden, William
  Three Investigators
Armstrong, Jennifer
  Dear Mr. President
  Fire-Us Trilogy
  Wild Rose Inn
Arthur, Robert
  Three Investigators
Asai, Carrie
  Samurai Girl
Asaro, Catherine
  Saga of the Skolian Empire
Ashby, R. S.
  Jackie Chan Adventures
Asimov, Isaac
  Foundation
  I, Robot
Asprin, Robert
  Myth Adventures
Ayres, Katherine
  American Girls: History
    Mysteries

B

Bach, Richard
  Ferret Chronicles
Bader, Bonnie (jt. author)
  Mary-Kate and Ashley:
    Adventures of Mary-Kate
    and Ashley
Baer, Judy
  Live from Brentwood High
  Sweet Dreams
Baglio, Ben
  Choose Your Own Adventure
Baker, Jennifer
  Class Secrets
  Clueless
  Dawson's Creek
  Enchanted Hearts

Baker, Richard
    Forgotten Realms—The Last
        Mythal
Baker, Susan
    Sweet Dreams
Bale, Karen A. (jt. author)
    Survival!
Ballard, Jane
    Sweet Dreams
Banim, Lisa
    Lizzie McGuire Mysteries
    Mary-Kate and Ashley: Two of
        a Kind
Banks, Iain M.
    The Culture
Barker, Clive
    Abarat
Barlow, Steve
    Outernet
Barnes, John
    The Thousand Cultures
Barnes-Svarney, Patricia
    Secret World of Alex Mack
    Star Trek: The Next
        Generation: Starfleet
        Academy
    Star Trek: Voyager: Starfleet
        Academy
Baron, Nick
    Endless Quest
Barondes, Jessica
    Sweet 16
Barron, T. A.
    Heartlight
    Lost Years of Merlin
Bates, Michelle
    Sandy Lane Stables
Baum, Lyman Frank
    Oz
Baum, Roger S.
    Oz
Beach, Lynn
    Phantom Valley
Bear, Greg
    Foundation
Beckett, Jim
    Choose Your Own Adventure
Bee, Coach Clair
    Chip Hilton Sports Series
Beecham, Jahnna
    Sweet Dreams
Beechen, Adam
    American Dreams (Aladdin)
Bell, Clare E.
    Ratha Quartet

Bell, Hilari
    Farsala Trilogy
Bellairs, John
    Anthony Monday
    Johnny Dixon
    Lewis Barnavelt
Benary-Isbert, Margot
    Lechow Family
Bender, Carrie
    Whispering Brook
Benford, Gregory
    Foundation
Benjamin, David
    The Sixth Sense: Secrets from
        Beyond
Bennett, Cherie
    Enchanted Hearts
    Mirror Image
    Pageant
    Smallville
    Sunset Island
    Teen Angels
    Trash
    University Hospital
Bennett, Joe (jt. author)
    Buffy the Vampire Slayer
        (Dark Horse)
Bentley, Karen (jt. author)
    Thoroughbred
Berman, Ron
    Dream Series
Bernard, Elizabeth
    Love Stories
Betancourt, Jeanne
    Cheer USA!
    Three Girls in the City
Bird, Isobel
    Circle of Three
Bisson, Terry
    X Files
Black, Jonah
    Black Book (Diary of a
        Teenage Stud)
Blackwell, Lawana
    Victorian Tales of London
Blackwood, Gary L.
    The Shakespeare Stealer
Blair, Margaret Whitman
    White Mane Kids
Blair, Shannon
    Sweet Dreams
Blake, Susan
    Cheerleaders
    Sweet Dreams

Blashfield, Jean
    Endless Quest
Block, Francesca Lia
    Weetzie Bat Saga
Bloss, Janet Adele
    Sweet Dreams
Blumenthal, Scott
    Dream Series
Bly, Stephen
    Belles of Lordsburg
Boal, Chris
    Buffy the Vampire Slayer
        (Dark Horse)
Boies, Janice
    Sweet Dreams
Bonham, Frank
    Dogtown Ghetto
Boraks-Nemetz, Lillian
    On Time's Wing
Boston, L. M.
    Green Knowe
Bova, Ben
    Asteroid Wars
    Orion the Hunter
Brand, Debra
    Sweet Dreams
Brandel, Marc
    Three Investigators
Brashares, Ann
    Sisterhood of the Traveling
        Pants
Bray, Libba
    Sweet 16
Brereton, Dan
    Buffy the Vampire Slayer
        (Dark Horse)
Bright, J. E.
    Love Stories: Super Editions
Brightfield, Richard
    Choose Your Own Adventure
    Choose Your Own Nightmare
    Mystic Knights of Tir Na Nog
    Young Indiana Jones
        Chronicles: Choose Your
        Own Adventure
Brin, David
    Foundation
Brinkerhoff, Shirley
    Nikki Sheridan
Brittain, C. Dale
    Yurt
Brockmann, Suzanne
    Troubleshooters
Brooke, Ali
    Love Stories

M

MacBain, Carol
  Sweet Dreams
McCafferty, Megan
  Jessica Darling
McCaffrey, Anne
  Acorna
  Pern
  Pern: The Harper-Hall Trilogy
McCaffrey, Todd (jt. author)
  Pern
McCay, William
  Three Investigators
McConnell, Ashley
  Angel
  Buffy the Vampire Slayer
    (Archway/Pocket)
McCorkle, Mark (jt. author)
  Kim Possible (TokyoPop)
McCrumb, Sharyn
  Ballad
McCusker, Paul
  Passages
McDaniel, Lurlene
  One Last Wish
McDevitt, Jack
  Priscilla Hutchins
MacDonald, James D. (jt.
    author)
  Valdemar: Mageworlds
McDonald, Megan
  American Girls: History
    Mysteries
Macdougal, Scarlett
  Have a Nice Life
McGowen, Tom
  Age of Magic Trilogy
  Endless Quest
  Magician Trilogy
McGraw, Eloise Jervis
  Oz
McGuire, Catherine
  Endless Quest
Machale, D. J.
  Are You Afraid of the Dark?
  Pendragon
McHugh, Elisabet
  Sweet Dreams
Mackall, Dandi Daley
  Degrees of Guilt
  Horsefeathers
  TodaysGirls.com
Mackel, Kathy
  Mike Pillsbury

McKinley, Robin
  Damar Chronicles
McKissack, Patricia C.
  Royal Diaries
McMurtry, Ken
  Choose Your Own Nightmare
McPhee, Phoebe
  The Alphabetical Hookup List
    Trilogy
Maguire, Gregory
  Hamlet Chronicles
Makris, Kathryn
  Sweet Dreams
Mangels, Andy
  Roswell High
Mantell, Paul
  The Jersey
Maravel, Gailanne
  Sweet Dreams
Marillier, Juliet
  Sevenwaters
Mariotte, Jeff
  Angel
  Buffy the Vampire Slayer:
    Buffy and Angel: The
    Unseen Trilogy
  Buffy the Vampire Slayer: The
    Xander Years
  Charmed
  Witch Season
Marsden, John
  Tomorrow
Marshall, Catherine
  Christy
Martin, Ann M.
  Baby-Sitters Club
  Baby-Sitters Club Friends
    Forever
  Baby-Sitters Club Mysteries
  Baby-Sitters Club Portrait
    Collection
  Baby-Sitters Club Super
    Specials
  California Diaries
Martin, Cory
  The O.C.
Martin, Les
  X Files
Martin, Michael A. (jt. author)
  Roswell High
Martin, S. R.
  Swampland Trilogy
Martindale, Chris
  Endless Quest

Mason, Lynn
  Alias
  Love Stories
  Love Stories: Super Editions
Massie, Elizabeth
  Buffy the Vampire Slayer
    (Archway/Pocket)
Matas, Carol
  The Minds Series
Matthews, Brett
  Angel (Graphic Novels)
Maxwell, Janet
  Sweet Dreams
Mead, Alice
  Junebug
Meeks, Dan (jt. author)
  Daystar Voyages
Metz, Melinda
  Buffy the Vampire Slayer
    (Archway/Pocket)
  Everwood
  Fingerprints
  Mary-Kate and Ashley:
    Adventures of Mary-Kate
    and Ashley
  Roswell High
  Sweet 16
Meyer, Carolyn
  Royal Diaries
  Young Royals
Mhan, Pop (jt. author)
  SpyBoy
Michaels, Fran
  Sweet Dreams
Michaels, Karen
  Love Stories
Mignola, Mike
  Hellboy
Miller, Lee (jt. author)
  Watching Alice
Millionaire, Tony
  Sock Monkey
Mills, Bart
  Beverly Hills, 90210
Mills, Claudia
  Losers, Inc.
Minsky, Terri
  Lizzie McGuire (TokyoPop)
Mitchell, Mark
  Are You Afraid of the Dark?
Mitchell, V. E.
  Are You Afraid of the Dark?
  Secret World of Alex Mack

Owens, Everett
  Love Stories: Super Editions
  X Files
Oz, Emily
  American Dreams (Aladdin)

P

Packard, Andrea
  Choose Your Own Adventure
Packard, Edward
  Choose Your Own Adventure
  Choose Your Own Nightmare
Page, Alexis
  Love Stories
Page, Katherine Hall
  Christie & Company
Pai, Helen
  Gilmore Girls
Paolini, Christopher
  Inheritance
Park, Anne
  Sweet Dreams
Parker, Daniel
  Countdown
  Sweet 16
  Watching Alice
  The Wessex Papers
Parkinson, Dan
  Dragonlance Dwarven
    Nations Trilogy
Parkinson, Siobhan
  American Girls: Girls of Many
    Lands
Pascal, Francine
  Fearless
  Sweet Valley High
  Sweet Valley High Senior Year
  Sweet Valley Junior High
  Sweet Valley Twins
  Sweet Valley Twins Super
    Chiller Editions
  Sweet Valley Twins Super
    Editions
  Sweet Valley University
  Sweet Valley University:
    Elizabeth
  Sweet Valley University
    Thriller Editions
Pascoe, Jim (jt. author)
  Buffy the Vampire Slayer
    (Dark Horse)
  Kim Possible (Chapter Books)

Pass, Erica
  Secret World of Alex Mack
Passarella, John
  Angel
  Buffy the Vampire Slayer
    (Archway/Pocket)
Paulsen, Gary
  Brian Robeson
  The Tucket Adventures
Paxson, Diana L.
  Wodan's Children
Peacock, Nancy
  TodaysGirls.com
Peck, Richard
  Blossom Culp
Pedersen, Ted
  Are You Afraid of the Dark?
  Cybersurfers
  Star Trek: Deep Space Nine
  Star Trek: Deep Space Nine
Peel, John
  Are You Afraid of the Dark?
  Diadem
  Eerie Indiana
  The Outer Limits
  Secret World of Alex Mack
  Star Trek: Deep Space Nine
    2099
Perl, Lila
  Fat Glenda
Perlberg, Deborah
  Mary-Kate and Ashley:
    Adventures of Mary-Kate
    and Ashley
Petrie, Doug
  Buffy the Vampire Slayer
    (Dark Horse)
Petti, Ken
  Zenda
Peyton, K. M.
  Flambards
Phelps, Lauren M.
  Sweet Dreams
Pieczenik, Steve (jt. author)
  Net Force
Pierce, Meredith Ann
  Darkangel Trilogy
  Firebringer Trilogy
Pierce, Tamora
  Circle of Magic
  Circle of Magic: The Circle
    Opens
  Daughter of the Lioness
  Immortals
  Protector of the Small

  Song of the Lioness Quartet
Pike, Christopher
  Cheerleaders
  The Last Vampire
  Spooksville
Pimentel, Joe (jt. author)
  Buffy the Vampire Slayer
    (Dark Horse)
Pines, Nancy
  Sweet Dreams
Pini, Richard (jt. author)
  ElfQuest
Pini, Wendy
  ElfQuest
Pinkney, Andrea Davis
  Dear Mr. President
Pittel, Jamie
  Sweet 16
Polcover, Jane
  Sweet Dreams
Pollotta, Nick
  Endless Quest
Pollowitz, Melinda
  Sweet Dreams
Ponti, James
  Journey of Allen Strange
Pratchett, Terry
  Bromeliad
  Discworld
Preiss, Pauline
  Mary-Kate and Ashley:
    Adventures of Mary-Kate
    and Ashley
Presser, Arlynn
  Love Stories
Prior, Natalie Jane
  Lily Quench
Pullman, Philip
  His Dark Materials
  Sally Lockhart Trilogy

Q

Quin-Harkin, Janet
  Enchanted Hearts
  Love Stories
  Sweet Dreams
  Sweet Dreams: On Our Own

R

Rabb, M. E.
  Missing Persons
Rabe, Jean
  Endless Quest
Raine, Allison
  Love Stories: Super Editions
Rand, Suzanne
  Sweet Dreams
Ransome, Arthur
  Swallows and Amazons
Reding, Jaclyn
  Highland Heroes
Redish, Jane
  Sweet Dreams
Reed, Teresa
  Moesha
Rees, Celia
  Celia Rees Supernatural
    Trilogy
  Witch Child
Rees, Elizabeth M.
  American Dreams (Avon)
  Heart Beats
  The Jersey
Reeve, Philip
  The Hungry City Chronicles
Reichman, Justin
  Dream Series
Reinsmith, Richard
  Endless Quest
Reisberg, Joanne A.
  The Young Americans
Reisfeld, Randi
  Clueless
  Love Stories
  T*Witches
Reiss, Kathryn
  American Girls: History
    Mysteries
Rennison, Louise
  Confessions of Georgia
    Nicolson
Reynolds, Anne
  Cheerleaders
Reynolds, Elizabeth
  Sweet Dreams
Reynolds, Marilyn
  Hamilton High
Richards, Ann
  Sweet Dreams
Richards, Cliff (jt. author)
  Buffy the Vampire Slayer
    (Dark Horse)

Richardson, Nancy
  Star Wars Junior Jedi Knights
Rinaldi, Ann
  Quilt Trilogy
Ritthaler, Shelly
  American Dreams (Avon)
Roberson, Jennifer
  Sword Dancer Saga
Roberts, Christa
  Alias
  Turning Seventeen
Roberts, Jeremy
  Eerie Indiana
Roberts, Katherine
  Echorium Sequence
Roberts, Laura Peyton
  Alias
  Clearwater Crossing
Roberts, Rachel
  Avalon 1: Web of Magic
  Avalon 2: Quest for Magic
Roberts, Shelly
  Avalon 1: Web of Magic
Robertson, William P.
  White Mane Kids
Rodda, Emily
  Deltora: Deltora Quest
  Deltora: Deltora Shadowlands
  Deltora: Dragons of Deltora
Roddy, Lee
  American Adventure
Rodriguez, K. S.
  Are You Afraid of the Dark?
  Dawson's Creek
Rogers, Mark E.
  Samurai Cat
Rogers, Mary
  Annabel Andrews
Ross, Carolyn
  Sweet Dreams
Rowling, J. K.
  Harry Potter
Royce, Easton
  Space Above and Beyond
  X Files
Ruditis, Paul
  Charmed
  Roswell High
Rue, Nancy N.
  Raise the Flag
Rusch, Kristine K. (jt. author)
  Roswell High
Rushford, Patricia H.
  Jennie McGrady Mysteries

Rushton, Rosie
  Fab 5
Ryan, Kevin
  Roswell High

S

Saal, Jocelyn
  Sweet Dreams
Saberhagen, Fred
  Berserker
  Book of the Gods
St. Pierre, Stephanie
  Sweet Dreams
Sale, Tim (jt. author)
  Buffy the Vampire Slayer
    (Dark Horse)
Salvatore, R. A.
  The Crimson Shadow
  The DemonWars
Sampson, Fay
  Pangur Ban
Sansevere, J. R. (jt. author)
  Tales of the Nine Charms
Santori, Helen
  Sweet Dreams
Sappey, Maureen Stack
  The Young Americans
Sarasin, Jennifer
  Cheerleaders
Sawyer, Kem Knapp
  White Mane Kids
Saylor, Steven
  Roma Sub Rosa
Scarborough, Elizabeth Ann
  The Fairy Godmother
Schooley, Bob
  Kim Possible (TokyoPop)
Schuler, Betty J.
  Sweet Dreams
Schultz, Mary
  Sweet Dreams
Schurfranz, Vivian
  Cheerleaders
Schwemm, Diane
  Love Stories
Scott, Kieran
  Love Stories
  Love Stories: Super Editions
Scott, Stefanie
  Moesha
Scrimger, Richard
  Nose

Seidman, David L.
  Are You Afraid of the Dark?

Selman, Matty
  The Jersey

Shahan, Sherry
  Eerie Indiana

Shan, Darren
  Cirque du Freak

Shands, Linda
  Wakara of Eagle Lodge

Shanower, Eric
  Oz

Shaw, Deirdre
  American Dreams (Aladdin)

Sheahan, Bernie
  Pacific Cascades University

Sheldon, Dyan
  Confessions of a Teenage
    Drama Queen

Sherman, Josepha (jt. author)
  Buffy the Vampire Slayer
    (Archway/Pocket)
  Endless Quest

Shetterly, Will
  Borderlands

Shusterman, Neal
  Shadow Club

Sieberetz, Barbara (jt. author)
  Dawson's Creek

Siegman, Meryl
  Choose Your Own Adventure

Silverberg, Robert
  Dragonflight Books
  The Majipoor Cycle

Simbal, Joanne
  Sweet Dreams

Simon, Morris
  Endless Quest

Simpson, Robert
  Mystic Knights of Tir Na Nog

Sinclair, Jay
  The Jersey

Sinclair, Stephanie
  Love Stories

Singleton, Linda Joy
  Cheer Squad
  Regeneration
  Sweet Dreams

Skurnick, Elizabeth
  Alias
  Love Stories: Super Editions

Skurnick, Lizzie
  Love Stories: His. Hers. Theirs

Skurzynski, Gloria
  National Parks Mystery

Slack, David
  Jackie Chan Adventures

Slade, Arthur G.
  Northern Frights

Sloan, Holly Goldberg
  Dream Series

Sloate, Susan
  Sweet Dreams

Smiley, Virginia
  Sweet Dreams

Smith, Carol
  TodaysGirls.com

Smith, Dean Wesley
  Roswell High

Smith, Gil Kane (jt. author)
  Chronicles of Conan

Smith, Jeff
  Bone

Smith, K. T.
  Beverly Hills, 90210

Smith, L. J.
  Dark Visions
  Forbidden Game
  Night World
  Secret Circle
  Vampire Diaries

Smith, Patricia Clark
  Royal Diaries

Snelling, Lauraine
  Golden Filly Series
  High Hurdles
  Red River: Red River of the
    North
  Red River: Return to Red
    River
  Secret Refuge

Snicket, Lemony
  A Series of Unfortunate Events

Sniegoski, Thomas E.
  Angel
  Angel (Graphic Novels)
  Buffy the Vampire Slayer
    (Dark Horse)
  Buffy the Vampire Slayer:
    Buffy and Angel
  The Fallen
  Outcast

Snow, Jack
  Oz

Snyder, Midori
  Dinotopia

Somtow, S. P.
  Dragonflight Books

Son, John
  First Person Fiction

Sook, Ryan (jt. author)
  Buffy the Vampire Slayer
    (Dark Horse)

Sorenson, Jody
  Cheerleaders

South, Sherri Cobb
  Sweet Dreams

Spector, Debra
  Sweet Dreams

Speregen, Devra Newberger
  Party of Five

Sprague, Gilbert M.
  Oz

Springer, Nancy
  Rowan Hood

Stableford, Brian
  Emortality

Stackpole, Michael A.
  DragonCrown War Cycle

Stainer, M. L.
  Lyon Saga

Stanek, Robert
  Ruin Mist: The Kingdoms and
    the Elves of the Reaches
  Ruin Mist Chronicles

Stanley, Carol
  Cheerleaders

Stasheff, Christopher
  A Wizard in Rhyme

Steiber, Ellen
  X Files

Stein, Joshua
  Dream Series

Steiner, Barbara
  American Girls: History
    Mysteries
  Sweet Dreams

Steinke, Ann E.
  Cheerleaders

Stevens, Janice
  Sweet Dreams

Stewart, Melanie
  Generation Girl

Stine, H. William (jt. author)
  Three Investigators

Stine, Megan
  House of Horrors
  Jackie Chan Adventures
  Mary-Kate and Ashley:
    Adventures of Mary-Kate
    and Ashley

Vernon, Rosemary
  Sweet Dreams
Vick, Helen H.
  Walker and Tag
Viguie, Debbie (jt. author)
  Wicked
Vinge, Joan D.
  Oz
  Psion
Voeller, Sydell
  Sweet Dreams
Voigt, Cynthia
  Bad Girls
  The Kingdom
  Tillerman Cycle
Von Moschzisker, Felix
  Choose Your Own Adventure
von Ziegesar, Cecily
  Gossip Girl
Vornholt, John
  Are You Afraid of the Dark?
  Buffy the Vampire Slayer
    (Archway/Pocket)
  Buffy the Vampire Slayer:
    Buffy and Angel
  Dinotopia
  Journey of Allen Strange
  Secret World of Alex Mack
  Star Trek: Starfleet Academy
  Star Trek: The Next
    Generation: Starfleet
    Academy

W

Wallace, Jim
  Choose Your Own Adventure
Wallace, Rich
  Winning Season
Wallach, Susan Jo
  Sweet Dreams
Wallens, Scott
  Sevens
Wallington, Aury
  The O.C.
Walls, Pamela
  Abby's South Seas Adventures
Ward, James Michael
  Endless Quest
Waricha, Jean
  Mary-Kate and Ashley:
    Adventures of Mary-Kate
    and Ashley

Warner, Chris
  Ghost
Warren, Andrea
  Sweet Dreams
Warriner, Holly
  Spell Casters
Washburn, Jan
  Sweet Dreams
Watson, Andi
  Buffy the Vampire Slayer
    (Dark Horse)
Watson, Jude
  Brides of Wildcat County
  Star Wars: Jedi Apprentice
  Star Wars Episode 1: Journals
Watt-Evans, Lawrence
  Obsidian Chronicles
Watts, Alycyn
  Sweet Dreams
Waugh, Sylvia
  Mennyms
  Ormingat
Weber, David
  Honor Harrington
Weber, Judith
  Cheerleaders
Wein, Elizabeth
  Arthurian-Aksumite Cycle
Weis, Margaret Baldwin
  Endless Quest
Weiss, Bobbi J. G.
  Are You Afraid of the Dark?
  Charmed
  Journey of Allen Strange
  Secret World of Alex Mack
  Smallville
  Star Trek: The Next
    Generation: Starfleet
    Academy
  Star Trek: Voyager: Starfleet
    Academy
Weiss, David Cody
  Are You Afraid of the Dark?
  Journey of Allen Strange
  Secret World of Alex Mack
  Smallville
  Star Trek: The Next
    Generation: Starfleet
    Academy
  Star Trek: Voyager: Starfleet
    Academy
Weiss, Jacklyn (jt. author)
  Charmed
West, Callie
  Love Stories

West, Cathy
  Jackie Chan Adventures
West, Nick
  Three Investigators
Weyn, Suzanne
  House of Horrors
Whedon, Joss (jt. author)
  Angel (Graphic Novels)
  Buffy the Vampire Slayer
    (Dark Horse)
Whelan, Gloria
  Angel on the Square
  Island Trilogy
White, Charlotte
  Sweet Dreams
White, Ellen Emerson
  Royal Diaries
White, John
  The Archives of Anthropos
White, T. H.
  Once and Future King
Whitman, John
  Mystic Knights of Tir Na Nog
  Star Wars Galaxy of Fear
Wilensky, Amy
  Love Stories
Wilhelm, Doug
  Choose Your Own Adventure
Wilkinson, Brenda
  Ludell
Willard, Eliza
  Jackie Chan Adventures
  Mary-Kate and Ashley Starring
    In . . .
Williams, Mark London
  Danger Boy
Williams, Tad
  Dragonflight Books
Willot, Rhondi
  Sweet Dreams
Wilson, Barbara
  Sweet Dreams
Wilson, Jacqueline
  The Girls Quartet
Wilson, Lynda
  On Time's Wing
Windsor, Barry (jt. author)
  Chronicles of Conan
Winfield, Julia
  Sweet Dreams
Winfrey, Elizabeth
  Love Stories
  Party of Five

TITLE INDEX

The series in which the title appears is shown in parentheses following the title. Series are listed in alphabetical order in the main section of this book.

A

The A-List (A-List)

Aaron Let's Go (Making Out)

Abandoned (Jennie McGrady Mysteries)

Abarat (Abarat)

Abarat: Days of Magic, Nights of War (Abarat)

Abby and the Best Kid Ever (Baby-Sitters Club)

Abby and the Mystery Baby (Baby-Sitters Club Mysteries)

Abby and the Notorious Neighbor (Baby-Sitters Club Mysteries)

Abby and the Secret Society (Baby-Sitters Club Mysteries)

Abby in Wonderland (Baby-Sitters Club)

Abby the Bad Sport (Baby-Sitters Club)

Abby's Book (Baby-Sitters Club Portrait Collection)

Abby's Lucky Thirteen (Baby-Sitters Club)

Abby's Twin (Baby-Sitters Club)

Abby's Un-Valentine (Baby-Sitters Club)

Abhorsen (Abhorsen)

Abner and Me (Baseball Card Adventures)

The Abominable Snow Monster (Graveyard School)

Abominable Snowman (Choose Your Own Adventure)

The Abominable Snowman of Pasadena (Goosebumps)

Above the Veil (The Seventh Tower)

Abraham Lincoln (Dear Mr. President)

The Absolute (Animorphs)

Absolute Zero (Hardy Boys Casefiles)

Accidental Dreams (The Lily Adventures)

Achieving Personal Perfection (Clueless)

Achingly Alice (Alice)

Acorna (Acorna)

Acorna's People (Acorna)

Acorna's Quest (Acorna)

Acorna's Rebels (Acorna)

Acorna's Search (Acorna)

Acorna's Triumph (Acorna)

Acorna's World (Acorna)

Across the Nightingale Floor (Tales of the Otori)

Acting on Impulse (Sweet Dreams)

Acting Up (Cheerleaders)

Acting Up (Hardy Boys Casefiles)

Action! (Nancy Drew: Girl Detective)

The Adept (The Adept)

The Adventurer (Highland Heroes)

The Adventures of Samurai Cat (Samurai Cat)

The Adventures of the Blue Avenger (Blue Avenger)

The Adventures of Tony Millionaire's Sock Monkey (Sock Monkey)

Aenir (The Seventh Tower)

Aerie (The Fallen)

African Safari (Young Indiana Jones Chronicles: Choose Your Own Adventure)

After the Storm (Heartland)

Aftermath (Remnants)

Aftershock (Mindwarp)

Aftershock (Star Trek: Starfleet Academy)

Aftershock (Sweet Valley High)

Against All Odds (Hardy Boys Casefiles)

Against the Odds (Sweet Valley High)

Against the Rules (Nancy Drew Files)

Against the Rules (Sweet Valley Twins)

The Agony of Alice (Alice)

Air Ferrets Aloft (Ferret Chronicles)

Aisha Goes Wild (Making Out)

Aisling (Indigo)

Alanna (Song of the Lioness Quartet)

The Alaskan Adventure (Hardy Boys)

The Alchemist's Cat (Deptford Mice Histories)

Alex Ryan, Stop That (Losers, Inc.)

Alex, You're Glowing! (Secret World of Alex Mack)

Alexandra the Great (Al (Alexandra))

Alice Alone (Alice)

Alice in April (Alice)

Alice In-Between (Alice)

Alice in Lace (Alice)

Alice in Rapture, Sort of (Alice)

Alice on the Outside (Alice)

Alice the Brave (Alice)

The Alien (Animorphs)

Alien Blood (Mindwarp)

Alien, Go Home! (Choose Your Own Adventure)

Alien Invasion from Hollyweird (The Outer Limits)

Alien Scream (Mindwarp)

Alien Terror (Mindwarp)

Alien Vacation (Journey of Allen Strange)

The Aliens Approach (Space Above and Beyond)

Aliens in the Sky (Spooksville)

All About Andy (Replica)

All About Love (Sweet Valley High Senior Year)

All But Alice (Alice)

All-Day Nightmare (Goosebumps: Give Yourself Goosebumps)

All I Want Is Everything (Gossip Girl)

All-Mars All-Stars (Slapshots)

The All-New Mallory Pike (Baby-Sitters Club)

April (Countdown)

April Fool! (Sweet Valley Twins)

April Fools' Rules (Mary-Kate and Ashley: Two of a Kind)

April Ghoul's Day (Graveyard School)

Aquatech Warriors (Tom Swift)

Arabian Challenge (Thoroughbred)

Arcade (Star Trek: Deep Space Nine)

Architects of Emortality (Emortality)

The Arctic Incident (Artemis Fowl)

The Arctic Patrol Mystery (Hardy Boys)

Are We in Love? (Sweet Valley High)

Are You Terrified Yet? (Goosebumps Series 2000)

Ariadne's Web (Book of the Gods)

Arin's Judgment (Passages)

The Ark (Lechow Family)

The Arms of Hercules (Book of the Gods)

Arms of Nemesis (Roma Sub Rosa)

Army of Terror (Star Wars Galaxy of Fear)

The Arrest (Sweet Valley High)

The Arrival (Animorphs)

The Arrival (Journey of Allen Strange)

Arrival (Smallville)

Artemis Fowl (Artemis Fowl)

As Ever, Gordy (Gordy Smith)

As I Am (Love Stories)

As if I Care (Sweet Valley High Senior Year)

As You Wish (Christy Miller: Christy and Todd: The College Years)

Ascendance (The DemonWars)

Ascendant Sun (Saga of the Skolian Empire)

Ascension (Water)

Ashes of Victory (Honor Harrington)

Ashleigh's Christmas Miracle (Thoroughbred)

Ashleigh's Diary (Thoroughbred)

Ashleigh's Dream (Thoroughbred)

Ashleigh's Farewell (Thoroughbred)

Ashleigh's Hope (Thoroughbred)

Ashleigh's Promise (Thoroughbred: Ashleigh)

Ashleigh's Western Challenge (Thoroughbred: Ashleigh)

Ask Annie (Sweet Dreams)

At All Costs (Nancy Drew and the Hardy Boys Super Mysteries)

At First Sight (Love Stories)

At the Crossing Places (Arthur Trilogy)

At the Earth's Core (Pellucidar)

Atalanta and the Arcadian Beast (Young Heroes)

Atlantis Station (Star Trek: The Next Generation: Starfleet Academy)

The Attack (Animorphs)

Attack of Apollyon (Left Behind—The Kids)

The Attack of the Aqua Apes (Fear Street: Ghosts of Fear Street)

Attack of the Beastly Baby-Sitter (Goosebumps: Give Yourself Goosebumps)

Attack of the Denebian Starship (Daystar Voyages)

Attack of the Graveyard Ghouls (Goosebumps Series 2000)

Attack of the Jack-O'-Lanterns (Goosebumps)

Attack of the Killer Ants (Bone Chillers)

Attack of the Killer Bebes (Kim Possible (Chapter Books))

Attack of the Killer Crabs (Spooksville)

Attack of the Living Mask (Choose Your Own Nightmare)

Attack of the Mutant (Goosebumps)

Attack of the Two-Ton Tomatoes (Eerie Indiana)

Attack of the Vampire Worms (Fear Street: Ghosts of Fear Street)

Attack of the Video Villains (Hardy Boys)

Attack on Petra (Left Behind— The Kids)

Atticus of Rome, 30 B.C. (The Life and Times)

Attitude (Making Waves)

Audacious (Brides of Wildcat County)

August (Countdown)

August Magic (Summer)

Aunt Weird (House of Horrors)

The Austere Academy (A Series of Unfortunate Events)

Autocrats of Oz (Oz)

Autumnal (Angel (Graphic Novels))

Autumnal (Buffy the Vampire Slayer) (Dark Horse)

Avatar (Angel)

Avatar (Indigo)

Awakening (Sweep)

The Awakening (Vampire Diaries)

The Awakening Evil (Fear Street: Fear Street Sagas)

Away Laughing on a Fast Camel (Confessions of Georgia Nicolson)

B

"B" Is for Bad at Getting Into Harvard (Raise the Flag)

Babe and Me (Baseball Card Adventures)

Babes in Boyland (Clueless)

Babes in the Woods (He-Man Women Haters Club)

Baby Be-Bop (Weetzie Bat Saga)

Baby Help (Hamilton High)

The Baby-Sitter (Baby-Sitter)

The Baby-Sitter Burglaries (Nancy Drew)

The Baby-Sitter II (Baby-Sitter)

The Baby-Sitter III (Baby-Sitter)

The Baby-Sitter IV (Baby-Sitter)

Baby-Sitters at Shadow Lake (Baby-Sitters Club Super Specials)

Baby-Sitters Beware (Baby-Sitters Club Mysteries)

Baby-Sitters' Christmas Chiller (Baby-Sitters Club Mysteries)

Baby-Sitters' European Vacation (Baby-Sitters Club Super Specials)

Baby-Sitters' Fright Night (Baby-Sitters Club Mysteries)

Baby-Sitters' Haunted House (Baby-Sitters Club Mysteries)

Baby-Sitters' Island Adventure (Baby-Sitters Club Super Specials)

Baby-Sitters on Board! (Baby-Sitters Club Super Specials)

The Baby-Sitters Remember (Baby-Sitters Club Super Specials)

Baby-Sitters' Summer Vacation (Baby-Sitters Club Super Specials)

Baby-Sitters' Winter Vacation (Baby-Sitters Club Super Specials)

Babysitting Blues (B.Y. Times)

The Back Door of Midnight (Dark Secrets)

Back in the Saddle (Saddle Club: Pine Hollow)

Back in the Saddle (Silver Creek Riders)

Back to Before (Animorphs: Megamorphs)

Back to School (Bone Chillers)

Back to the Stone Age (Pellucidar)

Backboard Fever (Chip Hilton Sports Series)

Backcourt Ace (Chip Hilton Sports Series)

Backfire (Virtual Reality)

Backstabber (Sweet Valley High Senior Year)

Backstage Romance (Sweet Dreams)

Bad (Fearless)

Bad, Badder, Baddest (Bad Girls)

The Bad Beginning (A Series of Unfortunate Events)

Bad Blood (Buffy the Vampire Slayer) (Dark Horse)

Bad Chemistry (Hardy Boys Casefiles)

Bad Dreams (Fear Street)

Bad Girl (Sweet Valley High Senior Year)

Bad Girls (Bad Girls)

Bad Girls in Love (Bad Girls)

Bad Hare Day (Goosebumps)

Bad Intent (Danger.com)

Bad Luck Filly (Thoroughbred)

Bad Medicine (Nancy Drew Files)

Bad Moonlight (Fear Street: Fear Street Super Chillers)

Bad News Babysitting! (Secret World of Alex Mack)

Bad News/Good News (Beacon Street Girls)

Bad Rap (Hardy Boys Casefiles)

Bad Sign (X Files)

Bad Spell in Yurt (Yurt)

The Bagpiper's Ghost (Tartan Magic Trilogy)

The Baker's Boy (Book of Words)

Balancing Act (Nikki Sheridan)

Baldwin from Another Planet (Clueless)

The Ballad of Frankie Silver (Ballad)

The Ballad of Sir Dinadan (The Denizens of Camelot)

Barbarians from the Isle (Winds of Light)

The Barking Ghost (Goosebumps)

Barnstormer in Oz (Oz)

Barnyard Battle (Sweet Valley Twins)

Barry (Wolfbay Wings)

The Baseball Card Conspiracy (Hardy Boys)

The Battle of Evernight (The Bitterbynde)

The Battle of Lookout Mountain (Bonnets and Bugles)

Battle of the Cheerleaders (Sweet Valley Twins)

Battlecry Forever! (Thoroughbred: Ashleigh's Collection)

The Battling Bucktails at Fredericksburg (White Mane Kids)

Battling the Commander (Left Behind—The Kids)

Batya's Search (B.Y. Times)

Bayou Blues (Dawson's Creek)

Bayside Madness (Saved by the Bell)

Be Afraid—Be Very Afraid! (Goosebumps Series 2000)

Be Careful What You Wish For (Goosebumps)

Be Mine (Sweet Valley High Senior Year)

Beaches, Boys and Betrayal (Summer)

The Beast Arises (Left Behind—The Kids)

The Beast from the East (Goosebumps)

Beast Is Watching You (Sweet Valley Twins)

Beast Must Die (Sweet Valley Twins)

The Beast under the Wizard's Bridge (Lewis Barnavelt)

Beastly Tales (Fear Street: Ghosts of Fear Street)

A Beautiful Place on Yonge Street (Harper Winslow)

Beauty and the Beach (Sweet Valley University)

Because I'm Worth It (Gossip Girl)

The Becoming (Daughters of the Moon)

Becoming Me (Diary of a Teenage Girl)

Before Gaia (Fearless)

The Beggar Queen (Westmark)

Begin Again (Remnants)

The Beginning (Animorphs)

The Beginning (Replica)

Behind Closed Doors (Sweet Valley University)

Behind His Back (Love Stories)

Behind the Great Wall (Young Indiana Jones Chronicles: Choose Your Own Adventure)

Behind the Mountains (First Person Fiction)

Behind the Veil (Royal Pavilions)

Behind the Wheel (Choose Your Own Adventure)

Believing the Dream (Red River: Return to Red River)

The Bell, the Book, and the Spellbinder (Johnny Dixon)

The Bellmaker (Redwall)

The Beloved Dearly (Beloved Dearly)

Ben Takes a Chance (Making Out)

Benched! (Alden All Stars)

Bending the Rules (Generation Girl)

Ben's in Love (Making Out)

Bernie and the Bessledorf Ghost (Bessledorf Hotel)

Bernie Magruder and the Bats in the Belfry (Bernie Magruder)

Bernie Magruder and the Bus Station Blow Up (Bernie Magruder)

Bernie Magruder and the Case of the Big Stink (Bernie Magruder)

Bernie Magruder and the Disappearing Bodies (Bernie Magruder)

Bernie Magruder and the Drive-Thru Funeral Parlor (Bernie Magruder)

Bernie Magruder and the Haunted Hotel (Bernie Magruder)

Bernie Magruder and the Parachute Peril (Bernie Magruder)

Bernie Magruder and the Pirate's Treasure (Bernie Magruder)

Berserker (Berserker)

Berserker: Blue Death (Berserker)

The Berserker Attack (Berserker)

Berserker Base (Berserker)

Berserker Fury (Berserker)

Berserker Kill (Berserker)

Berserker Lies (Berserker)

Berserker Man (Berserker)

Berserker Prime (Berserker)

The Berserker Throne (Berserker)

Berserker Wars (Berserker)

Berserkers: The Beginning (Berserker)

Berserker's Planet (Berserker)

Berserker's Star (Berserker)

Best Dressed (Lizzie McGuire)

The Best Friend (Fear Street)

The Best Friend 2 (Fear Street)

Best Friend, Worst Enemy (Holly's Heart)

Best Friends (Sweet Valley Twins)

Best Friends for Never (Clique)

Best Friends Forever (Mary-Kate and Ashley: So Little Time)

Best Friends Forever (Sweet Dreams: On Our Own)

Best Friend's Girl (Saved by the Bell)

Best of Enemies (Nancy Drew and the Hardy Boys Super Mysteries)

Best of Enemies (Sweet Valley High Senior Year)

The Best of the Best (Replica)

Bet You Can't! (Secret World of Alex Mack)

Bet Your Life (SpyBoy)

The Betrayal (Fear Street: Fear Street Sagas)

Betrayal (2099)

Betrayal: Week 6 (Sevens)

Betrayal at Cross Creek (American Girls: History Mysteries)

Betrayed (Cheerleaders)

Betrayed (Fearless)

Betrayed (Fingerprints)

Betrayed (Jennie McGrady Mysteries)

Betrayed By Love (Nancy Drew Files)

Bettypalooza (Clueless)

Between Madison and Palmetto (Maizon)

Between Worlds (Charmed)

Beverly Hills Brontosaurus (Dinoverse)

Beverly Hills, 90210 (Beverly Hills, 90210)

Beware Dawn! (Baby-Sitters Club Mysteries)

Beware of the Purple Peanut Butter (Goosebumps: Give Yourself Goosebumps)

Beware, Princess Elizabeth (Young Royals)

Beware the Babysitter (Sweet Valley High)

Beware the Bohrok (Bionicle Chronicles)

Beware the Fish! (Bruno and Boots)

Beware the Metal Children (The Outer Limits)

Beware the Shopping Mall! (Bone Chillers)

Beware the Snake's Venom (Choose Your Own Nightmare)

Beware, the Snowman (Goosebumps)

Beware the Wolfman (Sweet Valley High)

Beware the Wolfman (Sweet Valley High Super Thrillers)

Beware What You Wish (Charmed)

Beyond Dreams (Hamilton High)

Beyond Escape! (Choose Your Own Adventure)

Beyond the Burning Lands (Sword of the Spirits)

Beyond the Great Wall (Choose Your Own Adventure)

Beyond the Law (Hardy Boys Casefiles)

Beyond the River (The Young Underground)

Bhagavati (Blood of the Goddess)

Big Bad Bugs (Fear Street: Ghosts of Fear Street)

Big Brother's in Love Again (Sweet Valley Twins)

The Big Camp Secret (Sweet Valley Twins Super Editions)

BIG for Christmas (Sweet Valley Twins)

Big-League Break (Rookies)

The Big Night (Sweet Valley High)

Big Party Weekend (Sweet Valley Twins)

The Big Six (Swallows and Amazons)

Bigby's Curse (Endless Quest)

Bijapur (Blood of the Goddess)

The Bike Tour Mystery (Nancy Drew)

The Biker (Nightmare Hall)

Billie's Secret (Sweet Valley University)

The Billion Dollar Ransom (Hardy Boys)

A Billion for Boris (Annabel Andrews)

Billy (Wolfbay Wings)

Billy Baker's Dog Won't Stay Buried (Spinetinglers)

Bindings (Books of Magic)

Bingo Brown and the Language of Love (Bingo Brown)

Bingo Brown, Gypsy Lover (Bingo Brown)

Bingo Brown's Guide to Romance (Bingo Brown)

Birth of the Firebringer (Firebringer Trilogy)

Biting for Blood (Choose Your Own Nightmare)

Bitter Rivals (Sweet Valley High)

Black and White (Three Girls in the City)

Black Blood (The Last Vampire)

The Black Cauldron (Prydain Chronicles)

Black Dawn (Night World)

The Black Dragon (Tom Swift)

The Black Gryphon (Valdemar: Gryphon Trilogy)

Black Hearts in Battersea (Wolves Chronicles)

Black October (Ghost)

The Black Raven (Deverry)

The Black Stallion (Black Stallion)

The Black Stallion and Flame (Black Stallion)

The Black Stallion and Satan (Black Stallion)

The Black Stallion and the Girl (Black Stallion)

The Black Stallion Challenged (Black Stallion)

The Black Stallion Legend (Black Stallion)

Boy Crazy (Mary-Kate and Ashley: So Little Time)

Boy-Crazy Stacey (Baby-Sitters Club)

Boy. Friend. (Sweet Valley Junior High)

A Boy Friend Is Not a "Boyfriend" (Party of Five)

Boy Meets Girl (Sweet Valley High Senior Year)

The Boy Next Door (Fear Street)

The Boy Next Door (Love Stories)

Boy, Oh Boy! (From the Files of Madison Finn)

The Boy She Left Behind (Sweet Dreams)

Boy Trouble (Sweet Valley High)

The Boy Who Ate Fear Street (Fear Street: Ghosts of Fear Street)

Boyfriend Blues (Sweet Dreams)

The Boyfriend Dilemma (Fabulous Five)

The Boyfriend Game (Sweet Valley Twins)

The Boyfriend Mess (Sweet Valley Twins)

The Boyfriend War (Sweet Valley High)

Boys Against Girls (Sweet Valley Twins)

Boys Are Bad News (Cheer Squad)

Boys! Boys! Boys! (Popular)

The Boys of Summer (Sweet Valley University)

Boys Only Club (Fabulous Five)

The Bragging War (Fabulous Five)

Brain Juice (Goosebumps Series 2000)

The Brain Spiders (Star Wars Galaxy of Fear)

Brain Trust (Body of Evidence)

The Brave (The Contender)

Brave the Betrayal (EverWorld)

The Bravest Girl in Sharpsburg (White Mane Kids)

The Breadwinner (The Breadwinner Trilogy)

Break the Surface (Watching Alice)

Breakaway (Star Trek: The Next Generation: Starfleet Academy)

Breakdown (Remnants)

Breakdown in Axeblade (Hardy Boys)

Breakfast of Enemies (Sweet Valley Twins)

Breaking Away (Sweet Valley University)

Breaking Free (Heartland)

Breaking Loose (Alden All Stars)

Breaking the Fall (Thoroughbred)

Breaking the Rules (Saved by the Bell)

Breaking the Rules: Bailey (Party of Five)

Breaking Up (Fabulous Five)

Breakout! (Left Behind—The Kids)

Breakthroughs (The Great War)

The Brewing Storm (Charmed)

Brian's Hunt (Brian Robeson)

Brian's Return (Brian Robeson)

Brian's Winter (Brian Robeson)

Briar's Book (Circle of Magic)

Bridal Dreams (Thoroughbred)

Bride of the Living Dummy (Goosebumps Series 2000)

A Bridge Between Worlds (W.I.T.C.H.)

The Bridge in the Clouds (Magician's House Quartet)

The Bridge to Cutter Gap (Christy)

Bridie of the Wild Rose Inn, 1695 (Wild Rose Inn)

Brilliance of the Moon (Tales of the Otori)

Brilliant Doctor Wogan (Choose Your Own Adventure)

Bring Me a Dream (Eerie Indiana)

Bring the Boys Home (Bonnets and Bugles)

The Bristling Wood (Deverry)

The Broken Anchor (Nancy Drew)

Broken Angel (Sweet Valley High Senior Year)

Broken Days (Quilt Trilogy)

Broken Drum (White Mane Kids)

Broken-Hearted (Sweet Valley High)

Broken Hearts (Fear Street: Fear Street Super Chillers)

Broken Hearts (Lizzie McGuire)

Broken Promises (Nancy Drew on Campus)

Broken Promises, Shattered Dreams (Sweet Valley University)

Broken Sky # 1 (Broken Sky)

Broken Sky # 2 (Broken Sky)

Broken Sky # 3 (Broken Sky)

Broken Sky # 4 (Broken Sky)

Broken Sky # 5 (Broken Sky)

Broken Sky # 6 (Broken Sky)

Broken Sky # 7 (Broken Sky)

Broken Sunrise (Buffy the Vampire Slayer: Wicked Willow)

Brooke and Her Rock Star Mom (Sweet Valley Twins)

Brother Against Brother (Hardy Boys Casefiles)

Brother Assassin (Berserker)

Brother Enemy (Promise of Zion)

Brotherly Love (Christy)

Brothers at War (White Mane Kids)

Bruce's Story (Sweet Valley High)

Bruja (Angel)

A Brush with Love (Sweet Dreams)

BSC in the USA (Baby-Sitters Club Super Specials)

The Buccaneers (High Seas Trilogy)

The Bucktails' Antietam Trials (White Mane Kids)

The Bucktails' Shenandoah March (White Mane Kids)

Budding Star (Angels Unlimited)

Bueno Nacho (Kim Possible (Chapter Books))

Bueno Nacho and Tick Tick Tick (Kim Possible (TokyoPop))

Bugged Out! (Choose Your Own Nightmare)

The Bugman Lives! (Fear Street: Ghosts of Fear Street)

Building a Mystery (T*Witches)

Bully (Sweet Valley Twins)

The Bungalow Mystery (Nancy Drew)

Bureau of Lost (Eerie Indiana)

Buried Alive (Distress Call 911)

Buried Alive (National Parks Mystery)

Buried in Time (Nancy Drew and the Hardy Boys Super Mysteries)

Buried Secrets (Nancy Drew Files)

Buried Secrets (Smallville)

The Case of the Blackmail Boys (Baker Street Irregulars)

The Case of the Blue-Ribbon Horse (Mary-Kate and Ashley: Adventures of Mary-Kate and Ashley)

The Case of the Candy Cane Clue (Mary-Kate and Ashley: Adventures of Mary-Kate and Ashley)

The Case of the Captured Queen (Nancy Drew)

The Case of the Cheerleading Camp Mystery (Mary-Kate and Ashley: Adventures of Mary-Kate and Ashley)

The Case of the Cheerleading Tattletale (Mary-Kate and Ashley: Adventures of Mary-Kate and Ashley)

The Case of the Christmas Caper (Mary-Kate and Ashley: Adventures of Mary-Kate and Ashley)

The Case of the Cinema Swindle (Baker Street Irregulars)

The Case of the Clue at the Zoo (Mary-Kate and Ashley: Adventures of Mary-Kate and Ashley)

The Case of the Comic Crooks (Baker Street Irregulars)

The Case of the Cop Catchers (Baker Street Irregulars)

Case of the Cosmic Kidnapping (Hardy Boys)

Case of the Counterfeit Criminals (Hardy Boys)

The Case of the Creative Crime (Nancy Drew)

The Case of the Creepy Castle (Mary-Kate and Ashley: Adventures of Mary-Kate and Ashley)

The Case of the Criminal Computer (Baker Street Irregulars)

The Case of the Dangerous Solution (Nancy Drew)

The Case of the Disappearing Deejay (Nancy Drew)

The Case of the Disappearing Diamonds (Nancy Drew)

The Case of the Disappearing Diplomat (Baker Street Irregulars)

The Case of the Disappearing Princess (Mary-Kate and Ashley: Adventures of Mary-Kate and Ashley)

The Case of the Dog Camp Mystery (Mary-Kate and Ashley: Adventures of Mary-Kate and Ashley)

The Case of the Dog Show Mystery (Mary-Kate and Ashley: Adventures of Mary-Kate and Ashley)

The Case of the Easter Egg Race (Mary-Kate and Ashley: Adventures of Mary-Kate and Ashley)

The Case of the Fagin File (Baker Street Irregulars)

The Case of the Firecrackers (Chinatown Mystery)

The Case of the Flapper 'Napper (Mary-Kate and Ashley: Adventures of Mary-Kate and Ashley)

The Case of the Floating Crime (Nancy Drew)

The Case of the Flying Phantom (Mary-Kate and Ashley: Adventures of Mary-Kate and Ashley)

The Case of the Fun House Mystery (Mary-Kate and Ashley: Adventures of Mary-Kate and Ashley)

The Case of the Game Show Mystery (Mary-Kate and Ashley: Adventures of Mary-Kate and Ashley)

The Case of the Ghost Grabbers (Baker Street Irregulars)

The Case of the Giggling Ghost (Mary-Kate and Ashley: Adventures of Mary-Kate and Ashley)

The Case of the Goblin Pearls (Chinatown Mystery)

The Case of the Golden Slipper (Mary-Kate and Ashley: Adventures of Mary-Kate and Ashley)

The Case of the Great Elephant Escape (Mary-Kate and Ashley: Adventures of Mary-Kate and Ashley)

The Case of the Green Ghost (Mary-Kate and Ashley: Adventures of Mary-Kate and Ashley)

The Case of the Haunted Camp (Mary-Kate and Ashley: Adventures of Mary-Kate and Ashley)

The Case of the Haunted Holiday (Baker Street Irregulars)

The Case of the Haunted Maze (Mary-Kate and Ashley: Adventures of Mary-Kate and Ashley)

The Case of the Hidden Holiday Riddle (Mary-Kate and Ashley: Adventures of Mary-Kate and Ashley)

The Case of the High Seas Secret (Mary-Kate and Ashley: Adventures of Mary-Kate and Ashley)

The Case of the Hollywood Who-Done-It (Mary-Kate and Ashley: Adventures of Mary-Kate and Ashley)

The Case of the Hotel Who-Done-It (Mary-Kate and Ashley: Adventures of Mary-Kate and Ashley)

The Case of the Icy Igloo Inn (Mary-Kate and Ashley: Adventures of Mary-Kate and Ashley)

The Case of the Jingle Bell Jinx (Mary-Kate and Ashley: Adventures of Mary-Kate and Ashley)

The Case of the Lion Dance (Chinatown Mystery)

The Case of the Logical I Ranch (Mary-Kate and Ashley: Adventures of Mary-Kate and Ashley)

The Case of the Lost Song (Nancy Drew)

The Case of the Mall Mystery (Mary-Kate and Ashley: Adventures of Mary-Kate and Ashley)

The Case of the Missing Masterpiece (Baker Street Irregulars)

The Case of the Missing Mummy (Mary-Kate and Ashley: Adventures of Mary-Kate and Ashley)

Case of the Missing She-Geek (Lizzie McGuire Mysteries)

The Case of the Mystery Cruise (Mary-Kate and Ashley: Adventures of Mary-Kate and Ashley)

The Case of the Nutcracker Ballet (Mary-Kate and Ashley: Adventures of Mary-Kate and Ashley)

The Case of the Photo Finish (Nancy Drew)

The Case of the Psychic's Vision (Hardy Boys)

Chamber of Fear (Fear Street: Fear Street Sagas)

Champion's Spirit (Thoroughbred)

Championship Ball (Chip Hilton Sports Series)

Championship Summer (Alden All Stars)

The Chance Factor (Star Trek: Voyager: Starfleet Academy)

A Chance to Love (Sweet Dreams)

The Change (Animorphs)

The Change (The Outer Limits)

A Change of Heart (Sweet Dreams)

Changeling (Sweep)

Changeling Diapers (Journey of Allen Strange)

Changing Leads (Saddle Club: Pine Hollow)

Changing Loves (Cheerleaders)

Changing Times (B.Y. Times)

Channel X (Sweet Valley University Thriller Editions)

The Chaos Balance (Recluce)

Chaos Bleeds (Buffy the Vampire Slayer) (Archway/Pocket)

Charlie Bone and the Invisible Boy (Children of the Red King)

Charlie Bone and the Time Twister (Children of the Red King)

Charm School Mystery (Sweet Valley Twins)

Charmed Again (Charmed)

Charmed Life (Chrestomanci)

Chase (Fearless)

The Chase (Forbidden Game)

The Chase for the Mystery Twister (Hardy Boys)

Chasing the King (Dream Series)

Chasing the Wind (The Young Underground)

Chat Freak (TodaysGirls.com)

The Cheater (Fear Street)

Cheating (Cheerleaders)

The Cheating Heart (Nancy Drew Files)

Cheating Heart (Sweet Dreams)

Cheating on Anna (Sweet Valley Junior High)

Cheating to Win (Sweet Valley High)

Check It Out—and Die! (Spinetinglers)

Checkout Time at the Dead-End Hotel (Goosebumps: Give Yourself Goosebumps)

Cher and Cher Alike (Clueless)

Cher Goes Enviro-mental (Clueless)

Cher Negotiates New York (Clueless)

Cherokee Bat and the Goat Guys (Weetzie Bat Saga)

Cher's Frantically Romantic Assignment (Clueless)

Cher's Furiously Fit Workout (Clueless)

Cher's Guide to . . . Whatever (Clueless)

The Chessmen of Doom (Johnny Dixon)

Chestnut Ridge Acres (Whispering Brook)

The Chestnut Soldier (Gwyn Griffiths Trilogy)

Chicken Chicken (Goosebumps)

The Chief (The Contender)

Chief Honor (Lightning on Ice)

Child of an Ancient City (Dragonflight Books)

Child of the Hunt (Buffy the Vampire Slayer) (Archway/Pocket)

Child of the Owl (Golden Mountain Chronicles)

Child of the Prophecy (Sevenwaters)

Childhood's End (Oh My Goddess!)

Children of Fear (Fear Street: Fear Street Sagas)

The Children of Green Knowe (Green Knowe)

Children of Hope (Seafort Saga)

Children of the Mind (Ender Wiggin)

The Children's Crusade (Books of Magic)

Chile Death (China Bayles Mystery)

Chill (Making Waves)

Chindi (Priscilla Hutchins)

Chinese Dragons (Choose Your Own Adventure)

The Chocolate-Covered Contest (Nancy Drew)

The Chocolate Lover (Missing Persons)

The Choice (Daughters of the Moon)

The Choice (The Outer Limits)

Choice Summer (Nikki Sheridan)

Choke Hold (Hardy Boys Casefiles)

Chomper (Dinotopia)

Choosing Sides (Kids from Kennedy Middle School)

Choosing Sides (Nancy Drew Files)

Choosing Sides (Sweet Valley Twins)

The Chosen (Night World)

The Chosen (The Nine Lives of Chloe King)

Christie & Company (Christie & Company)

Christie & Company Down East (Christie & Company)

Christie & Company in the Year of the Dragon (Christie & Company)

Christina's Courage (Thoroughbred)

Christina's Shining Star (Thoroughbred)

The Christmas Countdown (Fabulous Five)

The Christmas Ghost (Sweet Valley Twins Super Chiller Editions)

Christmas in Oz (Oz)

A Christmas Without Elizabeth (Sweet Valley Twins)

Christy's Choice (Christy)

Chronically Crushed (Clueless)

Chronicles of Avonlea (Avonlea)

Chronicles of Pern (Pern)

Ciao, Sweet Valley (Sweet Valley Twins)

The Cinderella Game (Sweet Dreams)

Cindy's Bold Start (Thoroughbred)

Cindy's Desert Adventure (Thoroughbred)

Cindy's Glory (Thoroughbred)

Cindy's Heartbreak (Thoroughbred)

Cindy's Honor (Thoroughbred)

Cindy's Last Hope (Thoroughbred)

Cindy's Runaway Colt (Thoroughbred)

Circle of Evil (Nancy Drew Files)

Circle of Fire (American Girls: History Mysteries)

Circle of Fire (Fear Street: Fear Street Sagas)

The Clue of the Leaning Chimney (Nancy Drew)

Clue of the Screeching Owl (Hardy Boys)

The Clue of the Tapping Heels (Nancy Drew)

The Clue of the Velvet Mask (Nancy Drew)

The Clue of the Whistling Bagpipes (Nancy Drew)

The Clue on the Crystal Dove (Nancy Drew)

The Clue on the Silver Screen (Nancy Drew)

Clueless (Sweet Valley Junior High)

Clueless: A Novel (Clueless)

The Clues Challenge (Nancy Drew)

Clutch Hitter! (Chip Hilton Sports Series)

The Coalition of Lions (Arthurian-Aksumite Cycle)

Cobra Connection (Choose Your Own Adventure)

Cobra Threat (Sports Mystery)

Code Name Cassandra (1-800-Where-R-You)

Cody (Wolfbay Wings)

The Coffin (Nightmare Hall)

Cold as Ice (Nancy Drew Files)

Cold Case (Net Force)

The Cold Cash Caper (Hardy Boys)

Cold Fire (Circle of Magic: The Circle Opens)

The Cold People (Spooksville)

Cold Shoulder Road (Wolves Chronicles)

Cold Sweat (Hardy Boys Casefiles)

College Bound (Beverly Hills, 90210)

College Cruise (Sweet Valley University)

College Girls (Sweet Valley University)

College Weekend (Fear Street)

College Weekend (Sweet Valley High)

Collision Course (Hardy Boys Casefiles)

Colman (Wise Child)

Colonization (Colonization)

Colonization: Down to Earth (Colonization)

Colonization: Homeward Bound (Colonization)

Colonization: Second Contact (Colonization)

The Color of Her Panties (Xanth Saga)

The Color of Magic (Discworld)

Colors of Chaos (Recluce)

Come a Stranger (Tillerman Cycle)

Come What May (Heartland)

Comeback Cagers (Chip Hilton Sports Series)

Comedy of Errors (China Tate)

Comedy of Errors (Sweet Dreams)

Comet Crash (Choose Your Own Adventure)

Coming Back (Cheerleaders)

Coming Home (Heartland)

Common Enemy (Extreme Zone)

Competitive Edge (Hardy Boys Casefiles)

The Complete Short Stories, 1986–1989 (Concrete)

The Complete Short Stories, 1990–1995 (Concrete)

Computer Confusion (Saved by the Bell)

Computer Crunch! (Secret World of Alex Mack)

The Computer Takeover (Choose Your Own Adventure)

Conan and the Prophecy (Endless Quest)

Conan the Outlaw (Endless Quest)

Conan the Undaunted (Endless Quest)

Condition Critical (University Hospital)

The Confession (Fear Street)

Confessions of a Shopaholic (Shopaholic)

Confessions of a Teenage Drama Queen (Confessions of a Teenage Drama Queen)

Conformation Faults (Saddle Club: Pine Hollow)

Conqueror Worm (Hellboy)

Consequences (Books of Magic)

Consider Phlebas (The Culture)

The Conspiracy (Animorphs)

The Contender (The Contender)

The Contest (Everest)

Control (Outernet)

Control (X Files)

Control Freak (Sweet Valley High Senior Year)

The Cool Club (Mary-Kate and Ashley: Two of a Kind)

The Cool Crowd (Sweet Valley Junior High)

Coot Club (Swallows and Amazons)

Copper Canyon Conspiracy (Nancy Drew and the Hardy Boys Super Mysteries)

The Coral Coffin (Finnegan Zwake)

Count on Me (American Dreams) (Aladdin)

Countdown to Terror (Hardy Boys Casefiles)

Counterfeit Christmas (Nancy Drew Files)

Country Girl (Sweet Dreams)

Couple of April Fools (Hamlet Chronicles)

Courage of Falcons (Secret Texts)

The Courage to Live (Why Me?)

Course of Action (Saddle Club: Pine Hollow)

Courting Disaster (Nancy Drew and the Hardy Boys Super Mysteries)

Cousin War (Sweet Valley Twins)

The Coven (Sweep)

The Covenant of the Forge (Dragonlance Dwarven Nations Trilogy)

Cover Girl (Sweet Dreams)

Cover Girls (Sweet Valley High)

The Cowardly Lion of Oz (Oz)

Cowboy Kisses (Sweet Dreams)

Coyote Moon (Buffy the Vampire Slayer) (Archway/Pocket)

Crash Landing! (Sweet Valley High)

Crash Test Demons (Buffy the Vampire Slayer) (Dark Horse)

Crazy for Cartwheels (Cheer Squad)

Crazy for You (Sweet Dreams)

The Creature from Club Lagoona (Fear Street: Ghosts of Fear Street)

The Creature in the Teacher (Spooksville)

Creature Teacher (Goosebumps Series 2000)

Creature Teacher (Graveyard School)

Creatures of Forever (The Last Vampire)

Dance with Me (American Dreams) (Aladdin)

Dance with Me (Sweet Dreams)

Dancing in My Nuddy Pants (Confessions of Georgia Nicolson)

Dancing in the Dark (Sweet Dreams)

The Danger (Dive)

Danger at Anchor Mine (Choose Your Own Adventure)

Danger at the Wild West Show (American Girls: History Mysteries)

Danger Down Under (Nancy Drew and the Hardy Boys Super Mysteries)

Danger for Hire (Nancy Drew Files)

Danger in Disguise (Nancy Drew Files)

Danger in Disguise (On Time's Wing)

Danger in the Extreme (Hardy Boys)

Danger in the Fourth Dimension (Hardy Boys)

Danger on Parade (Nancy Drew Files)

Danger on the Air (Hardy Boys)

Danger on the Diamond (Hardy Boys)

Danger on the Great Lakes (Nancy Drew)

Danger on Thunder Mountain (American Adventure)

Danger on Vampire Trail (Hardy Boys)

Danger Time (Goosebumps: Give Yourself Goosebumps)

Danger Unlimited (Hardy Boys Casefiles)

Danger Zone (Distress Call 911)

Danger Zone (Hardy Boys Casefiles)

Dangerous (Brides of Wildcat County)

Dangerous Decisions and Hidden Choices (Summit High)

Dangerous Games (Nancy Drew and the Hardy Boys Super Mysteries)

Dangerous Games (Wolves Chronicles)

Dangerous Love (Sweet Valley High)

Dangerous Loves (Nancy Drew Files)

A Dangerous Path (Warriors)

A Dangerous Plan (Left Behind—The Kids)

A Dangerous Promise (Orphan Train Adventures)

The Dangerous Quest (Spooksville)

Dangerous Relations (Nancy Drew Files)

The Dangerous Rescue (Star Wars: Jedi Apprentice)

A Dangerous Ride (Thoroughbred: Ashleigh)

The Dangerous Transmission (Hardy Boys)

Dangers of the Rainbow Nebula (Daystar Voyages)

Danny (Love Stories: Brothers Trilogy)

Danny Means Trouble (Sweet Valley Twins)

Daphne (Sisters)

The Dare (Fear Street)

Dare to Scare (Mary-Kate and Ashley: Two of a Kind)

Daredevil Park (Choose Your Own Adventure)

Daredevils (Hardy Boys)

Darien's Rise (Passages)

The Dark (Phantom Valley)

Dark Angel (Night World)

Dark Ararat (Emortality)

The Dark Corner (Spooksville)

The Dark Design (Riverworld Saga)

The Dark Ground (Dark Ground Trilogy)

The Dark Hand (Jackie Chan Adventures)

The Dark Is Rising (Dark Is Rising)

Dark Lies (Extreme Zone)

The Dark Lord's Demise (The Archives of Anthropos)

The Dark Mage (Avalon 2: Quest for Magic)

Dark Magick (Sweep)

Dark Matter (X Files)

Dark Mirror (Angel)

Dark Moon (Firebringer Trilogy)

Dark Moon (Nightmare Hall)

Dark of the Moon (On Time's Wing)

The Dark One (Roswell High)

The Dark Portal (Deptford Mice)

Dark Quetzal (Echorium Sequence)

Dark Reunion (Vampire Diaries)

The Dark Rival (Star Wars: Jedi Apprentice)

The Dark Secret of Weatherend (Anthony Monday)

Dark Side of the Sun (Space Above and Beyond)

Dark Spell Over Morlandria (Daystar Voyages)

The Dark Stairs (Herculeah Jones)

The Dark Tower (Dark Tower)

Dark Vengeance (Charmed)

Darkangel (Darkangel Trilogy)

The Darkening (Buffy the Vampire Slayer: Wicked Willow)

Darkening Skies (Left Behind—The Kids)

Darkest Hour (Heartland)

Darkest Hour (The Mediator)

The Darkest Hour (Warriors)

Darkest Knight (Star Wars Young Jedi Knights)

Darkness, Be My Friend (Tomorrow)

Darkness Before Dawn (Hazelwood High)

Darkness Below (Bionicle Adventures)

Darkness Falls (Hardy Boys Casefiles)

Darkness Falls (X Files)

Darksong Rising (The Spellsong Cycle)

Darkspell (Deverry)

Darth Maul (Star Wars Episode 1: Journals)

The Dastard (Xanth Saga)

A Date with a Werewolf (Sweet Valley High)

Date with Death (Charmed)

A Date with Deception (Nancy Drew Files)

Dating (Cheerleaders)

Dating Game (Mary-Kate and Ashley: So Little Time)

The Dating Game (Sweet Valley High)

Daughter of Magic (Yurt)

Daughter of the Forest (Sevenwaters)

Daughter of Twin Oaks (Secret Refuge)

Daughters of Darkness (Night World)

Death Threat (Sweet Valley High)

Deathgame (Hardy Boys Casefiles)

Death's Door (Herculeah Jones)

Deathworld (Net Force)

The Deceived (Forbidden Doors)

Deceived (Jennie McGrady Mysteries)

December (Countdown)

The Deception (Animorphs)

Deceptions (Star Trek: The Next Generation: Starfleet Academy)

Deceptions (Sweet Valley High)

The Decision (Animorphs)

Decisions (Sweet Valley High)

The Deep (Dive)

The Deep End of Fear (Dark Secrets)

Deep in My Heart (Sweet Dreams)

Deep in the Jungle of Doom (Goosebumps: Give Yourself Goosebumps)

Deep Powder, Deep Trouble (X Games Xtreme Mysteries)

Deep Secrets (Nancy Drew Files)

Deep Trouble (Goosebumps)

Deep Trouble (Hardy Boys Casefiles)

Deep Trouble II (Goosebumps)

Deep Water (Buffy the Vampire Slayer) (Archway/Pocket)

Deep Wizardry (Wizardry) (Duane)

Deepsix (Priscilla Hutchins)

Defender (Foreigner)

The Defenders of the Dead (Star Wars: Jedi Apprentice)

The Defiant Hero (Troubleshooters)

Deleting the Net Threat (Summit High)

Delusions of Grandeur (Star Wars Young Jedi Knights)

The Demolition Mission (Hardy Boys)

Demolition Winter (Space Above and Beyond)

The Demon Apostle (The DemonWars)

The Demon Awakes (The DemonWars)

The Demon in the Teahouse (The Ghost in the Tokaido Inn)

Demon Lord of Karanda (Malloreon)

The Demon Spirit (The DemonWars)

Demon Witch (Ravenscliff)

The Demon's Den (Hardy Boys)

Demons Don't Dream (Xanth Saga)

The Departure (Animorphs)

Depth Charge (Journey of Allen Strange)

Derby Day (Thoroughbred: Ashleigh)

Derby Dreams (Thoroughbred: Ashleigh)

Derby Fever (Thoroughbred)

Deryni Checkmate (Chronicles of Deryni)

Deryni Rising (Chronicles of Deryni)

The Desert Thieves (Hardy Boys)

Designs in Crime (Nancy Drew Files)

Desperate Measures (Jennie McGrady Mysteries)

Desperate Measures (Nancy Drew and the Hardy Boys Super Mysteries)

The Desperate Search (American Adventure)

Destination Unknown (Remnants)

Destiny's Twins (T*Witches)

Detour for Emily (Hamilton High)

The Devil in Miss Urd (Oh My Goddess!)

Dew Drop Dead (Sebastian Barth)

Dial L for Love (Sweet Dreams)

Dial 'V' for Vengeance (Spy Girls)

Diamond Deceit (Nancy Drew Files)

The Diaries (Clearwater Crossing)

Diary of a Mad Mummy (Goosebumps: Give Yourself Goosebumps)

Dicey's Song (Tillerman Cycle)

Dido and Pa (Wolves Chronicles)

Die Bug Die (X Files)

A Different Path (W.I.T.C.H.)

Diggers (Bromeliad)

A Dilly of a Death (China Bayles Mystery)

Dino Sword (Danger Boy)

Dinosaur Island (Choose Your Own Adventure)

Dinosaurs Ate My Homework (Dinoverse)

Diplomacy of Wolves (Secret Texts)

Diplomatic Deceit (Hardy Boys Casefiles)

Dirty Big Secrets (Trash)

Dirty Deeds (Hardy Boys Casefiles)

The Disappearance (W.I.T.C.H.)

Disappeared (Alias)

Disappearing Acts (Herculeah Jones)

The Disappearing Floor (Hardy Boys)

Disaster for Hire (Hardy Boys Casefiles)

Discover the Destroyer (EverWorld)

The Discovery (Animorphs)

The Discovery (Dive)

Distance Runner (Thoroughbred)

The Diversion (Animorphs)

Diversity Alliance (Star Wars Young Jedi Knights)

Dixie's First Kiss (Sunset Island)

DJ's Challenge (High Hurdles)

The DNA Disaster (Tom Swift)

Do I Have to Paint You a Picture (Raise the Flag)

The Dog Ate My Homework (Bone Chillers)

Dog Eat Dog (Blue-Eyed Son Trilogy)

Dog Gone Mess (Mary-Kate and Ashley in Action)

Dollars and Sense (B.Y. Times)

The Dollhouse that Time Forgot (Eerie Indiana)

Dolphin Watch (Dinotopia)

The Dolphins of Pern (Pern)

Don't Answer the Phone (Sweet Valley University Thriller Editions)

Don't Bet on Love (Sweet Dreams)

Don't Count on Homecoming Queen (Raise the Flag)

Don't Cry for Yesterday (Why Me?)

Don't Eat the Mystery Meat (Graveyard School)

Dragonsinger (Pern: The Harper-Hall Trilogy)

The Dragonslayer (Bone)

Dragonsong (Pern: The Harper-Hall Trilogy)

Dragonwings (Golden Mountain Chronicles)

Drama Queen (Sweet Valley Junior High)

Draugr (Northern Frights)

Draven's Defiance (Passages)

The Drawing of the Three (Dark Tower)

Dread Mountain (Deltora: Deltora Quest)

The Dreaded Ex (Sweet Valley University)

The Dreadful Future of Blossom Culp (Blossom Culp)

Dream a Little Dream (Aloha Cove)

Dream Date (Sweet Dreams)

The Dream Date Debate (Mary-Kate and Ashley: Two of a Kind)

Dream Holiday (Mary-Kate and Ashley Sweet 16)

Dream On (Clearwater Crossing)

Dream Pony (Sandy Lane Stables)

Dream Prom (Sweet Dreams)

Dream Storm (Remnants)

The Dream Team (Mary-Kate and Ashley in Action)

A Dream to Follow (Red River: Return to Red River)

Dreamcrusher (Replica)

Dreamboat (Sweet Dreams)

Dreamfall (Psion)

The Dreaming Place (Dragonflight Books)

Dreams of Ships, Dreams of Julia (The Young Americans)

Dreamskate (Sweet Dreams)

Dreamwalk (Roswell High)

Drive You Crazy (7th Heaven)

Dropping Out (Sweet Valley University)

Drowned Ammet (Dalemark Quartet)

Drowned Wednesday (Keys to the Kingdom)

The Druid of Shannara (Shannara: Heritage of Shannara)

The Druid's Keep (Shannara: The Sword of Shannara)

The Drum, the Doll, and the Zombie (Johnny Dixon)

Drummer Boy at Bull Run (Bonnets and Bugles)

Drums of Autumn (Outlander)

Dual Identity (Net Force)

Ducky (California Diaries)

Ducky, Diary Two (California Diaries)

Ducky, Diary Three (California Diaries)

Dude Ranch (7th Heaven)

Dude with a 'Tude (Clueless)

Duel of the Masters (Endless Quest)

Duel on the Diamond (Alden All Stars)

Dugout Jinx (Chip Hilton Sports Series)

The Dummy (Nightmare Hall)

Dungeon of Doom (Hardy Boys)

Dungeon of Dread (Endless Quest)

Dungeon of Fear (Endless Quest)

Durango Street (Dogtown Ghetto)

The Dust Waltz (Buffy the Vampire Slayer) (Dark Horse)

Dustland (Justice Trilogy)

Dwight D. Eisenhower (Dear Mr. President)

Dying to Win (Jennie McGrady Mysteries)

Dying Young (Dear Diary)

Dylan's Choice (Thoroughbred)

E

E.B.E. (X Files)

The E-Mail Murders (P.C. Hawke Mysteries)

The E-Mail Mystery (Nancy Drew)

The Eagle and the Nightingales (Bardic Voices)

Eagle Strike (Alex Rider)

Eagle's Wing (Golden Filly Series)

An Ear for Danger (Three Investigators)

Earth Geeks Must Go! (Goosebumps Series 2000)

Earth Made of Glass (The Thousand Cultures)

Earthborn (Homecoming Saga)

Earthborn (Ormingat)

Earthfall (Homecoming Saga)

Earthly Possessions (Angel (Graphic Novels))

Earthquake! (Choose Your Own Adventure)

Earthquake! (Left Behind—The Kids)

Earthquake (Sweet Valley High)

Earthquake: San Francisco, 1906 (Survival!)

The East-West Contest (7th Heaven)

The Easter Egg Haunt (Graveyard School)

Easy Marks (Nancy Drew Files)

Eat Your Poison, Dear (Sebastian Barth)

Eaten Alive (Star Wars Galaxy of Fear)

Echoes in the Wind (Summerhill Secrets)

Echoes of Honor (Honor Harrington)

Echoes of the Well of Souls (Watchers at the Well)

Echoes of the White Giraffe (Sookan Bak)

Eclipse (Sweep)

Edge of Destruction (Hardy Boys Casefiles)

The Edge of the Cloud (Flambards)

Eerie in the Mirror (Eerie Indiana)

The Eerie Triangle (Eerie Indiana)

ElfQuest: Wolfrider (ElfQuest)

Egg Monsters from Mars (Goosebumps)

Eggs in One Basket (Mike Pillsbury)

Eight Is Enough (Holly's Heart)

The El Dorado Adventure (Vesper Holly)

Eldest (Inheritance)

Eleanor (Royal Diaries)

Election Connection (Journey of Allen Strange)

Elevator to Nowhere (Goosebumps: Give Yourself Goosebumps)

The Elf Queen and the King, Book 1 (Ruin Mist Chronicles)

The Elf Queen and the King, Book 2 (Ruin Mist Chronicles)

The Elf Queen of Shannara (Shannara: Heritage of Shannara)

Everest Adventure (Choose Your Own Adventure)

Every New Day (Heartland)

Everybody Say Moesha! (Moesha)

Everybody's Favorite, by Penny (The Broadway Ballplayers)

Everything Changes (Baby-Sitters Club Friends Forever)

Everything Changes (Heartland)

Everything Changes: Julia (Party of Five)

Evil Elizabeth (Sweet Valley Twins Super Chiller Editions)

The Evil Experiment (Star Wars: Jedi Apprentice)

The Evil House (Spooksville)

Evil in Amsterdam (Nancy Drew and the Hardy Boys Super Mysteries)

Evil, Inc. (Hardy Boys Casefiles)

The Evil Lives! (Fear Street: Fear Street Super Chillers)

Evil on Board (House of Horrors)

The Evil One (Phantom Valley)

The Evil Pen Pal (Choose Your Own Nightmare)

Evil Returns (The Vampire's Promise)

The Evil that Men Do (Buffy the Vampire Slayer) (Archway/Pocket)

Evil Thirst (The Last Vampire)

The Evil Twin (Sweet Valley High)

The Evil Twin (Sweet Valley High)

The Evil Twin (Trash)

Ex-Zack-Ly (Saved by the Bell)

Excession (The Culture)

Exchange of Hearts (Sweet Dreams)

Exhibition of Evil (Nancy Drew and the Hardy Boys Super Mysteries)

Exhuming Elisa (Ghost)

Exiled to Earth (Choose Your Own Adventure)

Exit, Stage Right (Saved by the Bell)

The Experiment (Animorphs)

The Experiment (Nightmare Hall)

Explorer (Foreigner)

The Explorers (Dinotopia)

The Exposed (Animorphs)

Exposed! (Beverly Hills, 90210)

Exposed (Fearless)

Exposed (Three Girls in the City)

Exposed: Week 2 (Sevens)

The Extreme (Animorphs)

Extreme Sisterhood (Clueless)

Eye of Eternity (Pyrates)

The Eye of the Fortuneteller (Fear Street: Ghosts of Fear Street)

Eye of the World (The Wheel of Time)

Eye on Crime (Hardy Boys)

The Eyes of the Killer Robot (Johnny Dixon)

Eyes of the Storm (Bone)

F

Fabulous Five Minus One (Fabulous Five)

The Fabulous Five Together Again (Fabulous Five)

The Fabulous Riverboat (Riverworld Saga)

The Face (Fear Street)

The Face in the Bessledorf Funeral Parlor (Bessledorf Hotel)

Face It (Sweet Valley University Thriller Editions)

The Face of Apollo (Book of the Gods)

The Face-Off Phony (Slapshots)

The Face on the Milk Carton (Janie)

Face the Fear (Mindwarp)

Face the Music (Diary of a Teenage Girl)

Face the Music (Heart Beats)

Face Up to Love (Sweet Dreams)

Faceless (The Lurker Files)

Faces in the Water (York Trilogy)

Faces of Terror (Fear Street: Fear Street Sagas)

Facing the Future (Left Behind—The Kids)

The Facts About Flirting (Mary-Kate and Ashley: Two of a Kind)

Faded Dreams (Live from Brentwood High)

Faery Lands Forlorn (Man of His Word)

Fair Play (American Dreams) (Aladdin)

Fair-Weather Love (Sweet Dreams)

Faith in a Long Shot (Thoroughbred)

The Faith Trials, Volume 1 (Buffy the Vampire Slayer) (Archway/Pocket)

Fake (Fearless)

The Fake Teacher (Don't Touch That Remote!)

The Falcon's Malteser (The Diamond Brothers)

The Fall (The Seventh Tower)

Fall (Witch Season)

Fall of a Kingdom (Farsala Trilogy)

Fall of Angels (Recluce)

The Fallen (The Fallen)

The Fallen (The Nine Lives of Chloe King)

Fallen Star (Thoroughbred)

Falling Apart (Sweet Valley High Senior Year)

Falling for Claire (Making Out)

Falling for Lucas (Sweet Valley High)

Falling for Ryan (Love Stories)

Falling in Love (Cheerleaders)

Falling in Love Again (Sweet Dreams)

Fallout (The Wessex Papers)

False Alarm (Hardy Boys Casefiles)

False Friends (Nancy Drew on Campus)

False Impressions (Nancy Drew Files)

False Memories (Buffy the Vampire Slayer) (Dark Horse)

False Moves (Nancy Drew Files)

False Notes (Nancy Drew: Girl Detective)

False Pretenses (Nancy Drew Files)

The Familiar (Animorphs)

A Family Apart (Orphan Train Adventures)

Family Secrets (Christy)

Family Secrets (Dear Diary)

Family Secrets (Sweet Valley High)

Fantasies (Beverly Hills, 90210)

Far From the Storm (The Young Underground)

Farewell, Dawn (Baby-Sitters Club)

Farewell to the Island (Island Trilogy)

Fisherman's Hope (Seafort Saga)

Five Alien Elves (Hamlet Chronicles)

The Five Paths (Circle of Three)

Flag in Exile (Honor Harrington)

Flambards (Flambards)

Flambards Divided (Flambards)

Flambards in Summer (Flambards)

Flame (Farsala Trilogy)

The Flaming Trap (American Adventure)

Flash Forward (Mindwarp)

Flavor of the Day (@CAFE)

Flee (Fearless)

Flesh and Blood (Hardy Boys Casefiles)

The Flickering Torch Mystery (Hardy Boys)

Flight (Smallville)

Flight into Danger (Hardy Boys Casefiles)

Flight of the Dragon Kyn (Dragon Chronicles)

Flight of the Phoenix (Mummy Chronicles)

Flight to Freedom (First Person Fiction)

Flirt in the Mirror (Mirror Image)

Flirting (Cheerleaders)

Flirting with Danger (Nancy Drew Files)

Flood (Med Center)

Flood: Mississippi, 1927 (Survival!)

Flowers in the Attic (Dollanganger)

Fly by Night (Spinetinglers)

A Fly Named Alfred (Harper Winslow)

Flying High (Angels Unlimited)

Flying High (B.Y. Times)

The Flying Saucer Mystery (Nancy Drew)

Flying Too High (Nancy Drew Files)

Focus on Love (Sweet Dreams)

Focus on This (The Real Deal)

Follow that Boy (Sweet Dreams)

Follow the Star (The Young Underground)

Follow Your Heart (Sweet Dreams)

Following My Own Footsteps (Gordy Smith)

Food Chain (Buffy the Vampire Slayer) (Dark Horse)

Fool for Love (Sweet Dreams)

Fooling Around (Sweet Valley University)

Footprints at the Window (York Trilogy)

Footprints Under the Window (Hardy Boys)

For All Time (Time Travel Quartet)

For Love or Money (Nancy Drew Files)

For Real (Turning Seventeen)

For the Love of Ryan (Sweet Valley University)

Forbidden Castle (Choose Your Own Adventure)

Forbidden Fountain of Oz (Oz)

Forbidden Love (Sweet Dreams)

Forbidden Love (Sweet Valley High)

Forbidden Secrets (Fear Street: Fear Street Sagas)

The Forbidden Stallion (Thoroughbred: Ashleigh)

Foreigner (Foreigner)

Forest Fire (Survival!)

Forest of Darkness (Endless Quest)

Forest of Fear (Choose Your Own Adventure)

Forest of Secrets (Warriors)

Forest of the Pygmies (Alexander Cold and Nadia Santos)

The Forests of Silence (Deltora: Deltora Quest)

Forged by Fire (Hazelwood High)

Forget Me Not (Aloha Cove)

Forget Me Not (Glory)

Forget Me Not (Mary-Kate and Ashley Sweet 16)

Forgetting (Cheerleaders)

The Forgotten (Animorphs)

Forgotten (Jennie McGrady Mysteries)

The Forgotten Filly (Thoroughbred: Ashleigh's Collection)

The Forgotten Forest of Oz (Oz)

The Forgotten Planet (Choose Your Own Adventure)

The Forsaken Crusade (Winds of Light)

Forsaken House (Forgotten Realms—The Last Mythal)

Fortress Draconis (DragonCrown War Cycle)

A Fortress of Grey Ice (Sword of Shadows)

The Fortune-Teller's Secret (Nancy Drew)

Fortunes of Love (Sweet Dreams)

Forty Thousand in Gehenna (Alliance-Union)

Forward the Foundation (Foundation)

Foul Play (Hardy Boys Casefiles)

Foul Play (Three Investigators)

Foundation (Foundation)

Foundation and Chaos (Foundation)

Foundation and Earth (Foundation)

Foundation and Empire (Foundation)

Foundation's Edge (Foundation)

Foundation's Fear (Foundation)

Foundation's Triumph (Foundation)

Fountain of Weird (Eerie Indiana)

The Fountains of Youth (Emortality)

Four and Twenty Blackbirds (Bardic Voices)

The Four Dragons (W.I.T.C.H.)

The Four-Headed Dragon (Hardy Boys)

Four Stupid Cupids (Hamlet Chronicles)

4Give & 4Get (TodaysGirls.com)

Fourth Down Showdown (Chip Hilton Sports Series)

The Fourth Goddess (Oh My Goddess!)

The Fowlers of Sweet Valley (Sweet Valley High)

The Fox Hunt Mystery (Nancy Drew)

Fragile Creatures (Concrete)

Frame-Up (Hardy Boys Casefiles)

Franken-Bobby! (Saved by the Bell)

Frankenturkey (Bone Chillers)

Franklin Delano Roosevelt (Dear Mr. President)

Freak (Fearless)

Freaked Out (Lizzie McGuire)

Freaky Friday (Annabel Andrews)

Free Fall (Alias)

The Ghost in the Tokaido Inn
(The Ghost in the Tokaido
Inn)

Ghost Light on Graveyard Shoal
(American Girls: History
Mysteries)

The Ghost Next Door
(Goosebumps)

Ghost of a Chance (Hardy Boys)

Ghost of a Chance (Sweet
Dreams)

The Ghost of Avalanche
Mountain (Goldstone Trilogy)

The Ghost of Blackwood Hall
(Nancy Drew)

The Ghost of Craven Cove
(Nancy Drew)

Ghost of the Jedi (Star Wars
Galaxy of Fear)

The Ghost of the Lantern Lady
(Nancy Drew)

The Ghost of Tricia Martin
(Sweet Valley High)

Ghost on the Net (Cybersurfers)

Ghost Riders (Ballad)

Ghost Roads (Buffy the Vampire
Slayer: The Gatekeeper
Trilogy)

Ghost Train (Choose Your Own
Adventure)

Ghost Wolf (Avalon 2: Quest for
Magic)

Ghostfire (Outcast)

Ghosts I Have Been (Blossom
Culp)

Ghosts of Vicksburg (White
Mane Kids)

Ghoul Friends (Fear Street:
Ghosts of Fear Street)

Ghoul Trouble (Buffy the
Vampire Slayer)
(Archway/Pocket)

The Giant Garden of Oz (Oz)

The Giant Horse of Oz (Oz)

The Giant Rat of Sumatra
(Hardy Boys)

The Gift (Fear Street: Fear Street
Seniors)

A Gift of Ice (Jimmy Fincher
Saga)

Gifted Touch (Fingerprints)

Gifts from the Heart (Sweet
Dreams)

Gimme Back My Brain
(Spinetinglers)

A Girl Called Al (Al (Alexandra))

Girl Talk (Mary-Kate and
Ashley: So Little Time)

The Girl They Both Loved
(Sweet Valley High)

The Girl Who Couldn't
Remember (Nancy Drew)

The Girl Who Cried Monster
(Goosebumps)

Girls, Girls, Girls (Black Book
(Diary of a Teenage Stud))

A Girl's Guide to Guys (Mary-
Kate and Ashley: So Little
Time)

Girls in Love (The Girls Quartet)

Girls in Pants (Sisterhood of the
Traveling Pants)

Girls in Tears (The Girls
Quartet)

Girls' Night Out (Saved by the
Bell)

Girls on Film (A-List)

Girls Out Late (The Girls
Quartet)

Girls R.U.L.E. (Girls R.U.L.E.)

Girls Under Pressure (The Girls
Quartet)

Give and Take (From the Files of
Madison Finn)

Give Me a Break (From the Files
of Madison Finn)

The Giver (The Giver)

The Glass Cat of Oz (Oz)

Glennall's Betrayal (Passages)

Glinda of Oz (Oz)

Glory (Glory)

Glory in Danger (Thoroughbred)

Glory in the Flower (Sterling
Family)

Glory's Rival (Thoroughbred)

Glory's Triumph
(Thoroughbred)

The Gnome King of Oz (Oz)

Go! (Love Trilogy)

Go Eat Worms! (Goosebumps)

Go for It, Patti! (Paxton
Cheerleaders)

Go for the Glory (Golden Filly
Series)

Go for the Gold! (Secret World
of Alex Mack)

Go, Girl, Go (Cheer USA!)

Go Jump in the Pool (Bruno and
Boots)

Go to Your Tomb—Right Now!
(Fear Street: Ghosts of Fear
Street)

Go West, Young Women
(Petticoat Party)

Goa (Blood of the Goddess)

God of the Golden Fleece (Book
of the Gods)

Goddess of the Night (Daughters
of the Moon)

The Godmother (The Fairy
Godmother)

The Godmother's Apprentice
(The Fairy Godmother)

The Godmother's Web (The
Fairy Godmother)

Gods of Fire and Thunder (Book
of the Gods)

Gods of Riverworld (Riverworld
Saga)

Gods of the Well of Souls
(Watchers at the Well)

Going Crazy Till Wednesday
(Brio Girls)

Going, Going, Gone! (Saved by
the Bell)

Going Home (Nancy Drew on
Campus)

Going Postal (Discworld)

Going Strong (Cheerleaders)

The Gold Medal Secret (Choose
Your Own Adventure)

Gold Rush Fever! (Secret World
of Alex Mack)

Gold-Rush Phoebe (Petticoat
Party)

The Gold Train Bandits
(American Adventure)

Gold Unicorn (Dragonflight
Books)

Gold Unicorn (Unicorn)

Golden Bees of Tulami
(Dogtown Ghetto)

The Golden Compass (His Dark
Materials)

Golden Girl (Sweet Dreams)

The Golden Globe (Star Wars
Junior Jedi Knights)

Golden Palaces (Royal Pavilions)

Goldstone (Goldstone Trilogy)

Golem in the Gears (Xanth Saga)

The Golem's Eye (The
Bartimaeus Trilogy)

Gom on Windy Mountain (Tales
of Gom in the Legends of Ulm)

Gone (Fearless)

Gone Too Far (Troubleshooters)

Good-Bye, Dressel Hills (Holly's
Heart)

Good-Bye, Elizabeth (Sweet
Valley University)

Good-Bye Is Not Forever (Aloha
Cove)

H

The Hand of the Necromancer (Johnny Dixon)

Hands Off! (Sweet Valley Junior High)

Hands Off My Crush-Boy! (Lizzie McGuire Mysteries)

Handy Mandy in Oz (Oz)

Hangman (The Sixth Sense: Secrets from Beyond)

The Hangman's Beautiful Daughter (Ballad)

Hangman's Root (China Bayles Mystery)

Happily Ever After (Sweet Dreams)

Happily Ever After (Sweet Valley High)

Happy Birthday, Dear Amy (Replica)

Happy Hauntings (Fear Street: Ghosts of Fear Street)

Happy Holidays, Jessi (Baby-Sitters Club)

Happy Mother's Day, Lila (Sweet Valley Twins)

Hard Cash (Hard Cash)

Hard Cash (Richard Steele Trilogy)

Hard Choices (Sweet Valley High)

Hard Lessons (Black Stallion: Young Black Stallion)

Hard to Get (Nancy Drew on Campus)

Hard to Resist (Love Stories)

Hardcourt Upset (Chip Hilton Sports Series)

Harpy Thyme (Xanth Saga)

Harry Potter and the Chamber of Secrets (Harry Potter)

Harry Potter and the Goblet of Fire (Harry Potter)

Harry Potter and the Half Blood Prince (Harry Potter)

Harry Potter and the Order of the Phoenix (Harry Potter)

Harry Potter and the Prisoner of Azkaban (Harry Potter)

Harry Potter and the Sorcerer's Stone (Harry Potter)

The Harvest (Buffy the Vampire Slayer) (Archway/Pocket)

Harvey Angell (Harvey Angell Trilogy)

Harvey Angell and the Ghost Child (Harvey Angell Trilogy)

Harvey Angell Beats Time (Harvey Angell Trilogy)

A Hat Full of Sky (Discworld)

Hatchet (Brian Robeson)

Hatchling (Dinotopia)

Haunted (Angel)

Haunted (Buffy the Vampire Slayer) (Dark Horse)

Haunted (Fear Street)

Haunted (Fingerprints)

Haunted (The Mediator)

Haunted (X Files)

The Haunted Baby (Choose Your Own Nightmare)

The Haunted Bridge (Nancy Drew)

The Haunted Burial Ground (Sweet Valley Twins Super Chiller Editions)

Haunted by Desire (Charmed)

The Haunted Car (Goosebumps Series 2000)

The Haunted Carousel (Nancy Drew)

The Haunted Cave (Spooksville)

The Haunted Fort (Hardy Boys)

The Haunted Heart (Enchanted Hearts)

Haunted House (Sweet Valley Twins)

Haunted House Hijinks! (Secret World of Alex Mack)

The Haunted Mask (Goosebumps)

The Haunted Mask II (Goosebumps)

The Haunted School (Goosebumps)

The Haunted Showboat (Nancy Drew)

The Haunted Starship (Star Trek: The Next Generation: Starfleet Academy)

The Haunted Wizard (A Wizard in Rhyme)

The Haunting (Forbidden Doors)

The Haunting of Drang Island (Northern Frights)

The Haunting of Horse Island (Nancy Drew)

Have You Heard About Elizabeth (Sweet Valley University)

Have Yourself an Eerie Little Christmas (Eerie Indiana)

Having It All (Cheerleaders)

Hawaii Five-Go! (Luna Bay)

Hayfoot, Strawfoot (White Mane Kids)

Head Games (Body of Evidence)

Head over Heels (The Jersey)

Head over Heels (Lizzie McGuire)

Head over Heels (Sweet Dreams)

Head over Heels (Sweet Valley High)

The Headless Bicycle Rider (Graveyard School)

The Headless Ghost (Goosebumps)

The Headless Ghost (Phantom Valley)

Headless Halloween (Goosebumps Series 2000)

Headstrong (Saddle Club: Pine Hollow)

The Healing of Crossroads (Crossroads Trilogy)

Heart and Soul (Clearwater Crossing)

Heart and Soul (Sweet Dreams)

Heart Breakers (Luna Bay)

A Heart Full of Hope (Christy Miller)

Heart of Avalon (Avalon 2: Quest for Magic)

Heart of Danger (Nancy Drew Files)

Heart of Ice (Nancy Drew Files)

Heart of the Hills (American Dreams) (Avon)

Heart of the Hunter (Fear Street: Fear Street Sagas)

Heart of the Pharaoh (Mummy Chronicles)

Heart to Heart (From the Files of Madison Finn)

Heart to Heart (Mary-Kate and Ashley: Two of a Kind)

Heart to Heart (Sweet Dreams)

Heart Trauma (University Hospital)

Heartbreak Hill (Sweet Dreams)

Heartbreaker (Sweet Valley High)

Heartfire (Tales of Alvin Maker)

Heartlight (Heartlight)

Heart's Blood (Pit Dragon Trilogy)

Hearts Don't Lie (Sweet Dreams)

Heartstrings (Sweet Dreams)

Heartthrob (Sweet Dreams)

Heat (Buffy the Vampire Slayer: Buffy and Angel)

Heat (Fearless)

Heat (Making Waves)

Hippolyta and the Curse of the Amazons (Young Heroes)

His and Hers (Sweet Dreams)

His Life as a . . . (Trigun Maximum)

His Other Girlfriend (Love Stories)

His Secret Past (Sweet Valley University)

Hit and Run (Fabulous Five)

Hit and Run (Misfits, Inc.)

Hit and Run Holiday (Nancy Drew Files)

Hit or Myth (Myth Adventures)

The Hitchhiker's Guide to the Galaxy (Hitchhiker's Trilogy)

Hits and Misses (Nancy Drew and the Hardy Boys Super Mysteries)

Hitting the Slopes (Generation Girl)

Hocus-Pocus (Mary-Kate and Ashley: Two of a Kind)

Hocus Pocus! (Secret World of Alex Mack)

Hocus-Pocus Horror (Goosebumps: Give Yourself Goosebumps)

Hogfather (Discworld)

Hold on Tight (Sierra Jensen)

Holding Fast (Heartland)

Holiday Homecoming (Thoroughbred: Ashleigh)

Holiday in the Sun (Mary-Kate and Ashley Starring In . . .)

A Holiday Memory (Heartland)

Holiday Mischief (Sweet Valley Twins Super Editions)

The Hollow Kingdom (Hollow Kingdom)

The Hollower (Angel (Graphic Novels))

Hollywood Hook-Up (Moesha)

Hollywood Horror (Nancy Drew and the Hardy Boys Super Mysteries)

Hollywood Noir (Angel)

Home Child (On Time's Wing)

Home for Christmas (Sweet Valley University)

A Home for Melanie (Thoroughbred)

Home Is Where Your Horse Is (Horsefeathers)

Home on Stoney Creek (Sarah's Journey)

Home Run Feud (Chip Hilton Sports Series)

The Homecoming (Black Stallion: Young Black Stallion)

Homecoming (Tillerman Cycle)

Homeless (Wild at Heart)

Homeward Heart (Pacific Cascades University)

Honor Among Enemies (Honor Harrington)

The Honor of the Queen (Honor Harrington)

Honus and Me (Baseball Card Adventures)

The Hooded Hawk Mystery (Hardy Boys)

Hoofbeats of Danger (American Girls: History Mysteries)

Hoofprints in the Snow (Thoroughbred)

Hoop City (Dream Series)

Hoop Crazy (Chip Hilton Sports Series)

Hope Happens (Clearwater Crossing)

The Horizontal Man (Finnegan Zwake)

The Hork-Bajir Chronicles (Animorphs: Animorph Chronicles)

The Horror at Camp Jellyjam (Goosebumps)

Horror Hotel (Fear Street: Ghosts of Fear Street)

Horror Hotel: The Vampire Checks In (Fear Street: Ghosts of Fear Street)

Horror House (Choose Your Own Adventure)

Horror of High Ridge (Choose Your Own Adventure)

Horrors of the Black Ring (Goosebumps Series 2000)

The Horse and His Boy (Chronicles of Narnia)

Horse Angels (Horsefeathers)

A Horse Called Raven (Black Stallion: Young Black Stallion)

A Horse Called Wonder (Thoroughbred)

Horse Cents (Horsefeathers)

A Horse for Christmas (Thoroughbred: Ashleigh)

A Horse for the Summer (Sandy Lane Stables)

Horse in Danger (Sandy Lane Stables)

A Horse of a Different Color (Horsefeathers)

The Horse of Her Dreams (Thoroughbred)

Horse Whispers in the Air (Horsefeathers)

Horsefeathers! (Horsefeathers)

Horsefeathers' Mystery (Horsefeathers)

Horsemen of Terror (Left Behind—The Kids)

The Host (X Files)

The Host Rides Out (Celia Rees Supernatural Trilogy)

Hostage! (Choose Your Own Adventure)

Hostage! (Sweet Valley High)

Hostages of Hate (Hardy Boys Casefiles)

The Hostile Hospital (A Series of Unfortunate Events)

The Hot-line Emergency (Fabulous Five)

Hot Pursuit (Danger.com)

Hot Pursuit (Nancy Drew Files)

Hot Summer Nights (Love Stories)

Hot Target (Troubleshooters)

Hot Tracks (Nancy Drew Files)

Hot Wheels (Hardy Boys Casefiles)

Hot Wheels (Three Investigators)

Hotline to Danger (Nancy Drew Files)

Hotshot on Ice (Alden All Stars)

The Houdini Whodunit (P.C. Hawke Mysteries)

House of a Thousand Screams (Fear Street: Ghosts of Fear Street)

House of Danger (Choose Your Own Adventure)

The House of Death (Sweet Valley University Thriller Editions)

House of Secrets (Summerhill Secrets)

House of Spies (White Mane Kids)

The House of the Vestals (Roma Sub Rosa)

House of Whispers (Fear Street: Fear Street Sagas)

House of Winter (Circle of Three)

The House on the Cliff (Hardy Boys)

House Party! (Moesha)

The House with a Clock in its Walls (Lewis Barnavelt)

How Could You Do This To Me, Mum? (Fab 5)

In Hot Pursuit! (Secret World of Alex Mack)

In Love (Cheerleaders)

In Love Again (Sweet Valley High)

In Love with a Prince (Sweet Valley High)

In Love with the Enemy (Sweet Valley High)

In Miranda, Lizzie Does Not Trust and The Longest Yard (Lizzie McGuire (TokyoPop))

In Plane Sight (Hardy Boys)

In Search of Andy (Replica)

In Search of Klondike Gold (On Time's Wing)

In Search of the Black Rose (Nancy Drew)

In Self-Defense (Hardy Boys Casefiles)

In the Circle of Time (Time Trilogy)

In the Dreaming (Circle of Three)

In the Face of Danger (Orphan Train Adventures)

In the Groove (NASCAR Pole Position Adventures)

In the Hand of the Goddess (Song of the Lioness Quartet)

In the House with Mouse! (Cheetah Girls)

In the Keep of Time (Time Trilogy)

In the Mummy's Tomb (Phantom Valley)

In the Name of Love (Nancy Drew on Campus)

In the Shadow of the Warlock (Shannara: The Sword of Shannara)

In the Spotlight (Heart Beats)

In the Spotlight (Nancy Drew on Campus)

In the Spotlight (No Secrets: The Story of a Girl Band)

In the Time of Dinosaurs (Animorphs: Megamorphs)

In There Be Thorns (Dollanganger)

In Time of War (Alex Balfour)

In Too Deep (Fear Street: Fear Street Seniors)

In Too Deep (Jennie McGrady Mysteries)

In Your Dreams (Sierra Jensen)

Inca Gold (Choose Your Own Adventure)

Incarnate (The Lurker Files)

Including Alice (Alice)

Incredible Madame Jessica (Sweet Valley Twins)

The Incredible Shrinking Stanley (Eerie Indiana)

Indigo Dying (China Bayles Mystery)

Infanta (Indigo)

Inferno (Indigo)

Inferno of Fear (Hardy Boys Casefiles)

Infiltration (Alias)

The Infinity Clue (Hardy Boys)

Inherit the Earth (Emortality)

Inherit the Witch (Charmed)

Inheritor (Foreigner)

Inhuman Fury (Extreme Zone)

Initiation (Circle of Three)

The Initiation (Nightmare Hall)

The Initiation (Secret Circle)

Inner Beauty and Best Dressed for Less (Lizzie McGuire (TokyoPop))

The Innkeeper's Daughter (American Dreams) (Avon)

The Innocent (The Outer Limits)

Inside the Illusion (EverWorld)

Inside UFO 54-40 (Choose Your Own Adventure)

Instant Boyfriend (Mary-Kate and Ashley: So Little Time)

An Instinct for Trouble (Nancy Drew Files)

Interesting Times (Discworld)

Into Battle (The Seventh Tower)

Into the Cold Fire (Daughters of the Moon)

Into the Danger Zone (Extreme Team)

Into the Dark (Fear Street)

Into the Dragon's Den (Abby's South Seas Adventures)

Into the Flames (The Young Underground)

Into the Jaws of Doom (Goosebumps: Give Yourself Goosebumps)

Into the Night (Troubleshooters)

Into the Storm (Left Behind—The Kids)

Into the Twister of Terror (Goosebumps: Give Yourself Goosebumps)

Into the Wild (Warriors)

Into the Wind (American Dreams) (Avon)

Into Thin Air (Nancy Drew Files)

Intrigue at the Grand Opera (Nancy Drew)

The Intruder (Roswell High)

Invader (Foreigner)

The Invaders (The Outer Limits)

Invaders from the Big Screen (Goosebumps: Give Yourself Goosebumps)

Invaders from Within (Choose Your Own Adventure)

Invaders of Planet Earth (Choose Your Own Adventure)

The Invasion (Animorphs)

Invasion (Journey of Allen Strange)

Invasion of the Body Squeezers, Part 1 (Goosebumps Series 2000)

Invasion of the Body Squeezers, Part 2 (Goosebumps Series 2000)

Invasion of the Killer Locusts (Daystar Voyages)

Invasion of the No-Ones (Spooksville)

The Invisible Intruder (Nancy Drew)

Invisible Me (Sweet Valley Junior High)

The Invitation (Books of Magic)

The Irish Rebellion (Young Indiana Jones Chronicles: Choose Your Own Adventure)

The Iron Grail (Merlin Codex)

The Iron Sceptre (The Archives of Anthropos)

Is This Apocalypse Necessary? (Yurt)

Is Underground (Wolves Chronicles)

Isaac Asimov's Caliban (Isaac Asimov's Caliban)

Isaac Asimov's Inferno (Isaac Asimov's Caliban)

Isaac Asimov's Utopia (Isaac Asimov's Caliban)

Isabel (Royal Diaries)

Isabel: Taking Wing, 1592 (American Girls: Girls of Many Lands)

Island Dreamer (Christy Miller)

Island Girls (Mary-Kate and Ashley: Two of a Kind)

Island of Doom (Choose Your Own Nightmare)

Island of Secrets (Nancy Drew Files)

Island of Time (Choose Your Own Adventure)

Islands of Intrigue (Nancy Drew and the Hardy Boys Super Mysteries)

Islands of the Black Moon (Tales of the Nine Charms)

The Isle of Illusion (Deltora: Deltora Shadowlands)

Isle of View (Xanth Saga)

Isolation (Remnants)

It Came from Beneath the Sink! (Goosebumps)

It Came from the Internet (Goosebumps: Give Yourself Goosebumps)

It Can't Happen Here (Sweet Valley Twins)

The It Guy (Sweet Valley High Senior Year)

It Had to Be You (Love Stories)

It Happened at Camp Pine Tree (Choose Your Own Nightmare)

It Must Be Magic (Sweet Dreams)

It Takes Two (Sweet Valley High Senior Year)

It's a Girl Thing (Holly's Heart)

It's a Prom Thing (Love Stories)

It's a Twin Thing (Mary-Kate and Ashley: Two of a Kind)

It's Different for Guys (Love Stories: Super Editions)

It's Magic (The Jersey)

It's My Life (Diary of a Teenage Girl)

It's My Life (Sweet Valley High Senior Year)

It's Not Easy Being Bad (Bad Girls)

It's Only a Nightmare (Goosebumps: Give Yourself Goosebumps)

It's Raining Benjamins (Cheetah Girls)

It's Snow Problem (Mary-Kate and Ashley: Two of a Kind)

It's the Thought That Counts (Saved by the Bell)

It's Your Move (Nancy Drew on Campus)

I've Already Forgotten Your Name, Philip Hall (Philip Hall)

I've Got a Secret (Sweet Valley High Senior Year)

J

Jack and the Beanstalker (Graveyard School)

Jack Pumpkinhead of Oz (Oz)

Jackaroo (The Kingdom)

Jackie and Jade Save the Day (Jackie Chan Adventures)

Jackie and Me (Baseball Card Adventures)

The Jade Monkey (Jackie Chan Adventures)

Jade's Secret Power (Jackie Chan Adventures)

Jahanara (Royal Diaries)

Jake and Christy (Love Stories: Prom Trilogy)

Jake Finds Out (Making Out)

Jamie (The Elliott Cousins)

Jana to the Rescue (Fabulous Five)

January (Countdown)

Jarka Ruus (Shannara: High Druid of Shannara)

Jason and the Gorgon's Blood (Young Heroes)

Jealous Feelings (Nancy Drew on Campus)

Jealous Lies (Sweet Valley High)

The Jedera Adventure (Vesper Holly)

Jedi Bounty (Star Wars Young Jedi Knights)

Jedi Under Siege (Star Wars Young Jedi Knights)

Jeepers Creepers (House of Horrors)

Jekyll and Heidi (Goosebumps Series 2000)

Jen Starts Over (B.Y. Times)

Jessi and the Awful Secret (Baby-Sitters Club)

Jessi and the Bad Baby-Sitter (Baby-Sitters Club)

Jessi and the Dance School Phantom (Baby-Sitters Club)

Jessi and the Jewel Thieves (Baby-Sitters Club Mysteries)

Jessi and the Superbrat (Baby-Sitters Club)

Jessi and the Troublemaker (Baby-Sitters Club)

Jessi Ramsey, Pet-Sitter (Baby-Sitters Club)

Jessica Against Bruce (Sweet Valley High)

Jessica and the Brat Attack (Sweet Valley Twins)

Jessica and the Earthquake (Sweet Valley Twins)

Jessica and the Money Mix-Up (Sweet Valley Twins)

Jessica and the Secret Star (Sweet Valley Twins)

Jessica on Stage (Sweet Valley Twins)

Jessica Quits the Squad (Sweet Valley High)

Jessica Saves the Trees (Sweet Valley Twins)

Jessica Takes Charge (Sweet Valley Twins)

Jessica Takes Manhattan (Sweet Valley High)

Jessica the Genius (Sweet Valley High)

Jessica the Nerd (Sweet Valley Twins)

Jessica the Thief (Sweet Valley Twins)

Jessica's Animal Instincts (Sweet Valley Twins Super Editions)

Jessica's Bad Idea (Sweet Valley Twins)

Jessica's Blind Date (Sweet Valley Twins)

Jessica's Cookie Disaster (Sweet Valley Twins)

Jessica's First Kiss (Sweet Valley Twins Super Editions)

Jessica's Lucky Millions (Sweet Valley Twins)

Jessica's New Look (Sweet Valley Twins)

Jessica's No Angel (Sweet Valley Twins Super Editions)

Jessica's Older Guy (Sweet Valley High)

Jessica's Secret (Sweet Valley Twins)

Jessica's Secret Diary (Sweet Valley High)

Jessica's Secret Diary Volume II (Sweet Valley High)

Jessica's Secret Diary Volume III (Sweet Valley High)

Jessica's Secret Love (Sweet Valley High)

Jessica's the Rock Star (Sweet Valley Twins)

Jessi's Baby-Sitter (Baby-Sitters Club)

Jessi's Big Break (Baby-Sitters Club)

Jessi's Gold Medal (Baby-Sitters Club)

Jessi's Horrible Prank (Baby-Sitters Club)

Jessi's Secret Language (Baby-Sitters Club)

Jessi's Wish (Baby-Sitters Club)

Jester in the Back Cover (Alden All Stars)

The Jester's Quest (Winds of Light)

Jingo (Discworld)

Joey Pigza Loses Control (Joey Pigza)

Joey Pigza Swallowed the Key (Joey Pigza)

John Quincy Adams (Dear Mr. President)

Johnny (Love Stories: Brothers Trilogy)

Johnny Chesthair (He-Man Women Haters Club)

The Joker's Revenge (Nancy Drew)

The Journey (Animorphs)

The Journey (Guardians of Ga'Hoole)

A Journey of Faith (Prairie River)

Journey to America (Platt Family)

Journey to Stonehenge (Choose Your Own Adventure)

Journey Under the Sea (Choose Your Own Adventure)

Joyride (Journey of Allen Strange)

Juanita Fights the School Board (Roosevelt High School)

Judgment Day (Left Behind—The Kids)

The Judgment of Caesar (Roma Sub Rosa)

Julia (Sweet 16)

Julian's Jinx (Spell Casters)

Julie (Julie of the Wolves)

Julie of the Wolves (Julie of the Wolves)

Julie's Wolf Pack (Julie of the Wolves)

July (Countdown)

July's Promise (Summer)

Jump Ship to Freedom (Arabus Family Saga)

Jumping to Conclusions (Sweet Valley Twins)

June (Countdown)

June Dreams (Summer)

Junebug (Junebug)

Junebug and the Reverend (Junebug)

Junebug in Trouble (Junebug)

The Jungle Pyramid (Hardy Boys)

Juniper (Wise Child)

Junkyard Jitters! (Secret World of Alex Mack)

Just Between Us (Mary-Kate and Ashley: So Little Time)

Just Don't Make a Scene, Mum! (Fab 5)

Just Friends (Clearwater Crossing)

Just like Lizzie (Lizzie McGuire)

Just like Sisters (Class Secrets)

Just like the Movies (Sweet Dreams)

Just Plain Al (Al (Alexandra))

Just Say Yes (Clearwater Crossing)

Just the Two of Us (Nancy Drew on Campus)

Just the Way You Are (Sweet Dreams)

Just Trust Me (Turning Seventeen)

Just Visiting (From the Files of Madison Finn)

Justice and Her Brothers (Justice Trilogy)

Justin and Nicole (Love Stories: Prom Trilogy)

K

Kabumpo in Oz (Oz)

The Kachina Doll Mystery (Nancy Drew)

Kaitlin's Wild Ride (Thoroughbred)

Kaiulani (Royal Diaries)

Kari (Sweet 16)

Kate Finds Love (Making Out)

Kathleen (American Girls: Girls of Many Lands)

Katie's Dating Tips (Fabulous Five)

Kazunomiya (Royal Diaries)

Keep Out, Claudia! (Baby-Sitters Club)

Keep the Faith (Clearwater Crossing)

Keeper (Dream Series)

Keeper Martin's Tale (Ruin Mist Chronicles)

Keeper Martin's Tales, Book 1 (Ruin Mist: The Kingdoms and the Elves of the Reaches)

Keeper Martin's Tales, Book 2 (Ruin Mist: The Kingdoms and the Elves of the Reaches)

Keeper Martin's Tales, Book 3 (Ruin Mist: The Kingdoms and the Elves of the Reaches)

Keeper Martin's Tales, Book 4 (Ruin Mist: The Kingdoms and the Elves of the Reaches)

The Keepers of the Flame (Fire-Us Trilogy)

Keepin' It Real (Sweet Valley Junior High)

Keepin' It Real: Bratz, the Video (Bratz)

The Keeping Days (Sterling Family)

Keeping It Real (Angels Unlimited)

Keeping It Real (Moesha)

Keeping Secrets (Mary-Kate and Ashley Sweet 16)

Keeping Secrets (Nancy Drew on Campus)

Keeping Secrets (Orphan Train Adventures)

Keeping Secrets (Sweet Valley Twins)

Kelly's Hero (Saved by the Bell)

Kenobi's Blade (Star Wars Junior Jedi Knights)

Kentucky Dreamer (Golden Filly Series)

The Kestrel (Westmark)

Kevin (Love Stories: Brothers Trilogy)

The Key in the Satin Pocket (Nancy Drew)

Kickoff to Danger (Hardy Boys)

The Kid from Courage (Dream Series)

Kidnapped! (Choose Your Own Adventure)

Kidnapped (Nightmare Hall)

Kidnapped! (Sweet Valley High)

Kidnapped by the Cult (Sweet Valley High)

The Kill (Forbidden Game)

Killer (Fearless)

The Killer (Regeneration)

Killer at Sea (Sweet Valley University Thriller Editions)

Killer Clown of Kings County (Bone Chillers)

Killer Computer (Spinetinglers)

A Killer on Board (Sweet Valley High)

Last Breath (Body of Evidence)

Last Breath (Nightmare Hall)

Last Chance (Fear Street: Fear Street Seniors)

Last Chance (Sweet Valley High)

Last Chance Quarterback (Alden All Stars)

Last Clue (Pyrates)

The Last Continent (Discworld)

Last Dance (Heart Beats)

Last Dance (Nancy Drew Files)

Last Date (Nightmare Hall)

The Last Hawk (Saga of the Skolian Empire)

The Last Hero (Discworld)

The Last Laugh (Hardy Boys Casefiles)

The Last Leap (Hardy Boys Casefiles)

Last Resort (Nancy Drew and the Hardy Boys Super Mysteries)

Last Run (Choose Your Own Adventure)

Last Seen in Massilia (Roma Sub Rosa)

Last Splash (Making Waves)

Last Summer with Maizon (Maizon)

The Last Tear (W.I.T.C.H.)

The Last Vampire (The Last Vampire)

The Last Wars (Ferret Chronicles)

Last Wish (Sweet Valley High)

The Last Word (Sweet Dreams)

Latin Nights (Heart Beats)

Laura of the Wild Rose Inn, 1898 (Wild Rose Inn)

Laura's Secret (Fabulous Five)

Laurie's Song (Sweet Dreams)

The Lavender Bear of Oz (Oz)

Lavender Lies (China Bayles Mystery)

Law of the Jungle (Hardy Boys Casefiles)

Laws of Nature (Prowlers)

The Lazarus Plot (Hardy Boys Casefiles)

Leader of the Pack (Oh My Goddess!)

Leading Lady (Victorian Tales of London)

Learning the Ropes (7th Heaven)

Leaving Home (On the Road)

Leaving Home (Sweet Valley High)

Left at the Altar (Sweet Valley High)

Left Behind (Sweet Valley Twins)

Left Out, by Rosie (The Broadway Ballplayers)

Legacy (Journey of Allen Strange)

The Legacy (One Last Wish)

Legacy (Sweep)

Legacy (Wicked)

Legacy of Lies (Dark Secrets)

Legend of Burning Water (Winds of Light)

The Legend of Luke (Redwall)

The Legend of Merlin (Charmed)

The Legend of Miner's Creek (Nancy Drew)

The Legend of the Ancient Scroll (Mystic Knights of Tir Na Nog)

The Legend of the Emerald Lady (Nancy Drew)

Legend of the Lost Gold (Nancy Drew)

Legend of the Lost Legend (Goosebumps)

Legend of the Zodiac (Jackie Chan Adventures)

Legends of Metru Nui (Bionicle Adventures)

The Lenski File (On Time's Wing)

Lessons in Love (Sweet Dreams)

Let Him Live (One Last Wish)

Let the Circle Be Unbroken (Logan Family)

Lethal Cargo (Hardy Boys Casefiles)

The Lethal Gorilla (P.C. Hawke Mysteries)

Let's All Kill Jennifer (Fear Street)

Let's Get Invisible! (Goosebumps)

Let's Party (Fear Street: Fear Street Seniors)

Let's Party (Mary-Kate and Ashley: Two of a Kind)

Let's Scare the Teacher to Death (Graveyard School)

Let's Talk Terror (Nancy Drew Files)

The Letter, the Witch, and the Ring (Lewis Barnavelt)

Letters from Atlantis (Dragonflight Books)

Letters from the Heart (Beacon Street Girls)

Letting Go (High Hurdles)

Leviathan (The Fallen)

Leyla (American Girls: Girls of Many Lands)

Liar (Fearless)

Liar, Liar (Nightmare Room)

License to Thrill (Spy Girls)

Life, the Universe and Everything (Hitchhiker's Trilogy)

Lifeguard Summer (Sweet Dreams)

Lifeline (Star Trek: Voyager: Starfleet Academy)

The Light Beyond the Forest (Arthurian Knights)

The Light Fantastic (Discworld)

A Light in the Castle (The Young Underground)

The Light of Meridian (W.I.T.C.H.)

Light on Quests Mountain (Endless Quest)

Lighthouse Legend (Dawson's Creek)

Lightning's Last Hope (Thoroughbred: Ashleigh)

Lights, Camera . . . (Nancy Drew: Girl Detective)

Lights, Camera, Action! (Saved by the Bell)

Lights Camera Action (Secret World of Alex Mack)

Lights, Camera, Die! (Spinetinglers)

Lights, Camera, Love (Sweet Dreams)

Lights, Camera, Love! (You're the One)

Lights Out (Fear Street)

Lights Out (From the Files of Madison Finn)

Lightsabers (Star Wars Young Jedi Knights)

Like Father, Like Son (Replica)

Like Gold Refined (Prairie Legacy)

Like Mother, Like Daughter (Gilmore Girls)

Likes Me, Likes Me Not (Mary-Kate and Ashley: Two of a Kind)

Lila's Music Video (Sweet Valley Twins)

Lila's New Flame (Sweet Valley High)

Lost Ninja (Choose Your Own Adventure)

Lost on Aquaria (Zenda)

Lost on the Amazon (Choose Your Own Adventure)

The Lost One (Daughters of the Moon)

The Lost Ones (Star Wars Young Jedi Knights)

Lost Places (Books of Magic)

The Lost Princess of Oz (Oz)

Lost Soul (Extreme Zone)

Lost Tribe (Choose Your Own Adventure)

Lost Wake (X Games Xtreme Mysteries)

The Lost Years of Merlin (Lost Years of Merlin)

Love (Fearless)

Love and Betrayal (Nancy Drew on Campus)

Love and Death (Angel)

Love and Death in London (Sweet Valley High)

Love and Kisses (Mary-Kate and Ashley Sweet 16)

Love and Murder (Sweet Valley University Thriller Editions)

The Love Bet (Sweet Valley High)

Love by the Book (Sweet Dreams)

Love Bytes (@CAFE)

Love Changes Everything (Love Stories)

Love Detour (Sweet Dreams)

The Love Factor (Mary-Kate and Ashley: So Little Time)

Love Happens (Love Stories: Super Editions)

Love Him Forever (Enchanted Hearts)

The Love Hunt (Sweet Dreams)

Love Hurts (Clearwater Crossing)

Love in the Air (Sweet Dreams)

Love in the Fast Lane (Sweet Dreams)

Love in the Wings (Sweet Dreams)

Love Is a Gift (Heartland)

Love Is in the Air (Mary-Kate and Ashley: So Little Time)

Love Letters (Sweet Valley High)

Love Letters for Sale (Sweet Valley High)

Love, Lies, and Jessica Wakefield (Sweet Valley University)

Love, Lies and Video (Trash)

Love Lies Bleeding (China Bayles Mystery)

Love-Lies-Bleeding (On Time's Wing)

The Love Line (Sweet Dreams)

Love Lines (Sweet Dreams)

Love Match (Sweet Dreams)

Love Me Always (Sweet Valley University)

Love Never Dies (Teen Angels)

Love Notes (Nancy Drew Files) (Campbell, Joanna)

Love Notes (Sweet Dreams) (Maxwell, Janet)

Love Notes (Sweet Dreams)

Love of Her Life (Sweet Valley University)

Love On-Line (Nancy Drew on Campus)

Love on Strike (Sweet Dreams)

Love on the Upbeat (Sweet Dreams)

Love on Wheels (Sweet Dreams)

Love or Fate (Goddesses)

Love Potion (Enchanted Hearts)

Love Potion (Sweet Valley Twins)

Love Potion, No. 9 (Oh My Goddess!)

Love Rules (Hamilton High)

Love-Set-Match (Mary-Kate and Ashley: Two of a Kind)

Love Song (Sweet Dreams)

Love Times Two (Sweet Dreams)

Love to Spare (Sweet Dreams)

Love Under Wraps (Everwood)

Love Without End (Teen Angels)

Lovebirds (Sweet Dreams)

Lovestruck (Sweet Valley High)

Loving and Losing (Nancy Drew on Campus)

Loving the Enemy (Sweet Valley University Thriller Editions)

Loyalties (Star Trek: The Next Generation: Starfleet Academy)

Lucas Gets Hurt (Making Out)

Luck Be a Lady (Charmed)

Luckiest Day of Your Life (Choose Your Own Adventure)

Lucky Bucky in Oz (Oz)

Lucky in Love (Sweet Dreams)

Lucky Thirteen (Replica)

Lucy (Sweet 16)

Lucy Takes the Reins (Sweet Valley Twins)

Lucy's Angel (7th Heaven)

Ludell (Ludell)

Ludell and Willie (Ludell)

Ludell's New York Time (Ludell)

The Lure of the Italian Treasure (Hardy Boys)

Lust (Fearless)

Luthien's Gamble (The Crimson Shadow)

Luv@First Site (TodaysGirls.com)

Lydia (Sisters)

The Lying Game (Class Secrets)

The Lyon's Crown (Lyon Saga)

The Lyon's Cub (Lyon Saga)

The Lyon's Pride (Lyon Saga)

The Lyon's Roar (Lyon Saga)

The Lyon's Throne (Lyon Saga)

Lyric's World (Star Wars Junior Jedi Knights)

M

The M.A.N.G.A. Affair (SpyBoy)

M.Y.T.H. Inc. in Action (Myth Adventures)

M.Y.T.H. Inc. Link (Myth Adventures)

Macdonald Hall Goes Hollywood (Bruno and Boots)

The Mad Gasser of Bessledorf Street (Bessledorf Hotel)

Mademoiselle Jessica (Sweet Valley Twins)

Mage Quest (Yurt)

Maggie (California Diaries)

Maggie, Diary Two (California Diaries)

Maggy, Diary Three (California Diaries)

The Magic and the Healing (Crossroads Trilogy)

Magic Casement (Man of His Word)

The Magic Chest of Oz (Oz)

The Magic Christmas (Sweet Valley Twins)

The Magic Dishpan of Oz (Oz)

The Magic Engineer (Recluce)

The Magic Labyrinth (Riverworld Saga)

Magic Master (Choose Your Own Adventure)

Magic Moments (Sweet Dreams)

The Magic of Oz (Oz)

Mary Anne and the Music Box Secret (Baby-Sitters Club Mysteries)

Mary Anne and the Playground Fight (Baby-Sitters Club)

Mary Anne and the Search for Tigger (Baby-Sitters Club)

Mary Anne and the Secret in the Attic (Baby-Sitters Club Mysteries)

Mary Anne and the Silent Witness (Baby-Sitters Club Mysteries)

Mary Anne and the Zoo Mystery (Baby-Sitters Club Mysteries)

Mary Anne and Too Many Boys (Baby-Sitters Club)

Mary Anne Breaks the Rules (Baby-Sitters Club)

Mary Anne in the Middle (Baby-Sitters Club)

Mary Anne Misses Logan (Baby-Sitters Club)

Mary Anne Saves the Day (Baby-Sitters Club)

Mary Anne to the Rescue (Baby-Sitters Club)

Mary Anne + 2 Many Babies (Baby-Sitters Club)

Mary Anne vs. Logan (Baby-Sitters Club)

Mary Anne's Bad Luck Mystery (Baby-Sitters Club)

Mary Anne's Big Breakup (Baby-Sitters Club Friends Forever)

Mary Anne's Book (Baby-Sitters Club Portrait Collection)

Mary Anne's Makeover (Baby-Sitters Club)

Mary Anne's Revenge (Baby-Sitters Club Friends Forever)

Mary, Bloody Mary (Young Royals)

Mary Is Missing (Sweet Valley Twins)

Mary's Rescue (7th Heaven)

Mary's Story (7th Heaven)

The Masked Monkey (Hardy Boys)

Maskerade (Discworld)

Masks (Wild at Heart)

Masquerade in Oz (Oz)

Master and Fool (Book of Words)

Master of Aikido (Choose Your Own Adventure)

Master of Judo (Choose Your Own Adventure)

Master of Karate (Choose Your Own Adventure)

Master of Kendo (Choose Your Own Adventure)

Master of Kung Fu (Choose Your Own Adventure)

Master of Martial Arts (Choose Your Own Adventure)

Master of Tae Kwon Do (Choose Your Own Adventure)

The Masterharper of Pern (Pern)

Masters of the Louvre (Young Indiana Jones Chronicles: Choose Your Own Adventure)

Mates, Dates, and Cosmic Kisses (Mates, Dates, and . . .)

Mates, Dates, and Designer Divas (Mates, Dates, and . . .)

Mates, Dates, and Inflatable Bras (Mates, Dates, and . . .)

Mates, Dates, and Mad Mistakes (Mates, Dates, and . . .)

Mates, Dates, and Sequin Smiles (Mates, Dates, and . . .)

Mates, Dates, and Sleepover Secrets (Mates, Dates, and . . .)

Mates, Dates, and Sole Survivors (Mates, Dates, and . . .)

Mates, Dates, and Tempting Trouble (Mates, Dates, and . . .)

Mattimeo (Redwall)

Matt's Story (7th Heaven)

Maui Mystery (Abby's South Seas Adventures)

Maverick Mania (Sports Mystery)

Max and Jane (Love Stories: Prom Trilogy)

Maximum Challenge (Hardy Boys)

Max's Choice (Sweet Valley University: Elizabeth)

May (Countdown)

May the Best Team Win (Saved by the Bell)

Maya's Divided World (Roosevelt High School)

Mayday! (Choose Your Own Adventure)

The Mayflower Project (Remnants)

Mayhem in Motion (Hardy Boys Casefiles)

The Maze (Dinotopia)

Maze of Shadows (Bionicle Adventures)

The Maze of the Beast (Deltora: Deltora Quest)

Me and Fat Glenda (Fat Glenda)

Me and My Little Brain (The Great Brain)

Me, Me, Me (Sweet Valley High Senior Year)

Mean Streak (Kids from Kennedy Middle School)

Meant to Be (Sweet Valley High Senior Year)

The Medusa Plague (Dragonlance Defenders of Magic)

Meet Me at Midnight (Sweet Valley High)

Meet the Austins (Vicky Austin)

A Meeting of Minds (The Minds Series)

Meets the Eye (Body of Evidence)

Melanie Edwards, Super Kisser (Fabulous Five)

Melanie's Double Jinx (Thoroughbred)

Melanie's Identity Crisis (Fabulous Five)

Melanie's Last Ride (Thoroughbred)

Melanie's Treasure (Thoroughbred)

Melanie's Valentine (Fabulous Five)

Melissa (Fab 5)

Meltdown (Mindwarp)

Meltdown (2099)

Meltdown: Week 4 (Sevens)

The Melted Coins (Hardy Boys)

Memories (Sweet Valley High)

The Memory of Earth (Homecoming Saga)

Men at Arms (Discworld)

The Mennyms (Mennyms)

Mennyms Alive (Mennyms)

Mennyms Alone (Mennyms)

Mennyms in the Wilderness (Mennyms)

Mennyms Under Siege (Mennyms)

The Merchant of Death (Pendragon)

Merchanter's Luck (Alliance-Union)

The Merchants of Souls (The Thousand Cultures)

Meredith (The Elliott Cousins)

The Merlin Effect (Heartlight)

Merlin's Destiny (Winds of Light)

Merry Go Round in Oz (Oz)

The Morning After (Sweet Valley High)

Mort (Discworld)

Mortal Engines (The Hungry City Chronicles)

Mortal Fear (Buffy the Vampire Slayer) (Archway/Pocket)

Mossflower (Redwall)

Most Likely to Deceive (Class Secrets)

Most Likely to Die (Nancy Drew Files)

Most Wanted (Danger.com)

Mostly Harmless (Hitchhiker's Trilogy)

Mother-Daughter Switch (Sweet Valley Twins)

Mother, Help Me Live (One Last Wish)

Mother, May I? (Remnants)

Motocross Mania (Choose Your Own Adventure)

Mountain Biker (Choose Your Own Adventure)

Mountain Light (Golden Mountain Chronicles)

Mountain Madness (Christy)

Mountain of Mirrors (Endless Quest)

Mountain Survival (Choose Your Own Adventure)

The Mountains of Majipoor (The Majipoor Cycle)

Mourning Song (One Last Wish)

Moving as One (Heart Beats)

Moving On (Everwood)

Moving Pictures (Discworld)

Moving Target (Nancy Drew Files)

Moving Up (Cheerleaders)

Moving Up (High Hurdles)

Mr. Nice Guy (7th Heaven)

Mr. Perfect (Sweet Dreams)

Mr Tucket (The Tucket Adventures)

Mr. Wonderful (Sweet Dreams)

Ms. Quarterback (Sweet Valley High)

Mud City (The Breadwinner Trilogy)

The Mummy Case (Hardy Boys)

The Mummy, the Will, and the Crypt (Johnny Dixon)

The Mummy Walks (Goosebumps Series 2000)

The Mummy Who Wouldn't Die (Choose Your Own Nightmare)

Murder at Monticello (Mrs. Murphy)

Murder by Magic (Hardy Boys Casefiles)

Murder in Paradise (Sweet Valley High)

Murder in the Holy Place (Left Behind—The Kids)

Murder on Ice (Nancy Drew Files)

A Murder on the Appian Way (Roma Sub Rosa)

Murder on the Fourth of July (Nancy Drew and the Hardy Boys Super Mysteries)

Murder on the Line (Sweet Valley High)

Murder on the Prowl (Mrs. Murphy)

Murder, She Meowed (Mrs. Murphy)

Murder to Go (Three Investigators)

Muses on the Move (Goddesses)

The Music Festival Mystery (Nancy Drew)

Music from the Heart (Sweet Dreams)

The Music Meltdown (Mary-Kate and Ashley in Action)

A Mustard Seed of Magic (Sterling Family)

Mutant Beach (Tom Swift)

The Mutation (Animorphs)

Mutation (Remnants)

Mutiny (Space Above and Beyond)

Mutiny in Space (Choose Your Own Adventure)

My Best Enemy (Sweet Dreams)

My Best Friend Is Invisible (Goosebumps)

My Best Friend's Boyfriend (Mary-Kate and Ashley Sweet 16)

My Best Friend's Boyfriend (Sweet Valley High)

My Best Friend's Girlfriend (Love Stories: Super Editions)

My Brother, the Ghost (House of Horrors)

My Deadly Valentine (Nancy Drew Files)

My Dentist Is a Vampire (Spinetinglers)

My Dream Guy (Sweet Dreams)

My Ex-Best Friend (Party of Five)

My First Love (Love Stories)

My Funny Guy (Sweet Dreams)

My Hairiest Adventure (Goosebumps)

My Name Is Chloe (Diary of a Teenage Girl)

My Name Is Evil (Nightmare Room)

My Perfect Guy (Sweet Valley Junior High)

My Perfect Life (Confessions of a Teenage Drama Queen)

My Perfect Valentine (Sweet Dreams)

My Secret Heart (Sweet Dreams)

My Secret Love (Sweet Dreams)

My Side of the Mountain (My Side of the Mountain)

My Sister the Supermodel (Mary-Kate and Ashley: Two of a Kind)

My So-Called Boyfriend (Love Stories)

My Son the Wizard (A Wizard in Rhyme)

My Teacher's a Bug (Spinetinglers)

Myself and I (Sterling Family)

Mysterious Boarder (Dawson's Creek)

The Mysterious Caravan (Hardy Boys)

Mysterious Doctor Q (Sweet Valley Twins)

The Mysterious Image (Nancy Drew)

Mysterious Love (Nikki Sheridan)

The Mysterious Mannequin (Nancy Drew)

Mystery at Chilkoot Pass (American Girls: History Mysteries)

The Mystery at Claudia's House (Baby-Sitters Club Mysteries)

Mystery at Devil's Paw (Hardy Boys)

The Mystery at Lilac Inn (Nancy Drew)

The Mystery at Magnolia Mansion (Nancy Drew)

Mystery at Moorsea Manor (Nancy Drew)

The Mystery at the Crystal Palace (Nancy Drew)

The Mystery at the Ski Jump (Nancy Drew)

Mystery By Moonlight (Nancy Drew)

The Mystery of Wrecker's Rock (Three Investigators)

Mystery on Makatunk Island (Hardy Boys)

Mystery on Maui (Nancy Drew)

Mystery on Skull Island (American Girls: History Mysteries)

Mystery on the Menu (Nancy Drew)

Mystery Train (Nancy Drew and the Hardy Boys Super Mysteries)

Mystery with a Dangerous Beat (Hardy Boys)

Mystify the Magician (EverWorld)

Myth Alliances (Myth Adventures)

Myth Conceptions (Myth Adventures)

Myth Directions (Myth Adventures)

Myth-ing Persons (Myth Adventures)

Myth-ion Improbable (Myth Adventures)

Myth-Nomers and Im-Pervections (Myth Adventures)

Myth-taken Identity (Myth Adventures)

Myth-told Tales (Myth Adventures)

N

N 2 Deep (TodaysGirls.com)

Naked (Fearless)

The Naked Sun (I, Robot)

Nancy's Mysterious Letter (Nancy Drew)

Narrow Walk (Nikki Sheridan)

Nasty the Snowman (Fiendly Corners)

The National Pageant (Pageant)

Natural Enemies (Nancy Drew Files)

Nechama on Strike (B.Y. Times)

Need for Speed (The Jersey)

Neela (American Girls: Girls of Many Lands)

The Negative Zone (Tom Swift)

Nemesis (Angel)

Nemesis (Indigo)

Nemesis (The Lurker Files)

Nerilka's Story (Pern)

Never Been Kissed (Mary-Kate and Ashley Sweet 16)

The Never-Ending Day (China Tate)

Never Give Up (Star Power)

Never Give Up (Sweet Valley High Senior Year)

Never Let Go (Sweet Valley High Senior Year)

Never Love a Cowboy (Sweet Dreams)

Never Say Die (Nancy Drew Files)

Never Say Goodbye (Sweet Dreams)

Never Say No (Sweet Dreams)

Never Tell Ben (Love Stories)

Never Trust Lara (Making Out)

The Never War (Pendragon)

Nevernever (Borderlands)

A New Beginning (Roswell High)

New Beginnings (Clearwater Crossing)

New Beginnings (Nancy Drew on Campus)

The New Boy (Fear Street)

A New Day Rising (Red River: Red River of the North)

A New Dimension (Zenda)

The New Elizabeth (Sweet Valley High)

A New Enemy (Jackie Chan Adventures)

The New Evil (Fear Street: Fear Street Cheerleaders)

The New Evil: Cheerleaders (Fear Street: Fear Street Super Chillers)

A New Fear (Fear Street: Fear Street Sagas)

New Found Land (Fireball)

The New Girl (Fear Street)

New Girl (Sweet Valley Twins)

The New, Improved Gretchen Hubbard (Kids from Kennedy Middle School)

The New Jessica (Sweet Valley High)

New Kid in School (Lizzie McGuire)

The New Kids (B.Y. Times)

New Lives, New Loves (Nancy Drew on Campus)

The New Me (7th Heaven)

The New Ron (Kim Possible (Chapter Books))

The New Ron and Mind Games (Kim Possible (TokyoPop))

New Threads in the Pattern (The Wheel of Time (Related Books))

The New Wizard of Oz (Oz)

New Year's Evil (Nancy Drew and the Hardy Boys Super Mysteries)

The New Year's Party (Fear Street: Fear Street Super Chillers)

New Year's Revolution! (Secret World of Alex Mack)

New York, Here We Come (Generation Girl)

New York, New York! (Baby-Sitters Club Super Specials)

New York Nightmare! (Secret World of Alex Mack)

The News Is Love (Sweet Dreams)

Newton's Cannon (The Age of Unreason)

The Next Passage (Animorphs: Alternamorphs)

A Nice Girl Like You (Sterling Family)

Nick and the Nerd (Love Stories: His. Hers. Theirs)

Nick's a Chick (The Jersey)

Nicolae High (Left Behind—The Kids)

The Night Fliers (American Girls: History Mysteries)

Night Games (Fear Street)

A Night in Terror Tower (Goosebumps)

Night in Werewolf Woods (Goosebumps: Give Yourself Goosebumps)

The Night Is for Hunting (Tomorrow)

Night Mare (Xanth Saga)

Night of a Thousand Claws (Goosebumps: Give Yourself Goosebumps)

Night of the Eye (Dragonlance Defenders of Magic)

Night of the Fireflies (Summerhill Secrets)

Night of the Gargoyle (House of Horrors)

Night of the Living Clay (Bone Chillers)

Night of the Living Dummy (Goosebumps)

Night of the Living Dummy II (Goosebumps)

O

Of Two Minds (The Minds Series)

Off the Wall (From the Files of Madison Finn)

Ogre, Ogre (Xanth Saga)

Oh, Brother! (Lizzie McGuire)

Oh, Buoy! (Luna Bay)

Oh, Promise Me (Sweet Dreams)

Ojo in Oz (Oz)

Old Friends, New Friends (Sweet Dreams: On Our Own)

Old Man's Cave (Bone)

Older Boy (Sweet Valley Twins)

The Older Guy (Love Stories: His. Hers. Theirs)

Olivia (Fab 5)

Olivia's Story (Sweet Valley High)

Olympic Dreams (High Hurdles)

Omega (Priscilla Hutchins)

The Omega Expedition (Emortality)

Ominous Choices (Left Behind—The Kids)

On Basilisk Station (Honor Harrington)

On Fortune's Wheel (The Kingdom)

On Her Own (Nancy Drew on Campus)

On Her Own (Sweet Dreams)

On My Own (Diary of a Teenage Girl)

On My Own (Sweet Valley High Senior Year)

On My Own: Bailey (Party of Five)

On the Bright Side, I'm Now the Girlfriend of a Sex God (Confessions of Georgia Nicolson)

On the Case (From the Files of Madison Finn)

On the Edge (Sweet Valley High)

On the Far Side of the Mountain (My Side of the Mountain)

On the Job (Lizzie McGuire)

On the Run (Left Behind—The Kids)

On the Run (Sweet Valley High)

On the Track (Thoroughbred)

On the Trail of Trouble (Nancy Drew)

On Thin Ice (Extreme Team)

On Thin Ice (Sweet Dreams)

Once on This Island (Island Trilogy)

Once Upon a Time (Sweet Valley High)

One Boy at a Time (Sweet Dreams)

One Boy Too Many (Sweet Dreams)

One Day at Horrorland (Goosebumps)

One Day You'll Know (Heartland)

One Evil Summer (Fear Street)

The One-Eyed Giant (Tales from the Odyssey)

101 Ways to Meet Mr. Right (Sweet Dreams)

One Is the Loneliest Number (Net Force)

One Last Kiss (Fear Street: Fear Street Sagas)

One Last Kiss (Sweet Valley University)

One of the Boys (Sweet Dreams)

One of the Gang (Sweet Valley Twins)

One Real Thing (Clearwater Crossing)

One Smooth Move (Extreme Team)

One Step Too Far (Party of Five)

The One That Got Away (Sweet Valley High Senior Year)

One Twin Too Many (Mary-Kate and Ashley: Two of a Kind)

One 2 Many (Sweet Valley Junior High)

One Wild Weekend (Saved by the Bell)

Only Make-Believe (Sweet Dreams)

Only the Lonely (From the Files of Madison Finn)

The Only Witness (Star Wars: Jedi Apprentice)

Only You—Sierra (Sierra Jensen)

Oops, Doggy, Dog! (Cheetah Girls)

The Ooze (Fear Street: Ghosts of Fear Street)

Open Season (Hardy Boys Casefiles)

Open Your Heart (Sierra Jensen)

Operation (Saved by the Bell)

Operation: Titanic (Nancy Drew and the Hardy Boys Super Mysteries)

Operation Evaporation (Mary-Kate and Ashley in Action)

Operation Love Match (Sweet Valley High)

Opportunity Knocks Twice (Brio Girls)

Opposites Attract (Sweet Dreams)

Orange Knight of Oz (Oz)

Orchard of the Crescent Moon (Gwyn Griffiths Trilogy)

The Order War (Recluce)

Oregon, Sweet Oregon (Petticoat Party)

The Origin (Buffy the Vampire Slayer) (Dark Horse)

Orion (Orion the Hunter)

Orion Among the Stars (Orion the Hunter)

Orion and the Conqueror (Orion the Hunter)

Orion in the Dying Time (Orion the Hunter)

The Orphan's Tent (Dragonflight Books)

The Other (Animorphs)

The Other Me (Sweet Dreams)

The Other Side of Dawn (Tomorrow)

The Other Side of Summer (Gilmore Girls)

The Other Wind (Earthsea)

The Other Woman (Sweet Valley University)

Otherwise Engaged (Nancy Drew on Campus)

Otto and the Bird Charmers (The Karmidee)

Otto and the Flying Twins (The Karmidee)

Our Lips Are Sealed (Mary-Kate and Ashley Starring In . . .)

Our Secret Love (Love Stories)

Our Town (X Files)

Out from Boneville (Bone)

Out of Bounds (Beacon Street Girls)

Out of Bounds (Nancy Drew Files)

Out of Control (Nancy Drew and the Hardy Boys Super Mysteries)

Out of Control (Sweet Valley High)

Out of Control (Troubleshooters)

Out of Line (X Games Xtreme Mysteries)

Out of Love (Sweet Dreams: On Our Own)

Pellucidar (Pellucidar)

Penalty Points (Saddle Club: Pine Hollow)

The Pentagon Spy (Hardy Boys)

The People of Sparks (City of Ember)

The Perfect Boy (Sweet Dreams)

The Perfect Catch (Sweet Dreams)

Perfect Challenge (Thoroughbred)

The Perfect Date (Fear Street)

Perfect Getaway (Hardy Boys Casefiles)

The Perfect Gift (Mary-Kate and Ashley: Two of a Kind)

The Perfect Girl (Sweet Valley High)

Perfect Girls (Replica)

Perfect Image (Thoroughbred)

The Perfect Match (Sweet Dreams)

The Perfect Plan (7th Heaven)

Perfect Planet (Choose Your Own Adventure)

The Perfect Plot (Nancy Drew Files)

The Perfect Pony (Sandy Lane Stables)

Perfect Shot (Sweet Valley High)

The Perfect Summer (Mary-Kate and Ashley Sweet 16)

Perfect Summer (Sweet Valley High)

Peril in the Bessledorf Parachute Factory (Bessledorf Hotel)

Perilous Seas (Man of His Word)

Perils of Love (Left Behind—The Kids)

The Personal Correspondence of Catherine Clark and Meredith Lyons (Liberty Letters)

The Personal Correspondence of Elizabeth Walton and Abigail Matthews (Liberty Letters)

The Personal Correspondence of Emma Edmunds and Mollie Turner (Liberty Letters)

The Personal Correspondence of Hannah Brown and Sarah Smith (Liberty Letters)

The Pet (Star Trek: Deep Space Nine)

Pet Store (Spinetinglers)

Petals on the Wind (Dollanganger)

Peter Duck (Swallows and Amazons)

The Phantom (The Last Vampire)

The Phantom Freighter (Hardy Boys)

The Phantom of 86th Street (P.C. Hawke Mysteries)

The Phantom of Pine Hill (Nancy Drew)

Phantom of the Auditorium (Goosebumps)

The Phantom of Venice (Nancy Drew)

Phantom Racer (Oh My Goddess!)

Phantom Submarine (Choose Your Own Adventure)

The Philadelphia Adventure (Vesper Holly)

Philip Hall Likes Me, I Reckon Maybe (Philip Hall)

Phoebe (Sisters)

Phoebe's Folly (Petticoat Party)

Phoebe's Fortune (Spell Casters)

The Phoenix Equation (Hardy Boys Casefiles)

Phone Fear (Spooksville)

Piano Lessons Can Be Murder (Goosebumps)

The Pictish Child (Tartan Magic Trilogy)

The Picts and the Martyrs (Swallows and Amazons)

The Picture of Guilt (Nancy Drew Files)

Picture Perfect (From the Files of Madison Finn)

Picture Perfect? (Generation Girl)

Picture Perfect (Saved by the Bell)

The Picture-Perfect Mystery (Nancy Drew)

A Picture-Perfect Prom (Sweet Valley High)

Picture Perfect Romance (Sweet Dreams)

Picture This (Lizzie McGuire)

Pictures of the Night (Egerton Hall Novels)

Pier Pressure (Luna Bay)

Pigeon Post (Swallows and Amazons)

Pillars of Pentegarn (Endless Quest)

The Pirates in Oz (Oz)

Pirates on the Internet (Cybersurfers)

Pirate's Revenge (Colonial Captives)

Pitchers' Duel (Chip Hilton Sports Series)

Pizza Zombies (Fiendly Corners)

A Place in the Heart (Aloha Cove)

A Place to Belong (Orphan Train Adventures)

Plainsong for Caitlin (American Dreams) (Avon)

Planet of Terror (Nightmares! How Will Yours End?)

Planet of the Dragons (Choose Your Own Adventure)

Planet Plague (Star Wars Galaxy of Fear)

Play (Have a Nice Life)

Play (Replica: The Plague Trilogy)

Play Ball! (Rookies)

Play It Again (From the Files of Madison Finn)

Play Me a Love Song (Sweet Dreams)

Play-Off Pressure (Rookies)

The Player of Games (The Culture)

Playing Dirty (Sweet Valley High Senior Year)

Playing for Keeps (Dawson's Creek)

Playing for Keeps (Love Stories)

Playing for Keeps (Sweet Dreams)

Playing for Keeps (Sweet Valley High)

Playing Games (Cheerleaders)

Playing Games (Mary-Kate and Ashley Sweet 16)

Playing Games (Sweet Dreams)

Playing Hooky (Sweet Valley Twins)

Playing the Field (Sweet Dreams)

Playing the Part (Fabulous Five)

Playing to Win (Sweet Dreams)

Playing with Fire (Hear No Evil)

Playing with Fire (Nancy Drew Files)

Playing with Fire (Sweet Valley High)

Playoff Champion (Choose Your Own Adventure)

Please Don't Die (One Last Wish)

Please Don't Eat the Teacher! (Dinoverse)

Please Don't Feed the Vampire! (Goosebumps: Give Yourself Goosebumps)

Please Forgive Me (Sweet Valley High)

Please, Please, Please (The Friendship Ring)

Please Reply! (TodaysGirls.com)

Please Say Yes (Sweet Dreams)

Point Blank (Alex Rider)

Poison (Med Center)

Poison in Paradise! (Secret World of Alex Mack)

Poison Pen (Nancy Drew Files)

Poisoned Paradise (Hardy Boys Casefiles)

The Poltergoose (Jiggy McCue)

The Pom-Pom Wars (Sweet Valley High)

The Pool of Fire (Tripods)

Pool Party and Picture Day (Lizzie McGuire (TokyoPop))

Pool Party Panic! (Secret World of Alex Mack)

Poor Lila (Sweet Valley Twins)

Poor Mallory! (Baby-Sitters Club)

Popover (Have a Nice Life)

Poppy (Fab 5)

The Popsicle Journal (Harper Winslow)

The Popular One (Love Stories: His. Hers. Theirs)

Popularity Contest (The Friendship Ring)

The Popularity Plan (Sweet Dreams)

The Popularity Summer (Sweet Dreams)

The Popularity Trap (Fabulous Five)

Portrait in Crime (Nancy Drew Files)

Portrait of Lies (TodaysGirls.com)

Portrait of Love (Sweet Dreams)

Po's Story (The Kin)

The Possessed (Dark Visions)

Possessed! (Choose Your Own Adventure)

Possession (Daughters of the Moon)

Powder Monkey (The Young Americans)

The Power (Secret Circle)

The Power Dome (Choose Your Own Adventure)

Power Drive (TodaysGirls.com)

The Power of Five (W.I.T.C.H.)

Power of Persuasion (Buffy the Vampire Slayer) (Archway/Pocket)

Power of Suggestion (Nancy Drew Files)

The Power of the Rat (Jackie Chan Adventures)

The Power of Three (Charmed)

The Power of Two (T*Witches)

Power Play (Alden All Stars)

Power Play (Hardy Boys Casefiles)

Power Play (Sweet Valley High)

Power Play: Trapped in the Circus of Fear (Goosebumps: Give Yourself Goosebumps)

Practice Makes Perfect (Sweet Dreams)

The Precipice (Asteroid Wars)

Precursor (Foreigner)

The Predator (Animorphs)

Predator and Prey (Prowlers)

Predator's Gold (The Hungry City Chronicles)

Prelude to Foundation (Foundation)

Prentice Alvin (Tales of Alvin Maker)

The Pretender (Animorphs)

The Pretender (Highland Heroes)

Pretending (Cheerleaders)

Pretenses (Sweet Valley High)

Pretty Please (Nightmare Hall)

The Price of Fame (Thoroughbred)

The Price of Love (Sweet Valley University)

Price of Silence (Live from Brentwood High)

The Price of the Stars (Valdemar: Mageworlds)

Priceless Love (Sweet Dreams)

Pride's Challenge (Thoroughbred)

Pride's Last Race (Thoroughbred)

Primary Inversion (Saga of the Skolian Empire)

Prime Evil (Buffy the Vampire Slayer) (Archway/Pocket)

Prime Time (Clearwater Crossing)

The Prime-Time Crime (Hardy Boys)

Prince (Wolfbay Wings)

Prince Caspian (Chronicles of Narnia)

The Prince in Waiting (Sword of the Spirits)

Princess Amy (Sweet Dreams)

The Princess Club (Christy)

The Princess Diaries (Princess Diaries)

Princess Elizabeth (Sweet Valley Twins)

Princess in Love (Princess Diaries)

Princess in Pink (Princess Diaries)

Princess in the Spotlight (Princess Diaries)

Princess in Waiting (Princess Diaries)

The Princess of Fairwood High (Homeroom)

The Princess of Pop (Truth or Dare)

The Princess Present (Princess Diaries)

The Princess Project (Princess Diaries)

The Princess, the Crone, and the Dung-Cart Knight (The Denizens of Camelot)

Prisoner of Elderwood (Endless Quest)

Prisoner of the Ant People (Choose Your Own Adventure)

Prisoner of Time (Time Travel Quartet)

Prisoner's Hope (Seafort Saga)

Prisoners of Peace (Star Trek: Deep Space Nine)

Private Eyes (Sweet Dreams)

Private Jessica (Sweet Valley University)

Private Lives (Net Force)

The Prize (Thoroughbred: Ashleigh)

Probability Moon (Probability)

Probability Space (Probability)

Probability Sun (Probability)

The Problem with Love (Sweet Dreams)

Process of Elimination (Nancy Drew and the Hardy Boys Super Mysteries)

Processing the Computer Conspiracy (Summit High)

Prognosis (University Hospital)

Program for Destruction (Hardy Boys)

Programmed for Love (Sweet Dreams)

Project Black Bear (China Tate)

Project Boyfriend (Sweet Dreams)

Project UFO (Choose Your Own Adventure)

Prom Date (Fear Street: Fear Street Seniors)

Prom Night (Sweet Valley High Senior Year)

Prom Princess (Mary-Kate and Ashley: Two of a Kind)

Prom Queen (Fear Street)

The Promise (Black Stallion: Young Black Stallion)

Promise Breaker (Promise of Zion)

A Promise Is Forever (Christy Miller)

Promise Me Love (Sweet Dreams)

Promise Me You'll Stop Me (Distress Call 911)

Promises (Star Wars Junior Jedi Knights)

Promises (Sweet Valley High)

Promises, Promises (Clearwater Crossing)

The Prophecy (Animorphs)

The Prophecy (Daughters of the Moon)

The Proposal (Animorphs)

The Proposal (Christy)

The Protester's Song (Misfits, Inc.)

Proving It (Cheerleaders)

Prowlers (Prowlers)

Psion (Psion)

Psychic Sisters (Sweet Valley Twins)

Public Enemy, Number Two (The Diamond Brothers)

Pulling Together (Cheerleaders)

Pumpkin Fever (Sweet Valley Twins)

Puppy Fat (Misery Guts)

Puppy Love (Sweet Dreams)

Pure Dead Brilliant (Pure Dead Magic)

Pure Dead Magic (Pure Dead Magic)

Pure Dead Wicked (Pure Dead Magic)

Pure Evil (Hardy Boys Casefiles)

Pure Poison (Nancy Drew Files)

Purple Prince of Oz (Oz)

Pursued (Jennie McGrady Mysteries)

Pursuing Amy (Replica)

The Pursuit (Alias)

Pursuit (Roswell High)

Pushed (Sevens)

Pushing the Limits (Generation Girl)

The Puzzle at Pineview School (Nancy Drew)

Pyramids (Discworld)

Q

Quantum Force (Tom Swift)

The Quantum Rose (Saga of the Skolian Empire)

Quarantine (Roswell High)

Quarantine (Star Trek: Voyager: Starfleet Academy)

Quarantine (X Files)

Quarterback Exchange (NFL Monday Night Football Club)

Queen Amidala (Star Wars Episode 1: Journals)

Queen Ann in Oz (Oz)

The Queen of Air and Darkness (Once and Future King)

Queen of Sorcery (The Belgariad)

The Queen of the Gargoyles (Bone Chillers)

Queen of the Sixth Grade (Kids from Kennedy Middle School)

The Queen of Vengeance (Oh My Goddess!)

Queen Sayoko (Oh My Goddess!)

Quest for Faith (The Viking)

Quest for the King (The Archives of Anthropos)

Quest for Treasure (Abby's South Seas Adventures)

The Quest of the Missing Map (Nancy Drew)

A Question of Guilt (Nancy Drew and the Hardy Boys Super Mysteries)

The Question of Magic (Age of Magic Trilogy)

Question Quest (Xanth Saga)

Questions of Love (Sweet Dreams)

A Quiet Strength (Prairie Legacy)

R

"R" for Revenge (Sweet Valley High)

R U 4 Real? (TodaysGirls.com)

The Race (Golden Filly Series)

Race Against Time (Nancy Drew)

A Race Against Time (Nancy Drew: Girl Detective)

A Race Against Time (Virtual Reality)

Race Forever (Choose Your Own Adventure)

Race Ready (NASCAR Pole Position Adventures)

Racing Hearts (Sweet Dreams)

Racing Hearts (Sweet Valley High)

Racing Image (Thoroughbred)

Racing Parker (Thoroughbred)

Racing Vacation (Sandy Lane Stables)

Racing with Disaster (Hardy Boys)

The Radiant Seas (Saga of the Skolian Empire)

Radical Moves (Hardy Boys)

Rage of Fire (National Parks Mystery)

Rags to Riches (Sweet Valley High)

Raid on Nightmare Castle (Endless Quest)

Rainbow Valley (Avonlea)

Raising the Bar (High Hurdles)

Rakkety Tam (Redwall)

Rama II (Rama)

Rama Revealed (Rama)

Rancher Ferrets on the Range (Ferret Chronicles)

Raptor Without a Cause (Dinoverse)

Rare Beasts (Edgar and Ellen)

Ratha and Thistle-Chaser (Ratha Quartet)

Ratha's Challenge (Ratha Quartet)

Ratha's Creature (Ratha Quartet)

Rays, Romance and Rivalry (Summer)

Reach for Tomorrow (One Last Wish)

The Reaction (Animorphs)

Ready? (Love Trilogy)

Ready, Shoot, Score! (Cheer USA!)

Rewolf of Oz (Oz)

Reyna's Reward (American Dreams) (Avon)

Rhythm of Love (Sweet Dreams)

Rich and Dangerous (Nancy Drew Files)

The Rich Girl (Fear Street)

Rich Girl in the Mirror (Mirror Image)

Rich in Romance (Sweet Dreams)

The Riddle and the Rune (Tales of Gom in the Legends of Ulm)

The Riddle in the Rare Book (Nancy Drew)

Riddle of the Prairie Bride (American Girls: History Mysteries)

The Riddle of the Ruby Gazelle (Nancy Drew)

Riddles of Love (Sweet Dreams)

Ride by Moonlight (Sandy Lane Stables)

The Riding Club Crime (Nancy Drew)

Riding to Win (Saddle Club: Pine Hollow)

Rigged for Revenge (Hardy Boys Casefiles)

The Right Combination (Sweet Dreams)

The Right Hand of Doom (Hellboy)

Rilla of Ingleside (Avonlea)

Rimrunners (Alliance-Union)

Rina's Family Secret (Roosevelt High School)

A Ring of Endless Light (Vicky Austin)

Ring of Fire (Buffy the Vampire Slayer) (Dark Horse)

Ring of Light (Circle of Three)

The Ringmaster's Secret (Nancy Drew)

Rinktink in Oz (Oz)

The Rise and Fall of the Kate Empire (Lizzie McGuire)

The Rise of the False Messiahs (Left Behind—The Kids)

The Rising Force (Star Wars: Jedi Apprentice)

Rising Star (Thoroughbred)

Rising Storm (Warriors)

Risk Your Life Arcade (Choose Your Own Nightmare)

Risky Assignment (Live from Brentwood High)

Rivals (Cheerleaders)

Rivals (7th Heaven)

The River (Brian Robeson)

The River at Green Knowe (Green Knowe)

River of Eternity (Riverworld Saga)

River of No Return (Choose Your Own Adventure)

River Quest (Dinotopia)

River Rats (Hardy Boys Casefiles)

Riverboat Ruse (Nancy Drew: Girl Detective)

Road Pirates (Hardy Boys Casefiles)

The Road to Camlann (Arthurian Knights)

The Road to Memphis (Logan Family)

The Road to Oz (Oz)

The Road to the Majors (Dream Series)

Road Trip (Diary of a Teenage Girl)

Road Trip (Sweet Valley High Senior Year)

The Roar of the Crowd (Winning Season)

The Roaring River Mystery (Hardy Boys)

The Roaring Twenties (Young Indiana Jones Chronicles: Choose Your Own Adventure)

Robbers and Robots (Endless Quest)

Robbery at the Mall (Sweet Valley Twins)

The Robin and the Kestrel (Bardic Voices)

Robots and Empire (I, Robot)

The Robots of Dawn (I, Robot)

The Robot's Revenge (Hardy Boys)

Roc and a Hard Place (Xanth Saga)

Rock and Roll Mystery (Choose Your Own Adventure)

Rock Jaw, Master of the Eastern Border (Bone)

Rock 'n' Revenge (Hardy Boys Casefiles)

Rock 'n' Roll Renegades (Hardy Boys)

Rock 'n' Roll Sweetheart (Sweet Dreams)

Rock On (Extreme Team)

The Rock Rats (Asteroid Wars)

Rock Star's Girl (Sweet Valley High)

Rocked Out (X Games Xtreme Mysteries)

The Rocky Road to Revenge (Hardy Boys)

Rocky Romance (Sweet Dreams)

Rogue Berserker (Berserker)

Rogues in the House and Other Stories (Chronicles of Conan)

Roll of Thunder, Hear My Cry (Logan Family)

Roller Hockey Rumble (Extreme Team)

Roller Star (Choose Your Own Adventure)

Rolling Thunder (NASCAR Pole Position Adventures)

Roman Blood (Roma Sub Rosa)

Romance on the Run (Sweet Dreams)

Romantically Correct (Clueless)

Rome (Love Stories: Year Abroad)

Romeo and Ghouliette (Bone Chillers)

Romeo and Two Juliets (Sweet Valley Twins)

Room 13 (Moondog)

The Roommate (Nightmare Hall)

The Roommate (Sweet Valley University Thriller Editions)

Rosa's Lie (Sweet Valley High)

Rose at Bull Run (The Young Americans)

The Rose Queen (Missing Persons)

Rosemary Remembered (China Bayles Mystery)

The Rosewood Casket (Ballad)

Rough Riding (Hardy Boys Casefiles)

Rough Stuff (Three Investigators)

Roughing It (Distress Call 911)

Round One (Popular)

Rowan Farm (Lechow Family)

Rowan Hood (Rowan Hood)

The Royal Book of Oz (Oz)

A Royal Kiss (You're the One)

Royal Pain (Kim Possible (Chapter Books))

Royal Pain (Sweet Valley University: Elizabeth)

Royal Pain and Twin Factor (Kim Possible (TokyoPop))

Scene of the Crime (Hardy Boys Casefiles)

Scene One, Take Two (Saved by the Bell)

Scent of Danger (Nancy Drew Files)

Scheming (Cheerleaders)

School Dance Party (Mary-Kate and Ashley Starring In . . .)

Scion of Cyador (Recluce)

The Scions of Shannara (Shannara: Heritage of Shannara)

Score (Have a Nice Life)

Scratch and the Sniffs (He-Man Women Haters Club)

The Scream (Forbidden Doors)

Scream Around the Campfire (Graveyard School)

The Scream Museum (P.C. Hawke Mysteries)

Scream of the Cat (Phantom Valley)

Scream of the Evil Genie (Goosebumps: Give Yourself Goosebumps)

Scream School (Goosebumps Series 2000)

The Scream Tea (Fear Street: Ghosts of Fear Street)

The Scream Team (Nightmare Hall)

Scream, Team! (Graveyard School)

Screamers (Hardy Boys Casefiles)

Screech in Love (Saved by the Bell)

Sea City, Here We Come! (Baby-Sitters Club Super Specials)

Sea for Yourself (Luna Bay)

Sea Glass (Golden Mountain Chronicles)

Sea of Suspicion (Nancy Drew Files)

Seal Island Scam (Girls R.U.L.E.)

Sealed with a Kiss (Holly's Heart)

Sealed with a Kiss (Mary-Kate and Ashley: Two of a Kind)

The Search (Left Behind—The Kids)

The Search (Regeneration)

Search for Aladdin's Lamp (Choose Your Own Adventure)

The Search for Cindy Austin (Nancy Drew)

Search for Senna (EverWorld)

Search for the Mountain Gorillas (Choose Your Own Adventure)

The Search for the Silver Persian (Nancy Drew)

The Search for the Snow Leopard (Hardy Boys)

Search the Amazon! (Choose Your Own Adventure)

Searching for Dragons (Enchanted Forest Chronicles)

Searching for Love (Sweet Dreams)

A Searching Heart (Prairie Legacy)

Seaside High (Aloha Cove)

Seaside Mystery (Choose Your Own Adventure)

A Season for Goodbye (One Last Wish)

A Season of Hope (Heartland)

Second Best (Life at Sixteen)

Second Best (Sweet Valley Twins)

Second-Best Friend (Holly's Heart)

Second Chance (Left Behind— The Kids)

Second Chance (Sweet Valley High)

Second Chances (Sweet Dreams)

Second Choices (Nikki Sheridan)

Second Evil (Fear Street: Fear Street Cheerleaders)

Second Foundation (Foundation)

Second Helpings (Jessica Darling)

The Second Horror (Fear Street: 99 Fear Street)

Second Sight (Circle of Three)

Second Sight (Mindwarp)

The Second Summer of the Sisterhood (Sisterhood of the Traveling Pants)

The Second Summoning (The Keeper's Chronicles)

Second Wind (Golden Filly Series)

The Secret (Animorphs)

The Secret (Fear Street: Fear Street Sagas)

Secret (Making Waves)

Secret Admirer (Dear Diary)

Secret Admirer (Fear Street)

Secret Admirer (Sweet Dreams)

Secret Admirer (Sweet Valley High)

Secret Agent Grandma (Goosebumps: Give Yourself Goosebumps)

Secret Agent on Flight 101 (Hardy Boys)

Secret at Cutter Grove (Abby's South Seas Adventures)

The Secret at Seven Rocks (Nancy Drew)

The Secret at Solitaire (Nancy Drew)

The Secret Bedroom (Fear Street)

Secret City (Pyrates)

Secret Clique (Replica)

The Secret Country (The Secret Country Trilogy)

Secret Crush (Mary-Kate and Ashley: So Little Time)

The Secret Gift (Highland Heroes)

Secret Identity (Sweet Dreams)

The Secret in the Dark (Nancy Drew)

The Secret in the Kitchen (China Tate)

The Secret in the Old Attic (Nancy Drew)

The Secret in the Old Lace (Nancy Drew)

The Secret in the Stars (Nancy Drew)

The Secret in the Stones (Tales of the Nine Charms)

Secret in the Willows (Summerhill Secrets)

The Secret in Time (Nancy Drew)

A Secret Life (Alias)

The Secret Life of Mary Anne Spier (Baby-Sitters Club)

The Secret Lost at Sea (Nancy Drew)

Secret Love Diaries (Sweet Valley University)

Secret Love Diaries: Elizabeth (Sweet Valley University)

Secret Love Diaries: Jessica (Sweet Valley University)

Secret Love Diaries: Sam (Sweet Valley University)

Secret Money (The Lily Adventures)

The Secret of Candlelight Inn (Nancy Drew)

The Secret of Mirror Bay (Nancy Drew)

The Secret of Mystery Hill (Choose Your Own Adventure)

Seven Crows (Buffy the Vampire Slayer: Buffy and Angel)

The Seven Songs of Merlin (Lost Years of Merlin)

Seven Spiders Spinning (Hamlet Chronicles)

Seventeen Against the Dealer (Tillerman Cycle)

Seventeen Wishes (Christy Miller)

Seventh-Grade Menace (Fabulous Five)

Seventh Grade Rumors (Fabulous Five)

The Seventh Sentinel (Dragonlance Defenders of Magic)

Seventh Son (Tales of Alvin Maker)

Sex (Fearless)

Sex? (Love Trilogy)

Shacked Up (Hard Cash)

Shacked Up (Richard Steele Trilogy)

Shades (Roswell High)

Shadow Academy (Star Wars Young Jedi Knights)

The Shadow Club (Shadow Club)

The Shadow Club Rising (Shadow Club)

Shadow Girl (Nightmare Room)

The Shadow in the North (Sally Lockhart Trilogy)

The Shadow in the Tomb and Other Stories (Chronicles of Conan)

The Shadow Killers (Hardy Boys)

Shadow Man (Danger.com)

Shadow of a Doubt (Nancy Drew Files)

Shadow of Honor (Net Force)

Shadow of the Hegemon (Ender Wiggin)

Shadow of the Sphinx (Charmed)

Shadow of the Swastika (Choose Your Own Adventure)

Shadow of the Well of Souls (Watchers at the Well)

Shadow over San Mateo (Golden Filly Series)

Shadow Puppets (Ender Wiggin)

The Shadow Rising (The Wheel of Time)

Shadow Self (Dear Diary)

The Shadow Sorceress (The Spellsong Cycle)

Shadow Tree (Glory)

Shadowed (Alias)

Shadowgate (Deltora: Dragons of Deltora)

Shadowland (The Mediator)

The Shadowlands (Deltora: Deltora Shadowlands)

Shadowmancer (Shadowmancer)

Shadows Beyond the Gate (Summerhill Secrets)

Shadows in the Glasshouse (American Girls: History Mysteries)

The Shadows of God (The Age of Unreason)

Shadows on Stoney Creek (Sarah's Journey)

Shadows on the Wall (York Trilogy)

Shadowsinger (The Spellsong Cycle)

The Shaggy Man of Oz (Oz)

Shakedown (Angel)

The Shakespeare Stealer (The Shakespeare Stealer)

Shakespeare's Scribe (The Shakespeare Stealer)

Shakespeare's Spy (The Shakespeare Stealer)

Shani's Scoop (B.Y. Times)

Shape-Shifter (Mindwarp)

Shape-Shifter: The Naming of Pangur Ban (Pangur Ban)

Shapes (X Files)

Shards of Alderaan (Star Wars Young Jedi Knights)

Sharing Sam (Love Stories)

Shark (Wolfbay Wings)

Shark Bite (Against the Odds)

Shattered (Sevens)

The Shattered Helmet (Hardy Boys)

The Shattered Peace (Star Wars: Jedi Apprentice)

Shattered Twilight (Buffy the Vampire Slayer: Wicked Willow)

Shatterglass (Circle of Magic: The Circle Opens)

The Shattering (Guardians of Ga'Hoole)

She Died Too Young (One Last Wish)

She Loves Me . . . Not (Sweet Valley Junior High)

She Walks These Hills (Ballad)

Sheer Terror (Hardy Boys Casefiles)

Shenandoah Autumn (White Mane Kids)

Shendu Escapes! (Jackie Chan Adventures)

She's Back (Sweet Valley Junior High)

She's Not What She Seems (Sweet Valley High)

Shield of Fear (Hardy Boys)

Shifting into Overdrive (Dawson's Creek)

The Shifting Sands (Deltora: Deltora Quest)

Shining's Orphan (Thoroughbred)

Ship of Ghouls (Goosebumps: Give Yourself Goosebumps)

Shipboard Wedding (Sweet Valley University)

The Ships of Earth (Homecoming Saga)

Shipwreck (Island)

Shiva in Steel (Berserker)

Shiver (Danger.com)

Shock (Fearless)

Shock Jock (Hardy Boys Casefiles)

Shock Waves (Nancy Drew and the Hardy Boys Super Mysteries)

A Shocker on Shock Street (Goosebumps)

Shoeless Joe and Me (Baseball Card Adventures)

Shoot the Works (Three Investigators)

Shop in the Name of Love (Cheetah Girls)

Shop 'Til You Drop . . . Dead (Goosebumps: Give Yourself Goosebumps)

Shopaholic and Sister (Shopaholic)

Shopaholic Takes Manhattan (Shopaholic)

Shopaholic Ties the Knot (Shopaholic)

The Shore Road Mystery (Hardy Boys)

Shore Thing (Mary-Kate and Ashley: Two of a Kind)

The Short Victorious War (Honor Harrington)

Short-Wave Mystery (Hardy Boys)

A Shot at Love (Sweet Dreams)

Sloppy Firsts (Jessica Darling)

Small Gods (Discworld)

Smile and Say Murder (Nancy Drew Files)

Smoke Jumper (Choose Your Own Adventure)

The Smoke Screen Mystery (Hardy Boys)

Smother Dearest (That's So Raven)

The Smugglers (High Seas Trilogy)

The Smuggler's Treasure (American Girls: History Mysteries)

Snag Him! (Love Stories: His. Hers. Theirs)

Sneaking Around (No Secrets: The Story of a Girl Band)

Sneaking In (Sweet Valley University)

Sneaking Out (Sweet Valley Twins)

Snow Day (Spinetinglers)

The Snow Spider (Gwyn Griffiths Trilogy)

Snowboard Racer (Choose Your Own Adventure)

Snowbound (Baby-Sitters Club Super Specials)

Snowbound (Nancy Drew on Campus)

So Cool (Sweet Valley High Senior Year)

So Long, and Thanks for All the Fish (Hitchhiker's Trilogy)

So Mote It Be (Circle of Three)

So Not Me (Sweet Valley High Senior Year)

So You Want to be a Wizard (Wizardry) (Duane)

Soap Star (Sweet Valley High)

Sober Faith (Payton Skky)

Soccer Star (Choose Your Own Adventure)

The Society (Forbidden Doors)

Sock Monkey (Sock Monkey)

Sock Monkey: The Glass Doorknob (Sock Monkey)

Sock Monkey: Uncle Gabby (Sock Monkey)

Sofia's Heart (American Dreams) (Avon)

Sold Out (Diary of a Teenage Girl)

The Soldier Boy's Discovery (Bonnets and Bugles)

A Solitary Blue (Tillerman Cycle)

Solitary Man (Angel)

The Solution (Animorphs)

Some Girls Do (Love Stories)

Someday, Some Way (Star Power)

Someone Dies, Someone Lives (One Last Wish)

Something Fishy at Macdonald Hall (Bruno and Boots)

Something M.Y.T.H. Inc. (Myth Adventures)

Something to Hide (Nancy Drew Files)

Something Wiccan This Way Comes (Charmed)

Something's in the Woods (Choose Your Own Nightmare)

The Son of Summer Stars (Firebringer Trilogy)

Son of the Black Stallion (Black Stallion)

Son of the Shadows (Sevenwaters)

Sondok (Royal Diaries)

A Song for Caitlin (Love Stories: Super Editions)

A Song for Linda (Sweet Dreams)

The Song of Red Sonja and Other Stories (Chronicles of Conan)

Song of Susannah (Dark Tower)

Song of the Dark Druid (Endless Quest)

Song of the Sea (American Dreams) (Avon)

Song of the Trees (Logan Family)

Song of the Unicorns (Avalon 2: Quest for Magic)

Song Quest (Echorium Sequence)

The Songcatcher (Ballad)

Sons from Afar (Tillerman Cycle)

Sons of Entropy (Buffy the Vampire Slayer: The Gatekeeper Trilogy)

Sooner or Later (Heartland)

Sophie (Fab 5)

The Soprano Sorceress (The Spellsong Cycle)

Sorcerers of Majipoor (The Majipoor Cycle)

Sorcerers of the Nightwing (Ravenscliff)

Sorceress (Witch Child)

Sorceress of Darshiva (Malloreon)

Sorority Scandal (Sweet Valley University)

Sorority Sister (Nightmare Hall)

Soul Music (Discworld)

Soul of the Bride (Charmed)

Soul Survivor (Body of Evidence)

Soul Trade (Angel)

Soulmate (Night World)

Soulmates (Sweet Valley Junior High)

The Source of Magic (Xanth Saga)

Sourcery (Discworld)

South of the Border (Young Indiana Jones Chronicles: Choose Your Own Adventure)

South Pole Sabotage (Choose Your Own Adventure)

Southern Fried Makeover (Clueless)

The Southern Girls (Pageant)

Space and Beyond (Choose Your Own Adventure)

Space Camp (Star Trek: Deep Space Nine)

Space Patrol (Choose Your Own Adventure)

Space Race (Ormingat)

Space Vampire (Choose Your Own Adventure)

Spark of Suspicion (Hardy Boys)

Sparks (Smallville)

Speaker for the Dead (Ender Wiggin)

Special Christmas (Sweet Valley High)

Special Someone (Sweet Dreams)

The Speckled Rose of Oz (Oz)

The Specter from the Magician's Museum (Lewis Barnavelt)

Speed (Smallville)

Speed Demon (NASCAR Pole Position Adventures)

Speed Times Five (Hardy Boys)

Speeding (Hard Cash)

Speeding (Richard Steele Trilogy)

Speedy in Oz (Oz)

The Spell (Forbidden Doors)

The Spell (Phantom Valley)

Spell Danger (Here Comes Heavenly)

A Spell for Chameleon (Xanth Saga)

Spell of the Screaming Jokers (Fear Street: Ghosts of Fear Street)

Standing Room Only (Saved by the Bell)

Star-Crossed Love (Sweet Dreams)

The Star Ghost (Star Trek: Deep Space Nine)

Star in Danger (Thoroughbred)

Star in the Mirror (Mirror Image)

Star Maps (American Dreams) (Aladdin)

Star of Shadowbrook Farm (Thoroughbred: Ashleigh's Collection)

Star Struck! (Sweet Dreams)

Star Wars (Choose Your Own Star Wars Adventures)

Star Wars: Return of the Jedi (Choose Your Own Star Wars Adventures)

Star Wars: The Empire Strikes Back (Choose Your Own Star Wars Adventures)

Stardust's Foal (Thoroughbred: Ashleigh)

Starfall (Star Trek: The Next Generation: Starfleet Academy)

Starpilot's Grave (Valdemar: Mageworlds)

Starring Jessica! (Sweet Valley High)

Starring the Baby-Sitters Club (Baby-Sitters Club Super Specials)

Starring You and Me (Mary-Kate and Ashley Sweet 16)

Starry Night (Christy Miller)

The Stars Asunder (Valdemar: Mageworlds)

Star's Chance (Thoroughbred)

The Stars from Mars (Slapshots)

Star's Inspiration (Thoroughbred)

The Starstone (Tales of Gom in the Legends of Ulm)

Starstruck (Thoroughbred)

Starstruck (Truth or Dare)

Start Here (Have a Nice Life)

Starting Over (Cheerleaders)

Starting Over (Sweet Valley High)

The State of the Art (The Culture)

Statue of Liberty Adventure (Choose Your Own Adventure)

Stay Away from the Treehouse (Fear Street: Ghosts of Fear Street)

Stay or Go (Sweet Valley High Senior Year)

Stay Out of the Basement (Goosebumps)

Stay Tuned for Danger (Nancy Drew Files)

Staying Pure (Payton Skky)

Staying Together (Cheerleaders)

Stealing Secrets (Cheerleaders)

Step on a Crack (Spinetinglers)

The Stepbrother (Fear Street)

Stepping on the Cracks (Gordy Smith)

The Steps Up the Chimney (Magician's House Quartet)

The Stepsister (Fear Street)

The Stepsister 2 (Fear Street)

Stepsisters (Sweet Valley High)

Sterling's Second Chance (Thoroughbred)

Steven and the Zombie (Sweet Valley Twins)

Steven Gets Even (Sweet Valley Twins)

Steven's Bride (Sweet Valley High)

Steven's Enemy (Sweet Valley Twins)

Steven's in Love (Sweet Valley Twins)

The Sting of the Scorpion (Hardy Boys)

Stinky Business (Don't Touch That Remote!)

A Stitch in Time (Quilt Trilogy)

Stitch of Courage (Trail of Thread)

Stock Car Champion (Choose Your Own Adventure)

The Stolen (The Nine Lives of Chloe King)

Stolen Affections (Nancy Drew Files)

The Stolen Diary (Sweet Valley High)

The Stolen Kiss (Nancy Drew Files)

Stolen Kisses (Love Stories)

Stolen Kisses (Sweet Dreams)

The Stolen Lake (Wolves Chronicles)

The Stolen Relic (Nancy Drew: Girl Detective)

The Stone Fey (Damar Chronicles)

The Stone Goddess (First Person Fiction)

The Stone Idol (Hardy Boys)

The Stones of Green Knowe (Green Knowe)

Stop, Don't Stop (Black Book (Diary of a Teenage Stud))

Storm Breaking (Valdemar: Mage Storms)

Storm Clouds (High Hurdles)

Storm of Wings (Dragonmaster)

Storm Rescue (Wild at Heart)

Storm Rising (Valdemar: Mage Storms)

Storm Warning (Valdemar: Mage Storms)

Stormbreaker (Alex Rider)

The Stowaway (Roswell High)

Stowaways (Star Trek: Deep Space Nine)

Straight-A Teacher (Holly's Heart)

Straight Up (Sweet Valley High Senior Year)

Stranded (Jennie McGrady Mysteries)

Stranded (Sweet Valley University)

Stranded: Death Valley, Circa 1850 (Survival!)

Strange Armor (Concrete)

Strange Bedfellows and Other Stories (Angel (Graphic Novels))

Strange Brew (Bone Chillers)

The Strange Case of Baby H (American Girls: History Mysteries)

Strange Memories (Nancy Drew Files)

Strange Message in the Parchment (Nancy Drew)

The Strange Power (Dark Visions)

Strange Times at Fairwood High (Homeroom)

The Stranger (Animorphs)

A Stranger at Green Knowe (Green Knowe)

A Stranger in the House (Sweet Valley High)

Stranger in the Mirror (Mirror Image)

Stranger in the Mirror (Phantom Valley)

The Stranger in the Shadows (Nancy Drew)

Stranger in Williamsburg (Sarah's Journey)

Stranger Online (TodaysGirls.com)

The Swamp Monster (Hardy Boys)

Swampland (Swampland Trilogy)

The Swarm (Star Wars Galaxy of Fear)

Sweet (Making Waves)

Sweet Dreams (Christy Miller)

Sweet 18 (Sweet Valley High Senior Year)

Sweet Kiss of Summer (Sweet Valley University)

Sweet Myth-tery of Life (Myth Adventures)

Sweet Revenge (Nancy Drew Files)

Sweet Sixteen (Buffy the Vampire Slayer) (Archway/Pocket)

Sweet Sixteen (Love Stories: Super Editions)

Sweetest Gift (Payton Skky)

Sweetheart, Evil Heart (Fear Street: Fear Street Seniors)

Swell Foop (Xanth Saga)

A Swiftly Tilting Planet (Time Fantasy Series)

Swiss Secrets (Nancy Drew Files)

Switched (Fear Street)

Switchers (Switchers)

Switching Channels (Eerie Indiana)

Switching Goals (Mary-Kate and Ashley Starring In . . .)

The Sword and the Circle (Arthurian Knights)

The Sword Bearer (The Archives of Anthropos)

Sword-Born (Sword Dancer Saga)

Sword-Breaker (Sword Dancer Saga)

Sword-Dancer (Sword Dancer Saga)

A Sword from Red Ice (Sword of Shadows)

The Sword in the Stone (Once and Future King)

Sword-Maker (Sword Dancer Saga)

The Sword of Bedwyr (The Crimson Shadow)

The Sword of Shannara (Shannara)

Sword of the Samurai Cat (Samurai Cat)

The Sword of the Spirits (Sword of the Spirits)

Sword-Singer (Sword Dancer Saga)

Sword-Sworn (Sword Dancer Saga)

Swords and Scimitars (Royal Pavilions)

The Swordsheath Scroll (Dragonlance Dwarven Nations Trilogy)

Sworn to Silence (Class Secrets)

Sympathy for the Devil (Oh My Goddess!)

T

Tag Against Time (Walker and Tag)

Tagged for Terror (Hardy Boys Casefiles)

The Taggerung (Redwall)

Tail of the Tip-off (Mrs. Murphy)

Take a Hike! (Secret World of Alex Mack)

Take Back the Night (Sweet Valley University)

Take Me On (Sweet Valley High Senior Year)

Take My Hand (Sierra Jensen)

Take Off (Impact Zone)

Taking a Stand (Generation Girl)

Taking Chances (Heartland)

Taking Chances (On the Road)

Taking Charge! (Generation Girl)

Taking Charge (Sweet Valley Twins)

Taking Over (Cheerleaders)

Taking Risks (Cheerleaders)

Taking Sides (Sweet Valley High)

Taking the Lead (Sweet Dreams)

Taking the Reins (Thoroughbred)

The Tale of Cutter's Treasure (Are You Afraid of the Dark?)

The Tale of the Bad-Tempered Ghost (Are You Afraid of the Dark?)

The Tale of the Blue Monkey (Fear Street: Ghosts of Fear Street)

The Tale of the Campfire Vampires (Are You Afraid of the Dark?)

The Tale of the Curious Cat (Are You Afraid of the Dark?)

The Tale of the Deadly Diary (Are You Afraid of the Dark?)

The Tale of the Egyptian Mummies (Are You Afraid of the Dark?)

The Tale of the Ghost Cruise (Are You Afraid of the Dark?)

The Tale of the Ghost Riders (Are You Afraid of the Dark?)

The Tale of the Horrifying Hockey Team (Are You Afraid of the Dark?)

The Tale of the Mogul Monster (Are You Afraid of the Dark?)

The Tale of the Nightly Neighbors (Are You Afraid of the Dark?)

The Tale of the Phantom School Bus (Are You Afraid of the Dark?)

The Tale of the Pulsating Gate (Are You Afraid of the Dark?)

The Tale of the Restless House (Are You Afraid of the Dark?)

The Tale of the Secret Mirror (Are You Afraid of the Dark?)

The Tale of the Shimmering Shell (Are You Afraid of the Dark?)

The Tale of the Sinister Statues (Are You Afraid of the Dark?)

The Tale of the Souvenir Shop (Are You Afraid of the Dark?)

The Tale of the Stalking Shadow (Are You Afraid of the Dark?)

The Tale of the Terrible Toys (Are You Afraid of the Dark?)

The Tale of the Three Wishes (Are You Afraid of the Dark?)

Tale of the Toa (Bionicle Chronicles)

The Tale of the Virtual Nightmare (Are You Afraid of the Dark?)

The Tale of the Zero Hour (Are You Afraid of the Dark?)

A Tale of Two Pipers (Charmed)

A Talent for Murder (Nancy Drew Files)

Tales of the Masks (Bionicle Chronicles)

Tales of the Slayers (Buffy the Vampire Slayer) (Dark Horse)

Tales Too Scary to Tell at Camp (Graveyard School)

The Talisman (Daughters of the Moon)

The Talismans of Shannara (Shannara: Heritage of Shannara)

Talking Back (Cheerleaders)

Talking It Over (B.Y. Times)

Talking to Dragons (Enchanted Forest Chronicles)

Tall Cool One (A-List)

Tall, Dark, and Deadly (Nancy Drew Files)

Tall, Dark, and Deadly (Sweet Valley High)

The Taming of the Pyre (Mystic Knights of Tir Na Nog)

Tanar of Pellucidar (Pellucidar)

Tanequil (Shannara: High Druid of Shannara)

Tangled Web (Nikki Sheridan)

Tangled Web (TodaysGirls.com)

Tankworld (Swampland Trilogy)

Taran Wanderer (Prydain Chronicles)

Target for Terror (Nancy Drew and the Hardy Boys Super Mysteries)

Tarot Says Beware (Herculeah Jones)

Tarragon Island (Tarragon Island)

Tartabull's Throw (Moondog)

Tarzan and the Tower of Diamonds (Endless Quest)

Tarzan and the Well of Slaves (Endless Quest)

Tarzan at the Earth's Core (Pellucidar)

A Taste for Terror (Hardy Boys Casefiles)

A Taste of Danger (Nancy Drew)

Tattoo of Death (Choose Your Own Adventure)

Te Amo Means I Love You (Sweet Dreams)

Teacher Creature (Bone Chillers)

Teacher Crush (Sweet Valley High)

Teacher's Pet (Sweet Valley Twins)

Teacher's Pet: Book 7: Maggie (Wild at Heart)

Team Player (The Jersey)

Team Player (Thoroughbred)

Teamwork (Sweet Valley Twins)

Tearing Me Apart (Sweet Valley High Senior Year)

Tears (Fearless)

Tears of a Tiger (Hazelwood High)

Tease (Making Waves)

Technical Foul (Winning Season)

Teen Angel (Roosevelt High School)

The Teen Model Mystery (Nancy Drew)

Teen Queens and Has-Beens (Truth or Dare)

Teen Taxi (Fabulous Five)

The Teens Time Forgot (Dinoverse)

Teetoncey (Outer Banks Trilogy)

Teetoncey and Ben O'Neal (Outer Banks Trilogy)

Tehanu (Earthsea)

Tell Me About It (Mary-Kate and Ashley: So Little Time)

Tell Me the Truth (Nancy Drew on Campus)

Telling (Hamilton High)

Telling Lies (Cheerleaders)

Tempestuous (Brides of Wildcat County)

The Templar Treasure (The Adept)

Temptation (Smallville)

Tempted Champions (Buffy the Vampire Slayer) (Archway/Pocket)

Ten-Boy Summer (Sweet Dreams)

Ten Seconds to Play! (Chip Hilton Sports Series)

Ten-Speed Summer (Sweet Dreams)

Tender Loving Care (Sweet Dreams)

Tender Mercies (Red River: Red River of the North)

The Tender Years (Prairie Legacy)

The Tenth Power (Chanters of Tremaris Trilogy)

Teresa (The Elliott Cousins)

A Terminal Case of the Uglies (Bone Chillers)

Terminal Shock (Hardy Boys)

Terrible Master Urd (Oh My Goddess!)

Terror (Fearless)

Terror at High Tide (Hardy Boys)

Terror in Australia (Choose Your Own Adventure)

Terror in the Sky (American Adventure)

Terror in the Stadium (Left Behind—The Kids)

Terror Island (Choose Your Own Adventure)

Terror on the Titanic (Choose Your Own Adventure)

Terror on Track (Hardy Boys Casefiles)

Terrorist Trap (Choose Your Own Adventure)

The Test (Animorphs)

The Test (Endless Quest)

The Test Case (Hardy Boys)

A Test of Mirrors (Zenda)

Thanks for Nothing (From the Files of Madison Finn)

That Certain Feeling (Sweet Dreams)

That Fatal Night (Sweet Valley High)

That Old Zack Magic (Saved by the Bell)

That's So Raven (That's So Raven)

Then (Remnants)

Theodore Roosevelt (Dear Mr. President)

There's a Ghost in the Boy's Bathroom (Graveyard School)

These Our Actors (Buffy the Vampire Slayer) (Archway/Pocket)

They Call Me Creature (Nightmare Room)

They Say (Eerie Indiana)

Thick as Thieves (Hardy Boys Casefiles)

Thicker than Water (Heartland)

Thief of Hearts (Body of Evidence)

Thief of Hearts: 1995 (Golden Mountain Chronicles)

Thief of Time (Discworld)

Thimble of Soil (Trail of Thread)

The Thing in the Closet (Spooksville)

The Thing Under the Bed (Bone Chillers)

Think I'll Just Curl Up and Die (Fab 5)

Think Like a Mountain (Concrete)

Thinking of You (Sweet Dreams)

Third Evil (Fear Street: Fear Street Cheerleaders)

The Third Horror (Fear Street: 99 Fear Street)

Third Planet from Altair (Choose Your Own Adventure)

Third Wheel (Sweet Valley Junior High)

The Thirst (Fear Street: Fear Street Seniors)

The Thirteenth Pearl (Nancy Drew)

This Boy Is Mine (Turning Seventeen)

This Can't Be Happening at Macdonald Hall! (Bruno and Boots)

This Rocks! (The Jersey)

This Side of Evil (Nancy Drew Files)

This Time for Real (Sweet Dreams)

Thomas Jefferson (Dear Mr. President)

Thorn Ogres of Hagwood (Hagwood Trilogy)

The Thoroughbred (Sweet Dreams)

The Threat (Animorphs)

The Threat Within (Star Wars: Jedi Apprentice)

Three Cheers for Love (Sweet Dreams)

Three Cheers for You, Cassie! (Paxton Cheerleaders)

Three Days, Two Nights (Sweet Valley Junior High)

Three Evil Wishes (Fear Street: Ghosts of Fear Street)

Three Girls and a God (Goddesses)

Three Girls and a Guy (Sweet Valley High Senior Year)

Three-Guy Weekend (Love Stories)

Three Princes (Love Stories: Super Editions)

Three-Ring Terror (Hardy Boys)

Three Rotten Eggs (Hamlet Chronicles)

3001 (2001)

Three's a Crowd (From the Files of Madison Finn)

Three's a Crowd (Sweet Dreams)

Three's a Crowd (Sweet Valley Twins)

Thrill (Making Waves)

The Thrill Club (Fear Street)

Thriller Diller (Three Investigators)

Throne of Zeus (Choose Your Own Adventure)

Through the Black Hole (Choose Your Own Adventure)

Through the Flames (Left Behind—The Kids)

Through the Veil (Circle of Three)

Thunder Falls (Dinotopia)

Thunderbird Spirit (Lightning on Ice)

Thyme of Death (China Bayles Mystery)

Tia in the Middle (Sweet Valley High Senior Year)

Tic-Tac Terror (Hardy Boys)

Tick Tock, You're Dead! (Goosebumps: Give Yourself Goosebumps)

The Ties that Bind (Star Wars: Jedi Apprentice)

Tiger Heat (Sports Mystery)

Tiger in the Sky (David Brin's Out of Time)

The Tiger in the Well (Sally Lockhart Trilogy)

Tiger, Tiger (X Files)

The Tiger's Apprentice (Tiger's Apprentice)

Tiger's Blood (Tiger's Apprentice)

Tik-Tok of Oz (Oz)

Tiki Doll of Doom (Bone Chillers)

Till Death Do Us Part (Nancy Drew Files)

Till the End of Time (Alex Balfour)

Timber Lane Cove (Whispering Brook)

Time After Time (Alex Balfour)

A Time of Exile (Deverry)

Time of Fear (Hear No Evil)

A Time of Omens (Deverry)

Time Out (Outernet)

Time Out for Love (Sweet Dreams)

The Time Shifter (The Outer Limits)

Time Stops for No Mouse (Hermux Tantamoq Adventures)

Time Terror (Spooksville)

A Time to Cherish (Christy Miller)

A Time to Die (One Last Wish)

Time to Fly (Wild at Heart)

Time Will Tell (Sierra Jensen)

The Tin Woodman of Oz (Oz)

'Tis the Season (Beverly Hills, 90210)

Titan Clash (Sports Mystery)

Titanic (Survival!)

To Catch a Thief (Sweet Valley High)

To Snoop or Not to Snoop (Mary-Kate and Ashley: Two of a Kind)

To the Blight (The Wheel of Time (Related Books))

To Your Scattered Bodies Go (Riverworld Saga)

Todd Runs Away (Sweet Valley Twins)

Todd's Story (Sweet Valley High)

Together Again (Cheerleaders)

Together Forever (Love Stories)

Together We Can Do It (Star Power)

Toilet of Doom (Jiggy McCue)

Toilet Terror (Bone Chillers)

The Tombs of Atuan (Earthsea)

Tommy Stands Alone (Roosevelt High School)

Tomorrow I'll Miss You (Aloha Cove)

Tomorrow, When the War Began (Tomorrow)

Tomorrow's Promise (Heartland)

Too Close for Comfort (Sweet Dreams)

Too Cool for School (Party of Five)

Too Good to Be True (Mary-Kate and Ashley: So Little Time)

Too Good to Be True (Sweet Dreams)

Too Good to be True (Sweet Valley High)

Too Hot to Handle (Dawson's Creek)

Too Hot to Handle (Sweet Valley High)

Too Hottie to Handle (Clueless)

Too Late (Sweet Valley High Senior Year)

Too Many Boys (Sunset Island)

Too Many Boys (Sweet Dreams)

Too Many Good-Byes (Sweet Valley Junior High)

Too Many Secrets (Jennie McGrady Mysteries)

Too Many Traitors (Hardy Boys Casefiles)

Too Much in Love (Sweet Valley High)

Too Much to Lose (Sweet Dreams)

Trouble on Cloud City (Star Wars Young Jedi Knights)

Trouble on Planet Earth (Choose Your Own Adventure)

Trouble Times Two (Hardy Boys)

Trouble with Aaron (Making Out)

The Trouble with Boys (That's So Raven)

The Trouble with Charlie (Sweet Dreams)

The Trouble with Flirting (Fabulous Five)

Trouble with Guys (Party of Five)

The Trouble with Toni (Sweet Dreams: On Our Own)

The Trouble with Weddings (Holly's Heart)

Troublemaker (Sweet Valley High)

Troublemaker (Sweet Valley High Senior Year)

Troubling a Star (Vicky Austin)

Truckers (Bromeliad)

True Believer (Make Lemonade Trilogy)

True Betrayer (Promise of Zion)

True Blue (Sweet Valley Junior High)

True Blue Hawaii (Clueless)

True Devotion (Uncommon Heroes)

True Enough (Heartland)

True Friends (Christy Miller)

True Honor (Uncommon Heroes)

True Identity (Pacific Cascades University)

True Romance (Silver Creek Riders)

True Thriller (Hardy Boys Casefiles)

True Valor (Uncommon Heroes)

Trumpet of Terror (Choose Your Own Adventure)

Trust (Fearless)

Trust Falls (The Wessex Papers)

Trust in Love (Sweet Dreams)

Trust Me (Fingerprints)

Trust Me (Love Stories)

Trusting Hearts (Sweet Dreams)

The Truth (Discworld)

The Truth (Regeneration)

The Truth About Love (Sweet Dreams)

The Truth About Me and Bobby V. (Sweet Dreams)

The Truth About Ryan (Sweet Valley University)

The Truth About Stacey (Baby-Sitters Club)

Truth and Consequences (Charmed)

Truth or Dare (Fear Street)

Truth or Dare (Mary-Kate and Ashley Sweet 16)

Truth or Dare (Sweet Valley University)

Truth or Die (Nightmare Hall)

Truth or Scare (Trash)

Truth Trap! (Secret World of Alex Mack)

Trying Out (Cheerleaders)

Tucket's Gold (The Tucket Adventures)

Tucket's Home (The Tucket Adventures)

Tucket's Ride (The Tucket Adventures)

The Tuesday Cafe (Harper Winslow)

Tug of War (Sweet Valley Twins)

The Tunnel Behind the Waterfall (Magician's House Quartet)

Tunnels of Blood (Cirque du Freak)

Turnabout (Roswell High)

Turns on a Dime (Goldstone Trilogy)

The 24-Hour War (Endless Quest)

24/7 (Love Stories)

2061 (2001)

Twice Upon a Time (Alex Balfour)

Twilight (The Mediator)

The Twin Dilemma (Nancy Drew)

Twin Switch (Sweet Valley Junior High)

Twins (Fearless)

Twins Get Caught (Sweet Valley Twins)

The Twins Go to College (Sweet Valley Twins Super Editions)

The Twins Hit Hollywood (Sweet Valley Twins)

Twins in Love (Sweet Valley Twins)

Twins in Trouble (B.Y. Times)

Twins' Little Sister (Sweet Valley Twins)

The Twins Take Paris (Sweet Valley Twins Super Editions)

Twist and Shout (Mary-Kate and Ashley: Two of a Kind)

Twist of Fate (Distress Call 911)

Twisted (Fearless)

The Twisted Claw (Hardy Boys)

The Twisted Tale of Tiki Island (Goosebumps: Give Yourself Goosebumps)

Two-Boy Weekend (Sweet Valley High)

Two Boys Too Many (Sweet Dreams)

Two for the Road (Mary-Kate and Ashley: Two of a Kind)

Two Hearts (Beverly Hills, 90210)

The Two of Us (Sweet Dreams)

Two Points for Murder (Nancy Drew Files)

2001 (2001)

2010 (2001)

Two-Timing Aisha (Making Out)

The Two Towers (Lord of the Rings)

Two's a Crowd (Mary-Kate and Ashley: Two of a Kind)

Two's a Crowd (Sweet Dreams)

Typhoon! (Choose Your Own Adventure)

Typhoon Island (Hardy Boys)

Tyrone's Story (Degrees of Guilt)

U

U.N. Adventure (Choose Your Own Adventure)

Ugly Little Monsters (Buffy the Vampire Slayer) (Dark Horse)

The Ultimate (Animorphs)

The Ultimate Challenge (Goosebumps: Give Yourself Goosebumps)

The Ultimate Enemy (Berserker)

The Ultimate Escape (Net Force)

Ultimate Risk (Thoroughbred)

Ultimate Scoring Machine (NFL Monday Night Football Club)

The Un-Magician (Outcast)

Unbridled Fury (Thoroughbred)

The Uncertain Path (Star Wars: Jedi Apprentice)

Vol. 1 (Kim Possible (TokyoPop))

Vol. 2 (Kim Possible (TokyoPop))

Vol. 3 (Kim Possible (TokyoPop))

Vol. 4 (Kim Possible (TokyoPop))

Vol. 5 (Kim Possible (TokyoPop))

Vol. 6 (Kim Possible (TokyoPop))

Vol. 7 (Kim Possible (TokyoPop))

Volcano! (Choose Your Own Adventure)

Voltage (X Files)

Volume 1 (Akira)

Volume 2 (Akira)

Volume 3 (Akira)

Volume 4 (Akira)

Volume 5 (Akira)

Volume 6 (Akira)

Volume 1 (Astro Boy)

Volume 2 (Astro Boy)

Volume 3 (Astro Boy)

Volume 4 (Astro Boy)

Volume 5 (Astro Boy)

Volume 6 (Astro Boy)

Volume 7 (Astro Boy)

Volume 8 (Astro Boy)

Volume 9 (Astro Boy)

Volume 10 (Astro Boy)

Volume 11 (Astro Boy)

Volume 12 (Astro Boy)

Volume 13 (Astro Boy)

Volume 14 (Astro Boy)

Volume 15 (Astro Boy)

Volume 16 (Astro Boy)

Volume 17 (Astro Boy)

Volume 18 (Astro Boy)

Volume 19 (Astro Boy)

Volume 20 (Astro Boy)

Volume 21 (Astro Boy)

Volume 22 (Astro Boy)

Volume 23 (Astro Boy)

Volume 1 (CLAMP School Detectives)

Volume 2 (CLAMP School Detectives)

Volume 3 (CLAMP School Detectives)

Volume 1 (Dragon Ball)

Volume 2 (Dragon Ball)

Volume 3 (Dragon Ball)

Volume 4 (Dragon Ball)

Volume 5 (Dragon Ball)

Volume 6 (Dragon Ball)

Volume 7 (Dragon Ball)

Volume 8 (Dragon Ball)

Volume 9 (Dragon Ball)

Volume 10 (Dragon Ball)

Volume 11 (Dragon Ball)

Volume 12 (Dragon Ball)

Volume 13 (Dragon Ball)

Volume 14 (Dragon Ball)

Volume 15 (Dragon Ball)

Volume 1 (Dragon Ball Z)

Volume 2 (Dragon Ball Z)

Volume 3 (Dragon Ball Z)

Volume 4 (Dragon Ball Z)

Volume 5 (Dragon Ball Z)

Volume 6 (Dragon Ball Z)

Volume 7 (Dragon Ball Z)

Volume 8 (Dragon Ball Z)

Volume 9 (Dragon Ball Z)

Volume 10 (Dragon Ball Z)

Volume 11 (Dragon Ball Z)

Volume 12 (Dragon Ball Z)

Volume 13 (Dragon Ball Z)

Volume 14 (Dragon Ball Z)

Volume 15 (Dragon Ball Z)

Volume 1 (Hellsing)

Volume 2 (Hellsing)

Volume 3 (Hellsing)

Volume 4 (Hellsing)

Volume 5 (Hellsing)

Volume 1 (Slayers)

Volume 2 (Slayers)

Volume 3 (Slayers)

Volume 1: Girls, Girls, Girls (Black Book (Diary of a Teenage Stud))

Volume 1: The Darkening (Buffy the Vampire Slayer: Wicked Willow)

Volume 2: Shattered Twilight (Buffy the Vampire Slayer: Wicked Willow)

Volume 2: Stop, Don't Stop (Black Book (Diary of a Teenage Stud))

Volume 3: Broken Sunrise (Buffy the Vampire Slayer: Wicked Willow)

Volume 3: Run, Jonah, Run (Black Book (Diary of a Teenage Stud))

Volume 4: Faster, Faster, Faster (Black Book (Diary of a Teenage Stud))

Voodoo Moon (Charmed)

The Voodoo Plot (Hardy Boys)

A Vote for Love (Sweet Dreams)

Voyage of Fear (Bionicle Adventures)

The Voyage of the Dawn Treader (Chronicles of Narnia)

Voyager (Outlander)

Voyager in Night (Alliance-Union)

W

The Wailing Siren Mystery (Hardy Boys)

Waiting (Cheerleaders)

Waiting for Stardust (Thoroughbred: Ashleigh)

Wake the Devil (Hellboy)

The Wakefield Legacy (Sweet Valley High)

The Wakefields of Sweet Valley (Sweet Valley High)

The Wakefields Strike It Rich (Sweet Valley Twins)

Walk in Hell (The Great War)

Walk on Water (Watching Alice)

Walker of Time (Walker and Tag)

Walker's Journey Home (Walker and Tag)

Wanted for Murder (Sweet Valley University Thriller Editions)

Wanted—Mud Blossom (The Blossom Family)

War! (B.Y. Times)

War Between the Twins (Sweet Valley Twins)

War Comes to Willy Freeman (Arabus Family Saga)

War of Honor (Honor Harrington)

The War of the Clones (Replica)

War of the Dragon (Left Behind—The Kids)

War of the Wardrobes (Mary-Kate and Ashley: Two of a Kind)

War with the Evil Power Master (Choose Your Own Adventure)

War with the Mutant Spider Ants (Choose Your Own Adventure)

Warehouse Rumble (Hardy Boys)

The Warning (Animorphs)

The Waste Lands (Dark Tower)

Whispers in Williamsburg (Sarah's Journey)

The Whistle, the Grave and the Ghost (Lewis Barnavelt)

Whistler in the Dark (American Girls: History Mysteries)

The White Dragon (Pern)

White Dragon of Sharnu, The (Daystar Voyages)

The White Gryphon (Valdemar: Gryphon Trilogy)

White Lies (Sweet Valley High)

White Lies and Barefaced Truths (Truth or Dare)

The White Mountains (Tripods)

The White Order (Recluce)

White Water (Wakara of Eagle Lodge)

White Water Terror (Nancy Drew Files)

Who Are You? (Choose Your Own Adventure)

Who Do You Love? (Love Stories)

Who Framed Alice Prophet? (Eerie Indiana)

Who Goes Home (Ormingat)

Who I Am (Diary of a Teenage Girl)

Who Is Carrie? (Arabus Family Saga)

Who Killed Harlowe Thrombey? (Choose Your Own Adventure)

Who Killed the Homecoming Queen (Fear Street)

Who Knew? (Sweet Valley University)

Who Loves Kate (Making Out)

Who's Been Sleeping in My Grave? (Fear Street: Ghosts of Fear Street)

Who's 'Bout to Bounce? (Cheetah Girls)

Who's to Blame? (Sweet Valley High)

Who's Who (B.Y. Times)

Who's Who? (Sweet Valley High)

Why I Quit the Baby-Sitter's Club (Bone Chillers)

Why I'm Afraid of Bees (Goosebumps)

Why I'm Not Afraid of Ghosts (Fear Street: Ghosts of Fear Street)

The Wiccan (Forbidden Doors)

Wicked (Fear Street: Fear Street Seniors)

The Wicked Cat (Spooksville)

Wicked for the Weekend (Nancy Drew Files)

Wicked Ways (Nancy Drew Files)

The Wide Window (A Series of Unfortunate Events)

Wild (Making Waves)

Wild Blood (Switchers)

Wild Boy (Rowan Hood)

The Wild Cat Crime (Nancy Drew)

Wild Child (Sweet Valley Junior High)

Wild Fire (Wakara of Eagle Lodge)

Wild Lies and Secret Truth (Summit High)

Wild Magic (Immortals)

The Wild One (Roswell High)

Wild Pitch (Alden All Stars)

A Wild Ride (Endless Quest)

Wild Ride (Extreme Team)

Wild Spirit (Black Stallion: Young Black Stallion)

Wild Things (Prowlers)

Wild Wheels (Hardy Boys Casefiles)

Wildfire (Left Behind—The Kids)

A Will to Survive (Hardy Boys)

Will Work for Fashion (Bratz)

The Willow Files, Volume 1 (Buffy the Vampire Slayer: The Willow Files)

The Willow Files, Volume 2 (Buffy the Vampire Slayer: The Willow Files)

Win, Lose, or Die (Nightmare Hall)

Win, Place, or Die (Nancy Drew Files)

A Wind in the Door (Time Fantasy Series)

The Wind Singer (The Wind on Fire)

Windchaser (Dinotopia)

Windows on the Hill (Summerhill Secrets)

Winds of Change (Valdemar: Mage Winds)

Winds of Fate (Valdemar: Mage Winds)

Winds of Fury (Valdemar: Mage Winds)

Winging It (Angels Unlimited)

Wings (Bromeliad)

The Wings of a Falcon (The Kingdom)

Wings of an Angel (Winds of Light)

Wings of Fear (Nancy Drew Files)

Wings of Love (Sweet Dreams)

The Wings of Merlin (Lost Years of Merlin)

Winner Take All (Hardy Boys Casefiles)

Winner Take All (Mary-Kate and Ashley: Two of a Kind)

Winner Takes All (Sweet Dreams)

The Winner's Circle (Golden Filly Series)

The Winners on the Roads (Pageant)

Winning (Silver Creek Riders)

Winning Isn't Everything, Lauren! 1994 (Paxton Cheerleaders)

Winning London (Mary-Kate and Ashley Starring In . . .)

Winter (Witch Season)

Winter Ball (7th Heaven)

Winter Carnival (Sweet Valley High)

Winter Dreams (Sweet Dreams)

Winter Hawk Star (Lightning on Ice)

Winter Holiday (Swallows and Amazons)

The Winter Prince (Arthurian-Aksumite Cycle)

Winter Race Camp (Thoroughbred: Ashleigh)

Winter Tidings (Prairie River)

Winter's Heart (The Wheel of Time)

Wipeout (Hardy Boys)

Wired (Fearless)

The Wisdom of War (Buffy the Vampire Slayer) (Archway/Pocket)

Wise Child (Wise Child)

The Wish (Nightmare Hall)

Wish You Were Here (Mrs. Murphy)

Wishes and Dreams (Mary-Kate and Ashley Sweet 16)

Wishing Horse of Oz (Oz)

Wishing on a Star (Cheetah Girls)

Wishing Season (Dragonflight Books)

The Wishing Stone (Spooksville)

Wrong Turn in the Fast Lane (Summit High)

Wrong-Way Romance (Sweet Dreams)

Wyrd Sisters (Discworld)

X

X Marks the Spot (X Files)

The Xander Years, Volume 1 (Buffy the Vampire Slayer: The Xander Years)

The Xander Years, Volume 2 (Buffy the Vampire Slayer: The Xander Years)

Xenocide (Ender Wiggin)

Xone of Contention (Xanth Saga)

Y

Yanked (David Brin's Out of Time)

Yankee Belles in Dixie (Bonnets and Bugles)

Yankee in Oz (Oz)

Yankee Spy (The Young Americans)

Year of Impossible Goodbyes (Sookan Bak)

The Year Without Christmas (Sweet Valley Twins Super Editions)

The Yearling (Black Stallion: Young Black Stallion)

The Yellow Feather Mystery (Hardy Boys)

The Yellow Knight of Oz (Oz)

Yon Ill Wind (Xanth Saga)

You Are a Genius (Choose Your Own Adventure)

You Are a Millionaire (Choose Your Own Adventure)

You Are a Monster (Choose Your Own Adventure)

You Are a Shark (Choose Your Own Adventure)

You Are a Superstar (Choose Your Own Adventure)

You Are an Alien (Choose Your Own Adventure)

You Are Microscopic (Choose Your Own Adventure)

You Can't Choose Your Family (Party of Five)

You Can't Scare Me! (Goosebumps)

You Know You Love Me (Gossip Girl)

The Young Black Stallion (Black Stallion)

The Young Unicorns (Vicky Austin)

Your Basic Nightmare (Sweet Valley High Senior Year)

Your Code Name Is Jonah (Choose Your Own Adventure)

Your Old Pal, Al (Al (Alexandra))

Your Turn—to Scream! (Spinetinglers)

You're a Brave Man, Julius Zimmerman (Losers, Inc.)

You're Dating Him? (Love Stories: His. Hers. Theirs)

You're Not My Sister (Sweet Valley University)

You're Plant Food! (Goosebumps: Give Yourself Goosebumps)

You're the One That I Want (Gossip Girl)

Yours for a Day (Sweet Valley Twins)

Yours Forever (Christy Miller)

Z

Zack in Action (Saved by the Bell)

Zack Strikes Back (Saved by the Bell)

Zack Zeroes In (Saved by the Bell)

Zack's Last Scam (Saved by the Bell)

The Zanti Misfits (The Outer Limits)

Zapped in Space (Goosebumps: Give Yourself Goosebumps)

Zappy Holidays! (Super Edition) (Secret World of Alex Mack)

Zenda and the Gazing Ball (Zenda)

Zip (Wolfbay Wings)

Zoey Comes Home (Making Out)

Zoey Fools Around (Making Out)

Zoey Plays Games (Making Out)

Zoey Speaks Out (Making Out)

Zoey's Broken Heart (Making Out)

Zombie Lover (Xanth Saga)

Zombie School (Goosebumps: Give Yourself Goosebumps)

The Zucchini Warriors (Bruno and Boots)

Genre/Subject Index

This index gives access by genre (in bold capital letters) and by subject, enabling you to find series by genre and to identify books that deal with specific topcis, such as horses or U.S. history.

ANIMAL FANTASY

Deptford Mice (5–8)

Hermux Tantamoq Adventures (5–8)

Joe Grey Mysteries (9–12)

Ratha Quartet (7–12)

Redwall (4–8)

Samurai Cat (10–12)

Animals *see also* specific kinds of animals (e.g., Cats) that may be real or anthropomorphic

Wild at Heart (4–7)

Appalachia

Ballad (10–12)

Arthurian legends

Arthur Trilogy (6–9)

Arthurian-Aksumite Cycle (7–12)

Arthurian Knights (6–8)

The Denizens of Camelot (6–9)

Lost Years of Merlin (6–10)

Merlin Codex (9–12)

Once and Future King (7–10)

Athens

The Life and Times (4–7)

Australia

Tomorrow (8–12)

Automobile racing

NASCAR Pole Position Adventures (5–8)

Baby-sitting

Baby-Sitter (6–8)

Baby-Sitters Club (4–7)

Baby-Sitters Club Friends Forever (4–7)

Baby-Sitters Club Mysteries (4–7)

Baby-Sitters Club Super Specials (4–7)

Baseball

Baseball Card Adventures (4–8)

Moondog (10–12)

Rookies (7–10)

Basketball

Hazelwood High (7–10)

Boxing

The Contender (6–8)

Canada

Avonlea (5–8)

Harper Winslow (6–9)

Cats

Joe Grey Mysteries (9–12)

Ratha Quartet (7–12)

Warriors (6–9)

Cheerleading

Cheer Squad (6–8)

Cheer USA! (6–9)

Cheerleaders (7–9)

Paxton Cheerleaders (6–8)

China

Golden Mountain Chronicles (7–8)

Chinese Americans

Golden Mountain Chronicles (7–8)

Christian life

Abby's South Seas Adventures (5–8)

Aloha Cove (7–10)

American Adventure (5–8)

Belles of Lordsburg (9–12)

Bonnets and Bugles (5–7)

Brio Girls (6–10)

China Tate (5–8)

Christy Miller (6–8)

Christy Miller: Christy and Todd: The College Years (9–12)

Clearwater Crossing (6–9)

Colonial Captives (6–8)

Diary of a Teenage Girl (9–12)

Forbidden Doors (7–9)

High Hurdles (4–7)

Holly's Heart (6–9)

Horsefeathers (7–10)

Left Behind—The Kids (6–10)

The Lily Adventures (8–10)

Live from Brentwood High (6–9)

Pacific Cascades University (8–10)

Passages (6–10)

Payton Skky (9–12)

Prairie Legacy (9–12)

Raise the Flag (7–10)

Red River: Red River of the North (9–12)

Red River: Return to Red River (9–12)

Sarah's Journey (10–12)

Sierra Jensen (6–8)

Summit High (7–10)

TodaysGirls.com (6–9)

Uncommon Heroes (10–12)

Winds of Light (6–8)

Clones and cloning

Regeneration (8–10)

Replica (6–9)

Replica: The Plague Trilogy (6–9)

2099 (5–8)

Clubs and gangs

Baby-Sitters Club (4–7)

Baby-Sitters Club Friends Forever (4–7)

Baby-Sitters Club Mysteries (4–7)

Baby-Sitters Club Super Specials (4–7)

Baker Street Irregulars (4–7)

Clique (6–9)

Dogtown Ghetto (6–8)

Hamlet Chronicles (4–7)

He-Man Women Haters Club (6–9)

Losers, Inc. (4–7)

NFL Monday Night Football Club (4–7)

Shadow Club (8–12)

Computers

@CAFE (7–10)

Cybersurfers (6–9)

Danger.com (6–9)

Net Force (7–10)

Outernet (6–9)

TodaysGirls.com (6–9)

2099 (5–8)

Virtual Reality (7–10)

Wizardry (7–12)

Crusades

Pagan (9–12)

Royal Pavilions (9–12)

Dancing

Heart Beats (7–8)

FANTASY (cont.)

CLAMP School Detectives (4–8)
Concrete (7–10)
Countdown (7–10)
The Crimson Shadow (7–12)
Crossroads Trilogy (8–12)
Dalemark Quartet (6–9)
Damar Chronicles (6–10)
Danger Boy (6–9)
Dark Ground Trilogy (6–9)
Dark Is Rising (4–8)
Dark Secrets (7–10)
Dark Tower (9–12)
Dark Visions (9–12)
Darkangel Trilogy (6–10)
Daughter of the Lioness (10–12)
Daughters of the Moon (9–12)
David Brin's Out of Time (6–8)
Deltora: Deltora Quest (4–7)
Deltora: Deltora Shadowlands (4–7)
Deltora: Dragons of Deltora (4–7)
The DemonWars (10–12)
The Denizens of Camelot (6–9)
Deptford Mice Histories (5–8)
Deverry (10–12)
Diadem (6–8)
Dinotopia (6–9)
Dinoverse (6–9)
Discworld (6–12)
Dragon Ball (7–10)
Dragon Ball Z (7–10)
Dragon Chronicles (6–9)
Dragon of the Lost Sea (6–9)
The Dragon Quartet (7–12)
DragonCrown War Cycle (10–12)
Dragonflight Books (7–10)
Dragonlance Defenders of Magic (9–12)
Dragonlance Dwarven Nations Trilogy (9–12)
Dragonmaster (9–12)
Earthsea (7–8)
Echorium Sequence (6–9)
ElfQuest (9–12)
Enchanted Forest Chronicles (4–7)
Enchanted Hearts (7–12)
Endless Quest (9–12)
EverWorld (7–12)
The Fairy Godmother (7–12)
The Fallen (8–12)

Farsala Trilogy (6–10)
Ferret Chronicles (7–10)
Fingerprints (7–10)
Fire-Us Trilogy (6–12)
Fireball (5–7)
Firebringer Trilogy (7–10)
Forgotten Realms—The Last Mythal (9–12)
Goddesses (6–9)
Goldstone Trilogy (5–7)
Green Knowe (4–8)
The Groo (6–12)
Guardians of Ga'Hoole (4–8)
Gwyn Griffiths Trilogy (4–7)
Hagwood Trilogy (6–9)
Hamlet Chronicles (4–7)
A Handful of Men (9–12)
Harry Potter (3–9)
Harvey Angell Trilogy (4–7)
Have a Nice Life (9–12)
Heartlight (6–9)
Help, I'm Trapped (5–8)
Here Comes Heavenly (6–8)
His Dark Materials (7–12)
Hitchhiker's Trilogy (7–12)
Hollow Kingdom (6–9)
Homecoming Saga (9–12)
Immortals (7–10)
Indigo (7–12)
Inheritance (6–10)
Jackie Chan Adventures (4–8)
The Jersey (4–7)
Jiggy McCue (4–7)
Johnny Dixon (5–8)
Justice Trilogy (5–8)
The Karmidee (4–7)
The Keeper's Chronicles (7–12)
Keys to the Kingdom (5–8)
Kim Possible (Chapter Books) (4–7)
Kim Possible (TokyoPop) (4–7)
The Kin (6–9)
The Kingdom (6–10)
Left Behind—The Kids (6–10)
Lewis Barnavelt (5–8)
Lily Quench (4–7)
Lionboy Trilogy (4–8)
Lord of the Rings (5–8)
Lost Years of Merlin (6–10)
The Lurker Files (6–10)
Magician Trilogy (4–7)
Magician's House Quartet (6–9)
The Magickers (6–10)
The Majipoor Cycle (10–12)

Malloreon (10–12)
Man of His Word (10–12)
The Mediator (7–10)
Mennyms (5–8)
Merlin Codex (9–12)
Mike Pillsbury (6–9)
The Minds Series (6–9)
Mindwarp (6–8)
Mirror Image (7–10)
Mummy Chronicles (4–7)
Mystic Knights of Tir Na Nog (5–8)
Myth Adventures (5–8)
NFL Monday Night Football Club (4–7)
The Nine Lives of Chloe King (9–12)
Northern Frights (5–8)
Nose (6–8)
Obsidian Chronicles (10–12)
Oh My Goddess! (10–12)
Ormingat (5–8)
Outcast (4–7)
The Outer Limits (6–8)
Outlander (11–12)
Oz (4–8)
Pangur Ban (5–8)
Pellucidar (7–12)
Pendragon (5–8)
Pern: The Harper-Hall Trilogy (10–12)
Phantom Valley (7–9)
Pit Dragon Trilogy (6–8)
Protector of the Small (5–8)
Prydain Chronicles (5–8)
Pure Dead Magic (5–8)
Pyrates (5–7)
Ravenscliff (7–10)
Recluce (10–12)
Rowan Hood (6–9)
Ruin Mist: The Kingdoms and the Elves of the Reaches (6–9)
Ruin Mist Chronicles (9–12)
Samurai Girl (6–10)
Secret Circle (7–10)
The Secret Country Trilogy (7–10)
Secret Texts (11–12)
Secret World of Alex Mack (5–8)
A Series of Unfortunate Events (3–7)
The Seventh Tower (6–9)
Sevenwaters (10–12)
Shadow Children (5–8)
Shadowmancer (7–12)

Shannara (10–12)

Shannara: Heritage of Shannara (10–12)

Shannara: High Druid of Shannara (10–12)

Shannara: The Sword of Shannara (6–12)

Shannara: The Voyage of the Jerle Shannara (10–12)

The Sixth Sense: Secrets from Beyond (5–7)

Slayers (7–10)

Smallville (7–10)

Sock Monkey (6–12)

Song of the Lioness Quartet (6–9)

Spell Casters (5–8)

The Spellsong Cycle (9–12)

Stravaganza (6–12)

Swampland Trilogy (7–10)

Sweep (8–10)

Switchers (6–9)

Sword Dancer Saga (10–12)

Sword of Shadows (10–12)

T*Witches (6–9)

Tales from the Odyssey (4–8)

Tales of Alvin Maker (8–10)

Tales of Gom in the Legends of Ulm (6–8)

Tales of the Nine Charms (6–9)

Tales of the Otori (10–12)

Tartan Magic Trilogy (4–7)

Teen Angels (9–12)

That's So Raven (6–8)

Tiger's Apprentice (6–9)

Time Fantasy Series (4–8)

Time Travel Quartet (6–10)

Time Trilogy (5–8)

Tom Swift (7–8)

Trigun Maximum (8–12)

The Underland Chronicles (4–8)

Unicorn (7–12)

Valdemar: Gryphon Trilogy (7–12)

Valdemar: Mage Storms (7–12)

Valdemar: Mage Wars (7–12)

Valdemar: Mage Winds (7–12)

Valdemar: Mageworlds (6–9)

Vampire Diaries (7–10)

The Viking (6–8)

Virtual Reality (7–10)

Walker and Tag (6–9)

Warriors (6–9)

Watchers at the Well (10–12)

Watcher's Quest (7–10)

Water (7–10)

Westmark (5–7)

The Wheel of Time (10–12)

The Wheel of Time (Related Books) (7–10)

Wicked (9–12)

The Wind on Fire (5–8)

Winds of Light (6–8)

Wise Child (6–8)

W.I.T.C.H. (5–8)

Witch Child (8–12)

Witch Season (9–12)

A Wizard in Rhyme (10–12)

Wizardry (7–12)

Wodan's Children (10–12)

Wolves Chronicles (4–8)

The Word and the Void (10–12)

X Files (5–10)

Xanth Saga (10–12)

York Trilogy (8–10)

Young Heroes (4–7)

Young Indiana Jones Chronicles: Choose Your Own Adventure (5–8)

Yurt (9–12)

Zenda (4–7)

Ferrets

Ferret Chronicles (7–10)

Folk and fairy tales

Egerton Hall Novels (9–12)

Enchanted Forest Chronicles (4–7)

The Fairy Godmother (7–12)

Once and Future King (7–10)

Football

NFL Monday Night Football Club (4–7)

Friendship

Al (Alexandra) (5–8)

Alden All Stars (4–8)

@CAFE (7–10)

Baby-Sitters Club (4–7)

Baby-Sitters Club Friends Forever (4–7)

Baby-Sitters Club Super Specials (4–7)

Beacon Street Girls (6–9)

Bratz (6–9)

B.Y. Times (4–8)

Christy Miller (6–8)

Egerton Hall Novels (9–12)

Fabulous Five (6–9)

The Friendship Ring (6–9)

The Girls Quartet (6–9)

Girls R.U.L.E. (6–8)

He-Man Women Haters Club (6–9)

Kids from Kennedy Middle School (5–7)

Maizon (6–8)

Moesha (6–8)

Paxton Cheerleaders (6–8)

Secret World of Alex Mack (5–8)

Silver Creek Riders (6–8)

Sisterhood of the Traveling Pants (6–9)

Sisters (6–8)

Sunset Island (6–9)

Swallows and Amazons (6–8)

Sweet Valley High (7–10)

Sweet Valley High Senior Year (7–10)

Sweet Valley Junior High (6–8)

Sweet Valley Twins (6–8)

Sweet Valley Twins Super Chiller Editions (6–8)

Sweet Valley Twins Super Editions (6–8)

Sweet Valley University (7–10)

Sweet Valley University Thriller Editions (7–10)

Tarragon Island (6–8)

Thoroughbred (4–7)

Three Girls in the City (6–9)

TodaysGirls.com (6–9)

Truth or Dare (7–10)

Turning Seventeen (7–10)

Wolfbay Wings (4–8)

Frontier and pioneer life

The Tucket Adventures (5–8)

Games

Dragonlance Defenders of Magic (9–12)

Dragonlance Dwarven Nations Trilogy (9–12)

Endless Quest (9–12)

Germany

Lechow Family (5–8)

Ghosts

Blossom Culp (5–7)

Green Knowe (4–8)

Haunting with Louisa (5–8)

Graphic novels/manga

Akira (8–12)
Angel (Graphic Novels) (8–12)
Astro Boy (8–12)
Bone (6–10)
Buffy the Vampire Slayer (6–10)
Chronicles of Conan (9–12)
Concrete (7–10)
Dragon Ball (7–10)
Dragon Ball Z (7–10)
ElfQuest (9–12)
The Groo (6–12)
Hellboy (10–12)
Hellsing (10–12)
Kim Possible (Chapter Books) (4–7)
Kim Possible (TokyoPop) (4–7)
Lizzie McGuire (TokyoPop) (4–7)
Oh My Goddess! (10–12)
Slayers (7–10)
Sock Monkey (6–12)
SpyBoy (6–9)
Star Wars: A New Hope—Manga (5–10)
Star Wars: Episode I The Phantom Menace—Manga (5–10)
Star Wars: The Empire Strikes Back—Manga (5–10)
Star Wars: The Return of the Jedi—Manga (5–10)
That's So Raven (6–8)
Trigun Maximum (8–12)

HISTORICAL

The Age of Unreason (10–12)
American Adventure (5–8)
American Dreams (9–12)
American Girls: Girls of Many Lands (4–8)
American Girls: History Mysteries (4–7)
Angel on the Square (6–9)
Arabus Family Saga (5–8)
Arthurian Knights (6–8)
Avonlea (5–8)
Belles of Lordsburg (9–12)
Bonnets and Bugles (5–7)
Boston Jane (7–10)
Christy (5–8)
Colonial Captives (6–8)
Dear Mr. President (5–7)

Flambards (7–8)
The Ghost in the Tokaido Inn (7–9)
Golden Mountain Chronicles (7–8)
Gordy Smith (5–7)
The Great Brain (5–7)
Highland Heroes (11–12)
Island Trilogy (6–9)
Julian Escobar (6–8)
Lechow Family (5–8)
Liberty Letters (7–10)
The Life and Times (4–7)
Logan Family (4–7)
Ludell (5–8)
Lyon Saga (6–9)
On Time's Wing (5–8)
Once and Future King (7–10)
Orphan Train Adventures (5–8)
Outer Banks Trilogy (5–8)
Pagan (9–12)
Petticoat Party (5–8)
Platt Family (6–9)
Prairie River (4–7)
Promise of Zion (6–9)
Quilt Trilogy (6–9)
Roma Sub Rosa (10–12)
Royal Diaries (3–7)
Royal Pavilions (9–12)
Sally Lockhart Trilogy (9–12)
Sarah's Journey (10–12)
Secret Refuge (9–12)
The Shakespeare Stealer (5–8)
Sookan Bak (5–8)
Sterling Family (6–8)
Survival! (5–8)
Trail of Thread (7–10)
The Tucket Adventures (5–8)
Victorian Tales of London (9–12)
White Mane Kids (6–10)
Wild Rose Inn (6–10)
Winds of Light (6–8)
The Young Americans (6–8)
Young Royals (6–9)
The Young Underground (5–8)

Holocaust

Promise of Zion (6–9)

HORROR

Angel (7–12)
Angel (Graphic Novels) (8–12)

Are You Afraid of the Dark? (5–8)
Baby-Sitter (6–8)
Bone Chillers (5–8)
Buffy the Vampire Slayer (6–10) (Archway/Pocket)
Buffy the Vampire Slayer (6–10) (Dark Horse)
Buffy the Vampire Slayer: Buffy and Angel (6–10)
Buffy the Vampire Slayer: Buffy and Angel: The Unseen Trilogy (6–10)
Buffy the Vampire Slayer: The Angel Chronicles (6–10)
Buffy the Vampire Slayer: The Gatekeeper Trilogy (6–10)
Buffy the Vampire Slayer: The Lost Slayer Serial Novel (6–10)
Buffy the Vampire Slayer: The Willow Files (6–10)
Buffy the Vampire Slayer: The Xander Years (6–10)
Buffy the Vampire Slayer: Wicked Willow (6–10)
Choose Your Own Nightmare (4–8)
Dark Visions (9–12)
Daughters of the Moon (9–12)
Dollanganger (8–12)
Eerie Indiana (5–8)
Extreme Zone (7–12)
Fear Street (7–10)
Fear Street: Fear Street Cheerleaders (7–10)
Fear Street: Fear Street Sagas (7–10)
Fear Street: Fear Street Seniors (7–10)
Fear Street: Fear Street Super Chillers (7–10)
Fear Street: Ghosts of Fear Street (4–8)
Fear Street: 99 Fear Street (6–9)
Fiendly Corners (5–8)
Forbidden Doors (7–9)
Forbidden Game (7–10)
Ghost (10–12)
Goosebumps (4–8)
Goosebumps: Give Yourself Goosebumps (4–8)
Goosebumps Series 2000 (4–8)
Graveyard School (4–7)
Hellboy (10–12)
Hellsing (10–12)
House of Horrors (5–7)
The Last Vampire (9–12)

Magic (cont.)

Shannara (10–12)

Shannara: Heritage of Shannara (10–12)

Shannara: High Druid of Shannara (10–12)

Shannara: The Sword of Shannara (6–12)

Shannara: The Voyage of the Jerle Shannara (10–12)

Song of the Lioness Quartet (6–9)

The Spellsong Cycle (9–12)

Tales of Alvin Maker (8–10)

Tartan Magic Trilogy (4–7)

Tiger's Apprentice (6–9)

Valdemar: Gryphon Trilogy (7–12)

Valdemar: Mage Storms (7–12)

Valdemar: Mage Wars (7–12)

Valdemar: Mage Winds (7–12)

Valdemar: Mageworlds (6–9)

Wise Child (6–8)

W.I.T.C.H. (5–8)

Media tie-in

Alias (8–12)

American Dreams (8–10)

Angel (7–12)

Angel (Graphic Novels) (8–12)

Animorphs (4–8)

Animorphs: Alternamorphs (4–8)

Animorphs: Animorph Chronicles (4–8)

Animorphs: Megamorphs (5–8)

Are You Afraid of the Dark? (5–8)

Beverly Hills, 90210 (7–10)

Bionicle Adventures (4–7)

Bionicle Chronicles (4–7)

Bratz (6–9)

Buffy the Vampire Slayer (6–10) (Archway/Pocket)

Buffy the Vampire Slayer (6–10) (Dark Horse)

Buffy the Vampire Slayer: Buffy and Angel (6–10)

Buffy the Vampire Slayer: Buffy and Angel: The Unseen Trilogy (6–10)

Buffy the Vampire Slayer: The Angel Chronicles (6–10)

Buffy the Vampire Slayer: The Gatekeeper Trilogy (6–10)

Buffy the Vampire Slayer: The Lost Slayer Serial Novel (6–10)

Buffy the Vampire Slayer: The Willow Files (6–10)

Buffy the Vampire Slayer: The Xander Years (6–10)

Buffy the Vampire Slayer: Wicked Willow (6–10)

Charmed (7–12)

Choose Your Own Star Wars Adventures (4–8)

Christy (5–8)

Clueless (6–9)

Dawson's Creek (7–12)

Dinotopia (6–9)

Eerie Indiana (5–8)

Everwood (7–12)

Gilmore Girls (7–10)

Jackie Chan Adventures (4–8)

Kim Possible (Chapter Books) (4–7)

Kim Possible (TokyoPop) (4–7)

Lizzie McGuire (4–7)

Lizzie McGuire Mysteries (4–7)

Lizzie McGuire (TokyoPop) (4–7)

Mary-Kate and Ashley: Adventures of Mary-Kate and Ashley (4–7)

Mary-Kate and Ashley: So Little Time (4–7)

Mary-Kate and Ashley: Two of a Kind (4–7)

Mary-Kate and Ashley in Action (4–7)

Mary-Kate and Ashley Starring In . . . (4–7)

Mary-Kate and Ashley Sweet 16 (4–7)

Moesha (6–8)

Mystic Knights of Tir Na Nog (5–8)

The O.C. (10–12)

Party of Five (7–10)

Saved by the Bell (6–8)

Secret World of Alex Mack (5–8)

7th Heaven (4–7)

The Sixth Sense: Secrets from Beyond (5–7)

Smallville (7–10)

Star Trek: Deep Space Nine (4–8)

Star Trek: Starfleet Academy (4–8)

Star Trek: The Next Generation: Starfleet Academy (4–8)

Star Trek: Voyager: Starfleet Academy (4–8)

Star Wars: A New Hope— Manga (5–10)

Star Wars: Episode I The Phantom Menace—Manga (5–10)

Star Wars: Jedi Apprentice (6–8)

Star Wars: The Empire Strikes Back—Manga (5–10)

Star Wars: The Return of the Jedi—Manga (5–10)

Star Wars Episode 1: Journals (4–8)

Star Wars Galaxy of Fear (4–8)

Star Wars Junior Jedi Knights (4–8)

Star Wars Young Jedi Knights (4–8)

That's So Raven (6–8)

X Files (5–10)

Mexican Americans

Dogtown Ghetto (6–8)

Mexico

Julian Escobar (6–8)

Mice

Deptford Mice (5–8)

Deptford Mice Histories (5–8)

Redwall (4–8)

Missing children

Janie (6–9)

Money

Hard Cash (9–12)

Shopaholic (10–12)

Monsters and creatures

Animorphs (4–8)

Animorphs: Alternamorphs (4–8)

Animorphs: Animorph Chronicles (4–8)

Animorphs: Megamorphs (5–8)

Are You Afraid of the Dark? (5–8)

Bone Chillers (5–8)

Choose Your Own Nightmare (4–8)

Eerie Indiana (5–8)

EverWorld (7–12)

Fiendly Corners (5–8)

Goosebumps (4–8)

Goosebumps: Give Yourself Goosebumps (4–8)

Goosebumps Series 2000 (4–8)

House of Horrors (5–7)
Magician Trilogy (4–7)
Mindwarp (6–8)
Spinetinglers (6–8)
Spooksville (5–8)
Star Wars Galaxy of Fear (4–8)
Swampland Trilogy (7–10)
Tales from the Odyssey (4–8)
Tom Swift (7–8)

Mountain climbing
Everest (6–9)

Multicultural
American Girls: Girls of Many
   Lands (4–8)
Cheetah Girls (6–9)
Daughters of the Moon (9–12)

Music
Bardic Voices (10–12)
Cheetah Girls (6–9)
Echorium Sequence (6–9)
The Spellsong Cycle (9–12)
Star Power (6–8)

MYSTERY
The Adept (10–12)
American Girls: History
   Mysteries (4–7)
Anthony Monday (5–7)
Baby-Sitters Club Mysteries
   (4–7)
Baker Street Irregulars (4–7)
Ballad (10–12)
Belltown Mystery (6–9)
Bernie Magruder (4–7)
Bessledorf Hotel (5–7)
Blossom Culp (5–7)
Body of Evidence (9–12)
China Bayles Mystery (9–12)
Chinatown Mystery (5–8)
Choose Your Own Adventure
   (4–8)
Christie & Company (5–7)
Danger.com (6–9)
The Diamond Brothers (5–8)
Eerie Indiana (5–8)
Finnegan Zwake (6–9)
The Ghost in the Tokaido Inn
   (7–9)
Hardy Boys (5–7)
Hardy Boys Casefiles (6–8)
Harvey Angell Trilogy (4–7)

Haunting with Louisa (5–8)
Hear No Evil (9–12)
Herculeah Jones (5–7)
Hermux Tantamoq Adventures
   (5–8)
James Budd (7–10)
Jennie McGrady Mysteries
   (7–10)
Joe Grey Mysteries (9–12)
Johnny Dixon (5–8)
Lizzie McGuire Mysteries (4–7)
Mary-Kate and Ashley:
   Adventures of Mary-Kate and
   Ashley (4–7)
Mary-Kate and Ashley in Action
   (4–7)
Misfits, Inc. (5–9)
Missing Persons (7–10)
Mrs. Murphy (10–12)
Nancy Drew (4–7)
Nancy Drew: Girl Detective
   (4–7)
Nancy Drew and the Hardy Boys
   Super Mysteries (7–9)
Nancy Drew Files (6–9)
Nancy Drew on Campus (7–10)
National Parks Mystery (5–8)
Nightmare Hall (6–9)
P.C. Hawke Mysteries (5–8)
Roma Sub Rosa (10–12)
Sally Lockhart Trilogy (9–12)
Sammy Keyes (5–8)
Sebastian Barth (5–7)
Sports Mystery (9–12)
Spy Girls (7–10)
Three Investigators (5–7)
Vicky Austin (4–7)
Vivi Hartman (6–10)
The Wessex Papers (9–12)
X Games Xtreme Mysteries (4–8)

Mythology
Book of the Gods (10–12)
Goddesses (6–9)
Merlin Codex (9–12)
Northern Frights (5–8)
Tales from the Odyssey (4–8)
Tiger's Apprentice (6–9)
Watcher's Quest (7–10)
Young Heroes (4–7)

Native Americans
Wakara of Eagle Lodge (6–9)
Walker and Tag (6–9)

Orphans
Orphan Train Adventures (5–8)
Winds of Light (6–8)

Owls
Guardians of Ga'Hoole (4–8)

Palestine
Promise of Zion (6–9)

Paranormal
Akira (8–12)
Dark Visions (9–12)
Fingerprints (7–10)
1-800-Where-R-You (7–10)
Psion (9–12)

Pirates
High Seas Trilogy (6–9)

Princesses
The Minds Series (6–9)
Princess Diaries (7–10)

REAL LIFE
A-List (9–12)
Al (Alexandra) (5–8)
Alden All Stars (4–8)
Aloha Cove (7–10)
The Alphabetical Hookup List
   Trilogy (9–12)
American Dreams (8–10)
American Girls: Girls of Many
   Lands (4–8)
@CAFE (7–10)
Avonlea (5–8)
Baby-Sitters Club (4–7)
Baby-Sitters Club Friends
   Forever (4–7)
Baby-Sitters Club Mysteries
   (4–7)
Baby-Sitters Club Portrait
   Collection (4–7)
Baby-Sitters Club Super Specials
   (4–7)
Bad Girls (6–9)
Beacon Street Girls (6–9)
Beverly Hills, 90210 (7–10)
Bingo Brown (4–7)
Black Book (Diary of a Teenage
   Stud) (8–12)
Black Stallion: Young Black
   Stallion (5–8)
Blue Avenger (7–10)
Blue-Eyed Son Trilogy (7–10)

REAL LIFE (cont.)

Bratz (6–9)

The Breadwinner Trilogy (6–9)

Brian Robeson (4–8)

Brides of Wildcat County (7–10)

Brio Girls (6–10)

B.Y. Times (4–8)

California Diaries (6–8)

Cheer Squad (6–8)

Cheer USA! (6–9)

Cheetah Girls (6–9)

China Tate (5–8)

Christy (5–8)

Christy Miller (6–8)

Christy Miller: Christy and Todd: The College Years (9–12)

Class Secrets (6–10)

Clearwater Crossing (6–9)

Clique (6–9)

Clueless (6–9)

Confessions of a Teenage Drama Queen (7–10)

Confessions of Georgia Nicolson (7–10)

The Contender (6–8)

Dawson's Creek (7–12)

Dear Diary (7–12)

Degrees of Guilt (7–10)

Diary of a Teenage Girl (9–12)

Distress Call 911 (7–10)

Dogtown Ghetto (6–8)

Don't Get Caught (6–9)

Don't Touch That Remote! (5–7)

Egerton Hall Novels (9–12)

The Elliott Cousins (7–8)

Everwood (7–12)

Fab 5 (7–10)

Fabulous Five (6–9)

Fat Glenda (4–8)

First Person Fiction (6–10)

The Friendship Ring (6–9)

From the Files of Madison Finn (6–8)

Generation Girl (7–10)

The Girls Quartet (6–9)

Girls R.U.L.E. (6–8)

Glory (6–9)

Golden Filly Series (6–9)

Goldstone Trilogy (5–7)

Gossip Girl (9–12)

The Great Brain (5–7)

Hamilton High (8–12)

Hard Cash (9–12)

Harper Winslow (6–9)

Hazelwood High (7–10)

He-Man Women Haters Club (6–9)

Heart Beats (7–8)

Heartland (4–7)

High Hurdles (4–7)

Holly's Heart (6–9)

Homeroom (7–10)

Horsefeathers (7–10)

Impact Zone (7–12)

Janie (6–9)

Jessica Darling (10–12)

Joey Pigza (5–9)

Junebug (4–7)

Kids from Kennedy Middle School (5–7)

Life at Sixteen (7–9)

Live from Brentwood High (6–9)

Lizzie McGuire (4–7)

Lizzie McGuire Mysteries (4–7)

Lizzie McGuire (TokyoPop) (4–7)

Logan Family (4–7)

Losers, Inc. (4–7)

Love Stories (7–10)

Love Stories: Brothers Trilogy (7–10)

Love Stories: His. Hers. Theirs (7–10)

Love Stories: Prom Trilogy (7–10)

Love Stories: Super Editions (7–10)

Love Stories: Year Abroad (7–10)

Love Trilogy (10–12)

Luna Bay (6–9)

Maizon (6–8)

Make Lemonade Trilogy (7–10)

Making Out (8–12)

Making Waves (9–12)

Mary-Kate and Ashley: Adventures of Mary-Kate and Ashley (4–7)

Mary-Kate and Ashley: So Little Time (4–7)

Mary-Kate and Ashley: Two of a Kind (4–7)

Mary-Kate and Ashley in Action (4–7)

Mary-Kate and Ashley Starring In . . . (4–7)

Mary-Kate and Ashley Sweet 16 (4–7)

Mates, Dates, and . . . (6–9)

Med Center (6–8)

Misery Guts (6–8)

Moesha (6–8)

My Side of the Mountain (4–8)

NASCAR Pole Position Adventures (5–8)

Net Force (7–10)

Nikki Sheridan (6–9)

No Secrets: The Story of a Girl Band (6–9)

The O.C. (10–12)

On the Road (6–10)

One Last Wish (6–9)

Pacific Cascades University (8–10)

Pageant (7–10)

Party of Five (7–10)

Paxton Cheerleaders (6–8)

Payton Skky (9–12)

Philip Hall (4–7)

Platt Family (6–9)

Popular (7–10)

Prairie Legacy (9–12)

Prairie River (4–7)

Raise the Flag (7–10)

The Real Deal (7–10)

Red River: Red River of the North (9–12)

Red River: Return to Red River (9–12)

Richard Steele Trilogy (9–12)

Roosevelt High School (9–12)

Saddle Club: Pine Hollow (6–8)

Sandy Lane Stables (5–8)

Sevens (6–12)

Shadow Club (8–12)

Shopaholic (10–12)

Silver Creek Riders (6–8)

Sisterhood of the Traveling Pants (6–9)

Sisters (6–8)

Star Power (6–8)

Summer (7–10)

Summit High (7–10)

Sunset Island (6–9)

Sweet Dreams (7–9)

Sweet Dreams: On Our Own (7–9)

Sweet 16 (7–10)

Sweet Valley High (7–10)

Sweet Valley High Senior Year (7–10)

Sweet Valley Junior High (6–8)

Sweet Valley Twins (6–8)

VALUES (cont.)

Holly's Heart (6–9)

Horsefeathers (7–10)

Jennie McGrady Mysteries (7–10)

Left Behind—The Kids (6–10)

Lightning on Ice (8–10)

The Lily Adventures (8–10)

Live from Brentwood High (6–9)

Nikki Sheridan (6–9)

Pacific Cascades University (8–10)

Passages (6–10)

Payton Skky (9–12)

Prairie Legacy (9–12)

Raise the Flag (7–10)

Red River: Red River of the North (9–12)

Red River: Return to Red River (9–12)

Sarah's Journey (10–12)

Secret Refuge (9–12)

7th Heaven (4–7)

Sierra Jensen (6–8)

Summerhill Secrets (6–8)

Summit High (7–10)

TodaysGirls.com (6–9)

Uncommon Heroes (10–12)

Victorian Tales of London (9–12)

Wakara of Eagle Lodge (6–9)

Winds of Light (6–8)

Weight control

Fat Glenda (4–8)

The Girls Quartet (6–9)

Witches and wizards *see also* Magic

Age of Magic Trilogy (5–9)

Books of Magic (9–12)

Charmed (7–12)

Chrestomanci (6–9)

Earthsea (7–8)

Enchanted Forest Chronicles (4–7)

Harry Potter (3–9)

Lewis Barnavelt (5–8)

Secret Circle (7–10)

Spell Casters (5–8)

Sweep (8–10)

T*Witches (6–9)

Wicked (9–12)

Witch (5–7)

Witch Child (8–12)

Witch Season (9–12)

A Wizard in Rhyme (10–12)

Wizardry (5–8)

Yurt (9–12)

Wolves

Julie of the Wolves (5–8)

World War II

Gordy Smith (5–7)

Platt Family (6–9)

The Young Underground (5–8)

BOOKS FOR BOYS

These series were selected for their appeal to boys.

Alden All Stars
Animorphs
Animorphs: Alternamorphs
Animorphs: Animorph Chronicles
Animorphs: Megamorphs
Anthony Monday
Baseball Card Adventures
Bingo Brown
Black Book (Diary of a Teenage Stud)
Black Stallion
Blue Avenger
Blue-Eyed Son Trilogy
Brian Robeson
Bruno and Boots
Chip Hilton Sports Series
Cirque du Freak
The Contender
Danger Boy
Don't Get Caught
Don't Touch That Remote!
Extreme Team
Fear Street
Fear Street: Fear Street Cheerleaders
Fear Street: Fear Street Sagas
Fear Street: Fear Street Seniors
Fear Street: Fear Street Super Chillers
Fear Street: Ghosts of Fear Street

Fear Street: 99 Fear Street
Fireball
Goosebumps
Goosebumps: Give Yourself Goosebumps
Goosebumps Series 2000
Gordy Smith
Graveyard School
The Great Brain
Hardy Boys
He-Man Women Haters Club
Help, I'm Trapped
High Seas Trilogy
Impact Zone
James Budd
The Jersey
Jiggy McCue
Joey Pigza
Johnny Dixon
Journey of Allen Strange
Lewis Barnavelt
The Magickers
Mars Year One
Mike Pillsbury
Misery Guts
Misfits, Inc.
Mummy Chronicles
My Side of the Mountain
Mystic Knights of Tir Na Nog

Nancy Drew and the Hardy Boys Super Mysteries
NASCAR Pole Position Adventures
Net Force
NFL Monday Night Football Club
Nose
Outcast
Outernet
Pendragon
Richard Steele Trilogy
Rookies
Slapshots
Slimeballs
Sports Mystery
SpyBoy
Sword of the Spirits
Tales of Gom in the Legends of Ulm
Three Investigators
Tom Swift
Tripods
The Tucket Adventures
The Viking
Walker and Tag
White Mane Kids
Winning Season
Wolfbay Wings
X Games Xtreme Mysteries
The Young Americans

BOOKS FOR GIRLS

These series were selected for their appeal to girls.

A-List
Abby's South Seas Adventures
Al (Alexandra)
Alice
The Alphabetical Hookup List
    Trilogy
American Dreams (Avon)
American Girls: Girls of Many
    Lands
American Girls: History
    Mysteries
Angels Unlimited
Avalon 1: Web of Magic
Avalon 2: Quest for Magic
Avonlea
Baby-Sitters Club
Baby-Sitters Club Friends
    Forever
Baby-Sitters Club Mysteries
Baby-Sitters Club Portrait
    Collection
Baby-Sitters Club Super Specials
Bad Girls
Beacon Street Girls
Black Stallion: Young Black
    Stallion
Boston Jane
Bratz
Brides of Wildcat County
Brio Girls
The Broadway Ballplayers
B.Y. Times
California Diaries
Cheer Squad
Cheer USA!
Cheerleaders
Cheetah Girls
Christie & Company
Christy
Christy Miller
Christy Miller: Christy and
    Todd: The College Years
Class Secrets
Clearwater Crossing
Clique

Clueless
Confessions of a Teenage Drama
    Queen
Confessions of Georgia Nicolson
Diary of a Teenage Girl
Egerton Hall Novels
The Elliott Cousins
Enchanted Hearts
Fab 5
Fabulous Five
Fat Glenda
The Friendship Ring
From the Files of Madison Finn
Generation Girl
Gilmore Girls
The Girls Quartet
Girls R.U.L.E.
Goddesses
Golden Filly Series
Heart Beats
Holly's Heart
Jennie McGrady Mysteries
Jessica Darling
Liberty Letters
Life at Sixteen
Lizzie McGuire
Lizzie McGuire Mysteries
Lizzie McGuire (TokyoPop)
Love Stories
Love Stories: Brothers Trilogy
Love Stories: His. Hers. Theirs
Love Stories: Prom Trilogy
Love Stories: Super Editions
Love Stories: Year Abroad
Love Trilogy
Ludell
Luna Bay
Maizon
Making Out
Making Waves
Mary-Kate and Ashley:
    Adventures of Mary-Kate and
    Ashley

Mary-Kate and Ashley: So Little
    Time
Mary-Kate and Ashley: Two of a
    Kind
Mary-Kate and Ashley in Action
Mary-Kate and Ashley Starring
    In . . .
Mary-Kate and Ashley Sweet 16
Mates, Dates, and . . .
Mirror Image
Moesha
Nancy Drew
Nancy Drew: Girl Detective
Nancy Drew and the Hardy Boys
    Super Mysteries
Nancy Drew Files
Nancy Drew on Campus
Nikki Sheridan
No Secrets: The Story of a Girl
    Band
1-800-Where-R-You
Pacific Cascades University
Pageant
Paxton Cheerleaders
Payton Skky
Princess Diaries
The Real Deal
Saddle Club: Pine Hollow
Sandy Lane Stables
Saved by the Bell
Secret Refuge
Shopaholic
Silver Creek Riders
Sisterhood of the Traveling Pants
Sisters
Spy Girls
Star Power
Sterling Family
Summer
Sunset Island
Sweet Dreams
Sweet Dreams: On Our Own
Sweet 16
Sweet Valley High
Sweet Valley High Senior Year

BOOKS FOR RELUCTANT READERS

These series were selected as those that would have the most appeal to reluctant readers.

Alden All Stars
Alex Rider
Alexander Cold and Nadia
   Santos
Angels Unlimited
Animorphs
Animorphs: Alternamorphs
Animorphs: Animorph
   Chronicles
Animorphs: Megamorphs
Are You Afraid of the Dark?
aby-Sitter
Baby-Sitters Club
Baby-Sitters Club Friends
   Forever
Baby-Sitters Club Mysteries
Baby-Sitters Club Portrait
   Collection
Baby-Sitters Club Super Specials
Beacon Street Girls
Beverly Hills, 90210
Bionicle Adventures
Bionicle Chronicles
Bone Chillers
Bratz
Brian Robeson
Bruno and Boots
Buffy the Vampire Slayer
   (Archway/Pocket)
Buffy the Vampire Slayer (Dark
   Horse)
Buffy the Vampire Slayer: Buffy
   and Angel
Buffy the Vampire Slayer: Buffy
   and Angel: The Unseen Trilogy
Buffy the Vampire Slayer: The
   Angel Chronicles
Buffy the Vampire Slayer: The
   Gatekeeper Trilogy
Buffy the Vampire Slayer: The
   Lost Slayer Serial Novel
Buffy the Vampire Slayer: The
   Willow Files
Buffy the Vampire Slayer: The
   Xander Years

Buffy the Vampire Slayer:
   Wicked Willow
California Diaries
Charmed
Cheetah Girls
Choose Your Own Adventure
Choose Your Own Nightmare
Choose Your Own Star Wars
   Adventures
Clique
Clueless
The Contender
Danger.com
Dinoverse
Dogtown Ghetto
Don't Get Caught
Don't Touch That Remote!
Eerie Indiana
Extreme Team
Fabulous Five
Fear Street
Fear Street: Fear Street
   Cheerleaders
Fear Street: Fear Street Sagas
Fear Street: Fear Street Seniors
Fear Street: Fear Street Super
   Chillers
Fear Street: Ghosts of Fear Street
Fear Street: 99 Fear Street
Fearless
Ferret Chronicles
Fiendly Corners
Fingerprints
Gilmore Girls
Goosebumps
Goosebumps: Give Yourself
   Goosebumps
Goosebumps Series 2000
Graveyard School
Have a Nice Life
He-Man Women Haters Club
Hear No Evil
Help, I'm Trapped
House of Horrors

Island
Jackie Chan Adventures
The Jersey
Jiggy McCue
Joey Pigza
Journey of Allen Strange
Kim Possible (Chapter Books)
Kim Possible (TokyoPop)
Lightning on Ice
Lily Quench
Live from Brentwood High
Lizzie McGuire
Lizzie McGuire Mysteries
Lizzie McGuire (TokyoPop)
Mars Year One
Mates, Dates, and . . .
Mike Pillsbury
Missing Persons
NASCAR Pole Position
   Adventures
National Parks Mystery
NFL Monday Night Football
   Club
Nightmare Hall
Nightmare Room
Nightmare Room Thrillogy
Nightmares! How Will Yours
   End?
Nose
1-800-Where-R-You
Princess Diaries
Secret World of Alex Mack
Slapshots
Slimeballs
Smallville
Spinetinglers
Spooksville
Star Trek: Deep Space Nine
Star Trek: Starfleet Academy
Star Trek: The Next Generation:
   Starfleet Academy
Star Trek: Voyager: Starfleet
   Academy

Star Wars: A New Hope—Manga

Star Wars: Episode I The Phantom Menace—Manga

Star Wars: Jedi Apprentice

Star Wars: The Empire Strikes Back—Manga

Star Wars: The Return of the Jedi—Manga

Star Wars Episode 1: Journals

Star Wars Galaxy of Fear

Star Wars Junior Jedi Knights

Star Wars Young Jedi Knights

Survival!

Swampland Trilogy

Sweep

Thoroughbred

Thoroughbred: Ashleigh

Thoroughbred: Ashleigh's Collection

TodaysGirls.com

The Tucket Adventures

White Mane Kids

Wild at Heart

Winning Season

Wolfbay Wings

X Files

X Games Xtreme Mysteries

The Young Americans

Young Indiana Jones Chronicles: Choose Your Own Adventure

DEVELOPING SERIES

These series did not include three titles at the end of 2004, but they had additional titles forecast for 2005 or were generating considerable interest.

Abarat
Angel on the Square
The Bartimaeus Trilogy
Beloved Dearly
City of Ember
Confessions of a Teenage Drama Queen
Dark Ground Trilogy
The Diamond Brothers
Farsala Trilogy
Forgotten Realms—The Last Mythal
Hagwood Trilogy
Inheritance
Jessica Darling
The Karmidee
The Life and Times
Lionboy Trilogy
Make Lemonade Trilogy
Merlin Codex
The O.C.
Ravenscliff
The Real Deal
Shadow Club
Shadowmancer
Stravaganza
Tarragon Island
Tiger's Apprentice
The Underland Chronicles
Witch Child

About the Authors

REBECCA L. THOMAS is an elementary school librarian, Shaker Heights City Schools, Shaker Heights, Ohio. She has taught at Kent State, received the distinguished service award from the Shaker Heights Teachers' Association, and serves or has served on several prestigious committees, including ALA's Caldecott Committee and the Penguin Putnam Committee. She is the author of three other books and contributing editor of a fourth title.

CATHERINE BARR, editor of such best-selling titles as *Reading in Series, From Biography to History*, and *High-Low Handbook*, is a freelance writer and publishing consultant based in Milford, New Jersey.